CENTRAL AMERICA
INSIDE OUT

CENTRAL AMERICA INSIDE OUT

The Essential Guide to Its Societies, Politics, and Economies

Tom Barry

GROVE WEIDENFELD

NEW YORK

Published by Grove Weidenfeld
A division of Grove Press, Inc.
841 Broadway
New York, NY 10003-4793

Published in Canada by General Publishing Company, Ltd.

Library of Congress Cataloging-in-Publication Data

Barry, Tom, 1950–
Central America inside out : the essential guide to its societies,
politics, and economies / Tom Barry.—1st ed.
p.   cm.
Includes bibliographical references and index.
ISBN 0–8021–1135–1 (alk. paper)
ISBN 0–8021–3260–X
(pbk. ; alk. paper)
1. Central America—Politics and government—1979– 2. Central
America—Social conditions—1979– 3. Central America—Economic
conditions—1979– I. Title.
F1439.5.B38   1991
972.805'3—dc20   90–29050
                              CIP

Manufactured in the United States of America
Printed on acid-free paper
Designed by Irving Perkins Associates
First Edition 1991
1   3   5   7   9   10   8   6   4   2

ACKNOWLEDGMENTS

This book, the product of two years of research, reflects the skill and commitment of the Resource Center staff. It draws extensively on the *Country Guide* series produced by the Resource Center in 1989–1990. I am especially grateful to Debra Preusch, the institute's executive director, for her interviewing and research assistance in Central America and for guiding this project along to its successful conclusion. Jenny Beatty, our production coordinator, oversaw the word processing, formatting, and proofing of the book, always with skill and good humor. For their careful editing work, I thank Connie Adler, Chuck Hosking, and Beth Sims. I would also like to acknowledge my appreciation for the research assistance provided by Jenny Beatty, Joan MacLean, Felipe Montoya, Debra Preusch, and Thomas Weiss. I also thank LaDonna Kutz for proofreading work and Gabrielle Miner for maintaining the Resource Center files in good order.

Others who helped in the preparation of portions of the manuscript include Martin Needler and Eric Shultz. Deserving of special acknowledgment are those who commented on various parts of the manuscript, including O. Nigel Bolland, Milton Jamail, Grant Jones, Karen Judd, Assad Shoman, and Dylan Vernon (Belize); Marc Edelman, Martha Honey, and Lezak Shallat (Costa Rica); Charles Kernigan, Thomas Quigley, and Mike Zielinski (El Salvador); Bob Stix (Guatemala); Steve Sefton, Phil Shepherd, and Zenaida Velásquez (Honduras); Larry Boyd, Judy Butler, William I. Robinson, and Richard Stahler-Sholk (Nicaragua); and Charlotte Elton, Richard Millet, George Priestley, and John Weeks (Panama). There are many others who deserve acknowledgment but go unmentioned here because of possible repercussions in Central America.

The chapter on Nicaragua was written in large part by Kent Norsworthy, who also coauthored the chapter on Honduras. He extends his special thanks to Yolanda, Marcelo, and Nelson, without whose patience and support his efforts would not have been possible.

CONTENTS

CENTRAL AMERICA
INSIDE OUT

INTRODUCTION

CENTRAL AMERICA: THE CRISIS THAT WON'T GO AWAY

Not too long ago Central America was known only for its bananas and the Panama Canal. The isthmus, which joins North and South America with its narrow bridge, is home to seven nations and twenty-eight million people. Situated in the northern tropics, it is a comparatively small place—a quarter the size of Mexico or about the same size and shape as the adjoining states of Florida, Alabama, Mississippi, and Arkansas (see Table One). Until the late 1970s the region was draped in obscurity; even the names of the Central American countries were unknown to most people living outside the region.

But beginning in 1979, the year that the Sandinistas finally overturned the Somoza regime in Nicaragua, there has been an increasing interest on the part of politicians, reporters, ideologues, and social activists in this long-ignored region. During the 1980s Central America became known as a region of civil wars, revolutions, and invasions; whenever Central America was mentioned, the word *crisis* inevitably followed.

Over the past twelve years Central America has become more familiar to U.S. citizens, too. Now elections and other local events in the region are often front-page news in the United States. Although familiarity has increased, Washington's interpretations of events and superficial news reporting have contributed to mistaken assumptions about the Central American crisis.

What exactly is this Central American crisis, and why won't it go away? Is it simply that the region is overpopulated or that it does not produce enough? Is it that Central Americans are drawn to violent solutions and have little understanding of democratic principles? Can the region's troubles be blamed on the meddling of the Yankee imperialists or foreign communists, or do internal factors alone explain the constant bloodshed and misery? Do all seven countries that share the isthmus also share the crisis?

To answer these and other questions it is necessary to dig deep inside the region, to look at Central America from the inside out. This means

5

studying the region's internal dynamics as well as its international relations. This book is an attempt to do just that.

In the following seven chapters, the reader is taken inside each country to see how the crisis affects the domestic politics, the military, and the economy of the seven nations. The impact of the crisis on the society and environment of each country is also examined. The various social sectors—churches, labor unions, and popular organizations, among others—are described and their roles analyzed. For each country there is also a discussion of U.S. foreign policy and assistance programs.

GOVERNMENT AND POLITICS

Entering the 1980s only Belize and Costa Rica had governments controlled by civilians. A decade later all the generals and *comandantes* were out of office, and representative democracy ruled the isthmus. In terms of political change, it was an extraordinary decade. Nicaragua experienced revolutionary change, Belize obtained its independence, and five countries underwent a successful transition from military to civilian governments—four with the cooperation of the military (El Salvador, Honduras, Guatemala, Nicaragua) and one as the result of an invasion (Panama).

Democratization was certainly one trend of the 1980s, but its significance was largely offset by the simultaneous militarization of the region. Although El Salvador, Honduras, and Guatemala no longer had generals as presidents, in each country the military remained the most powerful institution. Central America–style democratization moved forward while the armed forces expanded, civil wars raged, and human-rights abuses struck terror in the hearts of the citizenry. The rise of representative democracy and civilian rule in the region did little to ensure the peaceful resolution of internal political conflicts.

Elections and Political Parties

Even before the latest transition from military regimes to civilian governments, elections were regularly scheduled in most Central American countries. Using fraud and coercion, generals and dictators routinely won the elections. Although elections have become more open and less fraudulent, the political arena in Central America remains quite narrow; center-right and ultraconservative parties dominate the political arena, offering voters little ideological choice.

Political parties in Central America have, for the most part, been elite clubs associated with one or another faction of the oligarchy. They have little connection with the popular movement, and instead hand out jobs and favors to win votes. Apart from their control of certain government positions, Central American political parties have insubstantial national infrastructures, which usually lie dormant after the election passes. Once in power, the parties operate within limits firmly set by the armed forces and business elite. Because they count on little popular support, they do not risk defying their main sponsors.

Many parties still trace their origins to the Liberal and Conservative parties of the late 1800s—the Liberals being the modernizing force that challenged the economic and political power structure remaining from the colonial era. In some countries, political parties have traditionally been associated with a single wealthy family or group of families. In the case of Honduras, the Liberal and National parties were originally linked to competing banana companies. The armed forces in El Salvador and Guatemala formed their own political parties, while certain civilian parties in Nicaragua, Honduras, and Panama were closely associated with the military.

Communist parties, although usually not legally recognized, enjoyed popular support in the 1920s. Communist and other leftist parties established the region's first union and peasant leagues, led the first major strikes, and were the first to call for labor codes and minimum-wage laws.

With the fall of the Jorge Ubico dictatorship in Guatemala in 1944 and its replacement by ten years of progressive civilian governments, it appeared that Central America was entering a period of political modernization. But this experiment in progressive politics was cut short in 1954. A right-wing coup engineered by the CIA and supported by the United Fruit banana company, the Catholic Church, and the governments of Honduras and Nicaragua ushered in a new era of military regimes and counterinsurgency warfare in Central America.

In the 1960s the emergence of Christian Democratic parties represented another modernizing force in Central American politics. Led by student leaders and middle-class professionals, these new parties hoped to break the military-oligarchy monopoly on political power. The Christian Democratic parties of Guatemala, Honduras, and El Salvador were the first noncommunist parties to reach out to the rural population and labor unions with service and training programs.

The Christian Democrats, while reformists, are not socialists. They contend that capitalism can be strengthened and made more resistant to revolutionary challenges through political modernization and limited social and economic reforms. The Christian Democratic parties that won elections in El Salvador and Guatemala in the 1980s were center-right parties that had allied themselves with the armed forces. The Christian Democratic party of Honduras, the most progressive in the region, has never succeeded in gaining more than a few seats in the national congress. Panama's Christian Democratic party became the strongest member in the three-party ruling coalition established after the 1989 U.S. invasion.

Politics in Honduras, Belize, and Costa Rica are dominated by two-party systems that are more or less divided along liberal-conservative lines. During the 1980s the differences between these parties became less obvious, especially in economic matters. This is particularly true in Costa Rica, where the National Liberation party, a member of the Socialist International, pushed through a conservative readjustment program favoring the business sector.

In Honduras, the Liberal party entered into a devil's pact with Washington, agreeing to open its territory to the *contras* and U.S. troops in exchange for an infusion of U.S. economic and military aid. The Liberal party was replaced in February 1990 by the more conservative National party. In El Salvador, the oligarchy swung back into power with the March 1989 victory of the rightist ARENA party over the ruling Christian Democrats.

As in El Salvador, the Christian Democratic government in Guatemala, installed in 1986, gave the country a measure of political and economic stability. But deteriorating socioeconomic conditions for the poor, continued control by the armed forces, and the government's lack of commitment to social reforms all weakened the Vinicio Cerezo government. In both El Salvador and Guatemala, Christian Democratic parties came to power on the heels of the democratization process, but failed to bring even a small measure of peace and justice to their countries.

The Sandinista National Liberation Front (FSLN) launched a revolution in 1979 to rectify the structural injustices in Nicaragua. At the time it was thought that their victory against Somoza's National Guard would herald the success of armed guerrilla movements in Guatemala and El Salvador, while sparking leftist movements elsewhere in the region. Although the July 19, 1979, triumph of the Sandinistas raised the hopes of other leftist guerrilla forces, it also had the effect of galvanizing new counterrevolutionary alliances throughout the region.

Neighboring Central American nations, encouraged by Washington, joined together to isolate and destabilize the Nicaraguan revolution.

Democratization, certainly a step forward in the political development of Central America, was not the result of popular pressure. Instead, it was largely the product of a counterrevolutionary strategy pursued by the U.S. State Department and the region's armed forces and opportunistic politicians. By adopting the procedures of electoral democracy, the civil-military alliances in Guatemala, El Salvador, and Honduras gained international credibility and access to foreign assistance, while becoming less vulnerable to challenges from the militant left. In Panama, civilian rule was not the result of a popular rebellion but the product of a foreign invasion.

Nicaragua also moved toward democracy and civilian rule in the 1980s. The November 1984 general election was the first free election in the country's history. The resulting electoral mandate for the Sandinistas, however, was undermined by the U.S.-induced decision of the conservative opposition not to participate. The next time around the anti-Sandinista opposition coalition, cemented together by U.S. advisers and funds, won the campaign and forced the revolutionary government out of power. It remains to be seen if the electoral defeat of the Sandinistas in February 1990 proves a fatal blow to the advocates of revolutionary change in Central America, or if it was just a temporary setback.

At the end of the decade the forces of the New Right in Central America were gaining control throughout the region. They were swept to power on a tide of right-wing populism and on the promise of economic growth. Figures like Rafael Callejas of Honduras, Rafael Calderón of Costa Rica, Jorge Serrano of Guatemala, and Alfredo Cristiani of El Salvador were the representatives of the modernizing right. Politically they are virulent antisocialists, and economically they have adopted the principles of neoliberalism—a conservative business-oriented philosophy of development.

In the Reagan tradition, they preach the new gospel of antistatism and praise the justice of the marketplace. As Raúl Marín observed in the Central American magazine *Pensamiento Propio* (published in Managua), "It took them ten years to assimilate the doctrines of Ronald Reagan's 'conservative revolution,' and they now try to hide their old links with the *criollo* reactionaries. The failure of the reformist promises of counterinsurgency, the lack of leftist alternatives, and the corruption of traditional political systems have smoothed their way to power. But their greatest success is having been selected as Washington's favorites.

Where they are found wanting, the United States has injected millions of dollars and arms."[1]

Democracy Without the People

The democratization process, while having succeeded in installing civilian governments throughout the region, has not opened the door to governments that are "of the people, by the people, and for the people." Democracy, as practiced in Central America, has signified neither the peaceful resolution to political conflicts nor the reduction of economic injustice. To the contrary, the democratization process has been accompanied by intensifying civil wars, increasing foreign intervention, worsening socioeconomic conditions, and continued military control.

There is a made-in-the-USA flavor to the democratization process. Electoral campaigns have been turned into media battles shaped by Madison Avenue consultants, for whom image matters more than substance. For many Central Americans, democratization is superficial and unresponsive to their major concerns. Increasing abstentionism reflects a growing feeling that voting does not make a difference.

The elitist character of the region's political parties and government domination by the military and the wealthy obstruct a broader democratization process. For the hungry, landless, and poor, electoral democracy becomes a meaningless charade unless accompanied by social reforms. Worse still, democracy becomes indistinguishable from repression and dictatorship when government leaders preside over counterinsurgency wars, economic exploitation, and abusive armed forces.

After more than a decade of political turmoil, both democracy and revolution are still volatile forces in Central America. The challenge of revolution has not gone away because the structural problems that revolutionary forces address are still present. Despite a measure of democratization, those forces responsible for the region's desperate conditions—the military, the economic elite, and the U.S. government—have only grown stronger.

During the 1980s democratization proved to be a foundation for conservatism and counterinsurgency. It was used as a weapon against the broader demands of the popular and revolutionary movements. But democracy may prove a double-edged sword not so easily managed by those concerned with quelling popular unrest. There may be attempts by the military and private-sector elite to discard or subvert the democratization process if it eventually proves to be a threat to their control.

Guerrillas, opposition leftist parties, and popular activists are raising high the banner of democracy, demanding that they, too, be included in the political process and that democratic governments begin responding to popular sentiment. They want the process to be broadened and made more meaningful to the poor majority. At the same time, however, the left faces the challenge of making its own organizations more democratic. To reflect the democratic aspirations of the Central American people, leftist opposition movements, both armed and unarmed, must change their highly centralized and hierarchical organizational structures.

Negotiating a Peace

Primary to the political environment in Central America has been the regional peace process. At first Washington ignored the peace initiatives (1984–1986) of the Contadora Group (Mexico, Panama, Venezuela, and Colombia, with the support of Brazil, Argentina, Uruguay, and Peru), and later it obstructed them, fearing the Nicaraguan government would use the proposed accords to its own advantage. Contadora failed, but as the aggressive Reagan doctrine of military rollback lost momentum, the new Central American peace initiatives eventually took hold. The Central American peace accords, as formulated in the Guatemalan town of Esquipulas in August 1987, set the stage for the eventual demobilization of the *contras*.

Largely because the Sandinista government abided by the accords, the *contra* war finally came to a halt in early 1990. The other countries affected—Costa Rica, Honduras, El Salvador, and Guatemala—were less willing to abide by regional settlements. Costa Rica declined to join the Central American Parliament, and Honduras did not insist that the *contras* leave the country as stipulated in the accords. None of the three countries of the so-called Northern Triangle (El Salvador, Honduras, and Guatemala) seriously attempted to resolve conflicts through a commission of national reconciliation, and El Salvador and Guatemala declined to recognize the legitimacy of the guerrilla armies.

With the Sandinistas gone from the table, the regional peace process degenerated into a series of glorified press conferences in which the Central American presidents expressed their mutual goodwill and their common concern over the sad state of the region's economy. In 1990 the pesky issues of peace in Guatemala and El Salvador and increasing human-rights violations were quietly dropped in favor of petitions for foreign aid and empty promises to renew the regional integration process.

Although the regional peace process faded away after the Sandinistas lost control of the Nicaraguan government, the pressure subsequently mounted for peace settlements in Guatemala and El Salvador. Domestically, most social sectors had grown weary of the war, and the business community recognized that there was little hope for economic recovery if the conflicts persisted. Internationally, patience with the decade-long conflicts also wore thin, even in Washington, which for the first time voiced limited support for government negotiations with leftist rebels.

Essential to any eventual settlements will be the presence of multilateral verification mechanisms to ensure that both sides honor their commitments. More than simply witnessing the peace negotiations and demobilization schemes, the international teams need to have implementation powers. This was a lesson learned in Nicaragua when the *contras* refused to demobilize as planned and then raised their demands. Without any implementation power, the International Support and Verification Commission just sat out the process. International election-monitoring teams need to be present in any elections following negotiated settlements, but these elections should be free of the type of election meddling seen in Nicaragua, where the United States government injected millions into a party it shaped and guided.[2]

THE STATE OF THE ECONOMY

The rosy economic statistics of Central American development from 1950 to 1978 told of an economy moving forward at 5 percent or more a year. But those numbers did not tell the whole story. They disguised indications of a region on the verge of economic and political collapse. At the same time the economy was expanding, the region's weak agricultural and industrial foundations were beginning to crack. Agroexport production was leveling off, and the regional market was proving too small to sustain continued growth of domestic industries. Central American society was also exploding with new tensions and conflicts resulting from inequitable income and resource distribution.[3]

In 1978 the region began falling into a severe recession as the market for its exports shrank, agroexport prices dropped, imports became more costly, and the bills for foreign borrowing came due. The Central American countries were hit harder by the depressed international market than many other Latin American nations because of their exceptionally open economies and greater dependence on a few traditional exports.

Besides trade problems, the region confronted a debt crisis. During the 1970s capital-rich foreign lenders had encouraged governments to take out large loans with low interest rates. Instead of being put to productive use, the loans were largely lost to corrupt generals, politicians, and businessmen. At the same time that interest rates were rising and debts were accumulating, the volume and value of the region's exports began to fall. Governments that for years had used foreign loans to cover budget and trade deficits now found it impossible to pay them back. To complicate matters, few new loans were forthcoming.

The crisis caused by imbalances in the external sector was compounded by national and regional problems. The war in Nicaragua and the guerrilla insurgencies in Guatemala and El Salvador disrupted domestic and regional production. Underlying this political upheaval were structural weaknesses undermining the region's economic foundations. Agricultural productivity for most crops was lower than international standards, with food-crop yields reaching as little as one-third of the yields in the United States (see Table Two). Land-use patterns were such that only 15 percent of the region's arable land was being used for local food production, while as much as two-thirds of the fertile farmland of the Pacific coastal strip was used for extensive cattle ranches that produced beef for foreign markets. As a result, Central America could no longer feed itself or provide jobs for its large peasant population. As the population continued to increase and the region's agricultural frontier disappeared, landlessness increased to explosive proportions.

The region's dual agricultural system was breaking down. On the one side, the agroexport sector was battered by shrinking prices and markets, and higher costs for imported fertilizer, pesticides, and technology. The other side of the system—the small farm/*campesino* sector—could no longer produce the food the region needed. The peasantry faced the double crunch of increasing landlessness and fewer available jobs on the agroexport estates.

The industrial sector also was in crisis. The opening of the Central American Common Market (CACM) in the early 1960s had created a regional market for locally manufactured goods. From the start the region's industrialization had been based on an unhealthy dependence on imported inputs. It also developed behind high protective tariffs that kept competitive goods out of the country while permitting inefficient industries to prosper. As the wider economic crisis began to hit the region, the industrial sector found the regional and domestic markets, on which it wholly depended, closing up. Intraregional trade dropped 60 percent in the 1980s.

The Crisis Deepens

Since 1980 the economic crisis has worsened, aggravated by new factors: the destruction caused by war and foreign intervention, the impact of structural-adjustment programs, and increasing dependence on U.S. foreign aid.

Hardest hit by war was Nicaragua, which faced a U.S.-coordinated campaign of economic and military destabilization. In its presentation before the International Court of Justice (World Court), the Nicaraguan government asserted that the U.S. interference had cost the country more than $2 billion in material damages and lost income. In 1985 the World Court ruled in Nicaragua's favor and decided that the U.S. government should compensate the beleaguered nation for $370 million in direct damages.

Washington's 1987–1989 campaign of economic sanctions against Panama cost that country $2 billion in economic losses, in addition to at least $600 million in economic damages caused by the December 1989 U.S. invasion. The civil war in El Salvador has caused at least $2 billion in infrastructure damage, not including production losses resulting from the general chaos and insecurity of war.

Along with the debt crisis came structural-adjustment programs designed to close budget deficits and reduce external imbalances in trade and payments. In return for new foreign loans and aid from the World Bank, International Monetary Fund (IMF), and the U.S. Agency for International Development (AID), Central American governments agreed to make certain economic adjustments. Currency devaluation, austerity measures, price and trade liberalization, and increased promotion of export production have been the common features of structural adjustment. Structural-adjustment programs showed some signs of success in stabilizing the economy, particularly in Costa Rica. But throughout the region these programs lowered the living standards of the poor and middle classes as government services were cut back and prices of basic goods and services increased.

Both structural-adjustment measures and large injections of U.S. aid did help narrow fiscal deficits and ease the balance-of-payments crisis, but as the commitment of U.S. assistance declined, the Central American countries began to realize just how dependent they had become on Washington. Guatemala, El Salvador, Honduras, and Costa Rica all ranked among the top ten recipients of U.S. aid during the 1980s. This extraordinary flow of dollars to the region began to slow down in the late 1980s, however, and was expected to continue dropping in the early 1990s. As the region entered the 1990s, among the major signs of economic crisis and instability were the following:

- The external debt had almost doubled in the 1980s, to $25 billion by 1990, with annual debt service (interest plus principal repayments) representing 30 percent to 40 percent of annual export income in most countries. During the 1990s the region will need to find at least $2.5 billion each year to pay the annual interest on the debt.
- Four countries (Honduras, Panama, Nicaragua, El Salvador) entered the 1990s ineligible for new World Bank loans because of accumulated overdue debts.
- All countries in the region continue to experience serious trade deficits despite structural-adjustment programs and efforts to promote export production. Although the volume of exports increased during the 1980s, the value of those products declined because of low market prices for most agroexports.
- Continuing trade deficits ($1.5 billion regional trade deficit in 1988) and declining foreign assistance meant declining revenues for Central American governments by the end of the 1980s. This has been especially difficult because the tax bases of the governments in the region are among the lowest in the world.
- Per capita income during the 1980s fell 17 percent, pushing the countries back to 1970 income levels. Rather than advancing a decade, Central American nations lost two.
- Between 1980 and 1985, the number of Central Americans living in poverty increased from 60 percent to 65 percent, or 15.3 million people. Ten million of those could not even afford an adequate minimum diet.

Tough Political and Economic Decisions Ahead

During the 1980s the infusion of U.S. aid and the imposition of structural-adjustment programs failed to bring about economic stability and growth. The symptoms of the economic crisis stayed with the Central American countries as they entered the 1990s (see Table Three).

Economic recovery and equitable broad-based development will require more than structural-adjustment programs. Recovery and sustained growth are contingent upon military budgets being drastically cut, peaceful solutions to internal conflict being reached, the external debt being substantially reduced or forgiven, and new international commodity agreements being negotiated. To move the economy forward and to improve conditions for the poor majority, multibillion-dollar foreign-aid programs will also be necessary.

The economic policies adopted in the 1980s under pressure from foreign donors and the business elite should be reevaluated as the adverse consequences of many of these conservative policies become evident. Although the export-oriented agricultural and manufacturing sectors did benefit from these policies, the domestic economy and the welfare of the poor majority suffered. Similarly, the rush to privatize and slash the public sector may have resulted in some temporary financial stability, but it also cut essential social services and left the region's economic infrastructure in a state of disrepair.

Governments that committed themselves to conservative, free-market economics will have to come to terms with the growing marginalization of their population, particularly the peasantry. The bottom-line character of the neoliberal economic policies favored by Washington left large sectors of the population out of the economic-growth equation while promoting the interests of export-oriented investors and commercially viable farmers. Large sectors of the population were written off as a marginal underclass with little role in the modern economy.

With the continued decline in per capita food production and the rising cost of food imports, the Central American nations are now confronted with their inability to supply their citizens with adequate and affordable food supplies. To solve this food-security crisis, governments will need to continue the promotion of export production but will also be forced to address the production and distribution problems in their domestic food systems. In contrast to the almost exclusive emphasis during the 1980s on extraregional, mainly U.S., markets, more attention will have to be given to the fundamental importance of strong domestic and regional markets.

The economic prognosis for Central America is extremely poor, at least in the short term. To put the region on a stable economic path, tough economic and political decisions are called for. But at this time, despite the gravity of the crisis, there is little willingness to make such necessary decisions as forgiving the debt or redistributing resources.

WAR AND MILITARIZATION

At the start of the 1980s only Guatemala had an army capable of waging a protracted military campaign. The National Guard in Panama was organized more as a police force than a military unit and had little counterinsurgency or battlefield training. Costa Rica had no army, and its police had little training or weaponry. In Nicaragua, the feared National Guard had just been defeated, with its officers exiled or imprisoned, and the new army was a ragtag outfit of former guerrillas with little professional training. The Salvadoran armed forces had overwhelmed the weak Honduran military in a 1969 border war, but it was more skilled in breaking up demonstrations and torturing dissidents than in organizing a prolonged counterinsurgency campaign. With the encouragement of Washington, the Honduran armed forces had become the nation's most powerful and unified national institution. But the Honduran military lacked discipline and a strong morale, and had been badly beaten by its counterpart in El Salvador. The Belize Defense Forces were the adopted little brother of British troops and were too small to present any threat outside the country's borders.

By the end of the 1980s, this picture had changed dramatically. After a decade of U.S. intervention and regional conflict Central America had become considerably more militarized. In Panama, the National Guard had evolved into the Panamanian Defense Forces (PDF), which boasted two new battalions trained to defend the canal and crush local insurgencies. The PDF itself was crushed by the U.S. invasion of December 1989—the largest U.S. military action since the end of the Vietnam War—but reemerged during the U.S. military occupation as the Panamanian Public Force. Costa Rica, despite its proclaimed neutrality, hosted the southern front of the *contra* war in the early 1980s, and its security forces were reequipped and schooled in military operations by the U.S. Special Forces. Confronted with a CIA-instigated counterrevolutionary force, Nicaragua's Popular Sandinista Army (EPS) expanded to five times its original size with Soviet and Cuban aid, soaking up more than 50 percent of the government budget by the late 1980s. The Salvadoran military quadrupled its forces during the decade, but was still just barely able to hold its own in the country's protracted civil war. Honduras became a home for three armies—its own armed forces, the *contras*, and U.S. troops. Adopting the type of national-security doctrine practiced by the most brutal military regimes in Latin America and bolstered by a generous flow of U.S. military aid, the Honduran military and police forces more than doubled in the 1980s. The Guatemalan army tripled in size over the decade and set up military outposts in the most isolated reaches of the highlands.

Over the 1980s the collective strength of the Central American

armies had increased by some 125,000 troops, and the military accounted for about 40 percent of government expenditures in El Salvador, Nicaragua, Guatemala, and Honduras. The region became an
armed camp fortified with the latest in military weaponry.

After the resolution of the Nicaraguan conflict and as the newly
elected presidents of the Central American nations tried to find solutions to the economic crisis, antimilitary sentiment increased in the
region. Demands that the armies be cut back predictably raised the ire
of the generals, who alleged that increased leftist subversion required
continued high levels of military expenditures. Only in Nicaragua have
troop levels been substantially reduced. And even if all the current
conflicts were resolved and troop levels were significantly reduced, the
accumulated inventory of instruments of war would present a threat to
regional peace well into the next century.

Changing Fortunes of Guerrilla Struggles

The July 1979 Sandinista victory brought an end to armed insurgency
in Nicaragua and instilled new hope in leftist rebel forces in Guatemala
and El Salvador. However, despite repeated government claims that
these two guerrilla armies were on the run, the Guatemalan National
Revolutionary Unity (URNG) and the Farabundo Martí National Liberation Front (FMLN) in El Salvador were still presenting strong challenges to government armies at the start of the 1990s. In Honduras
small leftist guerrilla groups launched isolated attacks against U.S. and
Honduran armed forces during the 1980s. Although not representing
a serious threat, the actions of the Honduran guerrillas may be the
precursor of more extensive armed conflict in years to come, especially
if human-rights abuses continue and misery spreads.

The anti-Sandinista counterrevolutionary forces organized and supplied by the United States emerged as a serious threat in 1983 but were
largely defeated by 1988. Hanging on with U.S. funds, the *contras*
remained armed even after the FSLN had turned over the government
to the U.S.-backed National Organized Union (UNO) coalition.

Since the late 1980s the armed left in Central America has had to
confront dramatic political and economic changes in the region and
around the globe. The collapse of the socialist bloc, the steady weakening and isolation of Cuba, and the electoral defeat of the Sandinistas
did not bode well for guerrilla armies led by Marxist revolutionaries.
Clearly, leftist movements that sought to win power solely through
military means could count on little international support and would be
unable to depend on aid from socialist countries. Nevertheless, the

dissolution of the socialist bloc and the ill fate of revolutionary governments have not resulted in the demise of leftist guerrilla movements in
Central America. Although they are associated with international socialist networks and have received foreign training and logistical assistance, the URNG and FMLN have never been dependent on arms from
either the socialist bloc or Nicaragua, contrary to such repeated assertions by Washington.

SOCIETY AND ENVIRONMENT

War, political turmoil, and a faltering regional economy have taken a
heavy toll on the Central American society and environment. All the
main social indicators are falling as governments slash health and
education budgets and adopt economic policies that adversely affect
the poor. Civil strife and the economic crisis have caused more than two
million Central Americans to abandon their homes, nearly 90 percent
fleeing to Mexico or the United States.[4] At least 160,000 Central
Americans have suffered war-related deaths since 1980. Landlessness,
population pressures, and the drive to increase exports present a common threat to the region's already badly depleted natural resources.

At the heart of the social conflicts in rural Central America is the
grossly uneven distribution of land. The concentration of land in the
hands of ranchers and the agroexport elite forces the rural population
onto smaller and more eroded hillside plots. This lack of opportunity
has pushed *campesino* families from rural areas into urban slums.
About 44 percent of the region's population now lives in cities—a
number that will rise to more than 50 percent by the year 2000 if
current migration trends persist.[5]

The economic crisis means that thirteen of every twenty Central
Americans find themselves unemployed or underemployed. The minimum wage in Guatemala and El Salvador, adjusted for inflation, has
declined nearly 40 percent since 1980. As jobs become scarce and per
capita income declines, social indicators of health, nutrition, and education also worsen. In the face of widespread layoffs and brutal repression in some countries, labor unions have had an increasingly difficult
time protecting the interests of the workforce. Only in the public sector
has unionism expanded. A new threat to the labor movement has been
the rapid growth of owner-controlled *solidarista* associations promoted
by U.S. investors and local business owners.

This poverty and the associated lack of education contribute to the
region's population explosion. Since 1960 the population has doubled

and is expected to double again in twenty-five years if current growth rates continue. Research has indicated that only when families achieve economic security and infant mortality rates begin to decrease will population rates start to decline. Unfortunately, Central Americans in the 1980s saw their standard of living decline while infant mortality rates began to climb (see Table Four).

For every thousand live births in the United States, ten infants die in their first year. In Guatemala and other countries, nearly eighty infants die for every thousand live births. Of every thousand children that survive infancy, 120 die before they reach the age of five. Two-thirds of the region's children are malnourished. Forty percent of Central Americans have no access to organized health care, and 50 percent lack access to safe drinking water.[6] Guatemala, Honduras, Nicaragua, and El Salvador have the highest birth rates in Latin America, with women in these countries averaging six or more births. Although abortion is illegal, induced abortion is thought to account for the highest proportion of maternal deaths and is the most frequent cause of hospital admission.[7]

Chronic diseases related to human behavioral patterns (diet, smoking, stress, and accidents) are the major causes of death in North America, the Caribbean, and temperate South America, while the major causes of mortality in Central America are war and infectious diseases related to environment and nutritional status.[8] Panama, Belize, and Costa Rica are the exceptions to this pattern.

Adult illiteracy ranges from 45 percent in Guatemala to 7 percent in Costa Rica. This widespread lack of education is one reason for the region's deplorable state of health. Literate women, for example, are better able to act on health care instructions and typically give birth to healthier babies. Not only does illiteracy obstruct economic and social development but it also undermines the political process. With no education or ability to read, many rural Central Americans select candidates according to the color of their party banners.

The Religious Transformation of Central America

The turmoil and violence of the last decade has disrupted Central American society and resulted in the emergence of new social forces. Changing religious beliefs, rising crime, and cultural disintegration have been among the results. Capitalizing on the social chaos, pentecostal churches have drawn believers away from the Catholic Church in droves: At least one-third of Guatemalans now belong to evangelical churches. Although accelerated by the region's economic and political crisis, the religious transformation of Central America has deeper historical and social roots. The institutional Catholic Church, constrained by its rigid hierarchies, paternalistic traditions, and abstruse dogmas, has proved unable to respond to the new emotional and spiritual needs of the changing Central American society. For many, the Catholic Church represents the feudal past while the evangelical churches are part of a modernizing trend that preaches individual salvation.

The long-term political implications of this religious upheaval are difficult to predict. For the time being, the Catholic Church remains the most important social institution in Central America. In some countries, notably El Salvador and Guatemala, it has used this position of influence to advance peaceful solutions to conflicts and to speak forcefully on behalf of the disenfranchised. Except in Nicaragua, where Cardinal Obando y Bravo allied himself with the *contras*, the Church has not clearly positioned itself on one side of a violent conflict. For the most part, the Catholic Church has backed away from its former ties with the oligarchy and acted as a force for moderation and social peace, careful not to identify itself with the militant voices of the popular movements. The new evangelical churches, in contrast, have served as a popular foundation for political conservatism, most clearly illustrated by the Ríos Montt phenomenon in Guatemala. Over time, however, more progressive tendencies within the evangelical community might emerge and be able to steer the movement away from its present reactionary direction.

Women and a Changing Society

As elsewhere in the Third World, women are the poorest of the poor. They are disproportionately represented among the region's malnourished, illiterate, and unemployed. Despite the increasing number of women entering the workforce and the high percentage of female-headed households (about 20 percent), women are still commonly regarded as being only marginal participants in the economy. Women often are excluded from rural cooperatives and rarely are found among the leadership of labor unions. They are routinely paid less than men, and are commonly denied inheritance rights to land and excluded from the benefits of agrarian-reform programs.[9]

Since the 1920s women's organizations in Central America have been fighting for such causes as the right to vote, protective family codes, and fair employment practices. In the 1980s there was an explosion in women's organizing as part of the broader popular movement. Women formed human-rights organizations, peasant associations, popular-education groups, and squatters' organizations, as well as women's health centers and other organizations focusing on gender issues.

The Popular Challenge

Repression in the late 1970s and early 1980s laid waste to the popular movements in Guatemala and El Salvador, but by the mid-1980s peasants, workers, students, and other sectors began to establish new organizations. While falling short of their former strength, the popular movements in those two countries represent powerful voices for peace and economic justice. In Honduras, the popular sectors became increasingly organized in the late 1980s as they joined together in new coalitions to protest government austerity policies, U.S. intervention, and escalating repression.

In Nicaragua, the country's popular sectors largely identified with the Sandinista government, especially in the early 1980s. But as the economic crisis and war stretched into the late 1980s, popular discontent grew and anti-Sandinista groups emerged, most with U.S. backing. Following its electoral defeat in early 1990, the FSLN will again attempt to shape a broad popular movement that will return them to power. Key to the Sandinistas' success will be their willingness to democratize the party structure, open it up to new leadership, and make the party responsive to popular demands.

Only in Nicaragua is the popular movement so closely linked to a powerful political party. Elsewhere in the region, with the partial exception of El Salvador, the popular movement is largely marginalized from the political process, with the political parties representing more the personal and financial interests of their leaders than the concerns of the vast majority.

Although the popular sectors became increasingly organized in the late 1980s, these organizations failed to push forward an alternative political and economic agenda for the region. Generally, the popular movement in Central America is led by social activists and union leaders, often of leftist political persuasion. It supports democratization but calls for a more participatory democracy in which national and local policy-making reflect the pressing needs and concerns of poor people. In the eyes of many popular leaders, the present electoral democratization is just another elite game played by rich people in concert with the military.

It is the economy rather than politics on which the popular movements have focused their attention. Economic policy over the past decade has largely been an assault on those sectors of the population least able to defend themselves. While aware that structural adjustment programs are needed, the popular movement rejects the concept that what is good for the wealthy is good for the whole society. Instead it argues that what is good for the poor—higher wages, education, health services, agrarian reform—benefits the entire society by sharing the wealth and creating a larger class of consumers. As the obverse of the neoliberal model, the popular movement proposes an economic and political model based on the "logic of the majority."[10]

The popular movement may have the logic of the majority and the force of morality behind it, but that is not enough. It needs to develop a cohesive agenda that reaches out and incorporates that majority. Rather than being defensive and reactive, the popular movement must develop a mature and workable vision of society—a vision that effectively counters the simple but powerful logic of neoliberal philosophy. To increase its power to shape events in the region, the popular movement must also confront its own weaknesses: its sectarianism, its reliance on disproven Marxist formulas, its sexism and racism, the absence of grass-roots organizing, and the lack of internal democracy.

Threats to the Environment

As a bridge and transitional zone for tropical and temperate life forms from North and South America, Central America hosts some of the hemisphere's richest and most diverse ecosystems. This lush environment has been increasingly threatened by ecological degradation caused by deforestation, war-related destruction, soil erosion, pesticide contamination, and industrial pollutants.

The environmental crisis cannot be separated from the military, political, and economic crises in the region. War has devastated broad stretches of woodlands in Guatemala, El Salvador, Honduras, and Nicaragua. As part of wide-ranging counterinsurgency campaigns, soldiers murder forestry officials and park guards, scorched-earth sweeps level villages and farmlands, armies bulldoze penetration roads into isolated mountain regions, massive military maneuvers devastate remote and fragile environments, and military chiefs authorize unsustainable resource-extraction schemes to finance military spending or increase their personal wealth.[11]

As hunger and poverty spread and economic instability deepens, the cycle of resource exploitation, underdevelopment, political turmoil, and war intensifies. The cycle begins with the inequitable patterns of resource and income distribution, which result in widespread deprivation. Poverty and underdevelopment then contribute to rapid population growth and increased pressure on natural resources. The environment is being carelessly exploited both by agroexport interests ravenous for easy profits and by the poor population hungry to satisfy daily needs. As is becoming increasingly apparent, the depletion of Central America's resources far exceeds renewal rates.

This environmental crisis further destabilizes the regional economy, which leads to increased poverty and sharpening class divisions. All this fuels war and political turmoil, which in turn hasten the cycle of misery, underdevelopment, and resource depletion. In his valuable study on the Central American environment, H. Jeffrey Leonard writes, "The challenge for all countries of the region is to break out of this cycle of crisis and to forge a stable sociopolitical consensus conducive to long-term, sustainable economic development that benefits all socioeconomic groups."[12]

Deforestation, perhaps the worst symptom of the region's ecological degradation, is an ominously modern process. Virtually all of Central America was originally covered by forests, but less than 40 percent of the land area remains forested today and little primary forest is still standing. The region is undergoing one of the world's fastest deforestation rates; two-thirds of all the forests cleared since Central America was settled by the Spanish were razed after 1950.[13]

Central America is losing 500–1,000 square kilometers of its remaining tropical rain forests every year. The exceptions to this trend are Belize, where development pressures are not as high, and El Salvador, where all the primary forests are already gone.[14] Reforestation and the establishment of reserves are beginning to slow the fast pace of deforestation, but unless there are dramatic changes the forests outside the few established reserves will be gone in two decades (see Table Five). Regionally, only 7 percent of the deforested lands are replanted each year.[15]

New reserves and national parks are being established throughout the region. In Costa Rica, nearly 20 percent of the land area is classified as wildlands, but, as in other countries, the Costa Rican reserves are not being adequately protected. Because of the accelerated deforestation rate outside of strictly protected areas, Costa Rica may have little primary forest outside its national parks by the year 2000.

Deforestation is only the most dramatic sign of the region's environmental crisis. Wildlife and marine ecosystems are also under attack. Over the last decade, catches of the two commercially important species—lobster and conch—have dropped 41 percent and 27 percent, respectively.[16] Mangrove forests, which once lined the coasts, are

rapidly disappearing. Currently, all cat and monkey species are threatened, as are the tapir, river otter, white-tailed deer, manatee, highland
squirrel, and giant anteater.[17] Furthermore, destruction of the natural
environment is threatening both the native bird species and the many
migrating birds that winter in the region.

The disruption of the region's ecological balance also has a human
side. Polluted water is a leading cause of death in Guatemala, Honduras, and Nicaragua. Central America has few sewage-treatment systems, and most sewage is dumped untreated into rivers, lakes, and
coastal waters. Lead pollution from uncontrolled vehicle emissions,
industrial accidents, contamination of the groundwater with agro-
chemicals, and pesticide poisonings have become serious threats to the
quality of life in the region.[18]

The depletion and degradation of the region's natural resources also
present an immediate threat to the livelihood of most Central Americans. With few mineral resources and little industry, Central America
is, more than most regions, critically dependent on its natural resources. More than 55 percent of the workforce is found in the agricultural sector, and over half of its export income comes from
unprocessed agricultural products. The environmental crises of heavy
soil erosion, polluted water, and the rapid loss of watersheds are also
economic crises.[19] Throughout the region dozens of new environmental groups have formed to sound the alarm about the consequences of
continued environmental destruction. Some are calling for do-it-
yourself remedies such as tree-planting and water conservation, while
national environmental associations are calling for the creation of new
reserves and parks. Concerns about the degradation of the environment are also being expressed by *campesino* groups, popular coalitions,
and guerrilla forces.

U.S. FOREIGN POLICY AND ASSISTANCE PROGRAMS

With the Monroe Doctrine of 1823 the United States declared its
hegemony over the newly emerging Latin American republics. It was
not, however, until the 1860s that the United States cemented its complete domination of Central America. The British, who had claimed a
major role in the isthmus, retreated before the reckless advance of U.S.
filibusters, financiers, and marines. A transisthmian railroad was built
in Panama with U.S. capital, and in 1867 Washington violated a previous accord with Great Britain by arranging for exclusive rights of

transit across Nicaragua. Only the small colony of British Honduras remained under British control.

By the turn of the century the United States had begun a policy of economic imperialism as a result of its tremendous industrial growth. In Central America, banana enclaves were carved out of tropical forests, construction began on the Panama Canal, and new ports, utility companies, and railroads were launched by U.S. investors. Always ready to protect economic interests, Washington often resorted to gunboat diplomacy—the practice of sending in warships and marines to "protect American lives and property."

Augusto César Sandino, a scrappy Nicaraguan nationalist and guerrilla commander, led the first indigenous challenge to U.S. authority in the region. After seven years of counterinsurgency warfare, Sandino was finally stopped in 1934—not by the U.S. marines but by the treachery of Anastasio Somoza García. After inviting him to dinner, Somoza had Sandino murdered on his way home. Installed by the United States as the chief of the newly created National Guard, Somoza went on to establish a family dictatorship in Nicaragua that lasted until 1979.

The next major threat to perceived U.S. national interests came in 1950 in the form of a democratically elected government in Guatemala. Offended by the progressive policies of the Jacobo Arbenz government, particularly a modest land-reform program, the CIA teamed up with the United Fruit Company and Guatemalan rightists to topple the government in 1954. The new military government reversed the reforms and presided over several decades of repression and counterinsurgency—the hallmarks of government in Guatemala.

The next two decades were a time of steady economic growth in Central America. Cotton, sugar, and beef joined the traditional agroexports of coffee and bananas. The new Central American Common Market spurred intraregional trade and industrial development by raising new barriers to foreign imports and facilitating the marketing of locally produced goods. Predictably, however, much of the new development—known as import-substitution industrialization—was controlled by U.S. investors who moved their pharmaceutical, chemical, and other factories into the region.

Paralleling this new surge in U.S. investment and trade from 1955 to the late 1970s was an expanding U.S. foreign-aid program. Stunned by the Cuban revolution of 1959, Washington employed a two-pronged program of military and economic aid to ward off revolutionary threats in Central America. The region's military and police were shaped into professional security forces with U.S. aid and counterinsurgency training, while the CIA worked covertly with secret police and paramilitary units that became the feared death squads. In Guatemala, U.S. military advisers joined with the local military in a bloody counterinsurgency campaign in the 1960s that resulted in more than ten thousand dead.

Under the aegis of the Alliance for Progress, the Agency for International Development (AID) managed an array of economic-aid projects designed to promote economic and social development conducive to increased U.S. trade and investment. But AID's program was not limited to economic objectives. Especially after the New Directions foreign-aid legislation of 1973, health, education, and food-distribution programs designed to satisfy basic needs were initiated. Although humanitarian in nature, many of these programs were inaugurated with explicit political objectives, namely to pacify potentially rebellious Central American communities.

Central America Captures U.S. Foreign Policy Attention

It was not until the late 1970s, however, that Central America became a leading concern of U.S. foreign policy. The renegotiation of the 1903 Panama Canal Treaty raised the hackles of U.S. ultraconservatives such as Ronald Reagan. However, the new treaties signed in 1977 counted on the support of the U.S.-based multinational corporations and the foreign-policy establishment. Just as the controversy of the canal treaties was fading, the Sandinista challenge to the U.S.-backed Somoza dictatorship in Nicaragua once again focused U.S. foreign-policy attention on Central America. The Sandinista victory in July 1979 was closely followed by the outbreak of civil war in El Salvador and a major counterinsurgency campaign in Guatemala.

Suddenly there was serious trouble in "Washington's backyard." The Carter administration responded with increased U.S. aid and diplomatic initiatives, but it was the Reagan administration that made events in Central America a test of U.S. resolve to maintain its historic role as the world's policeman. Former Secretary of State Henry Kissinger asserted that "if we cannot manage in Central America, it will be impossible to convince threatened nations in the Persian Gulf and in other places that we know how to manage the global equilibrium."[20]

Once again, U.S. national security and interests were threatened by political changes in Central America, a region that represented just 2 percent of U.S. worldwide trade and investment. In persuading the U.S. public and Congress to support U.S. intervention in the region, President Reagan warned, "Soviet military theorists want to destroy our capacity to resupply Western Europe in case of an emergency. They want to tie down our attention and forces on our own southern border and so limit our capacity to act in more distant places."[21]

Asking for increased U.S. military aid to El Salvador in 1984, the president framed U.S. security interests this way: "Central America is America; it's our doorstep. And it has become the stage for a bold attempt by the Soviet Union, Cuba, and Nicaragua to install communism by force throughout the hemisphere. . . . This communist subversion poses the threat that 100 million people from Panama to the open border on our south could come under the control of pro-Soviet regimes."[22]

Kissinger Commission's Undue Optimism

More than anticommunist hyperbole was needed to secure full public and congressional commitment for the Reagan foreign policy in the region. To establish the foundation for his Central American policies, Reagan called together the National Bipartisan Commission on Central America (Kissinger Commission).

In its 1984 report, the Kissinger Commission contended that foreign-supported elements were using the region's widespread poverty and social injustice to gain popular support against the region's established governments. It argued that economic aid was needed to stabilize governments and spur development, while the objective of military assistance was "to create a shield to protect democratization and growth."[23] The White House immediately reformulated the commission's recommendations into the Central America Democracy, Peace, and Development Initiative Act, a legislative package of military and economic aid that was approved almost in its entirety by Congress. This initiative, which focused on El Salvador, Honduras, Guatemala, Costa Rica, and to a lesser extent Belize, was later extended past its original 1989 termination point to 1992.

During the 1980s Central America became the recipient of an extraordinary flow of U.S. foreign aid. The region ranked second after Israel in per capita economic aid and received 65 percent of all U.S. aid to Latin America and the Caribbean.[24] In the 1981–1990 period, Central America received more than $9 billion ($7.7 billion in economic aid and $1.6 billion in military aid), El Salvador being the leading recipient. Even much of the economic aid was security-related. In El Salvador, for example, three-quarters of the U.S. economic-aid package was used for war-related expenditures, according to the Arms Control and Foreign Policy Caucus of the U.S. Congress.

Bilateral aid is, however, only one dimension of intensified U.S. activity in the region (see Tables Six and Seven). Also part of the picture in the 1980s were major U.S. or joint military maneuvers, expanded trade and investment credit programs, U.S.-supported multilateral loans, and at least $390 million in military and other aid to the *contras*[25] (see Table Eight).

It was assumed that large injections of U.S. assistance would pacify the region by the end of 1986, allowing Central America to resume its former pace of economic growth. By the late 1980s the region would be experiencing, according to commission predictions, 3 percent annual per capita growth. This recovery would be based on an economic-stabilization program backed by AID and a development strategy that stressed private-sector initiatives and nontraditional export production.

As the region entered the 1990s, some progress had been made toward a peaceful settlement of the region's conflicts, but as a result of regional initiatives, not U.S. efforts. The thesis that the regional turmoil was largely directed and financed by foreign communist agitators had been proven false. There were no Soviet bases in Nicaragua, and there was no evidence of any substantial Soviet, Cuban, or Nicaraguan aid to the guerrilla forces in Guatemala or El Salvador.

It was the U.S. government, not the Soviet bloc, that had been fueling the militarization of the region during the 1980s by underwriting guerrilla insurgencies in Nicaragua, building new bases in Honduras, and carrying out an invasion of Panama. The Cubans and the Soviets had backed the Sandinistas' counterinsurgency campaign while the United States provided military aid to the six other nations in the region. Military aid to Nicaragua from Cuba and the Soviet Union was eliminated by late 1989, but U.S. military aid and advisers continued to flow to the region into the 1990s. Intended to provide a protective "shield" for fragile democracies and economic recovery, U.S. military aid has instead promoted military solutions to internal political conflicts and obstructed the full democratization of Central America. The Berlin Wall crumbled and the Cold War melted down, but U.S. intervention in Central America continued to be driven by anticommunist fears and imperialist logic.

The Kissinger Commission's economic projections proved to be wildly optimistic. Only in the case of Costa Rica was there positive per capita economic growth in the late 1980s. The unprecedented levels of U.S. aid may have provided Guatemala, Honduras, and El Salvador with a measure of short-term stability, but neither this assistance nor U.S. development programs sparked the predicted economic rebound.

What growth these countries did experience was exceeded by the rate of population growth. At the end of the 1980s, the region's per capita income had regressed to 1970 levels. Despite massive U.S. aid, private-sector investment remained stagnant and the value of the region's exports was no greater than it had been a decade earlier.

Washington did stand firmly behind the transition from military to civilian rule. Though a step forward, this democratization process has shown itself to be more procedural than substantive. Elections have been largely free of fraud, but left-of-center parties and organizations have been given little or no room in the electoral process. Although they have relinquished the formal reins of power, the armed forces in Guatemala, Honduras, and El Salvador have remained the superior partner in the military-civil alliances controlling those nations.

Hailed by Washington as "the decade of democracy," the 1980s were in fact the bloodiest period in Central American history. Elections followed constitutionally mandated schedules, voters went to the polls as planned, and presidential sashes passed on to opposition candidates. But all the while, civil wars raged, priests and nuns were massacred, popular activists disappeared, and Central Americans died in record numbers from war and poverty. Despite U.S. aid to strengthen the region's judicial institutions, no military or police officers were convicted and sentenced for human-rights abuses—except in Nicaragua.

Aid for Political and Economic Stabilization

Part of the problem with the U.S. economic-aid program has been how the funds were divided. Most aid came in the form of balance-of-payments assistance that neither the recipient governments nor the Central American people ever saw. This aid, largely in the form of Economic Support Funds (ESF), was simply recycled to pay the foreign debt and U.S. suppliers. Of the total aid package (1981–1990), ESF assistance comprised 62 percent. Another 11 percent was accounted for by the PL480 Title I food-aid program, also designed as balance-of-payments assistance. Development Assistance funds made up only 24 percent of the total package, with PL480 Title II distributive food programs accounting for the 3 percent balance.

Economic stabilization was clearly AID's top priority. Yet even when U.S. funds were marked for development, improving the lot of the poor and hungry was not the chief focus. Instead, reflecting Ronald Reagan's "trickle-down" economics, most of the U.S. development programs were designed to assist the private-sector elite on the theory that the more money the business community made, the better off the poor would be. New private investment would translate into new jobs, and the wealth would trickle down. In this region characterized by stark class divisions and a long tradition of oligarchic control, AID's promotion of a modernizing business class also came with the ideological conviction that "private enterprise produces liberty," a slogan propagated by AID-funded business lobbies.

Foreign aid means more than dollars. It is also leverage. Rather than using this leverage to promote social reforms, the U.S. government pressured recipient governments to adopt economic policies that favored foreign investors and the local business elite. Rather than insisting that governments enforce minimum-wage laws or extend social services, AID told governments to privatize public utilities, revise labor codes in favor of business interests, and encourage nonunion sweatshop manufacturing. Most harmful to the general public welfare, however, was the U.S. practice of making aid contingent on the implementation of structural-adjustment programs designed to close fiscal deficits and ease trade imbalances while encouraging governments to pay off their external debts. Because of their emphasis on austerity measures and integration into the global market, these programs have boosted the fortunes of the export-oriented business class while casting millions of Central Americans into economic desperation.

The broad outline of U.S. foreign policy in Central America over the past decade was for the most part a continuation of a long history of military intervention, imperial arrogance, anticommunist agitation, political manipulation, and the primacy of U.S. economic interests in the region. But there have also been distinct variations in U.S. foreign-policy strategy in Central America. Whereas in the past Washington was content with a triple alliance of local oligarchs, generals, and the U.S. Embassy to control the Central American countries, a slightly more sophisticated economic and political system was installed in the 1980s. No longer were the traditional oligarchies the favored allies of U.S. economic interests. Although not directly confronting the landed robber-barons (except as part of the counterinsurgency-motivated agrarian reform in El Salvador), Washington chose to promote a more modernizing private-sector elite as its political and economic allies. As in the past, however, the emphasis was not on the expansion of the local market but on exports, whether agricultural products or assembled manufactured goods.

Until recently, Washington was content to let the generals, together with the oligarchs, govern the string of republics. But popular challenges and international pressure no longer made that a viable option. Instead, Washington promoted—indeed funded—the transition to civilian rule. The new civilian administrations proved more credible and effective instruments of U.S. policy in the region. They blocked popular challenges while constraining neither the military nor the business classes. At first the U.S.-allied governments were simply pliable instruments of U.S. policy, but by the early 1990s the heads of state had themselves become, with a couple of exceptions, the advocates of the most conservative economic and political sectors in the region.

The United States entered the 1980s with the remnants of a Third World development policy that recognized the need for land reform, more extensive government social services, and basic-needs programs. It also acknowledged the necessity of support for domestic producers. But that commitment was largely discarded in favor of a philosophy of development that focused almost exclusively on business interests. What remained of the earlier concern for the lower classes were U.S.-funded social investment programs, including food distribution and temporary public-works projects, designed to soften the brutal impact of structural-adjustment programs. Charity and small development projects by churches and private voluntary agencies were also expected to pacify the marginalized sectors of peasants and unemployed slum residents.

Despite the changing economic and political picture in the world, evidence such as the invasion of Panama, an unwavering commitment to the Salvadoran military, and expanding intervention in narcotics trafficking demonstrates that Washington remains intent on controlling events in its backyard. Indeed, the breakup of the socialist bloc and fall of the Soviet Union as a preeminent world power gave it a newfound impunity to intervene as it would.

It is true that Washington is limited in how much economic aid it can use to control events in Central America. But it is getting more punch for fewer bucks. No longer preoccupied by Nicaragua, the United States has become less concerned about the social stability of other nations in the region, and consequently more apt to insist on the immediate implementation of harsh neoliberal measures. With neoliberal allies now installed in the national palaces, huge sums of U.S. aid are no longer needed to guarantee that the U.S. economic agenda is also the agenda of the region's governments. In fact, without such a large cushion of U.S. aid, governments are less able to resist pressure for structural adjustment from the World Bank and the International Monetary Fund.

In the face of a multipolar world of coalescing economic blocs, the United States is not backing away from its imperial past in Central America. Instead it finds itself compelled to reassert its dominance over trade and investment in the region because of the isthmus's new geoeconomic significance as the inevitable link between a Canada-U.S.-Mexico bloc and the rest of Latin America.[26]

Anticommunism has not yet been discarded as an imperative for U.S. intervention and control in the region. It now shares its place in the rhetoric of U.S. intervention, however, with the war against drugs, the fight to install and protect U.S.-guided democratic governments, and the crusade to break down all foreign barriers to U.S. trade and investment. The strategic use of political aid and economic pressure has become an important new weapon of U.S. foreign policy, but military measures have proved to be a ready alternative.

Consequences and Lessons

All the consequences of the past decade of U.S. foreign policy in Central America will not be entirely clear until later in the 1990s. It seems certain, however, that the economic and political crisis is not yet over—and may in fact worsen. Economically, the region became mired in a deep depression. The United States provided short-term economic stabilization, but its recovery formulas—privatization, export promotion, and structural adjustment—proved inadequate. By accentuating inequitable patterns of distribution and making countries more vulnerable to domination, these conservative remedies will likely contribute to the long-term instability of the region.

Central America clearly needs a large infusion of foreign aid and capital. To be effective, however, an economic-recovery program should not be linked to one donor nation's foreign policy. A multilateral effort that stresses regional solutions is needed instead. Sharply contrasting with the bilateral programs pushed by Washington that focus on each country's relationship with the United States, the European Community has sponsored regional programs to increase the food security of the entire isthmus and boost the Central American Common Market.

But foreign aid, even if managed multilaterally, will be largely wasted if the debt crisis and terms-of-trade crunch persist. As long as they are obligated to spend 30 percent to 40 percent of their export earnings on debt payments, the Central American nations will not be able to generate significant economic growth. The way to address the region's mounting balance-of-payments problem is not simply to inject dollars into the central banks of the Central American countries. Rather, the debt itself must be substantially reduced.

The development of Central America is also blocked by the shrinking world market and declining prices for unprocessed agricultural commodities. At the same time that Central American countries are facing smaller markets and lower prices for cotton, sugar, and other commodities, they are finding that the prices for essential imports such as medicines, fuel, machinery, and chemicals are rapidly rising.

With the encouragement of the United States and other foreign donors, the Central American nations have attempted to increase their export offering by focusing more on nontraditional exports, such as winter vegetables, flowers, and assembled clothing and electronic products. Although nontraditional exports have found new markets in the United States and other industrialized nations, the limits and weaknesses of this development strategy are becoming apparent. Generally, only the larger producers have access to the capital and technology necessary for the transition to nontraditional agricultural production. The increasing emphasis on export production and free trade has victimized the small basic-grain farmers by depriving them of government credits and market guarantees while forcing them to compete against cheap grain imports. Even those farmers who successfully cultivate nontraditional products are finding that they are often unable to market their produce because of increasing protectionism abroad and expanding competition from growers in other Central American countries and Mexico. Another problem is that such nontraditional exports as broccoli require large amounts of imported pesticides and fertilizer, thereby further draining foreign-exchange reserves.

In the manufacturing sector, the export-processing zones established to assemble jeans and bras for the U.S. market bring little foreign exchange into the region since none of the clothing parts or machinery used by these manufacturers is purchased within the country. They do provide employment but only at minimum wage and in union-free environments.

The production of nontraditional exports can certainly be part of the solution to the region's underdevelopment. But if the region is to resolve its economic crisis, this renewed emphasis on export production will have to be part of a more balanced development strategy that stresses regional cooperation, human rights, food security, debt relief, and better terms of trade.

If the United States and other industrialized nations are truly interested in the economic progress of Central America, they will need to find ways to pay higher prices for the region's coffee and bananas and to open their own markets to more Central American products. As it is, however, the United States in its crusade for global free trade has helped undermine the very international associations, such as the Union of Banana Exporting Countries, founded to give producer countries a fair price and has routinely erected its own tariff barriers to protect domestic producers, notably in the sugar and textile industries.

The electoral defeat of the Sandinistas in 1990 was tallied as a victory for U.S. policy and regional security. Washington's intervention did seriously set back the Nicaraguan revolution and other popular struggles in the region. During the 1980s, Washington also succeeded in bestowing on allied nations a certain degree of economic stability. Overall, though, the aggressive foreign policy of the United States appears to have done little to ensure the long-term economic and political stability of the region. In fact, the repression of popular challenges and the implementation of a narrowly conceived model of economic growth have restricted the region's options for development and progress. The insistence on military solutions and "magic of the marketplace" economics ensures that the crisis of Central America won't go away any time soon.

REFERENCE NOTES

[1] Raúl Marín, "La Nueva Derecha en Centroamérica," *Pensamiento Propio*, June 1990.

[2] "Whither Central America? Coopted Negotiation or Participatory Democracy," *Envío* (Central America Historical Institute), May 1990.

[3] Good sources on the Central American economy include Victor Bulmer-Thomas, *The Political Economy of Central America Since 1920* (Cambridge: Cambridge University Press, 1987); John Weeks, *The Economies of Central America* (New York: Holmes and Meier, 1985); and the Sanford Commission Report, *Central American Recovery and Development Task Force Report to the International Commission for Central American Recovery and Development*, William Ascher and Ann Hubbard, eds. (Durham, NC: Duke University Press, 1989).

[4] Sergio Aguayo, "Displaced Persons and Central American Recuperation and Development," *Central American Recovery and Development Task Force Report*, op. cit., p. 24.

[5] Inter-American Development Bank, *Economic and Social Progress in Latin America: 1989 Report* (Washington, D.C.: IDB, 1988).

[6] John Freiberger, "Health Care in Central America," *Central American Recovery and Development Task Force Report*, op. cit., p. 215.

[7] Inter-American Commission on Women, *Status of Women in the Americas at the End of the Decade (1976–1985): An Overview and General Strategy for the Year*

2000 (Washington, D.C.: United Nations/Organization of American States, 1985).

8 H. Jeffrey Leonard, *Natural Resources and Economic Development in Central America* (New Brunswick, NJ: Transaction Books, 1987), p. 47.

9 An excellent overview of women's status and problems in Central America is provided in Sally Yudelman, "Access and Opportunity for Women in Central America: A Challenge for Peace," *Central American Recovery and Development Task Force Report*, op. cit., pp. 235–54.

10 The term *logic of the majority* was popularized in Nicaragua but is also used to describe the agenda of the popular movements elsewhere in the region. For a longer discussion, see "Whither Central America? Coopted Negotiation or Participatory Democracy," loc. cit.

11 Robert G. Healy, "A Reconnaissance of Conservation and Development Issues in Central America," *Central American Recovery and Development Task Force Report*, op. cit., p. 140.

12 Leonard, op. cit., p. xv.

13 Ibid., p. 117.

14 Ibid., p. 119.

15 Ibid., p. 171.

16 Ibid., p. xii.

17 Environmental Project on Central America (EPOCA), *Green Paper No. 2* (San Francisco: EPOCA, 1986).

18 Healy, op. cit., p. 111.

19 For an excellent discussion of the connections between conservation and development, see Leonard, op. cit., p. 169–94.

20 *New York Times*, July 19, 1983.

21 "Strategic Importance of El Salvador and Central America," a March 10, 1983, speech by Ronald Reagan published as *Current Policy No. 464* (Washington, D.C.: United States Department of State, 1983).

22 "U.S. Interests in Central America," a May 9, 1984, speech by Ronald Reagan published as *Current Policy No. 576* (Washington, D.C.: United States Department of State, 1984).

23 *Report of the National Bipartisan Commission on Central America* (Washington, D.C.: U.S. Government Printing Office, January 1984).

24 K. Larry Storrs, "Central America's Economic Development: Options for U.S. Assistance," *CRS Review*, February 1989. Average per capita aid for Guatemala, Honduras, El Salvador, and Costa Rica in the late 1980s was $52, rising to $97 per capita for El Salvador, while Israel received $711 in per capita U.S. assistance each year.

[25] Arms Control and Foreign Policy Caucus of the U.S. Congress, *Previous U.S. and U.S.-Coordinated Aid to the Contras* (Washington, D.C., January 1988, updated November 1989).

[26] See Xavier Gorostiaga's preface to the Spanish edition of *Central America: The Future of Economic Integration*, George Irvin and Stuart Holland, eds. (Managua: CRIES, 1990).

TABLE ONE
Central America

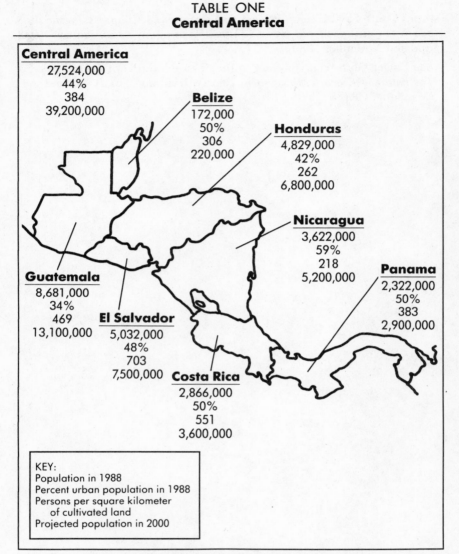

Central America
27,524,000
44%
384
39,200,000

Belize
172,000
50%
306
220,000

Honduras
4,829,000
42%
262
6,800,000

Nicaragua
3,622,000
59%
218
5,200,000

Panama
2,322,000
50%
383
2,900,000

Guatemala
8,681,000
34%
469
13,100,000

El Salvador
5,032,000
48%
703
7,500,000

Costa Rica
2,866,000
50%
551
3,600,000

KEY:
Population in 1988
Percent urban population in 1988
Persons per square kilometer
   of cultivated land
Projected population in 2000

SOURCES: Inter-American Development Bank, *Economic and Social Progress in Latin America: 1989 Report* (New York: 1989); H. Jeffrey Leonard, *Natural Resources and Economic Development in Central America* (New Brunswick, NJ: Transaction Books, 1987).

TABLE TWO
Average Yields of Principal Crops
Kilograms per Hectare 1979–1981

	Costa Rica	El Salvador	Guatemala	Honduras	Nicaragua	Panama	United States
Coffee	1,300	900	600	600	600	200	1,000
Sugar	53,200	73,400	68,900	33,700	72,600	54,200	84,200
Cotton	1,500	2,100	3,900	2,200	2,000	NA	1,500
Corn	1,600	1,900	1,500	1,000	1,100	1,000	6,500
Beans	500	800	700	500	800	300	1,600

SOURCE: Food and Agriculture Organizations, *Production Yearbook* (New York: 1981).

TABLE THREE
Economic Indicators

	Belize	Costa Rica	El Salvador	Guatemala	Honduras	Nicaragua	Panama
Top Exports	sugar textiles citrus	coffee bananas beef	coffee shrimp sugar	coffee cotton sugar	bananas coffee lumber	coffee cotton beef	bananas petroleum shrimp
External Debt (millions of dollars) 1988	95	4,100	1,913	2,647	3,045	7,220	5,400
Per Capita Debt (dollars) 1988	552	1,430	380	305	630	1,993	2,326
Per Capita Gross Domestic Product (dollars) 1988	1,284	2,235	955	1,502	851	819	2,229

SOURCES: Comisión Económica para América Latina y el Caribe, *Notas sobre la Economía y el Desarrollo*, December 1989; United States Department of Commerce, *Foreign Economic Trends: Belize*, April 1989; Inter-American Development Bank, *Economic and Social Progress in Latin America: 1989 Report* (New York: 1989); United States Information Agency.

TABLE FOUR
Social Indicators

	Belize	Costa Rica	El Salvador	Guatemala	Honduras	Nicaragua	Panama	United States
Life Expectancy (years at birth) 1988	69	76	59	60	65	62	73	75
Infant Mortality (per 1,000 live births) 1988	36	16	86	79	66	43	24	10
Deaths from Infectious and Parasitic Diseases (percent of total)	22.6	5.1	18.5	31.0	18.9	21.2	14.0	0.9
Literacy (percent) 1985	93	93	72	55	59	74	86	NA
Unemployment (percent) 1988	18	5	30	10	12	20	16	6
Rural Absolute Poverty (percent of families unable to afford adequate minimum nutritional requirements)	NA	40	70	60	77	57	55	13

SOURCES: United States Agency for International Development, *Congressional Presentation FY 1990, Annex III, Latin America and the Caribbean* (Washington, D.C.: 1989); Tom Barry, *Roots of Rebellion: Land and Hunger in Central America* (Boston: South End Press, 1987); Inter-American Development Bank, *Economic and Social Progress in Latin America, 1989 Report* (New York: 1989); *Encyclopedia of the Third World* (New York: Facts on File, 1987); *World Almanac* (New York: Scripps Howard, 1989); United States Department of Commerce, *Poverty in the United States* (Washington, D.C.: 1987); H. Jeffrey Leonard, *Natural Resources and Economic Development in Central America* (New Brunswick, NJ: Transaction Books, 1987).

TABLE FIVE
Natural and Human Environment

	Belize	Costa Rica	El Salvador	Guatemala	Honduras	Nicaragua	Panama
Primary Tropical Forest Remaining (square kilometers) 1983	NA	15,400	0	25,700	19,300	27,000	21,500
Rate of Loss of Forest (sq. km/year)	NA	600	0	600	700	1,000	500
Territory in Parks and Protected Areas (percent) 1984	NA	8.14	0	0.55	3.77	0.13	8.57
Population with Access to Safe Drinking Water (percent) 1984	62	82	51	45	44	53	82

SOURCES: Centro Agronómico Tropical de Investigación y Enseñanza, H. Jeffrey Leonard, *Natural Resources and Economic Development in Central America* (New Brunswick, NJ: Transaction Books, 1987).

TABLE SIX
U.S. Economic and Military Aid to Central America
1980–1991

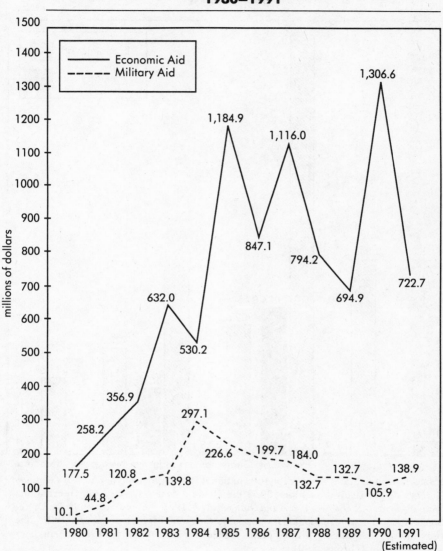

SOURCES: United States Agency for International Development, *U.S. Overseas Loans and Grants*, July 1, 1945–September 30, 1984; United States Agency for International Development, *U.S. Overseas Loans and Grants*, July 1, 1945–September 30, 1988; United States Agency for International Development, *Congressional Presentation, FY 1991, Summary Tables*; Pat Sommers, United States Agency for International Development, computer printout, February 1991.

TABLE SEVEN
U.S. Economic and Military Aid to Central America by Country
1980–1990

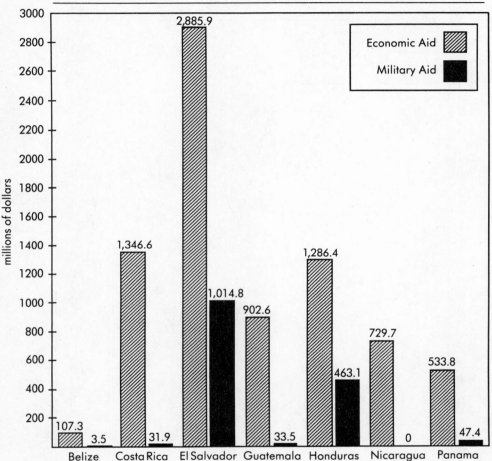

SOURCES: United States Agency for International Development, *U.S. Overseas Loans and Grants*, July 1, 1945–September 30, 1984; United States Agency for International Development, *U.S. Overseas Loans and Grants*, July 1, 1945–September 30, 1988; United States Agency for International Development, *Congressional Presentation, FY 1991, Summary Tables*; Pat Sommers, United States Agency for International Development, computer printout, February 1991.

TABLE EIGHT

Cumulative Multilateral and Bilateral Economic Aid to Central America 1981–1990
($ million)

| | Multilateral 1981–1988 | | | | Bilateral 1981–1990 | | | | | Total |
	IRBD & IDA	IDB	IMF	Total Multi-lateral	DA	ESF	PL 480	Other	Total Bi-lateral	
Belize	26	0	0	26	55	32	0	20	107	133
Costa Rica	164	658	157	979	156	989	176	27	1,348	2,327
El Salvador	65	530	120	715	675	1,699	461	0	2,835	3,550
Guatemala	228	547	236	1,011	266	407	189	31	893	1,904
Honduras	141	406	140	687	379	711	170	47	1,307	1,994
Nicaragua	55	140	0	195	3	67	2	1	73	268
Panama	380	372	0	752	95	593	6	0	694	1,446
ROCAP	0	23	0	23	318	113	0	0	431	454
Regional Total	1,059	2,676	653	4,388	1,947	4,611	1,004	126	7,688	12,076

ROCAP—Regional Office for Central America and Panama; IBRD—International Bank for Reconstruction and Development; IDA—International Development Association; IDB—Inter-American Development Bank; IMF—International Monetary Fund; DA—Development Assistance; ESF—Economic Support Funds; PL480—Food for Peace.

SOURCES: United States Agency for International Development, *U.S. Overseas Loans and Grants*, July 1, 1945–September 30, 1984; United States Agency for International Development, *U.S. Overseas Loans and Grants*, July 1, 1945–September 30, 1988; United States Agency for International Development, *Congressional Presentation, FY 1991, Summary Tables*; Pat Sommers, United States Agency for International Development, computer printout, February 1991; IMF data supplied by Center for International Policy, April 1990.

Chapter One
BELIZE

CHRONOLOGICAL HISTORY

1839   Central American Federation disintegrates; Guatemala claims to have inherited sovereign rights over Belize from Spain.

1840   Laws of England declared to be in force in Belize; Executive Council formed to assist superintendent. Spain does not attempt to reassert its authority.

1850   U.S.-British treaty; Britain agrees to refrain from occupying, fortifying, or colonizing any part of Central America. Britain claims that this treaty exempts Belize as a prior settlement.

1854   Formal constitution adopted, providing for Legislative Assembly. Belize is now "a colony in all but name."

1859   Guatemala recognizes British sovereignty but claims that it signed treaty because both parties agreed to build a road to the Caribbean coast.

1862   Officially declared a colony and recognized as part of the British Commonwealth with the name British Honduras.

1871   Status changed to crown colony under governor in Jamaica; Legislative Council with five official and four unofficial members.

1919   Blacks protest white rule in Ex-Servicemen's Riot.

1922   Establishment of the Civil Service Association.

1936   Constitution promulgated with elective principle. Property, income, and literacy qualifications restrict eligible voters.

1941   Mass meetings held, demands of adult suffrage and the right to elect the government.

        Labor unions legalized by colonial governor.

1945   "Belice" is defined as the twenty-third department in Guatemala's new constitution.

1950   Formation of People's United party (PUP).

1954   New constitution promulgated providing for universal adult suffrage and elected majority in Legislative Council.

1955   Semiministerial government introduced but governor keeps reserve powers. PUP begins thirty-year winning streak in all general and most local elections.

1958   Formation of National Independence party (NIP) as first political opposition to PUP.

1960   In a new constitution, a majority of the Executive Council is elected.

1961   Belize obtains associate-member status in the United Nations Economic Commission for Latin America. Belize turns down offer to become an "associate state" of Guatemala.

        Hurricane Hattie levels Belize City.

1964   Control of local government passes to Belize, with Great Britain retaining control over defense, foreign affairs, internal security, and terms and conditions of public service.

        Governor general appoints George Price as premier.

1972   Guatemala breaks off negotiations with Britain, and threatens war by mobilizing troops at the border. Britain sends a fleet and several thousand troops to the country.

1973   Name changes to Belize; Belmopan becomes the capital.

        Formation of the United Democratic party (UDP).

1975   Tension with Guatemala prompts Britain to send a squadron of Harrier jets to Belize. Britain allows Belize government to act in international matters.

        The first of a series of votes by the United Nations on Belize's right to self-determination, with the United States abstaining.

1977   Latin American countries begin to shift from siding with Guatemala to solidarity with Belize.

1979   Refugees from El Salvador and Guatemala begin to arrive.

1980   The United Nations passes a resolution demanding the secure independence of Belize before the next UN session in 1981. No country voted against the measure; Guatemala refused to vote.

1981   New constitution promulgated. Negotiations with Guatemala provoke riots and a state of emergency in Belize.

Belize becomes a fully independent member of the Commonwealth of Nations. The queen of England remains the ceremonial head of state.

Price first prime minister of independent Belize. Belize joins the United Nations and the Non-Aligned Nations.

1984   The UDP wins in landslide victory in parliamentary elections. Manuel Esquivel becomes prime minister.

1985   Esquivel government signs economic stabilization agreement with U.S. Agency for International Development (AID), which requires government to adopt neoliberal economic policies including privatization of public corporations and agencies.

1989   The PUP narrowly wins September parliamentary election (fifteen to thirteen seats) that returns George Price to the prime minister's office.

Sources for the chronology include O. Nigel Bolland, *Belize: A New Nation in Central America* (Boulder: Westview Press, 1986); Gerald Greenfield and Sheldon Maran, eds. *Labor Organizations in Latin America* (Westport, CT: Greenwood Press, 1987); and *Encyclopedia of the Third World* (New York: Facts on File, 1987).

TRENDS

- Unlike elsewhere in the region where right-wing parties were winning elections, Belize entered the 1990s with a government that had shifted slightly toward the left with the 1989 victory of the People's United party (PUP).
- Electoral democracy and a two-party political system have become entrenched in Belize, although other manifestations of democracy such as worker, farmer, and community organizing remain weak.
- Immigration of *mestizos* and Indians from neighboring countries and emigration of English-speaking Creoles (Afro-Belizeans) will continue to change the ethnic and cultural character of Belize and contribute to racial tensions.
- A marked increase in U.S. influence characterized the 1980s, but U.S. budget constraints and changing foreign-policy priorities will result in reduced U.S. aid and influence.
- Belize will remain deeply dependent on the international market, but the country's small population, large internal frontier, and its access to a variety of markets (Mexico, United States, Caribbean, Great Britain, and Central America) offer a measure of economic stability.

Belize, with its some 200,000 residents, is Central America's least populated nation. Known as British Honduras until 1973, Belize is a former British colony that won its independence in 1981. With its 8,867 square miles (about the same size as New Hampshire), the country is slightly larger than El Salvador. Not directly involved in the bloody conflicts affecting other Central American countries, Belize enjoys internal peace.

Belize remains largely undeveloped and unspoiled. It is a country of limestone soil and bush except for the Maya Mountains, which rise to 3,681 feet at their highest point in the south-central region along the Guatemalan border. At its greatest point Belize is only 174 miles long and 68 miles wide. While the wildlife population has long since been lost in most of the neighboring countries on the isthmus, the dense forests of Belize are still refuge for jaguars, tapir, crocodiles, and exotic bird species.[1] Regarded as a paradise by some and an uncarved jewel by others, Belize is often subject to devastating hurricanes, like Hurricane Hattie in 1961, which leveled Belize City and encouraged the colony to move its capital inland.

For many, Belize does have all the allure of a tropical island, but life is not easy for all Belizeans; large numbers of them leave for the United States to escape high unemployment, dead-end jobs, and empty futures. There is also rising concern that the land and natural resources of Belize are falling more rapidly into foreign hands.

Now after their second national election since independence, Belizeans are in the process of deciding the economic and political direction of their country.

GOVERNMENT AND POLITICS

Although independent, the country retains a place within the Commonwealth of Nations and an allegiance to the queen of England, who is the titular head of state. The prime minister and the cabinet—chosen from the majority party in the lower house of the legislature—constitute the executive branch of government, and a bicameral National Assembly forms the legislative branch. Modeled along the Westminster-Whitehall form of government, the twenty-eight-member House of Representatives is elected, whereas the eight-member Senate is appointed: five by the governor general on the advice of the prime minister, two by the leader of the opposition, and one by the Belize Advisory Council.[2] The prime minister and the appointed cabinet are all members of the National Assembly, making the legislative branch a close reflection of the ruling party. General elections must be called within five years but may be called earlier at the discretion of the cabinet or if the cabinet cannot muster enough votes to pass its programs.

The country is divided into six administrative districts (Belize, Cayo, Corozal, Orange Walk, Stann Creek, and Toledo). The districts are governed by locally elected seven-member town boards (with the exception of Belize City, which has a nine-member city council). Government on the local level is carried out with the assistance of village councils, which have no independent powers.

Although it was not until September 21, 1981, that Belize won its full independence, the country was self-governed from 1964 to 1981 with the British retaining control over foreign affairs, internal security, and defense. For those years of limited self-government and for the first three years of independence, George Price, the country's first prime minister, and the People's United party (PUP) were synonymous with government in Belize. After losing the 1984 national elections and spending five years as the political opposition, Price and the PUP returned to office in late 1989.

Political Parties

Politics in Belize has always been more a matter of personalities and degree of emphasis than a contest of ideological positions. Although the PUP has strong social-democratic leanings, it is also anticommunist and ambivalent about U.S. power in the region. The United Democratic party (UDP), the other leading political contender, is more conservative and pro-U.S. than the PUP, but during its rule (1984–1989) the UDP demonstrated the political maturity to make many domestic and foreign-policy decisions based on practicality rather than ideology. During the last half of its tenure, the UDP government demonstrated increasing awareness of the dangers of complete liberalization of the economy. The PUP administration has shown no sign of radically changing the economic policies promoted by the UDP, but the party has promised to place a greater emphasis on redistributing the benefits of economic growth—something that the UDP promised to do in its 1989 campaign.

People's United Party

From the mid-1950s to 1984, PUP politics in Belize were dominated by one man, George Cadle Price. A middle-class Catholic Creole who spent thirteen years in the United States studying for the priesthood, Price helped form the People's Committee in 1949, which became the PUP in 1950. From its earliest days the PUP relied heavily on the national infrastructure and activism of the Belizean labor movement led by the General Workers' Union (GWU).

Although basically social-democratic in practice, the PUP has encompassed three wings: left, right, and center. On the left were Said Musa and Assad Shoman, two British-educated lawyers who have been dedicated to a progressive social and economic vision of Belize since the 1960s. Both served as ministers in the PUP government, and have continually fended off red-baiting attacks. Shoman left the party to do grass-roots education through SPEAR (Society for the Promotion of Education and Research) while Musa became party chairperson. To

the right was Louis Sylvestre and Fred Hunter, who were also supporters of the Anti-Communist Society. They resigned from the party in
1984 and formed the all-but-moribund Belize Popular party.

Price, a formidable politician and excellent manager, has long been a
centrist, favoring what he calls "wise capitalism." A strong anticolonial-
ist, Price is also a firm capitalist, pushing both for a stronger local
capitalist class and increased economic ties with the United States.
Since the beginning Price has described the PUP's political orientation
as Christian democratic.

In its early days, Price and the PUP relied on the independence fight
to capture voters. But soon Great Britain also decided to back Belizean
independence, and the PUP relied less and less on voter mobilization
around nationalist issues. According to Assad Shoman, it became an
electoral machine with a personalized and paternalistic style of leadership that was out of touch with a changing society.[3] Still the party
counts on a strong base of faithful supporters who favor the social-
democratic vision that still lingers within the PUP.

Winning by a swing vote of about 5 percent, the PUP squeaked into
power in the September 4, 1989, election. The electoral shift back to
the PUP was confirmed by the party's subsequent sweep of all nine seats
of the Belize city council. The PUP's successful challenge to the UDP in
the 1989 national elections was based on the contention that the country had become more repressive and corrupt. Once again appealing to
nationalist sentiments, Price charged during the campaign that the
UDP had opened the doors to foreign speculators and that the persistently high unemployment rate proved Belizeans were not benefiting
from new investment projects.[4] The PUP campaigned on the slogan
Belizeans First.

As the country moves into a new decade, the PUP government will
shift to a more mixed economy, but will be careful not to threaten the
economic growth rates experienced during the late 1980s. Its maneuvering room will be limited now by the strong parliamentary opposition, placing a premium on party unity. For this reason, every elected
PUP representative was given a role in a ministry as either a full
minister or deputy.[5]

Immediately after regaining power, the PUP government abolished
the UDP-established secret police unit, reduced the government's control over the media, ended the controversial practice of selling Belizean
citizenship, and abolished the law that made libel a criminal offense. In
taking these measures, the PUP fulfilled its campaign promises while
establishing a more open and social-democratic direction for government.

Although the PUP did implement many of its campaign promises, the new government also adopted policies and programs for which it had previously criticized the UDP. When in opposition, for example, the PUP had cautioned the UDP government against the establishment of export-processing zones (EPZs). It also charges the UDP was allowing U.S. military engineers on a bridge-building exercise to establish a "beachhead" in the country. As the ruling party, however, the PUP approved legislation authorizing EPZs and also invited the U.S. military engineers, this time accompanied by twenty-five army medics, back to the country to repair the bridge.

United Democratic Party

The UDP again became the country's main opposition party in September 1989 after voters put the PUP back in power. In 1984, however, the party had offered Belizeans a "fresh breath" of politics, and Belizeans were ready to give it a chance.

Actually, the UDP was not that new or fresh. As a party, it had been contesting elections since 1973, and many of its political stars had been dueling in the political arena since the 1950s. It was founded in 1973 as an amalgam of three parties: the National Independence party (NIP), the People's Development Movement (PDM), and the Liberal party (LP). Internal disputes, weak support outside creole communities, and failure to back the independence movement, however, kept the UDP weak and without a strong popular base.

But changes in leadership and the emergence of Manuel Esquivel as party leader allowed the UDP to present a stronger, more self-assured party to the voters in 1984. No longer simply the opposition to the PUP, the UDP under Esquivel's leadership presented a conservative platform that stressed the need for foreign investment and private-sector solutions. "We want to see personal initiative and free choice become more a part of the pattern of the lives of individuals," said the UDP platform. The UDP gave Belizeans a more conservative government and one closer to Washington, although the differences between the two parties were mostly a matter of degree rather than of contrasting ideological positions.

When Esquivel called for a snap election in September 1989, many observers felt that he would certainly win based on the country's positive economic performance and the lack of new leadership in the PUP. The popular support of the government's increased distribution of tax revenues through highly visible development and road-construction projects was also thought to have favored its reelection. But the old campaigner George Price was ready with a strong platform and a couple of hot issues, notably popular chagrin at the UDP's selling of passports as a source of government revenue, and won a surprising victory.[6] While maintaining thirteen seats in the House of Representatives, the UDP once again assumed its former role as the opposition party.

In a postmortem evaluation of its electoral defeat, the UDP concluded that it had been weak in popular candidates but strong in terms of its economic record. With Dean Barrow leading the opposition, the UDP immediately began attacking the PUP government for its economic policies. It claimed that the new PUP budget showed no vision and contained no specific measures to "alleviate the lot of the poor." The budget, charged Barrow, confirmed the government's "absolute betrayal of its manifesto to 'restore national dignity.' " Retreating from its earlier conservative economic rhetoric, the UDP denounced the economic policies approved by the PUP, such as export-processing zones and a foreign ship registry, as being "radically capitalist."[7]

Foreign Policy and the Peace Process

The foreign policy of Belize is largely determined by its economic, political, and military links with the United States and Great Britain, and its geographical ties to both Central America and the Commonwealth Caribbean. In its fight for independence, Belize often looked to increased connections with the United States as an alternative to continued domination by Great Britain. The inclusion of Belize in the Caribbean Basin Initiative (CBI) has drawn the country closer to the U.S. vision of economic and political development. The PUP has promised to continue Belize's "special relationship" with the United States while forging new and similar ties with other industrialized countries.

Belize, however, has tried to maintain a certain independence from U.S. foreign-policy goals. While eager to receive increased aid, the country is fearful of being drawn too close to the U.S. military buildup in the region and being brought into the regional conflict. The Esquivel administration appointed an ambassador for the region, including Nicaragua, and in 1988 refused to endorse U.S. efforts to oust Panama's General Manuel Noriega.[8]

In the past, Belize has been excluded from regional accords. It played no direct role in the Central America peace process due both to its traditional self-imposed isolation from Central American politics and certain opposition from Guatemala if it had pushed for inclusion.[9] Rebuffed by the Central American Common Market (CACM) in 1968 and drawn culturally to the Commonwealth Caribbean, Belize joined the Caribbean Community (CARICOM). Although CARICOM membership has brought only limited economic benefits, it did serve to further the country's battle for independence.

Its relationship with Guatemala is Belize's longest-running foreign-policy issue. Guatemala's century-old claim on Belize has, in the past, caused serious internal political tensions in Belize. The continued presence of two thousand British troops in Belize is largely due to continuing tensions between Belize and Guatemala. A November 1988 incident in which a British vessel working off the Belizean coast was challenged by a Guatemalan gunboat increased tensions between the two nations. Since then relations between Belize and Guatemala have, as a whole, become considerably better. Although no final settlement is in the offing, the permanent Joint Commission established between the two countries did propose a solution to the unresolved border and territory conflict.

In the proposed settlement, Guatemala would recognize Belize's existing border claims while Belize would withdraw its claim to a twelve-mile international sea boundary, thereby allowing Guatemala easier access to its own coastal waters. National security considerations continue to be an issue, however. An agreement could mean the withdrawal of British troops, except for a British-maintained jet fleet and leave Belize vulnerable to future Guatemalan aggression.

The first foreign-policy victory for Foreign Minister Musa was the unanimous authorization by the Organization of American States (OAS) of full observer status to Belize. This was the first step toward becoming a full member, which occurred in early 1991. For the first time Guatemala supported Belize's request for entry to the OAS.

MILITARY

The Belize Defense Forces (BDF) were formed a year before independence with the merger of the Police Special Forces and the Belize Volunteer Guard. The BDF includes an army of about 555 soldiers (including a couple of female platoons), a maritime wing with forty marines and four patrol boats, and a fifteen-member air wing with two transport planes. In addition, there is a volunteer component of the BDF with some three hundred members. The BDF receives aid and training from Great Britain, the United States, and Canada, and has been commanded by British officers under the British Loan Service

Commandant program. Soon after returning to office, the PUP government announced that beginning in 1990, a Belizean will be the BDF commander. The BDF's officer corps includes a dozen or more officers on loan from the British armed forces.[10]

The BDF's main base is at the Price Barracks near the international airport. Among its main operations are joint border surveillance with the British troops, anti–drug smuggling activities, defense of the international airport, and assistance to the police forces in such areas as search-and-rescue and immigration control. The five-hundred-member Belize Police Force (BPF) is the country's main civilian police unit.

Although on a lesser scale than elsewhere in the region, human-rights violations and political repression exist in Belize. Illegal Central American refugees, poor urban youth, and non–English-speaking Belizeans are targets for police abuse. Called "aliens" by the government and the media, refugees have often been subjected to harsh treatment and unfairly accused of instigating violence and promoting the drug trade. Reported cases of police abuse declined from forty-one in 1988, six in 1989, and only one in the first half of 1990. The country's improving human-rights record has been tarnished by reports by the Human Rights Commission of Belize (HRCB) that the BPF's Special Branch detained and tortured a Guatemalan national and then turned him over to the Guatemalan military.

ECONOMY

Three features stand out about the Belizean economy: extreme openness, precarious external dependence, and small size. As a British colony, the country became accustomed to importing virtually everything it consumed. Although the country now has its own small industrial sector and food-production system, a heavy reliance on imports still characterizes the economy. As a result of all these imports, which range from U.S. wheat to Dutch condensed milk, Belize suffers an annual trade deficit of about $50 million. If unofficial trade with Mexico were included in balance-of-trade calculations, this deficit would be much higher. (Each week some two to three thousand Belizeans cross the border to purchase lower-priced goods in the Mexican border city of Chetumal.[11])

On the positive side, the country's foreign debt is the smallest in Central America—both in absolute terms and relative to export income. Unlike its less fortunate neighbors, 90 percent of its debt is held by multilateral and bilateral institutions rather than by private banks, which demand a higher rate of interest.

Agricultural exports provide 70 percent of the country's foreign exchange. Unprocessed agricultural commodities have long been the foundation of the Belizean economy, and a highly skewed structure of land ownership characterizes the agricultural sector. Only 10 percent to 15 percent of the potentially cultivable land, however, is being put to productive agricultural use.[12]

The country's small economic scale makes it ill-equipped to absorb even minor setbacks and downturns in the international market. Increased fuel prices or sinking sugar prices can have a disastrous impact on the $180 million economy. But there is also a positive side to having such a miniature economy; even small infusions of foreign economic aid or other sources of foreign income (tourism and remittances) can stabilize the country's finances.

Economically, independence came at a bad time for Belize. In the 1970s the country had enjoyed high sugar prices and an expanding world economy. Low sugar prices in the 1980s pushed the country to the edge of bankruptcy as foreign-exchange reserves dried up and the government's budget deficit widened. At a point when the government was struggling to meet its payroll and had only several weeks' worth of foreign exchange left in the Central Bank, the IMF came in with an emergency loan. Under the IMF agreement, the PUP government was forced to impose a series of austerity and contractionary measures, including tax increases, higher interest rates, and a wage freeze.

Burdened by a balance-of-payments crisis and a deficit-ridden budget, the PUP suffered a decisive electoral defeat in December 1984. The UDP swept into Belmopan with an economic development rhetoric that stressed private initiative, free markets, and export promotion. The economy under the UDP government was characterized by increased exports, increased U.S. trade and investment, and an infusion of multilateral and bilateral funds, which solved the balance-of-payments crisis and allowed the government to balance its budget. These features were offset by a continuing trade deficit, a marked decline in the search for public-sector solutions, and greater attention to increasing private-sector investment. The economy also saw increased private investment in citrus, cocoa, seafood, manufacturing, tourism, and nontraditional agriculture—almost all of which involved foreign, mainly U.S., capital. To attract more foreign exchange, the Price administration pushed through the International Business Companies (IBC) Act, modeled after similar laws in the Bahamas and the

British Virgin Islands, which allows international businesses to register for a fee in Belize without necessarily doing business in the country.

If the growth experienced in the second half of the 1980s is to continue into the 1990s, it will require a favorable international environment, particularly an expansive U.S. market. But economic growth does not necessarily translate into economic development and broad improvements in a country's living standards. For this to happen, appropriate economic policies are needed. In Belize, it is hotly disputed whether the private-sector policies first instituted by the UDP government are sufficient to spur widespread social and economic development or whether greater public-sector investment in such areas as health and education might also be needed. Most economic observers agree, however, that because of the country's limited internal market, exports are key to the development of Belize.

Agriculture

The agricultural economy of Belize was first dominated by logwood, then mahogany. Forestry lost its leading place in the Belizean economy in the 1960s, and now accounts for only 3 percent of export income. Sugar, originally dominated by British sugar giant Tate & Lyle, became the next major player in the economy. For more than three decades, sugar production has dominated the economy of northern Belize and provided as much as 60 percent of the country's export income. But falling prices and slashed U.S. sugar quotas in the early 1980s forced Tate & Lyle out and brought an end to the heady days when sugar was king.

Sugar exports, which account for about one-third of the country's export revenues, face an uncertain future. Low international prices and high production costs have caused many cane farmers and cane cutters to leave the industry, abandoning 30 percent of the farmland formerly devoted to sugar cane. However, several recent increases in the U.S. sugar quota and improving international prices in 1989 resulted in the increased production and export of sugar cane. In early 1990 Belize Sugar Industries reported its largest bulk shipment: 17,300 long tons of raw sugar destined for Canada.[13]

The citrus industry is the country's second most important agricultural activity. Although citrus is also grown in other areas, it is centered in the southeast where the country's two citrus-processing plants are located. The future is bright for the citrus industry in Belize. Frosts in Florida have caused citrus magnates to look elsewhere for orange juice concentrate, and the removal of the 30 percent import duty under the CBI provisions has made Belize look increasingly attractive. Most of the citrus produced on the 13,000 acres devoted to the industry is shipped to the United States to meet the increasing demands of U.S. juice drinkers.

The banana industry dates back to late last century when U.S. and British investors created banana enclaves in the south. But disease and hurricanes have always cut short the country's potential as a major banana exporter. In the mid-1980s, after numerous efforts, the banana industry was encouraged by rising prices and finally began taking off. A large stumbling block to industry growth is the lack of a good deep-water port capable of handling the cargo ships of Fyffes, the British subsidiary of the U.S. banana company United Brands. Efforts are under way to create such a port at Big Creek.

Crop diversification is the main theme of current agricultural development programs in Belize. The Caribbean Basin Initiative opened up the U.S. market to nontraditional agroexports from Belize, while the U.S. Agency for International Development (AID) has provided the funds to boost production of such exports as cocoa, spices, and mangoes. The AID and the UDP government combined efforts to encourage private investment in nontraditional production, but the results were disappointing. In mid-1987 the failure of the country's most prominent nontraditional export enterprise, Caribe Farm Industries, seriously deflated hopes for increasing exports of winter vegetables and fruit to the United States. While there is a great need for increased agricultural diversification, some critics feel that the current AID-government emphasis on nontraditional exports might be misplaced given the lack of commercial experience on the part of small farmers. These critics believe that a more balanced approach—one that pays equal attention to the local and foreign markets—would have a better chance of success. The potential for developing the domestic market has been amply illustrated by the local Mennonite community, which has created a thriving business supplying Belizeans with dairy products, vegetables, beans, and poultry.

As a country that imports nearly 25 percent of what it eats, there is much room for improvement in the food-production system. The country's small *milpa* (cornfields) farmers—mostly Indian and *mestizo*—have not been given a favored place in Belize's new agricultural development program. There are some six thousand subsistence or sub-subsistence *milperos* who grow mainly corn and beans in roadless areas and on mountain slopes. These small growers have little access to credit or technical assistance. Slightly above this class of *milpa* farmers is a group of small farmers (mainly *mestizo*) who produce basic grains for national consumption. The slash-and-burn method of farming practiced by these groups has deforested the hilly land they farm and threatens to cause erosion problems. Larger-scale operations include those of the Mennonite communities and a handful of large landholders (with more than two hundred hectares), who own as much as 60 percent of the country's productive agricultural land.[14] Although much of this land is held in speculation, some is used for ranching, sugar, citrus, bananas, and rice.

Industry and Tourism

Most of the goods consumed by Belizeans are imported, with industry representing only 20 percent of the national income, and most of this in the agroindustry sector (flour milling, citrus extraction, feed manufacture, etc.). Other important industries include brewing, soft-drink bottling, and textiles. But the low labor productivity and high wage levels relative to other Central American countries undermine the prospects for a booming export-oriented manufacturing sector in Belize. What is booming in Belize is infrastructure construction. A wide array of public-sector construction projects are under way with international financing.

The most important economic sector outside agriculture is the tourism industry, which has experienced a 15 percent growth rate in recent years. Tourism now ranks second to sugar production as a source of foreign exchange. The main tourist attraction is the country's spectacular barrier reef and the nearby cays (small islands). Approximately six hundred archaeological sites and the frontier quality of the Belizean environment are also tourist draws. Because of new interest in Belize as a tourist spot, several foreign companies are constructing hotels.

SOCIETY AND ENVIRONMENT

Popular Organizing and Labor

The kind of popular organizations of poor and working people seen elsewhere in Central America do not exist in Belize. For example, Belize does not have a history of peasant organizing nor does it have the kind of poor people's organizations that have sprung up in the urban slums of other Central American countries. There is, however, a small cooperative sector in Belize that took hold in the 1960s.

The country's trade union movement, which emerged in the 1930s, was instrumental in the Belizean struggle for independence and for adult suffrage. But the strength and militancy of the country's unions suffered from their close relationship with the state and the major political parties as well as from their own factionalism. Today, the labor movement is fragmented, disorganized, and powerless.

High unemployment (18 percent) and the seasonal nature of most agricultural work make labor organizing difficult, despite low wages, major price increases, and widespread job insecurity. It has been estimated that 11 percent of the workforce is organized.[15]

Although there is high unemployment in Belize, there are labor shortages in the agricultural sector, which is the largest and most dynamic part of the economy. The unwillingness of many Belizeans to work in the agricultural sector is largely explained by historical and economic factors. Because Belize has had neither a plantation economy nor a historical base of small farms, there exists no strong tradition of agricultural work. Early on, Creoles blocked from purchasing their own land tended to seek their fortunes in the cities. Many pursued education as a way to enter the civil service, while others found work as carpenters, blacksmiths, boatbuilders, and repairmen. Also, in part due to the efforts of labor unions, Creoles generally refuse to work for the extremely poor wages offered in the agricultural sector.

Belize does not have a general minimum wage, although minimum wages are set for certain occupations (domestic service, hotel work, and in places where alcohol is served). Wages for unskilled labor range from 90 cents to $1.70 an hour, with women receiving 30 to 40 cents less than men for comparable work.[16] Fringe benefits add about 15 percent to an employer's wage bills. All employees in workplaces of two or more workers are covered by social security protections and benefits.

Schools and Students

Belize's literacy rate of 93 percent reflects the country's commitment to providing its citizens with a basic education. Primary-school education (ages six to fourteen) is free and compulsory for all children. Girls constitute 49 percent of primary-school enrollment and 52 percent of secondary enrollment.[17]

The church school forms the foundation of the country's educational system. This system of government-subsidized denominational schools dates back to 1816 when the Church of England managed the country's first public school. Anglicans, Roman Catholics, and Methodists administer most of the country's primary schools, although in recent

years evangelical churches like the Assemblies of God have been opening schools. Compared with urban schools, rural education lags behind
in the quality of its teachers and facilities.

Secondary education is much more restricted. Only 60 percent of
primary-school graduates go on to the country's twenty-five secondary
schools. Eight of these high schools are operated by the government
and the rest are managed by churches. All primary and secondary
education in Belize follows the British examination system whereby
students are required to pass standardized exams before they pass onto
another level of schooling. Only a tiny elite goes on to receive a university education, and only 13 percent of Belizeans have received professional or technical training.[18]

Although the education system in Belize compares favorably with
others in Central America, there is much room for improvement. Functional literacy is much lower than the official figure, which reflects little
more than a familiarity with the alphabet and an ability to write one's
name. Government expenditures per student have been falling, and
there is little money available for adult instruction, technical training,
or higher education.

Communications Media

Although the media has never been severely repressed in Belize, the
government's traditional aversion to criticism and its attempt to control
the electronic media constrain free circulation of information and
ideas. The PUP, which had made easing government restrictions on the
media a major part of its successful 1989 campaign, moved quickly
after its election victory to fulfill its campaign pledge of a more open
media policy with unrestricted political dialogue. As it had promised,
the PUP moved to establish an independent broadcasting authority
called the BBN, similar to the British Broadcasting Corporation, to
control the country's TV and radio stations.

Soon after the 1989 elections the PUP-controlled legislature abolished the offense of criminal libel, under which the editor of the *Belize
Times* was repeatedly charged in 1987 and 1988.[19] Although the PUP
government has received good marks for its media policy, it was criticized for its failure to rescind an ordinance that gives the minister of
finance broad discretion to decide which information will be allowed to
enter the country.[20]

At least five weekly newspapers hit the streets of Belize City each
Friday, and most copies are gone before the week is up. Despite the wide

variety of newspapers, the quality of newspaper reporting is poor although it is steadily improving. News accounts are skimpy, and often border on slander. Most papers carry an undisguised political slant.

Only ten years ago, radio was probably the country's most influential media. Radio Belize, the country's only station, broadcasts in Spanish and English, and was renamed Belize Radio One by the UDP. The PUP government approved the longstanding application by Evan X. Hyde, owner of the *Amandala* newspaper, for a new radio station called Radio Krem. Hyde and his partners have also applied for a national frequency as well as a TV license.[21]

In the 1980s radio was replaced by television as the country's favorite medium. A new television program, hosted by representatives of the two opposing political parties, was authorized by the government. The government has required that 1 percent of TV broadcasting be local programming, but the lack of resources and training has stood in the way of producing programs locally. Recently, however, the government has been producing documentaries and other programs. In the more open climate following the PUP victory, a weekly interview program hosted by young leaders in each political party now airs.

The State of Health

Mobile clinics are only one indication that health care in Belize is a large cut above what is found in neighboring Central American countries. Although health statistics in Belize do not measure up to those of the industrialized world, Belizeans generally enjoy good health and access to health care facilities. Upon independence, the government declared that health was a "basic human right and a fundamental part of the development process." Government policy is that health services should be democratic, comprehensive, educational, participatory, and accessible.[22] About 75 percent of the population has access to government health services, which include seven public hospitals, rural clinics, and mobile clinics. However, about one-half of rural inhabitants still lack easy access to health services.[23]

Belize is relatively free of epidemic diseases, although malaria persists as a leading cause of hospital admission, especially in the Punta Gorda district in southern Belize. Although malnutrition is less prevalent than elsewhere in Latin America, the incidence in children under age one is about 8 percent, and for ages one to four, 19 percent. Malnutrition and severe deficiencies in calcium and vitamin A are much more common in rural areas, especially among the refugee population.

The widespread access of Belizeans to potable water is one reason for their generally good health. Almost the entire population in the eight main urban areas is supplied by public water systems, with 62 percent enjoying home connections. In rural areas, about 50 percent of residents have easy access to potable water. There are sewage systems in Belmopan and Belize City.

Although the health care system in Belize compares favorably with other countries in the region, it is not without problems. The country's nursing school teaches Belizean nurses the techniques of primary and preventive health care, but nurses receive poor wages and many leave the country to seek higher-paying jobs in the United States. This, together with the great strain on services used by refugees, has created a critical shortage of nurses in rural health posts. The number of Belizean doctors is increasing, but most are based in Belize City, leaving other district hospitals without the capability to perform surgery.[24] Private organizations such as Project Concern International and Project Hope have provided some additional access for Belizeans to health care, but many Belizeans are concerned that the country is becoming too dependent on these foreign agencies. Lack of medicines and funding plague government hospitals, and many Belizeans seek cheaper drugs and health care in Mexico.

The PUP had criticized the UDP administration's negligence of the country's health care system, and once in office promised to upgrade and extend health care services as well as promote preventive medicine and healthier life-styles. When explaining the new government's programs, Minister of Health Dr. Theodore Aranda said that health is "much more than the mere presence or absence of disease. It involves primary health care, attitude and behavior, environment, and satisfying basic human needs." To change what the PUP charged was the "Go to Mérida" health policy of the former government, the new administration has promised to increase the quality and availability of primary and secondary health care so that Belizeans will not have to travel to Mexico for treatment.[25]

Religion

In Belize, the dominance of the Catholic Church was not the result of Spanish colonialism but rather the product of immigration from Mexico and the development of a strong Church infrastructure by U.S.-based Jesuits. The Jesuits administer five of the country's twelve parishes and the prestigious secondary school, St. John's College. Roman Catholics, constituting almost 70 percent of the population in

1970, have lost significant membership to evangelical churches: Their numbers fell to 62 percent in 1980 and have been steadily decreasing since then, some say to as low as 50 percent.[26]

Belize hosts a small enclave of Mennonites, who speak a Low German dialect and do not proselytize. Mainline protestant churches have also lost members to new evangelical churches, mostly to the Assemblies of God. Also growing are such fundamentalist churches as the Baptists and the Seventh-Day Adventists. Other U.S.-based religious groups increasing their presence in Belize include Jehovah's Witnesses and the Church of Jesus Christ of Latter-day Saints (Mormons).

Spurring on the evangelical boom are an array of U.S.-based nondenominational Christian organizations that sponsor evangelical campaigns, feeding centers, church-building projects, and medical and dental programs. These include Youth with a Mission (YWAM), Campus Crusade for Christ, Feed the Children/Larry Jones' Ministries International, Christian Medical Associations (coordinated by Southern Baptist Mission), Amigos International, and Compassion International.

Since independence the evangelical boom has been one of the most striking changes in Belizean society. Bible institutes, corner churches, schools, media programs, and a wide range of social-service projects sponsored and financed by U.S. evangelical churches are changing the country's social fabric. Although the full significance of this change has not yet been examined, the evangelical churches exercise a conservative influence in terms of politics and social activism. The sheer numbers of denominations and sects also tend to undermine or obstruct the unity of communities, particularly Maya communities.

Women and Feminism

As in many other countries of the Third World, the United Nations declaration that 1975–1985 was the International Decade of Women sparked the development of a women's movement in Belize. Today, there are a half-dozen organizations concerned with women's rights and needs, ranging from a rural development group to one concerned about violence against women. The late 1970s were years of growing women's consciousness, and in 1979 the first women's organization, Belize Organization for Women and Development (BOWAND), was founded. In government, there is a Department of Women's Affairs as well as a government-sponsored National Women's Commission. Since 1982, the women's movement has sponsored a week of educational events to celebrate International Women's Day (March 8). The theme of the activities in 1989 was "Women + Men = The Key to the Future."

Leaders of women's organizations assert that extensive job discrimination and unequal pay levels are major problems facing Belizean women, many of whom head their families. Illegal abortions are another leading concern of the women's movement. More than 15 percent of the women hospitalized in Belize City are suffering from complications resulting from illegal abortions. Another concern is the lack of education about birth control. Contraceptive injections are a favored method of many women despite their sometimes serious side effects because "it's the only method husbands won't find out about," noted BOWAND's Diane Haylock.[27] Violence against women is a serious problem, but because of the efforts of various women's organizations, women are now talking more about the problem and reporting abuses to the police.

Ethnic Groups

For being so ethnically diverse, Belize is a remarkably cohesive society. Creoles constitute about 40 percent of the population, but are geographically concentrated in the Belize district, where two-thirds of them live. About a third of the population is *mestizo*, whose first language is Spanish. Ten percent of Belizeans are Amerindian, and about 7 percent are Garifuna. Whites constitute about 4 percent of the society. Another sizable minority is East Indian, many of whose ancestors were indentured to work on the sugar estates in the 1880s.

While English remains the language of business and politics, Spanish is becoming more widely spoken as the *mestizo* and Mayan populations increase. Garifuna and several Mayan communities speak their own languages, and Low German is spoken by the Mennonite settlements in Cayo and Orange Walk.[28] Creole is also being used more as a common language, although there are now both English and Spanish varieties of creole dialects.

The Mennonites in Belize trace their lineage back to villages in the Swiss Alps. They are members of a protestant sect that moved from northern Germany and southern Russia to Pennsylvania in the late 1700s, and to Canada a century later. Following World War I, some settled in Mexico. The Mennonites in Belize began immigrating in the late 1950s, mostly from Canada and Mexico. They own large blocks of land (about 145,000 acres) and insist on control of their own schools and financial institutions and on exemption from military service. Although they also insist on complete separation of church and state, their innovations in agricultural production and marketing have been felt throughout the country. The Mennonite community is divided into conservative and progressive wings.

Refugees and Outward Migration

The changing ethnic makeup of Belize is immediately noticeable on the streets of Belize City. Lining the main street are Spanish-speaking street vendors, refugees, for the most part, from Guatemala and El Salvador. This new immigrant population can also be found clearing their *milpas* in the Maya Mountains or working as temporary laborers picking oranges or cutting cane. They do the hardest and worst-paid agricultural work, and some have been hired to tend clandestine marijuana farms deep in the Belizean bush.

Since 1979 Belize has seen a steady stream of refugees from El Salvador and Guatemala. There are some 4,100 refugees registered with the United Nations in Belize, and 25,000 to 40,000 other undocumented Central American immigrants, mostly from Guatemala and El Salvador.[29] By the mid-1980s, popular resentment, particularly among the creole population, began to build against the so-called aliens. As the refugee flow has slowed down, the hysteria about the aliens has also diminished, but there is still widespread concern that the new immigrants are altering the social balance of the country. More than one in three Belizeans now speak Spanish as a first language.

Although Belize is a society of immigrants, it now is confronting a serious emigration problem. Although the standard of living is higher there than elsewhere in the region, Belize is an economic and cultural backwater compared with the United States. The country, even in the best of times, does not offer its young women and men the kind of wage, educational, and vocational opportunities available in the United States. As a result, over the last four decades a steady stream of Belizeans has headed to the economic colossus to the north. Today, an estimated one of every five, or 50,000 to 65,000 Belizeans, make their permanent home in the United States.[30]

Creoles have been the country's main emigrants, constituting an estimated 75 percent of the Belizean population in the United States.[31] Although no one factor explains this trend, their English-language skills certainly facilitate migrating and finding good work.

Nature and Environmentalism

Sparsely populated Belize remains largely forested and unspoiled. Deep within these tropical forests, there are more jaguars than in any other Central American country. Also found are large communities of endangered howler monkeys, tapir, and scarlet macaws, along with seven hundred kinds of trees and 533 kinds of birds.[32] Environmental initiatives in the 1980s by the government and private organizations have resulted in new nature reserves, legal protections for the environment, and an expanded environmental consciousness among Belizeans. The booming tourism industry and the pressure to speed up the country's pace of development, however, represent potential threats to the country's land and sea environments.

More than 70 percent of Belize is under some type of forest cover, and 44 percent of the country's primary forest is still standing. The timber industry, which provided the area's first link with international trade, has declined considerably since its heyday in the mid-1800s.[33] It now ranks seventh among the sources of foreign exchange. Less than one percent of the country's forests is cut annually. The government has established fifteen forest reserves covering 28 percent of the country. While most of these reserves are open to regulated tree cutting, about one-fifth of the reserves is permanently protected. One of the largest untouched rain forests in Central America is the Bladen Forest, a 135-square-mile stretch of forest in southwestern Belize. The government is considering a proposal to preserve this natural resource, which has the enthusiastic support of nearby communities.

The 1985 purchase of 700,000 acres by a consortium of investors, including Coca-Cola and its Refreshment Product Services subsidiary, sparked widespread concern from cattle and agribusiness industries about the threat to the country's tropical forests.[34] The failure of Coca-Cola to gain federally funded insurance for the project (due to the pressure of the Florida citrus industry) and an outcry by U.S. and local environmentalists caused Coca-Cola to reconsider and eventually squash its plans to convert its more than 192,000-acre share into orange groves. Coca-Cola having given 40,000 acres to the Audubon societies of Belize and Massachusetts and another 10,000 to the government, and having sold approximately 91,000 acres to two Belizeans, now owns only about 50,000 acres, which it has no immediate plans to develop. Although the immediate danger has passed, the vast tract of land is now subject to land speculation by Coca-Cola and the other U.S. investors—something the UDP government did nothing to control.

The Massachusetts Audubon Society together with its Belizean counterpart has spearheaded a major environmental initiative called the Program for Belize, which is a nonprofit Belizean corporation engaged by the government to develop policies and help write legislation for the management of the country's natural resources. It is funded by the Massachusetts Audubon Society, Nature Conservancy International, and World Wildlife Fund. Its director is Bill Burley, a former associate of the World Resources Institute in Washington.

The 240-kilometer barrier reef that runs the length of Belize (second only in size to the Great Barrier Reef of Australia) is a beautiful and economically important natural resource that the government is committed to protecting. At the same time, however, Belize is promoting the tourism industry, which threatens this fragile environment. The increasing number of divers has resulted in deterioration of the reef. Of particular concern to Belize is ocean liners anchoring on the far side of the reef, allowing passengers to enjoy a day of scuba diving and snorkeling, while the country receives no economic benefit. The seafood industry also represents a threat to the reef's marine life, which is showing signs of overexploitation.[35]

FOREIGN INFLUENCE

U.S. Foreign Policy

After independence, the U.S. economic relationship with Belize broadened substantially. At the same time, Washington moved to incorporate the country into its foreign-policy strategy for Central America and the Caribbean. In the 1980s the United States came to exercise an influential role in just about every aspect of political, social, and economic life in Belize. This influence ranged from an influx of Peace Corps volunteers to a U.S. military/civic action project, from establishing the country's economic policies to restructuring its educational institutions.

By mid-decade Belize ranked as the second largest per capita recipient of U.S. economic assistance in the Caribbean Basin (after El Salvador). Its embassy staff had grown to forty-seven, Peace Corps volunteers numbered more than 140, and a new Voice of America (VOA) transmitter was established in southern Belize. The increase in the official U.S. presence was paralleled by a flood of private U.S. organizations, churches, and businesses. With the embassy and the Agency for International Development (AID) leading the way, an array of evangelical missionaries, nongovernmental organizations (NGOs), and investors marched into this newly independent nation. Although there are not yet any Yankee Go Home slogans spray-painted around Belize City, irritation within Belize at the high-handed ways of the United States is growing.

U.S. Trade and Investment

The United States is Belize's leading trading partner and main source of foreign investment, purchasing more than half its exports and providing close to half its imports. Its proximity to the Gulf Coast ports of New Orleans and Texas has facilitated this domination. Most British goods are, in fact, transshipped through New Orleans. Other favorable factors in the U.S.-Belize trade relationship are the U.S. sugar quota and the duty-free provisions of the Caribbean Basin Initiative (CBI). During the 1980s the injection of U.S. economic assistance, which stipulates that funds be used to purchase U.S. goods and services, has also increased this dependence on U.S. trade. Belize's main exports to the United States are sugar, citrus, apparel, seafood, and wood products.[36]

Foreign investors have long played a commanding role in the Belizean economy. In the past, though, most of the major players have been British, including such large firms as Tate & Lyle and Barclays Bank. Throughout the last several decades, individual U.S. investors have claimed a stake in the country's tourism and agricultural industries. Among the largest U.S. investors are Hershey Foods Corporation (cacao growing and processing), Coca-Cola/Minute Maid (land ownership), Chase Manhattan (interest in Atlantic Bank), Prosser Fertilizer, Ramada Inns (Ramada Royal Reef Hotel), Texaco (petroleum distribution), Esso (petroleum distribution), Yalbac (ranching), and Williamson Industries (assembling Dixie Jeans for export).[37]

U.S. Economic Aid

From 1981 to 1983 AID funds were distributed to Belize through the Caribbean regional office, but just two years after independence, an AID mission was established in Belize, its headquarters located next to the U.S. embassy. Talks for a significantly expanded AID program began during the PUP government, but it was not until the UDP's Esquivel became prime minister that large sums of U.S. economic assistance began entering Belize. In terms of per capita U.S. aid, Belize was among the world's top recipients. From 1983 to 1989 Belize received more than $94 million in U.S. economic assistance.[38]

As elsewhere in Central America, AID channeled a high proportion of its aid through the private sector. Several new business organizations—including the National Development Foundation, Belize Export and Investment Promotion Unit, and Belize Institute for Management—were sustained entirely by AID grants. An array of U.S.

and local nongovernmental organizations also emerged as a result of AID funding.

Continued assistance from AID funds has been contingent on government compliance with conditions and policy changes. Generally, AID has insisted that the government liberalize its internal and external economy while using government programs and funds to promote increased private investment and export production. AID stipulated, for example, that the government undertake a "comprehensive review of the foreign trade and import-licensing practices to determine a set of policies which will promote economically efficient productive investment." It obligated the government to remove all controls on domestic prices and foreign trade while pushing the Esquivel administration to privatize parastatal corporations such as the Belize Marketing Board.

A large Peace Corps presence and scholarship and training programs are other aspects of the U.S. economic aid program for Belize. Under the Central America Peace Scholarship Program (CAPS), more than three hundred Belizeans are scheduled to receive education in the United States. In addition, regular training and exchange programs are managed by the United States Information Agency (USIA). Economic aid is also paying for an ambitious program to send all the country's secondary- and primary-school administrators for training in the United States.

After an initial infusion of aid in 1985 and 1986, U.S. economic commitments to Belize fell to about $10 million by 1988. The earlier Economic Support Funds (ESF) grants were eliminated, and AID's development assistance was down to $6 million in 1990. New U.S. budget restraints and diminished U.S. foreign-policy concern for Central America may lead to dramatic aid reductions and possibly the termination of U.S. economic assistance to Belize in the 1990s. In a 1990 document, "Policy Agenda and Strategy," AID acknowledged that it could no longer offer ESF transfers as inducements for policy change but planned to rely more on dialogue and the leverage that project assistance could provide. During the current Price administration, AID has continued to insist on policy reforms to reduce public-sector involvement in the economy and to promote export production and privatization.

U.S. Military Aid

Since 1981 the Pentagon has demonstrated steady interest in increasing its influence in Belize. It has pursued its interests through military assistance and training programs. Military engineers (from the Army

Reserve and National Guard) have coordinated a bridge-building project with AID,[39] and U.S. military medical-training teams have on at least two occasions sponsored training exercises with the Belize Defense Forces. According to the U.S. military attaché, these "civic action" exercises are designed mainly to promote goodwill but also to help train U.S. army engineers in a tropical setting.[40]

There are five U.S. military personnel permanently stationed in Belize. A military liaison officer works directly with the Belize Defense Forces while a U.S. military attaché advises the U.S. ambassador and the country's prime minister on defense matters.

REFERENCE NOTES

[1] U.S. Agency for International Development and Robert Nicolait & Associates, *Belize: Country Environmental Profile*, 1984.

[2] Government Information Service, "Belize Fact Sheet," 1987.

[3] Assad Shoman, "Belize: A Democratic Authoritarian State," paper presented to the Second Annual Studies on Belize Conference, Belize City, October 1988.

[4] *Belize Briefing*, August 1989.

[5] *Belize Briefing*, September 1989. Florencio Martin, the leader of the opposition from 1984 to 1989, lost his seat in the House of Representatives and was appointed by Price to the deputy prime minister spot. Said Musa won an easy victory from Dean Lindo and was appointed to head the ministries of Foreign Affairs, Economic Development, and Education.

[6] *Central America Report*, September 8, 1989; *Belize Briefing*, August 1989.

[7] Dean Barrow, "A UDP Response to the Budget," *Spearhead*, April 1990.

[8] "Belize Articulates Her Foreign Policy at the UN," *Belize Today*, October 1988.

[9] Carla Barnett and Assad Shoman, "Belize in Central America and the Caribbean: Peace, Development, and Integration," paper prepared for a conference in Belize, June 24–26, 1988.

[10] "The Belize Defense Force Now Ten Years Old," *Belize Today*, January 1988; interview by Debra Preusch with Bill Tillet, then permanent secretary in the Ministry of Defense, March 19, 1987.

[11] "The Recent Evolution of the Belizean Economy," *Central America Report*, March 4, 1988.

[12] *Belize: Country Environmental Profile*, op. cit., p. 83.

[13] *Belize Times*, April 15, 1990.

[14] Ibid.

[15] Lawyers Committee on Human Rights, *Critique: Review of the Department of State's Country Reports on Human Rights Practices for 1989*; and U.S. Embassy, "Foreign Economic Trends and Their Implications for the United States" (Washington: U.S. Department of Commerce, April 1989).

[16] O. Nigel Bolland, *Belize: A New Nation in Central America* (Boulder: Westview Press, 1986), p. 94.

[17] For an overview of the country's educational system, see C. N. Young, "The Educational System of Belize," unpublished report, 1988.

[18] *The Admission and Placement of Students from Central America* (Central America Peace Scholarship Program, P.I.E.R. Workshop Report, 1987).

[19] Ibid.

[20] SPEAR press release, March 5, 1990.

[21] Lawyers Committee on Human Rights, op. cit.

[22] Government Information Services/Pan American Health Organization, "Priority Health Needs," November 1985.

[23] Ibid.

[24] Interview by Debra Preusch with Dr. César Hermida of PAHO/Belize, May 2, 1989.

[25] Interview with Dr. Theodore Aranda in *Belize Today*, January 1990.

[26] Figures from the Belize census 1980 show the following percentage breakdown of religious preference: Roman Catholic, 61.7 percent; Anglican, 11.8 percent; Methodist, 6 percent; Mennonite, 3.9 percent; Seventh-Day Adventist, 3 percent; Pentecostal, 2.2 percent; Nazarene, 1.1 percent; Jehovah's Witnesses, 1 percent; Baptist, 0.9 percent; and others/not stated, 8.4 percent.

[27] Interview by Debra Preusch, May 2, 1989.

[28] An excellent overview of the ethnic origins of Belizean society is O. Nigel Bolland, *Colonialism and Resistance in Belize: Essays in Historical Sociology* (Belize: Cubola Productions, 1988).

[29] Estimates of undocumented refugees vary greatly. The U.S. Committee for Refugees in "World Refugee Survey: 1988 in Review" reports "25,000–40,000 other undocumented aliens." The UNHCR estimated between 15,000 and 25,000 undocumented refugees (*The Reporter*, April 30, 1989). A joint government-PAHO report ("Priority Health Needs," op. cit.) in 1985 estimated 10,000 to 15,000 undocumented Central Americans entered Belize between 1979 and 1985.

[30] The U.S. embassy estimates the Belizean population in the United States to be 50,000, but this appears to be an underestimate according to Dylan Vernon, "Belizean Exodus to the United States: For Better or For Worse,"

paper presented at the second annual Studies on Belize Conference, Belize City, 1988.

[31] "Belizean Exodus: Dominance of the Creole," *Spearhead*, March 1989.

[32] H. Jeffrey Leonard, *Natural Resources and Economic Development in Central America* (New Brunswick, NJ: Transaction Books, 1987); Georgia Tasker, "Some Wins, Some Losses," *Miami Herald*, October 9, 1988.

[33] O. Nigel Bolland, *The Formation of a Colonial Society: Belize, from Conquest to Crown Colony* (Baltimore: Johns Hopkins University Press, 1977), pp. 159, 175.

[34] Involved in the deal with Coca-Cola were two prominent Texas investors, Walter Mischer and Paul Howell, and Belizean businessman Barry Bowen.

[35] Leonard, *Natural Resources and Economic Development*, op. cit., p. 18.

[36] U.S. Embassy, "Foreign Economic Trends," op. cit.

[37] U.S. Embassy, "Investment Climate Statement: Belize," March 1989.

[38] U.S. Agency for International Development, *Congressional Presentation, FY1990, Annex III* (Washington, 1989).

[39] For two months in early 1987, the Army Corps of Engineers coordinated a bridge-building project over the Mullins River. AID supplied the materials while the U.S. military attaché supplied the men, equipment, and expertise. The project was arranged by the first PUP government, which gave the U.S. military a wish list of a half-dozen projects. Interviews by Debra Preusch with U.S. military liaison Terry Course and U.S. military attaché Lt. Col. John D. Skidmore, March 18, 1987.

[40] Ibid.

Chapter Two

COSTA RICA

CHRONOLOGICAL HISTORY

1821	Central American region declares its independence from Spain.
1870–1	New liberal constitution promulgated.
	First railroad opens Atlantic coast to banana production.
1910	Election of conservative Jiménez Oreamuno.
1919	Tinoco resigns; constitution of 1871 restored.
1934	Massive banana worker strike led by Communist party (PC).
1940	National Republican party (PRN) candidate Calderón Guardia elected in landslide.
1941	New labor code recognizes right to strike; broad social-security program established.
1942	Figueres Ferrer denounces President Calderón in radio speech and is sent into exile.
1944	PRN-PVP (Popular Vanguard party) coalition candidate Picado Michalski elected.
1948	Election won by Ulate Blanco of a coalition comprised of Democratic party (PD), Social Democratic party (PSD), and National Unification party (PUN). PRN wins majority in Congress, which annuls the presidential election results.
	Civil war breaks out; the 1948 "revolution."
	Figueres receives substantial U.S. support (and later admits to CIA connections).
	Picado overthrown by forces led by Figueres.
	Formation of the Junta of Second Republic, with Figueres acting as president.
1949	Ulate inaugurated as president.
	New constitution promulgated, which abolishes army, enfranchises women, and outlaws PVP. Catholicism declared official religion. Banks nationalized.

1951	Formation of National Liberation party (PLN) by Figueres.
1953	PLN candidate Figueres elected.
1958	PUN candidate Echandí Jiménez elected.
1962	PLN candidate Orlich Bolmarcich elected. Full relations broken with Cuba.
1966	National Unification Coalition candidate Trejos Fernández elected.
1970	PLN candidate Figueres elected. Antigovernment protest over U.S. interest denounced by government as being provoked by "communist elements."
1974	Use of the words *Marxist* and *communist* banned during pre-election period by Supreme Electoral Tribunal. PLN candidate Oduber Quiros elected.
1975	Trade relations with Cuba reestablished. PVP returned to legal status.
1977	Indigenous Bill establishes right of Indians to land reserves.
1978	Opposition Union candidate Carazo Odio elected; PVP-MRP gains three seats in legislative election.
1979	Support of the FSLN revolutionaries in Nicaragua.
1981	United States begins military aid and police training after fourteen-year lapse.
	Moratorium on debt payments.
1982	PLN candidate Monge Alvarez elected. Government asks seventeen Soviet diplomats to leave the country.
1983	Presence of *contras* on Costa Rican territory increases tension with Nicaragua.
	Israel begins security and intelligence training for Costa Rican police forces.
1984	Costa Rica seeks increase in military aid.
	Monge reaffirms Costa Rica's neutrality in U.S.-Nicaragua conflict, but U.S. opposition leads to resignation of foreign minister. Cabinet reshuffle, right-wing shift in government.
	Agreement with USIA initiates Voice of America broadcasts in northern Costa Rica.
1985	Arrival of U.S. military training team.
1986	Arias Sánchez of the PLN elected.

1987   Arias takes leadership role in regional peace initiatives in Esquipulas, Guatemala, which lead to signing of Esquipulas II peace accords by presidents of Costa Rica, El Salvador, Guatemala, Honduras, and Nicaragua. Arias is awarded the Nobel Prize for Peace.

Esquipulas peace accords go into effect. Costa Rica already meets most terms of compliance except for ratification of the Central American Parliament.

1988   A special request brought from the White House by Morris Busby, Arias approves use of Costa Rican territory to channel humanitarian aid to the *contras*.

Arias travels to Washington, meets with President Bush, and requests more aid.

The five Central American vice presidents meet in San José to discuss the Central American Parliament and agree to present a regional economic cooperation plan to the United Nations.

Guatemala accuses Costa Rica of noncompliance with the Esquipulas peace accords because it has failed to ratify the treaty to create the Central American Parliament.

Agreements with Nicaragua for joint patrol of common border.

1989   The former minister of public security is accused of being a collaborator of the illegal activities of the National Security Council and Oliver North. Former president Oduber admitted receiving one million *colones* for his electoral campaign from a U.S. citizen linked to drug trafficking.

Former president Monge denies allegations that he had accepted U.S. funding for "certain operations" in exchange for supporting the *contras* in Costa Rica.

John Hull, U.S. citizen and longtime resident of Costa Rica, is arrested by the Office of Judicial Investigations (OIJ) for crimes against the state. Eleven U.S. congressmen request that Arias intervene in the arrest and trial of Hull.

John Hull jumps bail and leaves for Miami.

Esquipulas peace talks held in El Salvador after four postponements. Arias reaffirms that the five Central American presidents were very explicit in their determination to dismantle the *contras*. Costa Rica says it will not keep the *contra* members unwilling to return to Nicaragua after they disband.

The other four Central American nations say they will go ahead with the Central American Parliament without Costa Rica, whose Congress has not yet ratified the plan.

1990   Social Christian Unity party (PUSC) candidate Calderón Fournier elected president.

1991   Costa Rica becomes 100th nation to join the General Agreement on Tariffs and Trade (GATT). Government imposes emergency measures to narrow the widening fiscal and trade deficit; workers join with small farmers to fight the government's deepening structural adjustment program.

Sources for the chronology include: *Encyclopedia of the Third World* (New York: Facts on File, 1987); *Conflict in Central America* (London: Longman Group Ltd., 1987); *Labor Organizations in Latin America*, Gerald Greenfield and Sheldon Maran, eds. (Westport, CT: Greenwood Press, 1987); and *Costa Rica: Balance de la Situación* (CEPAS, various issues).

TRENDS

- Privatization, government austerity, and free-market development strategies initiated by the National Liberation party (PLN) during the 1980s continue and are deepening under the Social Christian Unity party (PUSC) government headed by President Rafael Calderón.
- The gradual dismantling of the social-welfare state and the government's promotion of the private sector have resulted in deepening poverty and threaten to undermine the social peace and progress that previously characterized the country.
- President Calderón's government, caught between his populist rhetoric and his ideological commitment to conservative economic and political policies, may prove less able to maintain social peace than the more experienced and adroit PLN leaders.
- Popular movements and the left are weak, disunited, and without a persuasive and coherent platform of political and economic alternatives.
- Recovering from an economic crisis in the early 1980s, the government stabilized the economy by the end of the decade, using conservative structural-adjustment measures and supported by debt-reduction arrangements and large injections of U.S. economic aid.
- U.S. budget constraints and the electoral defeat of the Sandinistas in Nicaragua mean that Costa Rica will see declining economic aid from Washington, and changes in Eastern Europe also diminish hopes for increased European aid.

Costa Rica is different, and Costa Ricans are proud of it. Statistical indicators of literacy and living conditions explain only part of this difference. It is the other, unquantified qualities that set the *ticos* (common term for Costa Ricans) and their beautiful country apart: taxi drivers telling you to fasten your seat belt, warnings about smoking in public places, the diversity of cultural offerings, police stopping to help you change a tire, respect for lines, and a multitude of parks and recreation areas.

In many ways, Costa Rica resembles an industrialized nation. Consumerism is a cultural phenomenon and despite the atmosphere of freedom, there is a conformism, passivity, and relative absence of analytical thinking that reminds one of the United States. A strong democratic tradition and respect for human rights distinguishes Costa Rica from other countries in this turbulent region, but there is also a marked lack of independent community organization and political participation outside of the electoral process.

Costa Rica is primarily a mountainous area where cross-isthmus travel is difficult except on the few main highways. It is a small country, not quite as large as West Virginia. Among the most homogeneous societies in the world, 97 percent of Costa Ricans are of either European or *mestizo* stock, with little real distinction between the two. Some 2 percent of Costa Ricans are of African-Caribbean descent. Brought from the West Indies to build railroads and work on the banana plantations of United Fruit, black Costa Ricans were largely confined to the Atlantic coast region until the late 1940s when changes in the country's constitution and travel regulations removed their second-class status. Most still live in the area but the Atlantic coast is gradually losing its Caribbean character because of intermarriage and easier access from San José.

Costa Rica has achieved a 93 percent literacy rate, and higher education is of exceptional quality. Another distinction of Costa Rica, a country of 2.9 million inhabitants, is its relatively low population growth (2.7 percent compared with 3 percent or higher in the rest of the region).

Costa Ricans are proud of themselves and their nation, and rightly so. Yet this pride is often tinged with racism and an alienating elitism. Despite its many attractions, Costa Rica is not the paradise that government tourist brochures describe. Although the national park system is well advanced, rapid deforestation may mean the country will be importing wood by the end of the century. Hunger and poverty are not as widespread as elsewhere on the isthmus, but malnutrition is increasing and one-tenth of Costa Ricans live in absolute poverty. Paradoxically, more than one-third of adult women and one-fifth of adult men are also dangerously overweight.

Corner bars are almost as common in Costa Rica as the corner *pulpería* (general store). An estimated 17 percent of adult Costa Ricans have drinking problems. Crime is also rampant, to which the many barred windows and doors (even in the countryside) amply testify.

In Costa Rica, the government has traditionally taken itself seriously as a mediator between classes, and the resulting reforms have created the most egalitarian society in the region. Guarantees of education, pensions, and free health care represent opportunities rare elsewhere in Central America. Yet serious inequities in income and land distribution do exist and are getting worse.

Another myth that marks Costa Rica is that it is a land of peace: Its commitment to peace often seems more like a public-relations ploy than a shared political vision. The rise of right-wing paramilitary groups that count on government support, the increasingly violent response to popular organizing, the visible rise in militarization, and the country's warm relations with such countries as Taiwan, Israel, El Salvador, and the United States all tarnish the myth of peace that Costa Rica currently uses to promote foreign tourism and investment.

In 1981 Costa Rica achieved a less enviable distinction. An economic crisis put this touted paradise on the international financial map for being the first underdeveloped country to suspend debt payments. Although the worst of the crisis has passed, the consequences have already begun to reshape the nation. The commitment to broad social welfare within the limits of capitalism that began in the 1940s weakened in the 1980s under international pressure for debt payments and financial restructuring. As a result, large holes began appearing in the safety net carefully woven over three decades of government programs.

From 1982 to 1989 the U.S. Agency for International Development (AID) pumped more than $1.2 billion in economic aid into Costa Rica. Supplemented by large loans from the World Bank and the International Monetary Fund (IMF), this injection of foreign capital has permitted Costa Rica to survive its economic crisis. The foreign largesse that brought Costa Rica from the brink of collapse to a new period of economic growth had political foundations. The generosity of the United States and the multilateral banks can be at least partially explained by their interest in maintaining Costa Rica as a showcase of democracy and dependent capitalist development in a region where traditional political structures are crumbling.

But foreign aid and economic recovery came with a price: the imposition of harsh austerity measures, a restructuring of financial priorities, and a revamped development model. The "reforms" being imposed in the structural-adjustment process run contrary to the economic model of modernization led by the public sector, which has characterized Costa Rica since the early 1940s. A centerpiece of this modernization, the nationalized banking system, is being undermined, and once again the agroexport sector occupies a privileged place in the nation's eco-

nomic priorities. Also under attack is the country's social-services infrastructure, as ministry budgets are being trimmed and many public-
sector institutions are under foreign pressure to privatize. The resulting liberalization of the Costa Rican economy has attracted new private
investors, primarily foreign, who also insist on certain conditions for
financial commitment.

All of this is changing the ethos of Costa Rica. It is not happening
overnight, but Costa Rica is becoming visibly more stratified and divided. Without money available to buy land to appease the landless, the
government is responding to rural unrest with repression. Faced with
the prospects of unemployment or low-paying jobs, the urban poor are
responding with crime. Where negotiations and concessions once characterized the society, confrontations are becoming endemic.

Although it is clearly the international financial institutions that are
directing the restructuring, the international donors are working in
tandem with conservative political and business sectors. Throughout
the society, there is a right-wing populism that has allowed the process
to proceed without widespread public dissent. The domination of
Costa Rican political thought by two political parties and the rightist
media contributes to a superficial understanding of the severity of
these changes.

GOVERNMENT AND POLITICS

Government in Costa Rica is distinguished by its pervasive presence.
The degree to which the public sector has assumed responsibility for
social welfare (in terms of education, health, and social assistance
programs) is comparable to many European states. The Costa Rican
government is also economically active, having extended public-sector
control to such areas as banking, petroleum refining, and utilities.
Because of this broad participation in society and the economy, the
public sector has been labeled variously as a welfare, benefactor, or
interventionist state, and even as a socialist state.

Big government in Costa Rica began in the 1940s as part of the social
reforms initiated by the Social Christian government of Rafael Angel
Calderón Guardia. Such reforms as instituting a labor code, a system
of social security, and social assistance programs were an attempt to
modernize Costa Rican society. In its attempt to push through these
controversial reforms, the Social Christian government counted on the

backing of both the Catholic Church under Archbishop Víctor Sanabria and the communist Popular Vanguard party (PVP).

In 1948 another unlikely coalition overthrew the *calderonistas* after
complaints of a fraudulent election in which conservatives were denied
the presidency. The conservatives and Social Democrats, led by José
Figueres, teamed up to seize state power in what is fondly remembered
by some as the Revolution of 1948. In the eighteen months that followed, Figueres put a social-democratic imprint on Costa Rican government that has endured four decades.[1] The social reforms of the
calderonistas were preserved and extended while new measures, such as
the nationalization of banking and the abolition of the army, established the revolutionary thrust of the Figueres leadership. The social-
democratic character of the new Costa Rican state was further ensured
by the progressive nature of the 1949 constitution. As agreed, Figueres
ceded power in 1949 to the conservatives, led by candidate Otilio Ulate
Blanco. Four years later, Figueres won the presidency as leader of the
newly constituted National Liberation party (PLN).

For three decades, until the late 1970s, the government expanded,
with public-sector investment and spending occupying an ever-larger
role in the national economy. The bank nationalization of 1949 established the class character of state interventionism, which succeeded in
breaking the traditional economic hold of the agroexport oligarchy
while promoting new economic interests, including those of an emerging industrial sector and a rising middle class.

Subsidized credit was made available to these dynamic new interests,
and the public sector set in place an economic and social infrastructure
to accommodate their growth. In the 1960s government moved (with
some ambivalence) to facilitate the national economy's participation in
the Central American Common Market by providing industrialists with
protective tariffs and by opening up the country to U.S. transnationals.
The Costa Rican state became not only a promoter of economic modernization but also a participant. Various corporations were nationalized in the public interest, and in the 1970s government began to
promote economic growth by venture capital investment through a new
public corporation called CODESA (Costa Rica Development Corporation).[2]

The other side of state interventionism was the state as a popular
benefactor. An expansive bureaucracy was created to meet the education, health, and other basic needs of society. The government has
never encouraged independent organizing by the working class or
peasants, and in numerous cases has repressed such movements. But

rarely has it ignored popular demands. In the interests of pacifying class conflict, the state has often responded to social conflict with new social programs and new state agencies. In the 1960s it tried to alleviate the problem of increasing landlessness with the creation of the Lands and Colonization Institute. In the 1980s it attempted to assuage militant demands for low-income housing with the promise to build 80,000 new homes. In this way, the government has maintained social peace and eased class conflict while reinforcing its own legitimacy.

In the late 1970s the Costa Rican development model began to crack due to widening trade imbalances and budget deficits and deepening balance-of-payments problems. With the state no longer able to pay its bills, the conservative private sector attacked the entire social-democratic model. Leading the offensive were the World Bank, IMF, and AID—institutions that found willing, even enthusiastic allies within the country's business and political community. They have blamed most of the country's economic ills on excessive public-sector spending and state intervention in the economy.

It is unlikely that the conservative, free-market assault on the public sector will ever be fully implemented given the degree to which such reforms as nationalized banking, social security, public health, and public education have been integrated into Costa Rican society. However, the country's narrow economic base can no longer sustain this development model, which has led to a steady but gradual paring away of the social welfare state. By the year 2000 only skin and bones may remain of the protections and services offered by the government at the beginning of the 1980s.

Drugs and Corruption

Although government in Costa Rica is not characterized by the venality seen in such countries as Honduras, the integrity of politics and government in Costa Rica is increasingly being tainted by revelations of high-level corruption, influence-peddling, and associations with drug trafficking. The openness of Costa Rican society and the attractiveness of the country itself have long made it a favorite place of exile for international crooks and villains, from U.S. financier Robert Vesco to Mexican drug figure Caro Quintero to Hosjabar Yazdani, the former executioner for the shah of Iran. In 1989, the flight from Costa Rica of U.S. rancher and prominent *contra* supporter John Hull, charged with drug trafficking and gun running, also sullied the reputation of Costa Rica. By the end of his first year in office Calderón failed to fulfill his campaign promises to address the deteriorating socioeconomic conditions. As a result, the new administration was plagued by mounting urban and rural protests.

The international rogues who find a home in Costa Rica all count on favors from members of the political elite. This high-level corruption came under the glare of international attention in the late 1980s when high government officials and party officials were linked with reputed drug traffickers. A close associate of President Arias was arrested for laundering drug money, and it was revealed in the U.S. Congress that both of the country's leading political parties had accepted campaign contributions from the Noriega regime.

According to the U.S. Drug Enforcement Administration (DEA), a ton of cocaine and a thousand metric tons of marijuana are produced every month in Costa Rica, a country that also ranks high on the DEA's list of countries attracting drug money laundering.[3] In response 1990 saw antidrug operations by the DEA, the U.S. military, and the Costa Rican police increase sharply.

Structure of Government

The actual governing of Costa Rica is managed by a national government divided into three branches—executive, legislative, and judicial—with the executive branch exercising disproportionate control. Nonetheless, the Legislative Assembly is well developed and limits presidential power somewhat more than in other Latin American nations, although there still has been a history of excessive rule by decree. Lately, the Legislative Assembly has asserted more authority, for example, over the approval of foreign-aid agreements, out of concern that these package agreements often infringe on national sovereignty. The 1949 constitution, amended in 1969, limits the president and the deputies of the fifty-seven-member unicameral Legislative Assembly to four-year, nonsuccessive terms.

After two successive National Liberation party (PLN) administrations, the government passed into the hands of the rival Social Christian Unity party (PUSC) in May 1990. Rafael Angel Calderón succeeded President Oscar Arias after a narrow election victory in February 1990 in which he received 52 percent of the vote. The elections also gave the PUSC control of the legislature—twenty-nine seats for the PUSC against twenty-five for the outgoing PLN and three for smaller parties. This will be the first time since 1953 that the PLN has been relegated to minority status in the legislature. (After 1978 it was also a minority but joined a majority coalition with other minority members.)

Political Parties and Elections

In Costa Rica elections are an honored tradition. Election politics have found a place in the country's culture as an affirmation of Costa Rican democracy, with the whole society joining in the fiesta of flag-waving, car parades, and political debate. The candidates from the country's two leading political parties—the National Liberation party (PLN) and the Social Christian Unity party (PUSC)—always take center stage during this national celebration. The two parties have alternately held power over the last three decades.

Political democracy, characterized by regular elections and a tradition of social compromise, is deeply ingrained in Costa Rican society. Still, there is a superficial, almost frivolous quality about Costa Rican democracy that might eventually undermine its stability. Many Costa Ricans vote out of family tradition for the *calderonistas* or the *figueristas*, not out of any ideological conviction. In recent years political campaigns have become "*americanizadas*" as television campaign spots that play on emotions have come to dominate the electoral arena. In many ways, elections represent the outer limits of the democratic process in Costa Rica. Once the party flag-waving and actual voting are over, Costa Rican citizens tend to withdraw from the political arena, leaving professional politicians to manage the affairs of the nation.

Although Costa Rica is a very literate nation, there is an alarming intellectual conformity and lack of tolerance for ideological diversity in its society. A right-wing media is largely responsible for the deepening conservatism. Indeed, it is the media that set the bounds of acceptable political discourse. Also eating away at the honorable traditions of Costa Rican democracy is the propagation by the media, business elite, and AID of a neoconservative philosophy embodied in the slogan, Private Enterprise Produces Liberty.

National Liberation Party

The National Liberation party (PLN) is the party that presided over the institution of a reformist, benefactor state. But its standard bearers during the 1980s, Presidents Luis Alberto Monge and Oscar Arias, ushered in an era of structural reform and cutbacks in the public sector. Officially, the PLN is a social-democratic party and a member of the Socialist International. Its social-democratic ideals, however, have been largely shunted aside since 1982 in favor of economic policies advocated by the IMF, World Bank, and AID. Stopping short of complete capitulation, the PLN has not entirely embraced or enforced neoliberal solutions, choosing instead to implement a more pragmatic than ideological policy of economic reforms.

Costa Rican voters turned the PLN out of office in the February 1990 general elections after two terms in office. Presidential candidate Carlos Manuel Castillo, a respected economist and former government official, stressed his greater experience and capacity for the presidency while reminding voters that the PLN had led the country out of the economic crisis of the early 1980s. Taking the PLN campaign to the Costa Rican public, Castillo was handicapped by deteriorating socio-economic conditions for the country's poor, a background of party factionalism, public identification of the party with corruption and narcotrafficking, and the lack of a distinct political platform. Many citizens, including some of the party faithful, became increasingly disenchanted with the PLN because it had effectively dropped its long commitment to social-democratic developmentalism. As a result, the gap between the party leaders and the party's popular base widened ominously during the 1980s. A superior campaign by the PUSC, Castillo's lack of charisma, and voter concern that the PLN was establishing itself as the state party also contributed to Calderón's victory.

The close election, however, did not give a clear electoral mandate to the PUSC. With 47.2 percent of the vote and twenty-five seats in the Legislative Assembly, the PLN will likely form a strong opposition, especially if the party can overcome its internal differences. There are factions within the party who have opposed the conservative economic direction the party took during the 1980s, and the PLN also has been weakened by a split between those who supported Castillo and a smaller faction who supported Rolando Araya for the presidential nomination. It is possible that the progressive elements within the PLN will come to the forefront of the party to lead a populist attack against the new conservative government. By early 1991 three candidates were in the running for the PLN nomination for the 1994 presidential contest: Carlos Manuel Castillo; José Maria Figueres, son of former president José "Pepe" Figueres; and the popular Margarita Penon de Arias, wife of former president Oscar Arias.

Social Christian Unity Party

The Social Christian Unity party (PUSC), led by Rafael Calderón Fournier, represents the bloc of political parties that alternated in power with the PLN for the past forty years. Since 1977 the bloc has functioned as the PUSC, which is a coalition of four parties: the Republican Calderonista party (PRC), led by Rafael Calderón Fournier; the

Democratic Renovation party (PRD); the Christian Democratic party (PDC), led by Rafael Grillo Rivera; and the Popular Unity party (PUP), led by Cristian Tattenbach Iglesias. The PUSC backed Rodrigo Carazo in a successful bid for the presidency in 1978 but lost two successive election contests in the 1980s.

Although as a whole more conservative than the PLN, the PUSC encompasses two political tendencies: Historically this political bloc has incorporated the reformist tradition of the 1940s, but the ideological right and the private-sector elite have also found a home in the PUSC and have dominated its leadership and policymaking.[4] During the 1980s Calderón and other PUSC leaders were aggressively anti-Sandinista and criticized the PLN's failure to implement fully conservative structural-adjustment measures. The PUSC, which represents the more conservative and traditional members of the business elite, calls for complete and rapid financial restructuring and the dismantling of the reformist state.

The PUSC is a member of the International Democrat Union (IDU), established in 1983 as a global association of conservative political parties, including the Republican party in the United States. Both the PUSC and the IDU have benefited from U.S.-government funding channeled through the quasiprivate National Endowment for Democracy (NED). In Costa Rica, NED funds have gone to the Association for the Defense of Freedom and Democracy, a right-wing organization run by PUSC officials.

President Rafael Calderón Fournier is the son of expresident Rafael Angel Calderón Guardia (1940–1944), who introduced the country's labor code and social security system. As a consequence, the working class is viscerally pro-Calderón in memory of his father's alliance with organized labor against the conservatives. Calderón won the PUSC convention's nomination handily, demonstrating his firm control of the party.

A graduate of the University of Costa Rica Law School in 1972, Calderón never practiced law but devoted himself to politics. He served in the legislature from 1974 to 1978, and was foreign minister from 1978 to 1980. He unsuccessfully ran for president in 1982 and in 1986. He lost substantial support in 1986 because of what critics described as his "war-mongering" and was very careful not to make the same mistake in the latest round. In 1990, Calderón strongly endorsed regional peace initiatives and maintained his distance from the ultraconservative sectors critical of Arias's peace efforts.

Calderón, forty-one years old, was the less qualified but more attractive presidential candidate. During the campaign he adopted a populist rhetoric that made him the candidate of change and hope for those frustrated with PLN corruption, and for the poor and working people adversely affected by the PLN's conservative economic policies. Proving to be a skilled politician who could change with the times, Calderón presented himself as the "candidate of the poor" and promised to levy no new taxes, to create mechanisms that allow workers to share in company profits, and to make the government's low-income housing program less costly to beneficiaries. The populist content of the Calderón campaign, together with widespread dissatisfaction with the PLN, made the difference in the close election.

Even among the business community, many have questioned Calderón's ability to run the country; they worry that he could suddenly deviate in some unpredictable direction, reminiscent of the anti-IMF and pro-Sandinista behavior of the last PUSC president, Rodrigo Carazo. Although some political observers question the tenacity of Calderón's conservative politics, his circle of advisers is dominated by political and economic conservatives. The cabinet includes ministers who are, on the average, older and more conservative than those of the Arias administration and most come directly from industry and management. Calderón's political and economic advisers hail from the most conservative wing of the party and represent the strong influence of the *La Nación* group on the new administration.[5] The minister of the economy previously directed the AID-sponsored Costa Rican Coalition for Development Initiative (CINDE) investment-promotion organization. To head the Central Bank, Calderón chose a former IMF official. Calderón's appointment of twenty-three relatives to fill embassy, ministry, and other government posts has opened up the administration to charges of nepotism—a criticism that also hounded the Carazo administration.[6] The new administration won high praise from the World Bank, IMF, and AID for its willingness to implement harsh austerity measures and step up the pace of neoliberal structural adjustment.

Minor Political Parties

The bipartisan character of electoral politics was underlined by the 1990 national elections in which five small parties attracted only 1.3 percent of the presidential vote. Three other parties each won a single seat in the Legislative Assembly. These included People United (PU), which was an electoral coalition of the Popular Vanguard party (PVP) and the Costa Rican People's party (PPC), the two main leftist parties, and two regional parties from San José and Cartago.

The negligible showing of the minority parties means that they will lose their legal identity, which according to the electoral law requires a minimum of 1.5 percent of the vote. These parties also lost their chance to receive government campaign funding, which is given to parties obtaining more than 5 percent of the vote.

The February elections were another strong blow to the organized left in Costa Rica. Sectarian splits, personality fights, loss of their base among labor (particularly the banana workers), and their inability to distance themselves from their dogmatic past were among the factors undermining the ability of the leftist parties to establish a strong popular base. Another factor according to Rodrigo Gutiérrez, the legislator representing People United, is that the electoral system and bipartisan nature of Costa Rican politics do not give sufficient opportunity to small parties.

The new alliances and coalitions that emerged in the late 1980s signaled a period of renewal and change within the left, but it remains marginalized in Costa Rican society. It is a process that is unlikely to bear political fruit until well into the 1990s.[7]

Foreign Policy

The foreign policy of Costa Rica has traditionally reflected the Cold War orientation of U.S. foreign policy. There was some room created for an independent foreign policy during the Carter administration. This disappeared, however, with the advent of the Reagan White House. The Carazo administration's (1978–1982) support for the Sandinistas, its attempts to fortify relations among Third World nations, and its opposition to IMF structural adjustment created strains with the United States.[8] With Luis Alberto Monge as president, Costa Rica became the pliant ally that the Reagan administration needed for its campaign against Nicaragua. By the end of his administration, however, Monge was attempting to stave off U.S. pressure to support directly and openly U.S.-led military aggression against Nicaragua. As a defensive measure, President Monge mobilized popular support for the country's traditional "proclamation of neutrality."

Although President Arias shared Washington's virulent antisocialist and anti-Sandinista convictions, he saw the futility and counterproductive nature of the *contra* campaign. He petitioned Washington to dismantle the *contra* infrastructure in Costa Rica and began working with congressional Democrats on an alternative foreign policy for the region. Tensions rose between Arias and the White House, with the former advocating a strategy of negotiation and democratization, the latter maintaining its allegiance to the *contras*. This conflict led to Arias being repeatedly snubbed by President Reagan and then by Bush. President Arias, for example, was not invited to Bush's inauguration. The differences between the Arias administration and Bush were also clearly evident in the Costa Rican government's failure to applaud the U.S. invasion of Panama. Economic aid to Costa Rica was also trimmed by Washington and initiatives by the Arias administration to forge closer ties with Europe failed to open up substantial new sources of non-U.S. funding. Moreover, the abrupt changes in the Eastern European countries that began in 1989 will probably make it even more difficult for Costa Rica to attract Western European money. Even though U.S. economic support is decreasing, the Calderón government is very unlikely to take any steps that would endanger its now favored relationship with its powerful northern ally.[9]

Peace Process

As a candidate, Oscar Arias had promised the Costa Rican people that he would uphold the country's neutrality and support regional peace efforts. The growing refugee problem and Nicaragua's World Court suit against Honduras and Costa Rica, which was damaging Costa Rica's international reputation, were among the factors that pushed President Arias to offer his peace plan. Although the regional peace accords were a product of all five countries, President Arias did play a special role in guiding the process along, standing up to the Reagan administration along the way. For these efforts, Arias was awarded the Nobel Peace Prize.

Within Costa Rica, the accords signed in Esquipulas found support among both the pro-peace, leftist communities, and progressive social democrats alike. The media and conservative business community looked upon the peace accords skeptically and critically, feeling, as did the Reagan administration, that the proposal was being used by the Sandinistas to deepen their hold on the Nicaraguan government. More progressive elements within the business community welcomed the peace agreements, however, reasoning that they would result in a more stable business climate in the region. Although most popular sectors support the peace accords, widespread opposition emerged in 1988 to the Arias government for devoting more attention to international problems than to increasingly acute internal economic problems, such as the agricultural crisis.

President Calderón, who in the past adopted hard-line and militaristic positions, campaigned in 1989 and 1990 on a platform of peace. After assuming office, the new president moved to fulfill his campaign promise to push the Legislative Assembly to authorize the country's participation in the newly established Central American Parliament, a proposal that had languished in the legislature during the last years of the Arias government.

Human Rights

As might be expected, the human-rights situation in Costa Rica compares favorably with that of other countries in the region. However, the military and economic crisis that has assaulted Central America since the end of the 1970s has taken its toll on Costa Rica's reputation for liberty and democracy: Human-rights abuses, such as arbitrary detentions, physical abuse and torture by security forces, repression of dissent, and the intimidation of political activists, became more common in the 1980s.

The marked increase in human-rights violations was to some degree an outgrowth of the role played by Costa Rica in regional politics. Its willingness to join the U.S.-sponsored war against Nicaragua resulted in the same cycle of repression seen in other countries, although less extreme. This weakening of its vaunted neutrality has resulted in the rise of right-wing vigilante organizations and a related witch-hunt atmosphere directed at popular organizations and dissidents. Also closely related to the government's participation in the U.S.-sponsored anti-Sandinista campaign was the emergence of increased drug-trafficking and associated corruption.

Refugees, especially, felt the burden of increased political tension and the repressive behavior of the country's security forces. Those without papers were often arrested and detained for long periods without being charged. Other sectors hit hard by repression were squatter groups and banana workers. In an increasing number of cases, squatters were set upon by the private security forces of large landowners, many of them U.S. citizens.

Uniformed members of the security forces, however, are most responsible for most human-rights violations. The police justify arbitrary detentions, violent repression of demonstrations and squatter movements, and other human-rights violations as necessary to maintain order and protect national security. Although the Rural Assistance Guard (GAR) has been charged with most human-rights abuses, the most serious violations have been attributed to the police of the Office of Judicial Investigations (OIJ) and the Security and Intelligence Department (DIS).

Unlike elsewhere in Central America, there are no death squads, although small right-wing paramilitary organizations emerged during the 1980s. As a percentage of the total population, the paramilitary groups represent only the shadowy fringe of Costa Rican society, but these groups enjoy close ties within government and business. The Monge administration provided critical support and legal cover for the paramilitary groups whose members included senior government officials, including the minister of security. Although the Arias administration officially distanced itself from such organizations, the Free Costa Rica Movement (MCRL), a paramilitary squad, was said to have six members who held high positions in the Arias government. The paramilitary movement also received U.S. support; as members of government security groups, many received training from the U.S. Special Forces. Former Minister of Security Juan José Echeverria also revealed that the CIA has unofficially supported the paramilitary forces as well.[10]

With the ascent of the Central America Peace Plan and international attention focused on President Arias, the human-rights climate in Costa Rica improved noticeably. For the first time, Costa Ricans could talk about human-rights problems without being labeled "unpatriotic." Police roundups were suspended and arbitrary detentions by immigration authorities became less frequent.

But other more broadly defined human-rights problems deepened as the socioeconomic conditions for the poor continued to worsen. The Costa Rican Human Rights Committee has voiced concern about such matters as the deteriorating state of prisoner rights, the lack of freedom of expression due to right-wing control of the media, the government's failure to honor workers' collective-bargaining rights and to guarantee the basic needs of its citizens, and the repression of *campesino* and worker organizations, particularly in rural areas.

MILITARY

Security Forces

Soon after the 1948 civil war José Figueres abolished the army, bringing himself lasting distinction and giving Costa Rica its reputation as the "Switzerland of Central America." The decision to abolish the army was not "immaculately conceived," as Phillip Berryman noted; rather it came at the end of a war fought against a political coalition that had introduced the country's first social reforms. Figueres, who later would adopt and broaden the reforms first instituted by the Calderón government, abolished the army to eliminate a potential threat to the victorious National Liberation movement that he led.

Four decades later Costa Rica still does not have an army, but it does count on a rapidly growing police force, much of which has received military training. During the 1980s, the number of police in the country doubled. Not only did the actual number of police increase, but the new security forces were also created. At least nine different police agencies now exist. Under the supervision of the Ministry of Justice is the police force of the Office of Judicial Investigations (OIJ), while the Ministry of Public Security administers the Security and Intelligence Department (DIS), the Civil Guard (GC), the Metropolitan Police, Crime Prevention Unit (UPD), and the Office of Drug Control. For its part, the Ministry of Government controls the Rural Assistance Guard (GAR) and the immigration police, while traffic police answer to the Ministry of Transportation and Public Works. The most recently created police force is called the Special Investigation Police, which is yet another branch of the Ministry of Public Security.

Unlike most other Central American countries, where police and military come under a central command structure, each government ministry in Costa Rica controls its own respective security force. This absence of a common command has hindered the security forces from asserting more influence in Costa Rican society, but at the same time the disparate nature of the security forces renders them less accountable to public management. There is, for example, no one legislative committee that oversees the activities of all security forces. In 1988 the government created the Security and Police Council, with representatives from the president's office, the Ministry of Security, Ministry of Government, DIS, and Interpol in an attempt to address this responsibility. A problem of continuity exists in the security forces due to the persistence of the patronage system; all except for the top officers in the main security forces are dismissed when a new political power takes over government.

While other government agencies are shrinking, the ministries with police forces have experienced steady budget increases. In addition to larger tax allocations, Costa Rican security forces have been bolstered by international aid from such countries as the United States (providing 85 percent of the foreign aid), South Korea, and Taiwan for externally initiated military training and supplies, counterterrorism assistance, and narcotics programs.[11]

ECONOMY

Costa Rica's development bubble burst in 1980, when it found itself technically bankrupt and in the midst of the worst recession in its history. The crisis was brought on by the rising interest rates the country was paying on external debt—then the highest per capita debt in Latin America, most of which was owed to private U.S. banks. The basis of the financial crisis, however, was the country's development model: an agroexport economy dependent on a few traditional crops, a protected industrial and import-dependent sector, and a benefactor state based on borrowed money. Rising oil prices and increasingly unfavorable terms of trade brought Costa Rica to the brink of collapse.

The 1980s, then, were a period when the financial and development remedies—commonly called structural adjustments—fostered by the U.S. government and international financial institutions were tested on Costa Rica. These included austerity measures that trimmed the government's social-services budget, the privatization of public-sector institutions, export promotion, and the economic liberalization (meaning the end of subsidies, price controls, and protective pricing and tariffs) of trade and production.

By the mid-1980s Costa Rica had managed to shake the crisis. The country's debt payments were back on track, exports were increasing, unemployment was down, and it was experiencing positive economic growth. By the standards of other Central American countries, Calderón inherited an economy in good shape with a low inflation and unemployment rate, and positive per capita income growth. It remains to be seen, however, whether this stability is a temporary result of large injections of foreign capital or whether it is a more long-lasting base for future economic growth and development. Also in doubt is whether a development model that successfully spurs economic growth necessarily improves socioeconomic conditions or might actually exacerbate inequitable patterns of income and resource distribution.

International aid from the World Bank, U.S. Agency for International Development (AID), and the International Monetary Fund (IMF) have, for the time being, solved the earlier balance-of-payments crisis. While helping to restructure the Costa Rican economy, this aid has also played a major role in the restructuring of Costa Rican society.

In the 1980s income and resources in Costa Rican society have become more concentrated. The tax system has, for example, become increasingly regressive, relying heavily on indirect taxes (such as sales tax) rather than on direct taxes on income and property. Real wages have not reflected recent gains in national economic growth, and the social services originally designed to broaden the distribution of national income are being cut. A system of mini-devaluations at three-week intervals which depreciates the currency about 20 percent annually also disproportionately impacts on the buying power of the poor.

Privatization of the State

The privatization drive under way in Costa Rica entails the transfer of public-sector investment and infrastructure to private corporate investors. The most obvious manifestation of this new privatization effort has been the opening of the financial sector to private institutions. Foreign lending institutions would like to dismantle completely the nationalized banking system, which was set in place in 1949 to guarantee a more even distribution of income and resources. While few in Costa Rica are ready for such a frontal attack on what has been a centerpiece of their society, the ongoing financial restructuring is steadily eating away at the government banking system.

Selling off state corporations is another facet of privatization. Under a plan financed by AID, the subsidiaries of CODESA, the state development corporation, are being sold to private buyers. Other public-sector institutions have also been threatened with privatization, including the National Production Council (CNP) and the Costa Rican Electricity Institute (ICE).

The third aspect of privatization affects various state service agencies, ranging from road construction and low-income housing departments to the laundry service at state hospitals. Clinics, birth-control services, and agricultural assistance are also being shed by the state and in some cases offered to corporations or cooperatives established by former public-sector employees at government prompting.

Although the privatization process has just begun, the transformations are already changing the face and character of Costa Rica. As in austerity programs the world over, it is the poor who are hit hardest by these transformations, as the safety net established by the state is surrendered to a private sector more interested in profits than public welfare. In early 1990 AID based its assistance to the Calderón administration on further privatization of state institutions. AID also insisted that private banks be given greater access to Central Bank funds, a move that will surely further weaken the national banking system.

An array of government services and financial rewards are directed to new investors. The government is also spending more money on the export-promotion services of CENPRO (Export Promotion Center) and on the creation of export-processing free zones. In the meantime, the government is cutting back the budget of state institutions that benefit the broader Costa Rican society. CEPAS, a social and economic research center in San José, says that privatization "is not simply the dismantling of the state, but the redefinition of its functions."

Back to the Export Model

Government austerity and privatization are only one side of the restructuring. An equally dramatic revamping of the country's productive sectors is also under way. In accord with the economics of comparative advantage, the IMF, AID, and the World Bank have all insisted that there be an increased effort to promote exports that are competitively priced in the world market. Such items include labor-intensive textiles and electronic goods in the industrial sector, and vegetables, flowers, and other nontraditional crops in the agricultural sector. Export fever, which has spread from foreign lending agencies to the government and business elite, was promoted in Costa Rica with the slogan *Exportar Es Bueno* (It's Good to Export).

Although exports have increased, especially nontraditional ones, the country still suffers a persistent trade deficit. The benefits of increased nontraditional exports are counterbalanced by the many economic and social costs associated with the new emphasis on export production. Most nontraditional agroexport production is in the hands of foreign investors, while foreign companies produce all the country's nontraditional industrial exports. This production does mean new sources of foreign exchange, but resulting profits are mostly repatriated. The end products are also heavily dependent on imports that simultaneously deplete foreign exchange reserves. Growing blemish-free vegetables and flowers in the tropics requires vast amounts of pesticides. Likewise, the income generated by manufactured products must be measured against the cost of the foreign imports needed to assemble these items.

Problems That Will Not Go Away

An infusion of international funds in the early 1980s and a rescheduling of its debt did alleviate Costa Rica's immediate debt crisis, but the problem remains: The country's debt is too high to be repaid—about $4.2 billion or $1,500 for each Costa Rican. Like other similarly indebted Third World countries, Costa Rica has seriously considered declaring a moratorium on debt payments or making payments based on its ability to pay (linking debt payments to export income, for example). Rescheduling of its private debt—about 38 percent of the total—has stalled repeatedly, leaving creditor banks increasingly frustrated by the country's failure to honor its repayment schedules. In recent years, Costa Rica met only 40 percent of its debt-servicing commitments to private foreign creditors. The severity of the debt crisis has been somewhat alleviated, however, by debt swaps and debt buy-back deals engineered by Washington.

The rising cost of basic goods has severely undermined the enviable standard of living of most Costa Ricans. While structural-adjustment measures have improved trade balances, cut budget deficits, and increased rates of economic growth, it is clear that the living conditions of most Costa Ricans have eroded. As always, structural adjustments affect the poor disproportionately, from reduced corn price subsidies for peasant farmers to higher food costs for low-income urban dwellers. In 1982 during the initial shock of structural adjustments, a crisis developed when the unemployment rate rose to 15 percent.

Although the number of jobless has declined dramatically, inflation, low wages, and reduced government services continue to sound economic alarms for many Costa Ricans. Critics say that if the neoliberal policies persist, Costa Rica will be "Central Americanized"—meaning troubled by increased class polarization and conflict—by the end of the century.

On assuming office, the Calderón administration shocked the country with a drastic adjustment and austerity program that sent costs of basic services soaring. The government pledged to privatize all parastatal enterprises and to cut public spending while at the same time announcing a hike in the sales tax. It was the hope of the new government that the shock program would make further adjustments unnecessary and that inflation could be held to 20 percent for 1990. The financial adjustment program met with approval from the export-oriented business sector and the international lending institutions, but was denounced by the labor unions, which complained that wage rates were falling far behind living costs.

Producers for the domestic market—both in the agricultural and manufacturing sectors—have expressed concern that in the relentless search for fiscal equilibrium the government is giving rise to other, perhaps more serious economic and social problems. Rising costs for basic goods and services, relatively static wage rates, and inflation are constricting local market demand and impoverishing the population.

After a year in office, the Calderón administration could point to some positive economic indicators, such as a reduction in the external debt and a reduced fiscal deficit. The government's willingness to implement structural-adjustment measures gained it access to increased funds from the IMF and World Bank. But other problems persisted. The trade deficit widened as the value of exports declined and import costs increased. Higher than predicted inflation rates depressed consumer spending and kept wage levels far below the cost of living increases. Per capita economic growth declined from 2.8 percent in 1989 to 1 percent in 1990—a sign of a decelerating economy but one which was still performing better than any other in the region.

To address the country's economic problems, the Calderón administration showed no sign of deviating from its chosen course of neoliberal reforms and export promotion. In 1990 Costa Rica became the one-hundredth nation to join the General Agreement on Tariffs and Trade (GATT) and also became the second Central American country (after Honduras) to sign a free trade accord with the United States under President Bush's Initiative for the Americas. In early 1991 President Calderón announced emergency measures to stabilize the economy. Condemning the stabilization plan, the Permanent Workers Congress said the measures "strike hardest at those who can least afford it."

Agriculture

Agriculture is the heart and soul of Costa Rica, and its main source of income. About two-thirds of the country's economic activity revolves around agriculture. In the 1980s agriculture underwent an overhaul aimed at making local food production more efficient while increasing agroexports. This "sectoral adjustment," labeled Changing Agriculture, was imposed by international lending institutions with the consent and approval of the Monge and Arias governments.

The Changing Agriculture policy attempted to rectify two weaknesses of Costa Rican agriculture: (1) its overdependence on a few traditional agroexports, namely coffee and bananas; and (2) the perceived inefficiency and backwardness of the local food-producing sector. The government has addressed these concerns from the perspective of free-market and comparative-advantage economics, which is to say that it is promoting agricultural production that is competitive in the international market while reducing its support for nonexport crops.

Encouraged and financed both by the government and by international financial institutions, nontraditional agroexport production intensified in the 1980s. Yet virtually all of this new investment is in the hands of individual foreign investors and transnationals. Two transnational corporations, British American Tobacco and Philip Morris, control tobacco production and processing. Del Monte controls most pineapple, mango, papaya, chayote, and lemon exports. Including bananas, Del Monte's agroexports represent 9 percent of the country's total export production. United Brands controls palm oil production and exports, as well as the domestic production of margarine and shortening. More than 80 percent of fern exports, more than 50 percent of cut-flower production, and about 40 percent of macadamia nut exports are controlled by foreign investors.

Such issues as commodity prices and quality standards are out of the hands of local producers. Foreign-controlled export houses and traders decide how much and what standard of products to accept, often leaving bewildered farmers stuck with unmarketable produce. Several years ago the World Bank began promoting cocoa production among small farmers, but recently world market prices have nosedived leaving many farmers with large debts and no market for their nontraditional produce.[12] The stress on export crops has also directed credit and technical assistance away from small farmers, to the large commercial-level operations that have easier access to foreign markets.

The result has been turmoil and conflict in rural Costa Rica as basic-grain farmers discover they no longer have access to government credit and price guarantees. Unable to produce profitably under these conditions, these farmers are not planting enough beans, corn, and rice to feed the nation. The resulting food deficits are being met by increased grain imports, some channeled through U.S. food-aid programs. From 1985 to 1988, the production of rice, beans, corn, and sorghum has dropped substantially; rice production decreased from 244,000 to 157,000 metric tons, beans from 26,600 to 22,800, corn from 126,500 to 97,000, and sorghum from 71,400 to 18,700.[13]

The struggle of small basic-grain farmers points to major failings of the country's economic policies, but their protests also highlight the limitations of Costa Rican democracy. Ever since the country began promoting increased agroexport production in the 1950s this sector has been left out of the decision-making process. They have not been the only ones. The agricultural policies have also created increasing numbers of landless peasants, who during the 1980s became increasingly militant. Although no longer labeling its policy Changing Agriculture, the Calderón administration is committed to the same restructuring principles. To avoid the social upheaval in rural areas experienced by the previous two administrations, the new government intends to channel AID "social compensation" funds to the most rebellious communities.

The Rise of *Precarismo*

"A time bomb is ticking" in rural areas, asserted Rogelio Cedeño of the moderate Costa Rican Confederation of Democratic Workers (CCTD) labor confederation. "The nation's democratic tradition is in jeopardy because of the government's refusal to heed the call of rural Costa Ricans for the distribution of idle farmland."[14]

The problem of landlessness in rural Costa Rica heated up in the 1960s as the expanding agroexport economy, particularly the beef business, began cornering more of the country's agricultural lands. In an attempt to forestall rural unrest, the government with the support of AID created the Lands and Colonization Institute (ITCO), which has since been renamed as the Institute for Agrarian Development (IDA). Rather than pushing through an agrarian-reform program, ITCO concentrated on colonization and titling programs. But the agricultural frontier soon disappeared under the pressure of colonization, and landlessness became endemic in rural Costa Rica.

The response of landless peasants has been *precarismo*, or rural land squatting. It has been estimated that as many as one in six peasant families is part of this squatters' movement, which targets uncultivated estates.[15] The country's political and economic elite charge that the *precaristas* are "communist inspired" and have overseen harsh repression of the movement.

The Dessert Economy: Coffee, Bananas, Sugar

While nontraditional products now account for 30 percent of all agroexports, the main crops are still coffee and bananas. Coffee revenue, which alone accounts for almost 50 percent of the country's agricultural export income, is buffeted by the ups and downs of international prices and quotas. Costa Rica, however, is favored because of its high-quality coffee and ideal growing conditions.

In the 1980s foreign investors began to exert more control over the coffee sector. Liberalized laws allowed foreign traders to finance local exporters and processors, facilitating the purchase of shares in domestic exporting companies and coffee mills. Foreign companies that gained influence during the 1980s include Volkart, Jacobs, Lonrays, and Ruthfos. Together with local investors, Volkart opened the country's most modern coffee mill, Beneficio 2000, in late 1988.

Banana production occupies second place among agroexport crops. Foreign companies, led by RJ Reynolds (Del Monte/BANDECO) and Castle & Cooke (Standard Fruit/Dole), dominate the industry. Local growers do account for about one-third of production, but foreign companies control the packaging and export stages.

The sugar industry has regained its vigor with the rise in international prices and an increase in U.S. sugar quotas. Virtually all sugar exports go to the United States, and Costa Rica has also begun to export sugar-based ethanol to the United States. However, shrinking markets in the United States combined with rising production costs have precipitated a severe slump in the beef industry, which emerged in the early 1970s to meet rising U.S. demand for cheap, lean beef. Although beef consumption is declining in Costa Rica, chicken consumption has boomed. "Chickenburgers," fed on imported yellow corn, are sold at the many fast-food outlets in San José.

The forestry industry is facing a crisis that is in many ways self-induced. Ironically, while the Costa Rican government has been forward-looking in its creation of national parks, it has exercised few controls over deforestation. Despite new government regulations, the high deforestation rate continues. An incentive system does encourage private landowners to reforest, but the system encourages the planting of fast-growing trees rather than the precious hardwoods that are disappearing. As a result, the country may experience a shortage of wood for domestic use by the mid-1990s.

Industry

Costa Rica's industrial sector developed in the 1960s largely as a result of the Central American Common Market, which gave manufacturers a larger market for their goods. The country has two general categories of industrial investment: one that produces mostly for the local or regional market and another that simply uses Costa Rica as an export platform for textile and electronic goods produced with cheap, unorganized labor.

The fastest-growing manufacturing industries are in the food-processing, beverage, and tobacco sectors, which are largely controlled by U.S. transnational corporations. Costa Rican companies that depend on a high degree of imports have been adversely affected by devaluation and other restructuring measures that erode the protections under which companies catering to the internal market have thrived. Increased prices for imported petrochemicals have also resulted in a slowdown in the domestic production of chemical products, including fertilizers and insecticides.

The government reports more than seven hundred foreign firms doing business in Costa Rica. These range from companies manufacturing fishing lures to those assembling lingerie and costume jewelry under drawback incentive provisions. About one hundred companies operate under the drawback provisions of the U.S. 807 temporary admission program that permits companies to import assembled goods (like jeans and other clothing whose pieces are sewn together by foreign labor) duty-free into the United States. About thirty companies are located in the country's five free zones, where they benefit from having their workforce trained at the government's expense, either on or off the site. The textile industry has boomed in recent years. Between 1986 and 1988 the textile industry increased its number of workers from 14,000 to 35,000.[16]

Provisions of the Caribbean Basin Initiative and new government measures to attract foreign investors have created a small boom in foreign manufacturing investment in Costa Rica. Virtually all of this industrial production is of the export-processing variety, which means that there are few local inputs aside from the labor that assembles goods destined for foreign markets. In this investment climate, Costa Rica has become a world center for brassiere manufacturing, with companies like Maidenform and Lovable managing the international assembly and marketing arrangements. About one-fifth of the new ventures in the manufacturing sector are from Asia, mostly Taiwan.[17]

Tourism is the country's third major source of foreign exchange, after agriculture and industry. After a decline starting in 1979, the country is again filling up with tourists. There is also new foreign interest in tourism investment. This new mini-boom is attributed to the international attention given to Costa Rica as a result of Arias's Nobel Peace Prize and to recent favorable international publicity about the country's national park system.

SOCIETY AND ENVIRONMENT

Popular Organizing

Costa Rica does not have the tradition of popular organizing seen elsewhere in Latin America. The government's attention to the basic needs of poor and working people has in many ways obviated the need for the kind of community organizing that occurs in countries where there is little government concern for the broad social welfare.

The *campesino* movement has, since 1986, been the most militant and unified sector of the popular movement. Its militancy and increased radicalization reflect the government's lack of serious attention to its demands. As the movement has developed, its demands have broadened to include more than just specific sectoral concerns. The entire neoliberal trajectory has come under *campesino* criticism. The movement's ability to catalyze widespread opposition to these policies is limited, however, by its own tenuous unity and the deep divisions in style and perspectives that separate urban and rural Costa Ricans.

The government, and to a lesser extent the Catholic Church, has sponsored social services and created institutions that channel and coopt community organizing. In the early 1980s there was a surge of popular organizing as a result of the economic crisis. The PLN successfully pacified organized popular opposition by promising to contain food costs, increase housing construction, and lower proposed utility rate increases. To demonstrate its commitment to the poor, the Arias government, following the lead of the Monge administration, promised to provide low-income housing to 80,000 poor families. In the process COPAN, one of the most vocal popular organizations, made a deal with the government to direct no land occupations in return for a minor role in the administration of low-income housing. In the end, COPAN lost its independent voice and militancy and became part of the government's housing bureaucracy. Imitating the methods of the PLN, President Calderón and the PUSC also adopted a popular tone in the 1989–1990 electoral campaign, promising an expanded housing program, the creation of a national family institute, and the provision of subsidies for the poor. These promises, when combined with the movement's lack of leadership, help explain the absence of a strong popular response to the new administration's economic plan.

In the cooperative sector, the government maintains influence over cooperative organizing through two autonomous institutions: the Cooperative Bank and INFOCOOP (Institute for Cooperative Promotion). In Costa Rica there are three basic kinds of cooperatives: consumer, productive, and credit. Most cooperatives are more like capitalist businesses than true cooperatives where work and profits are shared. Government austerity measures have hit the cooperative sector hard, forcing many into bankruptcy as government subsidies are cut back. Particularly hurt by reduced government support are those rural cooperatives that produce basic grains; those producing for the export market or marketing such luxury items as cheese have been less affected.

Community groups are integrated into a network controlled by a state institution called DINADECO (National Directorate of Community Development), which channels government resources and training to local groups known as community development associations. Increasingly, however, more and more community groups are demanding genuine decision-making power and independence within this government-financed structure.

Reflecting on the state of popular organizing, political analyst Manuel Rojas Bolaños mused, "The popular movement does not appear willing to endure more restrictions [austerity measures and budget cuts], but since they lack an appropriate alternative, they move like blind worms, which upon running into tiny obstacles remove some of them while others force them to redefine their route, without ever knowing where they are going."[18]

Labor and Unions

The state of union organizing highlights yet another of the apparent contradictions in Costa Rican society: Although workers are not subject to the kind of repression seen in other parts of Central America, the union movement is weak and in decline.

The labor movement is characterized by the proliferation of small unions and the lack of labor unity. The country has more than 350 unions and seven union confederations. These confederations represent less than three-quarters of union members since 27 percent belong to independent unions.[19] Various attempts have been made to unify the disparate union confederations, the latest being the Permanent Workers Congress (CPT) formed in 1986. Costa Rican workers are generally better paid than their counterparts elsewhere in the region, but wages are still one-fourth to one-third the U.S. average.

Obstacles Facing Labor Unions

As the labor movement enters the 1990s it faces an array of obstacles, including effective loss of worker rights to collective bargaining; restrictive government policies; constraints imposed by the country's code of labor, whose benefits are applicable only to those labor conflicts judged legal by the country's Supreme Court; rise of the *solidarismo* movement; lack of effective labor movement unity; and continued ability of government to coopt sectors of the labor movement.

Collective bargaining is waning as a method for resolving labor conflicts. Direct agreements between workers and companies in lieu of collective bargaining arrangements are common in the private sector. The government has further restricted the strategy options of public-sector unions with the 1984 financial stability law, which additionally narrows the few instances when government institutions can negotiate directly with their employees.

Another threat to public-sector employees comes from the privatization of the government institutions for which they work. This issue is pressing since some 30 percent of the country's labor force and 65 percent of organized labor falls within the public sector.[20] Leading the opposition to privatization are workers of the Costa Rican Electricity Institute (ICE).

The founding of CPT in 1986, coalescing all the labor confederations, represents labor's strongest commitment yet to unity and common defense. Nonetheless, the government has proved adept in negotiating agreements with the public-sector associates of CPT. Although the agreements guarantee certain protections against further deterioration in wages, they offer no hope for the recuperation of real wages lost since the beginning of the economic crisis. Critics faulted CPT for its failure to lead the fight against the conservative restructuring that is eating away at hard-won social reforms. Instead it was the independent unions that mounted the most vocal opposition to the new government's economic plan. Beset with rising layoffs of public-sector employees and unable to agree on a "social pact" with the government, the CPT became more aggressive in its opposition to the country's structural-adjustment program during the Calderón administration's first year. A national front of labor unions and rural associations was formed to fight against the deepening neoliberal reforms.

Solidarismo Takes Off

Solidarismo is a philosophy of worker-owner cooperation formulated by Alberto Marten in Costa Rica in 1947. It is designed as an alternative to class confrontation, unionism, and collective bargaining. In practice, solidarismo takes the form of financial associations in which businesses and workers alike contribute to the formation of credit cooperatives and investment projects. The funds come from worker savings and investment by the company owner of the employee's future severance pay.

As a result of rapid growth in the 1980s, the solidarismo movement now includes more than 1,100 associations with more than 140,000 members and accumulated capital of over $30 million. The base of the movement has been the manufacturing sector in the San José metropolitan area, but since 1985 solidarismo has also made impressive inroads in agriculture, especially in the banana industry. The movement is also surging among commercial workers and lately has even established associations in the public sector. Over 90 percent of the country's U.S.-based transnationals, including Firestone, McDonald's, Coca-Cola, RJ Reynolds, IBM, and Standard Brands, sponsor *solidarista* associations.[21] One reason *solidarismo* is growing so fast is the foreign financial support it now receives. It not only receives support from transnational corporations but also from such sources as the U.S. embassy, the Konrad Adenauer Foundation, and AID.

Costa Rican labor confederations joined together in 1987 to create the National Union Commission on *Solidarismo* (COSNAS). Unions have also done extensive research and analysis of their adversary through the Service Commission for Labor Growth (ASEPROLA), labor's main source of information about *solidarismo*. *Solidarismo's* growth is not the only problem confronting the unions, though. They also find themselves battling the movement's increasingly aggressive attempts to undermine unions by collaborating with unionized companies and by arranging direct wage agreements with employers. Unions complain that companies fire unionized workers, for example, to make way for *solidarista* associations.

Solidarismo also faces internal opposition as members complain that the associations are undemocratic and lack adequate financial controls by worker representatives. Some observers predict increasing radicalization among the associations as companies fail to live up to promises to protect worker interests. There is also concern building among the *solidarista* associations that some companies may never be able to give retiring workers their severance pay due to poor investments and bankruptcies.

The benefits of *solidarismo* have not been all illusory. Aside from the reluctance to involve themselves in labor-management strife, workers often choose and stay with *solidarista* associations for some tangible rewards. They point to the cheap loans, savings plans, social events, and development programs offered by the associations.

Schools and Students

Costa Ricans enjoy the best public education system in Central America. The government spends approximately 5 percent of the national income on education, 1 percent higher than the standard recommended by UNESCO. As a result of this commitment to education, 93 percent of Costa Ricans are literate. A qualitatively superior system of higher education also distinguishes Costa Rica. Like many other Latin American nations, university-level institutions enjoy legal autonomy. This autonomy, which ensures freedom of expression and political activism, has been carefully observed, in contrast to other countries of the region.[22]

In contrast to postsecondary education, primary and secondary education, where learning is by rote, is mediocre to poor. One study found that 80 percent of students in sixth, ninth, and eleventh grades did not receive minimum passing marks on Spanish-language examinations. Although literacy is widespread, the average citizen has only an eighth-grade reading level.[23]

Recently, private institutions of higher learning have mushroomed. Most are very expensive, concentrate on business and the sciences, and are run like corporations. The Autonomous University of Central America (UACA), founded in 1975, is the leading private university. Actually, it is a collection of different departments (law, medicine, etc.) that function as separate profit-making enterprises. Founded by Guillermo Malavassi, a former professor at the University of Costa Rica, UACA was hailed as a procapitalist institution in contrast to the left-leaning sentiments that characterized the national centers of higher learning during the mid-1970s. Today, UACA continues to be a center for neoliberal thought, joined by an array of other private colleges, most of which also foster conservative views about education, politics, and economics.

Communications Media

Costa Rica enjoys a free press, but it is dominated by the ideological right. Although there is no censorship or suppression of the press, it is difficult to find news that is not colored by the stridently right-wing convictions of the owners of the major media.[24] The nation's largest daily newspaper, *La Nación*, sets the tone and direction of most news coverage in Costa Rica with its circulation of 75,000.

La Nación is more than a newspaper. It is a media complex that publishes a half-dozen magazines, including the prominent *Perfil* and *Rumbo*, and is linked to the cable station Cablecolor. Stockholders of *La Nación* also hold interests in the daily newspaper *La República*, Radio Monumental, and Radio Mil. *La Nación* is the country's preeminent source of news and opinion. The other media, especially the radio and television news, follow the lead of *La Nación* in reactions to news events and public policies. This is a phenomenon that close observers call the "news of consensus" in Costa Rica.

Sharing this conservative consensus are the two other dailies, *La Prensa Libre* and *La República*. Both newspapers emerged as alternatives to *La Nación*, but have moved to the right since their founding and now share its uncompromising conservatism. Three smaller papers— *Seminario Universidad, Esta Semana,* and *The Tico Times*—offer a more liberal view, but their influence is limited by their relatively small circulation.

Radio stations abound, yet offer little diversity, relying on regurgitated news from the three dailies. Radio Reloj boasts the most listeners, and it bolsters the conservative consensus sweeping Costa Rica with its daily news programs and its influential noon editorial called *La Opinión.* The news station Radio Monumental is at least as conservative, and faithfully reflects the rightist opinions of its owners. An exception to the conformity of the radio news is the Sunday morning program *La Patada* on Radio Sonora, which offers criticism in a humorous vein and a wide array of viewpoints. Many radio stations carry Voice of America (VOA) and other United States Information Service (USIS) programs in Costa Rica. VOA's *Buenos Días, América,* is fed to twenty-eight radio stations in Costa Rica, while some seventeen stations broadcast other VOA package programs.

The penetration in the 1980s of the media by the CIA and USIA raised concerns among many Costa Ricans. In an affidavit submitted to the World Court, former *contra* leader Edgar Chamorro testified that he had personally paid Central American journalists with CIA funds and was told by the CIA that the agency was bribing Costa Rican journalists to disseminate U.S.-produced information about Nicaragua and the *contras.* Carlos Morales, editor of *Seminario Universidad,* charged that at least eight journalists, including three top editors, received monthly CIA payments.[25]

Health

The good health of Costa Ricans—superior to that in many U.S. communities—is a product of a state-sponsored infrastructure of health services matched in Latin America only by Cuba. When compared with most other Central American countries, the advances in health made by Costa Rica are truly impressive. One indicator of the country's commitment to citizen health is its social security system, which covers three of every four Costa Ricans—easily the highest rate in the region. Latest statistics show infant deaths to be fewer than eighteen per thousand compared with seventy-nine per thousand in Guatemala. Life expectancy is high—seventy-six years—a rate approached in Central America only by Panama.[26]

Structural adjustment and resulting budget cuts during the 1980s took a serious toll on health services, however. The Family Assistance

Agency, a welfare and community development organization, was hard hit, suffering a budget reduction of one-third. The lack of funds reverberated throughout the health system, affecting disease prevention programs, child centers, feeding programs, and the installation of sanitary systems.

The statistics are not yet in for the 1980s, but health professionals predict a sharp decline in the nation's health status. Signs of this deterioration include a rise in contagious diseases such as measles and meningitis, increases in cases of hepatitis and diarrhea, and outbreaks of malaria and sexually transmitted diseases. Hospital directors and Social Security and Family Assistance officials state that the quality and availability of health services have substantially deteriorated over the last ten years. Medicines and hospital beds are in short supply; medical care, when available, has become routine and dehumanized. At least 10 percent of hospital patients acquire new diseases during their hospital care due to budget cuts in hospital sanitary services.

The shrinking welfare budget has also meant less government money for potable water systems, sewage treatment, and public health programs. As a result of the fewer wells and community water facilities being installed, the percentage of Costa Ricans with potable water and sanitary facilities inside their homes is declining for the first time. The lack of public funds for trash collection and sewage treatment has translated into increased water contamination. This has meant a general decline in public health and a rise in preventable diseases.

The privatization of the health-care system advocated by the business elite, and to a lesser degree by AID, has been only partially implemented. And those with the ability to pay have found private health-care services. For the poor, however, reduced government services simply mean no access to health care. The government—pressured by unions, leftist political parties, and the PLN's social-democratic wing—has tried to minimize budget cutting in health care. But as medical anthropologist Lynn Morgan observed, "The Costa Rican government's challenge will be to perform a political high-wire act: maintaining state control over the health system developed during the 1970s while not exceeding the austerity budget of the 1980s, yet without reducing services at a time when people need them the most."[27]

Religion

Although its base has been seriously undermined in the last twenty years by the evangelical movement, Catholicism still functions as the *de facto* state religion. The institutional Catholic Church has played a central role in shaping the social-democratic ideology in Costa Rica. It has been instrumental in legitimizing the social-welfare state, maintaining a lid on popular organizing, and propagating an ideology of anticommunism.

Harmony between rich and poor and between church and state has been the ideology promoted by the Church hierarchy. Its endorsement of the *solidarismo* movement, its promotion of such welfare organizations as CARITAS, and the integration of Catholic clergy into government institutions like INFOCOOP (the government's cooperative institute) exemplify this cautious theology.

Although the Church's ties with government strengthened in the 1980s, its hold on Costa Rican society has waned. As elsewhere in Central America, Catholics in Costa Rica are eclectic believers, whose most fervent expressions of faith are evoked during Holy Week and at baptism, marriage, or death of family members. More than 80 percent of Costa Rican Catholics do not attend mass regularly.[28] Within the Church, there do exist communities and clergy that espouse a theology of liberation, but the institutional Church isolates and represses this tendency while promoting a more spiritualistic religion.

Rise of Evangelical Movement

Evangelical churches, which accounted for 1 percent of Costa Ricans in 1949, have made rapid advances since 1965, encompassing about 16 percent of the population by the mid-1980s.[29] The recent boom in evangelicalism in Costa Rica is the direct result of advances by pentecostal churches, mainly Assemblies of God, Church of God, and the Pentecostal Holiness Church, which have been setting up churches since the early 1950s. Besides altering the theological mix in the country, pentecostal growth also has resulted in rival Catholic and more traditional evangelical churches adopting many of the tactics and the emotional nature of the pentecostals.

Generally, evangelical churches exert a conservative, pro-U.S. influence in Costa Rican society. In the late 1960s and early 1970s, a politically and theologically progressive faction of evangelicals did emerge, forming a base at the Latin American Biblical Seminary. But this new dynamism of ecumenism and religious social activism was eventually marginalized by most U.S. missionary societies, and has been largely unsuccessful in gaining a strong following among the evangelical community.

Outside this evangelical movement are numerous other religious groups, most of which have their origin in the United States. These include the Mormons, Jehovah's Witnesses, Theosophical Society, Baha'i, Unification Church, and the Society for Krishna Consciousness.

Nongovernmental Organizations

Nongovernmental organizations (NGOs) involved in development, business, and charitable activities proliferated in Costa Rica in the 1980s. Three factors to a large extent explain this rapid increase in nonprofit humanitarian and developmental activities: response to the government's failure to address deteriorating social and economic conditions; new attention to the NGO sector by AID and other foreign funding agencies; and a tendency to locate regional NGO headquarters in Costa Rica, a relatively stable and pleasant setting.

Beginning in 1985, AID increased its financial support of and direct involvement in NGOs. Through CINDE, a business NGO that was created and funded by AID, the agency began to channel funds to a growing number of NGOs. In 1987, CINDE/AID officially established the Costa Rican Association of Development Organizations (ACORDE) as a funding and coordinating organization for NGOs. The AID mission selected the members of ACORDE's board of directors. All are members of the country's business and professional elite with no previous NGO experience.

ACORDE operates on an annual budget of $3.8 million, all of which until 1989 came from AID. In 1989 ACORDE also began receiving grants from groups in West Germany (Hanns-Seidel Foundation and Agricultural Action), from the U.S.-based Resource Foundation, and from the Inter-American Development Bank (IDB).

AID's money goes to the more conservative NGOs in Costa Rica. Excluded from the AID-triggered NGO boom is a network of highly effective and innovative Costa Rica NGOs that sponsor popular education, community development, and research projects and which rely mainly on European funding.

Unlike in other Central American countries, where social conditions are more serious, the NGO sector in Costa Rica does not serve as society's safety net. The social infrastructure set in place by NGOs and churches elsewhere in the region is the public sector's domain here. As these government-sponsored welfare services are cut back, though, churches and NGOs are gradually moving into this type of social-assistance activity. Nevertheless, most NGOs continue to focus on specific objectives, such as family planning, business development, and technical assistance.

Women and Feminism

In its class character and articulated gender focus, the women's move-ment in Costa Rica resembles feminism in developed countries. Issues such as sexual preference, battering, job discrimination, and sexual harassment are publicly debated in Costa Rica. Employment of women in government has been quite impressive. Women have occupied many cabinet-level and even vice-presidential posts in sharp contrast to most of Costa Rica's neighbors in Latin America. Even though some were believed to be lesbians, they were not only tolerated but respected for the quality of their work. There are numerous feminist organizations that maintain a gender focus in their education and organizing. There are, however, few links between the women's movement and social-justice issues and struggles in Costa Rica.

As early as 1984 the country had a shelter for battered women, in contrast to the other Central American countries, which have none. Another indication of the degree to which women's rights are of con-cern to Costa Ricans is the ongoing effort to pass an equal-rights law. The country already has a highly advanced family code, which stipu-lates that a husband and wife have equal rights and equal duties. The code also provides equal recourse to divorce and allows divorce by mutual consent, thereby avoiding emotionally wrenching court cases.

Although women's rights are increasingly becoming part of social consciousness in the country, the overall situation of women has not greatly improved. Violence continues to plague women in Costa Rica. The number of cases of woman-battering has risen more than 200 percent since 1983. Rape has also increased, but convictions have remained few, in part due to a Costa Rican law that requires proof that a rape victim physically resisted her attacker.

Higher prices and lower wages in recent years have resulted in more women in the registered labor force (currently about 28 percent). Women generally receive lower wages than men do, and the rate of women working for less than minimum wage is three times the male rate.[30] Numerous projects exist to provide productive employment for women living in poor urban areas. Most of these projects, however, are cottage industries in which women sew clothing for substandard wages.

Birth control in Costa Rica is both a nationalistic and feminist issue, as well as a religious one. Many critics say that foreign agencies like AID and Planned Parenthood are undermining the sovereignty and dignity of Costa Ricans with their birth-control campaigns. Many Costa Rican feminists, however, assert that sterilization and other forms of birth control are a right. As a Costa Rican feminist publication stated,

"Women don't choose sterilization just because they are ignorant or are forced without consent. Social problems such as lack of employment, education, decent housing, medical services, and safe, secure contraception are decisive factors."[31]

The decrease in social services and the worsening economic conditions for the poor may account for the alarming number of adolescent mothers in recent years. Public health officials estimate that every fifty-two seconds a teenage girl gives birth. One-fourth of all Costa Rican women have their first child between fifteen and eighteen years of age, and 40 percent of the female adolescent population is not in school. These statistics indicate that previous advances in education and equal opportunity won by Costa Rican women may now be reversed by the new economic and political climate.[32]

Native People

Costa Rica is a largely *mestizo* society whose people have lighter skin tones than those of other Central American countries—a trait explained by the historical absence of a widespread native population. Today, there are fewer than 25,000 Indians in the country, most of whom live within the twenty-two Indian reserves established by the government.

Not only are these Costa Rican natives isolated from the dominant society, they are isolated from each other by both their geographical seclusion and their own cultural differences. A dozen ethnic groupings exist within the small Indian population, although only six native languages have survived the last five hundred years of colonization. As isolated as most Costa Rican Indians are, they have been reached by the dominant culture of the country. Although they may live without electricity and running water, Costa Rican Indians do live in a culture of soft drinks, junk food, and battery-powered TVs.

Costa Rica boasts a progressive policy regarding its native peoples. In 1977, the government passed the Indigenous Bill establishing the Indians' right to land reserves and authorizing measures to preserve native culture and language. But numerous Indian community leaders assert that the government has not adequately protected Indian land rights and treats the Indian people solely as a tourist attraction. As Baldomero Torres, a member of the Cabagra community commented, "We don't want to be treated as animals in a zoo, but we do need help to improve our poor living conditions."[33]

While the government is given much credit for promotion of Indian culture, it gets few good marks when it comes to preserving Indian land rights. On many reserves, the majority of land has fallen into the hands of "white" Costa Ricans. Non-Indian cattle ranchers and farmers have seized and fenced Indian land with impunity. Indians living in the extensive Talamanca Reserve, which straddles the border with Panama, are also threatened by increasing land speculation, mining, and petroleum exploration.

Economic development is an issue that now confronts the Indian communities of Costa Rica. At a time when many are taking steps to preserve their culture from further deterioration, they are also being faced with decisions about how best to promote their economic interests.

Refugees

Over the last couple decades, Costa Rica has served as a haven for Latin American political exiles. But it was not until the late 1970s, when thousands of Nicaraguans crossed the border to escape the widening repression unleashed by Somoza, that Costa Rica gained its present status as host to large concentrations of Central American refugees. Most of these Nicaraguans returned to Nicaragua after the Sandinista triumph, but their numbers were soon replaced by Salvadorans fleeing escalating violence at home. When the *contra* war heated up, and later as economic conditions worsened in Nicaragua, tens of thousands of Nicaraguans once again sought refuge in Costa Rica.

As of early 1989, there were 42,000 documented Central American refugees in Costa Rica, although only seven thousand were living in the country's half-dozen refugee camps sponsored by the United Nations High Commission on Refugees (UNHCR). Included in this official refugee population are some 6,200 Salvadorans, 2,500 Cubans, two hundred Guatemalans, twenty-five Hondurans, and seventy-five Panamanians. More than 33,000 Nicaraguans have refugee status in Costa Rica, as well as over one thousand Cubans. In addition, 150,000 to 200,000 undocumented refugees—most of them Nicaraguans—have found a temporary home in Costa Rica. The Salvadorans who sought refuge in Costa Rica entered the country in the early 1980s; most were women and children, and had personally experienced the terror of military counterinsurgency campaigns. The Salvadoran community in Costa Rica, which has been treated with both suspicion and caution by the government, has been prohibited from most forms of political activism and protest.

Environment

Costa Rica has the reputation in Central America for having taken the boldest steps to protect its environment. In many respects, this reputation is well deserved. The government is committed to protecting nearly a quarter of its national land area in national reserves and has recently instituted a logging moratorium. A series of environmental laws have been instituted to protect the country's diverse flora and fauna, which includes some 850 bird species and 1,200 types of orchids. The Costa Rican citizenry certainly lead the region in terms of environmental consciousness.

Although the environmental movement achieved significant gains in the last fifteen years, laws and good intentions have fallen short of effective protection and improvement. While legally established wildlands occupy some 25 percent (11 percent in national parks and 14 percent in protective status) of the country's land, less than half of this area is effectively protected. As a consequence, the reserves at the edges of the national parks are being exploited. The desire to clear land for farming and cattle-grazing, plus a voracious lumber industry, spurred until recently one of the world's highest rates of deforestation. The country has been losing about 106,000 hectares of forest each year—a rate that means by the year 2000 Costa Rica would have no wildlands outside its national parks. The government's Ministry of Mines and Energy has warned that Costa Rica may be importing wood within a decade if the deforestation rate continues.

Watershed deterioration as a direct result of deforestation presents an additional threat to the country's hydroelectric system, which produces most of the country's electric power. Reservoirs are silting up at a rapid rate due to soil erosion, costing the system hundreds of millions of dollars in lost revenues.

Pesticide abuse, once concentrated in such traditional agroexport crops as bananas and sugar, now poses a major environmental threat. With the recent focus on nontraditional exports, the major danger lies in uncontrolled pesticide use by producers of vegetables and flowers. Agricultural chemicals have all but exterminated armadillos, fish, and crocodiles along the Tempisque River. Humans also fall victim to pesticides. One study found that between 1978 and 1983 the number of farm workers poisoned by pesticides increased steadily, up to almost eight hundred cases a year. Although one has been proposed the country has no government agency that monitors food products for harmful chemicals and possible pesticide contamination.

Uncontrolled industrial dumping is also a major environmental hazard. Contamination of Pacific coast waters near Puntarenas by effluents from a government fertilizer plant (FERTICA) is one example of the lack of sewage and dumping regulation. Along the same coast around Puerto Quepos and Golfito, the banana companies have made a habit of dumping their toxic waste into the ocean.[34]

The government's efforts to create a large national park system stand at the center of the country's commitment to environmental protection. International conservation organizations have joined this effort through what has been called the Debt-for-Nature Swap program. These organizations (including the Nature Conservancy, World Wildlife Fund, and the World Fund for Flora and Fauna) purchase some of the nation's external debt from foreign banks usually at less than 20 percent of face value. The government's Central Bank then buys this debt with short-term government bonds, with the stipulation that the funds be used for conservation. More than $40 million has been invested in this innovative manner of debt settlement.

A major trend in protecting ecosystems is the plan to consolidate about two dozen protected areas into seven "megaparks" over the next five years. The integration of peasants and communities living within or on the borders of national parks into park planning and development has been another trend that distinguishes environmental protection in Costa Rica. The minister of natural resources called this concept "mixed management," which he said means "managing buffer zones as integral to the protected area, teaching rural people agroforestry, and training them as tourist guides."[35]

Not all parks in Costa Rica are government-owned. Some are managed privately, and cost as much as $75 a day to enjoy. This privatization of nature worries some Costa Rican environmentalists, who are also concerned about the explosion of an ecotourism industry largely controlled by foreigners. In the late 1980s there was a 50 percent increase in businesses catering to such avocations as bird watching and white-water rafting. The government, which has encouraged these new entrepreneurs, has begun to see the environment in terms of its ability to generate foreign exchange from international tourists.

Environmental organizations and experts abound in Costa Rica. Their recommendations and initiatives, however, often conflict with the country's model of economic development, in which extensive agroexport production depends on cheap land and labor. One encouraging sign is the emergence of community environmental initiatives. Examples include the Guapiles neighborhood association's concern with deforestation, the struggle by the Desamparados community to stop coffee-processing plants from dumping wastes in nearby rivers, and the growing interest among peasant farmers in organic vegetable production.

FOREIGN INFLUENCE

U.S. Foreign Policy

Costa Rica, a longtime ally of the United States, is often cited by Washington as a showplace of capitalist democracy. Although the Costa Rican government has often shown more independence than Washington would like, it has proved a reliable U.S. ally in the region on many occasions.

Costa Rica has also provided a friendly climate for U.S. investment and settlement, but it was not until the 1980s that it began receiving substantial monetary rewards from Washington, chiefly in return for Costa Rica's cooperation with the U.S. anti-Sandinista campaign. Costa Rica reluctantly allowed its territory to be used to mount the *contras'* southern front, and the country's media became a mouthpiece for U.S. anti-Sandinista propaganda. In violation of its own stated commitment to peace and neutrality, the government also permitted the United States to bolster the capabilities of the Costa Rican police forces.

Although the country's anti-Sandinista policy did cause some inconveniences for Costa Rica, such as societal disruption and deceptions associated with the *contra* presence, it also proved to be the salvation of an economy on the edge of bankruptcy. This trade-off, however, led to certain difficulties when Arias's less-than-compliant position led to cutbacks and delays in U.S. aid, designed to express U.S. displeasure.

Yet as long as Washington is concerned about leftist rebellion and threats to its traditional hegemony in Central America, it is likely that Costa Rica will receive favored treatment from Washington in such matters as debt renegotiations and economic-aid commitments. However, U.S. budget constraints and rising demands for aid from other quarters, such as the East European countries, will probably mean that Costa Rica in the 1990s will see its U.S. aid commitments steadily decrease from the unprecedented highs of the 1980s.

Costa Ricans continue to be receptive to U.S. influence, especially when it means dollars flowing into the economy. But accelerated U.S. intervention in the country's internal affairs, such as the shaping of Costa Rica's economic and foreign policies, has caused a dilemma for many Costa Ricans. A symbol of the deepening U.S. presence and influence is one that few have missed: the construction of an imposing, new fortresslike embassy that cost $11 million and houses 225 employees. Blocks away is an equally commanding new structure that houses the AID complex of offices. Some find this concrete demonstration of U.S. commitment to the country reassuring, while others see it as a self-indulgent manifestation of U.S. imperial might.

U.S. Trade and Investment

For the first-time visitor, the extent of U.S. influence in Costa Rica is startling: Menus in the classier restaurants are commonly bilingual; U.S. brand-name products are readily available; and there is a large U.S. community. For Sale signs for choice houses and property are frequently only in English. To many observers of Latin America, Costa Rica has become Americanized—in cultural values, style of dress, consumption patterns, and even political ideology. To a large degree, the dominance of U.S. trade and investment is responsible for this saturation of culture and values.

Trade with the United States dwarfs commercial relations with other countries. About 65 percent of the country's exports (mostly coffee, bananas, cacao, and beef) is sold in the United States and about 45 percent of its imports (chemicals, industrial raw materials, consumer goods, vehicles, machinery, and grains) comes from the United States.[36] Foreign investment pervades the economy and close to 60 percent of it comes from the United States.[37]

About three hundred U.S. firms do business in Costa Rica, accounting for $550 million worth of investment, according to the U.S. embassy.[38] More than one-third of these transnational corporations (TNCs) are in the manufacturing sector. The top five U.S. pharmaceutical corporations have operations in Costa Rica. Many TNCs take advantage of the country's cheap labor to assemble products as diverse as nuclear gauges, golf carts, yachts, and bird cages; Movie Star, Inc., produces underpants for export, Lovable manufactures a full line of women's underwear, and Consolidated Foods assembles bras. Costa Rica also has several clothing manufacturers that subcontract assembly work with large U.S. clothing companies. More than twenty TNCs either manufacture or distribute chemicals (mostly pesticides and fertilizers). Seven of the top twenty TNC food processors produce for the nation's internal market. Colgate-Palmolive markets toothpaste there and also manufactures candy, chocolates, and crackers through its subsidiary Pozuelo.

An impressive array of business equipment corporations, including IBM, Honeywell, Burroughs, ITT, and Xerox, market their products in Costa Rica. Five of the top eight accounting firms and the top two U.S. banks have offices, primarily to serve the other TNCs. Also in the service sector are McDonald's, Kentucky Fried Chicken, and Pizza Hut.

All three banana companies—Castle & Cooke, United Brands, and RJ Reynolds—have agribusiness operations, although United Brands pulled out of its banana investments in 1984 while retaining its palm oil investment. IU International has interests in sugar production, while Hershey and IC Industries are involved in the cocoa industry. Eight U.S. companies, including American Flower and Foliage, Inc., dominate the ornamental flowers and plants business.[39]

Tico businessmen express deepening resentment at their government's favored treatment of U.S. investors. Special incentives— including tax credit certificates and exemptions from import and export duties—available to U.S. investors are often not offered to local investors.

Another group selected for special treatment is the community of 7,000 foreign settlers (one-third from the United States) who qualify for pensioner status in Costa Rica. To qualify for this special status (or an associated one called *rentista*) a foreigner has to receive $600 to $1,000 monthly from sources outside the country. This person then has the right to import duty-free a car, electronic items, and other household goods that are prohibitively expensive for Costa Ricans due to steep import taxes.

Foreigners are not only enjoying the beauty of Costa Rica, they are also buying and fencing it. According to Terry Ennis, a realtor and director of the Pensioners Association, more than 60 percent of west coast beachfront property is now in the hands of foreigners.[40]

U.S. Economic Aid

Spread across a block of land on the outskirts of San José, the mammoth new Agency for International Development (AID) headquarters is surrounded by the luxury homes of the country's nouveau riche. One *Tico Times* reporter described the complex as "a monument to what some Costa Ricans are calling the parallel state."[41] The $10 million building is the center for the U.S. government's efforts to stabilize and privatize the Costa Rican economy.

The term *parallel state* became part of the common political vocabulary in 1988 when a close adviser to President Arias, economist John Biehl, charged that AID was creating an infrastructure of private-

sector institutions designed to undermine corresponding public ministries and agencies. The media and business elite were indignant, and
the adviser was quickly removed from government. But the term *parallel state* stuck, and for many Costa Ricans remains the most apt description of AID operations.

The focus of U.S. aid has been economic stabilization with very little
going to economic development. Virtually all the aid has come in the
form of balance-of-payments support (either through the Economic
Support Fund or the PL480 Title I food-aid program), designed to
improve the country's foreign-exchange reserves while giving the government a flexible source of local revenue.[42] Very little of the funds
pumped into the country has come from AID's Development Assistance budget. The U.S. economic aid package includes a Peace Corps
presence, a large scholarship program, and various credit and insurance arrangements sponsored by the departments of Commerce, Agriculture, and the Treasury.

Balance-of-payments support is the main thrust of AID's economic
stabilization plan for Costa Rica. Another level of U.S. strategy comes
into play, however, with the use of the local currency created by all the
U.S. dollars and food pumped into the domestic economy. For the most
part, AID has directed these funds into two interrelated strategies of
economic development: private-sector support and the promotion of
nontraditional exports. It is mainly here, in the allocation of these local-
currency funds, where the so-called parallel state has emerged.

Assisting the Private Sector

Although private-sector support has long been an element in AID's
development philosophy, the Reagan administration converted it into
the common denominator of the agency's development programs. In
Costa Rica, this thrust took two directions: a drive to privatize many
public corporations and agencies, and a multifaceted plan to bolster the
country's business elite.

The privatization strategy garnered widespread public sympathy for
its targeting of bureaucratic inefficiency and corruption prevalent in
many government institutions. The initial target was CODESA, a state
development corporation established in 1972. The tentacles of privatization have also made gestures toward the electricity company. Even the
National Production Council (CNP), the institution responsible for protecting the interests of grain producers and low-income consumers, has
been threatened with privatization. Asked why AID has not demanded that all government corporations be fully privatized, Neil Bil-

lig, the director of the agency's Private Sector Office, confided, "We're already twisting the government's arm as hard as we can. . . . We can't do it all, some are sacred cows."[43] AID's Private Sector Office has recognized that it must tread carefully and has adopted what it calls a "less inflammatory" and "low profile approach to further privatization."[44]

Closely associated with the privatization drive is an AID-backed plan to promote private banking in Costa Rica. As a condition for continued economic assistance, AID obligated the Costa Rican government to allow private banks to benefit from international lines of credit from foreign donors like AID and to permit those banks to accept individual deposits—both previously prohibited under the country's system of nationalized banking.

The result was a proliferation of private financial institutions, a surplus of credit at these banks, and a substantial tightening of credit available to poor and working people through the government's financial system. As Ottón Solís, the country's former planning minister (who resigned as a result of AID's success in undermining the country's nationalized banking system), chided, "One of the corollaries of democracy is the avoidance of the concentration of wealth, which is what the national banking system has helped this country to do. It is, in fact, a fundamental mode of being in this society." He has also stated that this subsidized support for private banking (more than 40 percent of the private banks' assets comes from AID credit lines) contradicts the private-enterprise and free-market standards proclaimed by AID and the advocates of Reaganism.[45] At the same time credit for small farmers and individual consumers can be obtained only at prohibitively high market rates (often over 30 percent).

The other part of AID's private-sector support effort has been support of business associations and the offer of incentives and subsidies to private investment. It is AID's contention that private-sector institutions need to take a more prominent role in forming economic policy and promoting investment in Costa Rica. Given the lack of a preexisting Costa Rican business organization capable of assuming this role, AID created the Costa Rican Coalition for Development Initiatives (CINDE), which AID has infused with tens of millions of dollars since 1983.

To AID critics, CINDE represents the paramount example of the *parallel state*. Rather than channeling agricultural assistance, investment promotion, credit, and industrial development funds through government institutions, AID chose to hatch a new organization to receive its grants. The government has an export-promotion agency called CENPRO, whose effectiveness has been limited by a small budget and low salaries. Rather than working to improve CENPRO, AID devised a component of CINDE, known as the Investment Promotion Program (PIE), to undertake the same functions. The difference is that PIE has a multimillion-dollar budget and can attract the best talent with salary levels comparable to those in the United States.

Other instances of this *parallel state* include the Private Agricultural and Agroindustrial Council (CAAP), which also budded as a branch of CINDE. CAAP's activities parallel those of the Ministry of Agriculture but are exclusively oriented to the promotion of agroexport production. There is also the AID-sponsored Costa Rica Highway and Road Association (which competes with the Ministry of Public Works and Transport) and the Private Investment Corporation (which assumes many of the functions of CODESA).

Addressing the issue of the *parallel state*, John Biehl observed, "They ended up with this fiction: When something is financed with Costa Rican taxpayers' money, it's public sector and inefficient. When the same thing is financed by U.S. taxpayers' money, it's private sector and efficient."[46] This sardonic remark was offered about the same time that an AID inspector general report highlighted the corrupt and often ineffective nature of AID-financed programs in Costa Rica. The report lambasted CINDE for lacking the managerial capacity to administer the large AID grants and for its inability to produce tangible results.

The success or failure of AID's intervention in Costa Rica is still open to debate. AID can point to a tripling of nontraditional exports, but the development impact of this achievement is undercut by two factors: Most of the investment in nontraditional export production is in the hands of U.S. investors who repatriate their profits; and nontraditional exports from the industrial sector are almost entirely assembly-type manufactured goods that provide little direct investment or value-added components to the Costa Rican economy. Although the injection of large sums of U.S. economic aid have indeed allowed Costa Rica to escape the clutches of financial bankruptcy, there is much uncertainty about whether the structural adjustments imposed by AID and other international institutions have equipped the country with the economic base and direction it needs for long-term stability.

Uncertain Future

Since the mid-1980s the level of aid received by Costa Rica has been declining. In 1985, Monge's last year in office, the country received more than $230 million. By the late 1980s the country could count on only $118 million in U.S. aid. The total aid package for 1990 was only

$75 million, with $48 million scheduled for 1991. Politics and economics have both figured into this pattern of decreasing U.S. aid.

The political tension between the Arias government and the White
House certainly was a factor in aid cutbacks in the late 1980s. But AID
never promised Costa Rica a future bankrolled by economic aid. After
more than a billion dollars in direct economic aid, in addition to an
infusion of multilateral assistance, the Costa Rican economy has
emerged from its earlier crisis. In AID's terms, it has been stabilized,
making it harder to justify the authorization of large aid packages.

It will also be more difficult to justify big chunks of Development Assistance to this middle-income country, especially when the foreign-aid
budget is falling and demands for U.S. aid have increased from Eastern
Europe, Panama, and Nicaragua. The U.S. installation of a new government in Panama in December 1989 and the electoral defeat of the
Sandinistas in February 1990 also meant that Costa Rica was no longer
as strategically important for Washington—further diminishing the
country's chances for a renewal of the high assistance levels of the 1980s.

U.S. Military Aid

After a lapse of fourteen years Washington began supplying military
aid and training to Costa Rica in 1981. At that time, former Ambassador to the United Nations Jeane Kirkpatrick insisted that Costa Rica
militarize its security forces as a condition for increased economic aid.
Both U.S. and Costa Rican officials have denied that U.S. military aid
undermines the country's professed commitment to neutrality and
demilitarization.[47]

Through the International Military Education and Training (IMET)
and Military Assistance Program (MAP), more than $30 million in aid
and $1 million in training was provided to the civil and rural guards
between 1980 and 1988. Costa Rican forces have received such items as
helicopters, jeeps, mortars, munitions, and a wide selection of high-
powered rifles. More than 1,200 members of Costa Rica's security
forces have been trained locally by U.S. Mobile Training Teams
(MTTs) in addition to some three hundred trained outside the country
in Panama and at Fort Benning, Georgia.

Civic action projects by U.S. National Guard and Army units have
become an annual event in Costa Rica. In 1989, some 750 U.S. soldiers
arrived to build bridges and roads in the isolated Osa Peninsula. This
civic action program, which the U.S. embassy dubbed Roads for Peace,
raised the ire of some Costa Ricans who complained that the presence
of U.S. soldiers, who are at times armed and dressed in combat uni-

forms, contributes to the increased militarization of the country. Besides road and bridge construction, U.S. military/civic action programs have also installed wells, repaired school buildings, and provided medical assistance. The programs have the dual purpose of generating goodwill toward the U.S. military and providing military engineer and medical units with valuable experience in tropical areas.

The Department of Defense lists four objectives of its security assistance to Costa Rica: to assist in economic stabilization and recovery; to modernize and professionalize the country's security forces; to enable Costa Rica to maintain surveillance of its borders and protect its territorial sovereignty; and to enable the security forces to respond to internal threats with discipline.[48]

With the sometimes halting cooperation of the Costa Rica government, Washington supported the southern front of the *contra* war along the country's northern border with Nicaragua. The corruption, intrigue, and depravity associated with that operation continues to plague U.S.–Costa Rica relations. A report on the 1984 La Penca bombing issued in late 1989 by the country's judicial authorities revealed the dirty underside of U.S. foreign-policy operations in the 1980s. The report blamed the bombing, which occurred at a *contra* camp in Nicaragua just across the Costa Rican border, on U.S. *contra* supporters, the CIA, and the FDN, which was the dominant *contra* group. Although targeting maverick *contra* leader Eden Pastora, the bombing killed three journalists attending a news conference and injured a dozen more, including Tony Avirgan. The report confirmed claims by Avirgan and Martha Honey that the CIA had formed a unit called the Babies within Costa Rica's Directorate of Intelligence and Security that took orders directly from the CIA. It also recommended that U.S. rancher/CIA operative John Hull and CIA operative Felipe Vidal be charged with first-degree murder for the bombing.

The most recent focus of U.S. military and police aid has been antidrug operations. U.S. Special Forces are training local guardsmen in antinarcotics field work, and U.S. DEA and Coast Guard agents have participated in joint antidrug operations with Costa Rican police along the Atlantic Coast and the Panama border.[49]

REFERENCE NOTES

[1] José Figueres, eighty-three years old, died on June 8, 1990, after a prolonged illness. During the 1980s Figueres, who in the past had collaborated with the CIA, was a staunch critic of U.S. policy in Nicaragua.

[2] See Manuel Rojas Bolaños, "Ocho Tesis sobre la Realidad Nacional," and Leonardo Garnier, "Crisis, Desarrollo, y Democracia en Costa Rica," in *Costa Rica: Crisis y Desafíos* (DEI and CEPAS, 1987); Diego Palma, "El Estado y la Desmovilización en Costa Rica," *Estudios Sociales Centroamericanos*, No. 27, 1980.

[3] *Central America Report*, July 6, 1990.

[4] Manuel Rojas Bolaños and Carlos Sojo Obando, "A la Tercera Va la Vencida," *Pensamiento Propio*, March 1990.

[5] Manuel Rojas Bolaños, "Costa Rica Showcase for Democracy and Economic Reformism," *Envío*, May 1990.

[6] *Mesoamérica*, June 1990.

[7] *Costa Rica: Balance de la Situación* (CEPAS), November–December 1988.

[8] Daniel García, "Costa Rica: La Subsidiaria Política Exterior," *Pensamiento Propio*, March 1990.

[9] Ibid.

[10] Jean Hopfensperger, "Costa Rica: Seeds of Terror," *The Progressive*, September 1986.

[11] Interview with Luis Guillermo Solís, vice-minister of foreign relations, quoted in the unpublished report, "Narcotics War: Going for the Gold" by Joel Millman (Institute of Current World Affairs), March 8, 1988.

[12] Sources for this section on export crops included: Wilmer Murillo, "Transnacionales Aumentan Su Poder Económico en Costa Rica," *La República*, October 28, 1988; *Costa Rica Agricultural Situation Annual 1988* (FAS).

[13] National Production Council (CNP), "Compendios Estadísticos Anuales," 1985–1988; CEPAS, *Costa Rica: Balance de la Situación* (CEPAS), April–May 1989.

[14] Abelardo Morales, "Democracia Rural Cede Terreno al Latifundio," *Aportes*, May–June 1984.

[15] Beatriz M. Villareal, *Precarismo Rural en Costa Rica* (San José: Editorial Papiro, 1983), p. 25.

[16] *Costa Rica: Balance de la Situación* (CEPAS), April–May 1989.

[17] Bruce W. Fraser, "Costa Rica Woos Foreign Investors," *Christian Science Monitor*, April 13, 1989.

[18] Bolaños, "Ocho Tesis Sobre la Realidad Nacional," in *Costa Rica: Crisis y Desafíos*, op. cit., p. 26.

[19] "El Movimiento Sindical en Cifras," *Panorama Sindical* (CEPAS), April 1988.

[20] *Foreign Labor Trends: Costa Rica 1987–88* (U.S. Department of Labor).

[21] Curtin Winsor, Jr., "The Solidarista Movement: Labor Economics for Democracy," *The Washington Quarterly*, Fall 1986.

22 Marc Edelman and Joanne Kenen, *The Costa Rica Reader* (New York: Grove Weidenfeld, 1989).

23 Ibid.; *Inforpress Centroamericana*, March 9, 1987.

24 Two valuable articles on media manipulation in Costa Rica are "The Continuing War: Media Manipulation in Costa Rica" by Howard Friel and Michell Joffroy in *Covert Action Information Bulletin*, Summer 1986; and "Back in Control" by Jacqueline Sharkey in *Common Cause Magazine*, September–October 1986.

25 Martha Honey, "Contra Coverage Paid for by the CIA: The Company Goes to Work in Central America," *Columbia Journalism Review*, March–April 1987. According to Morales, the eight journalists are each paid 30,000 *colones* monthly while the monthly salary of most Costa Rican journalists averages about 20,000 *colones*.

26 Main sources for this section: *World Health Statistics Annual 1988* (WHO) and "Caos Sanitario en el País" in *Costa Rica: Balance de la Situación* (CEPAS), August–October 1987.

27 Lynn M. Morgan, "Health Effects of the Costa Rican Economic Crisis," in Edelman and Kenen, *The Costa Rica Reader*, op. cit.

28 *Directorio de Iglesias, Organizaciones, y Ministros del Movimiento Protestante: Costa Rica* (San José: PROLADES, 1986).

29 Ibid.

30 CEPAL, *Diagnóstico de la Situación de la Mujer Centroamericana*, 1988.

31 Cited in "Sterilization in Costa Rica," an article by Abigail Adams in *Links* (NCAHRN), Winter 1987.

32 *Central America Report*, September 1, 1989.

33 *Seminario Universidad*, February 24, 1989.

34 Alexander Bonilla D., *Situación Ambiental en Costa Rica* (ASCONA), no date.

35 *The Amicus Journal*, fall 1988.

36 U.S. Embassy, "Business Fact Sheet," compiled June 1989.

37 Ibid.

38 The book value of U.S. investment is given at only $115 million by the U.S. Department of Commerce.

39 Most information on extent of U.S. corporate investment comes from The Resource Center, "Compilation of Corporations," 1985.

40 Interview by Debra Preusch, March 1989.

41 Lezak Shallat, "AID and the Parallel State," in Edelman and Kenen, *The Costa Rica Reader*, op. cit.

42 Both the ESF and Title I programs function as balance-of-payments support, either by injecting dollars directly into the national treasury (ESF) or shipping food commodities that would otherwise have required scarce dol-

lars to purchase (Title I). When the coveted foreign exchange (ESF) or food (Title I) is then sold to the private sector on the local market, the government obtains a sum of local currency equal to the value of the two programs.

[43] Interview by author with Neil Billig, AID's Private Sector Office, March 1989.

[44] U.S. Agency for International Development/Costa Rica Private Sector Office, "Three Year Strategy," January 25, 1988.

[45] Interview by author with Ottón Solís, March 1989.

[46] Lezak Shallat, "AID and the Parallel State," *The Costa Rica Reader*, op. cit.

[47] Martha Honey, "Undermining a Friend: The Impact of Reagan/Bush Policies in Costa Rica," (unpublished manuscript, July 1989).

[48] U.S. Department of Defense, *Congressional Presentation for Security Assistance, Fiscal Year 1989*.

[49] *Central America Report*, July 6, 1990.

Chapter Three

EL SALVADOR

CHRONOLOGICAL HISTORY

1821   Declaration of independence of Central America; the United Provinces of Central America continues to exist until 1838.

1838   Independence of El Salvador, but pro-Conservative interventions from Guatemala and pro-Liberal interventions from Honduras continue; interparty conflict, assassinations, revolutions.

1886   Stability under Conservative rule for next forty-five years. Communal lands privatized. Coffee becomes dominant crop, and coffee oligarchy consolidates into "Fourteen Families."

1913   Presidency alternates between Meléndez and Quiñónez families until 1927.

1922   Formation of the National Guard.

1931
Mar.   First honest elections; no clear popular winner; Congress elects Arturo Araujo, who begins reformist government.

        Depression wipes out market for coffee.

        Popular agitation led by Communist Party of El Salvador (PCS) under charismatic Augustín Farabundo Martí.

Dec.   Coup led by Minister of War General Maximiliano Hernández Martínez. His dictatorship continues until 1944.

        Martí organizes revolt but is captured first. Revolt occurs, especially among Indian peasants, easily put down.

1932   Up to 30,000 peasants rounded up and massacred in the *matanza*. Martí and PCS leadership publicly executed, PCS outlawed.

        Union organizing outlawed until 1944.

1944   Hernández Martínez overthrown by sit-down strike (Fallen Arms Strike).

Salvadoran Trade Union Reorganizing Committee (CROSS) builds underground union movement.

1945   Castro elected president.

1948   Revolt by reformist junior officers.

1950   New constitution promulgated.

Government party (PRUD) organized.

Presidential elections won by PRUD's Lieutenant Colonel Oscar Osorio. Over next six years, unions are legalized, social security, public housing, and electric power projects are begun.

1956   Lieutenant Colonel José María Lemus of PRUD becomes president after rigged elections. Repressive rule, repudiated by Osorio.

1960–1   Coup by reformist officers.

Conservative countercoup led by Lieutenant Colonel Julio Rivera. New government Party of National Conciliation (PCN, renamed from PRUD) wins all seats in Constituent Assembly.

Foundation of National Democratic Organization (ORDEN), a rural paramilitary network of informers and enforcers, by General José Alberto Medrano of military intelligence.

Formation of Christian Democratic party (PDC).

1962   Rivera elected president on pro–Alliance for Progress platform. Opposition parties boycott elections. New constitution adopted.

1964   José Napoleón Duarte of PDC elected mayor of San Salvador.

1969   "Soccer war" with Honduras over mistreatment of Salvadorans in Honduras and related issues lasts four days.

1970–1   Formation of Popular Liberation Forces (FPL). Formation of People's Revolutionary Army (ERP).

1972   Duarte and Guillermo Manuel Ungo of UNO apparently elected president and vice president, but results altered by electoral commission; Colonel Arturo Molina of PCN elected by Legislative Assembly. Nixon administration declines to use influence to assist Duarte.

Revolt led by reformist younger officers put down with two hundred deaths. Duarte arrested, tortured, exiled.

1974   Fraudulent legislative elections, all PCN candidates win. Formation of Unified Popular Action Front (FAPU).

1975   Formation of second mass organization, Popular Revolutionary Bloc (BPR), linked to FPL.

Formation of Armed Forces of National Resistance (FARN), linked to FAPU.

1976   President Molina attempts moderate land reform, abandoned when landowners threaten armed resistance.

1977   Monsignor Oscar Arnulfo Romero becomes Archbishop of El Salvador.

Assassination of Jesuit Father Rutilio Grande by a death squad apparently sponsored by security forces, the first of seven priests killed in next two years.

General Carlos Humberto Romero elected president in fraudulent election; more than two hundred peaceful protesters killed. Catholic Church boycotts inauguration.

1979   Escalating violence: kidnappings, assassinations, building seizures, and hostage-taking by guerrillas; repression and killings by government forces. More than six hundred political killings during year. Shafik Handal of PCS says armed revolt now necessary.

Oct.   General Romero overthrown by junior officers. First junta formed, including Guillermo Ungo and Lieutenant Colonels Majano and Gutiérrez. Progressive cabinet; Colonel José García defense minister.

United States begins increase in military and economic assistance.

1980
Jan.   First junta and cabinet resign, charging military noncooperation; Ungo goes into exile. Second junta formed, with Majano, Gutiérrez, and Christian Democrats.

Feb.   Banks nationalized and land reform decreed. Death-squad killings escalate.

Archbishop Romero writes letter to President Carter requesting halt of aid.

Mar.   Archbishop Romero assassinated while saying mass.

            Third junta formed with Duarte a member.

April   Formation of the Democratic Revolutionary Front (FDR) to
            coordinate leftist political opposition, which links up with
            FMLN.

May   Coup organized by Roberto D'Aubuisson fails. D'Aubuisson
            organizes Secret Anticommunist Army to coordinate death-
            squad activities.

Oct.   Formation of the Farabundo Martí National Liberation Front
            (FMLN) to coordinate guerrillas.

Nov.   Six FDR leaders killed.

Dec.   Four U.S. churchwomen raped and killed; U.S. military aid
            cut off.

            Third junta disbanded; Duarte becomes provisional president.

1981   Reagan takes office; U.S. military aid resumes.

            FMLN launches "final offensive."

            Head of land-reform institute and two U.S. advisers assassi-
            nated.

            D'Aubuisson organizes Nationalist Republican Alliance
            (ARENA).

1982
Mar.   Elections for Constituent Assembly, boycotted by left. Right-
            wing majority, though PDC largest single party.

            Alvaro Magaña elected president after United States blocks
            D'Aubuisson, who becomes president of Assembly.

1984   Presidential elections: Duarte beats D'Aubuisson in May
            runoffs, inaugurated in June.

            Duarte attempts peace talks with FMLN without prior con-
            sultation with the United States, but FMLN power-sharing
            demands are unacceptable to army and the United States.

1986   New military strategy to clear and hold areas one by one is
            unsuccessful.

            Formation of the National Unity of Salvadoran Workers
            (UNTS).

            New round of peace talks sabotaged by military violation of
            ground rules.

Oct.   Disastrous earthquake in San Salvador: 1,500 killed, 10,000
            families displaced, $1.5 billion damage.

1987

Oct.   Duarte proposes amnesty for political prisoners; Herbert Anaya of nongovernmental Human Rights Commission speaks out against the amnesty and is killed in death-squad fashion. Some political parties withdraw from the National Reconciliation Commission and FMLN talks are broken off as a result.

              Duarte bows and kisses the U.S. flag during a visit to the United States.

              Guillermo Ungo and Ruben Zamora return from exile to enter overt political activity; Zamora kisses the Salvadoran flag.

1988   Death-squad killings rise; FMLN increases military actions, sabotage, assassinations (especially of local officials).

              Catholic Church initiates National Debate for Peace; more than sixty organizations participate.

1989

Jan.   FMLN offers to participate in elections if they are postponed six months, dropping demand for prior participation in government and new military force.

Mar.   Presidential elections won by ARENA's Alfredo Cristiani, 53 percent, to 37 percent for PDC, and only 3.2 percent for Ungo (Democratic Convergence). FMLN ambiguous: calls for boycott, or spoiling ballot, or voting for Ungo. Turnout low.

Oct.   FMLN calls off talks with government after the bombing of FENASTRAS, the country's largest labor federation.

Nov.   FMLN launches major military offensive.

              Six Jesuit priests of the University of Central America, including the rector, are assassinated by the army.

1990

April   UN mediated peace talks begin.

Oct.   United States suspends one-half of military aid package.

1991

Jan.   Suspended U.S. military aid released by Washington.

Mar.   Assembly elections held.

Sources for the chronology include *El Salvador Election Factbook* (Washington, D.C.: Institute for the Comparative Study of Political Systems,

1967); Thomas P. Anderson, *Politics in Central America* (New York: Praeger, 1982); *Conflict in Central America* (London: Longman Group Ltd., 1987); Jan K. Black, *Sentinels of Empire* (Westport, CT: Greenwood Press, 1986); *Crisis in Central America* (Boulder: Westview, 1988); *Labor Organizations in Latin America*, Gerald Greenfield and Sheldon Maran, eds. (Westport, CT: Greenwood Press, 1987); *Central America Report*, March 3, 1989; *Central America Bulletin*, April 1989.

TRENDS

- Mounting international and local pressures pushed the Salvadoran government and military to the negotiating table but hard-line and ideologically extreme elements may obstruct a lasting negotiated solution to the conflict.
- The ARENA government, having promised to end the war quickly by military means and to revive the economy with private-sector remedies, is failing on both counts, resulting in increasing international isolation and widespread domestic dissent.
- The FMLN continues to demonstrate its political and military strength in its persistent challenge to the country's oligarchy and military, while new international and domestic conditions make a negotiated end to the conflict the preferred option.
- Despite rising repression, the popular movement continues to militate for a negotiated peace and economic justice, insisting on the necessity of incorporating its demands and its representatives into any postwar economic and political structures.
- By the end of the 1980s it became clear that the U.S. counterinsurgency strategy in El Salvador had reached a dead end, given the continuing military and political power of the FMLN guerrillas, the bankrupt economy, and the failure of the government to build a national consensus about the political and economic direction of the country.
- Socioeconomic conditions continue to worsen, with the country's future economic and political stability further threatened by signs of reduced U.S. commitment.

The war in El Salvador broke out in 1980 but it was a conflict that had been building for at least half a century. In the late 1920s a popular movement of students, workers, and peasants began coalescing around demands for basic political and economic rights. A U.S. Army officer visiting El Salvador in 1931 described the country this way: "There appears to be nothing between these high-priced cars and the oxcart with its barefoot attendant. There is practically no middle class. . . . Thirty or forty families own nearly everything in the country. They live in almost regal style. The rest of the population has almost nothing."[1]

After a civilian president, Arturo Araujo, proved unable to pacify this mounting internal dissension either with reforms or by repression, the country's vice president, General Maximiliano Hernández Martínez, took over the presidency. In 1932 the general unleashed a scourge of repression that is still referred to simply as the *matanza* or massacre. No one really knows how many died; the most common figure is 30,000 but some say that the army did not have enough bullets to kill more than 10,000. One of those killed was the communist leader Augustín Farabundo Martí, whose name and cause was assumed in 1980 by a guerrilla coalition called the Farabundo Martí National Liberation Front (FMLN).

The repression of 1932 had the desired effect of smothering the dissidents in a blanket of blood. But neither General Hernández Martínez nor any of the generals or colonels that later ruled the country did anything to alter the desperate circumstances of the rural poor or to open up the country's military-controlled political system.

At first look, not much had changed in the five decades that followed the *matanza*. At the end of the 1970s an army general was still in the Casa Presidencial; terror was still used to repress popular organizing; hunger and poverty were the lot of the large majority; and the economic elite or oligarchy was, if anything, more ostentatious in its display of wealth and privilege.

While the country's narrow political and economic divisions remained largely intact, Salvadoran society had been changing in many important and decisive ways. In the 1950s the economy began to diversify. Sharecroppers who worked the traditional *latifundios* were pushed off the land as estates were converted into more modern agricultural enterprises relying on seasonal peasant labor. Other small farmers were pushed off their plots as the agroexport economy expanded beyond coffee to include cattle, cotton, and sugar. El Salvador also began to industrialize, which created new tendencies within the oligarchy and gave birth to a larger working class. The changing economy also gave rise to an expanding middle class of professionals, technicians, small entrepreneurs, and bureaucrats.

New political and religious ideas that began to circulate challenged the traditions and structures of Salvadoran society. The alliance between the Catholic Church and the elite began to break down after Vatican II and the Medellín Conference of 1968 in which the poor were empowered and dignified by new Church teachings, which equated morality and social justice. The revolution in Cuba reverberated throughout the continent, giving leftist organizers and intellectuals new hope that radical change was indeed possible. The economic reformism and attention to rural problems promoted by President John F. Kennedy's Alliance for Progress, although not directly challenging the military and political elite, also stirred the winds of change. So too did the emergence of new political parties like the Christian Democratic party, which created new hope for the country's political and economic future.

In the 1960s and especially in the 1970s the popular sectors began breaking the silence of fear that had settled over the country after the 1932 bloodbath. Peasants demanded land, and workers a decent wage. The booming economy and the expanding reach of the electronic media created rising expectations among the country's downtrodden majority. As if overnight, in the mid-1970s it suddenly seemed that Salvadorans were organized and demanding change.

But neither the oligarchy nor the military were ready to budge. During the 1970s the political opposition was kept out of government by fraudulent elections, and the peaceful protests of students, workers, and peasants were brutally repressed. Political and social tensions reached an apex in 1979 and 1980. It was at this point that the FMLN was formed and the United States moved in to assist the Salvadoran state on its new path of political, military, and economic development.

Repression and uncompromising rule by the military and oligarchy had failed to keep the society pacified. In the 1980s a new combination of civilian rule, counterinsurgency, and halting economic reforms was tested. By the end of the decade, however, class divisions had widened, and what had initially seemed merely a police problem had widened into a civil war.

The war, whose stated purpose was to eliminate the guerrillas, targeted mostly the civilian population. Particularly hard hit were those workers, students, squatters, peasants, and displaced who tried to organize themselves to protect their rights and improve their conditions. From 1979 through 1989, 40,000 to 50,000 civilians died in the conflict, mainly at the hands of the U.S.-trained and supplied military.[2] The combined death toll for civilians and combatants was more than 70,000.

The nearly $4 billion in U.S. aid to El Salvador during the 1980s was justified on the premise that a small group of terrorists was obstructing the country's economic and political progress. But Washington recognized that El Salvador had more than a strictly military problem and that political and economic changes were needed if the Salvadoran state was to be stabilized. Besides building up the army and police, the U.S. government put in place a "democratization" program designed to ensure civilian and constitutional rule. Acknowledging that the economically precarious conditions of most Salvadorans constituted a breeding ground for subversion, Washington spent three of every four aid dollars in economic assistance and stabilization programs.

But neither military nor economic aid succeeded as the country became more militarized, the government grew more unstable, and the divisions between the poor and the rich became yet more extreme. By the end of the decade the cancer of insurgency had been neither neutralized nor removed. (In fact, the enemy's military capacity was greater than ever.) No part of the country's economic, political, or military system was secure from the subversion and even the country's most exclusive neighborhoods had at times become battlegrounds.

After a decade of U.S.-directed democratization and counterinsurgency, the Salvadoran army is more powerful and abusive than ever before, having quintupled in size and having been fortified by more than a billion dollars in U.S. military aid. No longer is the magnitude of its human-rights abuses constrained by the number of bullets it possesses. The military now counts on unlimited firepower and a formidable air force, all of which it uses freely against nonmilitary targets. Although a civilian now wears the presidential sash, the military reigns supreme.

By 1990 per capita income had fallen to one-quarter below the 1980 level. Unemployment was greater than 50 percent, and 45 percent of Salvadorans could not afford even a basic diet—let alone other necessities like health care and housing.[3] At least a third of the population is internally displaced or has been forced to flee the country because of the war. Sixty percent of the urban population and 90 percent of those living in the countryside do not have the economic resources to live in decent housing.[4] Around the major cities shantytowns of cardboard and other discarded materials have sprung up.

At the same time San Salvador saw a boom in the construction of luxury housing and commercial buildings. Services catering to the elite also prospered during the 1980s. A posh commercial center opened, and a new Pizza Hut and other fast-food places sprang up in wealthier neighborhoods. Smartly polished BMWs, Mercedes, and Cherokees—many with tinted windows and some armor-plated—line up for the drive-thrus at such favorite spots as Pop's and McDonald's. Although the economy as a whole was stagnating, U.S. aid and credits pumped billions of dollars into the highest reaches of Salvadoran society. This only further antagonized class divisions and exacerbated the civil war.

War has devastated this Massachusetts-size country of 5.3 million people. It is a war that reflects the country's sharp class divisions and its tradition of militarization. It is also an ideological standoff between those content with electoral democracy and those who want a fuller popular democracy, between those who want to reinforce the private-enterprise system and those who demand radical structural reforms. At the extremes of this divide are right-wing ideologues who embrace fascism and leftist revolutionaries committed to socialist solutions. But more than a civil war, the bloodletting in El Salvador has been a product of an unwavering U.S. commitment to defeat the FMLN and maintain this U.S. client state.

In late 1988 the FMLN announced a strategic offensive to force a negotiated end to the war. By allying itself with the economic demands of the poor and through new political and peace proposals, the FMLN hoped to solidify its base among the bottom 74 percent of society and increase its appeal among the middle sectors. In its view, control of the government by the right-wing ARENA party will only sharpen the contradictions and divisions within Salvadoran society. This, in the end, may only strengthen the FMLN's appeal to the workers, peasants, unemployed, and middle classes.

If there is to be a negotiated settlement to the conflict, it will be necessary for Washington and the Salvadoran government and armed forces to accept the FMLN as the powerful political and military force it has proven itself to be. The FMLN, in turn, will be expected to honor its stated commitment to participate in the electoral process once appropriate guarantees for its security are in place. But if a bilateral cease-fire and serious negotiations prove impossible, this war of attrition could continue at least through ARENA's term in office.

In 1990, ten years after it began, civil war remains the major issue facing El Salvador. But when the war finally ends El Salvador will confront a host of development problems. As one of the most densely populated nations in the world, El Salvador will have a difficult time both feeding itself and increasing its agricultural exports. Infrastructure damage from the war will present a serious impediment to economic modernization and growth. On the positive side, however, Salvadorans are an admirably industrious and organized population with a strong will to survive and progress.

GOVERNMENT AND POLITICS

Since 1979 the right and power to govern have come under serious challenge in El Salvador. The government of El Salvador is subject to the limits imposed by the military and the U.S. embassy and no policy decisions are made without first seeking the approval of these unofficial partners in government. Historically the military has administered government in El Salvador with the blessing of the dominant economic forces. Although the military relinquished formal power to civilians in 1982, it suffered little real loss of power. The authority of the army can be seen most clearly in rural areas, where zone commanders rule surrounding areas like personal fiefdoms. On a national scale, the military makes the key decisions about how the war is fought and how, or if, its end will be negotiated.

The three major centers of governmental power in the country, as set forth in the 1983 constitution, are the presidency, the Legislative Assembly, and the Supreme Court. Like other Central American countries (except for Belize), El Salvador has a unicameral legislature, whose sixty members are elected every three years. The majority political faction in the Legislative Assembly exercises power over the judiciary by appointing Supreme Court members. Local justices are then appointed by the Supreme Court.

The country is divided into fourteen administrative departments, whose governors and deputy governors are appointed by the president. The local level of government called the *municipio*, is governed, in principle, by an elected mayor and city council. During the late 1980s this system of local government was seriously disrupted as mayors became, quite literally, military targets of the FMLN. Out of fear, many mayors have not occupied their offices. New Assembly and mayoral elections took place March 1991, and the next presidential elections are scheduled for 1994.

Another key focus of influence is the Central Election Council (CCE), whose objectivity in vote-counting and regulation is often called into question by opposition parties. Constitutional government by elected civilian authorities became institutionalized in El Salvador during the 1980s. Civilian government and the electoral system were consolidated through five major elections and the peaceful transfer of power from one elected civilian to another in 1989—the first time in the country's history. But this U.S.-backed democratization has been weakened by a persistent decrease in the number of Salvadorans going to the polls and the failure of elected governments to resolve the country's two major crises: a widening civil war and worsening socioeconomic conditions.

Political Parties and Elections

The March 1989 election gave the presidency to Alfredo Cristiani and consolidated the right-wing ARENA party's power over the government. ARENA controlled the Supreme Court during all five years of the Christian Democratic presidency of José Napoleón Duarte. It also regained supremacy over the Assembly in 1988 after having lost to the Christian Democratic party (PDC) in the 1985 elections. The ARENA victory in 1989 came as no surprise. It had trounced the PDC in mayoral and Assembly elections the year before, winning 48 percent of the vote to the 35 percent of the Christian Democrats. ARENA broadened its electoral victory in 1989, gathering 54 percent of the vote to the 36 percent of the PDC. In addition, it controls 70 percent of the municipal seats.

On one hand, the successful transfer of the presidency represented the new strength of the electoral system in the 1980s; but on the other, the decreasing participation of voters in elections indicated an underlying weakness of this democratization process. More than 1,551,000 voters had gone to the polls in 1982 but only 1,003,000 cast ballots in 1989.[5] If the rate of abstention takes into account all 2.3 million potential voters, ARENA effectively obtained only twenty-two votes out of one hundred possible ones. If calculating only those registered to vote, ARENA won twenty-eight of every one hundred voters with an election identity card. But when considering only those who actually voted, ARENA won a clear majority: fifty-four votes of every one hundred cast.[6]

ARENA: The Party of the Right

The key figure in the creation of the Nationalist Republican Alliance (ARENA) in September 1981 and its maturation as a political party has been Roberto D'Aubuisson. In March 1980 D'Aubuisson, a former military intelligence officer, was arrested and briefly held for planning a coup against the Duarte-led junta. Formerly, D'Aubuisson had worked under General José Alberto Medrano, the founder of ORDEN (National Democratic Organization), a paramilitary network of informers and enforcers organized by the security forces to crush political discontent in rural areas. His coup attempt having failed, D'Aubuisson used the contacts he developed through ORDEN and his activities as an intelligence officer to lay the foundation of a new political party.[7]

As a new party, ARENA brought together oligarchs, rightists, conservative professionals, and military hard-liners around the themes of virulent anticommunism and nationalism. Although initially it had opposed the elections for Legislative Assembly scheduled for March 1982, ARENA later decided to enter the electoral contest and won 29 percent of the vote. Joining with the Party of National Conciliation (PCN), traditionally the party of the military, ARENA formed a right-wing coalition in the new Assembly, which elected D'Aubuisson Assembly president. Only pressure from the United States prevented the Assembly from naming him provisional president. In 1984 D'Aubuisson ran against Duarte for president but lost in the run-off election. The following year the PDC also won control over the Assembly.

A Face-Lift for the Election

After its defeat in the 1985 Assembly elections, ARENA began a process of party-strengthening in preparation for the 1988 and 1989 elections.[8] D'Aubuisson began grooming Alfredo "Fredy" Cristiani to represent the new public image of ARENA when he suggested that Cristiani be placed on the party's executive council in 1985. The next year Cristiani became party president although D'Aubuisson retained his position as "maximum leader." Cristiani, with his moderate image and no known death-squad connections, proved the perfect candidate for the United States.

Despite his status as a leading member of the country's narrow oligarchy and a representative of the far-right ARENA party, Cristiani was hailed by the White House and the U.S. Congress as El Salvador's new "moderate." Educated at the American School in San Salvador and later at Georgetown University, Cristiani speaks English flawlessly and projects himself as a political moderate.

Cristiani personifies ARENA's close connections with the agroexport oligarchy and the industrial bourgeoisie. Born into a wealthy family, he came into more wealth with his marriage to Margarita Llach—a member of one of the country's mythic fourteen oligarchic families. He is the epitome of the modern oligarch, owning such diverse interests as a pharmaceutical corporation in San Salvador and coffee estates in San Vicente. Cristiani also has been president of the Salvadoran Coffee

Exporters' Association (1977) and vice president of the National Private Enterprise Association (1977–1979).

Tendencies Within ARENA

Nationalism, anticommunism, commitment to private enterprise, and deep distaste for the liberalism and opportunism of the Christian Democrats have been the unifying principles of ARENA. Like any other political party, ARENA is not monolithic but composed of various factions and tendencies, some being more extreme than others.

Politically, there is a strong extremist faction comprising early D'Aubuisson loyalists and military hard-liners. These are the party's radical conservatives who will tolerate no compromise with the FMLN, calling for a quick military victory against the guerrillas no matter what the cost in human lives. It is within this extremist faction that ARENA's nationalist tendency is also most strong. Within the ranks of these radical conservatives there runs a strong neofascist current, manifested in the party's fist-to-heart salutes, the fanaticism of party youth, and its appeals to the defense of God and fatherland.

The ideological purity and fanaticism of the political extremists have been somewhat offset by the party's political pragmatists. Confronted with the difficulties of running a government, the pragmatist forces gained increased influence within ARENA. These realists recognize that any political, military, or economic solution promoted by the party must take into account the need to maintain international support. It was this faction that warned that a postelection outbreak of terrorism and massacres would destabilize the government by sparking wider popular opposition and cutting the country off from international sources of capital.

Shortly before his murder on November 16, 1989, Ignacio Ellacuria, rector of the University of Central America, described three tendencies with ARENA: the civilian tendency of Cristiani, the militarist tendency of D'Aubuisson, and the death-squad tendency. According to Ellacuria, "D'Aubuisson is not now responsible for the death squads because he understood the necessity of moderating his party to be able to win the elections."[9]

Cristiani and the more moderate ARENA supporters, associated primarily with the country's modernized business community, have seemed seriously interested in negotiating an end to the war. Cristiani recognizes that the success of his government and the future prospects of ARENA depend on his administration's ability to end the war, while the nonideological business community understands that economic growth is impossible as long as the war lasts. William LeoGrande has pointed out that unlike the traditional oligarchy the modernized private sector "believes that its economic interests can be safeguarded in a democratic system"—a belief reinforced by ARENA's resounding electoral victories in the 1980s.[10]

By late 1990, however, ARENA seemed to be losing support on all sides. Its failure to reactivate the economy and end the war frustrated its private-sector allies, while its willingness to continue the dialogue with the FMLN angered the hard-line factions of the army and the party. ARENA also found itself increasingly isolated internationally because of its inability to prosecute successfully the case against those responsible for the 1989 massacre of the Jesuit priests and the steady increase in human-rights violations, a situation that put it at odds with the United Nations. ARENA maintained its confrontational stance with the popular sectors and Catholic Church, further narrowing its already thin base of electoral support.

Rise and Fall of the Christian Democratic Party

The Salvadoran Christian Democratic party (PDC) holds classic Christian-democratic principles: a denial of the necessity of class conflict, and espousal of a populism and reformism that do not threaten established social and economic structures. The PDC has been a party preeminently of rising middle and working classes in urban areas, as well as rural people of all social levels. Although progressive in tone, the party's position was never antiimperialist, nor even clearly antimilitary, but it has always stood for the principle of civilian control. Its reformist reputation, combined with its flexibility and the prestige of its leader, José Napoleón Duarte, made it an ideal civilian partner for the military in the 1980s. The party's right wing took the formal reins of government with the formation of the second military-civilian junta in early 1980.

Since 1980 the party has seen its political base shrink steadily. Its left wing split off in early 1980, disgusted with the party's willingness to join the military-civilian junta. In each election since 1982 the number of votes cast for the PDC has dropped—from 590,000 in 1982 to 340,000 in 1989. Thrust into national office in 1980, for most of the decade the party was the willing, although at times uncomfortable, instrument for the U.S. counterinsurgency project.

Once in office Duarte made little effort to maintain his support among the U.S.-backed unions and peasant associations that had thrust him into the presidential seat. Instead, defeating the FMLN—the priority of the U.S. government and its allies in the Salvadoran military and elite—became the government's top priority as well. Earlier promises to push forward economic reforms and pursue peace negotiations fell aside. Duarte's economic policy, like that of the United States, became increasingly oriented toward the private sector, leaving the poor majority to face deteriorating socioeconomic conditions. During the Duarte administration, as government corruption soared to new heights, living standards kept falling, and human-rights abuses against labor leaders and popular activists continued unabated.

Disgusted with the subservience, corruption, and internal factionalism of the PDC, many voters joined with the right wing to push the Christian Democrats out of office. Much to the consternation of the U.S. embassy, ARENA in 1988 swept the local elections, gaining control over the Legislative Assembly and a clear majority of the municipalities. Only the presidential seat remained in the hands of the PDC, and that too became ARENA's in the March 1989 presidential elections.

Having lost its base of popular support as a party that stood for reforms and negotiated peace, the PDC presidential candidate Fidel Chávez Mena secured only 36 percent of the votes cast in the March 1989 contest. After the elections the PDC quickly adapted to its new role as the opposition party, seeing itself as the popular alternative in the 1991 Assembly elections. Reminiscent of the electoral alliances the party had formed in the early 1980s, the PDC promoted candidates from the National Campesino Workers Union (UWOC) and the Salvadoran Workers Union (CST) during the 1991 campaign.

Alliances on the Left

Foremost among Salvadoran leftist political forces are those of the FMLN. It is at once both a political and military organization. Although it does not yet have its own political party, the FMLN has offered to enter into the electoral arena in the event of a negotiated settlement to the war.

Since 1980 the main unarmed leftist organization has been the Democratic Revolutionary Front (FDR), formed in April 1980 immediately after the assassination of Archbishop Oscar Arnulfo Romero. In the months that followed virtually all the dissident groups in El Salvador—political parties, activist religious groups, mass popular organizations, unions, and peasant associations—joined the FDR, which went on to function in the 1980s as the diplomatic voice of the left opposition to the government. The FMLN-FDR alliance united the armed and unarmed left, although members of the FDR coalition sometimes have taken positions distinct from those of the FMLN. Despite continual rumors of its dissolution, circulated mostly by the U.S. embassy, the FMLN-FDR alliance has endured into the 1990s. There are three political parties included in the FDR: The National Revolutionary Movement (MNR) is a party primarily of intellectuals led by Guillermo Ungo. MNR is affiliated with the Socialist International and is a member of the Permanent Conference of Political Parties of Latin America (COPPAL). There is also the Popular Social Christian Movement (MPSC), a party formed in March 1980 when progressive members of the Christian Democratic party split in protest over the party's continued association with *de facto* military rule. Ruben Zamora, appointed as a minister in the first junta, is the secretary-general of MPSC. The final party in the FDR is the National Democratic Union (UDN), which formed in 1968 as a legal front for the outlawed Communist Party of El Salvador. Led by Mario Aguiñalda Carranza, the UDN maintains a socialist ideology.

The Democratic Convergence

The unarmed political left had previously denounced elections as part of a counterinsurgency strategy to put a democratic front on a repressive state apparatus. It reversed this policy in 1988 and decided to participate in the 1989 election campaign. FDR leaders Guillermo Ungo and Ruben Zamora returned to the country for the first time since 1980 and helped forge the Democratic Convergence (CD). The three political parties that comprised this new electoral coalition were MNR, MPSC, and the Social Democratic party (PSD), a party formed in 1987. Ungo was nominated as the presidential candidate, and the PSD's Mario Reni Roldán was nominated as vice president.

Even though the CD never harbored any illusion of winning the election, it did hope to do better both in the vote-counting and in the realm of popular mobilization. It had projected winning 10 percent to 15 percent of the vote, but collected only 3.8 percent, placing a sad fourth. The principal reason for this poor showing was the last-minute call by the FMLN, the CD's major support group, for an election boycott and a transportation stoppage on election day.

It was the position of the FMLN that the CD made the wrong choice when it decided to stay in the election campaign even after the government had rejected the FMLN's January 1989 peace proposal. Despite some bitter feelings after the elections, the FMLN contended that the FMLN-FDR alliance had in fact been strengthened by the mid-1989

FMLN offer to enter the electoral arena after a negotiated settlement.[11]

Another factor in the CD's failure to generate more popular support was the antielectoral position taken by many popular organizations. Not only were the Salvadoran people tired of the war, but they were also in large part tired of showcase elections, which had proven ineffective mechanisms for effecting needed social and economic reforms. Despite its weak showing in the 1989 elections, the CD's potential to draw votes in the future should not be discounted, given the extensive outreach work of its associated parties. The prospects of the CD and leftist parties also hinge on the FMLN's proposal to join the electoral arena, possibly forming a broad-based alliance with the CD. Given sufficient lead time for campaigning and proper international guarantees for their personal security, leftist politicians may eventually win control of the government.

In April 1990 when the FMLN and the government agreed to begin UN-moderated negotiations, there was widespread hope that a cease-fire would be signed by September 1990 and that the March 1991 elections would present an opportunity for peaceful change and reform. The peace talks, however, did not prove immediately fruitful and by late 1990 it was apparent that the March 1991 municipal and Assembly elections would proceed, as had previous elections, in the atmosphere of war. Opinion surveys in late 1990 showed widespread dissatisfaction with ARENA because of its poor economic performance and the rising repression. Concerned about its falling popularity, ARENA began to court the support of the Authentic Christian Movement (MAC), a rightist spinoff of the PDC, and the Party of National Conciliation (PCN).

President Cristiani's inability to deliver on his campaign promise to end the war and reactivate the economy increased the prospects for the candidates of the PDC and the leftist parties. Both the UDN and the Democratic Convergence were running well-known candidates from the UNTS leftist labor federation, raising the possibility for the first time that the popular movement would have a direct voice in the Legislative Assembly.

The Peace Process

The first talks between the FMLN and the Salvadoran government were held in October 1984 in La Palma, Chalatenango, several months after Duarte was inaugurated as president. A second meeting was held in November in La Libertad, at which the FMLN presented a broad peace proposal calling for the formation of a transition government, official recognition of guerrilla-held territory, and the fusion of the FMLN and the government's army. The proposal was dismissed by the Duarte government, which insisted that the FMLN lay down its arms and incorporate into the constitutionally regulated democratic process. Three years later in June 1987 the FMLN presented the government with a new proposal calling for the humanization of the war and the renewal of talks. This was also rejected by Duarte and the military.

Running parallel to the bilateral talks between the FMLN and the government have been the regional peace talks. The Central American peace process was set in motion in February 1987 at the Guatemala border town of Esquipulas. Although the Duarte government signed the Esquipulas accords, it made no serious efforts to end the civil war or to achieve internal peace. The Duarte government persisted in its demand that the guerrillas lay down their arms and join the ongoing political process.

Although they did not bring peace to El Salvador, the Esquipulas accords broadened the political space to permit FDR leaders Guillermo Ungo and Ruben Zamora to found the Democratic Convergence, and helped bolster popular and guerrilla pressure for a negotiated settlement. By 1988 calls for a settlement of the civil war echoed throughout the region—from the increasingly unified popular movement within the country to regional meetings of presidents and foreign ministers. With the winding down of the *contra* war against Nicaragua, El Salvador's civil war became the main impediment to regional peace.

In January 1989 the FMLN announced an innovative electoral proposal that demonstrated its new willingness to participate in the electoral arena. Dropping their long-held demand for a transition government, power-sharing, and the dismantling of the armed forces, the FMLN said that it would cease hostilities and abide by the results of a presidential election. But rather than participating in the upcoming March election, it proposed postponing the election until September, thereby gaining time to prepare an election campaign together with the FDR and the Democratic Convergence. The proposal apparently represented an attempt by the FMLN to align itself more closely with the demands for peace by the National Debate for Peace (a broad-based national dialogue begun by the Catholic Church) and other social forces. The proposal also revealed an increasing realization that there was little international support for a prolonged guerrilla war.

The January 1989 proposal was rejected by the Christian Democratic government, ARENA, and the military on the grounds that it would violate the Salvadoran constitution. The Salvadoran government charged that the proposal was little more than a ploy to advance the political and military projects of the FMLN. Like Washington, the Salvadoran government and military regarded the FMLN as a debilitated military force negotiating out of weakness.

Its political project rebuffed, the FMLN expanded and intensified its military project to undermine official claims that the guerrilla forces were simply isolated terrorist bands. Put on the political defensive by the bold electoral proposal of January 1989, the Salvadoran state also found itself increasingly on the defensive militarily. The FMLN, considering the March 1989 election "a fundamental political component of the low-intensity war strategy," called for a voter boycott and transportation stoppage, while pursuing its political goals through increased diplomatic initiatives.

The Tela Accords, signed in August 1989 by five Central American presidents (Belize and Panama did not participate), were a product of the forward momentum for peace created by the Esquipulas accords and new Sandinista initiatives in Nicaragua. The Salvadoran government, which had argued for the demobilization of the FMLN similar to that stipulated for the *contras*, was forced to back down from its insistence on symmetry between the *contras* and the FMLN and to sign the accords, which called for direct talks between the government and the FMLN. The Tela Accords, however, also called for the FMLN to lay down its arms, recognize the ARENA government, and incorporate itself in the country's political process.

FMLN and ARENA Maneuver to End War

Local, regional, and international pressure pushed both the FMLN and the new ARENA government to enter into talks following the ARENA victory and the Tela summit. Although the FMLN's proposals basically followed the outlines of its electoral proposal of January 1989, they also represented a hardening of its position. In its April 1989 proposal, for example, the FMLN insisted that ARENA declare itself to be a government of transition.

During later talks in Mexico and Costa Rica, the FMLN offered new compromises and initiatives that kept the new government on the defensive. Again dropping its previous demand for power-sharing, the FMLN stated its willingness to cease hostilities and convert, together with other dissident forces, into a political party that would campaign in Legislative Assembly and municipal elections. The FMLN said that it didn't seek a quota of power, but space and guarantees to compete for power. Besides its political offer, the FMLN also agreed in September 1989 to end its sabotage campaign, to terminate its use of antipersonnel mines, and to call a unilateral cease-fire during negotiations.

The FMLN peace proposal demanded the following in return: an end to all repression of the popular movement, reorganization of the judicial system, punishment of those responsible for the assassination of Archbishop Romero, advancement of the 1991 elections including an election for the now-appointed department governors, a purge of the abusive and criminal elements from the army, a reduction in the size of the army, an end to government economic programs detrimental to the poor, and respect for the 1980 agrarian reform. In addition, the FMLN suggested that further U.S. aid be used for the reconstruction of the war-devastated country.

When talks between the FMLN and the new government began in September 1989, it seemed to many that El Salvador was closer to peace than at any other time since the civil war broke out. But it remained difficult to visualize a negotiated end to the conflict. The army, which would necessarily have to approve any such settlement, declined to participate in peace talks and persisted in its illusion that the FMLN was at its "politically and militarily weakest point."

Rather than responding in kind to the FMLN's deescalation of the war by halting the use of sabotage and car-bombs and its unilateral cease-fire, the army took advantage of the lull in guerrilla strikes to mount its own offensive, trying to regain an upper hand in the war. Following the October 31, 1989, bombing of the FENASTRAS union federation headquarters, the FMLN unilaterally broke off the talks, charging that neither the government nor the army was seriously interested in putting an end to political violence. On the contrary, the military had unleashed a campaign of repression against popular organizations and those leaders suspected of FMLN links.

Less than two weeks later the FMLN launched its most daring offensive of the war. The army responded with aerial bombings of San Salvador *barrios* where the guerrillas were entrenched, causing many hundreds of civilian deaths and forcing the evacuation of 50,000 frightened residents. Although failing to break the military stalemate of the war, the offensive did demonstrate the FMLN's impressive military capacity and set in motion a new series of peace talks.

At their December 1989 summit the presidents of Guatemala, Honduras, Costa Rica, Nicaragua, and El Salvador again called for peace in the region. President Daniel Ortega of Nicaragua presented the FMLN's proposal, requesting an internationally supervised cease-fire, an end to human-rights violations—with international verification—

the removal of major military figures involved in human-rights abuses, and a "definitive" dialogue with the ARENA government. The proposal was rejected by Cristiani, and in a diplomatic setback for the FMLN, the five presidents hammered out a compromise statement that condemned the FMLN offensive, likened the FMLN to the *contras*, and supported peaceful resolutions to regional conflicts.[12] The FMLN condemned the summit declaration as one-sided and rejected the implication that a symmetry existed between it and the *contras*.

By early 1990, however, plans were being made for a new round of talks between the FMLN and the government under the auspices of the United Nations. Both sides promised they would not unilaterally break off the talks as the FMLN did following the October bombing of the FENASTRAS union headquarters. While international pressure might keep the two sides talking, it was still doubtful if the Salvadoran government and military would budge from their stubborn position that any peace settlement would have to conform to the dictates of the country's constitution and that the integrity of the Salvadoran armed forces was nonnegotiable. Nonetheless, hope for a negotiated settlement was bolstered by new U.S. congressional opposition to military aid and proposals that any further aid be conditioned on continuing negotiations and prosecution of those responsible for the November 16, 1989, massacre of six Jesuit priests and a mother and daughter.

Since its first electoral proposal in early 1989, the FMLN has made numerous concessions in the interests of obtaining a negotiated settlement, including dropping earlier demands for power sharing and integration of rebel and military forces; accepting elections as a legitimate path to gain political power; no longer demanding permanent control over territory based on military strength; and accepting the legitimacy of the constitution and elected government. These positions placed the FMLN closely in line with the sentiment of an expanding popular movement and war-weary population, giving the guerrillas new political strength and legitimacy.

In return to laying down its arms the FMLN has demanded that the armed forces be cleansed of its worst human-rights violators and that the military be reduced to the pre-1980 level (about 12,000). In addition it asked that the country's three security forces (National Guard, Treasury Police, and National Police) be separated from the military command structure and that the country's judicial system be substantially reformed. To allow its participation in the elections, the FMLN also has insisted that the country's election schedule be modified. These negotiating demands, especially those calling for the purging and reduction of military forces, closely paralleled those of the popular movement, the Catholic Church, and to some extent even the U.S. Congress.[13]

The suspension of U.S. military aid in late 1990 seemed to signal that the war was drawing to a close. The possibilities for peace seemed to suffer a severe cutback however when the State Department announced in January 1991 that this aid would be released following the March elections.

Finally, in late April, the two sides signed an accord that appeared to pave the way to an eventual peaceful conclusion to the war. The agreement signed in Mexico City under UN mediation called for important changes in the country's constitution in regard to the armed forces, the electoral system, human rights, and the judicial system. It was agreed, for example, that a "Truth Commission" would investigate human-rights abuses, that a new nonpartisan electoral commission would be established, and that a new police force under civilian authority would be formed. Negotiations were established to set the conditions and a date for a cease fire; these talks were to also consider other contested issues such as agrarian reform, the process of demobilization of both armies, and the purging of human-rights violators in the army.

Although the "Agreement of Mexico" seemed to make a negotiated settlement inevitable, numerous obstacles remained. Fearing a loss of privilege, the army immediately blocked a cease-fire agreement. Deep dissension among the right wing and sectors of the military also hindered the negotiations. Nonetheless, there was finally "light at the end of the tunnel," as the newly elected UDN assembly member observed. Although the agreement brought no immediate halt to U.S. military aid, there was strong sentiment in the U.S. Congress to convert the military assistance into economic aid or to use it to help integrate combatants into civilian life. Fidel Chávez Mena, leader of the Christian Democrats, warned: "After a cease fire and a formal peace, something much worse is going to occur here. That's the crisis of peace, when the true problems of this country will overwhelm."

Human Rights

Since 1980 human-rights monitoring groups have denounced El Salvador for the estimated 40,000 to 50,000 civilians who have been killed or have disappeared due to the country's security forces. Organizations like Amnesty International and Americas Watch have also charged the guerrilla forces with abuses but on a considerably smaller scale. Amnesty International describes El Salvador as a country where the "ordinary citizen has no protection when threatened with anonymous violence . . . as the police or the military themselves carry out death-squad killings."[15] In its 1988 report *Nightmare Revisited*, Americas Watch warned that the situation in El Salvador was on the verge of returning to the massive killings of the early 1980s.[16]

Denunciations by human-rights monitors contrasted greatly over the decade with the generally positive picture of the Salvadoran security forces painted by the U.S. government. However, in its monitoring and reporting of the human-rights situation, the U.S. embassy typically does not gather information itself, but uses press reports—reports that usually are based on army press releases.[17] The establishment press in the United States does little better, with the *New York Times* particularly failing egregiously in its responsibilities.[18]

A characteristic feature of human-rights violations in El Salvador is the coverups and obstructions of justice that result when the legal system is used to punish the perpetrators of abuses. Amnesties are declared, witnesses are intimidated, and judges are coopted. Uncooperative judges are killed, as are human-rights workers. Four of the founders of the nongovernmental Human Rights Commission of El Salvador (CDHES) were killed within ten years of the organization's founding.[19] On the other hand, no military or police officers have been tried and convicted of human-rights abuses against civilians.[20] Some enlisted soldiers have been convicted, principally where the victims were U.S. citizens.[21] It was widely hoped that the arrest in January 1990 of a Salvadoran colonel, two junior officers, and five soldiers for the November 1989 murder of six Jesuit priests, their housekeeper, and her daughter would lead to the first exception to this pattern.

Numerous human-rights organizations have emerged as part of the popular movement. These include the Human Rights Commission (CDHES), Committee of Mothers of the Disappeared (COMADRES), Federation of Committees of Mothers and Families (FECMAFAM), and the Christian Committee of the Displaced (CRIPDES). The State Department labels such groups "FMLN fronts" and dismisses their human-rights reports as "highly distorted" and "fabrications." CDHES, which has been nominated for the Nobel Peace Prize three times, is, according to the State Department, "the FMLN human-rights organization."[22]

Two organizations associated with the Catholic Church that document human-rights abuses and provide legal assistance to victims are Socorro Jurídico Cristiano and Tutela Legal. The Institute of Human Rights of the University of Central America (IDHUCA) also monitors human-rights violations and publishes reports. The government has its own Human Rights Commission (CDH) that focuses almost exclusively on charging the FMLN with human-rights abuses.

The human-rights situation worsened dramatically in late 1989. The United Nations General Assembly denounced the aerial bombing of civilian neighborhoods in San Salvador by the Salvadoran air force. The imposition of martial law, increased media censorship, the enactment of a new penal code, and the widespread arrest of union leaders, church activists, and representatives of popular organizations also resulted in international condemnation of the ARENA government. The penal code, which has been characterized as "fascist" by the Christian Democratic party, authorizes the arrest and imprisonment for up to four years of those found distributing or printing literature that subverts the public order. Finally, the massacre of the Jesuits on November 16, 1989, focused world attention on the deteriorating human-rights climate in El Salvador.

Six months following the Jesuit murders, the congressional Arms Control and Foreign Policy Caucus issued a report that challenged the military's ability to improve its human-rights practices. The report found that troops under fifteen of the military's top commanders were charged with committing serious human-rights crimes. It stated that "of the 14 commanders, whose troops reportedly committed abuses, 11 received U.S. training. This raises doubts about the military's ability to absorb U.S. training in human-rights principles or possibly about the relevance of the U.S. training."[23]

MILITARY

Despite more than $1 billion in U.S. military aid and substantial clandestine support by U.S. intelligence agencies, the Salvadoran military has never become the professional army its U.S. sponsors were hoping for. It remains a highly corrupt institution without the capacity to defeat an underequipped guerrilla army less than one-sixth its size.

The November 1989 offensive by the FMLN highlighted the shortcomings of the military. Despite many signs that the FMLN was preparing a general offensive, the army was unprepared for the breadth and intensity of the FMLN's campaign. The offensive demonstrated the army's inability to wage counterinsurgency war in the cities; only by relying on aerial bombings of poor neighborhoods was the military able to drive the guerrillas from their urban strongholds. The offensive also shattered the belief that the military had the upper hand in the war and that the FMLN was a guerrilla force in the process of disintegration. The military's difficulty in turning back daring advances by the FMLN seriously damaged its prestige and aggravated tensions within its ranks.

As it entered its second decade of war, the Salvadoran armed forces also faced serious political problems. In the United States, public opposition to U.S. military aid to El Salvador was growing stronger and there was new talk in Congress of imposing human-rights conditions on further aid. Also weakening the position of the military in the counterinsurgency war has been the inability of the Salvadoran government to sustain a project of national reconstruction and economic recovery. Upon assuming control of the government, the Cristiani administration, like the Duarte administration before it, attempted to shape a government that would offer a strong foundation on which to base a counterinsurgency war. But burdened by a deteriorating economy and presiding over a country where conditions for the poor seem only to worsen, Cristiani, like his predecessor, has proven inadequate for this strategic role. The government's association with extremist military and political elements, its failure to build coalitions with popular sectors, and its difficulty in attracting international support have undermined its value and effectiveness as a partner with the military in counterinsurgency.

Structure and Organization

The two main figures within the military are the minister of defense, selected by the president, and the chief of staff of the Salvadoran Armed Forces, chosen by the military hierarchy itself. The armed forces consist of the army, air force, and navy. Together they number some 55,000 officers and soldiers—almost quintuple the 1980 figures.[24] The army, comprising eight brigades, seven regional detachments, and thirty-three battalions, forms the bulk of the armed forces. Military reserves and a civil-defense force constitute auxiliary components of the armed forces.[25]

Also operating under military authority are the country's three main security forces: the National Guard, National Police, and Treasury Police. Founded in 1912, the National Guard is a rural gendarmerie that has traditionally functioned as a security force for plantation owners. The National Police, established in the mid-nineteenth century, maintains security on roads and highways. The newest service, the Treasury Police, was created in 1937 to enforce treasury regulations against smuggling and moonshining but has developed into a political and intelligence police force with associated death-squad and terrorist operations. During the war, the three police units have provided the main protection for San Salvador.

Two major weaknesses of the military are its reliance on forced recruitment and its system of automatic upgrading of officers (the *tanda* system). The constitution mandates universal military service, but legislation to structure a military draft has never been passed. To fill its ranks, the military forcibly recruits 12,000 to 20,000 poor youths annually. At movie theaters, soccer fields, and even schools, youths as young as fourteen are forcibly conscripted. Unless a family has money or connections to win their release, the young men are required to serve for two years, receiving about $80 a month. The weaknesses of the recruiting system are paralleled by deficiencies in the officer corps. Officers are largely the product of the Gerardo Barrios Military School, which graduates classes of junior lieutenants.[26] Each class, or *tanda*, then jointly rises in grade until reaching the rank of colonel. Bound by loyalty to their *tanda*, the officers mutually assist one another in what is, according to a U.S. military report, "a West Point Protection System gone berserk."[27] This system of advancement and solidarity means that officers rise to high positions regardless of merit or competence. Despite U.S. attempts to "professionalize" the Salvadoran armed forces, the *tanda* system dominates the hierarchical structure.

In October 1988 the thirty-fifth class, which graduated in 1966, rose to top positions within the armed forces. Known as the *tandona*, or big class, it had forty-five members, approximately double the normal size, and is known for its hard-line officers and extreme solidarity. Members of the *tandona* include ARENA's Roberto D'Aubuisson; Colonel Sigifredo Ochoa Pérez (retired), another ARENA leader named by President Cristiani to be head of the public corporation that generates electricity for the country; Colonel Juan Orlando Zepeda, appointed undersecretary of defense by Cristiani; Colonel René Emilio Ponce, appointed armed forces chief of staff in November 1988 and defense minister in mid-1990; Mauricio Staben, a battalion commander against whom charges of running a kidnapping racket for ransom were dropped "for lack of evidence" after members of the *tandona* had rallied in his defense; and Colonel Mauricio Vargas, the army's foremost counterinsurgency theorist and one of the few Latin American officers to have taught at the U.S. School of the Americas in Panama.

By 1989 the *tandona* had assumed control over ten of the fourteen military zones, five of seven military detachments, five of six prestigious brigades, the three police forces, and three of the military commands (intelligence, operations, and personnel). The implication of one member, Colonel Guillermo Alfredo Benavides, in the November 1989 murder of the Jesuits indicates cracks in the unity of the *tandona* and is a sign that the military high command might be willing to forsake one of its high officers in the interest of continued high levels of unrestricted U.S. aid.

Besides their anticommunist ideological underpinnings the Salvadoran armed forces have a vested financial interest in continuing the war. They have parlayed U.S. military aid into a small financial empire in El Salvador, comprising banks, real estate, insurance, and other business ventures.[28] Unlike the private sector as a whole, the health of military-related business depends on continuation of the war. The aid feeds the pervasive corruption within the armed forces. In the final analysis, the military's now-privileged position in government and society would be challenged by an end to the war.[29]

Paramilitary Groups

With names like the Secret Anticommunist Army, White Warriors Union, and the Revolutionary Anticommunist Extermination Action, death squads have terrorized the popular movement since the 1970s. These bands of heavily armed, uniformed men have kidnapped, tortured, and killed tens of thousands of Salvadoran labor leaders, church activists, students, suspected guerrillas, and community organizers. It would be a mistake, however, to categorize death-squad members simply as right-wing extremists, as the U.S. embassy does. In its 1988 report, *El Salvador: Death Squads—A Government Strategy*, Amnesty International concluded that the so-called death squads "are simply used to shield the government from accountability for torture, disappearances, and extrajudicial executions committed in their name. . . . Squads are made up of regular army and police agents under orders of superiors."

Just as the death squads should not be considered apart from the armed forces, neither should they be regarded simply as a domestic invention. There is good reason to believe that the emergence of death squads in El Salvador and throughout Latin America was directly related to U.S. counterinsurgency, intelligence, and police-training programs. One important source of supplies and training for anticommunist terrorism was the Agency for International Development's Office of Public Safety, which trained Salvadoran police and the National Guard between 1962 and 1975. The police-training program was established by President Kennedy to "counter communist inspired or

exploited violence and insurgency" and for the purposes of "detecting
and identifying individuals and organizations engaged in subversive
insurgency in its incipient state." The program instructed the Salvadoran police in such areas as intelligence systems, interrogation
systems, and even bomb-making.

The CIA was another major influence on the formation of military-
linked death squads. Together with U.S. Green Beret instructors, the
CIA conceived and organized ORDEN (National Democratic Organization), the rural paramilitary and intelligence network described by
Amnesty International as a movement designed "to use clandestine
terror against government opponents." Out of ORDEN grew the White
Hand, one of the first Salvadoran death squads.[30] The CIA also established ANSESAL, the elite presidential intelligence service that was
strongly suspected of death-squad links. In addition, the CIA and the
U.S. embassy have regularly shared intelligence information on leftists
and popular leaders with military and police intelligence units.[31]

With the reconstitution of the popular movement in the late 1980s,
death-squad violence again became common. The main targets of the
death squads are activists with popular organizations that the U.S.
embassy terms "FMLN fronts." Among the newly named death squads
are the National Movement for the Salvation of El Salvador, Revolutionary Anticommunist Extermination Action, Eastern Solidarity Action,
and the Central American Anticommunist Hand. In May 1989 the
most extreme elements within ARENA working with First Brigade
Commander Colonel Zepeda (later assigned to the Ministry of Defense), formed the Patriotic Defense Committee—a new open paramilitary organization—as an "integral front" against the FMLN. But
local pressure, especially from the Catholic Church, forced the government to disband the paramilitary group.

It is commonly believed in El Salvador that the rash of bombings of
popular organizations such as UNTS, COMADRES, and FEN-
ASTRAS are the work of special operations teams associated with
military intelligence. With CIA and Pentagon support, the old AN-
SESAL apparatus has been replaced with a sophisticated intelligence
network directed by the National Directorate of Intelligence (DNI),
which falls under the authority of the Ministry of Defense.[32] Other
intelligence organizations are the C-2 of the Combined General Staff of
the Armed Forces, which works directly with the D-2 or S-2 intelligence
units of the three security forces: National Police, Treasury Police, and
National Guard. The D-2 of the air force is also widely suspected of
coordinating the increased death squad–type activity in the eastern
reaches of San Salvador.[33]

Guerrilla Opposition

The Farabundo Martí National Liberation Front (FMLN) takes its name from Augustín Farabundo Martí, the leader of the 1932 insurrection, who was executed by the military. Now widely recognized as the strongest guerrilla army in Latin American history, the FMLN is the unified front of five guerrilla armies. The FMLN is, however, much more than an army with a political agenda. As the country's leading nongovernmental political force, the FMLN has demonstrated that political considerations generally guide its military strategy, not the other way around.

The five guerrilla organizations that constitute the FMLN are the Popular Liberation Forces (FPL), the People's Revolutionary Army (ERP), the Armed Forces of National Resistance (FARN), the Central American Revolutionary Workers party (PRTC), and the Armed Forces of Liberation (FAL). Until 1980 the four existing guerrilla groups were not armies but clandestine political organizations whose operations were largely limited to kidnapping oligarchs and political organizing among the mass popular organizations. But with the resignation of the progressive civilians from the first junta and intensified repression, the role of the armed resistance increased dramatically. In March 1980 the four armies (FPL, ERP, FARN, and PRTC) formed the Unified Revolutionary Directorate (DRU), which together with the FAL became the FMLN in October 1980.

During the 1980s and especially after 1983, the distinctions among the five organizations eroded, particularly at the command level. Although the different armies are still not completely integrated, they function under one five-member general command, which is the FMLN directorate. Divisions and different tendencies do exist, however, mainly at the field level. In 1989, for example, the FMLN general command reprimanded FAL commanders for unauthorized attacks against civilian targets in San Salvador. While the FMLN has been calling for peace negotiations since 1981, elements within the FPL at times regarded the call for negotiations as a tactical ploy aimed at setting the stage for an eventual military triumph rather than as a strategic goal of the guerrilla forces.[34] The bold peace initiatives and concessions offered by the FMLN leadership in 1989 and 1990 were a new source of discord in the guerrilla ranks, where some viewed the emphasis on a negotiated solution as selling out the original revolutionary demands.

The FMLN does not release information about its internal structure and numbers. It is, however, generally accepted that the number of organized full-time combatants has declined from its peak of some 12,000 in the early 1980s, when its ranks were swelled by thousands of refugees from the popular movement. At the end of the decade, the FMLN's forces numbered about 7,000. These troops were divided into guerrilla units that fight in areas where they live; regular units that move throughout the country; and special forces, which have long political and combat experience.[35] After the November 1989 offensive, the FMLN claimed that its ranks swelled with new recruits.

These full-time troops are supplemented by militias, including part-time combatants and auxiliaries. Militias are active FMLN supporters who, because of family and work commitments, cannot or do not wish to join the guerrilla forces but who significantly augment the FMLN's military capacity. In addition, these "weekend warriors" serve as important links between the FMLN and the popular organizations and are a key element in the insurrectional strategy.[36] Although not institutionally linked to the FMLN, militant popular organizations, popular power structures in rural areas, and large numbers of guerrilla sympathizers amplify the power of the FMLN.

FMLN Political and Economic Philosophy

The U.S. embassy characterizes the FMLN leadership as Marxist-Leninist ideologues, and it is clearly the case that the ideological foundation of the FMLN is Marxist-Leninist. As the civil war has evolved, however, the FMLN leadership has gradually backed away from earlier revolutionary dogmatism. No longer do they promise to install a socialist government after the military defeat of the Salvadoran armed forces.[37] Today the FMLN's rhetoric carries a more moderate tone, overflowing with assurances of its commitment to democracy, negotiations, pluralism, and broad class alliances. FMLN theoretician Joaquín Villalobos claims that reality, not ideology, is the FMLN's main guide for action. According to Villalobos, the FMLN "pursues an El Salvador that is open, flexible, pluralistic, and democratic in both the economic and political spheres."[38]

Unmistakably most Salvadorans are desperately poor—and this poor population is the main social base of the guerrilla army. The FMLN represents, however, more than a peasant war against the oligarchy. For most of the 1980s the thrust of guerrilla political organizing was in rural areas where its forces were based. The peasantry— downtrodden, repressed, and deeply cynical about reformist claims of the military and government—proved the natural allies of the revolutionary army. But the FMLN commanders also maintained their strong

roots in the unions, universities, political struggles, and popular movements of the cities. In the last few years, as the war extended into urban
areas, the FMLN has gone a long way toward renewing its links with the
newly energized urban popular movement. It has also sought to
broaden its appeal among the critically important middle class.

Although Marxism-Leninism remains the principal analytical tool of
the FMLN, there is also a strong foundation in progressive Christianity.
For many revolutionaries, the martyred Archbishop Oscar Arnulfo
Romero is their main hero and inspiration. Significantly, the Christian
base communities in Morazán were among the first recruits of the ERP
guerrilla army.[39] The FMLN's commitment to sexual equality and its
success in integrating women into the military and political leadership
are other prominent components of the guerrilla struggle.

When held in the context of the civil war, elections have always been
dismissed by the FMLN as part of a counterinsurgency strategy. Beginning in January 1989, however, the FMLN substantially altered its
demands for a negotiated settlement. It announced that it was abandoning its call for power-sharing in a transition government and was
ready to compete for power in the electoral arena once hostilities
ended.

Despite these offers to transfer its revolutionary struggle to elections,
there is concern in some sectors that the FMLN's new political program
is little more than a "communist trick." The FMLN replies that it has
been calling for a government of broad participation since 1983 and
that domestic and geopolitical realities would make a socialist regime in
El Salvador impossible, even if it were still committed to such a project.
The FMLN is not forsaking socialism but sees it as a long process.

The FMLN says it intends to develop a minimal program, which
includes an agrarian reform "since land is the fundamental factor in
the economy and the fundamental source of social conflict." Modifications in the country's economic structure and reforms to guarantee the
welfare of all Salvadorans are what the FMLN labels "economic democracy." It asserts that for political democracy to be meaningful, "people
must eat, become educated, and have access to health care."[40]

Guerrilla Strategy of War and Peace

The FMLN began its "strategic counteroffensive" in January 1989, a
new phase of war incorporating an expanded political project and a
wider military offensive. The new strategy, in preparation since 1986,
reflected wide agreement within the FMLN that a purely military
victory would be impossible because of the logistical superiority of the

armed forces and continued U.S. military aid. Instead, FMLN strategists predicted that the war would be brought to a close either by negotiations or by a popular insurrection in conjunction with a military offensive.

Insurrection has long been part of the FMLN strategy. In the first phase of the revolutionary struggle (1979–1981), hope was placed on a Nicaraguan-style popular insurrection that would be spearheaded by the FMLN army. That hope, however, was crushed by unprecedented repression aimed at eliminating the revolution's social base. The final offensive of December 1981 fell far short of FMLN expectations and resulted in a new resolve by the FMLN to establish itself as a formidable armed force, capable of conventional and unconventional warfare.

The next stage of the war began in late 1983 when the FMLN battalions began posing a serious military challenge to the armed forces. Recognizing the new military threat represented by the FMLN, the United States responded with increased military aid and training. But rather than leading to victory, the strategy led to a military stalemate. Quickly adjusting to the new air war and ground offensives, the FMLN switched its emphasis from large units and zones of control to smaller irregular units and a countrywide network of support and military action. Unable to respond in kind to military firepower, the FMLN developed a homespun weapons industry and seriously inhibited army mobility with extensive use of landmines. The FMLN's acquisition and successful use of surface-to-air missiles in 1990 proved a sharp setback to the Salvadoran military, which had become dependent on air transport and aerial strafing.

Another element in the guerrillas' strategy was sabotage aimed at the country's economic and transportation infrastructure. The objective was not only to debilitate the country's "economy of war," but also to keep army troops pinned down to guarding fixed positions such as bridges, dams, and the electrical system. Causing $2 billion in infrastructure damage, the FMLN's campaign of economic destabilization effectively counterbalanced Washington's aid for economic stabilization.

Essential to any insurrectional strategy is urban support—probably the FMLN's weakest point. But during the late 1980s, the FMLN made great strides in building an urban support network. It dramatically increased its urban military actions, even to the extent of launching attacks against military bases within San Salvador. The FMLN also encouraged the formation of an infrastructure of clandestine urban cells made up of the most radicalized members of the popular movement, which could spark wider insurrectional response. Rather than integrating all new militants into the guerrilla army, the FMLN has advocated locally initiated insurrectional activity.

In late 1989, as human-rights violations soared and the government stalled at the negotiating table, the FMLN launched a major offensive. Although it failed to ignite the "social explosion" the FMLN had hoped for, the offensive furthered the two-track strategy of the guerrilla command; it alerted Washington and the Salvadoran government that the FMLN was a powerful military force with impressive popular backing. And it broke the political deadlock and opened the way for UN-arbitrated peace negotiations. But while firmly committed to the peace process, the FMLN also threatened to launch new offensives if the government failed to negotiate seriously.

The military's intransigence during the peace talks, the weakening state of government, and the prospects of substantially reduced U.S. aid encouraged some elements within the FMLN to adopt a harder line regarding the negotiating process and to consider a military solution the only possible option. A negotiated solution to the conflict and FMLN's insertion into the electoral process under the security of international verification remained, however, the preferred option of the guerrilla directorate.

ECONOMY

The State of the Economy

The Salvadoran economy entered the 1990s in a precarious state.[41] Its principal characteristics were the following:

Costs of War: Since 1975 current expenditures for defense have increased ninefold, while the overall government budget has trebled. In 1988 nearly 45 percent of current government spending was for defense and security.[42] This prioritization of war spending has contributed to the budget deficit and inflationary problems and has led to budget cuts in the agriculture, education, and other government ministries. The war has also created serious obstacles to industrial and agricultural production because of the overall conditions of insecurity and damage to the nation's economic infrastructure.

War-related damage to the economy as a result of guerrilla sabotage is estimated to be more than $2 billion—about the same amount that the U.S. Agency for International Development (AID) has pumped into the country for economic stabilization. The Ministry of Planning estimated that the guerrilla offensive of late 1989 and the military's response caused $30 million in infrastructure damage and as much as $90 million in direct and indirect losses in economic production.[43]

Dependence on External Aid: Economic aid in El Salvador is not just a booster, but a central part of the economy. During the 1980s the U.S. government pumped almost $3 billion of U.S. economic aid into the country. Congressional sources have reported that 75 percent of the U.S. aid program was for war-related expenditures.[44] The $300 million in average annual economic assistance in recent years has been complemented by generous funding (more than $600 million between 1980 and 1988) from the Inter-American Development Bank (IDB), a multilateral bank controlled mainly by the United States.

Dependence on Remittances: Remittances from Salvadorans living abroad inject more dollars into the Salvadoran economy than either the coffee industry or the U.S. economic-aid program. A 1987 study by the University of Central America estimated that more than one-third of Salvadorans have family members in the United States. Those family members were sending an average of $188 dollars a month to relatives in El Salvador.[45] Estimates of total remittances range from $500 million to more than $1.3 billion annually. Only some $225 million of this is directed through official channels, the balance being exchanged on the thriving black market.

Falling Exports and Widening Trade Imbalance: The balance of trade has dropped precipitously, from a positive $112 million in 1980 to a projected negative $520 million in 1989. A sharp drop in coffee exports and an accompanying fall in coffee prices in 1989 meant that the country was importing a half-billion dollars more than it was exporting at the end of the decade. Some planners, like those at AID and the U.S.-funded Salvadoran Foundation for Social and Economic Development (FUSADES), have pinned their hopes on the growth of nontraditional exports, both industrial and agricultural. Despite tens of millions of dollars to promote such growth, nontraditional exports to countries outside Central America have increased only by about $15 million since 1979, while nontraditional exports to other countries in the region have been cut in half over the last decade.

If the economy is to grow, there needs to be a substantial increase in imports of intermediate and capital goods. During the several pre-1979 periods of economic expansion, the pace of economic growth was paralleled by a significantly faster rate of import growth. In other words, the possibilities of economic recovery depend a great deal on the country's import capacity. Declining export income, increasing debt service, and foreign aid dedicated to stabilization and not investment are all factors that contribute to the economy's increasing inability to afford imported intermediate and capital goods.[46]

Absence of Investment: Despite some early success at economic stabilization, the Salvadoran economy is once again sliding backward. During the 1979–1983 period, the economy experienced negative growth, but this was followed by a few years of cumulative economic growth that resulted from a sharp increase in U.S. economic aid. By the end of the decade, however, the economy was stagnating again. In per capita terms, the Salvadoran economy steadily declined in the 1980s (except for 1984) at the rate of 1 to 2 percent a year, and in 1989 Salvadorans found themselves living with an economy one-fourth smaller than in 1978 and a GNP lower than in 1965.[47]

Decreased public-sector investment and an all-but-dormant private sector explain this retrogression. Agriculture is experiencing continuing reverses; the construction industry, which boomed because of cheap credit and postearthquake building, has lost its momentum; and manufacturing has barely kept up with per capita growth.[48] The private sector has been the focus of AID efforts to energize the economy but its promotional efforts have fallen flat—understandable when one considers the insecurity and disruption resulting from the ten-year civil war.

Persistent Budget Deficits: When measured against many other Third World countries, the country's budget deficit is not extremely serious.[49] But when taking into account the tremendous influx of budget-balancing AID monies, the deficit is serious indeed. Despite constant U.S. efforts to plug the budget deficit with local currency generated from its balance-of-payments assistance (ESF and Title I aid), the gap seems only to grow wider.

Because more than 90 percent of the government's budget covers routine operating expenses (the public-sector investment budget is handled almost exclusively by the foreign donor-generated extraordinary budget), it is difficult to cut. Already public services have been cut to a minimum. Education's portion of the budget dropped from 35 percent to less than 20 percent during the 1980s, and public health expenditures were halved.[50] This means that it would be impossible to close the budget deficit without laying off thousands of public employees—which is exactly what the ARENA government started to do in late 1989.

Higher taxes and more efficient tax collection can also play a role in closing the deficit. The government is already heavily dependent on indirect or consumption taxes, which fall most heavily on the poor. There is little room to increase taxes in this area, although the Cristiani administration has attempted to push the limits of what the poor can bear by increasing utility rates and public-transportation costs. Despite the ARENA government's commitment to more efficient tax collection, it is unlikely to risk angering middle-class and wealthy supporters by raising property and income taxes or even strictly enforcing current tax laws.

Instead of increasing taxes on those who can best pay—the agroexport sector—the ARENA government's economic package included tax breaks for sugar and shrimp exporters and other tax breaks for producers of nontraditional exports. At the time ARENA took hold of the government, the shortfall between budget revenues and expenses was approaching 30 percent. Things were made worse by the fact that the outgoing government had already spent most of the first-quarter government revenues. Weak coffee production, the worst in thirty years, further aggravated the government's revenue problems. Given the continued drain caused by war-related expenses and the dismal state of the export economy, even small deficit reductions will prove extremely difficult.

Devalued Currency: Devaluation has been on the economic agenda of El Salvador for the last ten years. At the start of the 1980s, the *colón* was valued at two *colones* to the dollar. Pressure from the multilateral banks and a growing black market resulted in the creation of a legal parallel market by the Duarte government followed by an official devaluation in 1986, reducing the *colón*'s value to five to the dollar.

Devaluation pressure began building again in 1987 and a promise of devaluation became part of ARENA's economic platform. But once elected the new government decided to postpone indefinitely the promised devaluation. It was thought that a devaluation might provoke widespread disapproval and ignite a popular insurrection. Instead the Cristiani administration opted for what amounts to a gradual devaluation process or a "sliding" currency exchange in which importers are permitted to buy dollars on the black market for the going rate. A similar process was unleashed when President Duarte authorized a parallel exchange rate prior to the official devaluation in 1986.

FUSADES and other sectors of the business community tied to export production continue to push for a currency devaluation as severe as twelve *colones* to one dollar.

Deepening Poverty: Officially the government reports 30 percent unemployment, but estimates from the Ministry of Planning place unemployment and underemployment in urban areas at 50 percent and in rural areas at 71 percent. But even those with jobs generally cannot afford basic necessities. Since 1980, per capita national income has dropped by 25 percent while inflation raised the cost of living by 360 percent. Real wages have dropped by at least a third since the war began.

As a result of unemployment, depressed wages, and inflation, at least 45 percent of Salvadoran families in 1985 were considered living at or below absolute poverty levels, meaning they do not have enough income to cover basic food needs. Ninety percent of the population were living in relative poverty in the mid-1980s, meaning that they did not have the economic capacity to provide a dignified life for themselves and their family (housing, education, health care, etc.).[51] Those measures of poverty have significantly worsened in the last five years because of inflation, a weaker currency, and static wage levels. According to the Economic Commission on Latin America (ECLA), by the end of the decade 85 percent of the population was living in poverty and 66 percent in extreme poverty.

Rescuing the Economy

Given the magnitude and length of the civil war, the economic crisis in El Salvador cannot be addressed without also seeking an end to the war. Yet throughout the 1980s that is exactly what foreign donor and lending organizations (principally AID) and the country's private-sector elite have tried to do. The widely expressed belief has been that with proper stabilization, austerity, and investment-promotion measures, the economy could be rescued from stagnation.

Initially at least, ARENA breathed new life into the myth that the country's economic problems have economic solutions. It is ARENA's contention that the private sector has been stifled by reforms, bureaucracy, and excessive interventionism by Christian Democratic governments. In its campaign the party promised a "national rescue" of the depressed and dependent economy. Being a party largely of businessmen, it promised that an ARENA-run government would know how to promote private-sector growth. The private capital that had fled the country during the 1980s would come rushing back to the country, according to ARENA enthusiasts.

ARENA's formula for success is based on the tenets of neoliberalism, including privatization, deregulation, and the freeing up of prices, trade, and market forces. Its emphasis on free enterprise and the primacy of the international market paralleled the growth strategies proposed by FUSADES, an economic think tank and promotional organization funded almost entirely by AID.

Implementation of such policies, however, is constrained by the structural realities of the Salvadoran economy. Privatization of state enterprises, for example, is limited by the relatively low degree (about 18 percent) of state economic involvement. Contrary to the impression created by ARENA, there was no increase in government intervention in the economy under the Christian Democratic government. There is important state investment in such areas as the ports, airport, telecommunications, and electricity services, but these are the very sectors controlled by the military—and are largely off-limits.

Where privatization will have its greatest impact is in the rollback of the 1980 reforms: agrarian reform, nationalization of banking, and nationalization of trade. The scheduled reprivatization of five banks and nine other financial institutions will affect the distribution of credit, since the nationalized financial sector had been managing about 80 percent of the country's local credit. The main obstacle to this reprivatization of financial institutions is that they are heavily burdened with bad debt (mainly to large private enterprises), making them unattractive to private investors.

Along with the loosening of control over the value of the *colón*, liberalization of prices, dismissal of public-sector employees, and increase of interest rates were other economic measures announced by President Cristiani. In proceeding with its economic program, however, the new government's neoliberal principles are being tested by the pressures of running a government in the middle of the civil war. The Cristiani administration is aware that uncompromising neoliberalism might drive the middle class toward a leftist popular alliance while pushing the poor and workers, particularly in the cities, toward rebellion.

The Cristiani government is also aware that the government's stability depends in part on its image among the poor. To polish that image, Cristiani announced a series of social-assistance measures including expanded food-for-work projects, the creation of temporary public-works jobs for 20,000 unemployed workers, and a school-lunch program. In the August 1989 speech announcing these programs,

Cristiani described ARENA's economic model as a "social market economy" and referred to Pope John Paul II's notion of the economy as a "virtuous circle," which generates employment allowing workers to satisfy their needs.[52]

Grim Economic Prospects

There is, of course, little doubt that El Salvador needs to adjust its precarious economy. Policies are needed to diversify its exports, increase private investment, narrow the gap in the fiscal deficit, and adjust its external financial and trade imbalances. But domestic producers have criticized the economic adjustment program of the Cristiani administration as placing considerations of monetary stability over concerns for the stability and growth of the domestic market. Popular organizations, in turn, charge that the government's structural-adjustment program is biased toward the financial and export elite and hurts those who can least afford it.

Yet the most pressing economic crisis for El Salvador has not been government economic policy but the war; this was made clearer than ever for the ARENA government by the FMLN offensive of November 1989. The prospects of any plan for economic recovery or improved conditions for the poor are dismal when faced with the prospects of a continuing war.

Although ending the civil war is the necessary first step toward recovery, a postwar El Salvador would face a bleak economic landscape. It would likely be confronted with a sharp drop in U.S. aid as well as diminishing remittances from Salvadorans living in the United States as they return home. The problems of uncertain export revenues and deep structural inequities in the distribution of land and resources would remain. Even if these were corrected, this small environmentally ravaged country will not easily be able to meet the basic needs of its large population.

Agriculture: Foundation of the Economy

Agriculture is the heart of the Salvadoran economy, accounting for nearly a quarter of the national product and two-thirds of its export income, and directly employing a third of the workforce.[53] Actually, agriculture is a dual economy, sharply divided between export-oriented and local food production. Both sectors are facing severe difficulties; traditional agroexports declined more than 50 percent since 1979 while grain production has not been able to meet local demand. And prospects are not good for the 1990s. The end of the war would immediately result in increased agricultural production, but the country's producers would probably still be faced with low coffee prices, increasing international prices for fertilizer and pesticides, lack of credit and technical assistance for grain production and for small farmers, and the concentration of the best land in a relatively few hands.

Agroexports: Province of the Oligarchy

Historically, El Salvador has been the largest coffee producer in Central America, and the fourth largest in Latin America following Brazil, Colombia, and Mexico. But the disruption caused by the war has halved coffee production since the late 1970s. Nonetheless, coffee still dominates the agroexport sector, producing 60 percent of total export income, 90 percent of agricultural-export income, and some 25 percent of the government's tax revenues.[54]

Yet even the coffee industry is in trouble; it has been battered by low international prices, coffee rust, and bad weather. Another major problem has been the economic destabilization campaign mounted by the FMLN, which has targeted the warehouses and processing plants (*beneficios*) of the coffee elite.

More than coffee oligarchs are hurt by the debilitated state of coffee production. The many small coffee farmers are also hard hit, as are the tens of thousands of peasants who depend on seasonal work on the coffee plantations. The stability of the government itself is affected by the projected drop of $100 million in export earnings and $25 million in export tax revenues. A sensitive issue confronting the ARENA government is the degree to which it will privatize coffee marketing.

In 1980 the government nationalized coffee trade and established INCAFE as the government institute controlling all international marketing. In mid-1989 the Supreme Court declared INCAFE unconstitutional because it monopolized coffee exports. Subsequently the Legislative Assembly approved legislation opening up coffee marketing to private firms. It is likely, however, that the government will attempt to maintain its control over foreign revenues generated by the coffee trade. Any complete relinquishing of government and Central Bank controls over the coffee trade would result in reduced tax revenues and increased capital flight—the very reasons why coffee trade was nationalized in the first place.

Another sad story in the agroexport sector is that of the disappearing cotton industry. Cotton is grown mainly in areas disrupted by the war, but the feeble state of the cotton industry is also the result of the industry's heavy reliance on expensive inputs and the weak world market. El Salvador is no longer exporting much cotton, and the country has had to resort to importing vegetable oil formerly produced locally by the country's cotton gins. A large part of the country's effective demand for vegetable oil is now covered by the U.S. food-aid program.[55]

Sugar and shrimp production are the only export crops that have maintained or increased former production levels, although together they still account for less than 10 percent of agricultural exports. Sugar production is important for its role in the domestic economy, meeting the large internal demand and providing a major source of rural seasonal employment.

Much is being made over the need to diversify agricultural production in El Salvador. There is, however, little to show for the nontraditional agroexport projects administered by FUSADES and backed by AID and the Inter-American Development Bank (IDB). Besides shrimp, melons are the only significant new nontraditional agroexport. Cantaloupe and cucumber production are also being promoted but with discouraging results. Most of the small local demand for fruits and vegetables is met by imports from Guatemala. El Salvador is, as a result, a net importer of fruits and vegetables.

Death of the Agrarian Reform

The 1980 Land Reform Law was a key element of the "hearts and minds" strategy for defeating the guerrillas. It was thought that the land-redistribution program would simultaneously create a popular base for a centrist government, undermine the power of a reactionary oligarchy, and open the way for increased agricultural production. Ten years later the agrarian-reform program is being dismantled by the right-wing government.

Although the agrarian reform did give the peasantry increased access to land, credit, and technical assistance, on many counts, the program failed. It fell far short of providing the reform sector with the support it required. And while the AID project did fulfill its guarantees to compensate expropriated landowners, it left the beneficiaries burdened in debt and without adequate government extension services. Only one-quarter of the reform sector benefited from government credit during the 1980s, and most agree that beneficiaries will never be able to pay off the accumulated debt.[56]

In economic terms, the program has been a disaster too. Between

1980 and 1986 grain production dropped 56 percent in the reform sector, while falling just 6 percent in the nonreform sector. In export production, the reform sector showed an 11 percent drop in production against a negative 17 percent in the nonreform sector.[57] Still, the reform sector proved an important source of support for the Christian Democrats and gave credibility to a reformist image of the government, particularly through the critical 1981–1986 period of the U.S. counter-insurgency project.

Although it is unlikely that the ARENA government will seek to reverse completely the results of the land redistribution for fear of peasant reaction, it has begun to cut off public-sector support for the Phase I cooperatives and push for the dissolution of these cooperatives in favor of individually owned parcels. The new director of FINATA (one of the AID-funded sources of credit for the reform sector) declared his intention "to break with the communist system of agricultural land distribution."

Industry: Import Substitution to Export Processing

El Salvador, historically an industrial leader in Central America, has seen its industrial sector shrink as a result of falling internal consumption and sharp decreases in regional trade in the 1980s. Manufacturing, which currently contributes about 18 percent to the GDP (gross domestic product) and employs about 20 percent of the labor force, has not been adversely affected by the war nearly as much as agriculture and transport, although it has felt the effects of infrastructure sabotage and transportation disruptions.[58] Industry is concentrated in the San Salvador area, although there are other centers in La Libertad, Santa Ana, San Miguel, Usulután, and San Vicente.

While large enterprises controlled by the leading families employ a majority of the industrial workforce, microenterprises with fewer than five employees account for 95 percent of the country's businesses. These small businesses produce 16 percent of the industrial product and employ 45 percent of industrial workers.[59] So small are 75 percent of these enterprises that they provide only a subsistence income for the proprietor.

Whereas government industrial policy historically stressed both production for export and import substitution, AID and the multilateral banks are encouraging a shift away from import-substitution industry in favor of export-oriented production. Locally, this growth strategy is being directed by the AID-funded FUSADES.

The ARENA government has promised to place increased emphasis on the promotion of labor-intensive export manufacturing, particularly textiles. A key part of this strategy, promoted by the Trade and Investment Promotion Program (PRIDEX) of FUSADES, is to keep wages low to maintain the country's "comparative advantage" in relation both to other Third World countries and to industrial countries. Economic strategists at FUSADES see no reason why El Salvador, with its cheap, skilled labor force, cannot become the Caribbean Basin's number-one exporter of textiles.[60]

Although united behind the neoliberalism and free-market rhetoric of FUSADES and ARENA, the industrial sector has benefited from longstanding protectionist tariffs and tax exemptions on imports. Industry owners now fear that the elimination of protectionist measures will seriously reduce their profit margins, while opening up the country's market to foreign products. The Association of Salvadoran Industrialists (ASI) has therefore demanded that the government back off from its plan for the immediate imposition of neoliberal measures. ASI also wants the government to help local industries restructure their production capabilities to make industry more competitive on the international market. It will be difficult for the ARENA government, in desperate need for new tax revenues and with no extra funds to invest, to meet the demands of the country's important but inefficient industrial sector.[61]

SOCIETY AND ENVIRONMENT

The Popular Movement

El Salvador's backward and exploitative structures were challenged for the first time by peasant communities, labor activists, and communist organizers in the late 1920s. This popular threat to feudal rule of the famous "Fourteen Families" (*Los Catorce*) and their military protectors was crushed by the *matanza* of 1932. So thorough was the massacre that popular dissension was silenced for several decades.

It was not until the 1960s that a new popular challenge began to coalesce.[62] Cooperatives formed, workers organized, and the expanding middle class called for political change. A strong popular movement had formed by the late 1970s. In the process, though, the movement's leadership was radicalized, demanding not only reforms but a revolution to overhaul the society.

By 1980 the expanding popular movement represented a threat to the fragile government. To pacify this movement, the government announced political and economic reforms, including a land-distribution program. And when pacification failed, the military was quick to resort to repression. In the early 1980s, widespread repression left thousands of activists dead. The government's two-pronged counterinsurgency strategy of the early 1980s seriously weakened the militant popular movement and facilitated the creation of progovernment worker and peasant organizations supported by U.S. economic-aid programs. Activists from older popular organizations had either fallen victim to death-squad terror or had joined the ranks of the FMLN guerrillas.

From Squatters' Associations to Insurrectional Organizing

The popular movement began reemerging in the mid-1980s. Among the first to organize were the workers, peasants, and those displaced by the war. Signaling the important new role of the displaced in the popular movement, the Christian Committee of the Displaced (CRIPDES), founded in 1984, insisted that the internally displaced had the right to return to their former villages. Defying the military, CRIPDES helped displaced families to return home. And in 1986 it gave birth to the National Repopulation Coordinator (CNR), which not only helped the internally displaced resettle their communities but also worked closely with Salvadoran refugees returning from Honduras.

Following the 1986 earthquake, which had left 56,000 poor Salvadorans homeless, there was a new surge of urban organizing. Two groups, the Coordinating Committee of Communities (CCC) and the National Union of Disaster Victims (UNADES) joined the existing Committee of Marginal Communities (CCM) to represent and respond to the needs of the increasing number of urban Salvadorans who found themselves without homes and jobs.

The 1980s also brought an explosion of women's organizing and the formation of new human-rights groups. In addition, the cooperative movement showed signs of new life and strength in the 1980s. The Confederation of Cooperative Associates (COACES), a member of the National Unity of Salvadoran Workers (UNTS) popular coalition, became the coordinating alliance of most of the country's cooperatives. Threats to the agrarian reform spurred the 1990 formation of the Democratic *Campesino* Association (ADC).

In 1987 a new dimension of the popular movement took hold in conflictive rural areas where government services and representatives were almost nonexistent. Local and regional groups formed to take the place of absent or unresponsive government institutions and communities began forming their own committees to represent their interests and to carry out development and service projects. More than four hundred committees from the departments of Morazán, San Miguel, La Unión, Usulután, San Salvador, Santa Ana, and Ahuachapán came together in January 1989 to form PADECOES (*Patronato* for Communal Development in El Salvador).

Repression of the popular organizations increased markedly during the first year of the ARENA government. The offices of many popular organizations were bombed; others had their offices ransacked and leaders arrested and tortured. The repression that followed the FMLN offensive of November 1989 forced hundreds of activists into hiding. By March 1990, however, the popular movement had regrouped to protest the socioeconomic consequences of ARENA's economic policies and to renew the demands for a negotiated peace. Christian Democratic unions and peasant groups joined with leftist groups to oppose the Cristiani government. Bringing all the popular organizations together in their support for peace negotiations was the Permanent Committee of the National Debate (CPDN), which counted on the support of the Catholic Church and the progressive protestant churches.

Labor and Unions

Workers in El Salvador are known throughout the region for their industriousness and proclivity for organizing. At least half of the available workforce, however, is unemployed, and real wages have fallen by a third since 1980. The minimum wage is about 40 cents an hour in the city and 20 cents in the countryside, meaning that the average monthly earnings of a two-income family can only provide for half the minimum cost of a basic nutritious diet.[63]

Repression in the late 1970s and the early 1980s all but wiped out the overt functioning of trade unions and peasant associations allied with the antigovernment popular movement. Between 1980 and 1984, hundreds of labor leaders disappeared or were openly murdered. Although independent organizing was silenced, this was a period of rapid growth for groups sponsored by the American Institute for Free Labor Development (AIFLD). Not generally subject to the same level of repression, these groups formed the base of a new labor coalition called the Popular Democratic Unity (UPD). The UPD, which brought together several rural and urban organizations, served to build support for the Christian Democratic party while acting as an effective counterweight to the repressed organizations clustered on the left.

The founding in early 1986 of the National Unity of Salvadoran Workers (UNTS) marked a new beginning for a strong progressive labor movement in El Salvador.[64] In response to the creation of UNTS and the disintegration of UPD as a conservative coalition, the Duarte government, the U.S. embassy, and AIFLD quickly collaborated to form a progovernment confederation called the National Union of Workers and *Campesinos* (UNOC). UNTS and UNOC remained sharply at odds until late 1988 when UNOC began inching away from the politics of its AIFLD sponsors, joined the UNTS in the national dialogue and cautiously applauded FMLN proposals for a negotiated settlement to the war. Differences still remain, though. In the 1989 presidential elections UNOC stood solidly behind the Christian Democratic party while the UNTS encouraged voter abstention. Following the ARENA victory UNOC quickly moved closer to the antigovernment stance of the UNTS, joining a coalition with the leftist confederation in opposing ARENA's economic policies and calling for a negotiated settlement of the war.

Repression and Trade Status Controversy

During the 1980s two divergent positions existed within the U.S. labor movement regarding the situation of labor rights in El Salvador. The dominant position was that of the AFL-CIO and its U.S.-funded Latin American branch, AIFLD, which claimed that labor-rights conditions were improving and that the main threat to the rights of workers was the leftist insurgency and alleged popular front groups, including its rival UNTS. Another more critical position has been maintained by labor activists associated with the National Labor Committee in Support of Democracy and Human Rights in El Salvador, an organization founded by the presidents of numerous U.S. labor unions. The National Labor Committee calls for the end of all U.S. military aid to El Salvador. Besides calling for an end to U.S. military aid and AIFLD intervention, critics of U.S. and AFL-CIO policy in El Salvador demanded that the U.S. trade status with the country be revised. They insisted that trade sanctions, mandated by U.S. law for labor-rights violators, be invoked against the El Salvador government. The 1984 Trade Act denies countries preferential trade status, which El Salvador currently enjoys, if "such country has not taken or is not taking steps to afford internationally recognized workers' rights." Similarly, the Caribbean Basin Initiative (CBI) requires that the president assess the degree to which a country's workers "enjoy the right to organize and bargain collectively" when determining its eligibility for duty-free access to the United States.

ARENA's electoral victory and the new opposition status of the Christian Democratic party, with which the AFL-CIO has been associated, changed both the character of labor alliances and the role of the AFL-CIO. No longer protected by its ties with government, the AIFLD-funded UNOC began to feel the weight of repression and became more vigorous in its condemnation of human-rights abuses. At the same time UNOC, through its links with the AFL-CIO, petitioned for the suspension of U.S. trade preferences for El Salvador. By supporting such a measure of censure, UNOC opened itself to harsh condemnation by the government and the private sector.

Schools and Students

Official statistics show a 72 percent literacy rate in El Salvador with only 40 percent literacy in most rural areas.[65] Half the workforce has, at best, a third-grade education. The sad state of primary education has been aggravated by decreases in per capita government expenditures for education, which dropped 66 percent between 1978 and 1987.[66]

Until 1970 El Salvador had only one public university, the University of El Salvador (known as the National University), and one private university, the University of Central America (UCA). After the 1980 closure of the National University, there was an explosion of twenty-nine new universities, many started by opportunists of various kinds, although some of these failed to enroll any students. In 1988, the country's lawmakers approved army plans for the establishment of a military university.

The largest and oldest private university is the University of Central America operated by the Jesuits from Spain. Founded in 1965, the university is serious about faculty research and publishes nine academic journals, including three that have provoked virulent reaction by the military and the right: *Proceso, Estudios Centroamericanos,* and *Carta a las Iglesias.* In July 1989, shortly after the extreme right Crusade for Peace and Work accused UCA authorities of collaborating with the FMLN, the university's print shop was dynamited.

The military closed the National University in 1972 and again in 1976. Between 1980 and 1984 it was closed and occupied by troops. During the occupation the institution sustained about $20 million in damage to buildings, equipment, and books. The earthquake of October 1986 caused additional damage. An estimated $15 million in damage resulted from the military's efforts to drive the FMLN out of San Salvador in November 1989 when once more the university was closed down. It reopened in mid-1990 amid government threats to remove its autonomous status. At the same time the government was attempting to push through a new law that would encourage private enterprise to involve itself in the administration of public schools, a measure that sparked the vehement opposition by the newly formed Salvadoran Teachers Front (FMS).

Communications Media

Under the tight control of owners and advertising agencies, the country's media outlets have served mainly as the voice of the business sector, government, and military. This is especially true for the printed media, characterized by a reactionary tone and outdated production format. Beginning in the mid-1980s television news became increasingly aggressive and balanced, even to the extent of interviewing guerrilla commanders. Strict military control over the media and a national emergency broadcasting system (known as the *cadena* or chain) was instituted when a state of siege was imposed by the government in November 1989.

La Prensa Gráfica, founded in 1915, is the largest daily and has the most modern equipment of any of the nation's newspapers. A conservative newspaper, *La Prensa Gráfica* reproduces armed forces press releases as news and consistently refers to the FMLN as "terrorists." Although it is commonly considered a proregime newspaper, it is not as stridently reactionary as its main competitor, *El Diario de Hoy*.

El Diario de Hoy, founded in 1936, is owned by the Altamirano family, who also have interests in coffee and cotton. A voice of the oligarchy and the extreme right wing, it supports the D'Aubuisson tendency of ARENA and has given space to extreme right-wingers to discuss the possibility that Cristiani may be too moderate. The United States Information Agency (USIA) considers it "ultraconservative."

Like the two other leading dailies, *El Mundo*, founded in 1968, is owned by members of the country's oligarchy, notably the coffee grower Nathan Borja. An afternoon paper, it is distinctly less conservative than the morning papers and allows its editors more independence. Denied the advertising available to its older competitors, *El Mundo* found an important source of income in the paid advertisements from opposition public organizations such as trade unions and human-rights groups, but new prohibitions by the ARENA government have limited the publication of such information. During the

Cristiani administration, another small daily, *Diario Latino*, has become an important source of opposition news and opinion.

Radio, with its 4.3 million daily listeners, is the communications medium with the greatest outreach. Like the printed media, however, the largest stations are owned and operated by ARENA sympathizers, although the important Radio Sonora is somewhat more open than the others. The army runs its own station, Radio Cuscatlán. Radio broadcasters thought to be too liberal have been fired from their stations. An alternative source of news exists in the radio stations of the rebels, Radio Venceremos and Radio Farabundo Martí, which can be heard throughout the country daily. They provide cultural programs along with reports on political and military events, including government troop movements.

It used to be that television news was little more than a digest of official pronouncements and the latest tidbits from high society. But beginning in the mid-1980s television news programming, especially that of Channel 12, became among the best in Central America.[67] There are four commercial stations and two government stations. The news programs of Channels 6 and 12 have provided forums for political discussion, bringing together declared enemies into polite and informative debates. In a recent poll, 85 percent of Salvadorans with at least two years of high school said that their primary source of news was television.[68] Just five years earlier, radio had been cited as the main source of news.

The army's press office COPREFA plays a major role in formulating and controlling the news in El Salvador. All journalists have to apply to COPREFA, based in the military headquarters, for press cards; COPREFA also arranges or denies permits for journalists to travel to conflictive areas. When three journalists were killed in a twelve-hour period during the March 1989 elections, COPREFA claimed they were shot for ignoring commands by soldiers to stop for registration.

Health and Welfare

The government health-care budget has steadily declined, from 11 percent of total expenditures at the start of the decade to just 6 percent in 1989.[69] This has left the public health-care system in a dismal state. Government health posts are now without medicine or completely abandoned, and public hospitals are filthy, overcrowded, and short-staffed. Patients entering public hospitals are told to bring their own sheets, food, soap, toilet paper, surgical supplies, and sutures. There is a waiting list of some 20,000 people for elective surgery at the Rosales

Hospital. Only the military hospitals are fully equipped and well supplied.

Aside from the marked decline in government spending, the health-care situation is also still suffering from the closing of the National University from 1980 to 1984, which meant that no new doctors, nurses, dentists, or pharmacists were being trained. Today in El Salvador for every 10,000 people there are only 3.2 doctors, 2.1 nurses, and only twelve hospital beds.[70] Only 37 percent of Salvadorans have access to medical care according to a 1989 report from the Ministry of Planning. According to 1989 figures from the Ministry of Health, 75 percent of children under five years suffer from malnutrition and 43 percent of pregnant women suffer from anemia.

Clearly the war has not been good for the country's health. There are numerous health-care problems associated with the war: Food supplies are destroyed, distribution systems are interrupted, water supplies become polluted, transportation to health-delivery centers becomes difficult, and medical supplies run out. Death and injury, however, are the most immediate by-products of the conflict. In a repopulated village in Chalatenango, health promoters reported that of all the children who had died since 1980, nearly half had been killed by the army.[71]

Religion

Although the country's religion is traditionally Roman Catholicism, the constitution does not give Roman Catholicism any official standing as an established religion. In fact, the number of evangelicals in the country, primarily of the fundamentalist denominations, has been growing rapidly. The population is now estimated to be only about 81 percent Catholic. (As elsewhere in Central America, the common use in El Salvador of the term *evangelical* refers to all non-Catholic Christians, including pentecostals, fundamentalists, and mainline protestant denominations.) Archbishop Arturo Rivera y Damas and Auxiliary Bishop Gregorio Rosa Chávez are the most prominent and influential Church leaders. About 60 percent of the priests in El Salvador are natives, a higher percentage than in other Central American countries.

El Salvador has been strongly affected by the development of the progressive "theology of liberation" tendency within the Catholic Church. This tendency within the Church was expressed at the 1968 Medellín Conference of Latin American bishops, which called for a "preferential option for the poor." The institutional expression of this new tendency is the so-called base community, groups of people who worship, study, and on occasion take political action together. The study component often takes the form of consciousness-raising, with a progressive or even revolutionary emphasis.

The approximately 350 base communities that formed in El Salvador were early targets of repressive activity, with the assassination or disappearance of about six hundred members between 1979 and 1989. In the face of this repression, most base communities in rural areas disintegrated. Today Christian base communities are founded mostly in the poorer neighborhoods on the periphery of San Salvador and among the repopulation communities.[72]

The persecution of Catholic clergy and laity began in the 1970s as a reaction to the increased identification of the Church with the country's poor majority. The Jesuits were among the main targets of right-wing vigilante groups and the military. In March 1977 Father Rutilio Grande, a Jesuit working in Aguilares, was murdered for his commitment to the poor. Three years later Archbishop Oscar Arnulfo Romero was gunned down on March 24, 1980, while celebrating mass. The archbishop, whose political position had originally been moderate and passive, was gradually drawn into becoming the voice of the oppressed as repression grew. His weekly nationally broadcast homilies, in which he denounced terror and pleaded for social justice, made him a hero to many Salvadorans but also a target of the right-wing extremists.

Archbishop Rivera y Damas, appointed to replace Romero, has been more moderate and careful, not to mention a great deal less charismatic, than Archbishop Romero. He has toned down the outspokenness of the Church's newspaper and its radio broadcasts. The archbishop has, however, been a key figure in mediating between government and guerrillas and has worked to bring the more conservative provincial bishops around to his position in favor of a peaceful settlement.

With the March 1989 electoral victory of ARENA, relations between the Catholic Church and the armed forces sank to the lowest point since the 1980 assassination of Romero. Both the army and ARENA have frequently charged that clerics and Church organizations are linked to the FMLN, incensing the Church hierarchy.[73]

Tensions between the Church and the state reached a new high in November 1989 when the FMLN launched its offensive in San Salvador. The military reacted by arresting religious activists, searching churches and Church-sponsored refuges, and repeating charges that the Church was supporting the guerrillas. The threats and violence against the Church culminated in the November 16 massacre by the military of six Jesuits, their housekeeper, and her daughter. Immediately following the massacre Attorney General Eduardo Colorado sent a letter to the Pope asking him to withdraw from El Salvador all bishops who were "fomenting violence."

Evangelical Churches Show New Dynamism

Of all the evangelical missions and churches founded in El Salvador, nearly 50 percent have been opened in the past ten years. Since 1978 the annual rate of growth has ranged from 15 to 22 percent. Today about 18 percent of the Salvadorans are evangelicals. The country has more than 3,300 evangelical churches operated by seventy-nine evangelical denominations and sects.[74]

Although protestant missionaries began proselytizing in El Salvador nearly a century ago, the pace of evangelical growth has dramatically increased since 1978 with the Assemblies of God leading the way with its aggressive proselytizing and church-building campaigns. Other pentecostal churches, including Church of God, Church of Apostles and Prophets, and Prince of Peace, have also experienced sharp increases in members. Central American Mission, the largest nonpentecostal fundamentalist church, has not experienced the rapid growth enjoyed by the pentecostals. The socially-committed Lutheran Church has seen its congregation expand, even though the church has been harassed by the army. Other traditional protestant denominations with churches in El Salvador are the Baptist and Episcopal churches.

The Salvadoran evangelical movement did not rise independently from the crisis conditions but is largely a product of the increased U.S. evangelical presence. Televangelists such as Jimmy Swaggart and Pat Robertson have traveled to El Salvador to preach before massive crowds in the national stadium. Evangelical growth has also been fueled by the deepening dissatisfaction among middle- and upper-class Catholics over the influence within the Catholic Church of Christian base communities and other advocates of the theology of liberation.

Although the vast majority of Salvadoran evangelicals belong to pentecostal churches where conservative theology mixes easily with conservative politics, there does exist a significant sector of more liberal mainline protestant churches. The Lutheran church, the Episcopal church, and sectors of the Baptist church, for example, have offered important support to repopulating and repatriating refugees and assistance to community-organizing efforts that are often subject to harassment and violence by the military. Because of the efforts of this small but influential sector of the evangelical community, ecumenism has become an important social force in El Salvador, especially in comparison with the neighboring countries of Honduras and Guatemala.

Nongovernmental Organizations

During the 1980s there was a sharp increase in the social-service, relief, and development operations of nongovernmental organizations (NGOs) in El Salvador. These NGOs, both local and foreign, are sharply divided between those that receive funds from the U.S. government (mainly through the Agency for International Development) and those that have tried to maintain an independent posture.[75]

Because of the direct U.S. involvement in the unpopular war, whether to work with the U.S. Agency for International Development (AID) is a major issue for NGOs in El Salvador. Since 1980 AID has greatly expanded its work with NGOs and has sought to involve private organizations in a three-pronged strategy: pacification of the population (political demobilization and control), political and economic stabilization, and private-sector support.

Three-fourths of AID funding for NGOs in El Salvador goes to organizations dedicated to private-sector solutions of the country's economic and social problems. Most of this aid flows to FUSADES, which was established by AID. FUSADES has attempted to strengthen other private-sector organizations; promote nontraditional exports (light-assembly industries and winter vegetable/fruit production); pressure the government for investment incentives, exemptions, and lower taxes; and promote foreign investment. AID and FUSADES say that these "reforms" will lead to economic growth, the benefits of which will then trickle down to the impoverished majority.

Women and Feminism

The continuation of the war and the deepening of the economic crisis have had a particularly severe impact on Salvadoran women. During the 1980s the percentage of female-headed households rose dramatically and more women were forced to seek work and at the same time care for their families. But unemployment among women is some 20 percent higher than male unemployment, forcing many Salvadoran women to eke out a living in the country's rapidly expanding informal sector of markets and street vendors.[76]

State family-planning programs were first introduced in 1968 and are used reportedly by about one-third of women of childbearing age.

The birth-control pill is the most commonly used method; abortions are not permitted in publicly funded hospitals. The Catholic Church opposes artificial methods of birth control, and the government's strong support of family planning has caused some women to complain that government-run hospitals and public health centers exert intense pressure to limit family size. It has even been reported that hospital personnel are given a quota of sterilizations to perform. Certainly a lot of pressure to be sterilized is placed on women who go to hospitals to give birth, and one-half of the women using contraception report sterilization as the method.[77] Nevertheless, according to one report, abortion is the most common cause of death among women of child-bearing age.[78] Another study revealed that one-third of all beds in the gynecological wards of public hospitals are occupied by women suffering from serious complications from badly performed abortions.[79]

Responding to these and other problems, numerous women's organizations have emerged since the mid-1980s most of which are situated at the heart of the popular movement.[80] The Association of Salvadoran Domestic Workers (ADEMUSA), for example, works primarily with base communities and domestics and has played a major role in the campaign against forced recruitment of men for the army. The Association of Salvadoran Indigenous Women (AMIS) aims to promote the values of the country's native people and the use of traditional medicinal plants. The Association of Salvadoran Women (AMS) is a strong peasant organization of committees from more than one hundred rural communities, including those in conflictive areas. The National Coordinator of Salvadoran Women (CONAMUS) is closely linked to the labor movement, including the women of the ANDES teachers' union.

Historically, the most important women's organization in the popular movement was the Association of Women in El Salvador (AMES), which was formed in the late 1970s and is now closely associated with the FMLN and FDR. It organizes around a wide range of issues of interest to women in Salvadoran refugee camps in Honduras and in the controlled zones. In 1987 AMES became part of the Salvadoran Women's Union (UMS), which is a coalition of the five revolutionary women's groups associated with the FMLN.

On the right, there are three women's organizations associated with ARENA: Crusade for Peace and Work, Salvadoran Feminine Front, and the Foundation for the Integration and Development of Women (which receives U.S. government funds through the National Endowment for Democracy). The Pro-Solidarity Committee is an organization formed by the wives of army colonels.

Native Peoples

El Salvador was never a center of Amerindian civilization. The group first encountered by the Spanish conquistadors were the Pipils, a sizable population living in communities south and west of the Río Lempa. These were Nahuatl-speaking Indians related to Aztecs who had migrated from Mexico in the eleventh century. Resistance by the Pipils kept the Spanish from colonizing the territory until 1539, when the native rebellions were finally crushed.

In the country's northwest lived the Pokoman Indians, the original settlers of El Salvador and closely related to the Mayan people then living in Honduras, Guatemala, and Yucatán. Also living in El Salvador at the time of the conquest were the Lenca Indians, who lived in the area to the north and east of the Río Lempa.[81]

There are no reliable figures on the percentage of El Salvador's current Indian population. The figures range from 6 percent to 20 percent.[82] What is certain is that the Indian population of El Salvador is not very visible, a circumstance that can be traced back to the *matanza* of 1932. The repression of the popular insurrection was a genocidal act aimed specifically at El Salvador's Indian population. In the belief that Indians were the backbone of the rural rebellion, General Maximiliano Hernández Martínez specifically ordered his troops to kill anyone obviously Indian, as indicated by clothing style and other outward features. As the word spread about what was happening, Indians hastened to adopt outward signs of belonging to the majority *mestizo*. Indian dress was dropped, hair was cut and only Spanish was spoken in public.[83]

Still spoken in El Salvador are two indigenous languages—Nahuatl (also known as Pipil) and Lenca—although the number of Indians speaking Nahuatl as their first language is rapidly dwindling. During the 1980s there has been a revival of Indian identity promoted by two groups: ANIS (National Salvadoran Association of Native People) and the Salvadoran Association of Democratic Indigenous People (ASID). ANIS was closely associated with the American Institute for Free Labor Development in the early 1980s. Frustrated with the Christian Democrats and disgusted with the political control exercised by AIFLD, ASID split off from ANIS in 1985 to join the UNTS popular alliance. There is also a government-affiliated organization called MAIS, which promotes traditional Indian cultural activities through the mass media and government-sponsored events.

Refugees and the Displaced

At least a quarter of the population has fled the country as refugees or been internally displaced from their homes as a result of the civil war. Estimates of the number of those displaced from their homes but still living in the country range from 200,000 to 500,000.[84] Most of the internally displaced are rural families fleeing the war, but there are also thousands of families displaced by the 1986 earthquake and most recently those displaced by fighting and bombardment in San Salvador.

Salvadoran refugees have fled principally to the United States, Mexico, and other Central American countries. As many as 750,000 Salvadorans have emigrated, mostly illegally, to the United States since the war broke out in 1979. Up to 250,000 have found new homes in Mexico, and some 50,000 to 100,000 Salvadorans are now living elsewhere in Central America because of the war. The largest concentration of Salvadoran refugees within Central America has been in Honduras, where 39,000 found refuge in United Nations camps. Only a small portion of those Salvadorans living outside the country has been officially treated as refugees. Joint UN and host government programs have established refugee programs in the other Central American countries and in Mexico, the largest program being in Honduras.

Counting those who came to the United States before the beginning of the civil war, there are some one million Salvadorans living in the United States. About 160,000 Salvadoran illegal immigrants have applied for amnesty under the provisions of the law; between 3,000 and 4,000 a year apply for political asylum.[85] The Immigration and Naturalization Service (INS) and the State Department are unsympathetic to Salvadoran requests for political asylum following the U.S. government rule that, despite the letter and spirit of applicable law, takes the view that only political refugees from left-wing and communist governments are legitimate. In 1988, for example, the INS approved 68 percent of the requests for political asylum from Nicaraguans but only 4 percent from Salvadorans.

Many Salvadorans settle in Mexico, where they constitute half of Mexico's illegal immigrants. Subject to petty extortion from Mexican police and officials, these refugees living in Mexico are commonly forced to find work under miserable conditions for much lower pay than a Mexican worker would accept.

A Displaced Nation

Homelessness and landlessness have deep historical roots in densely populated El Salvador. But the numbers of displaced really began to escalate in the late 1970s as a result of the repression by General Romero's military government. The outbreak of the civil war in 1979–1980 resulted in yet another wave of refugees and displaced families seeking to escape the army's rural counterinsurgency campaign. The counterinsurgency war—complete with scorched-earth tactics, aerial bombing, and forced relocations—has caused a massive displacement of the Salvadoran population. A major upsurge in internal refugees resulted from the initiation in 1983 of the National Plan, a counterinsurgency campaign in San Vicente. Another jump in the displaced population came in the wake of the military's 1985 Operation Phoenix against guerrilla-controlled areas of the Guazapa volcano. More than 10,000 families were displaced by the earthquake that shook San Salvador in 1986.

The massive dislocations that resulted in November 1989 from the FMLN offensive and the army's harsh response further aggravated the crisis of the displaced in El Salvador. At least 50,000 Salvadorans were displaced in the last two months of 1989, mainly by indiscriminate military bombing of poor neighborhoods. The intensified fighting of late 1989 also created a new group of displaced: those U.S. citizens and wealthy Salvadorans who left for the United States when the conflict reached the wealthy enclaves of San Salvador.

As the war dragged on in the 1980s, the displaced and refugee communities began a resettlement or repopulation movement. Tired of living in refugee camps outside El Salvador and squatter settlements within the country, the homeless Salvadorans organized to return home, even if it meant returning to conflictive areas. By mid-1990 most of those refugees who had been living in UN camps in Honduras had returned to El Salvador as part of self-organized massive repatriations. Similarly, displaced communities within the country had returned to their former villages. Those returning from Honduras worked closely with the Catholic Church and two popular organizations, the Christian Committee of the Displaced (CRIPDES) and the National Repopulation Coordinator (CNR). The resettlement communities have been targets of attacks and repression by the military, which considers these organized communities to be guerrilla supporters.

The massive human displacement caused by the war disrupted the economy and society of rural El Salvador. On a macroeconomic level, however, the large number of Salvadorans living in the United States has helped stabilize the economy because of the increasing importance of remittances. In the late 1980s the repopulation of formerly abandoned villages with displaced families and refugees returning from Honduras, most of whom are vocal advocates of negotiated settlement, has tended to increase the pressure for a negotiated settlement to the war.

Ecology and Environmentalism

El Salvador is a spectacularly beautiful land of lakes and volcanoes, which also boasts some of the world's longest uninterrupted beaches.[86] The native people knew it as *Cuscatlán*—Land of the Jewel. But for all the beauty still found here, El Salvador is the country in Central America with the most severely degraded environment. Erosion, which affects at least 50 percent of the country, has created a national agricultural crisis.[87] And the tropical bird known as the quetzal is extinct in El Salvador as are most of the formerly abundant species of cats and monkeys that once made this country their home.

There is also a human side to the ecological devastation. When torrential rains caused the hills of Monte Bello to give way, more than a thousand squatters and displaced people were buried under forty feet of mud. Only one-tenth of the rural population has easy access to clean drinking water, and sewage and waste is quickly contaminating the groundwater in San Salvador. High concentrations of DDT have been found in cow's and mother's milk and in beef.[88]

The tropical forests that once covered the country have been cut down to make room for agroexport production and for subsistence agriculture of the large peasant population. Primary forests now cover only 3 percent of the national territory. Together with secondary growth, natural vegetation covers only 7 percent. Severe erosion causes an annual topsoil loss of 20 percent.[89] According to the United Nations' Food and Agricultural Organization, El Salvador is undergoing a process of desertification.

During the 1970s, cases of pesticide poisoning averaged between 1,000 and 2,000 a year nationwide. Salvadoran environmentalists say that fifty children died from pesticide contamination in one San Salvador hospital alone.[90] In the urban areas, there are problems with smog, pollution of water supplies by industrial effluents, and improper disposal of human waste. It has been estimated that only 15 percent of rural residents and 38 percent of urban dwellers are served by sewage-disposal systems.

The war has contributed in various ways to the degradation of the environment. Bombing by the Salvadoran air force, which includes napalm and white phosphorus, as well as the infamous shrapnel-throwing "daisy-cutter" bomb, has set off fires that destroyed wilderness and cultivable land, and contributed to floods and landslides.

The government, through its Department of National Parks and Wildlife and other agencies, has begun some conservation projects, especially since international financing for such projects is available. With only 2 percent of the country left with any significant remaining forest cover, little of El Salvador is regarded as suitable for preservation in parks.[91] The government has set aside about 50,000 acres for reserves and parks but no timetable has been set. Thus far only six protected areas covering 15,000 acres have been established.

FOREIGN INFLUENCE

U.S. Foreign Policy

The State Department outlined the main principles and features of U.S. foreign policy in El Salvador in its January 1989 statement "El Salvador: The Battle for Democracy," making the following observations:[92]

- The U.S. government supports the process of democratic transition in El Salvador. The most recent example of this policy's success was the peaceful transfer of power after the March 1989 elections.
- The chief threat to democratic transition is the FMLN, which is a Marxist-Leninist coalition guided and financed by Cuba, Nicaragua, and the Soviet Union and determined to seize power by military means. The FMLN is characterized as a terrorist organization.
- There is a large centrist political base in El Salvador, which is on attack from both political extremes. These extremes are marginal elements that are relevant only because of their use of violence.
- Human-rights violations have steadily diminished from the early 1980s, largely because of increased professionalism of the security forces and the lack of government/army support for right-wing extremists.
- U.S. military aid is necessary to permit the Salvadoran armed forces to protect the fragile democratic institutions against the FMLN terrorists. The success of these local armed forces in repelling and isolating the FMLN military obviates any need for the introduction of U.S. combat troops.

• U.S. economic aid is necessary to stabilize the economy. This economic stabilization is accomplished through balance-of-payments assistance and through programs to promote private-sector investment. Other smaller economic-aid programs address the basic needs of the poor through food distribution, health and education programs, low-income housing projects, and care for the displaced. Economic aid also directly supports the democratization process through support for elections, the judicial system, and nongovernmental democratic organizations.

A year later these "truths" of U.S. foreign policy in El Salvador were increasingly being called into question. The November 1989 FMLN offensive shattered the assumption that the guerrillas were an insignificant political and military force. In early 1990, for example, General Maxwell Thurman acknowledged that the Salvadoran army was not capable of defeating the FMLN.[93] The end of the Cold War and the Sandinista–Soviet Union alliance made untenable the former arguments that U.S. national interests were directly threatened in Central American conflicts. The murder of the Jesuits, the inability of the civilian government to control the military, and antipopular positions adopted by the right-wing ARENA government also weakened the White House's contention that the United States was protecting democracy and reform in El Salvador.

By early 1990 the Bush administration's foreign policy in El Salvador seemed limited to short-term strategizing designed to weather new congressional challenges and to fortify the embattled ARENA government. It clung to badly worn and discredited formulas and appeared incapable of seriously reevaluating and revising its foreign policy in El Salvador. Recognizing that a military victory was unlikely, the White House began leaning toward a negotiated end to the conflict. But it appeared unwilling to make the hard decisions necessary for a peaceful resolution—namely, drastically cutting military assistance and using its leverage to force the Salvadoran government to make necessary concessions to the FMLN.[94]

After a decade of U.S. military and economic intervention in El Salvador, Washington could point to only one real achievement. Its intervention in the civil war had kept the FMLN-FDR out of power, albeit at a high cost in Salvadoran lives. On the economic side, the U.S. economic-stabilization program was successful only in that it kept a bankrupt government afloat. It failed, however, to spark promised economic growth.

Perhaps the greatest failure of U.S. foreign policy was its apparent inability to recognize and respond to the class nature of the conflict. The 1980 reforms had represented a superficial but still meaningful attempt to address the war's underlying causes. Despite persistent rhetoric about its commitment to improving socioeconomic conditions, U.S. policy had, in practice, allied itself with the rich. Its unqualified support for the ARENA government, the party of the oligarchy, high-lighted as never before Washington's class alliances in El Salvador.

The main product of U.S. foreign policy was the continuation of war. Without U.S. economic and military aid, the counterinsurgency war could not have been sustained. The long-term consequences of this intervention will be severe. During the 1980s the country became extremely dependent on U.S. economic aid, which approached $1 million a day. Having grown accustomed to a steady supply of dollars and food aid, El Salvador would face severe food-production and fi-nancial crises if the U.S. commitment faded. Still more ominous is the future of the 55,000-member armed forces and the mountains of weaponry and aircraft that someday will be left behind by departing U.S. military advisers.[95]

Still, the old myths have continued to surround U.S. foreign policy in El Salvador. The State Department proclaimed that "the center has held" in El Salvador as the oligarchy, the military, and the right wing were consolidating their control.[96] But in embracing ARENA, Wash-ington only demonstrated how desperate it was to keep its counter-insurgency project alive.[97] By 1990 the U.S. commitment to the counterinsurgency war was being tested by rapidly changing global politics, U.S. budget deficits, rising concerns about human-rights viola-tions, and the increasing realization both in Washington and El Sal-vador that the war could not be won.

Reflecting the eroding bipartisan consensus on U.S. foreign policy in El Salvador, congressional Democrats proposed that U.S. military aid be cut by half and that all aid be terminated if the Salvadoran govern-ment declined to negotiate an end to the conflict. Aid would also be cut if the Jesuit priests' murderers were not brought to justice or if there were a military coup. Along with this evidence of new congressional support for a negotiated solution, there were also proposals that Wash-ington, instead of providing military aid, channel assistance through the National Endowment for Democracy (NED) to "strengthen demo-cratic legal and political institutions." However, in failing to terminate military aid immediately after the murder of the Jesuits, both the White House and Congress demonstrated their willingness to hang on to old premises rather than committing themselves to more realistic and nonmilitary policy directions.

Almost a year after the Jesuit murders, Congress, frustrated by the lack of action on that case, voted to withhold 50 percent of the military aid requested by the Bush administration. For the first time, the vote sent a clear signal to the Salvadoran military that it could no longer count on steady U.S. backing for its program of militarism and repression. Only a few months later the Bush administration released the suspended aid in response to the deaths of two U.S. soldiers, who were apparently executed by FMLN troops. Ever since the suspension of the full military aid package, the Bush administration had been looking for an opportunity to renew it. Congressional opposition to U.S. military aid to El Salvador noted that the release of military aid offered a clear signal to the Salvadoran government that Washington was not greatly concerned about the Cristiani administration's failure to prosecute the perpetrators of the 1989 massacre of the Jesuit priests.

U.S. Trade and Investment

The United States dominates the country's foreign trade and investment. About 70 percent of the country's exports go to the United States and 40 percent of its imports come from the United States.[98] With $95 million in direct investment in El Salvador, the United States accounts for 48 percent of total registered foreign investment of $196 million in the country.[99]

The major U.S. investors in El Salvador, in order of economic significance, are Esso Standard Oil, Kimberly-Clark, AVX Ceramics, Crown Zellerbach, Texaco Caribbean, Chevron, and Foremost-McKesson. Other U.S. corporations with substantial investment are National Cash Register, Phelps Dodge, Cargill, and Minnesota Mining & Manufacturing (3M).[100] Panama and Japan are the next largest investors after the United States, followed by Canada. The Japanese have substantial investment in the textile industry; Bayer of Canada dominates the agrochemical industry; Shell Oil is also a major presence.

In recent years the only economic sector in which direct U.S. investment has increased has been in the service industry. McDonald's is one of several U.S. fast-food firms operating in the country, the luxury hotels are owned by U.S. firms, Taca Airlines is largely U.S.-owned, and U.S. advertising and consulting firms do an active business in El Salvador. AID-funded infrastructure-repair projects and its development-assistance programs have also brought U.S. firms to the country.

As part of an effort to increase foreign investment, AID pressured the Salvadoran government to pass the 1986 Export Promotion Law and the 1988 Foreign Investment Development and Guarantee Law, both of which give preferential tax treatment to new foreign investors. AID is also funding the expansion of the San Bartolo free trade zone and the creation of a new privately owned industrial zone for export-processing factories.

U.S. Economic Aid

For most of the 1980s, between $300 million and $320 million in U.S. economic assistance annually entered El Salvador through the AID mission in San Salvador. About two-thirds of this annual allotment arrived in the form of Economic Support Funds (ESF), with the balance split between Development Assistance and PL480 food aid. This aid exceeds the Salvadoran government's own contribution to its budget. The large injection of direct AID assistance was complemented by other sizable foreign-aid programs, including those of the U.S. Department of Agriculture's Commodity Credit Corporation (CCC), the Overseas Private Investment Corporation (OPIC), Trade Investment Insurance Program of the Export-Import Bank (Eximbank), as well as millions of dollars channeled through AID's regional and Washington offices for labor programs, disaster preparedness, business strengthening, and a variety of other programs. In addition, hundreds of millions of dollars have been directed to El Salvador in the last ten years through the Inter-American Development Bank and the World Bank.

In describing U.S. assistance programs, there is the immediate difficulty in defining what is truly "economic" and what should be considered military or political aid. In its reports on U.S. economic aid in El Salvador, the Arms Control and Foreign Policy Caucus of the U.S. Congress has rejected State Department statements that most U.S. aid to El Salvador is economic. Instead, the caucus has more correctly defined most AID assistance (about 75 percent) as "war-related."[101]

Economic stabilization has been one of the chief goals of U.S. economic aid. It has also been one of the most successful elements of AID's program in war-torn El Salvador. Economic stabilization refers basically to the effort to keep the government and the economy afloat by alleviating the country's foreign-exchange shortage and resulting balance-of-payments crisis. By pumping about a million dollars a day into the country, AID relieves the government of the debt-servicing pressures and dollar shortages that plague other Third World nations. During the 1980s El Salvador has ranked among the top half-dozen countries receiving ESF and Title I stabilization aid.[102]

Political stabilization and pacification (or population control) represent another major thrust of economic-assistance programming in El

Salvador. In the context of a civil war, the "development" objectives of the Agency for International Development have been interpreted primarily according to the imperatives of the U.S. counterinsurgency project. Economic-aid programs are designed to complement the strictly military aspects of counterinsurgency. As it did in Vietnam, AID funds and manages this "other war."[103]

While striving to keep the economy stable, AID has also played a leading role in seeking to establish a pro-U.S. political stability in the country. The U.S. government calls this political focus of economic aid "democratization." Recognizing that a key ingredient of counterinsurgency is the existence of a government capable of maintaining a wide base of national and international support, the U.S. government lent its support to the establishment of a Christian Democratic government that could claim centrist and moderate credentials. It also financed an elaborate electoral system to give credibility to U.S. assertions that El Salvador is a democratic republic fighting off a challenge by antidemocratic left-wing terrorists.

Although initial support for popular reforms diminished, AID did not lose sight of the importance of winning Salvadoran hearts and minds for the counterinsurgency project. Rather than addressing the structural injustices of the society, however, AID chose after 1983 to stress programs aimed at controlling the rural population through pacification strategies. Several new government agencies were created for the purpose of pacifying the increasing displaced population and the communities in conflictive zones. These AID-funded agencies included the National Commission for Aid to the Displaced (CONADES) and the National Commission for the Restoration of Areas (CONARA).

Yet another aspect of political stabilization is the "institution-building" support AID and the Department of Justice have offered to a variety of governmental and nongovernmental institutions in El Salvador. Most of this aid is administered by AID's Office of Democratic Initiatives. To refurbish the democratic image of the government, AID in 1984 launched several projects to strengthen the country's judicial system by offering training courses and creating a Special Investigative Unit (SIU) and a Judicial Protection Unit. As part of its democratization program AID also finances the Revisory Commission on Salvadoran Legislation, which works with the National Assembly in reviewing and revising laws, regulations, and procedures of the country's judicial system.

After six years of funding Washington had little to show for this judicial project: Human-rights abuses by security forces were still not being investigated or prosecuted and the judicial system remained hostage to military and political control. Since the program was introduced, no military officer has been successfully prosecuted for human-rights abuses. It is clear that the program has not addressed the fundamental weakness of the judicial system: its lack of independence from the military.[104]

U.S. Military Aid

U.S. assistance to El Salvador does not fit easily into the two major aid categories: military and economic. Most economic aid is war-related, even food-aid and development programs. Even using the Pentagon's own limited definition of military aid, this category is quite substantial. Since 1980 more than $1 billion in U.S. military aid has been used to keep the Salvadoran armed forces trained, equipped, and on the battlefield. This does not include the costs of maintaining U.S. advisers in the country, nor the various logistical and intelligence services provided by the U.S. Southern Command, the CIA, Defense Intelligence Agency (DIA), or National Security Council (NSC).

Although not officially designated as military aid, the United States also provides support and training for Salvadoran security forces. Congress terminated AID's controversial international police-training program in 1974, but special congressional waivers have allowed Washington to sponsor several police-assistance and training programs in El Salvador. Through AID and the Justice Department, programs train and supply special criminal and judicial police units and prison police. Since 1983 the country's police forces have received training as part of the State Department's Anti-Terrorist Assistance (ATA) program.[105] Beginning in 1985 the ATA program was complemented by a much larger program designed to combat urban "terrorism." As part of the U.S. government's counterterrorist assistance to El Salvador, three special units of the Salvadoran security forces were trained: Special Antiterrorist Force, Liberator, and Lightning Battalion.[106]

The lack of clarity about the full extent of U.S. military commitment to El Salvador is best illustrated by Washington's claim that there have been only fifty-five U.S. military advisers in the country at any one time, while U.S. military sources place that figure closer to 150.[107] Salvadoran military sources place the figure at three hundred. In addition, Salvadoran military sources estimate that for each U.S. military adviser there is at least one other U.S. adviser connected to the CIA, DIA, or NSC working in intelligence or security operations.[108] A major recipient of covert U.S. aid is the National Directorate of Intelligence (DNI), which is a large intelligence and special operations center financed by the CIA.[109]

Some 6,000 Salvadoran troops were trained at the U.S. Army's School of the Americas during the 1980s. Within the country, the contingent of U.S. military advisers is coordinated by the Military Group (MilGroup). An Operations and Training Team (OPATT) is assigned to each Salvadoran brigade. Officially, they do not engage in combat themselves, but sometimes it becomes clear that the official story disguises the truth. A 1988 recommendation for awarding medals to two marines was turned down by a review board at U.S. Southern Command when it was determined that the marines had organized and led a counterattack against a guerrilla unit that had attacked the Sixth Infantry Brigade in Usulután.[110] More than advisers, U.S. officers have provided intelligence to the Salvadoran air force, allowing them to pinpoint targets for aerial bombardment.[111]

Military aid requests in the 1980s were regularly couched in language about the necessity of defending the country's fragile democracy against a communist conspiracy and of allowing the country to rebuild its economy in the face of guerrilla terrorism. An emergency grant of $5.7 million in military aid requested by President Carter in late 1979 set off the present era of U.S. military intervention in El Salvador. Called the "decisive battle for Central America" by the Reagan administration, within a few years the counterinsurgency war in El Salvador was supported annually by more than $80 million in direct military aid.

The Bush administration backed its request for a continued high level of aid on the grounds that "U.S. security assistance contributes to regional stability. It also promotes professionalism, respect for human rights, self-sufficiency, and deference to civilian leadership." According to the administration, U.S. military aid is needed because "the guerrillas continue to reject conciliation that would be keyed to elections." Not only is the aid needed, but the Pentagon says it has also proven successful. "The armed forces have become increasingly successful in countering ever-changing guerrilla tactics." Military aid in 1988 and 1989 was "aimed principally at sustainment," and 1990 aid is necessary for "the replacement and reconditioning of essential equipment, particularly helicopters."[112] Rising congressional frustration with the recalcitrant Salvadoran military and the stalemated war make large commitments of U.S. military aid in the future doubtful.

REFERENCE NOTES

[1] Quoted in Kenneth J. Grieb, "The United States and the Rise of General Maximiliano Hernández Martínez," *Journal of Latin American Studies*, November 1971, p. 152.

[2] Communication with Americas Watch, January 23, 1990.

[3] Segundo Montes, Florentín Meléndez, and Edgar Palacios, *Los Derechos Económicos, Sociales, y Culturales en El Salvador* (San Salvador: IDHUCA, May 1988).

[4] Housing figures from FUSADES, cited in *Proceso*, August 30, 1989.

[5] Total votes by election: 1982: 1,551,687; 1984: 1,419,493; 1985: 1,101,606; 1988: 1,083,812; and 1989: 1,003,153. *Proceso*, April 5, 1989.

[6] *Proceso*, April 12, 1989.

[7] Philip L. Russell, *El Salvador in Crisis* (Austin: Colorado River Press, 1984), p. 90.

[8] Evidence of the success of ARENA's party-building maneuvers was apparent in 1988 when the party won nineteen additional seats in the Assembly while the PDC lost eleven. ARENA also gained control of 178 municipalities while the PDC lost 174.

[9] *Latin American News Update*, January 1990.

[10] William M. LeoGrande, "After the Battle of San Salvador," *World Policy Journal*, Spring 1990, p. 350.

[11] Interview by Terry Karl with Salvador Samoya, "Negotiations or Total War," *World Policy Journal*, Spring 1989, p. 331.

[12] President Cristiani went into the San Isidro Coronado summit of December 10, 1989, intent on condemning Nicaragua for having allegedly supplied arms to the FMLN. On the defensive because of reports that a Nicaraguan plane carrying arms had been shot down in El Salvador, President Ortega signed the accord condemning "the armed and terrorist actions of the irregular forces of the region" and calling for the FMLN to lay down its arms apparently in an effort to keep the regional peace talks alive.

[13] Foreign policy analyst William LeoGrande observed, "Ironically, the FMLN's demands for military reform do not conflict fundamentally with stated U.S. policy aims. On the contrary, if civilian democracy is what Washington truly wants in El Salvador, these reforms are essential to achieving it. In addition, Washington has a vested interest in reducing the size of the military once the war is over, since the United States has to foot the bill for it." LeoGrande, *World Policy Journal*, op. cit., p. 351.

[14] Tom Gibb and Frank Smyth, *El Salvador: Is Peace Possible—A Report on the Prospects for Negotiations and U.S. Policy* (Washington Office on Latin America, April 1990).

[15] Amnesty International, *El Salvador: Death Squads—A Government Strategy* (New York: October 1988).

[16] Americas Watch, *Nightmare Revisited: 1987–1988* (New York: 1988).

[17] Americas Watch, *The Civilian Toll: 1986–1987* (New York: 1987).

[18] Edward S. Herman, "Disinformation as News Fit to Print," *Covert Action Information Bulletin*, Winter 1988.

[19] Walt Spencer, "Herbert Ernesto Anaya Sanabria: 1954–1987," *Links* (National Central America Health Rights Network), Winter 1987.

[20] Americas Watch, *Nightmare Revisited*, op. cit.

[21] Ibid.

[22] U.S. Department of State, *Country Reports on Human Rights Practices for 1988* (Washington, D.C.: February 1989), pp. 564–565.

[23] Arms Control and Foreign Policy Caucus, U.S. Congress, "Barriers to Reform: A Profile of El Salvador's Military Leaders," May 21, 1990.

[24] U.S. military advisers have described the pre-1980 Salvadoran armed forces as "a militia of 11,000 that had no mission" that "acted historically as a blight on the political system." While the army claims now to have about 50,000 men, the FMLN say that number is inflated, the real number being 36,000 to 38,000.

[25] The proclaimed number of civil-defense members also appears inflated, given the self-acknowledged failure of the army to organize the population in conflictive areas to take up arms or to establish paramilitary groups.

[26] The United States has attempted unsuccessfully to reform the officer corps, while also attempting to develop a cadre of noncommissioned officers, regarded as essential for small unit operations. But the concept of noncommissioned officers is alien to the military establishment, which "consists of the commissioned officer elite above and short-service peasant conscripts below." Only 10 percent of the noncommissioned officers trained in the United States reenlist for another term. Ltc. A. J. Bacevich, Ltc. James Hallums, Ltc. Richard White, and Ltc. Thomas Young, John F. Kennedy National Security Fellows, "American Military Policy in Small Wars: The Case of El Salvador," paper presented at the John F. Kennedy School of Government, March 22, 1988.

[27] Ibid.

[28] Joel Millman, "El Salvador's Army: A Force Unto Itself," *New York Times Magazine*, December 10, 1989.

[29] Gibb and Smyth, *El Salvador*, op. cit., p. 17.

[30] Another death squad associated with ORDEN was Regalado's Armed Forces (FAR), run by Dr. Antonio Regalado who turned a Boy Scout troop into a death squad. The FAR and other death squads were coordinated by ANSESAL, which was directed by military intelligence specialist D'Aubuisson.

Later, Regalado was selected by D'Aubuisson to run the special protection unit, which had its headquarters in the Constituent Assembly building. Regalado was fingered by a fellow collaborator as the man who shot Archbishop Romero. Douglas Farah and Tom Gibb, "Confessions of an Assassin," *Mother Jones*, January 1989.

31 Allan Nairn, "Behind the Death Squads," *The Progressive*, May 1984. Also see Jim Naureckas, "Death Squad Strategy Was Made in U.S.A.," *In These Times*, January 13–19, 1988; and Michael McClintock, *The American Connection: State Terror and Popular Resistance in El Salvador* (London: Zed Books, 1985).

32 See interview with Colonel Juan Orlando Zepeda in Max Manwarring and Court Prisk, eds., *El Salvador at War: An Oral History* (Washington, D.C.: National Defense University Press, 1988), pp. 310–314.

33 Chris Norton, "Spectre of Terror in El Salvador," *Christian Science Monitor*, April 21, 1989.

34 LeoGrande, *World Policy Journal*, op. cit., p. 336.

35 *NACLA Report on the Americas*, September 1989, p. 19.

36 Kenneth Freed, "Weekend Warriors Aid Salvador Rebels' Strategy," *Los Angeles Times*, November 2, 1988.

37 According to the FMLN platform of 1981, the revolutionary democratic government, after defeating the military-civilian junta representative of the oligarchy and reformist plans of the United States, would establish along with the working class, the *campesinos*, the "advanced" middle classes, democratic parties, and honest army officials a "democracy for the popular masses." Among the political measures taken would be the disarmament and dissolution of all the security and defense forces, the abolition of the three state organisms, and the restructuring of "municipal power," which was to be converted into a real organ of popular power. A sole popular army would be created and the new government would break the economic, political, and military dependence on the United States, establish relations with socialist countries, and be incorporated into the Movement of Non-aligned Nations. "Special Report: A New FMLN Project," *Central America Report*, September 22, 1989.

38 Joaquín Villalobos, "A Democratic Revolution for El Salvador," *Foreign Policy*, Spring 1989; Joaquín Villalobos, "El Estado Actual de la Guerra y sus Perspectivas," *Estudios Centroamericanos*, March 1986; and Villalobos, "Popular Insurrection: Desire or Reality?" *Latin American Perspectives*, Summer 1989.

39 *Central America Report*, September 22, 1989.

40 Ibid.

41 For this analysis of the economy, the author relied extensively on the monthly reports circulated by the American Friends Service Committee ("El

Salvador Notes") and two UCA publications: *Proceso* and *Realidad Económico-Social.*

42 Alexander Segovia, "Límites y Dilemas de la Política Económica en un País en Guerra," *Realidad Económico-Social,* November–December 1988; Montes et al., *Los Derechos Económicos,* op. cit., p. 165.

43 *Proceso,* December 6, 1989.

44 Senator Mark Hatfield, Representative Jim Leach, and Representative George Miller, *Bankrolling Failure: United States Policy in El Salvador and the Urgent Need for Reform: A Report to the Arms Control and Foreign Policy Caucus* (November 1987).

45 Segundo Montes, "La Crisis Social Agudizada por la Crisis Política Salvadoreña, la Migración a los Estados Unidos," *Estudios Centroamericanos,* October 1987.

46 *Realidad Económico-Social,* November–December 1988.

47 *Situación Actual y Perspectivas de la Economía y la Integración,* CEPAL, June 9, 1989.

48 The only major new construction projects scheduled are those related to the military (new Armed Forces Pension Fund building) or to U.S. government projects (new U.S. embassy compound and new buildings for the AID-funded FUSADES and the industrial training center of the Salesians).

49 El Salvador's 3 percent to 4 percent budget deficit/national-income ratio falls safely under the 5 percent maximum recommended by the International Monetary Fund (IMF).

50 *Proceso,* May 10, 1989.

51 Montes et al., *Los Derechos Económicos,* op. cit., p. 8.

52 *Facing Reality in El Salvador: Cristiani's First 100 Days* (Philadelphia: NARMIC/AFSC, November 1989), p. 11.

53 *El Salvador: Agricultural Situation Report* (Washington, D.C.: Foreign Agricultural Service/U.S. Department of Agriculture, March 31, 1989).

54 Ibid.

55 Ibid., p. 7; Rachel Garst and Tom Barry, *Feeding the Crisis: U.S. Food Aid and Farm Policy in Central America* (Lincoln: University of Nebraska Press, forthcoming).

56 See "Reforma Agraria," *Coyuntura Económica* (Instituto de Investigaciones Económicas, UES), January–February 1989.

57 *Proceso,* September 13, 1989.

58 U.S. Department of Commerce, *Foreign Economic Trends and Their Implications for the United States,* pp. 4–5; U.S. Embassy, San Salvador, "Investment Climate Survey"; *Encyclopedia of the Third World 1987,* p. 640.

59 *IDB Annual Report* (Inter-American Development Bank, 1987).

[60] Interview by Tom Barry with Carlos Palacios, director of PRIDEX, February 1989.

[61] "Los Industriales Desprotegidos Frente al Ajuste," *Proceso*, August 23, 1989.

[62] Important sources on the popular movement include Segundo Montes, *Estructura de Clases y Comportamiento de las Fuerzas Sociales* (San Salvador: IDHUCA, 1988) and *Problemática Urbana, Movimiento Popular y Democracia en el Area Metropolitana de San Salvador, 1986–1988*, Documento de Trabajo (San Salvador: Coordinación Universitaria de Investigación Científica, UES, September–October 1988).

[63] *El Salvador: Critical Choices—A Special Report by the National Labor Committee in Support of Democracy and Human Rights in El Salvador*, June 1989.

[64] For the best detailed breakdown of union federations see Montes, *Estructura de Clases*, op. cit.

[65] *The Advancement and Placement of Students from Central America*, P.I.E.R. Workshop Report, 1987 (Washington, D.C.: National Association of Foreign Student Affairs, 1987); *CIA World Factbook 1988*.

[66] *Central America Report*, June 16, 1989.

[67] Lindsey Gruson, "Salvador TV Dares to Tell the News," *New York Times*, September 27, 1988.

[68] U.S. Embassy, San Salvador, *Country Data: El Salvador*, January 1, 1989.

[69] "A Ten Year War on Health," *Links* (NCAHRN), Spring 1989.

[70] Figures from Ministry of Planning, cited in *Proceso*, August 30, 1989.

[71] Alan Myers and Adrienne Epstein, "Passage to Chalatenango," *Links* (NCAHRN), Winter 1988–1989.

[72] *Central America Report* (London), Summer 1989.

[73] Colum Lynch, "Salvadoran Church, State Tensions Rise," *Washington Post*, June 24, 1989.

[74] For a thorough treatment of religious groups and nongovernmental organizations (NGOs) in El Salvador, see *Directory and Analysis: Private Organizations with U.S. Connections—El Salvador* (Albuquerque: Resource Center, 1988).

[75] Data on AID funding to NGOs supplied to Resource Center by AID in communications of September 12, 1987, and April 5, 1988. For a complete breakdown see *Directory and Analysis: Private Organizations with U.S. Connections—El Salvador*, op. cit., p. 7.

[76] *Diagnóstico de la Situación de la Mujer Centroamericana* (CEPAL, September 1988).

[77] Marilyn Thomson, *Women of El Salvador: The Price of Freedom* (London: Zed Books, 1986), pp. 36–38.

78 "Gathering Strength" (London: El Salvador and Guatemala Human Rights Committees).

79 Thomson, op. cit., p. 27, which cites T. Monreal et al., "Abortos Hospitalizados en El Salvador," *Salud Pública en México*, May–June 1977, pp. 387–395.

80 For an overview of women's issues and organizing in El Salvador, see New America Press, eds., *A Dream Compels Us: Voices of Salvadoran Women* (Boston: South End Press, 1989).

81 Jenny Pearce, *Promised Land: Peasant Rebellion in Chalatenango El Salvador* (London: Latin American Bureau, 1986), pp. 12–17.

82 Indians are not a census category, and definitions are arbitrary. The highest figure, of 20 percent, was cited by Helen Schooley in *Conflict in Central America* (London: Longman Group Ltd., 1987). Many other estimates refer back to estimates made in authoritative works of forty years ago. The *CIA World Factbook 1988* reports 10 percent, and *Encyclopedia of the Third World 1987* gives 6 percent.

83 Theodore MacDonald, "El Salvador's Indians," *Cultural Survival Quarterly*, Vol. 6, No. 1, Winter 1982; Thomas P. Anderson, *Matanza* (Lincoln: University of Nebraska Press, 1971), p. 17; Richard N. Adams, *Cultural Surveys of Panama, Nicaragua, Guatemala, El Salvador and Honduras* (Detroit: Ethridge, 1957), p. 504.

84 United Nations High Commission on Refugees, Information Paper, International Conference on Central American Refugees (CIREFCA), Guatemala City, May 29, 1989; *Central America Bulletin*, December 1988; U.S. Government Accounting Office, *Central America: Conditions of Refugees and Displaced Persons* (Washington: March 1989).

85 Robert Pear, "A Letter from Duarte Urges U.S. to Temporarily Accept Refugees," *New York Times*, September 11, 1988.

86 H. Jeffrey Leonard, *Natural Resources and Economic Development in Central America* (New Brunswick: Transaction Books, 1987).

87 Because of the exceptionally high quality of the volcanic soil in El Salvador, much of the cropping is on hillsides. As erosion becomes more severe, the country's food production and agroexport systems are increasingly endangered.

88 Leonard, op. cit.

89 Bill Hall and Daniel Faber, "El Salvador: Ecology of Conflict," *Earth Island Journal*, Summer 1989.

90 Ibid.

91 Leonard, op. cit., p. 119.

92 U.S. Department of State, "El Salvador: The Battle for Democracy," *Department of State Bulletin*, January 1989.

[93] Michael Gordon, "General Says Salvador Can't Defeat Guerrillas," *New York Times*, February 9, 1990.

[94] LeoGrande, *World Policy Journal*, op. cit., p. 353. LeoGrande notes that the Republican right, most strongly represented in the NSC staff and in the office of the vice president, remains confident of a military victory although it recognizes the need for at least the appearance of a negotiating process to pacify Congress.

[95] For a provocative discussion of the regional implications of a strong and uncontrolled Salvadoran military, see Bacevich, Hallums, White, and Young, "American Military Policy in Small Wars," op. cit.

[96] U.S. Department of State, "El Salvador: The Battle for Democracy," op. cit.

[97] For further discussion of U.S. foreign policy, see Sam Dillon, "Dateline El Salvador: Crisis Renewed," *Foreign Policy*, Winter 1988–1989; Ricardo Stein, "Civil War, Reform, and Reaction in El Salvador," in *Crisis in Central America* (Boulder: Westview, 1988); Chris Norton, "U.S. Salvador Policy: Spell It Unsalvageable," *In These Times*, February 1989.

[98] U.S. Embassy, San Salvador, *Foreign Economic Trends and Their Implication for the United States: El Salvador* (Washington, D.C.: U.S. Department of Commerce, March 1989; CEPAL, *Current Situation and Economic Perspectives*, June 19, 1989.

[99] U.S. Embassy, San Salvador, "Update of Investment Climate," July 13, 1988.

[100] Ibid.

[101] Senator Mark Hatfield, Representative Jim Leach, and Representative George Miller, *U.S. Aid to El Salvador: An Evaluation of the Past, A Proposal for the Future* (February 1985), and *Bankrolling Failure*, op. cit.

[102] For a more thorough treatment of AID's stabilization strategy see Tom Barry and Debra Preusch, *The Soft War: The Uses and Abuses of U.S. Economic Aid in Central America* (New York: Grove Press, 1988).

[103] The term *other war* was first used by officials of the Johnson administration to describe the nonmilitary aspects of the Vietnam war, which were managed by AID, military/civic action teams, and NGOs. See ibid.

[104] *Elusive Justice: The U.S. Administration of the Justice Program in Latin America*, Report on the Workshop Sponsored by the American University Law School of International Service and the Washington Office on Latin America, May 1990.

[105] Lionel Gómez, former director of the Agrarian Reform Institute (ISTA), informed U.S. Senator Tom Harkin that at least six of the eighteen Salvadoran officers being trained by the Anti-Terrorism Assistance program had death-squad links. *In These Times*, August 20, 1986.

[106] Barry and Preusch, *The Soft War*, op. cit., pp. 181–183; *Underwriting Justice* (Lawyers Committee for Human Rights, April 1989).

[107] Ibid.

[108] *NACLA Report on the Americas*, July 1989.

[109] According to Colonel Juan Orlando Zepeda, former director of military intelligence, "The DNI receives most of its aid from the Central Intelligence Agency. The CIA provides some support to the C-2 [Intelligence Division of Combined General Staff], such as direct training. But the whole product, the handling of sources, such as communications, traffic analysis, and equipment, is handed over to the DNI." Manwarring and Prisk, op. cit.

[110] Alfonso Chardy, "Two U.S. Advisors Played Role in Salvador Battle," *Miami Herald*, January 19, 1989.

[111] Frank Smyth, "Caught with Their Pants Down," *Village Voice*, December 5, 1989, reported monitoring radio conversations in which the U.S. military command center in San Salvador instructed the Salvadoran air force to "hit" an area several blocks "north of the church."

[112] U.S. Department of Defense, *Congressional Presentation for Security Assistance Programs FY1990* (Washington, D.C.: 1989).

Chapter Four

GUATEMALA

CHRONOLOGICAL HISTORY

1821–2 Central American region declares its independence from Spain and is annexed to Mexico.

1823 Independence from Mexico as United Provinces of Central America.

1830 After four years of civil war, Morazán takes Guatemala City, becomes president of United Provinces of Central America.

1839 Central American Federation disintegrates.

1859 Guatemala signs treaty recognizing British sovereignty of Belize.

1901 United Fruit Company arrives in Guatemala.

1920–1 Estrada Cabrera overthrown; United States intervenes militarily. In the elections that followed the Central America Unionist Party elected, but with U.S. encouragement, a second coup installs military government.

1931 Ubico elected; purge of leftists and repression of unions for the next thirteen years.

1944 Ubico forced to resign; "October Revolution" breaks out and victorious forces sponsor new elections.

1945 Reformist candidate Juan José Arévalo is elected president.

1949 Francisco Javier Arana, chief of the armed forces, is assassinated soon after announcing his candidacy for president.

1950 Jacobo Arbenz Guzmán elected president. Agrarian reform carried out over the next four years.

1954 CIA's Operation Success topples Arbenz government; Carlos Castillo Armas of the National Liberation Movement (MLN) takes power.

Expropriated lands returned to former owners; all unions disbanded; thousands of people are killed.

1955 Castillo Armas confirmed as president.

1957   Castillo Armas assassinated; Vice President Luis Arturo
        González named provisional president. Presidential elections
        turn into riots, military takes control of government and
        names Guillermo Flores Avendano as head of state.

1958   New elections won by conservative Michael Ydigoras
        Fuentes.

1960   Failed U.S. invasion of Cuba is launched from Guatemalan
        and Nicaraguan soil.

1961   Belize turns down an offer to become an associate state of
        Guatemala.

1962   Formation of the M-13 and Rebel Armed Forces (FAR) guer-
        rilla groups after a failed coup attempt by a group of refor-
        mist officers.

1963   Army removes Ydigoras and names Defense Minister Al-
        fredo Enrique Peralta president.

1966   PR candidate Julio César Méndez Montenegro is elected
        president.

        U.S. Special Forces participate in Operation Guatemala, a
        counterinsurgency campaign led by Araña Osorio, which
        kills more than 8,000 people. Appearance of the White
        Hand and other right-wing death squads, which are be-
        lieved to be responsible for more than 30,000 deaths over the
        next seven years.

1970   MLN candidate Carlos Araña Osorio elected president.

1974   Right-wing candidate Kjell Laugerud García elected presi-
        dent in apparently fraudulent victory over Ríos Montt.

1976   Earthquake leaves 22,000 dead, one million homeless, and
        Guatemala City partially destroyed.

1977   U.S. aid rejected by Guatemala because of human-rights
        requirements.

1978   National elections leave no candidate with clear majori-
        ty; PR-PID-CAO candidate General Romeo Lucas García
        elected president by the National Congress.

        U.S. bans arms sales to Guatemala.

1980   Security forces kill twenty-seven CNT leaders; repression
        forces most unions underground.

1981   Army carries out major counterinsurgency offensive in Chimaltenango; 1,500 Indian *campesinos* are killed in a two-month period.

1982   USAID distributes $15.5 million in economic aid.

         PID candidate General Angel Aníbal Guevara wins national elections; a junta of army officers seizes power before Aníbal is installed. New junta unveils its National Development and Security Plan. After three months the junta is disbanded and its leader, retired General Efraín Ríos Montt, takes power. A month later a state of siege is declared.

         World Council of Churches reports that the government is responsible for the death of more than nine thousand people in the previous five months.

1983   United States resumes supplying spare military parts.

         Evangelical Ríos Montt alienates business, army, as well as the Catholic Church; Defense Minister General Oscar Humberto Mejía Víctores seizes power in military coup, and initiates "model villages" program.

1984   Constituent assembly convenes to formulate new constitution.

         The World Council of Indigenous Peoples accuses the military of systematic extermination of the Indian population.

1985   Resumption of official U.S. economic and military aid.

         Formation of the Mutual Support Group (GAM), which brings international attention to the plight of the disappeared; a founder is assassinated.

         Christian Democrat Marco Vinicio Cerezo Arévalo wins national elections.

1986   West Germany gives more than $175 million in bilateral assistance over the next three years.

1987   Presidents of Costa Rica, El Salvador, Guatemala, Honduras, and Nicaragua sign Esquipulas II peace accords.

         Army massacres twenty-two peasants in Aguacate and blames it on guerrillas, and military announces "Year's End" offensive to wipe out insurgency.

1988   Catholic bishops release a pastoral letter entitled "The Cry for Land."

         "Year's End" offensive called off after major casualties incurred and failure to stamp out guerrillas becomes obvious.

Two coup attempts fail to unseat Cerezo government.

1989   Failed coup attempt.

1990   The general elections in November marginalize the govern-
          ing Christian Democratic party along with such traditional
          rightist parties as the National Liberation Movement (MLN),
          pushing the leaders of two new right-wing parties, Jorge
          Carpio Nicole of Union of the National Center (UCN) and
          Jorge Serrano Elías of Movement of Solidarity Action (MAS),
          into the run-off elections in January 1991. On December 2
          the army massacres fifteen Indians in Santiago Atitlán. U.S.
          terminates military aid, citing the Santiago Atitlán massacre
          and the previous murder of U.S. citizen Michael Devine.

1991   Jorge Serrano of MAS wins resoundingly in the presidential
          run-off election on January 6 and takes office a week later.

Sources for the chronology include *Encyclopedia of the Third World* (New
York: Facts on File, 1987); *Conflict in Central America* (London: Long-
man Group Ltd., 1987); *Crisis in Central America: Regional Dynamics and
U.S. Policy in the 1980s* (Boulder: Westview Press, 1988); *Labor Organiza-
tions in Latin America*, Gerald Greenfield and Sheldon Maran, eds.
(Westport, CT: Greenwood Press, 1987); and "Facts of the Matter"
(Central America Education Project, Summer 1987).

TRENDS

- The country's political parties and governmental institutions will prove unable to broaden and stabilize the democratization process begun in the mid-1980s because of their failure to assert effective control over the military and oligarchy and to represent the interests of the poor majority.
- The early successes of the military's National Security and Development strategy are now disintegrating as the guerrilla insurgency intensifies, popular discontent rises, and the civilian government fails to produce long-term economic and political stability.
- The tenuous economic recovery of the late 1980s is likely to crumble in the early 1990s as international aid dries up and persistent trade imbalances and debt-servicing problems bankrupt the external sector, while inflation and deepening poverty continue to drag down the domestic economy.
- Though expanding, the popular movement lacks the power to negotiate peaceful resolutions to its many economic and social-justice demands, and instead is kept weak and disjointed because of government repression and human-rights violations.
- The U.S.-Guatemala relationship continues to be characterized by ambivalence and instability: Although Washington firmly supports the counterinsurgency war and remains committed to the reactionary private sector, it is unable to supply sufficient economic and military aid to guarantee the stability of the government and the military, due to congressional budget and human-rights concerns.

Guatemala, the northernmost country on the Central American isthmus, is with close to 9 million inhabitants the region's most populous nation. About the size of Kentucky, Guatemala is at once the most beautiful and most terrifying country in this turbulent region. Its spectacular Mayan ruins, majestic volcanoes, misty highlands, and the persistence of native people and cultures make Guatemala a wonder-

land for tourists. But a pall of terror hangs over this country as a result
of almost four decades of repression and military control.

The story of modern-day Guatemala actually begins in 1944, the
year when long-time dictator General Jorge Ubico retired and a successor regime was overthrown by a reformist alliance of military officers, students, professionals, businessmen, and politicians.[1] For ten
years, Guatemala experimented with democracy, social reforms, and
economic modernization. A violent coup supported by the CIA, right-
wing politicians, the Catholic hierarchy, and the oligarchy brought that
period to an abrupt end in 1954. For the last thirty-five years the
country has suffered the legacy of that abortion of democracy and
reform.

The 1954 coup carried out by Colonel Carlos Castillo Armas and his
CIA backers brought back oligarchic and military control in Guatemala, which quickly melded with the ideology of anticommunism
and national security. Many hoped that the 1985 elections that brought
the Christian Democrat Vinicio Cerezo into the National Palace would
return Guatemala to the path optimistically initiated in 1944 by Juan
José Arévalo and the October Revolution and bring relief to a country
darkened by decades of right-wing extremism, military rule, and oligarchic conservatism.[2]

The principal protagonists of the 1954 coup—Guatemala's right
wing and the reactionary agroexport oligarchy as well as the United
States—still loom as major obstacles to real change in Guatemala. The
oligarchy and the extreme right-wing political parties in league with
army factions are vigilant against creeping socialism, threatening and
even occasionally attempting coups to keep the country in line with
their authoritarian beliefs. The U.S. government, while no longer such
a principled opponent of agrarian reform, would consider any serious
reform movement in Guatemala as a threat to its own security. Since
1983, Washington has supported the army's project for political stabilization, focusing its economic aid on bolstering the private-sector elite
and export economy.

Life has always been lived on the edge in Guatemala and is becoming
even more precarious. For most Guatemalans, increasing human-
rights violations and repression are of less concern than the constant
suffering inflicted by the society's grossly uneven economic structures.
More Guatemalans die of preventable diseases than as a result of
political violence. During the 1980s the standard of living declined 20
percent.[3] Each year, moreover, 42,000 children die of preventable or
curable diseases.[4] Although Guatemala has moved forward politically,

it remains entrenched in its benighted systems of land tenure and labor exploitation.

A small but growing guerrilla movement presents a persistent challenge to this society of generals and oligarchs. The leftist guerrilla coalition calls for revolutionary changes in the nation's economic structures and a broadening of democracy. Failure of the government and army to modernize the economy and politically stabilize the country could result in a widening civil war. A brutal, almost genocidal, counterinsurgency campaign smashed the guerrilla movement in the early 1980s, and the transition to civilian rule in 1986 was accompanied by widespread hope that finally the pall of military terror could be shaken off and the society could begin to address its many inequities. By 1990, however, those hopes had largely faded as human-rights abuses spread, the civilian politicians proved to be corrupt and opportunist, and dire poverty remained the common condition.

GOVERNMENT AND POLITICS

Although military rule is a tradition in Guatemala, so are elections.[5] Every four years, the military selected its candidate, held an election, and declared its candidate the winner. By the early 1980s, this system began breaking down as elements within the military began to question the validity and wisdom of government by direct military rule. In 1982 a group of dissident officers led by General Efraín Ríos Montt (retired) seized the National Palace and ousted the handpicked successor of former president General Romeo Lucas García. A month after the coup, the military government took a decidedly new approach to the counterinsurgency war. While continuing the scorched-earth tactics of the predecessor regime, the Ríos Montt government began to incorporate a developmental and nation-building side to the military effort.

This new vision was outlined in the National Security and Development Plan (PNSD), decreed as law in April 1982. According to this plan, "The war is to be combated on all fronts: on the military and the political, but above all on the socioeconomic. The minds of the population are the principal objective." The PNSD addressed four problem areas undermining national stability:

1. Political Stability: the need to legitimize the government on local and international levels. To do this, the military recog-

nized that it needed to take steps to return government to a legal framework, meaning a new constitution, elections, and the revival of political parties.

2. Economic Stability: the need to pull the country out of economic recession and to address the severe poverty of the rural population.
3. Psycho-Social Stability: the need to contain the advances of the guerrillas among peasants, Indians, and the illiterate.
4. Military Stability: the need to defeat the armed subversion.[6]

The PNSD set the guidelines for the evolution of government in the 1980s. It established politics as an extension of war, and government as an instrument of a national-stability project defined by the military. The plan for security and development moved Guatemala away from a military-controlled "national security state" to a national security civilian government, also controlled by the military.[7]

The Ríos Montt coup injected a new dynamism into the military's response to the guerrilla threat and popular rebellion in the highlands. As president, Ríos Montt attempted to legitimize his government by establishing a Council of State with representatives from various social sectors. Ríos Montt was not, however, the ideal coordinator for the military's stabilization efforts. His evangelical religious convictions alienated many important elements of Guatemalan society and did little to break down the country's international isolation.

A year and a half after the coup that installed Ríos Montt as president, the National Palace was the scene of another military coup in August 1983. This time Ríos Montt was replaced by his minister of defense, General Oscar Humberto Mejía Víctores, which put the traditional military hierarchy back in command. They immediately began the process of instituting formal civilian rule—one of the principles of the PNSD. Elections for the Constituent Assembly were held in 1984, and a new constitution was approved. In late 1985 the military sponsored fraud-free elections for the presidency and seats in the new National Congress. President Vinicio Cerezo received the blue presidential sash from General Mejía Víctores in January 1986, and began his five-year presidential term backed by the military high command and by a clear majority of Christian Democrats in the newly constituted unicameral National Congress.

The critical role of the military in setting the democratization process in motion has never been in doubt. There was, however, widespread hope that the Cerezo government would take measures to build popular support for government and would seek more independence from the military. What feeble attempts the Cerezo government did take to meet popular economic demands were blocked by the private sector and opposing right-wing parties. As a result, the Cerezo government's support base steadily eroded, making it increasingly dependent on the continued goodwill of the military high command.

Serrano Takes Office

The ruling Guatemala Christian Democratic party (DCG) went into the 1990 election campaign badly divided and with its popular support steadily declining. As a result, this center-right party and its presidential candidate Alfonso Cabrera fared poorly at the polls in the November 1990 general elections, opening the way for the leaders of two right-wing parties, the Union of the National Center (UCN) and the Movement of Solidarity Action (MAS), to contend for presidential office in the run-off election on January 6, 1991.

MAS's candidate Jorge Serrano Elías won 68 percent of the run-off vote, badly defeating UCN's Jorge Carpio Nicole. Serrano took office on January 14, 1991, and became the second consecutive democratically elected president in the country's history. Although decidedly beating his opponent, Serrano's victory did not represent a national consensus. Of the 3.2 million registered voters, 55 percent abstained, compared to a 44 percent rate in the first round in November 1990 and 34 percent in the 1985 presidential election. Considering the large numbers of adults who are not even registered to vote and those rural residents who go to the polls only because they think that voting is still obligatory, the high abstention rate understates the degree of popular disillusion with the electoral process in Guatemala.

The triumph of Serrano (who had placed third in the 1985 presidential contest) can be largely explained by the backing of the losing parties in the first round elections and by his support within the evangelical community. Serrano stayed out of the fray of accusations that characterized other campaigns and many Guatemalans saw him as preferable to the newspaper magnate Jorge Carpio, whose lavish campaign expenditures alienated voters. Serrano also gained voter sympathy as a result of his prominent participation in the peace-making efforts of the National Reconciliation Commission.

Serrano, a forty-five-year-old civil engineer, was affiliated with the Christian Democrats during the 1970s. During the Ríos Montt regime he served as the president of the Council of State. A member and former director of the fundamentalist Elim church, he is married to Magda Bianchi, whose brother Roberto Bianchi is a leader of the

Church of the Word (Verbo) with which Ríos Montt is closely associated.

Like the other presidential candidates, Serrano ran on a platform advocating expanded neoliberal reforms. He is a leading member of the International Democratic Union, a conservative political association that includes the U.S. Republican party. Serrano's own conservative political and economic beliefs were largely reflected in the cabinet appointees, who were drawn from the private sector and many of the parties that supported his candidacy. The obvious exception was the appointment of Mario Solórzano of the Democratic Socialist party (PSD) to be the new labor minister. The appointment of Solórzano was an apparent attempt to boost support for the government among the popular sectors and to draw the labor movement into a "social pact" with the government and private sector.

Serrano moved into the national palace at a time when Guatemala was becoming increasingly isolated at the international level because of continuing human-rights abuses by the country's security forces. The five years of civilian rule had not helped to decrease these abuses or to institute better government control over the security forces, as international human-rights monitors had earlier hoped. Just prior to Serrano's inauguration, Americas Watch issued a report ranking Guatemala just behind Colombia in human-rights violations, noting that the difference between the two countries was that the Colombian government was making "enormous efforts" to restore peace. In 1990, the UN Human Rights Commission placed Guatemala "for the tenth consecutive occasion, in third place among the 19 countries where the situation of forced disappearances is critical."

The inability of the Guatemalan government to control human-rights violations committed by the security forces and associated death squads will have economic implications for the new government unless it can persuade the United Nations and other international donors that the country's human-rights climate will improve substantially. Accordingly, Serrano attempted to establish his independence from the military in his first months as president, but the army proved to have the ultimate word in the appointment of the new defense chief and interior minister.

In addition to concerns about the country's international image and about the dominant power of the military, Guatemala also faced severe economic problems at the start of the Serrano administration. The new government was confronted with large fiscal and trade deficits compounded by dwindling foreign-exchange reserves. Inflation was soaring, and the neoliberal remedies promised by Serrano would only make matters worse for the poor majority.

Serrano entered office with a weak political base. Counting on only eighteen of the 116 seats in Congress, the ruling MAS party was forced into a tenuous alliance with the Christian Democrats, the National Advancement party (PAN), and the Guatemalan Republican Front (FRG). This alliance elected Catalina Soberanis, former labor minister and a stalwart Christian Democrat, as president of the Congress. The UCN had the most congressional seats (forty-one followed by twenty-eight seats controlled by the Christian Democrats), but was passed over for all leadership positions in the legislative body.

The State of Politics

Most political parties in Guatemala are found on the right side of the political spectrum. These rightist parties range from the National Liberation Movement (MLN), the long-time standard bearer of anti-communist politics, to the Union of the National Center (UCN), which poses as a centrist party but leans decidedly to the right. In between are a number of other rightist parties that are commonly little more than platforms for their current leaders. During the 1990 elections the right wing was marked by disunity and the absence of a clear vision of the future. Suffering its worst crisis in thirty-five years, the organized right has found itself dangling without a popular base and out of touch with the political thinking of both the army and private sector. In a quandary of ideology and organization, the right wing has found itself unable to adapt to the political changes brought on by the military-sponsored democratization process.

Since the late 1940s anticommunism—more visceral than rational—has been the driving force of the political right in Guatemala. But in the era of *glasnost*, anticommunism as an ideology does not stir the blood of the party faithful as in the past. In the new political rhetoric adopted by the army and government, terrorism is posed as the main threat to democracy. But unlike the military, rightist parties have failed to modernize their political tactics. Like a defective phonograph needle, the extreme right remains stuck in its decades-old rut, expounding on the communist threat to national security. Formerly at the center of power in Guatemala, the old political right now faces hard times. It finds itself on the outside of political and economic decision-making, left with only a few seats in the National Congress and conspiring on the sidelines with isolated factions of the military and oligarchy.

Although the economic right does not have its own political parties, it does boast powerful economic organizations, notably the Coordinating Committee of Agricultural, Commercial, Industrial, and Financial Associations (CACIF), and to a lesser extent the Free Business Chamber (*Cámara de Libre Empresa*) and the *Cámara Empresarial* (CAEM).[8] By no means does the entire business elite fully share the faith in neoliberal economics. But the entire business community does share the conviction in the primacy of the business sector. This economic right, comprising both the neoliberal purists and the more pragmatic elements of CACIF, had difficulty finding an appropriate electoral instrument within the political right.

The notorious old party of the extreme right, the National Liberation Movement (MLN) is directed by Mario Sandoval Alarcón, alleged godfather of the Central American death squads. As leaders of the coup that overthrew the Arbenz government, the rabidly anticommunist MLN has long been looked on with favor by the traditional agroexport oligarchy and rightist factions within the military. Under Cerezo the debilitated MLN charged that the DCG government served as a front for international communism, asserting that the Cerezo government was fomenting social discontent as the first step in a civil war that would open up the country to communism. By 1990 the MLN had toned down its extremist rhetoric, mimicking the evolution of the ARENA party in El Salvador. During peace talks with the Guatemalan National Revolutionary Unity (URNG) in May 1990, Sandoval Alarcón surprised observers by adopting an extremely conciliatory and friendly position, apparently with an eye to broadening vote support for the extreme right.

Founded in 1983 by *El Gráfico* publisher Jorge Carpio Nicolle, the Union of the National Center (UCN) is the country's second most powerful party, after the DCG. Benefiting from its ability to propagate publicity through the country's second largest newspaper and characterized by its right-wing populism, the UCN quickly achieved the national prominence and outreach that other rightist parties lacked.

To the left is the Democratic Socialist party (PSD). The PSD disbanded following the assassination of its founder Alberto Fuentes Mohr and fifteen other party activists during the Lucas García regime but reestablished itself in 1985 to take advantage of the political opening afforded by the democratization process.[9] Associated with the Socialist International, the PSD is more a social-democratic party than a socialist one. The party leader is Mario Solórzano, who represents the more conservative or centrist faction of the party and favors a reformist rather than a socialist political philosophy.

The Guatemala Christian Democratic party (DCG) is the only political party that can be considered centrist. The DCG was founded as a
rightist party in 1955, in the shadow of the 1954 coup. For the last
twenty years, however, the party has assumed a reformist image, posing
as the centrist alternative between revolutionary change and extreme
right-wing reaction. It has been consistent in its call for the modernization of capitalism as "a better way to fight communism."[10]

Despite its support for social reforms, the DCG has remained strictly
an electoral party, eschewing coalitions with the popular movement.
Although it has lost dozens of party activists to political repression, the
DCG has been steadfast in its commitment to the electoral path. In fact,
the pursuit of political power increasingly distanced the party from the
popular movement, shifting it ever closer to the very elements of
society responsible for the country's main social ills.

In its years as the ruling party the DCG, directed by Cerezo, was
characterized by its political astuteness, its adept international public
relations, and its opportunism. Benefiting from a generous supply of
international aid and goodwill, the Cerezo government managed to
keep the other political parties off-balance and divided. The successful
ascent to power of the DCG and Vinicio Cerezo was due largely to its
opportunistic alliance with the military and sectors of the right wing.
From its earliest years, the DCG formed alliances with such ultraright
parties as the Anti-Communist Unification party (PUA) and has a long
tradition of backing military candidates for president. In 1974, General Efraín Ríos Montt, the presidential candidate of a reformist coalition that included the DCG and the social-democratic parties of
Fuentes Mohr and Manuel Colom Argueta, was denied the presidency
in a fraudulent election. Despite this experience, the DCG persisted in
its quest for political power, fielding candidates again in 1978 and
1982, thereby bestowing a continued credibility to the electoral process.

Its status as ruling party greatly strengthened the DCG. As the
government party, the DCG was able to build a network of supporters
linked to jobs and government programs. In marked contrast to its
main competitor, the Union of the National Center (UCN), the Christian Democrats established a relatively strong party infrastructure in
rural Guatemala. Yet its position in government exposed the basically
conservative and opportunistic nature of the party, considerably undermining initial popular enthusiasm.

As in El Salvador, the Christian Democrats in Guatemala began to
splinter before the end of their first term in office. Most of the controversy resulted from Cerezo's efforts to promote the candidacy of major
party figure Alfonso Cabrera for the 1990 elections. A reputation of

corruption and association with narcotraffickers handicapped Cabrera as did his uncharismatic, party-hack image. Supporters of party founder René de León Schlotter complained that the nominating process was fraudulent and refused to recognize the legitimacy of the Cabrera candidacy. Besides the bitter dispute between the Cabrera and de León factions, the party also suffered from the emergence or resuscitation of party offshoots, including the Popular Alliance-5, whose secretary-general was forced into exile by death threats, and the Movement for the Recuperation of the Christian Democrat's Ideological Identity.

About twenty parties nominated candidates for the November 1990 elections. The beginning of the campaign was marked by a saturation of television and radio publicity. It was also distinguished by its absence of ideological debate and concrete political platforms. The floating of the *quetzal* and the conservative economic measures adopted by the government left the right wing with little ammunition for a strong ideological campaign. The DCG, in effect, had taken the wind out of the right wing's sails. But by adopting the right wing's program and ignoring popular demands, the DCG has had a more difficult time projecting itself as a centrist party.

The superficial nature of Guatemalan democratization became more apparent during the 1990 campaign. The political parties were based on personal ambitions rather than on ideas or a commitment to democracy. Despite the country's debilitated state, there was no substantial debate about the nation's economic direction, military control, or social reforms. Neither was there any link between the political parties and the rising chorus of demands from popular organizations.

Foreign Policy

Although not formally acknowledged, Guatemala's foreign relations have long been closely aligned with the United States. As the country's main investment and trading partner and its chief source of financial aid, the United States has maintained a large degree of economic and political hegemony over Guatemala. With the exception of the Carter years in the 1970s, there has been a confluence of interests that has conditioned relations between the two nations. The United States is the country's main agroexport market, its main supplier of imports, and its principal supplier of investment capital. Especially since the mid-1950s, the United States has been Guatemala's principal partner in economic development, both in the agroexport sector and in the import-substitution industrial sector. Politically, both countries consider their national interests threatened by any serious rise in leftist popular opposition.

In 1983, having successfully waged its counterinsurgency campaign, the Guatemalan military was ready to pursue a strategy of economic and political stabilization. The military's program largely paralleled measures proposed by Washington, the European Community (EC), and the multilateral banks: transition from military to civilian rule, economic reactivation based on foreign aid, structural adjustment, and export promotion. These new Guatemala initiatives dovetailed nicely with the U.S. strategy of surrounding Nicaragua with U.S.-backed "democratic" republics.

While Guatemala's domestic policies closely matched the U.S. strategy for the region, the same was not always true with the foreign policy of "neutrality" adopted by the Mejía Víctores regime in 1983. This policy called for nonintervention in the internal affairs of other Central American nations and giving priority to resolving Guatemala's internal problems and its international isolation. President Cerezo renewed this policy, calling it "active neutrality." Armed with a foreign policy of "active neutrality," the Cerezo government was an early advocate of the Central American peace process, creating some apparent conflict with Washington.[11]

Active neutrality served Guatemala well in its campaign to improve its international image and enhance its democratic credentials. It was, however, a policy that was in practice not strictly followed. As relations improved with the United States, the Guatemalan military and civilian government began to provide covert aid for the Nicaraguan *contras*. According to a CIA memo, Guatemala agreed to provide clandestine logistical support and training for the *contras* in return for Washington's efforts to refurbish the country's international standing.[12] International arms shipments for the *contras* were channeled through the Guatemalan army, *contras* were trained at the Pólvora Special Counterinsurgency School in northern Petén, and the *contras* used Guatemala as a base for their political operations, which included a political training center established at the Francisco Marroquín University.[13]

Guatemala's involvement in armed conflict beyond its borders also extended to the civil war in El Salvador. During the Salvadoran guerrilla offensive of November 1989, an unspecified number of counterinsurgency specialists and advisers were sent to El Salvador, one of whom was held by Salvadoran guerrillas when they captured the Sheraton hotel in San Salvador.[14] Asked about this collaboration, Chief of Staff Manuel Callejas replied, "The Guatemalan army has always collaborated with the Salvadoran army, and that situation will not change."[15]

There have long been close relations between the extreme right in Guatemala, particularly the National Liberation Movement (MLN), and the right-wing ARENA party in El Salvador. This regional right-wing alliance may have been responsible for the death-squad killing in January 1990 of Héctor Oquelí, secretary general of El Salvador's National Revolutionary Movement, and Gilda Flores, a lawyer associated with Guatemala's Social Democratic party.

Peace Process

The Cerezo government initially played a key role in arranging regional talks among the five Central American presidents (Panama and Belize did not participate). Cerezo's ambitions to win international acclaim as a regional peacemaker were thwarted, however, by the more aggressive efforts of President Oscar Arias of Costa Rica. Revelations of Guatemala's support for the Nicaraguan *contras* and the superficial manner in which the Guatemalan government implemented the peace accords contrasted sharply with Cerezo's proclamation of regional neutrality and commitment to peaceful solutions.

The provisions of the Esquipulas II peace accords, ratified by Guatemala in August 1987, were only superficially implemented within the country. In keeping with the accords, the Cerezo government did declare a political amnesty, but its main beneficiaries were military officers who participated in a May 1988 coup attempt against the government. Refugees returning from Mexico or displaced persons rounded up by the army have also been given amnesty but only after the military coerced them into signing amnesty declarations stating their repudiation of the guerrillas. Criticizing this use of amnesty, Americas Watch complained that "rather than opening a way for an individual to participate in political life, the acceptance of amnesty attaches to that individual the stigma of subversive association, which is extremely dangerous in Guatemala."[16]

As specified in the Esquipulas II peace accords, a national dialogue was initiated under the auspices of the newly established National Reconciliation Commission (CNR), which received strong support from the Catholic Church. Representatives of the country's major political parties, churches, and popular organizations were represented in the CNR. But the relevance and impact of the organization was undermined from the start by its failure to incorporate representatives of the URNG guerrilla coalition and groups of Guatemalan exiles who also petitioned for the right to participate. The failure of the military and the business coalition CACIF to join the dialogue also foiled the CNR's efforts to promote peace and justice.[17]

For all its limitations, the popular movement, represented by the Labor and Popular Action Unity (UASP), regarded the national dialogue as an opportunity to raise demands in a public forum sanctioned by the government. Dialogue participants and observers took advantage of the forum to establish links with each other and to forge a common strategy. The popular movement, however, approached the national dialogue mindful that past attempts to reach national accords over such issues as wages and human rights had been repeatedly sabotaged by other government agreements with the private sector and the army.

International pressure brought the Cerezo government to agree to discussions with the URNG guerrilla coalition in October 1987, but this dialogue quickly lapsed due to right-wing reaction in Guatemala. The URNG continued to express interest in reopening talks but was repeatedly rebuffed. It was not until early 1990 that a series of talks between the URNG and the country's political parties, private groups, and popular organizations was initiated. In March 1990 delegations from the URNG and CRN met in Oslo where it was decided that the CRN and the URNG would meet with the country's key economic, social, and political groups. The intent of these talks was to lay the foundation for direct negotiations between the rebels and the government and military.

Neither the government nor the military has indicated, however, that it would seriously consider a negotiated end to the conflict. It has been the government's unbending position that there can be no substantive talks until the guerrillas lay down their arms and incorporate themselves into the "democratic" process. The CNR has also insisted that any accords reached with the URNG be "within the limits of the constitution." For its part, the URNG has insisted that any negotiated solution to the conflict will have to include measures that effectively address the country's underlying social and economic problems. The guerrilla leadership stated that it is not considering joining the electoral framework but is working toward the establishment of a "true democracy."

The URNG called for a boycott of the 1990–1991 elections. At least in the first months of the Serrano administration, there was widespread hope that President Serrano, who had participated so prominently in the National Reconciliation Commission, could move the country toward peace. In his inaugural address, he spoke of his desire to accelerate the dialogue process and offered to negotiate unconditionally with the rebels.

Human Rights

Extensive human-rights violations have been a constant in Guatemala for almost four decades. As the intensity of popular organizing and guerrilla insurgency increases, the level of infractions tends to increase. Violations also tend to increase during preelection campaigning. The country saw diminished human-rights abuses in the main urban center during the short reign of Ríos Montt at the same time that massive terror ruled in the countryside. Following the 1986 inauguration of Vinicio Cerezo there was a marked reduction in human-rights violations. By the end of the decade, however, politically related deaths and disappearances had once again become an almost everyday occurrence.

Human-rights monitoring groups like Americas Watch and Amnesty International repeatedly condemned Guatemala for gross abuses of human rights during the 1980s. Declining to accept official explanations that human-rights violations were the exclusive work of extremist political groups, the international monitors charged that the police and military were themselves responsible for most violations.[18]

Until early 1990, the U.S. State Department had backed official claims that the civilian government was successfully improving the human-rights climate. In its 1988 human-rights reports, the State Department commended the government for establishing a human-rights office and sponsoring programs to improve the judicial system. The report asserted that the government itself was not to blame for the "infrequent" and "isolated" politically motivated violations that did occur.[19]

While the horror of the human-rights climate in Guatemala has long received international attention, only in recent years has the issue been publicly discussed within the country. Much credit for this goes to the Mutual Support Group (GAM), which despite the torture and disappearance of several of its own directors and members has persisted in denouncing abuses and demanding justice for past violations. The death of a GAM founder in 1985 was attributed by the army to a "lamentable accident." President Cerezo advised the group, 90 percent of whom are rural Indian women, "to stop acting macho" and "forget the past."

Other groups that have brought attention to human-rights issues are CONAVIGUA (National Coordinator of Guatemalan Widows), CERJ

(Council of Ethnic Communities Runajel Junam), and CIEPRODH (Center for Investigation, Study, and Promotion of Human Rights). Besides denouncing human-rights abuses, CERJ aims "to advance the goals of democracy, justice, and dignity of the Mayan peoples while fighting racial discrimination."

Government initiatives to investigate human-rights violations have served more to polish the image of the government than seriously to address the issues. The human-rights commission created by the Cerezo government was constrained by a low budget ($200 a month) and fear of accusing the military of any abuses. In its first year, the commission received nine hundred denunciations of human-rights violations but did little or nothing to investigate those cases.

The commission's existence was cited by the Cerezo government as an example of its commitment to resolve the human-rights problem. The government also repeatedly referred to the training that the Guatemalan judiciary received from Harvard Law School's Center for Criminal Justice as proof that the government was working to improve the investigation and prosecution of political and common crimes. In television advertising, it claimed that the training program—funded by the U.S. Agency for International Development (AID)—was helping to correct the human-rights situation in rural areas. According to Americas Watch, however, the judiciary demonstrated no inclination to prosecute cases of human-rights violations. Furthermore, denunciations of human-rights violations are passed from the human rights commission to the Ministry of Defense or to the National Police, "in most cases, the same institutions from which the plaintiffs seek redress."[20] In mid-1990, Harvard withdrew from the program charging that the country's failure to prosecute human-rights abuses "is plainly a failure of political will and not capacity."[21]

By the fifth year of the Cerezo administration the deteriorating human-rights climate was causing increasing problems for the government. The August 1989 assassinations of Christian Democratic leader Danilo Barrillas and banker Ramiro Castillo, followed by a wave of disappearances and deaths of student leaders, signaled an escalation in the level of death-squad terror and resulted in condemnations of political violence from all quarters. Shocked by the Barrillas and Castillo killings, private-sector leaders began to complain that the deepening climate of terror was undermining their ability to do business.

Accusations by the U.S. embassy in early 1990 that the Cerezo government was doing little to clamp down on human-rights abuses shocked the Cerezo government. While the government and the military blamed the increasing violations on the guerrillas, right-wing extremists, and narcotraffickers, the State Department for the first time since 1985 focused on the responsibility of the armed forces and the government. The January 1990 murder of Salvadoran socialist leader Héctor Oquelí and Guatemalan lawyer Gilda Flores of the Democratic Socialist party sparked strong international rebuke for the country's human-rights climate. The case was immediately compared to the massacre of six Jesuit priests in El Salvador two months before.

MILITARY

Security Forces

The Guatemalan armed forces—incorporating the military wisdom of U.S., Israeli, Taiwanese, and Argentine advisers—seriously set back the guerrilla insurgency of the early 1980s with ruthless violence and sophisticated pacification techniques. Not only has the Guatemalan army demonstrated a remarkable ability to combine "security" and "development" in its counterinsurgency efforts, but it has also successfully carried out a nation-building project that further strengthened the Guatemalan state. Notably, the military conducted this multifaceted campaign without large infusions of foreign assistance, in marked contrast to neighboring El Salvador.

As successful as counterinsurgency in Guatemala has been and as invincible as the military may appear, the stability and security of the Guatemalan state still remain in question for the following reasons:

- Despite massive killing of dissidents and the militarization of society, the army has failed over the last three decades to rid the country of the guerrilla threat. Its claims to have finished off the guerrillas have proven to be wishful thinking. By the late 1980s, the guerrilla movement was once again seriously challenging the power of the military at the same time that the popular movement was gaining new strength and visibility. National security, as defined by the army and its advisers, seems to be an unachievable goal. As a result, counterinsurgency has become a permanent state of affairs.
- The army's apparent success in gaining control over the rural population is related more to its use of terror than to the performance of its civic-action and psychological-operations teams. Since 1954 the security forces have eliminated successive generations of leaders, activists, and educators, leaving communities largely unorganized and de-

prived of social and political foundations. But the resulting void in popular political education and experience has not meant that the army and government have been able to shape the kind of supportive social base necessary for national stability, nor has this constant repression succeeded in keeping a lid on popular organizing.

• Counterinsurgency theorists generally recognize that deteriorating socioeconomic conditions create a base for insurgency. Despite a widespread commitment for a developmentalist side of counterinsurgency, the military has been unable to conceptualize and implement the kind of projects that would indeed alter the socioeconomic circumstances of the countryside. Instead, the development component of counterinsurgency has been translated into welfare-type projects that depend on the continued flow of supplies and funds from foreign governmental and nongovernmental donors.

• The military high command guided a nation-building project designed to create a modernized state capable of responding politically, socially, and economically to revolutionary insurgence. Although successful in establishing the structure of a modern state, the army's nation-building efforts have so far failed to cement the kind of national-unity pact needed to support its broad vision of counterinsurgency. The key sectors that would be included in such a pact—the Catholic Church, worker and peasant organizations, the business community, and the political parties—each has refused, for different reasons, to offer the required support. Even significant elements within the armed forces have rejected the modernization vision of the military high command, which stresses the need for a civilian government and a more open political atmosphere.

• Continued repression and military control of the civilian government have undermined the government's credibility and dashed hopes that political modernization would bring peace, stability, and progress. As public enthusiasm for the "democratization" process has waned, the potential for widespread social turmoil and armed rebellion has increased.

• The capacity of the military to wage an offensive war has been increasingly undermined by its lack of funds, supplies, and equipment, particularly aircraft.

Structure of the Armed Forces

There are three armed forces in Guatemala: army, navy, and air force. The army, with more than 40,000 troops, is the dominant element in this tripartite defense structure. In contrast, the navy has only 1,200 members (including six hundred marines) and the air force only 850 (including five hundred conscripts).

In the last few years, the army has mounted a nationwide publicity campaign about the values of military service. Officially, military service is the duty of all Guatemalan males; in fact, universal military service is a myth, as is voluntary recruitment. Generally, only the sons of the rural poor serve in the ranks of the army and they are, for the most part, recruited forcibly. Typically, army trucks arrive in a village on market days and the feast days of patron saints, with the local military commissioner signaling which youth should be recruited.

For the last fifteen years, the Guatemalan armed forces have increasingly integrated themselves into the private sector and the national oligarchy. The Military Social Welfare Institute (IPM) and the Army Bank are the center of this newfound financial status, but the tentacles of martial economic power extend much further. Among the public-sector corporations that fell under military control in the 1970s and early 1980s were INDE (National Electrification Institute), Aviateca national airline, Aurora international airport, GUATEL (national telephone company), and Channel 5 television station. In addition, the military controls such state agencies as the National Reconstruction Committee (CRN), CONE (National Emergency Committee), National Geographic Institute, and FYDEP (Petén development directorate, which is now being dismantled).

The Soft Sell

Since the April 1982 release of the National Security and Development Plan, the military has been committed to pursuing what could be called the "soft" side of counterinsurgency. This is not to say that the army has shirked from military offensives designed to defeat the insurgency while keeping the rural population terrified and passive; massacres, torture, random terror, and aerial bombardments continue as part of a campaign to guarantee national security. These "hard" tactics, however, are now usually combined with measures designed to pacify, to some degree, the guerrillas' rural base of support. As the military began to gain a firmer hold on the embattled highlands in 1982 and 1983, this other side of counterinsurgency received increasing attention. The various aspects of this soft sell of national security include

• Pacification of the population in conflict zones through civic action projects, model villages, reeducation and psychological operations, food distribution, and development projects.

- Modernization of the Guatemalan state through a process of "democ-ratization."
- Limited reforms designed to broaden the financial base of govern-ment (tax increases) and pacify popular demands (wage hikes, land sales programs, increased social services).

The S-5 teams from the Civil Affairs section are responsible for pacification efforts. These teams are composed of soldiers specially trained in the areas of social services, psychological techniques, and ideological indoctrination. Usually nonuniformed, they function as a fifth column for the military in contested zones. Their work includes intelligence gathering; reeducation of displaced persons and refugees; coordination of the projects of government ministries in targeted zones; and, in general, implementation of the "development" side of counterinsurgency. In addition to coordinating development, Civil Affairs also manages the army's extensive psychological operations. It is called upon to "create an efficient leadership, which permits the forma-tion of local leaders to spread the doctrinal elements of counterin-surgency strategy. The leadership must incorporate social promotion and community organization to arrive at integral community develop-ment."[22]

Splits Within the Military

The Guatemalan armed forces have long been torn by tactical differ-ences and divisions between the ranks. A long-running source of ten-sions has been the split between those favoring developmental and nation-building programs and those committed to a strictly military approach to maintaining national stability. For example, the National Reconstruction Committee (CRN), created in 1976, was largely a proj-ect of the army developmentalists. In the early 1980s the adoption of the National Security and Development Plan (PSND) represented a fusion of the two approaches to counterinsurgency and a moderation of tensions between the two camps. But as the guerrillas began to recuperate their former strength and the civilian government became less capable of forging a national consensus, earlier differences be-tween the reformist and hard-line approach began to resurface.

The unity of the Guatemalan military has also been weakened at times by splits between junior and senior officers. The military crisis of 1983 aggravated this division and resulted in the coup by younger officers led by Efraín Ríos Montt. This split became apparent again in the late 1980s as the younger officers who were on the front lines of the counterinsurgency war grew increasingly frustrated with the military high command directing the war. They resented the luxuries available to these senior officers, who were not directly involved in the increasingly dangerous counterinsurgency campaigns. In many cases, the internal divisions in the military assume an ideological form when in fact the dispute has more to do with the division of privileges and perks.[23]

By the second year of the Cerezo administration these divisions within the armed forces began to represent a serious threat to its cohesiveness. In May 1987 a military faction calling itself the Officers of the Mountain, began to publish clandestine communiqués critically analyzing the government and Minister of Defense General Hector Alejandro Gramajo. The Officers of the Mountain challenged Gramajo's contention that the counterinsurgency war had been reduced to a police action against isolated bands of terrorists. From their battlefront perspective, these military dissidents knew that the guerrilla offensive was still causing large numbers of casualties. The reemergence of the *Campesino* Unity Committee (CUC) peasant group and the presence in the country of opposition figure Rigoberta Menchú irked the Officers of the Mountain, who felt that the fighting forces were getting short shrift in this pretentious new democracy. While members of the high command and officers in the city were well off, the dissidents charged that the combatants were not getting the aid they needed to fight the war successfully.

Although not taking full responsibility for the various 1988–1989 coup attempts, the clandestine Officers of the Mountain were certainly among the rebel ranks. The coups appeared to be negotiating maneuvers rather than serious attempts to seize state power. Although these intrigues did not succeed in breaking the alliance between the Cerezo government and the military high command, many of the rebel officers' demands were respected, including the cancellation of a political agreement with the UASP; removing the URNG from the political dialogue; increased spending for military supplies; the reinsertion of military officers into key positions in the public administration; increased military control over police forces; and maintenance of civil patrols.

The Officers of the Mountain and other right-wing elements within the armed forces have received direct backing and encouragement from ultraright political and economic factions. Significantly, the coup attempts and threats of 1988–1989 were not condemned by the leading voices of the private sector. Instead, the destabilizing impact of the attempted coups served the immediate interests of the private sector in that both the government and the army hardened their position against popular demands for wage increases and price freezes.

Civil Patrols

Civil patrols have been the army's main instrument in maintaining the militarization of the Guatemalan countryside. First formed in Alta Verapaz in 1976 and expanded in mid-1981 by the Lucas regime, the Civilian Self-Defense Patrols became a central element in the counter-insurgency strategy of the Ríos Montt government aimed at breaking guerrilla links with the population. By late 1984 there were more than 900,000 members of the civil patrol system. Supposedly a voluntary movement, the civil patrols were in fact obligatory. All males sixteen years or older were required to "volunteer" several days a week to serve in these military-directed patrols. Failure to volunteer meant being branded a guerrilla sympathizer and often resulted in imprisonment and torture at the local army base. Beginning in 1983, civil patrols became a ubiquitous part of rural life, as they began to maintain guard posts in most villages to monitor the movement of visitors and villagers alike.

Although civil patrols are no longer as extensive and numerous as they were in the early 1980s, they remain an important element in the military's counterinsurgency operations in the most conflictive zones. In some communities, they function as paramilitary squads that terrorize the local population. In army offensives in the highlands, civil patrols are ordered to seek out and destroy settlements of displaced families associated with the Communities of Population in Resistance (CPR) and to enter into direct conflict with guerrilla units. The disbanding of the civil patrols is one of the major demands of the country's human-rights groups and *campesino* associations. The right wing and the army, however, are calling for the extension of the civil patrol system into the cities, where guerrillas have mounted new antimilitary actions.

Police Divisions

The National Police, with 9,500 members, is the principal police organization. The 2,100-member Treasury Police (*Guardia de Hacienda*) enhances its influence by working closely with the army's G-2 intelligence command.

Under the Cerezo government, the National Police was the favored recipient of considerable foreign training and supplies from the United States, Spain, West Germany, and other European countries. This aid raised concerns among sectors of the military that the Cerezo government was creating a source of armed power independent of the military. This conflict was resolved at least temporarily when, following the May 1988 coup attempt, the government agreed both to increase efforts to resupply the military and to cede control over the National Police to the military. The militarization of the police deepened in 1989 when an army general replaced a civilian as minister of justice.

The creation of SIPROCI (Civil Protection System) in 1988 also allayed fears in the military that the government was crossing over into the security business. This police unit, incorporated directly under the army's high command, places the Mobile Military Police (PAM), civil patrols, National Police, and Treasury Police under military coordination and control. The tradition of army control of the Guatemalan police continued into the Serrano administration with the January 1991 appointment of Colonel Mario Enrique Paiz Bolaños to head the National Police.

Paramilitary Groups

Death squads in Guatemala are part of the country's security apparatus. The country has a long history of private right-wing paramilitary units operating in conjunction with at least some elements of the military and police. Military-sanctioned paramilitary violence was responsible for much of the repression inflicted on the left and the popular movement arising from the 1954 coup. A second surge of paramilitary violence, coordinated largely by the MLN, arose as part of the counterinsurgency campaigns of the 1960s. The two major death squads of this period were the White Hand and the New Anti-Communist Organization. Some sources report that death squads killed between 30,000 and 40,000 people from 1966 to 1973.[24]

After a brief respite, paramilitary killings and disappearances rose again in the late 1970s and early 1980s. In 1983, with the incorporation of the civil patrol system, the armed forces counted on a new dimension of paramilitary activity. Death-squad violence did decrease during the first year of the Cerezo administration but increased dramatically by the end of the decade. At first Cerezo and the military high command blamed the rise in disappearances and killings on common criminals and leftist terrorists. By the turn of the decade, however, both the government and the military charged that right-wing extremists and narcoterrorists were behind the scourge of death-squad killings of student leaders, politicians, and community activists. International human-rights groups and even the U.S. ambassador complained, however, that the government was doing little or nothing to control the paramilitary violence and was to some degree implicated itself in the rash of murders and disappearances of the 1988–1989 period.

The army's Presidential Department of Communications, located next to the National Palace, has long been considered one of the most important links between the military and paramilitary activities. The army's intelligence (G-2) agents, who work closely with the National Police and the Department for Criminal Investigations (DIC), are regarded as directly responsible for death-squad operations.

Guerrilla Opposition

The origins of guerrilla warfare in Guatemala can be traced to a failed military coup by reformist officers in 1962. The rebel officers then began guerrilla warfare and were joined by revolutionaries from the Guatemalan Communist party. This guerrilla effort was quickly crushed but its survivors regrouped in late 1962 to form the Rebel Armed Forces (FAR), which harassed the army until 1969 when its remnants straggled into exile in Mexico.

After a period of reflection and analysis, two new guerrilla organizations—Guerrilla Army of the Poor (EGP) and the Organization of People in Arms (ORPA)—emerged in the 1970s and were later joined by FAR. Unlike the 1960s when the emphasis was on forming *focos* or centers of guerrilla operation that would ignite widespread revolutionary war, the new guerrilla fronts placed more emphasis on popular education and the political formation of peasant communities.

This new strategy proved successful in mobilizing widespread support for revolutionary objectives. But the newly formed guerrilla armies were neither sufficiently organized nor prepared for the terror that descended upon them and upon the communities where they were working (mainly in the villages of the northwestern highlands, the northern transverse strip, and the Petén). Although they met their popular education objectives, the revolutionary forces had not advanced to the stage where they were able to incorporate large numbers of peasants into guerrilla units. Nor were they strong enough to defend the Indian communities from the army's wholesale butchering.

The army's counterinsurgency campaign, which reached its height from 1981 through 1983, crushed the unarmed resistance movement and seriously weakened the guerrilla forces themselves. The brunt of the 1981–1983 war was aimed at destroying or disrupting the guerrillas' unarmed rural support base. This campaign came on the heels of several years of intensive repression in both rural and urban areas against popular organizations, development groups, and community organizations.

Although the guerrilla armies survived, they could no longer count on ample popular support. The army had clearly made its point: Any support for the "terrorists" would be dealt with in the cruelest fashion, which often meant eliminating entire villages. While fear was certainly the main factor in breaking the strong links between the guerrillas and Indian communities, disillusionment, fed by army propaganda, also contributed to diminishing revolutionary sentiment. Many felt that the guerrillas had promised more than they could deliver and had failed to protect them when violence struck. The army's developmentalist and democratization strategies also helped to isolate the guerrilla armies.

Who They Are and What They Want

Since 1982 four guerrilla forces have been united in the Guatemalan National Revolutionary Unity (URNG), which functions as both the diplomatic and military command of the armed revolutionary movement. While Marxism-Leninism has been the dominant ideological tendency within URNG, there are also strong liberation-theology and social-democratic tendencies. Depending on the guerrilla army, the combatants are largely Indian and many have joined the armed struggle because of their Christian perspective.

The four guerrilla armies that compose URNG often operate under common field commands and in some cases have mounted joint operations. They are, however, distinguished by different geographical areas of concentration and varying political philosophies. The EGP, which established itself in the highlands in 1972, operates mainly in northern Quiché and Huehuetenango. FAR, the oldest guerrilla army, concentrates on the south coast and the Petén, although it is also active in the highlands. ORPA began operations in 1972 and, after years of education and organizing, launched its first military operation in 1979. Its base is found in Sololá, San Marcos, and Quezaltenango, and to a much lesser extent in Chimaltenango, and Totonicapán. Its commander is Rodrigo Asturias (also known as Gaspar Ilom), son of the famed Guatemalan novelist Miguel Angel Asturias who wrote *Men of Corn* and *El Señor Presidente*. The fourth component of URNG is the Guatemalan Workers party (PGT) Central Committee, which rejoined the guerrilla coalition in early 1989 after splitting off in 1983.

The five main points of URNG's revolutionary platform are elimination of repression and guarantees of life and peace; distribution of property of the very wealthy, agrarian reform, price controls, and the allowance of reasonable profits; guarantee of equality between Indians and non-Indians; equal representation by patriotic, popular, and democratic sectors in the new government, equal rights for women, protection for children, and guarantees of freedom of expression and religion; and national self-determination and a policy of nonalignment and international cooperation.

The sketchy nature of the URNG's political platform has made the URNG a mysterious entity in many respects. Its failure to present a more detailed platform for political and economic change may also explain its failure to develop a strong base of support among the popular sectors, the popular movement, and those Guatemalans of progressive political tendencies. As it entered into the peace talks in 1990, the URNG's exact political and economic demands remained unclear.

The Military Front

Military and political initiatives by URNG have proved the continued viability of the guerrilla movement. The URNG has not pretended to wield a military force capable of directly confronting the Guatemalan army with major offensive operations. Instead of direct confrontation, it has waged an escalating war of attrition relying mainly on ambushes, sabotage, and attacks on isolated military outposts.

Despite military claims that the guerrillas are simply isolated bands of terrorists, the URNG has demonstrated its ability to mount geographically diverse and well-coordinated military operations. In 1988 it launched its first joint offensives involving all four guerrilla armies, and the number of its operations doubled in 1989. By 1990 the URNG had forces active in twelve departments and the country's two largest cities. The URNG claims that it is slowly accumulating forces so that at the proper political opportunity it will be able to launch a major offensive. Boasts by the military that it defeated the guerrillas have repeatedly proven to be false. Stalled army offensives in the highlands and lightning guerrilla attacks in Guatemala City and Quezaltenango in the late 1980s testified to mounting URNG strength. Government estimates put the number of guerrillas at fewer than one thousand, while other more objective sources estimate that there are 1,500 to 2,000 guerrillas.[25] The URNG itself reports 3,500 to 4,000 combatants.[26]

Talking About Peace

Speaking for URNG, Pablo Monsanto, the commander of FAR, stated that the guerrilla armies are fighting for "a neutral, independent country able to decide for itself its destiny and not one subjected to the interests of other nations."[27] The primary goal is to negotiate a solution to the conflict, he emphasized. The military tactic of wearing down the army is viewed as essential to the political goal of forcing the army and government to the negotiating table.[28]

Since 1985, the URNG has called for negotiations to resolve the conflict. It has also demanded the right to participate in the national dialogue that was created as a result of the Esquipulas II peace accords. With the exception of a brief meeting in October 1987, all the URNG's offers were ignored or dismissed by the government until April 1990, when diplomatic and military initiatives by the URNG and international pressure resulted in the government's agreement to open a dialogue with the guerrilla command. There is, however, little real hope that the guerrilla conflict will soon be brought to a conclusion, either by political or military means. For the government and the military, counterinsurgency has become, after more than twenty-five years of fighting, a type of governance and a way of life.

ECONOMY

During the 1960s and until the late 1970s the Guatemalan economy was boosted by 5 percent or greater annual growth rates. But a slump in the world market combined with escalating internal political turmoil resulted in a sharp economic downturn that burdened the country with negative growth rates until 1987. Bolstered by a sudden influx of multilateral and bilateral aid, the Cerezo government managed to pull the economy out of its recession.

At the beginning of the 1990s the economy was inching forward at a rate of 2 percent to 4 percent a year. The country had experienced some new investment in nontraditional agricultural and industrial production, but overall the value of the country's exports was no greater than in 1980.[29] Conditions for the country's poor majority deteriorated in the 1980s as the prices of basic goods rose dramatically, unemployment and underemployment affected more than half of the workforce, and wages remained below poverty levels. As a result of these years of negative or slow growth, per capita income in Guatemala was no greater than it was in 1970. Some 87 percent of the population was living in poverty, up from 79 percent in 1980, and half the country's families could not even afford a minimally adequate diet let alone other necessities.[30] The minimum wage—about $1.16 a day in early 1990—

provides less than a worker needs to cover basic needs. In the 1980s, all the social indicators of adequate housing, health, education, and nutrition declined. Meanwhile, wealth is becoming more concentrated. Between 1970 and 1984, the percentage of national income captured by the top 20 percent increased from 45.5 percent to 56.8 percent.

Having ruled out the feasibility of structural reform measures, the Cerezo government chose to address widening social inequity with handout programs financed by foreign private and government agencies. It backed away from demands for substantial increases in the minimum wage, price controls on basic goods, agrarian reform, assistance to small farmers, and protection of workers' right to organize. Although with the support of the army it did push through higher income and production taxes, most attempts to institute measures that would adversely affect the private-sector elite were only halfheartedly pursued or quickly dropped. All things considered, the Christian Democratic government proved to be more concerned with short-term economic growth statistics than the broader public welfare. Although the economy had achieved a modicum of stability by 1990, there was little hope that socioeconomic conditions would improve under the selected model of growth that stressed private-sector investment and export production.

The economic prospects for the 1990s are less than hopeful despite the small measure of growth and stability achieved in the late 1980s. Among the major characteristics and weaknesses of the economy as it enters the new decade are

- Reliance on large injections of bilateral and multilateral foreign aid, which are now steadily declining.
- A widening trade imbalance owing to increased imports and a disappointing export trade.
- Deterioration of domestic and regional markets due in large part to austerity measures and an almost exclusive emphasis on extra-regional exports.
- A $2.8 billion (1989) external debt, which has led to a worsening debt-service crunch as interest rates rise and short-term debt comes due.
- Continued heavy dependence on agroexports (about 75 percent of total exports) in a time of depressed world prices for its main exports, especially coffee.
- A tax burden that is one of the lightest in the world, which prevents tax increases needed for funding of government social services, forc-

ing the government to rely on bilateral and multilateral aid for virtually all public-sector infrastructure projects.

- A reactionary private sector dominated by agroexport-based oligarchs who obstruct the kind of reforms (agrarian reform, expanded labor rights, higher minimum wages, and increased direct taxes on income and property) that would contribute to a modernization of the economy and a broadening of the internal market.
- Dependence on public-sector spending to bolster the economy while private-sector investment remains low.
- Continuing pressure to step up the pace of currency devaluation.
- Dramatic worsening of conditions for the poor majority in the face of unprecedented inflation.

Agriculture

The country's economic mainstay continues to be the agricultural sector, which accounts for about 25 percent of national income, employs 58 percent of the active workforce, and provides 75 percent of the country's foreign exchange.

Perhaps more clearly than in any other Central American country, there are really two agricultural economies. The dominant economy is one of commercial estates located mostly along the fertile south coast and also in the north in the department of Izabal. The extreme concentration of land and an export orientation characterizes this dominant agricultural economy. Paralleling the agroexport economy is a system of peasant agriculture, characterized by small plots of land devoted to subsistence farming. These two economies, while markedly different, are interdependent. The peasant economy of *minifundios* (small parcels) serves to keep wage rates low in Guatemala by enabling many peasants to survive and feed themselves during the off-seasons, while working temporarily during the harvest seasons for substandard wages paid by the agroexport estates.[31]

To fight for better conditions and higher wages the *Campesino* Unity Committee (CUC) was formed in 1980. After mounting a general strike of farm labor on south-coast plantations, CUC was driven underground. CUC emerged in 1988 to renew its struggle and joined the UASP popular coalition. CUC has become an important voice in the widening popular movement.

Land Reform

No other issue in Guatemala is so volatile as the use and ownership of land. It is an issue that sparked a 1954 CIA-sponsored coup and gave rise to death squads and civil war. As Guatemala enters the 1990s, the inequities resulting from skewed patterns of land ownership and use continue to divide society and stifle economic development.

Despite harsh repression, the issue of land reform will not go away. Less than 2 percent of the landowners own 65 percent of the farmland—the most highly skewed land-tenure pattern in Latin America. This land-tenure situation is compounded by the fact that most postage-stamp plots of land straddle mountain slopes while the richest land is held by the largest producers. According to AID about a third of the population lives on farms too small or too lacking in quality soil to support a family.[32]

Such conditions explain the widespread support among Guatemalan peasants for the guerrilla forces in the early 1980s. But peasants and guerrillas are not the only ones who see the need for agrarian reform. Reversing its former position, the Catholic Church called for better land distribution in a 1988 pastoral letter, "The Cry for Land." Even AID has concluded that the country needs agrarian reform, although it recognizes that political conditions within Guatemala make it unfeasible.

In 1986 Padre Andrés Girón and his Pro-Land Peasant Association once again put agrarian reform on the national agenda. A year before, presidential candidate Vinicio Cerezo had promised the National Agricultural Union of Guatemala (UNAGRO) that his government would not institute an agrarian reform. He said he would not even mention land reform because "to use the term in this country causes emotional reactions." Shortly after Cerezo's inauguration, Girón led 16,000 *campesinos*, mainly from the south coast, to the National Palace to demand that the government distribute land to the landless. Even though Girón's movement was only demanding that the government redistribute land purchased from private owners, not expropriate it, the Pro-Land organization stirred vitriolic opposition from UNAGRO and large landowners.

The government did eventually respond favorably to the Pro-Land Movement. But while several estates were sold to the Girón organization this token measure fell far short of the great need and could scarcely be termed an agrarian reform. Instead it represented an extension of a land-sales program financed by AID and implemented by the Penny Foundation with the approval of UNAGRO. As an added onus, the Girón movement, rather than paying the foundation, had to pay the government at higher than market value prices.

Nontraditional Exports

Nontraditionals, which account for about 10 percent of total agroexports, face many of the same problems of more established agroexports like coffee and cotton, such as oscillating prices and shrinking markets. The oscillations of the world market are compounded for nontraditional agroexport producers because the markets for which they produce are generally smaller. There is also more risk involved since nontraditional exports usually spoil more quickly. The risks to the farmer's health are greater too. One such problem is that these crops commonly require more frequent applications of fertilizer and pesticides, which means high-level chemical exposure for the farmer.

There is little doubt that the agricultural sector needs to diversify, but it is a development path fraught with difficulties. While diversification into fruit and vegetable production was boosted by the Caribbean Basin Initiative (CBI), Guatemalan producers have discovered that the U.S. market is a fickle creature. Competition from nontraditional agroexport sectors in other Caribbean Basin countries, mainly the Dominican Republic and Costa Rica, also narrows the market for Guatemalan products. Protectionism by U.S. producers and new consumer concerns about pesticide-saturated produce cast a further shadow over the future of diversification attempts.

Although nontraditional agroexports often spell high profit margins, they also involve high costs of production. It costs a producer of snow peas about $4,000 a hectare, compared with only $250 to $375 (ranging from manual to mechanized production) a hectare for corn or $750 to produce a hectare of coffee using modern agricultural inputs and machinery.[33] While AID poses nontraditional agroexport production as an alternative for Guatemalan farmers, it is generally a gamble only affordable to commercial-level farmers, not the hundreds of thousands of peasant farmers that cultivate the country's poorest land.

Food Production

The production of basic grains (corn, beans, and rice) for human consumption has failed to keep pace with population growth in Guatemala. During the 1980s the production of corn for the local market increased at an annual rate of about 1 percent while the population increased 3 percent or more each year. As a result of this declining per capita production, Guatemala has become a net importer of basic grains.[34] Neither can Guatemala meet its need for dairy products; the country has the lowest rate of milk production in Latin America, providing an average daily per capita allotment of only two table-spoons.

Farmers have little incentive to grow basic grains despite this shortfall in production. Food imports from the United States undercut the local market and keep prices low. Since 1984, Guatemala has received an increasing amount of U.S. food aid. The Guatemalan government does have a policy of food security with the stated objective of promoting local food production, but it has not been enforced. In fact, the government has welcomed increasing food aid to ease budget deficits and to pacify targeted social sectors (urban slums and displaced families in conflict areas) with food aid. Both the army and the government share the concern that food shortages and high food prices will increase social tensions. But rather than initiate the kind of sectoral adjustment needed to prioritize food production, food aid and cheap food imports have provided a short-term avoidance mechanism.[35]

Industry and Tourism

Although Guatemala's is the most developed manufacturing sector in Central America, industry accounts for only 16 percent of national income. The country has no heavy industry, and the bulk of manufacturing is found in food-processing and beverages, while pharmaceuticals manufactured by foreign companies lead the list of industrial exports.

Very few manufacturing firms employ many Guatemalans. Only one hundred companies employ more than one hundred workers, and now most of these firms operate at much less than full capacity. As elsewhere in the region, local industry, operating for a long time under protectionist tariffs, is now threatened by structural-adjustment measures.

With AID's encouragement and financing, there is a new emphasis on export-oriented manufacturing plants or *maquilas*. Government incentives and tax exemptions resulted in a rapid increase in clothing exports in the late 1980s, but the benefits of such assembly manufacturing to the local economy are few. Some 220 textile plants do provide employment, albeit at low wages in nonunion shops, but since all the inputs are imported the overall economic impact of these sweatshops is minimal. Many local investors are also skeptical about the long-term potential for this export-oriented manufacturing. For example, one Guatemalan industrialist found that after two years of exporting textiles to the United States he was being squeezed out of the market by investors in the Dominican Republic.[36] Confidence in textiles was also deflated by a 1989 reduction in the U.S. import quota.

Because Guatemala's public sector is one of the smallest in the world (about 10 percent of the gross domestic product), privatization of state enterprises is not the heated issue that it is in other Latin American nations. This, however, has not stopped AID and other international lenders from calling for the privatization of public-sector corporations. The first company targeted was Aviateca airline, 75 percent of which was purchased by foreign investors. Foreign donors and CACIF have also pressured the government to privatize the telephone company (GUATEL), the national railroad system (FEGUA), and the electricity company (INDE).

One of the most hopeful signs for the economy during the late 1980s was the steady growth of tourism. The improved international image of Guatemala was the main factor behind the tourism boom, which also benefited from increased publicity about the tropical rain forests and Mayan ruins. Foreign investors, like Club Med (which is considering establishing an "archaeological villa" near Tikal), have expressed increasing interest in profiting from this upswing in tourism.

SOCIETY AND ENVIRONMENT

Popular Organizing

The 1954 coup and subsequent repression of the organized popular movement cast Guatemala into a political winter. It was not until the early 1970s that the popular movement began to recuperate. But it was soon crushed by the military and associated death squads. The repression was so complete that by 1983 there was little evidence of any popular organizing.

Gradually, however, a popular movement began to reemerge as the counterinsurgency war subsided and the country moved to refurbish its international image. One of the first groups to surface was the CUSG labor confederation, which counted on U.S.-government support. In 1985 the founding of the Mutual Support Group (GAM), a human-rights advocacy organization, and the UNSITRAGUA labor confederation set the foundations for the creation of a small but steadily expanding progressive movement that gave the popular sectors a voice to challenge the government, oligarchy, and military.

In late 1987 the country's unions and other popular organizations entered a common popular coalition called Labor and Popular Action

Unity (UASP) to present a united front in the face of repression and government unresponsiveness. The leading member of this new popular coalition was the UNSITRAGUA labor confederation, but it was based on the collective strength of the entire popular movement. Members of UASP included two human rights groups (GAM and CONAVIGUA), two student organizations (AEU and the secondary students' organization, CEEM), numerous unions (UNSITRAGUA, FESEBS, CUSG, STINDE, STEG, FENASTEG, and *Luz y Fuerza*), a progressive religious association called the Monsignor Romero Group, the CUC peasant association, and the CERJ.

In 1988 UASP presented a list of demands to the National Reconciliation Commission that constituted a platform for moderate social change in Guatemala. This statement incorporated a wide range of demands, from respect for human rights and an end to sexual harassment and discrimination to a moratorium on external debt payments.

Increasingly, however, during the late 1980s those who dared to join the struggle for social change disappeared or were killed. Students, peasant activists, unionists, journalists, and community organizers became victims of a rising scourge of antipopular terrorism. Still the popular movement courageously pushed on although it never regained the strength it had in the 1970s. There were few victories other than the determination to stand up to the oligarchs, generals, and politicians. When the unions and popular coalitions sat down to negotiate accords with the government and private sector, the accords they reached were routinely violated. And when they went out on strike or dared to confront directly the perpetrators of human-rights abuses, they were brutally repressed.

The history of the popular movement in Guatemala has been silenced by decades of repression. As new leaders rise, they are killed or exiled. Not only has the popular movement been cut off from its leaders but also from its base. Guatemalans have internalized the long campaign of terror and fear, the consequences of any form of organizing. But deepening poverty, the hunger of their children, the indignity of living without rights, and the courage of selfless activists has kept the movement alive.

The isolation of the popular movement from the country's political parties, the guerrilla movement, and the peace process have contributed to its lack of impact. Remarkably few links exist between the popular organizations and the political parties, and their demands have not found a place in the electoral arena despite the decline in the country's socioeconomic conditions. Both the armed and popular movements suffer from the absence of a strong infrastructure of support and the lack of a well-defined platform of political and economic change. As a result, their efforts only rarely complement one another, keeping both movements relatively weak. Although the popular organizations certainly have supported negotiations to end the war, they have had neither the strength nor political vision to assert themselves as a principal force in forging peace and developing a new social order.

Labor and Unions

Being a worker in Guatemala means living on the edge of survival. The daily minimum wage for an agricultural worker is $1.20. Other workers are supposed to receive at least $1.70 but most do not collect even this bare minimum, a wage far below the $5.00 a day that a family requires to meet its basic needs. Yet many Guatemalans who do work for these substandard wages count themselves among the fortunate, mindful of the high unemployment rate.

Few Guatemalan workers are organized into unions. Although only about 4 percent of the Guatemalan workforce belong to unions, this is the highest rate since before the 1954 coup, when as many as a third of the workers were organized. Repression is the main obstacle to labor organizing, but it is not the only one. An antiquated labor code, an unresponsive Ministry of Work, the large pool of cheap labor, and the growth of *solidarista* associations are among the impediments faced by unions.[37]

Nonetheless, the Guatemalan labor movement steadily intensified in the 1980s, especially after 1983 when organizing was once again officially permitted. The main growth occurred among government and municipal employees, who were not granted the right to organize until 1986. Continued repression and union-breaking tactics have slowed the movement's advance in the private sector. In the face of strikes and occupations by unions, numerous factories have simply closed then reopened with newly hired employees who are included in management-sponsored *solidarista* associations. Private companies, especially after the May 1988 coup attempt, have been able to rely on ready police support. In contrast, unions find that neither the police nor Ministry of Labor will act to protect worker rights or to enforce court decisions favorable to the workers.

At the end of the decade, the labor movement comprised three major confederations and one smaller one (formed in late 1988), various independent unions, and a few peasant associations.[38] Unions were further divided into different coalitions of the broader popular movement. The two popular alliances are UASP and COSU (Unitary

Union Coordinator), which was formed in 1988 by the Christian Democratic CGTG labor federation as a progovernment counterpart of UASP.

The Confederation of Guatemalan Trade Union Unity (CUSG) originated on May Day 1983 with the official blessing of the Ríos Montt government. A principal reason for its founding was to qualify Guatemala for the benefits of the Caribbean Basin Initiative. The main affiliation of CUSG is the American Institute for Free Labor Development (AIFLD). CUSG, the best-financed confederation in Guatemala, offers instruction in "free trade union" principles at local and U.S. workshops to any unionist willing to attend. Its base is mostly among rural associations formed to receive inexpensive agricultural inputs and to benefit from community development projects sponsored by AIFLD and AID.[39] In the 1990 electoral campaign CUSG threw its support behind the center-right UCN.

The Union of Guatemalan Workers (UNSITRAGUA) was founded in February 1985 and is identified with the most progressive sectors of the labor and popular movement. Among its strongest unions are CAVISA (Central American Glass Company Workers Union), STECSA (Coca-Cola Bottling Company Trade Union), and STUSC (San Carlos University Workers Union). UNSITRAGUA is concentrated in the industrial sector and secondarily in banking and services, with little outreach in the public sector. Yet the influence of UNSITRAGUA extends beyond the confederated unions. As the most progressive confederation, it has opened up political space for all unions.

The General Confederation of Guatemalan Workers (CGTG) is the Christian Democratic labor confederation that was formally established in April 1986 although it had been in the works since 1982. Based largely on public-sector unions, CGTG was closely tied to the Christian Democratic government.

The 1980s have also seen the growth of worker groups called *solidarista* associations. *Solidarismo* is a philosophy of labor/ownership that was formulated in Costa Rica in 1947, where it has received important support from the Catholic Church, big business, and more recently AID. In practice, *solidarismo* takes the form of financial associations in which workers and businesses form credit cooperatives, food services for workers, and investment projects. Most of the capital used for these projects comes from employee savings and the investment by the company owner of severance pay due to each worker. It is supported by businesses as an alternative to class confrontation, unionism, and collective bargaining.

Promoted by U.S. and local corporations and financially backed by

AID, *solidarismo* is regarded as the best response to the threat of union-ism. It is also being promoted by the army and landowners to combat rural unrest. In rural areas, the members are sometimes armed or work with the army to protect their association against leftist insurgents. By the end of the decade the country had some 280 *solidarista* associations with 80,000 members.[40]

Schools and Students

Education is a privilege in Guatemala. With a 55 percent literacy rate, Guatemalans are the least educated society in Central America. Among children ages seven to fourteen, four of every ten do not attend school. Of those who do attend, only 20 percent finish the sixth grade. It is estimated that by the early 1990s, fewer than 40 percent of Guatemalans will be literate.

The student movement, decimated during the Lucas García years, started to come back to life in 1983. The Guatemala Association of University Students "Oliverio Casteneda de León" (AEU), the elected student organization, is attempting to reclaim its former role in the popular movement.

Being a student activist, however, is a risky undertaking. The AEU has been forced to adopt elaborate security measures in response to a frightening history of persecution of AEU leaders. The disappearance of the AEU's executive committee in 1984 forced the organization underground. In 1987, its executive secretary was murdered. Despite the repression, AEU emerged from the shadows in 1988 and joined the UASP popular coalition. AEU activism encompasses economic-justice issues, human-rights concerns, labor solidarity, and student issues. On the University of San Carlos campus, AEU provides critical support for the workers' union, while aggressively demanding better quality educa-tion and more socially relevant studies. In 1988 it stood firmly behind a strike by secondary students who had organized for better school facilities and an increased education budget.

The new student activism, however, was met by renewed repression. In March 1989, the entire AEU government council received death threats, with repression against student activists reaching a new peak in August 1989, when twelve students disappeared. By September 1989, only three of the sixteen members of the AEU directorate remained; the others were killed, missing, exiled, or in hiding.

Communications Media

During the first couple years of the Cerezo government there were signs that the country was increasing its press freedoms after years of military rule. In early 1988 two new magazines were established: *Crónica*, a weekly magazine in the style of *Newsweek* and *Time*, and the short-lived *La Epoca*, which featured investigative reporting and critical political analysis. Television news took on new life, and reporters could travel to any region of the country without government permission.

By mid-1988, however, hopes for increasing press freedom in Guatemala came crashing down. In June heavily armed men broke into the *La Epoca* offices, burglarized it, and then firebombed it. Also destroyed was the office of the news agency ACEN-SIAG (closely associated with *La Epoca*).

For many close observers of Guatemala, the forced closing of *La Epoca* was inevitable given the restricted nature of journalism in the country. Others saw the paper as the litmus test of democratic freedoms under the new civilian government. While there was no official censorship under the civilian government, a system of self-censorship was blatantly violated by *La Epoca*. In Guatemala, as in many other countries, reporters and editors do not criticize the military or engage in investigative reporting that would challenge established power structures.

Guatemala has two major daily newspapers, *La Prensa Libre* and *El Gráfico*, with two smaller progressive dailies, *Diario La Hora* and the recently established *Siglo XXI*. There is also a government daily, *Diario de Centro América*, which has traditionally simply reproduced government notices and decrees. The two leading dailies have become bitter enemies of the Christian Democratic government, *La Prensa Libre* more over ideology, *El Gráfico* for purely political reasons. Shallow reporting, bad writing, and unattractive layout characterize both papers.

Radio reaches more Guatemalans than any other media. Radio Fabulosa, the country's most influential station, boasts a chain of affiliated stations throughout the country. Altogether, some one hundred radio stations operate in Guatemala. Virtually all radio news is produced by independent news services that buy time on individual stations that are called *radioperiódicos*. There is less military, government, or private-sector control over radio than any other media, although self-censorship reigns here as well.

The State of Health

Guatemala is often considered the most beautiful country in Central America. It is the most populous nation and also the richest in terms of natural resources. Excluding Panama, it is the wealthiest country in terms of aggregate gross national product. At the same time, though, the Guatemalan poor are the most deprived and least healthy citizens on the isthmus. According to a 1982 UNICEF study, Guatemala has the lowest "physical quality of life" index in Central America, and the third lowest in Latin America, after Haiti and Bolivia.[41]

So severe and widespread are hunger, malnutrition, and illness that they can only be described as a type of social violence. Even at the height of the counterinsurgency campaign in the early 1980s, more Guatemalans were dying of malnutrition and preventable disease than through political violence.

Guatemala is the Central American nation with the least amount spent on health care per person. Only 45 percent of Guatemalans have access to safe water supplies; only 34 percent have regular access to health services.[42] In Guatemala City, half the population has no daily access to a toilet and three of four children under five are malnourished.[43]

The overall averages, as appalling as they are, hide the alarming disparities between Indian and *ladino* health. The life expectancy for non-Indian men is sixty-five years, and sixty-four years for non-Indian women. But Indian males can expect to live only forty-eight years, and Indian women only forty-seven years.

Guatemalan health-care facilities are of notoriously poor quality. Two government agencies, the Ministry of Public Health and Social Assistance (MSPAS) and the Guatemalan Social Security Institute (IGSS), administer the government's constantly diminishing health-care budget. And while there is a social security system, it covers only 12 percent of the total population, or one-quarter of the active workforce. But even if a person is covered by social security or does have some income to pay for health care, the country's clinics and hospitals are extremely underbudgeted, understaffed, undersupplied, and unable to take care of an increasing patient load. In fact, most rural health posts have no medicines. Guatemala does have a large number of hospital beds when compared with other Central American countries, yet most of these beds are in private hospitals, beyond the reach of the impoverished majority. Actually, only the wealthy and the military enjoy reasonably good health care.

Stepping in to fill the health-care gap in Guatemala have been numerous foreign humanitarian and religious organizations. But this private source of health care has been largely ineffective in combating the country's deplorable state of health. One exception is the Maryknoll project in Huehuetenango, which for the last twenty-five years has been training health-care promoters. Like other programs that incorporate a certain degree of community empowerment and popular education, the Maryknoll project was hit hard by counterinsurgency terror, as over 160 promoters either fled the country, quit, or were killed from 1981 to 1989.

Medical workers run great political risk in Guatemala, as doctors, nurses, medical students, and health-care promoters are targets for repression. Medical neutrality is not respected by the government, which has failed to ratify the Geneva Convention on the safety of medical personnel. From 1980 to 1988, there were 125 cases of serious violations of medical neutrality, including the killing and disappearance of medical students, health professionals, and patients (abducted from medical facilities and killed). During this same period, some five hundred health promoters were killed or reported missing.[44]

Religion

The Roman Catholic Church is the country's major religious institution. As such, it has played a major role not only in the religious and cultural aspects of Guatemalan life, but also in such diverse areas as politics, community development, social services, and refugee relief. Catholic clerical and lay initiatives have often served as important models for the development programs of many other private organizations and even a few government agencies.

The Church under Archbishop Próspero Penados del Barrio moved sharply away from its previous conservatism. The new social voice of the institutional Church became obvious with the March 1988 release of the pastoral letter, "The Cry for Land." The pastoral letter's call for land distribution sorely angered the national elite while lifting the hopes of the poor that the Church would become an ally in the struggle for justice. A year later, the Bishops' Conference issued another strong statement, called the Declaration of Cobán, concerning the country's deplorable economic and social conditions. The bishops charged that the country's "economic structure increases the wealth of the privileged sector [while making] the majority of Guatemalans even poorer." Furthermore, they noted that "more than a few Guatemalans have lost their faith in the possibility of an authentic democratic process."[45]

This voice of social criticism is welcome in a country where so many other voices have been silenced. However, though the prophetic or denunciatory voice of the Church is present, the church hierarchy is still largely conservative in respect to its support for the popular struggle. The Church's most socially committed and activist elements have been either forced out of the country or isolated within the institution; lay organizations like the Delegates of the Word continue to exist, but their work is largely limited strictly to pastoral functions.

In the late 1980s, repression against the Catholic clergy escalated. At the same time the Church was again becoming a target for military repression, it was involving itself more in seeking an end to the war and a resolution of social tensions. The Catholic church joined with the evangelical community in sponsoring the ecumenical National Campaign for Life and Peace.

The Rise of the Evangelicals

Protestantism and evangelicalism have a stronger base in Guatemala than in other Central American countries. Since the mid-1970s, the evangelical faiths have been increasing at an unprecedented rate— about 12 percent a year—and show no signs of abating. According to a July 1987 survey by SEPAL (Evangelization Service to Latin America), approximately 31.6 percent of the Guatemalan population is evangelical. Within the country, there are 9,298 evangelical churches, almost one church for every 906 Guatemalans. Even the Catholic Church now acknowledges that 35 percent of the population is evangelical.[46]

The neopentecostal churches and ministries are the most obvious and vocal in the evangelical community, owing to their presence in urban areas and their largely professional and middle-class congregations. Most of these are nondenominational and identify themselves not as "evangelical" but as "Christian" churches, thereby increasing their access to Catholics and former Catholics. But it is the older, mostly fundamentalist churches, such as the Assemblies of God, Central American Mission, Church of God, Nazarenes, Baptists, and Presbyterians, that constitute the backbone of the evangelical church in Guatemala. These denominations reach into the most isolated rural areas. The message of personal salvation of the evangelical churches and their often apocalyptic vision have found a niche in communities beset with poverty and wracked by violence. Their strong defense of the family and attacks on drunkenness and other vices have also endeared them to rural communities. The emotional support provided by the church community plus the entertainment generated by almost nightly activities also attract adherents.

While the evangelical movement is largely conservative, some small and relatively isolated sectors, mainly associated with traditional denominations, have adopted the social interpretations of the theology of liberation. Others are already in the process of breaking with the paternalistic style of social work and encouraging development projects with more self-determination. Significantly, several church-based social programs have formed an umbrella group to coordinate and further promote development projects by evangelical churches.

Nongovernmental Organizations

Nongovernmental organizations (NGOs), mainly from the United States, serve as a "privately" sponsored social infrastructure in this country where government services are so notoriously lacking. Guatemala hosts more foreign NGOs than any other Central American country. Among the first NGOs to come to Guatemala were AID-financed groups like CARE, Project Hope, Pan American Development Foundation, and Partners of the Americas, which came to the country as part of the Alliance for Progress in the 1960s.

Following a stagnant period during the Lucas García regime, economic aid from the United States has steadily increased. In 1982 AID distributed only $15.5 million in total economic aid, but by 1989 more than $147 million in aid dollars flowed into the country. Guatemala has experienced a similar increase in U.S. food aid, which swelled from $5.6 million in 1982 to $29.7 million in 1989. A substantial part of this new aid has been channeled into NGO programs. The NGOs' role in aid distribution really began in 1983 when the U.S. Congress prohibited AID from granting new aid to the military government. To keep economic aid flowing into Guatemala, AID distributed funds to NGOs through the National Reconstruction Committee and other intermediaries. With government approval, AID has directed most of its development and relief money into the embattled highlands.

In recent years, AID and U.S. Information Agency (USIA) dollars have been instrumental in the formation and expansion of numerous private-sector lobbying groups, think tanks, and business associations in Guatemala. Although the stated purpose of this aid is to foster the growth of democratic institutions, many feel that the assistance is going only to elite groups and to those that support U.S. foreign policy in the region. AID-funded business organizations, for example, generally exert a reactionary presence, strongly opposed to government plans to increase taxes, redistribute land, and meet the wage and social demands of popular organizations and unions.

Private groups, both local and foreign, have often served the interests of the military's counterinsurgency campaign. A nexus for NGO-government-military cooperation in rural pacification is the National Reconstruction Committee (CRN). Together with the closely associated army's Civil Affairs division, the CRN coordinates NGO activity in most conflictive areas. AID has channeled local currency funds to CRN-coordinated NGO projects involving such groups as World Vision, Project Hope, Food for the Hungry, and the archdiocesan CARITAS.[47] As part of its coordinating role, the CRN has also attempted to serve as a registry and clearinghouse for NGOs in Guatemala, although numerous NGOs have simply refused to cooperate.

A small number of NGOs work directly with the military in pacification programs. These include such right-wing groups as the Air Commandos Association, Knights of Malta, Food for the Hungry, Americans for a Free Central America, Carroll Behrhorst Development Foundation, PAVA, and the National Defense Foundation, in addition to numerous evangelical groups like Youth with a Mission and the Summer Institute of Linguistics. The Air Commandos Association, for example, works directly under military supervision in the Quiché area providing medical services, and Food for the Hungry collaborates with Army Civil Affairs in facilitating relocation of displaced Indians into model villages. Also integrated into the military's game plan are several openly right-wing U.S. NGOs, like Friends of the Americas and CAUSA.

There are many other NGOs whose humanitarian and development work has little if anything to do with counterinsurgency operations. But even much of this NGO activity has political implications. The CARE and SHARE food-for-work projects in Guatemala City were explicitly designed to forestall urban unrest that might be unleashed as a result of the Cerezo government's economic-stabilization plans, for example.

Most NGO activity in Guatemala is characterized by its paternalistic, welfare nature, in contrast to a style of NGO assistance more supportive of community organizing and popular education. Several NGOs do attempt to explore the limits imposed by repression by sponsoring such projects, but on the whole NGO work in Guatemala has a charitable character that serves to pacify people and attempts to mollify the social costs of counterinsurgency. The most progressive NGO activity is sponsored by European agencies and, to a lesser extent, by progressive protestant churches and Catholic orders in the United States.

Women and Feminism

The women's movement in Guatemala is the least developed in Central America, in terms of organizing at the popular level and among educated women. This is largely attributable to the high level of repression that has beset the country for over thirty-five years. The highly divided nature of Guatemalan society, both in class and race, and the low level of schooling are other factors.

In 1975 at the beginning of a new stage of popular organizing, the Women's Solidarity in Action committee flowered briefly. Another short-lived attempt to organize women was the National Women's Union (UNAMG), which disbanded shortly after its founding in 1980 due to the intensifying violence of the Lucas García regime. Other women's organizations did exist but were mostly associations of upper-class women who met for charitable or professional purposes rather than to organize for social change.

The Cerezo government opened up political space for serious popular organizing, and women took advantage of this opportunity to form human-rights organizations and groups concerned specifically with the situation of women. In addition, the new administration's placement of women in high government positions played a role in increasing feminist consciousness in Guatemala. The Mutual Support Group (GAM), a human-rights organization directed principally by women, has succeeded in focusing international concern over continued human-rights violations and the plight of widows.

In 1988 GAM was joined by another women's human-rights organization called CONAVIGUA (National Coordinator of Guatemalan Widows), whose directors and members are mostly Indian widows of the murdered and disappeared. According to Rigoberta Menchú, an opposition representative, CONAVIGUA is "the first organization in all the 500 years of Guatemala that was born of indigenous women. It is an organization so powerful that the indigenous women can channel the convictions of thousands of other Guatemalan women."[48]

Another significant step forward for the women's movement in the 1980s was the creation in 1986 of the GRUFEPROMEFAM, a women's organization linked to the UNSITRAGUA union confederation. The success of the First Conference of Guatemalan Women Workers, which GRUFEPROMEFAM sponsored in 1989, encouraged the organization to make more links with the popular movement and to strengthen its ties with the women's movement in other Central American countries. Its slogan is, Together Always for the Unity of Our Families and for a Better Society.

During the 1980s many women sought outside income (since 1981, the proportion of women in the official workforce rose from 13 percent to 24 percent), but most were forced to take such menial jobs as street vendors in urban areas. Illiteracy is more widespread among Guatemalan women than among their male counterparts, and it has been estimated that only 25 percent of Indian women can read and write. The majority of the country's refugees and internally displaced are women.[49]

Native People

The Indian people of Guatemala constitute the majority group; estimates of native people in Guatemala range from 38 percent (government statistics) to 70 percent, but most sources indicate that Indians constitute at least half of Guatemalan society. Descendants of the Mayan civilization, they are divided into twenty-one different language groups.

Today, although the numerical majority, Guatemalan Indians are relegated to the margins of society. Isolated in terms of language and politics, their exploitation is a cornerstone of the national economy. Guatemala's agroexport system has been built on the backs of cheap Indian labor. Tourism, the country's second largest source of foreign exchange, is also largely dependent on the native community.[50]

The continued cultural survival of indigenous groups in Guatemala has been threatened mainly by the ongoing counterinsurgency war and its strategy of ethnocide. In 1984, the World Council of Indigenous Peoples accused the military of pursuing a "policy of systematic extermination of the Indian population of Guatemala."[51] In response to these accusations of ethnocide, the military claims that it focuses its counterinsurgency campaign in the highlands only because that is the stronghold of guerrilla support. Critics, however, charge that only the racism of Guatemalan society can explain the wholesale horror of the war that has eliminated more than four hundred Indian villages.[52]

Massacres of Indian communities thought to be sympathetic to leftist guerrillas (themselves largely Indian) are only one element of this ethnocide. As part of its pacification plan, the army has attempted to restructure and reprogram Indian communities. Development poles, model villages, strategic reeducation camps, penetration roads, obligatory civil patrols, and the encouragement of evangelical proselytizing are all part of the army's overall plan to undermine Indian communities and to assert the dominance of "the national identity." The psychological action plan for the Ixil Triangle, an area in northern Quiché, states that the purpose of pacification is "to capture the mentality of the Ixils to make them feel part of the Guatemalan nation."[53]

Cultural survival is also a matter of economic survival. Without agrarian reform, there is no longer enough land to support the Indian population, which continues to grow despite the persecution. The lack of land is forcing entire Indian families to relocate to the urban slums, initiating the loss of cultural identity. Large sectors of Indian society are living in a state of shock brought on by the economic and political crisis. They have been displaced from their homes, have lost their families, and are being subjected to a systematic military campaign of psychological operations.

In the late 1970s, the army suddenly realized that the Indians of the highlands were quickly becoming an insurgent population. The socio-economic conditions, particularly the land crisis, certainly provided cause for rebellion. But it was a combination of the new social teachings of the Church, the focus on cooperative formation by many foreign development groups, and the popular education programs of the guerrillas that sparked what the army considered to be a widespread Indian revolt. What was so threatening, from the army's point of view, was the way whole communities suddenly seemed to adopt an organized posture in the face of deteriorating socioeconomic conditions.

It was not until the late 1960s that Guatemalan insurgents recognized the revolutionary potential of the Indian majority. When the guerrilla forces resurfaced in the late 1970s, the focus of their organizing was on the Indian communities of the *Altiplano*. The three major organizations—Guerrilla Army of the Poor, which targeted northern Huehuetenango and Quiché; Revolutionary Organization of People in Arms, which organized in Sololá and San Marcos; and FAR, which established its base in the Petén—took more care this time in promoting Indian leadership and presenting the revolutionary struggle in terms of Indian interests.

Although more conscious of racism and the need to integrate Indians into the struggle, the guerrilla leadership has had trouble developing a policy dealing with ethnic issues. Guatemalan National Revolutionary Unity (URNG), the guerrilla coalition, currently places high priority on what it calls "ethnic-national questions," while cautioning against the dangers of Indian nationalism. URNG defines the revolution as a war on two fronts: "The situation of the Indian as both oppressed and exploited, in which class contradictions are linked to ethnic-national contradictions is what gives the Guatemalan revolution its special character."[54] Many Indians feel, however, that the guerrilla leadership still clings to old models. As one critique proposed, "The revolution must be a political method, through which the popular masses decide their destiny, not an already decided system. The Indian must play a protagonist role, a role not won as a concession, but rightfully owned."[55]

Refugees and the Internally Displaced

The military coup of 1954 marked the beginning of the diaspora of Guatemalans. Until 1980, most of those fleeing the country were *ladino* activists and politicians. The 1980s, however, marked a decade of mass Indian emigration. A people who for so long has clutched tenaciously to its land fled on foot before the advancing terror that swept across the highlands. Political violence has forced an estimated 500,000 to 1 million Guatemalans to abandon their homes over the last ten years.[56] Most of those fleeing the country head north to Mexico, with many continuing on to the United States or Canada. One measure of this refugee population is the number of Guatemalans living under United Nations protection. In Mexico, some 40,000 Guatemalans inhabit UN-sponsored camps, while in Belize there are 1,200, in Honduras, 380, and in Nicaragua, 400. But the majority of those who have fled Guatemala are not tabulated as official refugees. Instead, they live and work in the shadows as undocumented residents, mainly in Mexico and the United States.

The large numbers of refugees in Mexico proved embarrassing to the Guatemalan army and the Cerezo government. The refugees are clear testimony to the savagery of the country's armed forces, and their fear of returning home indicates that conditions have not substantially improved under the civilian government. In response, the Cerezo government in 1986 created the Special Commission to Aid Repatriates (CEAR) as a government agency to work with the United Nations to facilitate the repatriation of refugees. In 1988 the agency increased its role to include supervising the resettlement of the internally displaced.

CEAR has had limited success in persuading Guatemalans to come home. Each year CEAR claims that there will be an influx of repatriates but continued fear keeps most refugees from leaving the camps in Mexico. Increasingly, CEAR's work has been with displaced persons, most of whom have been driven from mountain hideouts by army offensives. Unable to weed out the guerrillas, army counterinsurgency units have focused attention on the displaced, mostly in the Ixil Triangle area. Once out of the mountains and in army hands, these displaced Indians are subjected to the army's psychological-operations campaign, which includes "civic and democratic education," housing in resettlement villages, and the distribution of food and medical services.

Displaced Guatemalans have also formed their own organizations. Those still living outside areas of military control have organized the Communities of Population in Resistance (CPR), a council of displaced communities in the northern highlands that have resisted army attempts to resettle them in military camps and model villages.[57] Other displaced Guatemalans organized the National Council of the Displaced (CONDEG) to protect their interests and rights in the face of continuing military hostility.

Nature and Environmentalism

Guatemala is famous for its environmental beauty and wealth. As the northernmost point of the isthmian bridge between the two American continents, the country hosts an extraordinary ecological diversity. Its habitats support 250 species of mammals, 664 of birds, 231 of reptiles, and 220 of freshwater fish. Such food crops as maize, runner beans, tomatoes, and cocoa all originated in the historic Mayan civilizations of Mexico and Guatemala.[58] According to some botanists, Guatemala hosts the richest and most diverse flora in Central America, with some 8,000 species of vascular plants. It is, however, an environment devastated by unequal patterns of land distribution, distorted patterns of land use, a counterinsurgency war, and a struggle for survival by the peasant population.

The facts of environmental destruction are as horrifying as the data on ecological diversity are impressive. The country is losing its remaining forest cover at the rate of 2.3 percent a year, mainly for fuel-wood, which supplies two-thirds of the country's home energy costs. Some 65 percent of the country's original forest cover has been destroyed, most in the last three decades. As a result, an estimated 25 percent to 35 percent of the land is considered eroded or seriously degraded.[59] The country's rich mangrove forests, potentially a bountiful source of shrimp and fish, are rapidly being raped by reckless development with 40 percent of the mangroves having seriously degenerated since 1965.[60]

Hydroelectric power has also brought ecological, financial, and human catastrophe to Guatemala. Financed by the World Bank and the Inter-American Development Bank (IDB), hydroelectric projects like the infamous Chixoy Power Plant have forced thousands of peasant families off their land, leaving in their wake massive deforestation and evaporative water loss without providing the promised cost-efficient energy. These projects also account for about half the country's external debt.

War is another enemy of the environment. Scorched-earth tactics and aerial bombing have left scars across the face of the highlands and the Petén. In some areas, so much of the forest has been destroyed by the war that local peasants can no longer find enough wood for cooking and heating. The boom in war-related road building, funded by AID and other foreign donors, represents a serious threat to the environment in conflict zones. AID, the World Food Program (which sponsors food-for-work road-building programs), and the government call them farm-to-market routes, but for the army these are penetration roads that link the most isolated areas to military bases.

A new environmental threat is the U.S.-sponsored War on Drugs, which involves widespread spraying of vegetated areas with glycophosphate herbicides such as Round-Up. Although Guatemala does not even appear on the UN's list of drug-growing nations, the Drug Enforcement Administration (DEA) and the State Department have used DEA planes for extensive aerial spraying of areas of the Petén and the highlands since 1987. The spraying, which supposedly targets marijuana and poppy-growing areas, has elicited protests from affected communities, which report deaths, illnesses, and nondrug-crop losses as a result of the program. In early 1988, the spraying was briefly halted after reports of more than a dozen related deaths in San Marcos and the Petén, but it soon resumed. Critics in Guatemala claim that in addition to Round-Up, such restricted-use chemicals as paraquat, malathion, and EDB have also been used in the defoliation campaign.

FOREIGN INFLUENCE

U.S. Foreign Policy

There has existed a long-term sharing of foreign-policy interests between Guatemala and the United States, the natural result of U.S. predominance in trade and investment in the Guatemalan economy. Relations were shaken in 1977 by the Carter administration's insistence that Guatemala improve its human-rights standing. During this brief period links between the two countries weakened, and Guatemala sought aid from other countries, including Israel and Argentina. Nevertheless, U.S.-Guatemala relations were never completely broken, and small levels of economic and military aid continued.[61]

Relations began to warm again after President Reagan took office. New commercial arms deliveries were approved by the White House, which also sought to persuade Congress to increase economic aid and renew direct military aid.[62] As the military began to wind down its campaign of terror and the country began to move toward civilian rule in 1984, close U.S. ties with Guatemala were gradually renewed.

Although Democratic party critics of Guatemala's human-rights practices kept the Reagan administration from supplying the country with large quantities of military aid, U.S. economic assistance was steadily increased and direct military aid was renewed in 1986. According to AID, "In terms of U.S. interests in Central America, Guatemala occupies a key position because it has the largest population and strongest economy in the region and has only recently returned to democratic government. The success of democracy and of free-market based economic reform will have a profound effect on the entire region and act as a brake on Marxist-Leninist expansionism."[63]

Since 1983 the United States has supported a program of political and economic stabilization, complementing a similar effort sponsored by the Guatemalan military. Among the elements of U.S. support have been the following:

- Large injections of balance-of-payments economic assistance.
- Development assistance and local currency funding to support the military-controlled pacification campaign in the conflict areas.
- An economic-growth strategy based on the promotion of private-sector investment, particularly in nontraditional exports.
- Increasing military aid and arms sales to support the army's counter-insurgency efforts and to link it more firmly to the United States.
- Support for the "democratization" process through economic-aid programs that finance the election process, policy think tanks, police training, judicial reform programs, and new business associations.
- Financial and diplomatic backing for generous multilateral aid programs from the World Bank, Inter-American Bank, and International Monetary Fund and related efforts to improve the international standing of Guatemala.

During the 1980s U.S. foreign policy backed the transition from military to civilian rule and at the same time increased support for the Guatemalan armed forces. Like the Guatemalan army itself, Washington decided that the best guarantee for political and economic stability would be a civilian-military alliance in which civilian political parties administered the government while the army devoted itself to internal security. By the end of the decade, however, the limits of this policy were becoming more evident.

The "democratization" process had lost much of its domestic and international credibility because of the corrupt and unprincipled behavior of the Christian Democratic administration and its utter failure to assert civilian authority over military power. The failure of the army's National Security and Development Plan to crush the guerrillas and pacify the rural population caused cracks in the military's internal cohesiveness, resulting in several attempted coups by dissident officers. With the crumbling of the military's plan for national stability came a rise in human-rights abuses, not only against the popular movement but also against reformist political and business leaders.

The likely decrease of U.S. aid in the early 1990s will further test the weak foundation of Guatemala's political and economic stability. Budget cutbacks and declining U.S. foreign-policy concern with Central America mean that Guatemala cannot count on the large injections of U.S. aid it experienced in the late 1980s. This, combined with likely reductions in Western European and multilateral assistance, will exacerbate tensions within the country.

Washington will remain committed to ensuring Guatemalan stability in the 1990s. But with less funding available and with its political and economic stabilization strategies already tested, the United States will have a more difficult time influencing the country's future. In the early part of the decade, U.S.-Guatemala relations will most likely be strained by certain contradictory aspects of U.S. policies, including the following:

- New drug enforcement measures—a new source of support for the military and police—will increase tensions as the involvement of the security forces in drug activities comes to light.
- Friction may increase as Washington expresses concern for the deteriorating human-rights climate, while at the same time it continues to insist on the need to support the army's counterinsurgency war.
- U.S. support for economic stabilization, conservative free-market economics, and structural adjustment will continue to aggravate social tensions while Guatemala attempts to deal with its deteriorating socioeconomic conditions.

U.S. Trade and Investment

No other Central American country, with the exception of Panama, has attracted so much U.S. trade and investment. The United States is Guatemala's leading trading partner, purchasing 41 percent of its exports and providing 39 percent of its imports. According to the U.S. Department of Commerce, new trade and investment guarantees provided by the U.S. Eximbank and OPIC accelerated U.S. trade with Guatemala in the late 1980s.

Approximately four hundred U.S. firms have investments in the country, ranging from small tourist businesses to large transnational corporations like United Brands and RJ Reynolds. Ninety of these companies are among the top five hundred corporations in the United States.[64] According to the Commerce Department, U.S. investors account for 75 percent of the foreign investment in the country with the the top U.S. investors in Guatemala being Castle & Cooke, Goodyear, and Texaco.[65] In recent years, U.S. economic-aid programs and free-market reforms promoted by AID have encouraged new U.S. investment in export-oriented manufacturing operations and in agricultural production covered by the tariff exemptions of the Caribbean Basin Initiative (CBI).

Investors in agriculture are mostly small U.S. agribusiness companies involved in the production and processing of nontraditional agroexports. Many of these have received loans from an AID-financed corporation called the Latin American Agribusiness Development Corporation (LAAD). Among the better-known U.S. agribusinesses operating in Guatemala is RJ Reynolds, which owns the Del Monte banana plantations near Puerto Barrios on the Atlantic coast. Goodyear cultivates rubber plantations, and Ralston Purina runs a variety of agroindustries including a feed mill. Other food-processing giants in the country include Warner Lambert (gum manufacturing), Beatrice (snack foods), Coca-Cola (instant coffee), and Philip Morris (cigarettes).

Seventeen of the top twenty U.S. pharmaceutical firms are active in the country, as are the top ten U.S. chemical firms, which manufacture pesticides. All five top petroleum corporations have distribution outlets in the country and the State Department once called Guatemala "the plum of Central America" because of its potential oil reserves. The slow rate of extraction, however, has dampened investor enthusiasm.[66]

U.S. Economic Aid

Although U.S. military aid was halted in 1977, modest levels of U.S. economic aid continued to flow to Guatemala during the Lucas García and Ríos Montt regimes. In the early 1980s, this aid—averaging about $15 million a year—was an important, and in some cases the only, source of support for military-sponsored development programs in the northwestern highlands.[67] As Guatemala moved toward civilian rule in the mid-1980s, the Reagan administration successfully pressured Congress to increase substantially economic aid to Guatemala. By 1989 Guatemala had become the seventh-largest recipient of U.S. economic aid in the world.

During the 1980s Guatemala received almost $800 million in AID funding. About 50 percent of this aid came in the form of balance-of-payments support either through the Economic Support Funds (ESF) or the Title I food-aid program. This money provided crucial foreign financial support for the institutional reordering and "democratization" plan initiated by the military high command in 1984. The ESF and Title I programs were used by AID to back an economic stabilization program for the Cerezo government and to push through conservative structural-adjustment measures such as currency devaluation and private-sector support programs. In addition to ESF and food aid, Washington has funded Development Assistance projects and determined how the Guatemalan government could spend the local currency generated by U.S. balance-of-payments support.

Private-Sector Support

Since 1983 AID has tried to prop up and stimulate the private sector with a dizzying array of development programs, including Agribusiness Development, Private Sector Development Coordination, Private Enterprise Development, Private Sector Education Initiatives, Micro-Enterprise Development, Micro-Enterprise Promotion, and Entrepreneurial Development. In addition, private-sector business organizations, especially those that promote export production, have been favored recipients of AID dollars. The private sector also stands first in line to receive local currency funds generated by AID's Title I and ESF programs.

AID's Private Enterprise Development project illustrates its elite approach to international development. It is a $10 million project that channels funds to the AID-created Chamber of Entrepreneurs and several other business organizations. According to AID, this is the flagship project of its Strengthening the Private Sector action plan. Part of this project is paradoxically titled Private Sector Initiatives, although the impetus for the project comes largely from AID.

One of the most serious problems facing Guatemala, according to AID's 1986 *Country Development Strategy Statement*, is the "gradual decline in the rate of food production." Nonetheless, AID has chosen to promote nontraditional agroexports and discourage local grain production, with the conviction that increased exports will not only ease the country's balance-of-payments situation but also create employment opportunities for the rural poor.

To fill the gap created by declining per capita food production, AID has dramatically increased the levels of food aid and encouraged the country to import basic grains produced in the United States. In

Guatemala, AID has sponsored numerous agricultural development projects, all of which aim to promote agroexport production. These projects, including Highlands Agricultural Development, Small Farmer Diversification Systems, and Agribusiness Development, have been at least partially responsible for Guatemala's increase in nontraditional agroexports.

Democracy Strengthening

For AID, democracy-strengthening includes financing the electoral process itself, supporting public forums to discuss national issues, promoting U.S. scholarships and civic education programs, upgrading and financing the country's judicial system, and training police. As with other AID projects, democracy-strengthening, at least on paper, addresses many areas of real need. Yet, as with so many other AID projects, the money spent often ends up being counterproductive because of AID's failure to consider structural obstacles to change and development. Also undermining even the best of projects are the underlying political goals of the U.S. economic program. This has been especially true with its democracy-strengthening programs, which, rather than promoting democracy, have advanced the antidemocratic political agenda of the army.

Indeed, the democratization of Guatemala has been a success, but mostly in terms of its showcase features. The electoral process, which AID financed through the Inter-American Center for Electoral Assistance and Promotion (CAPEL), went smoothly. Based upon the democratization/counterinsurgency project used in El Salvador, a succession of assembly, municipal, and presidential elections were held, with the promotional and logistical aspects of this process paid for largely by AID and USIA.

Beyond the electoral process itself, the U.S. government has created and financed institutions designed to support this display of democracy. This has involved the financing of an array of study centers and forums whose objective is to popularize a language and ideology of democratization. The three major think tanks working on these issues and funded by the United States are the Center for Political Studies (CEDEP), the Association of Social Studies (ASIES), and the Center for Social and Economic Studies (CEES).

In addition to supporting these think tanks (ranging from center to extreme right), the U.S. government is also a main source of funding for study and propaganda centers serving business and conservative labor in Guatemala. The study center of the AIFLD-sponsored CUSG labor confederation, for example, depends entirely on USIA and AID funding. The Chamber of Free Enterprise, a branch of the economic New Right, utilizes U.S. economic aid to sponsor forums on political organizing for the business elite. Two other business organizations—Chamber of Entrepreneurs (CAEM) and Guatemalan Development Foundation (FUNDESA)—also rely on U.S. funding for publications and studies that promote the business sector's vision of democratization.

AID has also directly supported political training programs for the country's business sector and political parties. Through the National Endowment for Democracy (NED), for example, U.S. funds have been channeled to the Academy for Liberty and Justice, an organization closely associated with the Movement of Solidarity Action (MAS) of Jorge Serrano.[68]

AID chose *Amigos del País*, a three-hundred-year-old organization of the traditional oligarchy, to implement its popular education project for rural Guatemala. Called the Private Sector Education Initiative Project, it publishes a newspaper called *Roots: The Friendly Voice of the Campesino* in cooperation with the Chamber of Industry. The new AID-funded *Altiplano* Institute, based in Quezaltenango, is one of several AID projects designed to propagate pro-U.S. and conservative political values among the most promising young Indians. The Central America Peace Scholarship Program does its part by bringing thousands of young Guatemalans to the United States to acquaint them with the "American way."

Although AID is prohibited from using economic aid to support military programs, the supply of AID-donated food and housing supplies for model villages in the early 1980s circumvented this regulation. Also in violation was a more recent AID accord, through its Office of Disaster Assistance, to supply and train the army's National Emergency Committee community promoters in disaster response and prevention.

Most AID support for military-related programs has, however, been more indirect. For the most part the infusion of U.S. aid into rural areas has been directed to the very areas that the military has itself targeted for "development" programs designed to control and pacify Indian communities.[69]

U.S. MILITARY AID

Strong ties between the two countries' security forces were established as a result of the U.S.-sponsored coup in 1954 and strengthened with the army's civic action programs and counterinsurgency campaign in the 1960s. The Reagan administration steadily solidified its links to the Guatemalan military and although U.S. military aid did not approach the levels received by Honduras or El Salvador, Guatemala became a substantial recipient by the end of the decade.[70]

After 1986, U.S. military aid and training increased, but always with the congressional restriction that the assistance be of a nonlethal variety. Recognizing that the U.S. Congress would support military aid only if it were couched in the language of democracy-strengthening, both the civilian government and the military high command of Guatemala pleaded that U.S. aid was essential to preserve the country's democratic process. In trips to Washington, President Cerezo told U.S. lawmakers that he needed U.S. military aid not so much to fight the counterinsurgency war but to demonstrate to the military that the civilian government was on its side. Military leaders, in turn, told Congress that U.S. military aid strengthened those within the armed forces who supported Cerezo and the United States.

For its part, the Pentagon claimed that its "austere" assistance program in Guatemala "will contribute to regional stability by providing limited counterinsurgency matériel and training."[71] Although technically nonlethal, U.S. military aid, which consisted mostly of helicopters, vehicles, and aircraft supplies and support, was exactly the type of assistance the Guatemalan armed forces needed most to pursue their counterinsurgency war.

In addition to congressionally approved aid, the Pentagon found a variety of other ways to support the Guatemalan military, including increased commercial arms sales, road building and military/civic action programs, and critical air-transport support. Logistical air support, supplied mainly from the Palmerola Air Base in Honduras, began in 1987 and has repeatedly been used to assist counterinsurgency operations and military-controlled refugee resettlement operations in the Petén and in the northern reaches of Quiché. At least one U.S. pilot died and nine airmen were injured in several crashes resulting from these logistical operations.[72]

The United States gradually stepped up its military/civic action programs in the 1980s. The first signs of this nonlethal but counterinsurgency-related activity were the medical programs sponsored by the Tropical Medicine Program of the Jungle Warfare School in the Panama Canal area. In November 1988, only three months after the massacre of twenty-two peasants in the village of Aguacate, uniformed and armed members of the National Guard participated in a civic action program in the department of Chimaltenango only a short distance from the village. The program, jointly sponsored by AID and the health ministry, was largely a public-relations effort that involved teeth-pulling and aspirin distribution by the U.S. soldiers. In 1989 the Army Corps of Engineers began a major road-building project in Sololá designed to give the Guatemalan army access to the isolated, guerrilla-controlled areas around Lake Atitlán.

Military training teams have traveled to the country to maintain aircraft and train counterinsurgency troops. The Pentagon has provided U.S. military personnel to train Guatemalans to fly A-37B attack planes as well as to help repair the military's C-47 transport aircraft.[73] Forty members of the U.S. Special Forces were sent from Fort Bragg in 1988 to train the country's elite and notorious *kaibiles* (counterinsurgency forces) at their jungle base in the Petén. Such apparent violations of congressional restrictions were commonly regarded as attempts by the Pentagon to test the depth of U.S. congressional concern about repression and human-rights abuses in Guatemala.

Colt Industries' sale in early 1989 of $13.8 million worth of M-16 assault rifles to the Guatemalan army sent the clearest signal: Not only were relations warming, but Guatemala itself had decided to increase its dependence on the United States. As part of its modernization drive, the Guatemalan army was switching from reliance on Israeli arms to U.S.-manufactured weapons. Following closely on this highly controversial deal, the State Department authorized the sale of an A-37B counterinsurgency plane for a nominal sum, which critics called a giveaway. It was noted that these sales violated congressional restrictions and the Pentagon's own stated commitment to provide only non-lethal training and aid to the country's armed forces.

Although on a much smaller scale than in the past, the United States is again training Guatemalan police forces, which are under the direct control of the military. Police are being trained under Administration of Justice and Drug Enforcement Administration (DEA) programs. In the last several years, DEA has steadily increased its presence in Guatemala, and now has an annual operating budget of over $1 million for the country. Despite the continued implication of the police forces in serious human-rights violations, U.S. aid pays for a variety of police training programs both inside Guatemala and in the United States.[74]

The presence of General Fred Woerner, then commander of the U.S. Southern Command, as an honored guest at the Army Day celebrations in Guatemala in mid-1989 marked the degree to which Washington was interested in increasing its influence and contacts with the Guatemalan armed forces. Woerner presided over a ceremony in which thirty-two U.S. trucks were delivered to Defense Minister Gramajo.

While continuing to push for increased military aid, the Pentagon has also sought to support the Guatemalan military in more indirect forms, such as rearming the country's troops with U.S. weapons provided through commercial channels. In providing this multifaceted support, Washington hoped to maintain the Guatemalan military as a cohesive force capable of maintaining the upper hand in the counterinsurgency war. The precarious military and political situation in El Salvador presents an additional incentive to keep the Guatemalan armed forces strong and stable.

In late 1990, as a result of the December 2 massacre in Santiago Atitlán, the killing of U.S. citizen Michael Devine, and the lack of government commitment to the protection of human rights, the U.S. State Department canceled U.S. military aid to Guatemala. During the Cerezo government, U.S. military aid had jumped from $5.4 million in the mid-1980s to more than $9 million by the end of the decade. Due to rising human-rights abuses, Washington reduced the aid package to $3.3 million in 1990. It is likely that U.S. military aid will be resumed under the new Serrano government, unless human-rights abuses by the military continue to increase.

REFERENCE NOTES

[1] Jim Handy, *Gift of the Devil* (Boston: South End Press, 1984). Handy's book provides an excellent history of Guatemala.

[2] Stephen Schlesinger and Stephen Kinzer, *Bitter Fruit: The Untold Story of the American Coup in Guatemala* (Garden City, NY: Doubleday, 1982); Susanne Jonas and David Tobis, *Guatemala* (NACLA, 1974); Blanche Cook, *The Declassified Eisenhower: A Divided Legacy of Peace and Political Warfare* (Garden City, NY: Doubleday, 1981); Jonathan Fried, Marvin E. Gettlelman, Deborah T. Levenson, and Nancy Peckenham, eds., *Guatemala in Rebellion: Unfinished History* (New York: Grove Press, 1983).

[3] U.S. Embassy, *Foreign Labor Trends: Guatemala* (Washington, D.C.: U.S. Department of Labor, 1989).

[4] Figures from Ministry of Health reported by Teleprensa, Guatemala City, June 16, 1988.

[5] *Guatemala: Elecciones de 1985* (Inforpress Centroamericana, October 1985); Network in Solidarity with the People of Guatemala, *Democracy or Deception? The Guatemalan Elections 1985*.

[6] For a more complete description of the PNSD, see *La Politica de Desarrollo del Estado Guatemalteca 1986–1987* (Guatemala City: AVANCSO, 1988), pp. 4–5.

Also see George Black, "Under the Gun," *NACLA Report on the Americas*, November 1985.

7 This concept of "national security civilian governments" was articulated by Franz Hinkelammert, director of the Department of Ecumenical Investigations (DEI) in Costa Rica. Cited in *Guatemala: Security, Development, and Democracy* (Guatemalan Church in Exile, 1989), p. 16.

8 Marcie Mersky, "Empresarios y Transición en Guatemala," unpublished report for CSUCA, November 1988.

9 Interview with Mario Solórzano, May 8, 1987; Partido Socialista Democrático, *Construcción del Partido Socialista Democrático y Desarrollo del Proceso de Democratización* (undated).

10 For an excellent description of the origins of the Christian Democratic party, see James Painter, *Guatemala: False Hope, False Freedom* (London: CIIR/Latin America Bureau, 1988), pp. 58–78. Much of this section on the DCG is drawn from information and analysis in the Painter book.

11 For a valuable analysis of "active neutrality" see *Política Exterior y Estabilidad Estatal*, AVANCSO Cuadernos de Investigación, No. 5, January 1989.

12 *New York Times*, May 17, 1989.

13 "U.S. Noose Around His Neck," *CERIGUA*, October–November 1989.

14 *La Prensa Libre*, November 16, 1989.

15 *El Gráfico*, November 14, 1989, cited in *CERIGUA*, October–November 1989.

16 Americas Watch, *Closing the Space: Human Rights in Guatemala* (New York, November 1988), p. 104.

17 For a critique of the national dialogue see: "National Dialogue: Reconciling the Poor to Their Poverty," *Entre Nos*, April 1989; *Information Bulletin* (Guatemala Human Rights Commission, USA), September 1989.

18 Amnesty International, *Guatemala: Human Rights under the Civilian Government* (New York: June 1989); Americas Watch, *Closing the Space: Human Rights in Guatemala* (New York: November 1988); "Human Rights in Guatemala," *News from Americas Watch*, Spring 1990.

19 U.S. Department of State, *Country Reports on Human Rights Practices for 1988* (Washington: 1989). For an excellent critique of the State Department's human rights reporting see Human Rights Watch and Lawyers Committee for Human Rights, *Review of the Department of State's Country Reports on Human Rights Practices for 1988* (New York: July 1989).

20 Americas Watch, *Closing the Space*, op. cit.

21 *Prensa Libre*, July 23, 1990.

22 Colonel Enríquez, in *Guatemala: Security, Development, and Democracy*, op. cit., p. 6.

23 For a discussion of splits within the army see Allan Nairn, "Guatemala During the Cerezo Years," *Report on Guatemala*, September 1989.

24 *Guatemala: Elecciones de 1985*, op. cit.; Gabriel Aguilera Peralta and Jorge Romero Imery, *Dialéctica del Terror en Guatemala* (Costa Rica: Editorial Universitaria EDUCA, 1981).

25 International Institute of Strategic Studies, *The Military Balance 1988–1989* (London: 1988).

26 Interview with Commander Rodrigo Asturias, *Latin America News Update*, August 1990.

27 *Central America Report*, September 2, 1988.

28 *Central America Report*, January 13, 1989.

29 Traditional exports are considered cotton, sugar, bananas, coffee, cardamom, beef, and petroleum. All other exports are called nontraditionals.

30 Hector Gross Spiell, "Report on Guatemala" (United Nations Commission on Human Rights, January 1990).

31 Thomas Melville, "Land Tenure in Guatemala," *Guatemala* (Guatemala News and Information Bureau), November–December 1986; "Girón Lights the Fuse: Land Problem in Guatemala," *Central America Report*, July 11, 1986.

32 Development Associates, *Land and Labor in Guatemala: An Evaluation* (Washington: U.S. Agency for International Development, 1982).

33 U.S. Department of Agriculture, "Guatemala: Agricultural Situation," March 1, 1989.

34 Ibid.

35 For an overview on food production and food security see Rachel Garst and Tom Barry, *Feeding the Crisis: U.S. Food Aid and Farm Policy in Central America* (Lincoln: University of Nebraska Press, 1990).

36 Raúl Marín, "Mitos y Miedos de la 'Nueva Derecha,'" manuscript, November 9, 1988.

37 U.S. Embassy, *Foreign Labor Trends Guatemala 1986–1987*.

38 Gerald Michael Greenfield and Sheldon Maran, eds., *Latin American Labor Organizations* (Westport, CT: Greenwood Press, 1987).

39 Using AID funds, AIFLD covers CUSG's $267,000 annual budget while USIA monies channeled through AIFLD and the Free Trade Union Institute (FTUI) support CUSG's study center, established in 1985 to support the democratization process. The AID mission in Guatemala supports AIFLD through its Agriculture Production and Marketing Service Project, which aims "to strengthen the capacity of farm unions to furnish needed service to their members."

40 *Central America Report*, January 12, 1990.

41 UNICEF, *Dimensions of Poverty in Latin America and the Caribbean*, 1982, cited in Painter, *Guatemala: False Hope, False Freedom*, op. cit., p. 3.

42 Joseph Breault, "Health on Horseback," *Links* (NCAHRN), Fall 1988.

43 See *Links*, Summer 1986 and Summer 1987.

44 *Reading the Vital Signs*, 1988.

45 *The Clamor for Land: A Collegial Pastoral Letter by the Guatemalan Bishops' Conference* (Guatemalan Church in Exile, May 1988); Penny Lernoux, "Bishops Take Courageous Stand," *National Catholic Reporter*, October 7, 1988.

46 Roy Wingegard, "Primer Reporte General del Crecimiento y Distribución de la Iglesia Evangélica de Guatemala," January 1988.

47 *Informe Anual de Actividades: 1984* (Area de Cooperación Nacional e Internacional, CRN).

48 *Report on Guatemala*, November–December 1988.

49 *Informe de La Cuarta Conferencia Regional Sobre la Integración de la Mujer*, CEPAL, October 31, 1988; *Situación de la Mujer en Guatemala*, Ciencia y Tecnología para Guatemala, March 1987.

50 Luisa Frank and Philip Wheaton, *Indian Guatemala: Path to Liberation* (EPICA, 1986).

51 Alex Michael, "Indigenous Peoples in the Guatemalan Struggle," *Report on Guatemala*, January–March 1989.

52 George Lovell, "From Conquest to Counterinsurgency," *Cultural Survival Quarterly*, Vol. 9, No. 2, 1985; Neil Boothby, "Uprooted Mayan Children," *Cultural Survival Quarterly*, Vol. 10, No. 4, 1986.

53 "Operación Ixil," *Revista Militar*, September–December 1982; Chris Krueger, "Re-education and Relocation in Guatemala," *Cultural Survival Quarterly*, Vol. 10, No. 4, 1986.

54 *Report on Guatemala*, January–March 1989, op. cit.

55 *Report on Guatemala*, January–March 1989, op. cit.

56 *World Refugee Survey: 1988 in Review*, U.S. Committee on Refugees, 1989, p. 34.

57 For a compilation of statements made by the CPR see Guatemalan Church in Exile, *Offensive of the People: Campesino Against Campesino*, July 1989.

58 Jim Burchfield, "Natural Resources Under Siege: The Environmental Costs of Counterinsurgency," *OSGUA Newsletter* (Chicago), Spring 1989.

59 H. Jeffrey Leonard, *Natural Resources and Economic Development in Central America* (New Brunswick, NJ: Transaction Books, 1987), p. 119.

60 Burchfield, op. cit.

61 For information about levels of military assistance during the 1977–1986

period, see, Allan Nairn, "The Guatemala Connection," *The Progressive*, May 1986.

[62] For a discussion of U.S.-Guatemala relations during the Carter and Reagan administrations see Robert Trudeau and Lars Schoultz, "Guatemala," in Morris Blachman et al., eds., *Confronting Revolution: Security Through Diplomacy in Central America* (New York: Pantheon, 1986).

[63] U.S. Agency for International Development, *Congressional Presentation FY1990, Annex III* (Washington, D.C.), p. 88.

[64] Resource Center, "Compilation of Corporations," 1986.

[65] U.S. Embassy, *Business Fact Sheets*, November 1988.

[66] Tom Barry and Debra Preusch, *The Central America Fact Book* (New York: Grove Press, 1986), pp. 245–248.

[67] For a thorough treatment of AID support for counterinsurgency-related projects during this period, see Tom Barry, *Guatemala: The Politics of Counterinsurgency* (Albuquerque: Resource Center, 1986).

[68] David Corn, "Foreign Aid for the Right," *The Nation*, December 18, 1989.

[69] Tom Barry and Debra Preusch, *The Soft War: The Uses and Abuses of U.S. Economic Aid in Central America* (New York: Grove Press, 1988), pp. 107–144.

[70] Allan Nairn, "Fattan Más: During the Cerezo Years," *Report on Guatemala*, June 1989. U.S. General Accounting Office, *Military Sales: The United States Continuing Munition Supply Relationship with Guatemala* (Washington, D.C.: January 1986).

[71] U.S. Department of Defense, *Congressional Presentation for Security Assistance Programs FY1989* (Washington, D.C.), p. 169.

[72] "U.S. Noose Around His Neck," op. cit.

[73] Charles Lane, "Step by Step, the U.S. Moves In," *Newsweek*, July 24, 1989.

[74] These include the Criminal Investigations Training Assistance Program (ICITAP), the State Department's Anti-Terrorist Assistance program, and DEA programs.

Chapter Five

HONDURAS

CHRONOLOGICAL HISTORY

1821   Honduras declares its independence from Spain as part of the Central American Federation.

1838   Honduras becomes independent republic.

1880   Tegucigalpa named national capital.

1899   The first banana concession is granted to the Vaccaro brothers, later to become Standard Fruit Company.

1905   U.S. troops land in Honduras for the first of five times during the next twenty years.

1907   U.S. banana merchant Sam Zemurray forms the Cuyamel Fruit Company.

1912   Trujillo Railroad Company wins contract to build a railway, beginning United Fruit Company's involvement in Honduras.

1923–5 Presidential elections won by General Tiburcio Carias Andino, who is prevented from taking office. Carias's forces take Tegucigalpa; new elections won by Paz Baraona. New constitution promulgated.

1929   United Fruit purchases Cuyamel for $32 million.

1932   Carias begins sixteen-year dictatorship.

1948   Carias steps down; Nationalist Party Juan Manuel Gálvez elected president.

1954   Elections won by Ramón Villeda Morales of Liberal Party; Vice President Julio Lozano Díaz seizes power.

        Successful strike by banana workers leads to widespread organizing among other workers.

1956   Constituent elections overturned by coup; military junta led by Roque I. Rodríguez assumes power.

1957   Villeda Morales elected president; new constitution promulgated; new labor codes and social security law adopted.

1963   Shortly before finishing his term, Villeda is ousted by army coup led by Colonel Oswaldo López Arellano.

1969   "Soccer War" with El Salvador over mistreatment of Salvadorans in Honduras and related issues lasts four days.

1971–2 Ramón Ernesto Cruz elected president, but is deposed shortly thereafter; Lopez returns to power.

1974   Hurricane Fifi leaves 12,000 dead and 150,000 homeless.

1975   "Bananagate" scandal: United Brands pays a "high government official" a $1.25-million bribe for a reduction in banana taxes and saves $7.5 million.

        López is overthrown and Juan Alberto Melgar Castro takes power.

1976   Border conflicts with El Salvador; OAS intervenes.

1977   Las Isletas banana cooperative destroyed by soldiers who arrive in Standard Fruit's railroad cars.

1978   Melgar ousted after drug-related allegations surface; General Policarpo Paz García assumes power.

1979   President Carter strengthens ties to Honduras after the fall of Somoza in Nicaragua.

1980   "Soccer War" officially ends with signing of treaty with El Salvador.

1981   Liberal Party candidate Roberto Suazo Córdova elected president, the first civilian president in more than two decades. General Gustavo Alvarez retains power as chief of staff.

        First U.S. military advisers arrive in Honduras; joint U.S.-Honduran naval and air maneuvers.

1982   Alvarez instigates change to constitution, which reduces presidential authority; Constituent Assembly approves Honduras's sixteenth constitution.

        Newsweek reveals that U.S. Ambassador John Negroponte in control of *contra* operations against Nicaragua.

1983   U.S. training base opens at Puerto Castilla. Joint U.S.-Honduran Big Pine I and II military and naval maneuvers begin.

1984   Alvarez ousted by younger officers and goes into exile; General Walter López Reyes named commander-in-chief of the armed forces.

Sixty thousand demonstrators in Tegucigalpa and 40,000 in San Pedro Sula protest U.S. presence in Honduras. Honduran government halts U.S. training of Salvadoran soldiers at Puerto Castilla.

1985   Liberal party candidate José Azcona Hoyo declared winner of presidential elections although National Party candidate gains most votes.

1987   Costa Rican President Arias takes leadership role in regional peace initiatives, meets with representatives from El Salvador, Guatemala, and Honduras in Esquipulas, Guatemala.

1989   Esquipulas peace talks held in El Salvador after four postponements.

Rafael Callejas wins November presidential election.

1990   Newly inaugurated President Callejas imposes new structural-adjustment plan and devalues currency.

1991   Rebel officers take over air force base in January in challenge to new Commander-in-Chief Luis Alonso Discua.

Sources for the chronology include *The Central America Fact Book* by Tom Barry and Debra Preusch (New York: Grove Press, 1986); *Conflict in Central America* (London: Longman Group Ltd., 1987); *Encyclopedia of the Third World* (New York: Facts on File, 1987); *Crisis in Central America: Regional Dynamics and U.S. Policy in the 1980s* (Boulder: Westview Press, 1988); *Labor Organizations in Latin America*, Gerald Greenfield and Sheldon Maran, eds. (Westport, CT: Greenwood Press, 1987); *Honduras: State for Sale* by Richard Lapper and James Painter (London: CIIR/Latin American Bureau, 1985).

TRENDS

- Having made the transition from direct military rule to civilian governments in the 1980s, Honduras is now confronting the limitations of this narrow "democratization" process, as the military continues to be the country's most powerful institution, the political parties make little effort to represent majority interests, and new "reforms" serve business interests rather than the increasingly impoverished population.
- Large infusions of U.S. economic aid and related support allowed Honduras to avoid a sharp economic downturn during the 1980s, but the combination of reduced aid, accumulated trade and budget deficits, and structural adjustment measures signal a severe economic crisis in the early 1990s.
- Repression of the expanding popular movement by the military and police forces continues to deepen, contributing to new demands that the national security budget be severely reduced.
- Popular organizing, historically limited to pockets of worker and *campesino* groups focusing on economic demands, is expanding to include a wide array of human-rights organizations, community groups, women's associations, and national coalitions that are challenging the country's political and military policies. Infighting and a lack of a cohesive political agenda obstructs the unity and effectiveness of the popular movement.
- Because of the continuing volatile political and military situation in neighboring countries, Washington still regards Honduras as a platform for intervention. But reduced U.S. military and economic aid, rising nationalist sentiment, and tensions over the Honduran military's involvement in the drug trade will further complicate and endanger the U.S.-Honduras alliance.

Honduras, long relegated to the backwater of Central American politics and economy, was pushed and pulled forward in the 1980s into a new position of prominence. Suddenly, Hondurans found their country being hailed as an "oasis of peace," as a "model of democratization," and as "pivotal in U.S. policy toward Central America." Centrally located on the isthmus and bordering three countries experiencing violent political conflict, Honduras was selected by Washington as a stable platform for its interventionism in the region.

About the size of Ohio, Honduras is a largely mountainous country of 4.8 million. Honduras has access to two oceans, through the Gulf of Fonseca on the Pacific side and Caribbean ports on the Atlantic side. Ethnically, the country is largely homogeneous; more than 90 percent of its citizens are *mestizo*.

Although in the geographical center of Central America, Honduras has had the reputation of being the exception to the region's history of brutal repression. Unlike neighboring states where class tensions and political disputes have been marked by violence, in Honduras compromise and smooth community relations have been favored over confrontation, peaceful solutions over bloodshed. This tradition was severely tested in the 1980s as Honduras was thrust into the regional turmoil. Wars raged across the border in three of its neighboring states, and in two of those conflicts Honduras took an active partisan role.

Per capita income, which currently stands at less than $800 a year, declined in the 1980s. Only one in ten Hondurans has what resembles a secure job. Even those holding jobs often cannot afford to meet their basic needs since most unskilled laborers earn less than $2 a day. During the decade the purchasing power of Honduran workers dropped 30 percent. The cost of basic goods rapidly increased in late 1989 and early 1990, so much so that the standard fare of many Hondurans, beans and shredded cabbage on a tortilla, has become unaffordable for many.

During the 1980s Honduras became an increasingly polarized and violent society. As a result, the country's popular sectors have become more organized and militant. A popular movement of unions, peasant associations, and student groups, which has formed an important part of Honduran society since the mid-1950s, gained a new dimension in the 1980s with the appearance of human-rights organizations, popular coalitions, and spontaneous community organizing. The popular movement's demands have expanded from strictly economic and sectoral concerns to broader national issues such as militarization and foreign policy. Disappearances, arrests, and torture have not had the intended effect of silencing these dissidents. As in Guatemala and El Salvador, the cycle of repression and radicalization seems to widen and sharpen of its own momentum.

Thrust into the geopolitical limelight during the 1980s, the historical flaws of the Honduran development process have acquired tragic
new dimensions. The characteristics of the 1980s—dependency and
subservience of the Honduran state, a paranoiac fear of its neighbors,
militarization of politics, lack of a strong national identity, absence of a
dynamic entrepreneurial spirit, unprincipled and narrowly based political parties, and pervasive corruption—were not products of the
Reagan era but of deeply rooted problems that have long obstructed
the political, social, and economic development of Honduras.

During the 1980s Honduras played the perfect foreign-policy pawn,
a role for which it was rewarded, although the U.S. dollars that the
Honduran government and military received often fell short of what
they demanded. Throughout the 1980s Honduras skillfully exploited
its acquiescence to U.S. foreign-policy concerns to wrest continuing aid
commitments from Washington while hedging on commitments to
devalue its currency, privatize its state enterprises, and institute harsher
austerity measures. By so doing, the government managed to maintain
a small measure of its historical commitment to the politics of social
compromise.

Throughout the 1980s the country's acute internal problems were
pushed into the background. The institutionalization of electoral politics and the anticommunist frenzy generated by the purported threat
of a Nicaraguan invasion served to downplay the seriousness of Honduran underdevelopment and poverty. Meanwhile, the vast influx of
U.S. dollars in economic aid, *contra* support, and military assistance
kept the economy and government afloat while fortifying and enrich-
ing the armed forces and business elite.

Honduras, however, faces a more uncertain and troubled future in
the 1990s. Despite the electoral defeat of the Sandinistas in Nicaragua,
the continuing presence of leftist threats in El Salvador and Guatemala
necessitate that Washington maintain Honduras as a close ally and
platform for U.S. intervention. But U.S. budget constraints and
changing foreign-policy priorities mean that Honduras will receive less
in return for its cooperation. No longer can the government depend on
a U.S. economic bailout, and the Honduran military will also find its
budget cut back as U.S. military aid dwindles and *contra* money disap-
pears.

Domestic tensions are likely to rise as foreign aid drops and new
austerity measures and business-oriented "reforms" take effect. Despite
the election of three civilian presidents, the promise of democracy and
civilian government faded in the 1980s as politicians oversaw the militarization of the country, the loss of national sovereignty, and the

absence of social reforms. As elsewhere in Latin America, a popular challenge to the formal democracy in Honduras will likely characterize the country's future political arena. In the 1990s Honduras may find that the sharp social conflicts that have come to the forefront in surrounding countries will further complicate the task of governing in this desperately poor nation.

GOVERNMENT AND POLITICS

Although the military and the United States are powerful behind-the-scenes actors, Honduras has succeeded in erecting a civilian state apparatus, backed up in theory by constitutional principles, responsible for carrying out policy decisions.[1] The current Honduran constitution—the fourteenth magna carta since independence in 1838—is the product of a National Constituent Assembly elected in 1980. While the Assembly worked on the document for more than a year and a half, it introduced few substantial changes from the structure and pattern of government inherited from previous decades. Formal power is concentrated in a highly centralized state apparatus headed by a strong executive branch. Although in spirit the constitution subscribes to the principle of separation of powers, the executive dominates both the legislative and judicial branches. Likewise, the potential for autonomy at the local level has been blocked by centralization of authority.

The executive branch presides over the burgeoning state apparatus and the assignment of posts in the public sector, the core of political patronage for the parties. By 1984 there were an estimated 70,000 employees working for the national government. Traditionally, following each change in government, the victors rewarded thousands of supporters with state jobs. As a sign of the changing times, the administration of President Rafael Callejas sent dismissal notices to some six thousand public employees in early 1990. But this time the vacancies were not filled by National party militants and campaign workers; the president's austerity package planned an across-the-board reduction of 10 percent in the public workforce.

The 1989 elections brought 128 representatives to the unicameral National Congress where they serve four-year terms. Historically in Honduras the Congress rarely challenges executive authority; the "new democracy" of the 1980s was no exception.

The judicial system is administered by a nine-member congressionally appointed Supreme Court. The Supreme Court is empowered to intervene in cases involving questions of constitutionality. In practice, the court's effectiveness and independence have been circumscribed by party loyalty, executive influence, widespread corruption, and the continuing impunity of the military.

The government structure is rounded out by 289 municipal representatives and the highly politicized National Election Board, responsible for overseeing all electoral matters. Voting is mandatory for all citizens, with the exception of active military personnel, who are not allowed to vote. Only the president is elected by direct vote. Congressional and municipal seats are assigned on the basis of party slates and vote proportions. Labor unions and other popular organizations have called for democratic reforms in the electoral legislation to allow voters directly to choose candidates for Congress and local posts, as opposed to the current, more restrictive system of party slates.

Political Parties and Elections

Party politics in Honduras has historically been dominated by *caudillos* (strongmen), with ideology taking a back seat to questions of personalism and influence.[2] Although newer generations of Honduran politicians have attempted to modify this tradition somewhat, it remains essentially the same. This was especially apparent during the 1989 presidential campaign, which relied far more on imagery and machine politics than ideology or a programmatic platform.

The two dominant political forces, the Liberal party (PL) and the National party (PN), emerged around the turn of this century. Both had close ties to the U.S. fruit companies that dominated national life and politics: The PN was close to the United Fruit Company, while the Liberals were partisan to the Cuyamel Fruit Company.

Through a complex series of legal obstacles, as well as through traditional loyalties among the population, the Liberals and Nationals have all but made it impossible for newer parties to challenge their predominance. With the revolutionary left outlawed and moderate or progressive forces small and marginalized, party politics remains dominated by the two big parties, whose stances on the major issues of the day are not substantially different. As a result, since the 1950s popular organizations and trade unions have played an essential role in pressing the demands and grievances of the worker and peasant majorities.

The founding members of the National party (PN), who split from the Liberals in 1902, were closely tied to large landed interests and historically the party has allied itself with the armed forces. Today the party represents conservative sectors of the business class and the state bureaucracy, and it continues to wield voting power among conservative sectors of the peasantry. Its current leader, the articulate Rafael Leonardo Callejas, won the November 1989 elections with more than 50 percent of the vote. The forty-eight-year-old Callejas is one of the youngest presidents in Honduran history.

Callejas, an agricultural economist, banker, and investor who was educated in the United States, has expanded the traditional political machine—essentially peons voting for the landlord's party—to include a neoconservative movement. This movement is the Honduran version of a New Right, involving many young, first-time voters.

Although the PN led by Callejas does not have a strong ideological definition, it is decidedly to the right of center on the Honduran political spectrum and enjoys close ties with the ruling ARENA party in El Salvador and other right-wing forces in Central America.[3] Under the leadership of Callejas, who adopted the slogan of Change for his electoral campaign, the party moved away from its rural, autocratic origins to incorporate young technocrats and urban businessmen.[4] The new president succeeded in unifying the three main factions of the National party and also managed to increase the disunity of the Liberal party by appointing several Liberals to government offices.

Traditionally, the Liberals had a broader support base than their National party rivals, including a sector of conservative landowners, small farmers and the rural middle class, the more progressive urban-based professionals, and some bankers and businesspeople. The Liberal party historically has advocated curbs on the military's role in national life and greater government intervention in the economy, especially through limited land reform, job creation through public investment, and expansion of social services.

But the Liberal governments of the 1980s broke with the party's historical image, presiding over a massive military buildup, curbing reform initiatives, and at least partially carrying out harsh austerity measures demanded by the U.S. Agency for International Development (AID) and the International Monetary Fund (IMF). Progressive forces within the party have been increasingly marginalized.

The Liberal party still has some progressive factions. There is a modernizing faction based among the north coast industrialists who belong to the Liberal Alliance of the People (ALIPO) faction. There is another weak faction to the left of ALIPO, the Liberal Democratic Revolutionary Movement (M-LIDER), which espouses social-democratic positions and has been an outspoken voice against the *contra* and U.S. military presence. Representatives from all three factions vied for the 1989 Liberal party nomination, with Carlos Flores Facussé, one of the wealthiest men in the country, eventually winning.

Two minority parties have enjoyed minor representation in Congress in the 1980s but have yet to build a national challenge to Liberal-National dominance. Together in 1989 they won less than 3.5 percent of the vote. One is the center-left Innovation and Unity party (PINU), which in 1988 affiliated itself with the Social Democratic International. The PINU was first formed in 1970 but did not acquire legal status until 1978. As a result of the 1989 elections, the PINU has two deputies in the National Congress. The other minority party is the Christian Democratic Party of Honduras (PDCH). Similar in name only to the parties in El Salvador, Guatemala, and elsewhere in Latin America, Honduran Christian democracy grew out of *campesino* movements and post–Vatican II "Popular Church" social and educational projects of the late 1960s through the mid-1970s. Together with the more centrist PINU, the PDCH often acts as the "conscience" of the Honduran Congress by exposing corrupt, illegal, and unpatriotic actions of the powers that be. Receiving fewer votes in 1989 than in the previous elections, the PDCH lost its two representatives in Congress.

Elections in the Eighties

Honduras is a prime example of the limitations of using the presence of elections as a yardstick of democracy. Under the elected civilian governments of the 1980s, Hondurans witnessed a reduction of traditional political space, a dramatic increase in repression and human-rights abuses, and the decrease of options for peaceful change and reform.[5] The policies adopted during this period, particularly in the key areas of the economy, defense, and foreign relations, were often at odds with popular sentiments on the issues.

Throughout this period the Hondurans' confidence in elections as a vehicle for authentic democratization and empowerment has eroded. In 1981 Hondurans enthusiastically participated in the first direct elections for president in more than twenty-five years. The winner, Liberal party candidate Roberto Suazo Córdova, a country doctor and rancher, was given an overwhelming mandate based on ambitious campaign promises to meet a series of popular demands.

Four years later many factors had led to widespread disenchantment with the government. Among them were Suazo's cozy relations with the military and the United States; his abandonment of proclaimed Honduran neutrality regarding conflicts in the region; rampant corruption; attempts to unconstitutionally prolong his stay in office; and the deteriorating economic situation. All of this contributed to the electoral victory of Liberal party rival José Azcona, with the assumption that he would discontinue the unpopular policies of his predecessor and return to the traditional stances of the party. Azcona also made explicit campaign promises to rid Honduras of the *contra* presence during his term in office. Four years later the *contras* were still camped in Honduras, human-rights violations were again on the rise, and popular discontent over the government's economic policies had sharpened.

In 1989 the electorate once again expressed its disappointment over the previous administration, this time by voting National party candidate Callejas into office. Although voting is technically mandatory, abstention was calculated at more than 23 percent of the electorate, up 6 percent from the 1985 elections in a clear expression of growing apathy.[6]

Although he counts on a large public mandate, with a 51 percent to 43 percent victory over the Liberals, and on a large majority in Congress, Callejas assumed office in January 1990 under difficult circumstances.[7] Under pressure from AID, the World Bank, and the IMF, Callejas immediately moved to devalue the national currency and implement further austerity measures, moves that generated a popular outcry, particularly among public-sector workers. Although the National party has largely succeeded in burying its longstanding image as the "civilian wing of the armed forces," Callejas himself was a founding member of the Association for the Progress of Honduras (APROH), the far-right organization set up by General Gustavo Alvarez in 1983 to act as a civilian-military pressure group. He also served as a high-level official in the military governments of the 1970s.

The first major disappointment with the new government came with Callejas's announcement of cabinet appointments in early 1990. Callejas had been publicly stressing his intentions to form a "government of national reconciliation," based on a consensus among the country's principal political and social forces. Although the new president gave representatives of the defeated Liberal party three seats in the leadership of the National Congress, as well as three of the nine Supreme Court magistrates, all key ministries are in the hands of close Callejas associates. Significantly, the top three economic positions, ministers of the economy and treasury and president of the Central Bank, all went to technocrats from Callejas's inner circle who have worked closely with AID.

The new administration called itself the government of national harmony, although there was no real attempt to reach out to the popular sectors. A strong consensus was, however, reached with the private-sector elite as represented by COHEP (Honduras Private Enterprise Council), which was in accord with the administration's policies of structural adjustment, currency devaluation, and export promotion. The Chamber of Commerce and Industry, which represents the interests of producers oriented to the local market, was less enthusiastic about the new government's program of structural adjustment.

The new administration benefited from the repatriation of the Nicaraguan *contras*, the lack of a unified popular movement with a viable political agenda, and the strong support of AID and international financial institutions. But as the austerity and structural-adjustment measures began to take hold, the Callejas government found itself beset by a series of strikes protesting its economic program and demanding substantially higher wages. The stability of the Callejas administration will depend primarily on its ability to control this rising popular discontent and to demonstrate positive economic results from structural readjustment. The government's stability is also linked to the institutional stability of the military, which is wracked by numerous internal divisions.

Foreign Policy

The fundamental dynamic in Honduran foreign policy over the past fifteen years has been the tendency of the civilian and military leadership to define national interests as a function of U.S. strategy for Central America.[8] As a result, traditional adversaries were transformed into "allies" (El Salvador); new "enemies" emerged (Nicaragua); and a country described in 1982 as an "oasis of peace" was turned into a perpetual base for two foreign armies (the U.S. and the *contras*) and a temporary training site for a third (Salvadoran). This "denationalization" of foreign policy led to a growing outcry among the public and important institutions of Honduran society while isolating the country internationally. By the end of the 1980s combined pressures forced the government to reconsider the key issue of *contra* presence in Honduran territory.

It was in large part due to Honduras's strategic location at the center of the Central American isthmus that the theoretical cornerstone of Honduran foreign policy was defined at the beginning of this century as perpetual neutrality vis-à-vis conflicts in the rest of Central America. Formally, the principle of neutrality has never been abandoned. But in practice it has been progressively distorted and stripped of its content by the string of military governments that have ruled during most of this century, and more recently by increasing alignment with the United States. By the mid-1980s Honduran foreign-policy concerns had for the most part been reduced to mere reflections of U.S. regional strategy.

The intermingling of U.S. and Honduran foreign-policy interests goes back to the banana-empire days when the fruit companies' control over local politics ensured that the nation's foreign policy would not stray too far from Washington's desires. Although more nationalist-minded sectors have since emerged and the relationship with the United States has become much more complex, the pattern has not been broken. Honduran collaboration with the United States in the 1954 overthrow of the Arbenz government in Guatemala and in anti-Castro adventures in the 1960s find their counterparts in more recent years in the *contra* war and support for the Salvadoran military's campaign against the FMLN guerrillas.

As the Central American crisis deepened over the 1980s, Honduran foreign policy shifted through several overlapping phases. Early in the decade the country was converted into the principal staging ground for the Reagan administration's regional counterrevolution. The installation of *contra* bases on Honduran territory and collaboration between the Honduran and Salvadoran armed forces in the war against the FMLN were the most salient manifestations of this new regional role. Beginning with the Contadora peace negotiations in 1983 and later with the Esquipulas II peace accords of 1987, the country's cooperation with U.S. interventionism became increasingly embarrassing and untenable. Honduras's persistent stalling tactics during the process of regional negotiations led to a deterioration of the country's image in Central America and internationally. By 1988 a combination of pressures forced the government to shift its position on the *contra* presence and to provide at least lukewarm support for efforts to demobilize the *contra* army. Honduras's constant vacillations about the demobilization indicate, however, that this change in policy is due more to political expediency and realpolitik than to any fundamental questioning of its overall relationship with the United States.

Peace Process

Prior to the August 1987 Esquipulas II peace accords, Honduras, along with El Salvador, acted repeatedly in concert with the United States to scuttle peace initiatives in the region. Recent exceptions to this pattern correspond to intense internal and international pressures to demobilize the Honduras-based *contra* army. As for other aspects of the peace process, such as national dialogue and respect for human rights, the country has made little if any progress as its leaders insist that such clauses "do not apply to Honduras."

In 1986 and 1987 severe military defeats suffered by *contra* forces inside Nicaragua erased any remaining hopes for a *contra* military victory and brought thousands of *contra* fighters back to their bases in southern Honduras. Popular pressures inside Honduras to expel the *contras* were reaching unmanageable levels. Anti-*contra* sentiments began to be expressed by the military, the traditional political parties, and the business elite—some of whom felt that Honduras had received far too little U.S. aid in return. By the time of the Esquipulas II peace accords in late 1987, the Iran-*contra* scandal in Washington and the near end of the bountiful Reagan years made Honduran leaders increasingly fearful that they would be left to pick up the pieces of the *contra* debacle.

But it was not until the February 1989 Costa del Sol summit that Azcona accepted that demobilization terms would be determined by the five presidents. The turnaround was due primarily to Washington's refusal to accept Honduran demands that the United States assume ultimate responsibility for the disarming and relocation of the *contras*.

Another round of Honduran stalling was followed by an August 1989 meeting in Tela, Honduras, when the five presidents agreed on a concrete demobilization plan to be carried out by December 5, 1989, under the auspices of a UN peace-keeping force. The December deadline passed unmet, however, because for two reasons demobilization was difficult for Honduras. First, the Bush administration, in open opposition to the deadlines specified in the peace accords, pressured Honduras into accepting the presence of the bulk of *contra* forces until after the February 25, 1990, elections in Nicaragua. The original Esquipulas II peace accords, as well as subsequent agreements on postponing the deadline, all called for the *contras* to demobilize and return to Nicaragua before the elections, a stance that Washington never accepted. Second, the peace plan called for "voluntary" demobilization, yet most *contras* simply refused to leave, even in the wake of the electoral victory of the U.S.-backed UNO coalition in Nicaragua, when Washington, the Sandinistas, the UNO, and Honduras urged them to go. By the end of March 1990, with all support lines cut off, most of the remaining *contras* began to trickle back into Nicaragua, albeit without disarming.

In the immediate aftermath of Esquipulas, there was widespread optimism in Honduras that, in addition to expulsion of the *contras*, the peace process would contribute to greater political openings, a drop in human-rights abuses, and some form of national reconciliation to off-set the growing polarization. Just weeks after the August 1987 signing of the accords, the Honduran Bishops' Conference issued a declaration in support of the treaty, calling on the Azcona government to move swiftly in the formation of a National Reconciliation Commission (CNR). The document affirmed that, among other issues, the CNR should promote a deepening of the democratic process through greater popular participation, ensure an end to human-rights abuses, and examine the refugee situation.[9]

But it was not until two days before the November 5 deadline stipulated in the treaties that the government officially formed the CNR. Over the next two years, the CNR held several meetings but the government's lack of enthusiasm inhibited the CNR from playing a very aggressive role.

Human Rights

The state's role in violations of human rights is nowhere proven more clearly than in the case of Honduras. Overwhelming evidence indicates that it is the military, not right-wing vigilantes, who carry out the violations. The initial wave of abuses took place from 1982 to 1984 when the armed forces were led by General Alvarez. It was under the aegis of policies implemented by Alvarez that the isolated occurrences that had characterized the 1960s and 1970s—the murder and torture of trade-union and peasant organizers, arbitrary detentions, and several massacres—were replaced by a systematic policy, practiced selectively and clandestinely, of domestic repression. By the time of his ouster in March 1984, Alvarez had presided over 214 political assassinations, 110 disappearances, and 1,947 illegal detentions.[10]

Widespread hopes that the departure of Alvarez would lead to an improvement and the prosecution of at least some of those involved were short-lived. After a brief period of relative decline in human-rights violations, since 1986 a resurgence in both the frequency and intensity of abuses has approached the extreme levels experienced in the first years of the decade. Independent human-rights monitoring organizations report that disappearances have largely been supplanted by political assassinations.

The violations of the early 1980s were aired in the judicial arm of the OAS, the Inter-American Court on Human Rights (IACHR) after years of official denials, refusals to investigate, and simple obstructions of justice.[11] Three cases were brought to trial on behalf of the families of disappearance victims by the OAS's human-rights monitoring and legal action team, the Inter-American Commission on Human Rights. While the commission prosecuted only three cases involving four individuals (two Hondurans and two Costa Ricans) who had "disappeared" with the help of Honduran security forces during the 1981–1984 period, it had to prove that the Honduran state "conducted or tolerated the systematic practice of disappearance" during that period.[12]

After tense and lengthy proceedings the IACHR found the Honduran state guilty in the two cases involving Hondurans (verdicts of July 29, 1988, in the Manfredo Velásquez case and January 20, 1989, in the Saul Godínez case) but was forced to dismiss the case involving two Costa Ricans for lack of evidence. Honduras nevertheless has the distinction of being the only Latin American state ever convicted in a court of law for the crime of disappearance.

The independent monitoring organization Committee in Defense of Human Rights (CODEH) has been the target of ongoing harassment, including armed attacks on its offices, infiltration by government agents, repeated public death threats against its leaders, and the assassination of Miguel Angel Pavón, president of CODEH's San Pedro Sula chapter, in January 1988. While the government waged a campaign to portray Pavón's death as the result of an internal power struggle, a former member of the Honduran security forces reported that his colleagues in the "death squad" were responsible for the killing.

The U.S. embassy and State Department have come under severe criticism from international human-rights monitoring groups for their role in attempting to discredit organizations like CODEH whose work involves exposing and documenting abuses. The Honduran government's own human-rights watchdog, the Inter-institutional Commission for Human Rights (CIDH), is composed of representatives from several state agencies and ministries who continue to be paid by their respective employers, plus four salaried investigators. In mid-1989 CIDH was reportedly considering suspending its activities because it had still not received its budget allocations from the government.

The unabated pattern of human-rights violations, compounded by the inefficiency of the judiciary system and CIDH, have led Hondurans to form several independent organizations designed to pressure the government and military for greater respect of human rights. CODEH, formed in 1981, is the most active and prominent. With disappearances becoming commonplace in 1982, relatives of some of the victims formed the Committee of Families of the Detained-Disappeared (COFADEH). The group was instrumental in bringing the landmark IACHR case to trial in 1987.

MILITARY

Security Forces

As is typical throughout Latin America, the military traditionally served as a police force to squelch worker and *campesino* unrest, usually on the basis of personal relations between local barracks commanders and plantation or factory owners. In 1946 General Tiburcio Carias created a separate force to carry out that function, a body that eventually evolved into the Public Security Forces (FUSEP). It was from his position as chief of FUSEP that Colonel Gustavo Alvarez rose to become commander-in-chief of the entire armed forces in 1982 and was promoted to the rank of general.

The armed forces are formally divided into four major service branches: the army, the air force, the naval force, and FUSEP. Although the bulk of police and internal security functions reside with FUSEP and the police forces it controls, the army has also been used extensively for these purposes. Estimates on the total number of full-time members of the combined armed forces range from 23,700 to 30,000.[13]

The army expanded from a few thousand troops in the 1970s to an estimated 15,000 by 1989.[14] With the addition of two new brigades in early 1989, one artillery and one infantry, the army now has five such units stationed around the country. Although much of Honduras is rugged, mountainous territory, the army's arsenal includes some ninety tanks.[15]

Led by a fleet of thirty-seven combat jets out of a total fleet of 120 aircraft, the Honduran air force is considered the most powerful in Central America.[16] Washington's repeated stalling on delivery of a promised fleet of a dozen F-5 supersonic jet fighters—the first of which were delivered in December 1987 and the last in January 1990—was a longstanding point of friction between the two countries. With a smaller and less combat-hardened army than Guatemala, El Salvador, and Nicaragua, and with a *contra* army almost as large as its own camped on its territory, Honduras regarded superiority in air power indispensable. While other Central American countries have concentrated on using air power to support counterinsurgency efforts, the Honduran air force is equipped and trained for offensive operations against installations in other countries.

The naval force, which essentially functions as a coast guard, is small and equipped with only nine patrol boats. It is, however, the focus of increased attention under the aegis of the War on Drugs.

FUSEP is controlled by army officers and is subordinated to the Ministry of Defense, although it has its own general staff and a separate organizational structure. In addition to its regular police units, FUSEP controls the treasury police, the traffic police, and a counterinsurgency unit known as the Cobras. The Honduran equivalent of the FBI, the National Investigations Division (DNI), formed in 1976, is also formally under the control of FUSEP. The DNI carries out routine criminal detective work, as well as surveillance and intelligence operations. In total, there are some 4,500 members of the various police forces controlled by FUSEP.[17]

The intelligence section of the armed forces, known as the G-2 and functioning under the command of the joint chiefs of staff, is primarily responsible for keeping tabs on political opponents and military personnel. This secret police unit created and operates Battalion 3/16—the official death squad—and carries out propaganda campaigns against domestic opposition groups, critics, and dissenters. Although Battalion 3/16 is directed by intelligence officers, it recruits its operatives from numerous forces such as FUSEP, the DNI, and the immigration service. The operatives remain at their jobs as a cover to restrict knowledge of the unit's existence even within the military institution.

National Security Doctrine and Militarization

The constitution of 1957 eliminated civilian authority over the military, transferring ultimate control of the institution to the chief of the armed forces, who was given the right to disobey presidential orders that he considered unconstitutional.[18] This formal authority provided a legal basis for the political independence and autonomous institutional development of the military and set the stage for its subsequent incursions into all areas of national affairs.

The poor performance of Honduras in a brief war with El Salvador in 1969, the revolutionary upsurges in Central America in the late 1970s—particularly the 1979 Sandinista victory in Nicaragua—together with Washington's selection of Honduras as a base camp for the Nicaraguan *contras*, thrust the militarization process into high gear. The chief Honduran architect of this process was General Gustavo Alvarez, whose tenure at the head of the armed forces officially lasted from January 1982 until March 1984. Alvarez was guided by the principles of the national-security doctrine, to which he was exposed during extensive training in Argentina, and through the Argentine military advisers he brought in to work with Honduran officers. From his post as commander-in-chief of the armed forces, Alvarez initiated a process of militarization that continued unabated throughout the decade, introducing profound changes in Honduran society and politics along the way. In essence, the Honduran conception of national-security doctrine entails the substitution of traditional notions of geographical and territorial enemies and borders for ideological ones. As such, the armed forces' mandate to provide territorial defense against enemy armies, particularly the Salvadoran, was subordinated to a new military project of ideological defense against subversion and communism.

Internally this meant engaging in a preventive war against the nascent Honduran revolutionary left, popular organizations, and in the extreme, anyone considered potentially subversive by the security forces. According to Honduran analysts, "here national-security doctrine implies the elimination of all those considered to be socially dysfunctional. In other words, both common criminals and political dissidents are subject to physical elimination."[19] In the international realm it meant collaborating with the United States in its *contra* war against Nicaragua and with the Salvadoran armed forces against the FMLN.

The Honduran armed forces entered the 1990s subject to increasing internal and external pressures. Conflicts within the institution became evident in early 1990 with the naming of a new commander-in-chief. The appointment of Colonel Arnulfo Cantarero, an ally of the outgoing General Humberto Regalado, angered members of the powerful graduating class of officers called the sixth promotion. Other factions within the military have objected to the corruption and arbitrary promotions by the high command.

The military has also faced rising criticism by the popular movement and some politicians for its role in drug-trafficking, embezzling military aid, repression, and forcible recruiting. In a time of budget cutbacks and privatization of state enterprises, the large sums of government revenue devoted to the armed forces and the military's control of such institutions as the post office, telecommunications company, civil aviation, merchant marine, customs, and immigration have come under new criticism. Responding to a proposed legislative measure to abolish mandatory military service, army chief Cantarero warned, "Do not corral the tiger, nor tease him." The military has also warned that increasing communist subversion, both armed and disguised as popular opposition groups, necessitates a strong and ever-vigilant armed forces. At the same time, however, the military has taken steps to improve its image, calling itself the "New Armed Forces" and involving itself in food-production and road-building projects.

Forced to resign in late 1990, Canterero was replaced by General Luis Alonso Discua. The immediate favoritism toward fellow members of his training group, the sixth promotion, sent shock waves through the entire institution and reverberated throughout Honduran society. Roberto Mendoza Garay, one of the colonels dismissed by the new commander-in-chief, seized control over the main air force base in Tegucigalpa together with other disgruntled officers. This challenge to Discua's authority was settled peacefully in January 1991, but talk of a constitutional crisis and other military rebellions swept through Honduras. A proposal by the Party of Innovation and Unity in January 1991 to eliminate the position of commander-in-chief and to assert more civilian control over the military received a warm hearing in the Honduran Congress but was vehemently rejected by General Discua. With this constitutional crisis heating up and with internal unrest growing over the dominance of the sixth promotion, the specter of a military coup cast a dark shadow over the country's prospects for economic stabilization and continued democratization.

Paramilitary Groups

Most analysts agree that Honduras does not have paramilitary groups in the sense of organizations truly separate of and independent from the armed forces. The bulk of the evidence relating to human-rights violations shows that units that belong or are closely linked to the military carry out the political abduction and murders, and systematically use torture on common as well as political prisoners. In general, use of the term *death squad* in the Honduran context is an attempt to distract attention from the military's systematic extralegal use of force in countering a broad range of perceived threats to national security.

The military usually denies formal involvement with any of these groups. One exception is Battalion 3/16, the group most often referred to as a Honduran death squad.[20] Formed under the jurisdiction of the intelligence branch of the Honduran military during the rule of General Alvarez, Battalion 3/16 has been accused by human-rights monitoring organizations as the main group responsible for the wave of disappearances and extrajudicial killings that took place in the early 1980s.

Three additional groups are shrouded in even more secrecy and controversy: the Anticommunist Action Alliance (AAA), the Free Honduras Movement, and the Honduran Committee for Peace and Democracy. Most active of the three is the AAA, which also made its appearance under Alvarez. After several years of inactivity, the AAA resurfaced in April 1988 following a wave of anti-U.S. demonstrations and the subsequent crackdown by the military. At that time, it distributed thousands of flyers bearing the names and photographs of twenty-two persons said to be "poisoning the ideological spirit of Honduran youth." The list included national leaders from student groups, unions, and human-rights organizations.[21] In January 1989 the AAA took out paid advertisements on several television and radio stations vowing to kill five prominent Hondurans in retribution for the killing of General Alvarez earlier that month.[22]

The human-rights group CODEH refers to these groups as "ghost organizations," whose activities are actually sponsored by the Military Technical Projects (PROMITEC), a unit run by the armed forces general staff, which specializes in psychological warfare. The human-rights group says it has documentary evidence linking the AAA to the military.[23]

Guerrilla Groups

Despite conditions similar to those that gave rise to the revolutionary left in neighboring El Salvador and Guatemala, Honduras has never confronted a sustained challenge from a guerrilla insurgency. In part, this is due to the success of the relatively sophisticated and intensive repression carried out in the early 1980s, which decimated the left-wing organizations through assassinations, disappearances, and exile. Others point to the left's inability to present a coherent alternative capable of capitalizing on widespread popular discontent, as well as the Honduran state's strategy of cooptation and the use of limited reforms aimed at neutralizing the influence of progressive individuals and organizations.

Although guerrilla groups have claimed responsibility for many of the bombings and armed attacks against U.S. military personnel that have taken place since 1981, at least some of these appear to be the work of the Honduran military itself. In March 1989 several leaders of the Honduran popular movement publicly asserted that the military was behind a recent series of bombings and death threats, which they called part of a "psychological war which seeks to create panic and justify repression against those who defend Honduran sovereignty, peace, and human rights."[24] Others cite accounts linking the military to incidents such as the bombing of a Peace Corps office and the San Pedro Sula shooting of several U.S. soldiers, both in 1988, as evidence of growing antagonism among members of the armed forces toward the United States.[25]

In the absence of a revolutionary alternative, a revised leftist agenda has been taken up by social and popular organizations including the FUTH labor federation, the CNTC peasant league, the COL-PROSUMAH teachers' union, and the Honduran Patriotic Front (FPH), as well as several secondary and university student groups.

Most of the left's leaders who managed to escape the repression of the early 1980s fled into exile. In June of 1983 five of the remaining guerrilla groups announced the formation of an alliance called the National Unitary Direction of the Honduran Revolutionary Movement (DNU). Most of the groups emerged in the late 1970s as offshoots of the Honduran Communist party (PCH), the Marxist-Leninist splinter group (PCH-ML), or from radical student groups. The DNU includes Cinchoneros Popular Liberation Movement (MPL), Morazanist Front for the Liberation of Honduras (FMLH), Revolutionary Workers Party of Central America (PRTC), and Lorenzo Zelaya Popular Revolution-ary Forces (FPR). After eight months of negotiation four exiled leaders of the DNU returned to Honduras after living ten years in Nicaragua. The former guerrillas pledged to continue working for revolutionary principles but promised to abandon the armed struggle.

Although polarization and social hardships in Honduras are likely to deepen under the administration of National party president Callejas, the omnipotence of the Honduran and U.S. military and intelligence networks make the appearance of an armed revolutionary movement unlikely in the coming years.

ECONOMY

The State of the Economy

In a region known for its poverty and underdevelopment, Honduras has traditionally been the poorest and least developed. The country's agrarian-based economy is highly dependent on export earnings from a few crops and on the handful of foreign companies that dominate productive activity. Meanwhile, most Hondurans continue to survive as subsistence farmers living largely outside the market economy.

Successive governments over the past three decades have intro-duced policies aimed at modernizing the economy and putting it on the path to more sustainable growth. As a result, the country's export production diversified to include coffee, beef, cotton, and nontradi-tional fruits and vegetables, and the domestic industrial sector ex-panded. Between 1960 and 1980 Honduras experienced average annual growth rates of more than 5 percent. This growth, however, did not generate significant internal development, but instead led to an increased foreign domination of the economy and an exacerbated inequality among the population. Declining terms of trade, a slump in the international economy, and an accumulated debt burden combined with internal factors to contribute to an economic downturn in the early 1980s.

The economy stagnated during the 1980s as economic growth rates rarely equaled the country's rate of population growth. Large infusions of U.S. economic and military aid kept the economy and the government above water, allowing the country to postpone measures to deal with serious imbalances in its domestic and foreign accounts. It has been estimated that foreign funds, mostly from Washington, financed 60 percent of the government's budget deficit, which topped 10 percent for most of the decade.

The Liberal party governments of the 1980s managed to avoid the implementation of a thoroughgoing neoliberal structural-readjustment program, which was advocated by the U.S. Agency for International Development, the World Bank, and the IMF. Due to overriding foreign-policy concerns, chiefly the need to maintain Honduras as a stable base for *contra* operations, Washington kept aid flowing to the country despite its failure to devalue the currency, raise interest rates, privatize state corporations, remove tariff barriers, and significantly reduce its fiscal deficit. Parts of the structural-adjustment programs were introduced—including some austerity measures and initiatives to increase exports—but it was not until the early 1990s with the advent of the Callejas administration that the complete adjustment program was imposed.

The Suazo and Azcona administrations feared that devaluation and further cuts in government services and employment would threaten the country's fragile political stability. But even without the full implementation of structural adjustment, socioeconomic conditions continued to worsen. At the end of the 1980s the principal trends afflicting Hondurans were

- **Increasing poverty:** The number of Hondurans living in poverty has risen to an alarming 68 percent of the population, 56 percent of whom cannot even cover basic food needs.[26] According to the World Health Organization, three of every four Hondurans suffer from some degree of malnutrition.[27]
- **Rising unemployment:** Official unemployment was 12 percent in 1988 but estimates of combined unemployment and underemploy-

ment run as high as 70 percent of the economically active population. Only one in ten Hondurans holds a steady job.

- **Declining wages:** Although annual inflation has been kept under 10 percent, purchasing power of wage earners dropped sharply over the last ten years. Average real wages have fallen every year since 1981, and the real value of the minimum wage fell more than 40 percent in the 1980s.[28]
- **Increasing income inequalities:** Prior to the economic crisis of the 1980s, which clearly exacerbated existing income inequalities, the wealthiest 20 percent of the Honduran population received nearly 60 percent of all income, while the poorest 20 percent subsisted on just 4 percent of national income.[29]

Although dependent on U.S. economic aid and suffering from large budget deficits and overall lack of dynamism, the Honduran economy in the 1980s did enjoy a relatively low rate of inflation, a fairly high domestic savings rate, and a fixed exchange rate. The tenuous economic stability that characterized Honduras for most of the 1980s was shattered by early 1990. Washington withheld $70 million in economic aid during the last year of the Azcona administration, citing the failure of the government to abide by bilateral accords. Confronted by an empty national treasury and a gaping budget deficit, the Callejas administration embraced an uncompromising neoliberal reform program aimed to close the budget deficit and regain the good graces of Washington and the multilateral banks.

Callejas proved successful in his bid to attract new multilateral loans but was unable to halt planned reductions in U.S. economic aid. Although new agreements with the World Bank and IMF gave the new government a needed lift, the Callejas administration's economic reforms shocked and depressed the domestic economy. The cost of living and doing business soared as the local currency (*lempira*) continued sinking, charges for utilities and government services increased, and domestic prices and international trade were liberalized. The steep increase in international oil prices as a result of the Middle East crisis also fueled the rising rate of inflation.

Although these adjustment measures hurt the poor, the workers, and most businesses producing for the domestic market, they proved a boon for the export sector. It was not, however, immediately clear that the improved environment for export production would result in increased private investment and an improved balance of trade. Six months after Callejas took office, capital flight and a low rate of private investment continued to plague the increasingly unstable economy. The new government also faced a new wave of social unrest when it failed to fulfill promises to consider the interests and demands of the popular sectors in economic policymaking.

Nontraditionals and Privatization

To some extent, the strategies of exporting nontraditional agricultural products and privatizing state businesses, ostensibly designed to pull Honduras out of its misery, serve only to exacerbate existing problems of poverty and inequality. Most of the profits generated by the ambitious export strategies of the 1980s remained in the hands of the foreign companies that continue to dominate the economy, or went to the handful of Honduran entrepreneurs who have been willing to take the investment risks.[30]

The growing trend toward privatization—spurred by a special law passed by the Honduran Congress in early 1989—also stands disproportionately to benefit foreign investors. By 1990 ten state businesses worth about $27 million had been sold to private investors and another forty-seven companies were up for sale.[31] Many companies are sold to foreign enterprises at a fraction of their market value to cover debts. In 1989, for example, debt-equity swaps financed the takeover of an abandoned paper plant by the Costa Rican–based company Scott Paper, while the Nelsin Group of Seattle bought a foundry and Wellington Hall purchased a furniture factory. The government is currently looking for buyers for the national airline, SAHSA, and the business association COHEP has called for privatization of services including water, electricity, and communications.

The most pressing short-term problem for the new Callejas government was the shortage of foreign-exchange reserves. In the long term, the only way for the new government to overcome the liquidity crisis was to negotiate a new agreement with the IMF to free up loans, credits, and assistance from AID and international lending institutions. Callejas implemented a package of structural-adjustment measures in March 1990 aimed at paving the way for negotiations on such an agreement.

The most drastic and unpopular step was a 100 percent devaluation followed by an apparent policy of minidevaluations. Other aspects of Callejas's economic plan included tax hikes on sales, leases, imports, exports, and fuel; the elimination of some tax exemptions and privileges for diplomatic missions, nongovernmental organizations (NGOs), the armed forces, cooperatives, and unions; additional export incentives, and the reduction or abolition of protectionist tariffs.

During the 1980s the Honduran government was under pressure from AID, the IMF, and the World Bank to adopt a full-scale structural-adjustment program. But for Washington the country's strategic value took precedence over demands for devaluation and austerity measures. Elements of the proposed structural-adjustment program were instituted but the Azcona government feared that implementation of the entire program would lead to social upheaval. By 1990 declining U.S. economic aid and the desperate need for injections of World Bank and IMF loans persuaded the government to accede to international and domestic pressures for a thoroughgoing program of structural adjustment.

There was little doubt that a serious economic restructuring was in order. The currency was overvalued, exports had stagnated, local industry was inefficient, the treasury was bare, and state enterprises had been pillaged by government, military, and business figures. The structural-adjustment program imposed by the Callejas administration promised to remedy these and other problems. But other structural weaknesses of the economy were not addressed. In fact, the structural-adjustment program tended to tighten the hold of transnational corporations over the economy and aggravate class tensions. Adjustment measures that stressed exports further discouraged the production of food and goods for the local market and failed to spur significant new investment and export production.

Agriculture

As in most of Central America, agriculture in Honduras is the single most important contributor to the GDP, as well as to export earnings and employment.[32] Although hard times for farmers have induced steady migration to urban areas during the 1980s, the majority of the population still lives in the countryside.[33]

Overall, Honduras enjoys a relatively low population density, but this is deceptive because only about one-fifth of the country's land is suitable for agriculture. The bulk of the good land—generally, the fertile low-lying valleys and coastal plains—is owned by large Honduran agroexport farmers or transnational companies. Food for local consumption is generally produced by peasants with small plots of low-quality land, usually on marginal steep and rocky mountainsides. The agricultural sector generally is characterized by low yields owing to inefficiencies at all levels. Only one in five farms in Honduras is worked by its owner; the rest are exploited under a variety of arrangements, from sharecropping, tenant farmers, and squatters, to the traditional *ejido*, or municipal lands.[34]

Although the concentration of land and wealth is less extreme than in neighboring Guatemala and El Salvador, both land ownership and rural income are highly skewed in Honduras. Approximately half of the rural population is considered essentially landless; many of those who do own lands are living on plots too small and of too poor quality even to meet subsistence needs. A full 55 percent of the farming population work plots smaller than five acres generating a net per capita income of less than $70 a year. At the other extreme, 510 people own farms larger than 1,700 acres with a corresponding per capita income of almost $15,000.[35]

Honduran agricultural exports remained fairly steady throughout the 1980s. Bananas provided more than one-third of the country's total export revenues, followed by coffee, which accounted for approximately one-fifth. The next three most important items—wood, beef, and seafood—each contributed less than 5 percent of export earnings. Honduras continues to be one of the largest exporters of bananas in the world, with "yellow gold," owned almost exclusively by transnational companies, accounting for a whopping 44 percent of the country's agricultural export earnings in 1987.[36]

Unlike bananas, production of and income from coffee remain in Honduran hands and most of the country's 45,000 producers are small growers. Although coffee has played an important role as a source of employment and has been prioritized as an alternative to dependence on bananas, minimal levels of technical assistance and credit contribute to Honduras having the lowest productivity and average yields in the region. Fluctuating international market prices and unfavorable export quotas have made coffee production increasingly risky. Export revenues have fallen each year since 1986 despite increased volumes.

Production of nontraditional exports, such as pineapples, melons, cucumbers, cardamom, black pepper, and ornamental flowers, has been promoted, in order to break dependence on the longstanding big earners like bananas and coffee. Although some of the new projects have fared well, others have proved a dismal failure.

The other side of the agroexport push is the declining per capita production of basic grains and increased food imports.[37] Honduras, which was once self-sufficient in food production, is now forced to import basic foodstuffs each year. Noting that Honduras is producing less and that *campesinos* are abandoning the countryside, Juan Antonio

Aguirre of the Inter-American Institute for Agriculture Cooperation (IICA) said that Honduras faces a "terrifying future" if corrective measures are not taken. He said that the country's current agricultural crisis will become truly catastrophic in the 1990s.[38]

During the 1980s the true dimensions of the agricultural crisis were somewhat hidden and distorted by the large U.S. food-assistance program. Through the PL480 Title I program, Honduras received $15 million to $19 million annually in food imports. The program eased the country's balance-of-payments crisis by allowing it to increase its grain imports without having to expend scarce foreign exchange. It also helped ease urban unrest by keeping wheat-flour products available and relatively low-priced.[39]

Although the food-aid program has temporarily disguised the severity of the agricultural crisis, it has seriously impacted local food production. The influx of relatively cheap foodstuffs has left little incentive for local grain producers and has acted to change consumption patterns. An AID-contracted study found that wheat imports (95 percent of which are covered by the food-aid program) have undermined the market price of corn for farmers, who as a result are cutting back on corn production.[40] Because wheat has become relatively cheaper and often more easily available, Hondurans have changed their diet to include more wheat products.

Despite the harsh poverty and inequitable distribution of land and wealth in the Honduran countryside, land-reform programs have been a major stabilizing factor since the early 1960s.[41] Nonetheless in the last few years the modest reform efforts begun in the 1960s and extended in the mid-1970s have ground to a halt and the growing problem of landlessness threatens to break the fragile peace in the 1990s.

Finding all other avenues closed, the well-organized peasantry has responded with direct action in the form of land occupations. The state has responded ambiguously to *campesino* land invasions. On occasions, it has simply turned a blind eye or invited *campesino* leaders to negotiate settlements of claims through the National Agrarian Institute (INA). But the most common response has been to send in the army. Many peasants participating in such actions have been jailed, tortured, and killed by the military or by the landowners' private guards. Repressive legislation passed in 1982 defines land invasions as "terrorist acts."

Meanwhile, with genuine land reform on ice since the 1970s, the government has instead pushed a land-titling program. Many *campesino* organizations see this AID-sponsored program as a way of dividing the peasantry. Its major thrust is to provide legal claim to lands that farmers have been working for years—in some cases for generations—

as a way to facilitate access to credit. The program thus completely fails
to address the most pressing problem in the countryside, that of the
tens of thousands of *campesino* families with no land at all.

Industry and Finance

Honduras has the smallest industrial sector in Central America. Little
of its industrial output is marketed outside the region except for the
textiles and other products assembled by the country's few export-
oriented assembly-manufacturing plants. Industry employs about 14
percent of the Honduran labor force and accounts for a quarter of the
country's GDP, while manufactured goods contribute one-fifth of export earnings. Economically, mining, forestry, tourism, and construction are all relatively marginal.

More than half of all manufacturing enterprises are small, family-
owned shops with fewer than ten employees. A full 40 percent of
Hondurans employed in manufacturing are classified as artisans, not
factory workers. The country's large, modern factories are in the hands
of foreign companies or the Honduran business elite. The country's
two major banana companies are also among the largest manufacturers. Castle & Cooke produces soap, plastic products, cans, boxes,
and cement; United Brands makes rubber, plastics, margarine, and
vegetable oil.

The protected regional markets erected under the provisions of the
Central American Common Market (CACM) did stimulate significant
growth of Honduran industry in the 1960s, but the boom years did not
last long. With the onset of recession in the early 1980s, industry began
a decline from which it has still not recovered. Virtually all manufacturing subsectors have stagnated or declined during the 1980s as a result
of contracting internal demand, closing off of regional export markets,
tight credit, and rising import prices. Structural-adjustment programs
that liberalize foreign trade and pull down tariff barriers represent a
further threat to local industries that cannot compete with foreign
products.

While the local manufacturing sector is stagnating, there has been
some growth in export-oriented manufacturing. In 1976 the government opened the doors of the Puerto Cortés free zone as part of a
policy to attract foreign investment in industry. Enterprises investing in
space at the industrial park may import raw materials and semifinished
products without tariffs or duties and freely reexport finished goods,
and profits are exempt from taxation. But a variety of constraints have
resulted in less than expected growth. By 1987 the free zone had

attracted only nineteen firms, many of which were clothing manufacturers from South Korea, Taiwan, and Hong Kong seeking to transfer to sites like Honduras, where they could take advantage of low labor costs and avoid U.S. import quotas.[42]

Honduras remains convinced that such reassembly-for-export ventures hold promise, and accordingly four additional industrial parks are under construction, like the Puerto Cortés park on the north coast. The country hopes to attract investment to the parks from 160 firms and generate 30,000 jobs between 1990 and 1995.[43]

SOCIETY AND ENVIRONMENT

Popular Organizing

The first peasant organizations, like the country's first unions, resulted largely from the work of organizers associated with the Honduran Communist party. One of the first peasant associations was the Central Committee of Peasant Unity, founded in the mid-1950s and later reorganized as the National Federation of Honduran Peasants (FENACH). From the beginning, FENACH was targeted by the security forces. In 1963, after a military coup that overthrew the Ramón Villeda government, FENACH's offices were destroyed and its leaders imprisoned.

Along with the military and the church, the AFL-CIO and the Inter-American Regional Labor Organization (ORIT) were also preoccupied with the FENACH's leftist activism. In 1962 the National Association of Peasants (ANACH) was formed to counteract the influence of FENACH within the peasantry and to assert "democratic" control over the incipient peasant movement. Traditionally ANACH, which is a member of the Confederation of Honduran Workers (CTH), has exerted a conservative influence but in recent years has adopted some of the more confrontational tactics of other peasant groups and has joined in coalitions with leftist union federations. Its long-time president, Julín Méndez, has served as a congressional deputy with the social-democratic Innovation and Unity party (PINU).

The National *Campesino* Union (UNC), founded in 1970, has also been a strong influence among the Honduran peasantry. Having strong roots within the social-Christian movement, UNC grew out of the Social Christian Peasant Association (ACASCH) and is a member of the Workers General Central (CGT). Like the CGT, factions of the UNC have become closely associated with the National party.[44] It has alienated itself from other forces within the peasant movement by making separate deals with the National Agrarian Institute and the military.

The most dynamic and progressive peasant federation during the late 1980s was the National Union of Rural Workers (CNTC), founded in 1985 mainly from split-offs from ANACH and UNC. This peasant confederation includes the National Union of Peasant Cooperatives (UNACOOPH), National Authentic Union of Honduran Peasants (UNCAH), Unitary Federation of Peasant Cooperatives (FUNACH), and Front of Independent Honduran Peasants (FRENACHINH). The U.S. embassy charges that CNTC has a Marxist bent because of its working relationship with the leftist FUTH labor federation, but its politics would better be described as progressive social-democratic.[45] Like other sectors of the popular movement, CNTC has been weakened by sectarian splits, corruption, and infighting.

The Honduran Peasant Organization (OCH) was formed in July 1989 in a split from the UNC. The Coordinating Committee of Peasant Organizations (COCOCH), which includes CNTC, ANACH, UNC, and the Federation of Honduran Agrarian Reform Cooperatives (FEC-ORAH), is the latest attempt to unify the divided peasant movement.

Two popular coalitions were formed in the 1980s. The Coordinating Committee of Popular Organizations (CCOP), founded in late 1984, brings together unions, peasant associations, student organizations, and groups of slum dwellers. Among the organizations included in the CCOP coalition are the Union of Electrical Workers (STENEE), the United Revolutionary Front (FRU) at the national university, the United Federation of Honduran Workers (FUTH), and the Visitación Padilla Women's Committee. CCOP has strongly condemned repression of the popular movement and has consistently expressed opposition to U.S. intervention in Central America.

A more recently formed popular coalition is the Unified Popular Alliance (APU), formerly known as the Francisco Morazán Patriotic Committee. The APU, which is interested in offering an electoral alternative to the country's popular sectors, also represents a variety of popular organizations, including the Texaco refinery union, the Organization of Honduran Peasants (based in the north), League of Patriotic Women, the FUR, and the Committee of the *Ejidos.*[46] Like CCOP, APU organizations and leaders have been subject to police and military repression. A third popular coalition is Popular Unity, a San Pedro–based coalition that serves as a coordinated front for ten popular organizations. In general, the popular movement in San Pedro Sula is more dynamic than the one based in Tegucigalpa. In late 1989 most

sectors of the popular movement signed a document called the Platform of Struggle, which was designed to rally popular organizations
around a single agenda of social change. Although the popular sectors
have taken some steps to form coalitions, these efforts continue to be
undermined by political sectarianism, personality differences, absence
of serious grass-roots organizing, police infiltration, and internecine
violence. These and other factors obstruct the kind of unity necessary
to confront the escalating repression and deteriorating socioeconomic
conditions.

The popular movement enters the 1990s without a cohesive political
strategy. In the 1980s numerous leftist guerrilla organizations attempted to mount a violent challenge to the established order, following the model of the Sandinista guerrillas in Nicaragua and the
revolutionary forces in Guatemala and El Salvador. A decade later the
Honduran guerrillas seem doomed to isolation and failure by their
own dogmatism and lack of understanding of the country's political
conditions, as well as by the military's effective campaign of repression.
Hondurans' continued adhesion to the traditional political parties
makes it clear that to become an effective force the popular movement
must expand its own political education work and adopt an electoral
strategy.

Labor and Unions

Since landmark strikes in 1954 the Honduran union movement has
been seen as the region's largest and strongest.[47] Currently about 15
percent of the total workforce and 40 percent of urban workers belong
to unions.

Honduran unions and peasant organizations have fought hard for
their position as influential actors on the national political scene; over
the past thirty years the government has been forced to pay attention to
their demands, and several have tried to integrate them into broad
coalitions. But sectarian practices, opportunistic leadership, and attempts to divide the movement have often diluted its strengths. In
addition, despite legal gains won by unions—such as a progressive
labor code and minimum-wage legislation—enforcement has largely
paralleled the government and private sector's ability to pay, and has
been limited to the small, modern sector of the economy that employs
skilled labor. Particularly with the onset of the economic crisis of the
1980s, there has been widespread noncompliance; wage-earners who
have seen their purchasing power shrink year after year since 1981
have been the ones forced to assume the burden of structural adjust-

ment of the economy. In the absence of strong popular coalitions and alternative political parties, the union movement has led the opposition to U.S. intervention in the country's internal affairs and to the debilitating structural-adjustment program.

In 1964 most of the federations associated with the American Institute for Free Labor Development (AIFLD)—including the most powerful of the banana workers' unions and the largest peasant organization, ANACH—came together to form the Confederation of Honduran Workers (CTH). The CTH was the dominant force in legal union activities throughout most of the 1960s and 1970s and, despite recent challenges by newer groups, it remains the largest confederation in Honduras today with an estimated 142,000 members. CTH-affiliated unions can be found in almost all sectors of the economy. Among the most important federations and unions affiliated with CTH are the National Association of Public Employees (ANDEPH), ANACH, the SITRATERCO banana workers union, FESITRANH, and FEC-ESITLIH.

The second national confederation, the Workers Central General (CGT), was formed in 1970 but was refused legal recognition until 1984. Originally linked to the more conservative sectors of the Christian Democratic party, conflicts over strategy and patronage have divided both the leadership and the base of the CGT since its founding. Today, the CGT enjoys close ties with the National party. In fact, several of the confederation's leaders stepped down in order to run for office on the National party slate in 1989, including one of Callejas's three vice president designates, Marco Tulio Cruz. The CGT leaders-turned-politicians have come out in support of Callejas's strategy of "selling" Honduras to foreign investors, insisting that it is the only way to create new jobs. The core of CGT membership, however, has adopted a more critical stance. The CGT claims to represent 120,000 members, two-thirds of whom come from the peasant groups of the UNC. Affiliated with the Latin American Workers Central (CLAT) and the World Federation of Labor (WCL), CGT unions have received assistance from several Western European social- and Christian-democratic foundations.

The more radical, class-oriented United Federation of Honduran Workers (FUTH), an alliance of unions associated with the Marxist-Leninist Community party (of Maoist orientation) and the Honduran Communist party, was formed in 1981 and awarded legal status in 1989. The FUTH claims 30,000 workers. Although this makes it by far the smallest of the three national confederations, the FUTH's vocal stance on burning political issues—together with the fact that its membership works in strategic areas of the economy such as the Central Bank, the National University, electricity and water companies, and construction—has given the group a high profile. In recent years FUTH has sought, with varying degrees of success, to overcome its sectarian tendencies and build alliances with the CTH and CGT.[48]

The latest addition among the labor confederations is the Independent Federation of Honduran Workers (FITH) founded in 1985 as a split-off from the CGT. Based in San Pedro Sula, FITH member unions include municipal-workers unions and small industrial unions.

Divisions and infighting, in some cases over legitimate political and ideological differences, in others the product of deliberate policies pursued by management and the government, continue to characterize the Honduran union movement. The three major confederations stand worlds apart on many issues. Nonetheless, growing hardships brought on by the economic crisis and austerity policies have led to increasing levels of unity within the movement.

Both the transnationals and Honduran businessmen have embraced *solidarismo* as an effective way of combating traditional trade unionism and of assuring a more compliant workforce. Well established in Costa Rica, the *solidarismo* movement seeks, with the likely support of the Callejas administration, to replace existing unions with worker-owner financial associations.[49]

Schools and Students

Until the late 1950s education in Honduras was the exclusive privilege of those among the middle and upper classes who could afford to send their children to private schools. The reformist government of Ramón Villeda Morales (1957–1963) introduced public education and began an ambitious school construction program. According to the Honduran constitution, primary education (ages seven to fourteen) is obligatory and free. Despite this constitutional guarantee, education remains a privilege in Honduras because of the lack of schools, the poor quality of public education, and the prohibitive cost of educational materials.

Illiteracy is widespread in Honduras, affecting more than 40 percent of the total population and 84 percent in most rural areas.[50] A third of Hondurans do not have any formal schooling.[51] In many isolated areas of Honduras there are no accessible schools, or instruction extends only through the third grade.

Even when educational opportunities do exist, the quality of instruction is poor for the following reasons: inadequate teacher training, low pay for teachers, backward teaching methods, corrupt and unqualified administration, and lack of adequate buildings and teaching materials. The country's teachers union has raised demands for a 400 percent salary increase. Some teachers are not even paid regular wages but are part of government food-for-work programs.

The National Autonomous University of Honduras (UNAH) is the central higher educational institution in the country. Founded in 1847, UNAH has some 30,000 students enrolled. Supported by the military, rightest groups gained control of UNAH in the mid-1980s and continue to engage leftist groups in armed confrontations. There are three private universities: the tiny José Cecilio del Valle University established in Tegucigalpa in 1978; the Central American Technological University (UNITEC) founded in 1987 in Tegucigalpa; and the University of San Pedro Sula (USPS).

AID began funding USPS in the 1980s to "provide a political counterweight to the traditionally leftist-dominated National University." Through its grants AID is shaping USPS as a business-oriented university with "curriculum emphasis in the skills areas most needed for improving Honduras' competitiveness in world markets: management, finance, international marketing, business law, and the physical and agricultural sciences." AID is also exploring the possibility of arranging a joint program with a U.S. university, which "could also act as a 'brain trust' for Honduran industry through consulting work and research."[52]

Communications Media

Because of the high illiteracy and low income of the population, radio is the medium with the greatest outreach. There are more than one million radios in the country, with some 3.5 million weekly listeners.[53] The first radio station in the country was established in 1929 by the United Fruit Company in Tela. The two largest radio networks in the country are HRN—The Voice of Honduras, and Radio América, which is owned by the leader of the PINU and often broadcasts news about worker and peasant issues. Radio Honduras is the government station. Both the Catholic Church and the evangelical community have radio stations, but unlike the evangelical station, the Radio Católica chain of transmitters has relatively little religious programming.

All television stations are privately owned and based either in San Pedro Sula or Tegucigalpa. Television was introduced in 1959, and about one-quarter of Hondurans now have access to television sets. Emisoras Unidas dominates television broadcasting, but Vica Televisión, which is owned by the Sikaffy family and other business investors in San Pedro Sula, is becoming increasingly competitive.[54]

Tiempo, arguably the country's most influential daily newspaper, is owned by Jaime Rosenthal, a banker and the controversial second vice president during the Azcona government. Based in San Pedro Sula, *Tiempo* is the country's most liberal newspaper; unlike the other papers, it has often criticized the military and police and regularly publishes liberal opinion articles. *La Prensa*, also based in San Pedro Sula, has close links with the commercial and industrial interests of that city; its editorial direction is conservative, extremely anticommunist, and pro–United States. *El Heraldo*, based in Tegucigalpa, is conservative and often closely reflects the opinions of the military and the National party. *La Tribuna*, based in Tegucigalpa and linked to the new industrial sector of the city, reflects the opinions of the orthodox Liberal party and is considered moderate and nationalistic in its editorial direction.

Repression, dependence on U.S. sources and programming, an environment of corruption and payoffs, poor technical quality, and the control of the media by oligarchic interests are all factors explaining the dismal state of news reporting in Honduras. The practice of self-censorship is also a serious problem. Honduran poet Roberto Sosa states that "in Honduras open censorship does not exist, but rather a more subtle form of censorship: self-censorship. Honduran reporters have not actually disappeared. But they have disappeared as thinking and inquisitive journalists, and this is worse. They are like zombies."[55]

Media owners and journalists have been careful not to cross an invisible line of what can and cannot be reported, especially about the *contras* and the military. When journalists do cross the line they are subject to arrest, harassment, blacklisting, and violence. Foreign journalists, particularly those who inquired too deeply about the relationship between the *contras* and Honduran military, have been deported or refused permission to enter the country.

The State of Health

The country's abject poverty is reflected in its deteriorating state of health. According to the Pan American Health Organization, health conditions in Honduras are among the worst in the hemisphere, and a recent study by the United Nations Fund for Children (UNICEF) revealed that malnutrition among Honduran children has worsened in the last two decades.[56] It is estimated that at least 12,000 Honduran children die each year, about thirty-six daily, from preventable illnesses.

The 1989 UNICEF study determined that 25 percent of Honduran families suffer from protein deficiency, 70 percent have inadequate iron intake, and 62 percent show calorie deficiency.[57]

Widespread malnutrition and the lack of access to potable water and sanitation facilities are the main factors in the country's low life expectancy (64.6 years) and high infant mortality (66 per 1,000 live births according to official estimates and 157 per thousand in rural areas according to a January 1989 report by the country's teaching hospital).[58] In 1988 only one-third of Hondurans had easy access to potable water and 50 percent did not have even the most rudimentary system for human waste disposal.[59]

In several areas of the country, severe malnutrition affects a quarter of the children entering first grade.[60] In rural areas, 77 percent of the population cannot afford food to provide them with minimal nutritional requirements.[61] Malnutrition, which had lessened in the 1960s and 1970s, worsened in the 1980s. Dr. Fidel Barahona, a Ministry of Public Health official, warned in 1988 that because of increasing malnutrition, coming generations of Hondurans would be mentally and physically less developed.[62]

Infectious and parasitic diseases are the leading causes of death and gastritis, enteritis, and tuberculosis are the country's main health problems according to the Ministry of Health. Health care is out of financial and geographic reach for most Hondurans. In the most isolated rural areas there are no doctors or nurses. Although government health clinics do exist, they are often little more than empty buildings without medicines or medical equipment. Another pressing problem is the lack of medicines in public health facilities. The ever worsening foreign-exchange crisis and new austerity measures have meant that there is less money available to import needed drugs. Even when hospitals do have medical supplies, they quickly disappear due to the widespread practice of stealing drugs from government health-care facilities to sell to private drugstores.[63]

The Ministry of Health has concluded that only 40 percent to 50 percent of the population has access to health-care services and that only 11 percent of the population is protected by the Honduran Institute of Social Security—despite constitutional guarantees of health care and social-security services.[64]

Religion

Although the Roman Catholic Church has enjoyed more than four and a half centuries in Honduras, it has never developed into a strong, indigenous institution.[65] Instead, it is one of the most dependent churches in Latin America. A symptom of this external dependence is the large number of expatriate clerics. Of the some 292 priests working in Honduras, only about seventy are natives.[66]

For the Catholic Church, the last three decades have been a time of rapid change and constant challenge.[67] The Catholic hierarchy, encouraged by the Vatican, began a concerted effort to consolidate and strengthen the institutional church and in 1959 called for an ambitious evangelization campaign to make the many Hondurans who were only culturally tied to the Catholic faith into practicing Catholics. The call went out from the Vatican to churches throughout the world to send missionaries and financial assistance to Honduras. Priests, brothers, and nuns from the United States, Spain, Canada, and France arrived in Honduras to carry out this mission of church-building and evangelization. By the late 1960s the number of dioceses had tripled, with most of them presided over by foreign-born bishops. The new missionaries confronted a nation of deeply religious people, but also one where superstition and magic were at least as important as Church dogma.

As the Church reached out to rural areas, it found a sea of illiteracy, poverty, and disease. As part of its evangelism, the Church tackled these tough socioeconomic problems with literacy and social-service programs. To a large extent, the Church's interest in improving *campesino* literacy was a direct outgrowth of its attempt to teach catechism; rural illiteracy was seen as a main obstacle to bringing Church doctrine to the rural poor.

As social conditions worsen in Honduras, the Church is gradually becoming an outspoken, albeit polite, critic of the government and the military. And once again there are signs that prophetic or socially committed priests are becoming a stronger force within the Catholic Church. As a result, repression against the clergy, particularly in poor rural areas, has intensified.

One factor that pushed the Church to assume a more critical posture was the arrival of refugees from Guatemala and El Salvador. The diocese of Santa Rosa de Copán denounced the Honduran military's repression of this refugee population. The local bishop assumed part of the responsibility of caring for the Salvadoran refugees, with CARITAS—the Catholic Church's relief arm—providing the refugees with food and other services. The diocese's refugee committee has played an important role in drawing national and international attention to these refugees. The killing of two CARITAS workers by the Honduran security forces induced the national Church hierarchy to condemn repressive conditions.

The government's acceptance of the right-wing, Unification Church—backed APROH, along with the worsening economic conditions in the country, the new militarism fueled by the United States, and the failure of the Suazo and Azcona governments to address the needs of the nation's poor, have also caused the institutional Church to become more outspoken about social issues in the 1980s. The creation of Church groups such as the Christian Movement for Justice and the continuing involvement of the clergy with refugees in rural areas have pushed the Church to assume a more committed social role in Honduran society too.

Protestant Churches and the New Evangelicals

In the 1980s evangelical churches and organizations emerged not only as a major religious force but also as sponsors of many social-service programs. *Evangélicos* (protestant groups), most of which receive U.S. supplies and financing, have exerted a significant conservative political influence on Honduras. Between 1978 and 1985 the number of evangelicals in Honduras doubled, and today approximately 12 percent of Hondurans profess to be evangelicals.[68] Only a small number of these belong to mainline protestant denominations such as the Lutheran church.

Today the largest evangelical churches in the country are the Assemblies of God, the Southern Baptists, and the Central American Mission. Most evangelical churches in Honduras are closely linked to U.S. denominations and groups, although churches based in Guatemala and El Salvador are also quickly gaining influence.

The pentecostal and neopentecostal groups, most of which are new to Honduras, have often been more aggressive politically than the older evangelical organizations. Indeed, many of them came to Honduras explicitly to fight communism. They chose Honduras because of the *contra* war and because they regard the country as a front line against communism. Allen Dansforth, for instance, the U.S. director of World Gospel Outreach, regards social assistance as a weapon against the spread of world communism.

There is, however, a sector of progressive evangelical organizations that is concerned about social-justice issues and that supports ecumenism. The Christian Development Commission (CCD), for example, has a reputation for effective, community-based development work. It is also true that although the hierarchy of most evangelical churches is very conservative, evangelical pastors on the local level are more concerned about social-justice issues.

Nongovernmental Organizations

Largely because of the country's important role in recent U.S. foreign policy, there was a rapid rise in nongovernmental organizations (NGOs) involved in development, refugee relief, business promotion, and social-service operations. Since 1980 the number of NGOs in Honduras has tripled, and most of this increase was in U.S. private and church organizations funded by the U.S. government.[69] Nowhere in Central America was the boom of NGOs linked to the United States so pronounced as in Honduras during the 1980s.

In the 1960s and early 1970s, several NGOs financed by the U.S. Agency for International Development (AID) also began operating in Honduras. These organizations were mostly involved in providing technical assistance, channeling credit, distributing food, or in the case of the American Institute for Free Labor Development (AIFLD), trying to establish a strong conservative pro-U.S. labor sector. Starting in 1962, AIFLD worked through the National Association of Honduran Peasants and the Confederation of Honduran Workers. Later, AID funds were also channeled to the Federation of Honduran Agrarian Reform Cooperatives. Most recently, AID has also channeled funds to the National *Campesino* Union, historically one of the more militant rural organizations.

The meteoric rise in the number of NGOs operating in Honduras in the last decade is almost totally attributable to AID. AID says it supports NGOs because they promote pluralism in Honduran society and are more efficient than government agencies. One common concern in Honduras is that AID itself is defining the boundaries of this pluralism. Most AID development funds go to groups that focus on entrepreneurship, export production, or paternalistic community development. Excluded from AID's funding programs are grass-roots peasant associations, militant trade unions, progressive development organizations, and human-rights groups.

Since 1980 AID has been responsible for creating at least ten organizations to promote the interests of the private business sector, particularly those entrepreneurs and investors involved in export production. AID funds also go to established business chambers like the Honduran-American Chamber of Commerce.

AID also directs funds to an array of service and development groups. AID funding resulted in the rapid expansion of a small umbrella organization for Honduran NGOs called FOPRIDEH (Federation of Private Development Organizations of Honduras). As AID funding to FOPRIDEH declined in 1989 and 1990, the organization adopted a more independent and politically progressive character.

Significantly, it is generally only those NGOs not receiving AID money that have maintained ties and work closely with the more progressive and independent peasant, worker, and community organizations. These NGOs rely mostly on European funding and stress that development work must be done in association with self-organized poor people's organizations.

Women and Feminism

In a region where women are generally consigned to inferior status in society, Honduran women are among the most abused and exploited. Statistics give some indication of the severity of discrimination against women. Approximately 40 percent of women have no schooling. Only 44 percent of children in primary school are female.[70] Of high school and university graduates, only 25 percent are women. Twenty-five percent of the paid workforce are women, yet almost half of all children are born to single mothers who head households.[71] Only one of the 134 deputies in the National Congress is a woman.[72]

Yet there is another reality not adequately portrayed by statistical data. In a society where base *machismo* is pervasive, women are often regarded as little more than sexual prey and cheap labor. The daily newspapers feature pinups to sell papers, and the political parties show seminude women dancing to sell their candidates. Sexual abuse and rape of young girls by male family members and neighbors is common. Indeed in many poor urban *barrios* few girls make it beyond their early teens without becoming sexual victims.

Irresponsible paternity is a common problem in Honduran society, one particularly widespread in rural areas. A study by the Overseas Education Fund found that 41 percent of the homes in twenty-nine Tegucigalpa neighborhoods were headed by women.[73] In rural Honduras, few people in this male-dominated culture marry because of expense. And when they do marry, peasant men commonly leave their wives and children to start new families elsewhere and only rarely feel responsible for the sustenance of all their offspring.

Fertility is the third highest in Latin America, and at least half of Honduran children are born out of wedlock.[74] Adding to the problem is that only about one-third of Hondurans use contraceptives, and abortion is illegal (as it is throughout Latin America with the exception of Cuba). Illegal abortions are available, but many women often resort to self-inflicted abortions.[75] Complications from botched abortions are one of the five leading causes of women's death in Honduras.[76] One of the most common means of birth control is sterilization, which many women have done without consulting their mates.

Legal protections against sex discrimination are not well developed and are only rarely enforced in Honduras. As the last Latin American country to grant women the right to vote (1954), Honduras has taken only limited steps to protect the rights of women. Single, childless women have no adjudicative land rights, whereas all males over sixteen years of age have such rights. When a landowner dies, his land passes directly to his oldest son—not to his widow, unless otherwise arranged. The country's penal code exempts husbands of culpability in cases of assault, battery, and even murder if his wife is caught in an adulterous act.[77] Only in 1984 did the country's family code give rights to children born out of wedlock, an important step in enforcing paternal responsibility.

Yet Honduras has a long and proud history of women organizing for their rights.[78] The Women's Culture Society, founded in 1923, was the nation's first women's organization. With close links to the communist-led Honduran Union Federation, the society led the fight for political and economic rights of Honduran women, with a special focus on the families of banana and mine workers. The Federation of Honduran Women's Associations was founded in 1950 to lead the fight for women's suffrage.

The Honduran Federation of Peasant Women (FEHMUC), founded in 1978, is one of the few female peasant organizations in Latin America. FEHMUC grew out of the rural Housewives' Clubs (CAC) within CARITAS (the Catholic Church's social-service organization) and the social-Christian peasant movement. Claiming that FEHMUC was becoming increasingly conservative and classist, a left-leaning faction split off in 1987 and founded the Council for Integrated Development of Peasant Women (CODIMCA). The League of Patriotic Honduran Women (LIMUPH), founded in 1988, works in the poor urban *barrios*. Another new women's organization is the Visitación Padilla Women's Committee, which has protested the U.S. military buildup and *contra* presence in Honduras, and has petitioned the National Congress to pass a law that would establish severe legal penalties for violence against women. Other organizations include the Center of Women's Studies, associated with the Liberal party; the Association of University Women; and a professional women's organization called the Committee for the Defense of Women's Rights (CLADEM).

Ethnic Groups and Native People

To a large degree Honduras is an ethnically homogeneous society with the population being about 90 percent *mestizo* (mixed Indian and Spanish). The remaining population is made up of 7 percent pure Indian, 2 percent black, and one percent Caucasian.[79] Spanish is the national language although Carib and Mayan dialects and English Creole are also spoken.

Honduras has two different black ethnic groups. The Antillean blacks, who live on the north coast and the Bay Islands, are descendants of laborers imported from Belize, the Cayman Islands, and Jamaica to work on the banana plantations. Along the Atlantic coast and on the Bay Islands there are communities of Garifuna, also known as Black Caribs; these are descendants of African slaves who found refuge among the Carib Indians in Saint Vincent, an island of the Lesser Antilles. Eventually these blacks became the dominant ethnic group on the island, and their own culture and language became mixed with those of the Carib Indian. There are some 70,000 Garifuna living in Honduras, most of whom are very poor.[80]

The indigenous population at the time of the Spanish conquest has been calculated at about 800,000, although other estimates rise as high as 1.4 million or more.[81] However, even before the conquest, Mayan civilization was in decline; the magnificent Copán religious and political center had been abandoned before the Spanish arrived. Estimates of the current Amerindian population in Honduras range from 157,000 to 450,000.[82]

There are two general groups of Honduran Indians: the settled agricultural communities of the west and the aboriginal Indians of the northern lowlands. Of the former group, the most important tribe is the Lenca, with the Chorti, Chorotega, and Pipil Indians also represented. Although most speak Spanish, they still retain cultural and religious traits that set them apart from the dominant *mestizo* population.[83] The Pipils, living mainly in the isolated La Mosquitia region and in Olancho and Yoro, are sometimes called the Forest Indians. They include the Miskito, Pech (Paya), Sumo, and Jicaque (Torpán) tribes. Because they are so isolated, they are less acculturated than those living in western Honduras.

Refugees and the Internally Displaced

Honduras is largely a host country rather than a source of refugees. Increasingly, however, Hondurans are leaving the country, mainly for

economic reasons but also because of increased human-rights violations. One indication of this is the increasing number of Hondurans
who are seeking political asylum in the United States.[84]

On the border of three countries torn by war, Honduras has been a
country of refuge for Guatemalans, Salvadorans, and Nicaraguans.
Approximately 60,000 refugees were under the care of the United
Nations High Commission on Refugees (UNHCR) by the mid-1980s
but the winding down of the *contra* war and mass repatriations of
Salvadorans have resulted in a steadily decreasing refugee population.
In addition to those refugees with official refugee status, Honduras is
host to an estimated 250,000 undocumented Central Americans,
many of whom are war refugees.[85]

Environment

The long disregard for the environment has created an ecological crisis
in Honduras, the consequences of which are just beginning to be
understood. In the south, desertification is well under way and may be
irreversible. The combination of wood-cutting and unsustainable agricultural practices, particularly in the cotton and cattle industries, have
denuded vast sections in this region. The result has been decreasing
rainfall and agricultural yields and widening food shortages. In the
rush to exploit the nation's forest reserves, roads have been bladed into
tropical forests, opening these areas not only to clear-cutting but to
colonization by land-hungry peasants and the abusive cattle industry.

Honduras is slowly waking up to the environmental crisis, but there is
still little environmental control. Honduras, for example, serves as a
regional export platform for parrots and other exotic wildlife. The few
cloud forests in Honduras continue to disappear at a rapid pace. And
the landscape has been raped so thoroughly that there is little hope for
Honduras to cash in on the booming international ecotourism business.

Forest cover in Honduras decreased from 63 percent in 1960 to 36
percent in 1980, and the country continued to lose 3.6 percent of its
remaining forests annually through the 1980s.[86] Most of the primary
hardwood forests that once covered parts of Honduras are now gone,
replaced by a secondary growth of pine, which is threatened by rapid
deforestation. At the current loss rate, the mature pine trees will be
completely gone in ten years and all the country's woodlands will vanish
in twenty years.[87] Cattle ranching, the timber industry, peasant colonization, and forest fires are among the main causes of this rapid deforestation. According to an archaic homesteading law, ranchers are
given title to land they clear and graze. The large cattle ranchers, a

powerful and reactionary group have forced small farmers off the land and blocked all attempts at regulation. Cattle ranchers also regularly pay landless peasants to clear forested lands to make room for future pastures. The timber industry is, however, the major culprit.

The use of DDT is still widespread in Honduras and high levels of DDT residues have been found in the fat tissues of many Hondurans. A 1981 study in Choluteca, a rice and cotton region in southern Honduras, showed that 10 percent of those living in the area showed high levels of intoxication.[88] In 1989 at least 129 Hondurans died from pesticide poisoning. Each year Honduras imports about $22 million in pesticides, but only 15 percent of the country's farmers receive any form of technical training in the proper use of these chemicals.[89] Not only are pesticides deadly for farmers but the country's food supplies have been found to carry high concentrations of these agrochemicals.

About 30 percent of Honduran land is currently dedicated to cattle ranching, including much of its limited fertile farmland.[90] Foreign-aid programs, including those of the U.S. Agency for International Development (AID) encourage the growth of this industry, despite its contribution to the country's serious deforestation and erosion problems. The spread of cattle across the Honduran landscape is a major factor in the country's declining per capita grain production. To meet the increasing demand for basic grains from the country's rapidly increasing population, small farmers have cleared new land. There were important gains in productivity made in the 1960s, but these have mostly been lost in the past two decades as the quality of the soil declines.

Overfishing also has had negative environmental and economic consequences. The conch population, for example, has been so depleted that there is no longer enough conch for either commercial exploitation or local consumption. The lobster and shrimp industries have also been severely affected. Honduran fishermen are often criticized for their practice of killing the endangered manatees in Guatemalan and Belizean waters and selling the meat of these large aquatic mammals in the Honduran market.

The deteriorating conditions in rural Honduras have resulted in the most rapid urbanization rate in Central America; the percentage of people living in urban areas rose from 18 percent in 1950 to 40 percent in 1985.[91] Forty years ago Tegucigalpa was a quaint town of 75,000. Today there are more than one million people living in this jungle of traffic jams, crime, and human desperation. The pine-clad hills that once surrounded the capital city have long since been stripped bare to make room for tens of thousands of wooden shacks. For the most part, these hovels lack basic water and sanitation services and although electricity is generally available few can afford the monthly charges. A survey by the National Water and Sewer Service found that of the 392 neighborhoods in Tegucigalpa, 219 are considered "marginal" because of their lack of basic services.[92]

Less than a third of the city's population has drinking water within their homes, and the rank-smelling Choluteca River is the only sewage system for many. There is a booming water-for-sale business in Tegucigalpa in which water of questionable quality is sold to desperate slum dwellers. Shifting cultivation, road building, and deforestation is undermining the nearby Los Laureles watershed and causing a rapid buildup in sedimentation in the reservoir that provides the city with 60 percent of its drinking water. Elsewhere in the country, the two new hydroelectric projects under construction, El Cajón and El Níspero, are already suffering from erosion problems related to the deforestation of surrounding watersheds. Floods are another problem. The peak runoff from steep watersheds is estimated at ten times more than when the mountains were heavily forested.[93]

FOREIGN INFLUENCE

U.S. Foreign Policy

During the 1980s large sums of U.S. economic assistance kept the economy afloat, and large allocations of U.S. military aid kept the armed forces acquiescent in the face of the "democratization" process and the expanding *contra* presence. In exchange, Washington relied on Honduras for close cooperation in its war of destabilization against Nicaragua. Honduras also became a base for a U.S. military buildup in which the Pentagon constructed an extensive infrastructure of air fields, bases, and radar sites in the country.

Washington will most likely remain committed to maintaining Honduras as a base for regional operations and intervention for many years to come, but the alliance faces a rocky future in the 1990s. Budget constraints, the fading Cold War, the Sandinista electoral defeat, and a rising chorus of funding demands from Nicaragua, Panama, and the Eastern European countries will make it more difficult for Washington to find sufficient funds to keep Honduras content with its present role. Total aid is expected to decline over the next few years, and as this flow of dollars slows, nationalistic and anti-U.S. tensions will sharpen.[94] These tensions will be also aggravated by the austerity measures and currency devaluation that the Callejas administration is likely to impose as a result of U.S. and IMF pressure.

Democracy, development, and stability have been the oft-repeated U.S. goals in Honduras. But after ten years of militarization on one hand and aid and intervention on the other, these goals still seem distant. In fact, rather than moving Honduras forward, the mix of U.S. policies and programs in Honduras appears to have sown the seeds of economic and political instability accompanied by repression and polarization. This failure can be attributed in part to the contradictory and misdirected character of U.S. economic and military assistance. But it also derives from the fact that Washington's interest in Honduras has been mainly a product of U.S. foreign-policy concerns in Nicaragua, El Salvador, and Guatemala.

The Bush administration seems determined to repeat and extend the mistakes of the previous administration. Rather than backing away from a one-sided commitment to the private sector, the new administration has deepened this commitment, with the U.S. embassy openly allying itself with the Honduras Private Enterprise Council (COHEP) and the narrow business interests of the National party.[95]

U.S. Trade and Investment

Ninety percent of the foreign investment in Honduras comes from the United States.[96] The United States is also the country's leading trading partner, supplying 39 percent of its imports and purchasing more than 50 percent of its exports.[97] The leading exports to the United States are fruit (bananas and citrus), coffee, seafood (shrimp), vegetables, and beef. Honduras, in turn, buys machinery, agricultural chemicals, and basic grains from the United States.

The book value of U.S. investment in Honduras is estimated to be $250 million, with the top three investors being United Brands, Castle & Cooke, and American Pacific Mining.[98] Close to three hundred U.S. companies do business in Honduras, including sixty of the top five hundred corporations in the United States.[99]

All three major U.S. banana companies have operations in Honduras. United Fruit and Standard Fruit's plantations date back almost one hundred years; RJ Reynolds (Del Monte) is a newcomer to the banana business. Castle & Cooke, owner of Standard Fruit, also produces pineapples and African palm oil and is experimenting with the production of winter vegetables. United Brands has African palm estates and cattle ranches in addition to its banana plantations.

The top three U.S. banks, Citicorp, BankAmerica, and Chase Manhattan, conduct business in Honduras. Citicorp has interests in Banco de Honduras while Chase Manhattan owns part of Banco Atlántida. In the manufacturing sector, Kimberly-Clark makes toilet paper, Beatrice produces snacks, Sterling Drug manufactures pills, United Brands makes plastics and vegetable oil, and Castle & Cooke is the country's major beer and soft-drink processor.[100] Among the other major industries dominated by U.S. investment are oil refining (Texaco), mining (American Pacific/AMAX), beef and poultry production, insurance, shrimp cultivation, and animal-feed production. The industrial parks in Puerto Cortés and Choloma, in the department of Cortés, have attracted a score of U.S. manufacturers, including Christian Dior, which produce apparel and other goods for the U.S. market.

Pressured by AID, the Honduran government has increased the incentives offered to foreign investors in the 1980s. Designed primarily to stimulate nontraditional export production by foreign investors, new measures include partial or total exemption from export taxes; the right to hold dollar-denominated accounts in the country; and easy capital repatriation. Honduran capitalists, resenting the privileged place given U.S. investors, succeeded in reducing major tax breaks that were suggested in the 1989 foreign investment law supported by AID.

Honduran businesses have also resisted U.S. efforts to liberalize all foreign trade. AID insists that trade liberalization (dropping all tariff barriers) would make Honduran industry more competitive but local businessmen protest that an increasing influx of foreign goods is killing domestic industries. Not only do new consumer products threaten local businesses but used clothing and shoes from the United States are flooding into the local market.

Most new U.S. investment in Honduras has been attracted by the provisions of the Caribbean Basin Initiative (CBI) and assorted U.S. government programs to promote export production. Several new business-promotion organizations funded by AID, including the Foundation for Investment and Export Development (FIDE) and the National Council to Promote Exports and Investment (CONAFEXI), offer generous lines of subsidized credit and marketing assistance to companies exporting to the United States. As a result of these efforts, U.S. imports of apparel from Honduras more than doubled and total U.S. imports of manufactured goods increased by 90 percent between 1983 and 1988.[101]

U.S. Economic Aid

During the 1980s Honduras ranked among the top ten recipients of U.S. economic assistance. Between 1981 and 1990 Honduras received

$711 million in ESF (Economic Support Funds), $370 million in Development Assistance, and $152 million in U.S. food aid. Not only did Honduras experience an unprecedented influx of economic aid during the 1980s, but for the most part this aid came in the form of direct grants rather than loans. Before 1984 grants composed only 30 percent to 40 percent of the U.S. economic-aid package, but between 1984 and 1988 more than 85 percent of U.S. economic aid consisted of grants.

The U.S. Agency for International Development (AID) has not used its economic-aid package to help Honduras tackle its deep structural problems such as land tenure patterns and declining per capita grain production. Nor has it insisted that the government and oligarchy develop strategies to meet the basic health, educational, and income needs of the country's impoverished majority. Instead AID has concentrated on implementing the macroeconomic and private-sector solutions that aggravate and accentuate the deep social and economic divisions in Honduras.[102]

AID has not only deepened the country's economic dependency; it has also further debilitated the country's governmental and non-governmental sectors. Through its agricultural, health, educational, finance, and other development programs, AID has created a "shadow government" in Honduras. Outside consultants have been placed in most ministries, and the government has become accustomed to turning to AID and the U.S. embassy for consultation and approval of most economic and political decisions. The same U.S. influence and control has come to pervade the nongovernmental sector as well—from the smallest social-service organizations to the country's largest business associations.

More than half of U.S. economic aid to Honduras during the 1980s has been in the form of ESF grants, which are primarily used to relieve the country's foreign-exchange crunch. Honduras qualifies for such a large commitment of ESF aid because the Pentagon and the State Department consider Honduras to be critical to U.S. security interests. The PL480 Title I food-aid program functions the same way in that it saves the country from using its limited foreign exchange to buy U.S. wheat.

At the same time that ESF and Title I ease the country's balance-of-payments crisis, they also provide the government and the private sector with a source of local currency to fund AID-approved programs. When private-sector importers and wheat mills buy U.S. dollars and U.S. wheat from the government, the local currency (*lempiras*) they use to make purchases is divided among government ministries, private development groups, and AID itself, according to agreements AID makes with the government.[103]

The basic thrusts of AID's economic-stabilization plan are to impose austerity measures on the Honduran economy that will cut budget deficits and allow the government to meet its debt payments, and to place private investment in export production at the center of the country's development strategy. According to this strategy, once the economy is stabilized and exports begin picking up, the benefits of growth will trickle down to the poor. But as AID has acknowledged, "implementation of a stabilization program will probably lower living standards and may well increase unrest among the country's already impoverished people in the short term."[104]

AID has had mixed success in forcing Honduras to implement its stabilization plan. Austerity measures have been set in place, and increased resources and incentives have been directed to the private sector. But as of early 1990 Honduras still had not devalued its currency, budget deficits remained high, and privatization had proceeded at a slower pace than AID demanded.

Outside the government, the private sector is the favored recipient of AID funds.[105] The economic assistance goes either directly to business associations or to development and social-service organizations that sponsor private-sector solutions to social and economic problems. The business community is also the main beneficiary of AID-generated credit and of policy reforms stipulated in economic-assistance agreements with the government.

Democracy-Strengthening Assistance

In the 1980s the U.S. government launched a new type of economic aid called "democracy-building" or "democracy-strengthening" assistance. Funds for these democracy projects are channeled through AID and the National Endowment for Democracy (NED), a government-funded private organization founded in 1983. In Honduras the democracy-strengthening projects have ranged from managing voter registration and the election process to training political leaders.

AID has funded virtually the entire electoral process in Honduras. It funds the National Registry of Persons and the National Elections Tribunal, the two institutions responsible for the registration of voters and management of the electoral process. The November 1989 presidential election was entirely paid for by U.S. taxpayers, including the paper and pens for and printing of the ballots; the voting tables and curtains for the voting booths; international observers; the election return system and monitoring center; and the labor to manage the elections.

AID paid for not only the mechanics of the election but also for the three-part civic-awareness campaign that preceded the voting. AID sponsored a six-month general education campaign in 1988 "designed to raise the awareness of the public about the advantages of the democratic system" and a 1989 voter-registration campaign and a second education campaign devoted to presenting "key issues and the presidential candidates' positions." Also sponsored were radio and television debates and newspaper summaries of candidate positions.[106]

The country's judicial and legislative institutions have also been included in AID's democracy-strengthening. Judges and legislators have been trained by AID consultants and provided with a wealth of written materials and information services. Although AID notes that the Honduran Congress and Supreme Court have been traditionally weak institutions, its institution-strengthening projects do not address or even mention the principal cause of their debility and lack of independence: the overriding power of the armed forces. Also considered part of AID's democracy program in Honduras is the Central America Peace Scholarship Program through which more than four thousand Hondurans will be schooled or trained in the United States by 1992.[107]

U.S. Military Aid

Between 1946 and 1980 Honduras received a total of $30.4 million in U.S. military loans and grants. Beginning in mid-1980 U.S. military assistance to Honduras rapidly increased, rising from $4 million in fiscal year 1980 to a high of $77 million in 1984. This rapid growth in U.S. military interests in Honduras was made possible by a 1982 amendment to a 1954 bilateral accord. It specifically allowed the United States to upgrade three major airfields and an unspecified number of smaller airstrips. The agreement was expanded again in 1988 to allow the United States to build a major radar station on the north coast.

Under consideration by the Honduran government is a revised military agreement—the third protocol of the 1954 agreement—which would permit the United States to build permanent military facilities in the country, owned by Honduras but run by U.S. forces. The agreement would also allow U.S. aircraft and ships to enter the country without prior permission from Honduran authorities.

The proposal has elicited strong opposition from popular sectors and President Callejas has said he opposes the establishment of permanent U.S. military installations in the country. The U.S. Embassy, however, stresses that the current GI presence contributes $45 million annually to the economy, a point that the government and private sector are certain to consider in evaluating the continuing U.S. military presence. The Foreign Ministry has asserted that having U.S. troops in Honduras "is still justified" because "fighting could possibly resume" in El Salvador and Honduras and the situation in Nicaragua is "very unstable."[108]

The three elements of the U.S. military assistance program are Foreign Military Sales (FMS); Military Assistance Program (MAP); and International Military Education and Training (IMET). During the 1980s most U.S. military aid (89 percent) was allocated under the MAP grant program. In 1990, however, the Department of Defense (DOD) switched its military assistance to the FMS program, and then placed all the FMS under the category of forgiven grant rather than the usual concessional sales.[109] Even in 1990, when the *contras* were under international pressure to dismantle and the Nicaragua government was abiding by the regional peace accords, the DOD request said that a continued large military-aid program was "critical to military modernization and professionalization to counter the Sandinista threat."[110]

During the 1980s the only Latin American country to receive more military training under the IMET program was El Salvador. The IMET program provided military education to 9,500 Honduran military officials in the United States and other locations from 1980 to 1989.[111] In addition to the IMET training at the U.S. army School of the Americas (in Panama and after 1985 at Fort Benning, Georgia), Honduran troops were trained by Mobile Training Teams (MTTs) of U.S. Special Forces (Green Berets), which entered the country for short periods to train entire units in counterinsurgency tactics and other military skills.

Outside the three main categories of military aid (MAP, FMS, IMET), the Honduran military benefited from an array of other U.S. military-aid programs. Under the Overseas Security Assistance Management Program, the United States stationed military managerial personnel in Honduras. In the 1980s nearly $2 million was authorized each year for this management program.[112] Honduras has also benefited from DOD military construction grants, which financed the construction and maintenance of foreign military bases. (Once constructed, the base is turned over to the host country, but the U.S. military retains access and perusal rights to the facility.) In 1987 and 1988 more than $4.1 million was spent each year for U.S. military construction in Honduras.[113]

In 1985 Congress authorized an exemption for Honduras and El Salvador from the prohibition of using U.S. aid for foreign police forces. In Honduras, $2.8 million was authorized for the program to supply the Honduran Public Security Forces (FUSEP) and other national police with training, riot-control gear, weapons, vehicles, and communications equipment.[114] Aid to the Honduran police has also been provided under the Anti-Terrorism Assistance program, which is managed by the State Department's Bureau of Diplomatic Security. Other police training has been sponsored by the International Criminal Investigative Training Assistance Program (ICITAP) run by the U.S. Justice Department.

The U.S. military-assistance program in Honduras is supporting the Honduran Force Modernization Plan—a plan to increase the strength and mobility of the Honduran armed forces.[115] Among the plan's specific objectives are developing an effective counterinsurgency capacity, bolstering the army's ability to patrol the Salvadoran border, and building a deterrent force for national defense. Extensive U.S. support has also been given for psychological operations, intelligence, and civil affairs. The most expensive component of U.S. aid has been DOD support for the Honduran air force. In 1987 the United States agreed to replace the country's Super Mystere jet fleet with twelve highly sophisticated F-5 jet fighters.[116] The United States also provided two C-130 transport aircraft for remote operations support. It is upgrading the country's fleet of A-37 aircraft as well.[117]

U.S. Military Facilities and Maneuvers

More than simply a recipient of generous U.S. military aid and training, Honduras in the 1980s became a U.S. military outpost. The Enrique Soto Cano Air Base (formerly Palmerola) outside Comayagua, constructed in 1983, is operated by the Honduran air force but functions as the nerve center of U.S. military operations in Honduras. Stationed at the huge base is Joint Task Force Bravo (JTFB), a contingent of 1,100 U.S. troops and about half that number of Honduran soldiers. JTFB, which is a joint U.S. army and air force command, coordinates U.S. military operations as well as the joint operations of U.S. and Honduran forces.

Joint maneuvers with the Honduran military have been conducted since 1965, but the frequency and scale of these training exercises picked up in the 1980s. Using DOD general funds, the Pentagon launched a series of more than six dozen military maneuvers that brought tens of thousands of U.S. troops (regular forces and the National Guard) to Honduras. The maneuvers, according to the DOD, have the following broad objectives: help develop Honduras's defenses; improve readiness skills of U.S. forces in deploying overseas; and demonstrate U.S. commitment to the democratic nations of the region.[118] In practice, these exercises trained U.S. invasion forces for the Central American climate and terrain and built up a military infrastructure along the Nicaraguan border. A related objective was to provide an infrastructure of logistical support for the *contras*.

Since 1983 Honduras has experienced an almost unbroken series of joint maneuvers. Besides playing out invasion and defense strategy, the maneuvers are designed to militarize Honduras. As part of the military games and training exercises, roads have been built, airfields constructed, barracks erected, tank traps dug, radar stations established, and ocean ports upgraded.[119]

REFERENCE NOTES

[1] Unless otherwise cited, all material in this section is based on James A. Morris's excellent study of Honduran politics. See "The State and Elections" in James A. Morris, *Honduras: Caudillo Politics and Military Rulers* (Boulder: Westview Press, 1984), pp. 60–73.

[2] More details on the history of Honduran political parties and their internal factions can be found in Morris, ibid., pp. 74–78; Margarita Oseguera de Ochoa, *Honduras Hoy: Sociedad y Crisis Regional* (Tegucigalpa: CEDOH/ CRIES, 1987), pp. 98–112; Richard Lapper and James Painter, *Honduras: State for Sale* (London: CIIR/Latin American Bureau, 1985), pp. 7–10; and "Elecciones Otra Vez," *Boletín Informativo*, CEDOH, October 1989, pp. 8–12.

[3] "Un Cristiani para Honduras?" *Pensamiento Propio*, November 1989, p. 36.

[4] American Friends Service Committee, "Honduras into the 1990s," April 1, 1990.

[5] Good accounts of the elections held in Honduras since 1980 can be found in Leyda Barbieri, "Honduran Elections and Democracy: Withered by Washington" (Washington, D.C.: Washington Office on Latin America, February 1986), and Morris J. Blachman, William M. LeoGrande, and Kenneth Sharpe, *Confronting Revolution: Security Through Diplomacy in Central America* (New York: Pantheon Books, 1986), pp. 129–130 and 151–152.

[6] *Boletín Informativo*, December 1989, p. 1.

[7] As a result of the 1989 elections, the National party candidates will occupy 73 percent of the municipal and mayoral posts, including Tegucigalpa and San

Pedro Sula, and the party will have seventy-one representatives in Congress to the Liberals' fifty-five.

[8] An outstanding analysis of the roots of Honduran foreign policy and the major issues confronting the country from 1975 to 1985 is Ernesto Paz, "The Foreign Policy and National Security of Honduras," in Mark B. Rosenberg and Philip L. Shepherd, eds., *Honduras Confronts Its Future: Contending Perspectives on Critical Issues* (Boulder: Lynne Rienner Publishers, 1986), pp. 181–209.

[9] *Honduras Update*, October 1987, p. 2.

[10] *Boletín Informativo*, October 1984, cited in Alison Acker, *Honduras: The Making of a Banana Republic* (Boston: South End Press, 1988), p. 122.

[11] For one account of the court proceedings, see Americas Watch, "Honduras: Without the Will," 1989, pp. 69–77.

[12] The evidence singled out the Battalion 3/16 as the chief security force responsible for the crimes. A wealth of information on the methods used by Battalion 3/16, its links with the CIA and *contras*, the location of clandestine jail cells, and the Honduran officers involved may be found in "A Death Squad Defector's Story," in Americas Watch, "Human Rights in Honduras: Central America's Sideshow," 1987, pp. 126–143.

[13] The lower figure is cited in *The Military Balance, 1988–1989* (London: The International Institute for Strategic Studies, 1989), p. 198. The higher figure was cited for 1988 in "Informe Especial: Distensión No Pasa por Centroamérica," *Inforpress Centroamericana*, December 7, 1989.

[14] Cited in U.S. Embassy, "Handbook on Honduras: Democracy, Defense, Development, Diplomacy, and Drug Control" (Tegucigalpa: Fall 1988).

[15] Raúl Sohr, *Centroamérica en Guerra* (Mexico: Alianza Estudios, 1989), cited in *Inforpress Centroamericana*, December 7, 1989.

[16] George Thomas Kurian, *Encyclopedia of the Third World, Third Edition* (New York: Facts on File, 1987). This source cites twenty-five combat aircraft, to which must be added the twelve F-5 fighters acquired in 1989. Total of 120 aircraft cited in U.S. Embassy, "Handbook on Honduras," op. cit.

[17] U.S. Embassy, "Handbook on Honduras," op. cit.

[18] The main sources consulted for the national-security doctrine and militarization in Honduras were *NACLA Report on the Americas*, January-February 1988; *Honduras: Fuerzas Armadas 1988, Contrainsurgencia Interna y Disuasión Regional* (Mexico: Instituto de Investigaciones Socioeconómicas de Honduras, 1988); Oseguera de Ochoa, op. cit., pp. 53–63; and "Military Impact Indicators," *Honduras Update*, March 1987, pp. 1–3.

[19] *Boletín Informativo*, CEDOH, July 1989, p. 3.

[20] Accessible accounts of the activities of Battalion 3/16 include George Black, "Dirty Hands in Honduras: The Many Killers of Father Carney," *The Nation*,

January 23, 1988; *New York Times*, June 5, 1988; and Julia Preston, "Honduras Accused of Death Squad Operations," *Washington Post*, November 1, 1988.

21 See COHA, "12th Annual Report on Human Rights in Latin America," December 25, 1988, and "Surge la 'Triple A' en Honduras," *Boletín Informativo*, April 1988, p. 16.

22 See *News from Americas Watch*, March 1989.

23 See CODEH, "The Situation of Human Rights in Honduras: 1988" (Tegucigalpa: February 1989); and *Boletín Informativo*, April 1989, p. 4.

24 Cited in *Boletín Informativo*, March 1989.

25 See Roger Burbach, "Restive Honduran Military, Ready to Bite the Hand that Feeds It," *Pacific News Service*, January 23, 1989.

26 Figures from Interamerican Children's Institute, cited in *Hondupress*, August 22, 1989.

27 Cited in *Honduras Update*, March 1987, p. 6.

28 *Economic and Social Progress in Latin America: 1989*, Inter-American Development Bank, p. 14.

29 *CEPAL Review*, April 1984.

30 The performance in the 1980s of Honduras's top four nontraditional exports, which together account for more than 25 percent of income from all nontraditionals, has been mixed: palm oil has grown substantially, pineapple and fruit conserves have increased modestly, and manufactured wood products have seen a dramatic decrease. Eva Paus, ed., *Struggle Against Dependence: Nontraditional Export Growth in Central America and the Caribbean* (Boulder: Westview Press, 1988), p. 125.

31 *Business Latin America*, November 27, 1989, p. 379.

32 Agriculture employs more than 50 percent of the labor force, its share of the GDP is 27 percent, and agricultural products account for 58 percent of export revenues. See George Thomas Kurian, *Encyclopedia of the Third World*, op. cit., p. 855; and *Economic and Social Progress in Latin America: 1989 Report*, Inter-American Development Bank.

33 In 1988 some 59 percent of the population lived in rural areas, down from 65 percent in 1980 and 70 percent in 1974.

34 *Encyclopedia of the Third World*, op. cit., p. 855.

35 This information is taken from Honduras background material supplied to Peace Corps volunteers, 1985, pp. 15–17.

36 U.S. Agricultural Attaché Report, #HO-9002, "Honduras Agricultural Situation," April 4, 1989, p. 25.

37 Food and Agricultural Organization, *Food Security in Latin America and the Caribbean*, June 1984; Tom Barry, *Roots of Rebellion: Land and Hunger in Central America* (Boston: South End Press, 1987).

[38] *Hondupress*, April 18, 1989.

[39] For a full treatment of the objectives and consequences of the U.S. food-aid program see Rachel Garst and Tom Barry, *Feeding the Crisis: U.S. Food Aid and Agricultural Policy in Central America* (Lincoln: University of Nebraska Press, forthcoming).

[40] Roger Norton and Carlos Benito, "Evaluation of the PL480 Title I Program in Honduras," Winrock International for AID-Honduras, 1987.

[41] For one good analysis of the agrarian-reform program, see Medea Benjamin, "Campesinos: Between Carrot and Stick," in *NACLA Report on the Americas*, January–February 1988, pp. 22–30.

[42] "El Modelo Asiático No Es una Solución," *Pensamiento Propio*, September 1988.

[43] *Heraldo*, May 12, 1989, cited in *Boletín Informativo*, May 1989, p. 5.

[44] *Boletín Informativo*, CEDOH, November 1988.

[45] U.S. Embassy, *Foreign Labor Trends: Honduras* (Tegucigalpa: U.S. Department of Labor, 1987).

[46] Other APU members include the COPEMH Defense Front, Black Fraternal Organization of Hondurans, Coordinating Block of Patronatos, Workers Union of the Institute of Professional Instruction, Housing Institute Union, Progressive Student Front-April 30, and the Industrial Packaging Union.

[47] Two comprehensive accounts of Honduran trade unions are Mario Posas, "El Movimiento Sindical Hondureño Durante la Década de los Ochenta," CEDOH Special Edition, No. 44, October 1989; and Neale J. Pearson, "Honduras," in Gerald Michael Greenfield and Sheldan L. Maran, eds., *Latin American Labor Organizations* (Westport, CT: Greenwood Press, 1987), pp. 463–494.

[48] For an excellent overview of the Honduras labor movement see Mario Posas, "El Movimiento Sindical Durante La Década del Ochenta," *Honduras Especial* (CEDOH), October 1989, No. 44.

[49] For more information on *solidarismo* in Honduras, see CEDOH Special Edition, October 1989, pp. 11–13; and *Central America Report*, December 9, 1988, pp. 382–383.

[50] Ministry of Public Education, cited in *Tiempo*, June 14, 1989.

[51] National Census of Population and Dwellings, 1988, sponsored with the support of the UN Population Fund.

[52] U.S. Agency for International Development, *Honduras: Country Development Strategy Statement FY1986* (Washington, D.C.: AID, May 1984), p. 23.

[53] U.S. Embassy, "Honduras," January 1, 1989.

[54] Ibid.

[55] Comité de los Periodistas de los Estados Unidos, *La Prensa Hondureña: Un*

Periodismo del Silencio (Tegucigalpa: Escuela de Periodismo de UNAH, 1984).

56 Rosa Morazán, "Malnutrition: The Child's Side of the Crisis," *Hondupress*, December 15, 1989; *Encyclopedia of the Third World*, op. cit.

57 Morazán, op. cit., citing UNICEF study.

58 U.S. Agency for International Development, *Congressional Presentation FY1990, Annex II, Latin America and the Caribbean* (Washington, D.C.: AID, 1989).

59 *Tiempo*, May 11, 1988, quoting Minister of Health Rubén Villeda Bermúdez.

60 *Primer Censo Nacional de Talla en Escolares de Primer Grado* (Ministerio de Educación Pública, 1987).

61 Tom Barry, *Roots of Rebellion*, op. cit., p. 16, citing CEPAL and AID statistics.

62 *Tribuna*, November 8, 1988.

63 *Centroamérica Hoy*, May 17, 1989.

64 Dr. Carlos Godoy Arteaga, *El Sistema Unico de Salud y Seguridad Social* (Tegucigalpa: self-published, 1988), p. 9.

65 This section on religion is excerpted from *Directory and Analysis: Private Organizations with U.S. Connections—Honduras* (Albuquerque: The Resource Center, 1988).

66 *Tribuna*, August 21, 1989.

67 For a history of the Catholic Church in Honduras see José María Tojeira, *Panorama Histórico de la Iglesia en Honduras* (Tegucigalpa: CEDOH, 1986).

68 World Vision, "Analysis de la Realidad Nacional de Honduras," 1988.

69 *Directory and Analysis: Private Organizations with U.S. Connections—Honduras*, op. cit.

70 Acker, op. cit.

71 Melba Reyes, "Situación de la Mujer en Honduras," *Paz y Soberanía*, March 6, 1988.

72 *Encyclopedia of the Third World*, op. cit.

73 Cited in Dolly Pomerieau, "Women in Honduras," *Honduras: A Look at the Reality* (Hyattsville, MD: Quixote Center, July 1984).

74 Reyes, op. cit.

75 Nancy Peckenham and Annie Street, "Women: Honduras' Marginalized Majority," in *Honduras: Portrait of a Captive Nation* (New York: Praeger, 1985).

76 *Hondupress*, December 6, 1989.

77 Reyes, op. cit.

78 Peckenham and Street, op. cit.

79 *Encyclopedia of the Third World*, op. cit., p. 849.

80 Melanie Counce and William Davidson, "Indians of Central America 1980s," *Cultural Survival Quarterly*, 1989, Vol. 13, No. 3, pp. 38–39.

[81] Linda Newson, *The Cost of Conquest: Indian Decline in Honduras Under Spanish Rule* (Boulder: Westview Press, 1986).

[82] The high estimate comes from the Consejo Asesor Hondureño para el Desarrollo de las Etnicas Autóctonas (CAHDEA); the lower estimate was reported in Counce and Davidson, op. cit.

[83] *Encyclopedia of the Third World*, op. cit., p. 849.

[84] Of the 27,500 asylum requests processed by the U.S. Immigration and Naturalization Service (INS) in Texas during the last half of 1988, 11 percent of the applicants were Hondurans. *Washington Report on the Hemisphere*, February 1, 1989.

[85] Figures for January 1989 from United Nations High Commission on Refugees, "Information Paper," International Conference on Central American Refugees, Guatemala City, May 29–31, 1989.

[86] H. Jeffrey Leonard, *Natural Resources and Economic Development in Central America* (New Brunswick, NJ: Transaction Books, 1987), pp. 99, 120.

[87] JRB Associates, *Honduras: Environmental Profile* (Washington, D.C.: AID, 1982).

[88] Leonard, op. cit., pp. 146, 149.

[89] *Hondupress*, October 5, 1981.

[90] Leonard, op. cit., p. 99.

[91] United Nations, "Estimates and Projections of Urban, Rural, and City Populations, 1950–2025," Department of International Economic and Social Affairs, 1985.

[92] *Hondupress*, September 28, 1989.

[93] Ibid., p. 135.

[94] For discussion of Honduran nationalism see David Ronfeldt, *U.S. Involvement in Central America: Three Views from Honduras* (RAND Corporation, July 1989).

[95] During the early 1980s COHEP resisted the complete implementation of AID's neoliberal remedies and AID directed most of its private-sector support assistance through a new breed of export-oriented business associations, most of which were created by AID. But AID never broke the hegemony of COHEP, and there was a realignment between AID and COHEP that opened the way for AID funding of COHEP beginning in 1988. For more background see Tom Barry, *Rain of Dollars* (Albuquerque: The Resource Center, 1986), and Benjamin Crosby, "Crisis y Fragmentación: Relaciones entre los Sectores Público-Privado en Centroamérica" (Latin American and Caribbean Center, Florida International University, May 1985).

[96] U.S. Embassy, *Foreign Economic Trends and Their Implications for the United States* (Washington, D.C.: U.S. Department of Commerce, June 1989).

[97] Ibid.

[98] U.S. Department of Commerce, "Business Fact Sheets: Honduras," June 1989.

[99] Resource Center Compilation of Corporations (Albuquerque: The Resource Center, 1986).

[100] Ibid.

[101] *CBI Business Bulletin*, November–December 1988.

[102] For a more thorough examination of AID in Honduras and Central America see Tom Barry and Debra Preusch, *The Soft War: The Uses and Abuses of U.S. Economic Aid in Central America* (New York: Grove Press, 1988) and Philip Shepherd, "The Honduran Economic Crisis and U.S. Economic Assistance: A Critique of Reaganomics for Honduras," unpublished manuscript.

[103] Estimated ESF local currency expenditures for 1988 were divided into four categories: $26.3 million for Public Development Activities, $37.5 million in Private Sector Programs, $11.7 million for the Public Sector Recurrent Budget, and $6.8 million for the AID Trust Fund. Figures from AID's "FY1990 Annual Budget Submission."

[104] U.S. Agency for International Development, *Honduras: Country Development Strategy Statement FY1986* (Washington, D.C.: AID, May 1984), p. 5. The statement continues, "The painful and wrenching adjustments that will take place during the retrenchment will temporarily dash the hopes of many for improved living standards. Low-income rural families will see their earnings diminish to the extent that the cost of transportation, imported agricultural inputs, and consumer goods rise in relation to the prices they can obtain for their products. The urban unemployed are the most likely to give up hope and look for solutions that threaten political stability. . . . Thus, some of our assistance must be aimed at helping the government minimize social unrest during this difficult period."

[105] Planning Minister Francisco Figueroa in 1987 revealed that 50 percent of the local currency created by ESF payments went directly to the private sector and that the government did not exercise any control over these grants. *Tribuna*, March 24, 1987.

[106] U.S. Agency for International Development, *Honduras Project Paper: Strengthening Democratic Institutions*, 1987, Project No. 522–0296.

[107] U.S. Agency for International Development, *Congressional Presentation, FY1990, Annex III* (Washington, D.C.: AID, 1989), p. 107.

[108] *Washington Report on the Hemisphere*, July 11, 1990.

[109] Honduras has an overdue FMS debt from the 1970s of $9 million. U.S. Government Accounting Office, *Security Assistance: Update of Programs and Related Activities* (Washington, D.C.: GAO, December 1988), p. 21.

[110] U.S. Department of Defense, *Congressional Presentation for Security Assistance Programs FY1990* (Washington, D.C., 1989), p. 161.

[111] Between 1946 and 1986, some 3,100 Honduran officers and enlisted men received training at the U.S. army School of the Americas.

[112] U.S. Government Accounting Office, *Security Assistance: Update of Programs and Related Activities* (Washington, D.C.: GAO, December 1988), p. 52.

[113] Ibid., p. 54.

[114] Ibid., p. 59.

[115] In 1983 the DOD formulated a "Force Modernization" plan for Honduras that called for an annual U.S. military aid commitment of $100 million for four years. U.S. Embassy, "U.S. Military Activities in Honduras" (Tegucigalpa: February 1984).

[116] The $74.5 million military-assistance package included ten FE-5 fighter jets and two F-5 training aircraft. These Mach 1.1 supersonic jets are superior to any other aircraft in Central America and replace the French Super Mysteres, which had been the most sophisticated in the region. See "Statement of Edward L. King before the Subcommittee on Arms Control and Scientific Affairs and Western Hemispheric Affairs," May 19, 1987.

[117] U.S. Embassy, "Handbook on Honduras," op. cit.

[118] U.S. Department of Defense, "Training U.S. National Guard Engineers in Honduras: 'General Terencio Sierra,' " 1986.

[119] *Honduras: A U.S. Base for Intervention* (Philadelphia: NARMIC/American Friends Service Committee, March 1989); and *Honduras: Fuerzas Armadas 1988* (Mexico: Instituto de Investigaciones Socioeconómicas de Honduras-INSEH, 1989).

Chapter Six

NICARAGUA

CHRONOLOGICAL HISTORY

1821   Central America declares its independence from Spain.

1852   Liberals and Conservatives finally agree to name Managua as the capital.

1855   In order to secure the rights to a canal for the United States, mercenary William Walker hires an army, invades Nicaragua, and declares himself president. Walker reestablishes slavery in the country and is subsequently recognized by Washington.

1857   Walker is overthrown and constitutional rule reestablished.

1860   Under the Treaty of Managua, part of the Atlantic coast is declared a reserve under British protection, although Nicaraguan sovereignty over the region is recognized.

1893   Nationalist José Santos Zelaya comes to power.

1894   U.S. troops intervene four times in the next five years.

1905   The British relinquish all claims to the Mosquito Coast in the Harrison-Altamirano Treaty, granting certain protections to Miskito and Creole populations.

1910–11 U.S. troops intervene. United States places Nicaragua under customs receivership, controlling the country's revenues for the next thirty-eight years.

1912   U.S. marines begin twenty years of repeated occupation of Nicaragua.

1916   Bryan-Chamorro Treaty confirms Nicaragua's status as U.S. protectorate.

1926   U.S. marines land and occupy the country almost continuously until 1933, mounting what would become Central America's first counterinsurgency war against a peasant army, led by Augusto C. Sandino, the "General of Free Men."

1932   Liberal Juan Batista Sacassa elected president.

1933   After failing to defeat Sandino's guerrilla army, the marines withdraw, having established the Nicaraguan National Guard with Anastasio Somoza García as commander-in-chief.

1934   Sandino is murdered.

1936   Sacassa removed by Somoza's forces; presidential election won by Somoza.

1950   Somoza reelected; new constitution promulgated.

1956   Somoza assassinated; National Assembly selects his son Luis to complete the term in office.

1957   Luis Somoza elected president.

1961   Carlos Fonseca, Tomás Borge, and Silvio Mayorga form the *Frente Sandinista de Liberación Nacional* (FSLN).

1967   Luis Somoza dies; his brother Anastasio Somoza Debayle elected president.

1971   Congress dissolves itself, abrogates the constitution and transfers executive power to President Somoza pending new constitution.

1972   Earthquake devastates Managua; Somoza named chairman of National Emergency Committee and declares martial law.

1974   Somoza reelected.

1977   Martial law lifted.

        Major FSLN offensive.

1978   Pedro Joaquín Chamorro, editor of *La Prensa* and leading opposition figure, is assassinated.

        FSLN commando seizes National Palace.

        FSLN-led insurrection takes Masaya, León, Chinandega, and Estelí for several days.

1979   FSLN units take León and Matagalpa, and begin march on Managua. The FSLN triumphantly enters Managua and installs a revolutionary government.

1981   United States cuts off $9.8 million in food aid to Nicaragua. Washington suspends all bilateral aid to Nicaragua, but continues support to private sector and Catholic Church.

        Reagan administration authorizes $19 million to destabilize Nicaraguan government, giving the CIA a green light to organize ex–National Guard members into a counterrevolutionary (*contra*) army based in Honduras.

1982   Some 10,000 Miskitos flee to Honduras.

          Following *contra* destruction of two bridges in the north, the
          government declares a state of emergency.

          U.S. Congress approves $24 million in covert aid to the *con-
          tras*.

1983   The Contadora Group, formed by Mexico, Venezuela, Co-
          lombia, and Panama, declares an avoidance of the outbreak
          of war between Nicaragua and Honduras to be the initial
          focus of its negotiating mission.

          First large-scale invasion of *contras* from Honduran territory.
          In the United Nations, Nicaragua denounces U.S. support
          for the *contras*.

          U.S. Treasury Department announces official policy of op-
          posing all multilateral loans to Nicaragua.

          Patriotic Military Service (draft) instituted.

          The *contras* launch their Black September offensive. *Contra*
          offensive deepens with heavy fighting in the north and
          south, eight aerial attacks, and sabotage actions against the
          ports of Corinto and Sandino.

1984   CIA and Pentagon units assist the *contras* in the mining of
          Nicaraguan harbors in gross violation of international law.
          Seven ships are damaged by the mines. The International
          Court of Justice orders the United States to suspend the
          mining of Nicaraguan ports and support for the *contras*.

          Nicaragua agrees to proposed Contadora peace plan; Rea-
          gan administration asks Honduras, El Salvador, and Costa
          Rica to demand changes in the plan.

          Nicaragua holds first free elections in history. The FSLN's
          candidate Daniel Ortega is elected to a six-year term with 67
          percent of the vote against six opposition parties. Reagan
          denounces the elections as a sham.

1985   Economic stabilization package implemented.

          White House declares trade embargo against Nicaragua and
          U.S. Congress approves $27 million in "humanitarian" aid to
          the *contras*.

1986 $100 million *contra* aid package approved by U.S. Congress.

1987   New constitution signed.

CENTRAL AMERICA INSIDE OUT

350

Presidents of Costa Rica, El Salvador, Guatemala, Honduras, and Nicaragua sign the Esquipulas II peace accords.

The government announces an end to all prior censorship of the media.

1988   Nicaragua announces its disposition to enter into direct talks with the *contras* and lifts the five-year state of emergency.

Provisional government-*contra* cease-fire signed in Sapoá.

After another round of dialogue with the government, the *contras* break off peace talks.

Hurricane Joan passes through Nicaragua, leaving an estimated $800 million in damages.

1989   The Costa del Sol summit of Central American presidents calls for the elaboration of a plan to disband the *contra* army. U.S. Congressional Bipartisan Accord results in the approval of $49.75 million in nonlethal aid to keep the *contras* intact.

In compliance with the Costa del Sol accords, Nicaragua's media and electoral laws are modified.

Sept.   Nicaraguan Opposition Union (UNO) selects *La Prensa*'s Violeta Chamorro and the Liberal party's (PLI) Virgilio Godoy to lead the opposition ticket in the 1990 presidential elections. U.S. Congress approves overt aid for the UNO campaign.

Following a sharp escalation in *contra* attacks against civilians, the government suspends its unilateral cease-fire and launches an offensive. Representatives from the government and *contras* meet face-to-face for the first time in more than a year to work out a plan for *contra* demobilization.

1990   Violeta Chamorro wins February 25 election with nearly 60 percent of vote. Chamorro inaugurated in April and FSLN assumes new role as opposition party.

Sources for the chronology include Gerald Greenfield and Sheldon Maran, eds., *Labor Organizations in Latin America* (Westport, CT: Greenwood Press, 1987); "Chronology of Key Events in the Atlantic Coast, 1979–89," *Envío*, April 1989, p. 30; "For the Record: Chronology of Nicaragua's Compliance," *Central America Bulletin*, June 1988, pp. 8–9; *Conflict in Central America* (London: Longman Group Ltd., 1987), pp. 68–70; Tom Barry and Debra Preusch, *The Central America Fact Book* (New York: Grove Press, 1986), pp. 312–318.

TRENDS

- Rather than stabilizing Nicaragua, the Sandinista defeat and the end of the war gave rise to new conflicts between economic classes and political factions, with Nicaraguan society facing the specter of prolonged instability.
- Unable to attract substantial sums of foreign aid and faced with the limits of its own economic plan, which emphasizes liberalization and privatization, the government is finding that economic recovery is as elusive as ever. Cuts in government services and the rollback of the social gains of the revolution, combined with the economic slump, are resulting in unprecedented levels of unemployment, hunger, and misery.
- The UNO coalition will undergo repeated fragmentation and re-configuration as it faces both its own centrifugal tendencies and the tough political and economic challenges of governing.
- The FSLN faces the task of redefining itself to fulfill its three roles of revolutionary front, a democratic opposition party, and leader of the popular movement. Divisions within the party and the popular movement make this a difficult challenge, but the historical prag-matism and maturity of the FSLN will likely keep the party strong.

Ask Nicaraguans how they would compare themselves with their Central American neighbors and you are likely to be hit with a chorus of boasts and pejoratives. Not unlike their neighbors, Nicaraguans (known as *Nicas* or *pinoleros*) consider themselves distinct. The 3.5 million inhabitants of the largest country in Central America are proud of what sets them apart, and often reject things foreign. Some of the Nicaraguans' sense of independence and nationalism can be attributed to the country's long history of resistance to U.S. domination, dating back to the struggle against the adventurism of U.S. filibuster William Walker in the 1850s and to the guerrilla war waged by Augusto César Sandino against the U.S. marines in the 1920s and 1930s.

351

Decades of dictatorship, followed by eight years of war, and U.S. financial aggression have taken a heavy toll: Underdevelopment and poverty pervade the physical landscape throughout Nicaragua. Although the Sandinistas attempted to reduce inequalities through the redistribution of national wealth and income, they eventually realized that a small pie can be cut only so many times. In stark contrast to neighboring Costa Rica, and to a lesser extent Guatemala and El Salvador, even the most basic infrastructure is conspicuously absent. Outside of the cities there are few paved roads, other than the deteriorated two-lane highways that link the capital with Pacific ports and border crossings. Access to safe water is still a luxury; in Managua, less than half the population enjoys running water in their homes, in the countryside less than one in ten.[1] Outside of urban offices and the wealthier *barrios*, telephone service is practically nonexistent.

The political history of Nicaragua throughout most of this century has been dominated by two forces: *somocismo* and *sandinismo*. The guerrilla struggle of nationalist hero Augusto César Sandino in the 1920s and 1930s succeeded in forcing the United States to withdraw its contingent of occupying marines. Sandino's subsequent murder at the hands of Anastasio Somoza García, who had been installed by the departing marines at the head of the Nicaraguan National Guard, paved the way for more than forty years of Somoza family rule over the country—the longest and one of the most corrupt dictatorships in Latin American history.

The Sandinista Front for National Liberation (FSLN) based its fight against the dictatorship on the thinking and actions of Sandino. The essential elements of Sandino's campaign, rescued thirty years after his death by the FSLN, included antiimperialism, the quest for national dignity and sovereignty, and a commitment to the worker and peasant majority. On this basis, the Sandinista guerrilla struggle proposed to overthrow the dictatorship, dismantle the exploitative structures and institutions of *somocismo*, break the country's dependence on the United States, and move toward the construction of a more just social and economic order.

Like the initial period after the 1979 Sandinista victory, Nicaragua in 1990 was enveloped in powerful changes. The National Organized Union (UNO—formerly Nicaraguan Opposition Union) government led by President Violeta Chamorro, in its drive to arrest the economic decline and reestablish agroexports and the private sector as the economy's motor force, has presided over a sometimes gradual, sometimes violent process of rolling back the revolutionary transformations of the 1980s.[2]

GOVERNMENT AND POLITICS

The FSLN, which began in 1961, was guided by its Historic Program, a statement of objectives for a post-Somoza society drafted in 1969. The document called for a system based on political pluralism, a mixed economy, and international nonalignment. It stressed a democratic society and a political pluralism within the framework of the "hegemony of the popular classes."[3] Perhaps, therefore, the most important changes to accompany the demise of the dictatorship were a fundamental reorientation of social priorities in favor of the poor and disenfranchised, a redefinition of values, and a redistribution of political power. For the Sandinistas, the guiding principle in political and economic decisions was the struggle to transform social and economic relations in the interests of the majority of the population. This led the FSLN to construct a concept of political pluralism as "participatory democracy" together with elements of traditional "representative democracy."

Thus while there was a strong commitment to political pluralism, it was clearly limited by its subordination to the class-based transformations of the revolutionary project. First, to the extent that representatives of the bourgeoisie felt their class interests threatened by the predominance of popular hegemony, they simply withdrew their political or economic support and participation from the project. Second, the FSLN invariably closed off political spaces to those who were seen as interested not in contributing to the new system, but in undermining or overthrowing it. These limits greatly influenced events during the formative years of the post-Somoza government.

With the departure of Somoza, the Sandinistas attempted to provide continuity to the pretriumph alliance by forming a coalition government, led by the Government Junta of National Reconstruction (JGRN). The five-member JGRN comprised three Sandinistas, including coordinator Daniel Ortega, and two representatives of the bourgeoisie, industrialist Alfonso Robelo and Violeta Chamorro, widow of one of the anti-Somoza struggle's martyrs, newspaper publisher Pedro Joaquín Chamorro.

The JGRN, in turn, formed a cabinet, in which key economic ministries were given to representatives of the private sector. It also formed a Council of State as a transitional, colegislative branch of government. Seats in the council were distributed to mass organizations, economic interest groups, and professional, political, and social associations. The biggest single block was accorded to the Superior Council of Private Enterprise (COSEP), a conservative alliance of industrialists, financiers, and large-scale agricultural and commercial groups.

In early 1980 the JGRN and the leadership of the FSLN expanded the total number of seats in the council from thirty-three to forty-seven, with the new ones awarded to recently formed popular organizations identified with the Sandinistas. The decision triggered a governmental crisis and the first major shakeup in the anti-Somoza alliance. Seeing their legislative strength diluted by the expansion of seats, the COSEP bloc pulled out of the council. Early in 1980 Chamorro resigned from the junta, citing health reasons. Robelo resigned in April stating his opposition to the redistribution of council seats.

The Robelo and Chamorro resignations symbolized the decision among important sectors of the bourgeoisie to try to influence the shape and the structures of the emerging governmental system from the legal and extralegal opposition, rather than sharing power with the Sandinistas. Robelo left the country shortly after to become a leader of the *contrarevolucionarios* or *contras*. Chamorro remained inside Nicaragua as publisher of the U.S.-funded *La Prensa*, the newspaper that served as the mouthpiece of the anti-Sandinista opposition.

In the wake of national elections held in 1984, both the structure of the provisional government and the informal nature of the coalition were dissolved. The Council of State gave way to a National Assembly in which all members were elected according to their party affiliation. The Assembly, where Sandinista candidates won some two-thirds of the seats, was charged with drawing up a constitution as the country's constitutive legislative branch. The JGRN gave way to a formal executive branch, in the presidential mold, headed by the victorious candidates President Daniel Ortega and Vice President Sergio Ramírez.

With the executive and legislative branches in place, attention turned in 1985 to drafting a new constitution. The *somocista* constitution was scrapped after the insurrection, and the country had been guided juridically by outdated legal codes, legislation passed and put into effect without a constitutional framework, and by presidential decree. Throughout 1985 and 1986, the 202 articles of the new constitution were drafted with the assistance of a lengthy process of nationwide *cabildos abiertos* (town meetings). These public gatherings, presided over by representatives from the constitutional commission of the National Assembly, were used as key forums to enrich the draft constitution through direct, popular input.[4]

The document provides constitutional protection for the broad democratic rights introduced since 1979. It also legally enshrines the structures of participatory democracy alongside representative democracy, and constitutionally sanctions many of the fundamental social and economic transformations undertaken since then. For instance, it guarantees the traditional liberties, such as freedom of speech, assembly, and movement, as well as legally proscribing gender, racial, ethnic, and religious discrimination. Access to health care, education, a decent wage, and other social and economic benefits are considered constitutional rights in themselves, restricted only by the material limits of society. The document elevates the mixed economy—in which private, state, cooperative, and mixed enterprises are to coexist—to the constitutionally prescribed economic structure. In addition to providing the constitutional framework for periodic elections, as held in 1984 and 1990, it mandates that the population has the right, and the duty, to participate in decision-making at all levels of society.[5]

The formal structure of the government itself also is enshrined in the constitution. The system is essentially a hybrid, drawing on different aspects of the Latin American, Western European, and United States models.[6] Similar to many Latin American countries, national government is divided among four branches: executive, legislative, judicial, and electoral. The executive branch, which enjoys broad formal powers, consists of the president and vice president, elected by direct popular vote for a six-year term, together with an appointed cabinet.

Legislative power resides with a ninety-member National Assembly, elected by universal adult suffrage (above sixteen years) under a system of proportional representation.[7] Like the executive, assembly members serve six-year terms. Legislators are elected from each of nine political-administrative regions in numbers roughly proportionate to the population of each region.

An independent judicial branch headed by a seven-member Supreme Court is appointed by the National Assembly on the basis of nominations made by the president's office. The president then designates which of the seven will preside over the court. The five-member Supreme Electoral Council, an independent branch of the government, is charged with administering and overseeing elections.

Political Parties and Elections

In 1980 the provisional government announced that national elections would be held in 1985. The decision was harshly criticized by the right wing and by Washington, both of which called for elections to be held immediately. The governing junta argued that holding elections at such an early date would represent a major diversion of energies and resources at a time when the top national priority should be economic reconstruction.

In the absence of a single opposition party or leader who could act as a magnet to attract popular support, anti-Sandinista forces—with the United States providing funding, guidance, and logistical support— engaged in intense efforts beginning in 1983 to build broad opposition coalitions. The Nicaraguan Democratic Coordinator (CDN) was consolidated in 1983 with a view toward presenting a united opposition front and a single presidential candidate in the elections, by that time scheduled for November 1984. The CDN, which would later go on to form the core of UNO, was dominated by far-right politicians and COSEP, although other groups had formal representation in the alliance. The bulk of the country's more independent-minded center and center-right parties, however, maintained their distance from the CDN.

Urged on by the Reagan administration, the CDN's political parties eventually boycotted the 1984 elections. After months of internal squabbling, Arturo Cruz, a banker and one-time member of the provisional government junta, was named CDN presidential candidate only to withdraw from the contest after a four-day campaign.

Despite Washington's attempts to bolster support for the *contra* project through the electoral boycott and *contra* military efforts to impede voters from going to the polls, the balloting was held according to schedule without the CDN. On November 4, 1984, 76 percent of registered voters cast their ballots. The FSLN won 67 percent of the vote and six opposition parties representing the right, center, and left split the remainder.[8]

According to the constitution, the next general elections were to be held in November 1990. In the framework of the Esquipulas peace negotiations, however, the Sandinista government decided to move up the date for elections by ten months to February 1990; reform the country's electoral legislation to conform with the opposition's main demands; pass a new media law; and open up the entire electoral process to extensive international observation. These and other initiatives were made in exchange for commitments by the other Central American countries to collaborate in disbanding the *contras*. By May 1989 Nicaragua had fulfilled its side of the bargain even though effective *contra* demobilization still was blocked by the intransigence of *contra* leaders and U.S. foot-dragging.

Under the watchful eyes of more than one thousand international observers—all sides agreed that this was the most closely scrutinized electoral process in history—Nicaraguans cast their votes on February 25, 1990. The upset victory gave UNO presidential candidate Violeta

Chamorro 54.7 percent of the popular vote to Daniel Ortega's 40.8 percent for the FSLN. In terms of percentage, the UNO presidential victory was closely paralleled in races for the National Assembly, and UNO candidates swept thirty-two of the municipal races in large cities and towns to the FSLN's ten.[9] Although several voting locations had to close down due to *contra* activity, more than 86 percent of all registered voters went to the polls, up from 76 percent in the 1984 elections. The observer missions—headed by the United Nations, the Organization of American States, and the Carter Center—unanimously testified to the fairness and integrity of the polling process and the vote count.

Within days of the elections, dozens of theories had begun to circulate regarding the reasons behind the electoral results.[10] In many ways, it was apparent that the vote was more a plebiscite-type rejection of the FSLN's reelection bid than an expression of active support for the UNO program or for the parties belonging to the alliance. Many Nicaraguans simply voted for a change. Above all, "changing the country" boiled down to two things: ending the war and reversing economic decline. During the campaign, UNO successfully portrayed itself as the only party that could bring peace—with the *contras* and with the United States—to a populace that had been devastated and exhausted by war. Likewise, the economic deterioration suffered by the majority of Nicaraguans had become so acute that UNO's promises of prosperity, and of the turnaround in relations with Washington necessary to achieve it, were difficult to resist. President Bush had promised to lift the economic embargo if Chamorro won, and there was a general sensation that a UNO victory would result in a generous flow of U.S. aid. Some evidence indicates that a significant portion of the electorate saw the United States as the prime factor behind the war and the economic crisis and voted for UNO on the conviction that it would get the United States off Nicaragua's back.[11]

Political Factionalism

The history of Nicaragua's traditional political parties is replete with infighting and divisions.[12] Between independence in 1821 and World War II, nearly all Nicaraguans with a preference were either Liberals or Conservatives. The major conflicts of the day, which often led to coups, civil wars, and foreign interventions, were kept within these two parties. A few new parties came on the scene in the 1940s in an effort to challenge Somoza's domination, but it was not until the 1980s that the political map was fundamentally recast. With the onset of the Sandinista revolution, some parties entered into national unity alliances with the FSLN.[13] Others became part of the counterrevolutionary forces based in Honduras and Costa Rica. But most parties began a process of subdividing that lasted throughout the decade. By the deadline for party registration for the 1990 election (June 1989), the number of parties had risen to twenty.

So splintered was the opposition that a U.S.-funded delegation sent to evaluate prospects for unifying the disparate groups described it as "centrifugal in dynamic [and] fratricidal in outlook."[14] Faced with this ominous panorama, the United States stepped in to, in the words of one State Department official, "micromanage the opposition" with the goal of unifying the anti-Sandinista forces.[15] Their efforts met with mixed results until June 1989, with the formation of the fourteen-party UNO coalition and the nomination of Violeta Chamorro as the group's presidential candidate two months later. Despite the creation of UNO, though, factionalism persistently remained even after the elections. In terms of the principal ideological currents, the Conservatives, Liberals, Social Christians, and Social Democrats each had representatives from at least two different factions elected to the National Assembly on the UNO ticket in 1990.[16] Two days after Chamorro assumed office UNO itself suffered a major internal division with eight parties supporting the hard-line stance of Vice President Virgilio Godoy and six backing the more moderate positions of Chamorro.

Until the end of the 1980s the multiplicity of parties meant that the center of Nicaraguan opposition was not in the hands of a political party or coalition. Instead, the opposition was managed by a newspaper (*La Prensa*), a cardinal (Obando y Bravo), and a businessmen's association (COSEP). Even UNO's upset victory at the polls in 1990 was hardly the product of the coalition's parties' organizational strength. With the exception of the Communists and Socialists, nearly all parties in UNO had been formed after 1985, albeit on the basis of long-standing traditional political currents, and had weak or nonexistent organizational bases and no proven independent electoral base.[17]

The secondary role played by the parties during UNO's electoral campaign was carried over into the new Chamorro government. The president, her top advisers, and nearly all cabinet ministers had no party affiliation. The parties initiated efforts to build new social bases on the basis of their presence in the municipal governments and in the National Assembly.

UNO: A Difficult Transition

High-level teams from the outgoing and incoming governments, led by Antonio Lacayo for UNO and Sandinista army chief General Hum-

berto Ortega for the FSLN, negotiated a seven-point transition protocol to guide the transfer of power from the FSLN to UNO. Signed on
March 27, 1990, after a month of tense negotiations, the pact promoted respect for the existing constitutional order, including the state
apparatus and armed forces, which had been built up since 1979. The
signing of the protocol was seen as a landmark event, both because it
served to defuse the short-term threat of civil war and because it
constituted the foundation for the first democratic transfer of government in Nicaragua's history.

The right wing within UNO had a radically different vision of what
the transition should look like. They argued that UNO's election victory gave them the mandate to impose their program regardless of the
consequences and of the FSLN's demands for the security of its supporters. However, the more moderate sectors of the Chamorro group
clearly recognized that in the absence of minimal guarantees for security and stability, the transfer of power itself would be jeopardized. But
the transition protocol also reflected the deeper motivation among
Chamorro's inner circle—their sharp ideological differences with the
FSLN notwithstanding—to break the cycle of victors and van-
quished.[18] Breaking that cycle was seen not as a concession to the
Sandinistas but as the only practical way to move toward the political
and social stability necessary for implementing UNO's program of
economic recovery and development.

By the end of UNO's first one hundred days in office, the coalition's
diverse factions had jelled into two distinct groupings. One sector, led
by President Chamorro, was characterized by a moderate and tempered approach to resolving the country's pressing problems. The
second sector, more ideological and extremist in vision, was headed by
Vice President Virgilio Godoy and included the group of far-right
political parties from UNO. The leadership of COSEP had, for the
most part, thrown its weight behind the Godoy faction. Although differences existed over a wide array of issues, the most important factors
separating the two factions were their stances vis-à-vis the Sandinista
opposition and the scope and pace of change needed to roll back the
social and economic transformations undertaken after 1979.

Although both factions shared an anti-Sandinista outlook and
agreed on the need to isolate and weaken the FSLN, major differences
emerged over how to achieve these goals. The pragmatists believed that
to govern and implement the UNO program, Chamorro would have to
assure a minimum of stability by working through peaceful means and
within the bounds of certain national realities. The fact that the FSLN
represented more than 40 percent of a highly politicized and well-

organized population constituted the foremost of those realities. Essentially the Chamorro group felt that in the short run the government could tolerate a legitimate Sandinista opposition and that the best way to neutralize *sandinismo* was through a protracted campaign waged principally in the ideological terrain aimed at coopting, dividing, and domesticating the FSLN. The Godoy faction and COSEP, by and large, shared the radically different view that implementing UNO's program required the swift and total elimination of *sandinismo*, through violent means if need be.

On April 26, 1990, when Chamorro's new cabinet reported for its first day of work, there was no room left for speculation: Not a single representative from the pre-election Political Council formed by the UNO parties or from COSEP occupied a ministerial post.[19] Vice President Godoy was given no specific functions within the government and was even denied an office in the presidential office complex. The overwhelming majority of ministerial positions was given to professionals and technocrats with little prior experience in politics and no party affiliation. The three most delicate assignments, the ministries of Defense, Presidency, and Interior, went respectively to Chamorro herself, to her son-in-law and closest adviser Antonio Lacayo, and to Carlos Hurtado, Chamorro's cousin and a close associate of her number-two adviser Alfredo César. Much of the rest of the cabinet came from the Commission for the Reconstruction and Development of Nicaragua (CORDENIC), a think tank formed in 1988 to facilitate debate on policy alternatives for the eventual peacetime reconstruction of Nicaragua, which Chamorro had repeatedly consulted during the campaign.[20]

Monopoly control over the cabinet gave the Chamorro group the upper hand in the central government apparatus and the executive branch. A shuffling of the Supreme Court in late July 1990 served to bring the judicial branch under effective control of the presidency as well.[21] But in the National Assembly, the municipal councils, and at the grass-roots level, UNO's right-wing parties—bitter opponents of Chamorro on a long list of major issues—clearly had the upper hand. On at least two occasions during Chamorro's first five months in office, the right's most prominent leader, Vice President Godoy, was involved in what the government interpreted as incipient movements toward a coup d'état.[22]

COSEP, by any standards a major power bloc within UNO, was in a unique position. Having spearheaded political opposition to the Sandinistas during the 1980s, COSEP shared the resentment of the Political Council's party leaders at having been brushed aside in Chamorro's cabinet appointments. But COSEP's stance toward the government was also motivated by concerns outside the realm of politics. As the country's main organization of capitalists, it had expected that the UNO electoral victory would result in the rapid privatization of the state sector of the economy, a process in which most of the spoils would be divided up among COSEP members. The government's cautious and methodological posture regarding privatization proved to be a major disappointment.

The Chamorro group's tenuous hold on power was further complicated by the ambiguous posture adopted by the Catholic Church hierarchy and by the United States. Although for different reasons and at different times, both had largely embraced a strategy of alternately playing the Chamorro and Godoy factions off against each other, and at other times of throwing their support to both.

The FSLN: Challenges for the 1990s

The electoral defeat threw the Sandinistas into the ranks of the political opposition and obliged the FSLN to identify and correct the errors that had contributed to its stunning loss at the polls; redefine its identity as a party; and devise a new program and strategy capable of simultaneously defending the revolutionary gains of the 1980s and paving the way for retaking the reigns of government through elections, scheduled for 1996.

The FSLN's distancing from the masses did not occur overnight. Methods for decision-making and leadership styles within the party—which defined itself as the "vanguard of the Nicaraguan masses"—had remained fundamentally unaltered over the course of three decades.[23] The centralized leadership and vertical, top-down organizational methods (which had been adopted in the 1960s and 1970s in order to operate as a clandestine movement against Somoza) were maintained and reinforced during the 1980s in the face of U.S.-sponsored aggression against the revolutionary process. Outside of the nine-member National Directorate, and its adjunct Sandinista Assembly—a consultative body comprised of 105 leading party militants—there was little room for direct, grass-roots participation in the definition of the strategic issues and tasks confronting the FSLN. Although there was hardly a shortage of debate and discussion among the party's estimated 12,000 members, once the National Directorate handed down its position on a given issue the entire party was expected to close ranks. Unity within the party was seen not just as an important goal, but as a prerequisite for survival. The FSLN also lacked democratic electoral procedures for selecting personnel for internal posts, and leaders at all levels of the party and affiliated mass organizations were appointed by those in the corresponding sector of the Sandinista hierarchy.

During the first several months of the Chamorro administration, Sandinista ranks were full of effervescent debate on how to revitalize the party. During this period no formal divisions appeared, but conditions clearly indicated the potential for a serious bifurcation. More than the question of historical tendencies or differences over interpreting the electoral defeat, the main issues of dispute centered on where the party should head in the immediate future. One group felt that the future of *sandinismo* lay in rebuilding a broad popular consensus with a view toward capturing a majority in the 1996 elections. Adherents to this perspective believed that tactics and alliances should be subordinated to the prevailing conditions of the country. Such a viewpoint implied occasional support for the Chamorro government—for example, in its efforts to isolate the UNO right wing. It also meant that the FSLN might advance political projects that appealed to those broad sectors of the electorate that had seen UNO as a centrist alternative.

Other members of the FSLN, including many of those close to the trade-union movement, were inclined to a more orthodox revolutionary perspective. These militants wanted the Sandinistas to place themselves at the head of the most radicalized sectors of the masses in their struggles to resist the antipopular policies of the government.

Rather than a neat lining up of Sandinista forces behind two alternative approaches, differences of opinion among both the leadership and the base on a number of key issues brought about a more fluid situation. These issues are:

- Maintaining the current party leadership versus a thoroughgoing modernization of the party, including new leaders. The latter position called for the "historic" Sandinista leadership, including at least some members of the current National Directorate, to step down to advisory positions. In June 1990 it was decided that all party leadership positions, including the National Directorate, would be filled by secret ballot elections.
- New social alliances for rebuilding the FSLN. Some Sandinistas called for rebuilding the worker-peasant alliance by reaching out to all forces, including ex-*contras* and UNO supporters, negatively affected by government policy.
- The FSLN's place on the political spectrum and its international profile and alliances. This new identity was to include a definition of the anti-imperialist struggle appropriate to the 1990s.

- The type of economic model to advocate. Possible options included state-centered versus decentralized alternatives, orthodox stabilization versus a basic needs approach, and so on.

Although many of these delicate issues will have to be resolved in practice, the FSLN is attempting to carry out the process of redefinition and reorganization in the most orderly fashion circumstances will allow. The June 1990 assembly of FSLN militants agreed to sponsor the first-ever party congress, which will be held in July 1991. Preparatory discussions for the congress will take place at the grass-roots level, and local assemblies are responsible for electing delegates. The congress itself is to be a public event open to all Nicaraguans.

Human Rights

As promised in the campaign, one of the Chamorro government's first acts after taking office was the approval of an unconditional general amnesty covering all Nicaraguans accused of political violations and common crime linked to political conflicts, whether in or out of prison. In practice the move was largely symbolic; because of the post-Esquipulas political freedom and a similar amnesty law passed by the lame-duck Sandinista administration, there were virtually no political prisoners left in Nicaragua.[24] During Chamorro's first months in office, reports of human-rights abuses were confined primarily to the murder of several FSLN activists at the hands of former *contras* and UNO extremists, and allegations of police misconduct against both FSLN and UNO supporters during the tense strike-related events of May and July 1990.

One lingering human-rights problem that the Chamorro government refused to resolve was the fate of *contra* kidnap victims, the Nicaraguan equivalent of the "disappeared." An organization formed in mid-1988 composed of family members of the kidnapped presented the National Commission for the Promotion and Protection of Human Rights (CNPPDH) with a list of 863 names of kidnap victims, including details of when and where they were taken. The *contras* have consistently denied any responsibility, arguing that all members of the Nicaraguan Resistance joined voluntarily, a position echoed by Cardinal Obando on the repeated occasions that the victims' family members solicited his assistance. Having spent years exhausting all avenues, in mid-1990 the families of the kidnapped resolved to seek assistance and authorization to visit the locations used as *contra* camps in Honduras to search for their relatives' remains in burial sites.

Many international observers feared a bloodbath in the wake of the July 1979 Sandinista victory, expecting Nicaraguans to take revenge against the National Guard, who had relied on brute force and repression to prop up the Somoza dictatorship. Despite widespread sentiment that those convicted of the most heinous crimes should face a firing squad, one of the new government's first acts was to abolish the death penalty. Captured Guard members were tried and most sentenced to the legal maximum of thirty years in prison. After serving less than one-third of their terms, all but a handful were pardoned and released from jail in 1989, even though many of their former comrades-in-arms continued to wage war against the country.

The treatment of the ex–Guard members was powerful testimony to the Sandinistas' commitment to respect human rights. In sharp contrast to its northern neighbors, government-sponsored or -condoned death-squad activity and the disappearance or assassination of opposition political leaders were conspicuously absent under the Sandinistas. In equally sharp contrast, the Sandinista government systematically investigated reports of human-rights abuses and punished those members of its security forces found guilty of misconduct.[25]

Despite the Sandinista government's policy of respect for human rights and its attempts to put the policy into practice, the Reagan administration and its allies inside Nicaragua repeatedly fabricated stories of Sandinista strong-arm tactics and repression of the opposition. Dozens of issues were taken up in the effort to portray Nicaragua as, in Reagan's words, a "totalitarian dungeon." However, the sweeping accusations did not hold up under examination by international human-rights organizations.

This is not to say, however, that the Sandinista government and its security forces were blameless. Wartime conditions took a heavy toll, and organizations like Amnesty International and Americas Watch reported incidents of maltreatment of prisoners, violations of international laws of wartime conduct, arbitrary detentions, and police brutality.[26]

As peace began to emerge toward the end of the 1980s, those who had charged the Sandinistas with using the war as a convenient excuse to crush political dissent were left with few arguments. Shortly after the August 1987 signing of the Esquipulas II peace accords, censorship of the press was suspended and both *La Prensa* and Radio Católica were allowed to reopen. The January 1988 lifting of the state of emergency restored *habeas corpus*, eliminated the special tribunal system set up to try ex–Guard members and those accused of counterrevolutionary activities, and established strict time limits on incommunicado and

pretrial detentions. Later that year, 985 *contra* collaborators were released from prison. In March 1989 the National Assembly granted a
pardon for 1,894 ex–Guard members who had been imprisoned since
1979. In preparation for the 1990 elections, the few remaining restrictions on opposition organizing and demonstrations were liberalized or
eliminated.

In mid-1990 the newly formed Nicaraguan Human Rights Center
(CENIDH) became the Nicaraguan affiliate of the regional umbrella
group, Commission for the Defense of Human Rights in Central America (CODEHUCA), whose affiliates are structured along guidelines
laid down by the United Nations. Although CENIDH maintains no
formal links with the FSLN, its general orientation has remained pro-
revolutionary. CENIDH follows the lead of CODEHUCA in adopting
broad definitions of human rights and governmental responsibility,
including concepts such as the social and economic rights of peoples.

The Permanent Commission on Human Rights (CPDH) was
founded in 1977. The group's board of directors are either members
of, or are closely linked to, the far-right parties of the UNO coalition.
Frequently cited in U.S. State Department reports on human-rights
violations by the Sandinistas, the CPDH (backed by the National Endowment for Democracy) often relied on questionable sources and
distorted its conclusions to conform with the guidelines of the broader
anti-Sandinista campaign.[27] Aware of the risks of appearing too progovernment, under the UNO administration the CPDH dedicated new
energies to building an image of independence.

The *contra* factions of the Nicaraguan Resistance (RN) had their own
human-rights agency, the Nicaraguan Human Rights Association
(ANPDH). The ANPDH received more than $5 million in U.S. funds as
its share of *contra*-aid packages. With the installation of the Chamorro
government, the ANPDH moved its operations to Managua and, like
the CPDH, was slated to receive new U.S. government funding. In
addition to these nongovernmental organizations, the National Assembly also has its own human-rights commission.

MILITARY

As an institution, Somoza's hated National Guard, installed by the U.S.
marines before they abandoned Nicaragua in 1933, virtually disintegrated following the 1979 Sandinista victory.[28] With the Guard so
closely linked to the dictatorship and to the United States, the FSLN

never entertained notions of institutional reform or of incorporating Guard members into new ranks; a new army had to be built from scratch. In this case, it meant building a professional army from the ragtag guerrilla columns that had fought the revolutionary war and led the popular insurrection.

The FSLN's original plan was to build a small, well-trained standing army, the EPS, backed by a larger, citizen-based militia, the Sandinista People's Militia (MPS). Formation of the initial army units began immediately, and the militias were officially inaugurated in February 1980. By the first anniversary of the revolution the MPS counted on some 100,000 volunteers, mainly workers and peasants, ranging in age from sixteen to sixty.

With the advent of the aggressive Reagan government in 1981, the EPS accelerated preparations for resisting a possible invasion, largely through a quantitative expansion of the militias. In mid-1983, with *contra* aggressions on the rise, a draft, known as the Patriotic Military Service (SMP) was instituted. The draft called for obligatory military service for males between the ages of seventeen and twenty-five and voluntary service for women. In an effort to spread the defense burden as equally as possible across the population, there were no exemption categories (although exceptions were made on a case-by-case basis for religious, family, and scholastic reasons). Unlike most countries in the region, even sons of the wealthy had to serve. The regular draft was backed up by the reserves (SMP-R) starting in 1985. More than 450,000 adults enlisted in the reserves, 175,000 of whom were actually mobilized.[29]

The draft was instrumental in allowing the military to defeat the *contra* forces during 1986 and 1987, thus paving the way for the peace process. Nonetheless, the draft had an enormously high social cost, with consequent political repercussions for the FSLN. Unpopular from the beginning, the draft became a rallying cry for the opposition, a cry that struck a responsive chord in many Nicaraguan homes. As is often the case in a protracted war, the most challenging phase turned out to be the end. As peace drew nearer in 1988 and 1989, the population grew increasingly resentful of the draft and the continued need for sacrifices. Overconfident of its chances for victory at the polls, the FSLN resisted suspending the draft until the promised *contra* demobilization became a reality. As expected, President Chamorro suspended the draft immediately upon taking office.

As Chamorro took office the EPS and militias constituted Nicaragua's land-based army. Security forces under the authority of the Defense Ministry also included the air force and navy. The small air force had no jets, relying for the most part on its fleet of Soviet-supplied helicopters, a vital asset used for ferrying troops and supplies into isolated regions during the *contra* war. The navy essentially functioned as a coast guard force, and counted on about a dozen patrol boats. With no minesweepers at the time, the navy had to rely on fishing vessels and tugboats dragging nets to remove mines following the 1984 U.S. mining of Nicaragua's harbors. Nicaragua later received light minesweepers from North Korea.

The EPS Under Chamorro

From the outset, the right-wing sectors in UNO, the *contras*, and the United States advocated eliminating the EPS as an institution and replacing it with a new force under a different mandate with its ranks comprising mostly ex-*contras*.[30] The accord worked out by the FSLN and Chamorro left the EPS intact with FSLN leader General Humberto Ortega at its head. In exchange for respecting the integrity of the EPS and the Ministry of the Interior—which in practice meant leaving intact the command structure and internal rules of the institutions—Chamorro received three concessions. First, the security forces would be "depoliticized": No member of the armed forces would be allowed to hold a leadership position in a political party and all parties would be free to proselytize among the rank and file. Second, the government would have exclusive authority for naming the ministers of defense and interior, thus bringing these institutions under civilian control. Third, the EPS would be significantly reduced in size.

In the context of the Esquipulas II peace accords, Nicaragua had committed itself since 1988 to a reduction in the size of its armed forces and weapons stock to a mutually agreeable Central American standard. By September 1989 the size of the permanent army had already been reduced by 30 percent and Nicaraguan officials spoke of plans to move toward a model similar to that of neutral countries like Switzerland, with a small full-time force backed up by ongoing compulsory reserve service.[31] But plans to cancel the draft and to make further reductions among the standing army and reserves were put on ice in the face of the *contras'* boycott of the demobilization accords and their continued refusal to accept a cease-fire.

On June 11, 1990, the day after the official *contra* demobilization, General Humberto Ortega delivered to President Chamorro a new plan for EPS troop reductions. Ortega's plan, and the Esquipulas-inspired reasonable balance-of-forces argument upon which it was based, were accepted by the Chamorro government.

For both the EPS and the government, the planned reductions entailed benefits and risks. Chamorro needed reductions to free up revenues for spending in other areas. In the 1988–1990 period, 40 percent to 60 percent of the national budget went to defense; the government estimated that anticipated army reductions would save the country $12 million to $15 million annually. On the other hand, 40,000 former soldiers would be thrown into an economy that already suffered from a 40 percent unemployment rate.

Guerrilla Opposition

At least until the serious military setbacks in 1986 and 1987, the bulk of those who joined the *contras* never harbored illusions about their goal. They sought to overthrow the Nicaraguan government militarily and eliminate all traces of *sandinismo* and the revolution from the country.[32]

In the initial period, 1981–1982, the *contras* were dominated by former Guard members.[33] From their bases in Honduras, small groups of *contras* launched incursions into the northern border regions aimed at destroying key infrastructure targets and terrorizing rural communities thought to be sympathetic to the Sandinistas. In 1983 a reorganized and expanded *contra* army took the initiative, launching three large-scale offensives in the northern and southern border regions, the central highlands, and the Atlantic coast. The following year brought more of the same, this time with greater direct participation by U.S. forces, particularly in sabotage operations along the coasts and in the mining of Nicaragua's harbors.

During the mid-1980s the initial *contra* strategy of seeking the Sandinistas' military defeat gradually gave way to a new formula, framed within the precepts of low-intensity warfare, which were then rapidly gaining adherents in the Pentagon and CIA. The *contras* concentrated increasingly on waging a grinding war of attrition, whose aim—in concert with diplomatic, ideological, and economic aggressions sponsored by Washington—was to erode support for *sandinismo* among the population and ultimately make the revolution cave in on itself.

The new approach proved to be much more effective. As the military conflict dragged on and the economic crisis worsened, the FSLN began to lose legitimacy among the population as key initiatives boomeranged. Despite advances in the political terrain, the military situation for the *contras* was increasingly bleak. The strategic military defeat inflicted by the EPS in 1986 and 1987 left the *contras* with few possibilities for retaking the initiative through military means. Under the auspices of the Esquipulas peace plan, the Sandinista government and *contras* entered into negotiations aimed at establishing a cease-fire and eventually a definitive end to the hostilities. While many *contras* were anxious to put an end to the war through the negotiations process and several *contra* leaders signed a preliminary cease-fire with the Nicaraguan authorities at Sapoá in March 1988, the top *contra* leader Colonel Enrique Bermúdez, with full backing from the United States, opposed the negotiation process. The ensuing conflicts threatened to bring about the disintegration of the *contra* movement itself. Thousands of *contras* simply gave up and returned to civilian life in Nicaragua or joined the ranks of the undocumented in the United States and Central America. Many formed "dissident" *contra* groups opposed to Bermúdez's uncompromising positions, while others, including several top leaders, decided to join the electoral battle inside Nicaragua.

By the time the electoral campaign got under way in late 1989, the most intransigent sectors of the *contra* leadership, including Bermúdez, had been displaced; their places were taken by a younger generation of *contra* field commanders who had risen through the ranks during the 1980s. Like the majority of the *contra* troops, the new leaders, under the command of Israel Galeano, were mostly of *campesino* origin.[34]

In preparation for the 1990 elections, the bulk of the *contra* forces were sent from their bases in Honduras into the Nicaraguan countryside. Their mission was to intimidate FSLN supporters and to campaign for the UNO ticket among the peasantry, while simultaneously rekindling the embers of war. In response, the government—with a view toward defending against the military attacks and safeguarding the electoral process—canceled the unilateral cease-fire it had maintained since the signing of the Sapoá accords a year and a half earlier. Then, in a strategic public-relations coup, UNO capitalized on the FSLN's decision by campaigning as "the party of peace."[35]

Demobilization: The Last Good-bye?

The timetable worked out by the Central American presidents under the auspices of the Esquipulas peace plan initially called on the *contras* to finalize the process of demobilization by December 1989, nearly three months before the scheduled general elections. With firm U.S. backing, the *contras* effectively resisted all pressures to disband, brandishing the argument that their continued existence was the only guarantee that the Sandinistas would hold fair elections and respect the results. Within days of UNO's upset victory, however, it became clear that the *contra* leadership had more ambitious goals.

Representatives of President-elect Chamorro, the Nicaraguan Catholic Church hierarchy, the army, and the UN- and OAS-sponsored groups responsible for overseeing the demobilization—the United Nations Observer Group in Central America (ONUCA) and the International Commission for Support and Verification (CIAV)—entered into a lengthy and complex process of negotiations with the Nicaraguan Resistance (RN). Playing on Chamorro's fear of renewed war, the RN extracted a series of hefty concessions from the government. Four months after the first agreements had been signed, ONUCA officially declared the process complete. They reported that a total of 19,256 contras had been demobilized.

The rural payoff for the contras was the right to form several semi-autonomous areas of rural economic development called "development poles" in remote areas of central and southeastern Nicaragua. According to the May 30, 1990, agreement, the poles could be placed in twenty-three locations totaling 3,280 square miles of Nicaraguan territory. The poles will be patrolled by the new security force, the contra-based POI-RN. The POI-RN is slated to receive training from Spanish and Venezuelan security teams.

Contras who decide to relocate to the poles will be granted direct representation in local governments. They also may send delegates to act as high-level advisers in the central government ministries whose work involves the poles (Construction, Health, Labor, Agrarian Reform, and Repatriation). In addition to the government's commitment to prioritize social and development projects and job-creating investments in the poles, $47 million in aid from the $300 million package approved by Congress is earmarked specifically for demobilized contras and their family members who repatriate from Honduras. Contra widows and families will receive pension benefits.

In practice, the poles got off to a slow start, and the ultimate fate of the contras remains uncertain. In the immediate aftermath of demobilization, individual contras went in several different directions. Most were eager to return to their families and farms. About one in ten chose to remain at the sites where the development poles were to be established. Still others began work with the new contra political party, the Nicaraguan Resistance Civic Organization.[36] Several former contra leaders participated in discussions with the Union of Nicaraguan Growers and Ranchers (UNAG), a pro-Sandinista organization of farmers and peasants. The talks were aimed at uniting peasants irrespective of their political or ideological leanings or past affiliations in the face of growing landlessness and negative fallout from Chamorro's agrarian policies.

Some ex-*contras* took advantage of the tensions unleashed during the July 1990 general strike to take up paramilitary activity in support of the extreme right within the UNO coalition. Ex-*contras* quickly turned up in the ranks of the National Salvation Committees, which Vice President Virgilio Godoy was busy organizing. According to press reports, some two thousand armed *contras* remained in the Honduran department of Olancho, not far from the border with Nicaragua.[37] Despite these ominous signs there were few indications that the *contras* had any chance of fully reviving themselves as an organized force.

ECONOMY

The mixed-economy model of the Sandinista government envisioned ownership in industry and agriculture divided among the state, small producers (including cooperatives), and a capitalist sector. Within a context of popular hegemony, the mixed economy would guarantee a place for all, regardless of ideological or political preferences, as long as a commitment to production was maintained.[38] According to the plan, the government would effect a redistribution of income and property while expanding consumption levels for the popular sectors. Agrarian reform and a state-controlled banking system and foreign-trade apparatus were established to facilitate the redistribution.

The Sandinistas' effort to transform the economy was hindered by several factors, however. The fight against Somoza had left much of the country's productive infrastructure in ruins. Also, Somoza and his associates looted the Central Bank vaults before fleeing, leaving the treasury bankrupt.[39] Even before the onset of the war and U.S. financial aggression, the web of economic constraints meant that, according to the World Bank, "per capita income levels of 1977 will not be attained, in the best of circumstances, until the late 1980s."[40]

Between 1980 and 1984, blessed with relatively generous levels of international economic assistance (the cutoff of U.S. aid notwithstanding) and widespread popular enthusiasm and participation in the new revolutionary programs and institutions, economic performance was quite positive. Government investment for reconstruction averaged 20 percent of GDP, far above the Central American average, and many areas of the economy were successfully reactivated. Significant gains were registered in consumption levels and in the extension of basic social services such as education and health care. Agrarian reform, along with flexible credit and technical-assistance policies, benefited thousands of formerly landless farmers and agricultural workers and helped the country move toward its goal of self-sufficiency in basic-grain production.[41]

But parallel to these positive developments were also troublesome signs. A web of interrelated factors, some tied to mistakes committed by the Sandinistas, others related to factors beyond their control, increasingly influenced the development of the economy. Although some within the government began to sound the alarm, no one envisioned the magnitude of the economic crisis that would emerge a few years down the road.

First, the costs and stresses of the reconstruction period demonstrated the limits of trying to apply economic planning in a mixed economy dominated by small and medium private producers and the commercial sector. Changes in the government's alliance strategy, made in order to satisfy the demands of diverse economic groups, often produced counterproductive results. Second, Nicaragua's ambitious efforts to transform the economy took place at a time when international conditions were wreaking havoc throughout the Third World. Contracting markets, deteriorating terms of trade, dwindling sources of external financing, and mounting foreign debt hampered Nicaraguan development. Third, and most important in terms of constricting the government's maneuvering room, was the war and U.S. financial aggression. Ongoing destruction caused by *contra* attacks and sabotage and by U.S. economic warfare, including a trade embargo, loan cut-offs, and the 1984 mining of Nicaragua's ports, extracted a high price. At its peak, the national defense effort involved a full 20 percent of the economically active population, 40 percent of the gross national product, and 60 percent of the national budget.[42]

In the face of these adverse circumstances, the government's response essentially boiled down to implementing a series of stopgap measures, while postponing the difficult choices. An increasingly unmanageable budget deficit was sustained year after year, covered through the printing of unbacked currency notes. The cost was a growing chain of macroeconomic distortions, a skyrocketing debt, uncontrollable hyperinflation, and, most important politically, a precipitous decline in living standards for the country's already poor majority.

The government's attempts to confront the imbalances behind the economic crisis brought mixed results. In 1985, the year the U.S. trade embargo was declared, the Sandinistas imposed austerity measures and prioritized military spending. Three years later, the government launched its "shock" package, which in many ways resembled plans adopted in other countries at the behest of the International Monetary Fund (IMF). Aside from the immediate goal of reducing inflation, the thrust of the 1988 adjustment package, executed in two phases, was to create a framework and context in which the economy could recuperate over the long run. Spearheaded by a 3,000 percent monetary devaluation and a currency swap, the new package of reforms included the virtual elimination of subsidies, reductions in the government budget (including defense, health, and education) and the curtailment of new investments in strategic development projects. Other measures were a tightening of credit conditions, indexing of interest and exchange rates to adjust them to inflation, additional restrictions on imports, and a near-total elimination of wage and price controls, which further strengthened the market orientation of the economy.

The austerity package brought unprecedented hardships to an already poverty-stricken population. Real per capita income fell to levels of the 1940s. Although some Nicaraguans saw the war and U.S. aggression as the ultimate causes of the economic crisis, the predominant sentiment by 1990 was one of exasperation.

When the Chamorro government stepped in, most of the toughest measures involved in instituting structural adjustments had already been taken. The measures adopted by the Sandinistas had at least partly succeeded in addressing some of the macroeconomic distortions that had brought on the crisis in the first place. By the end of 1989 both hyperinflation and the fiscal deficit had been substantially reduced, and export levels had begun to recuperate. Although problems still abounded, UNO inherited an economy ripe for recovery.

UNO's Program: "Recovery, Reconstruction, and Prosperity"

The newly installed government opted immediately to push full steam ahead with the most confrontational aspects of the economic recovery plan designed by the Central Bank president, Francisco Mayorga. The "Mayorga Plan" aimed to completely eradicate inflation through harsh austerity measures and the introduction of a new, freely convertible currency, the *córdoba oro*, pegged to the dollar. It also hoped to recover production levels of the late 1970s through the large-scale reduction of the state apparatus, the privatization of all state-owned businesses, and the gradual privatization of the banking system. Unlike the Sandinistas who attempted to include labor in economic decisions, UNO simply imposed its austerity measures. The offensive was multipronged: twice-weekly currency devaluations; massive public-sector layoffs; elimination of subsidies; and initiatives aimed at turning state farms over to private producers.

The quick reaction of Nicaragua's organized labor movement and popular sectors took the government by surprise. The first showdown came in May with a strike by public-sector employees, and this was followed by a nationwide general strike in July 1990. The government's ambiguous posture in both strikes—initially confrontational responses, followed by conciliatory gestures, negotiated settlements, and then systematic violation of those settlements—fueled resentment among the unions and their supporters. The chief union demands were for job stability and workers' inclusion in the process of defining how economic policy would be implemented. Over time the unions became increasingly convinced that the government would not, or could not, negotiate in good faith. While continuing to push for a national dialogue on economic policy, union representatives increasingly expressed the view that the only demands the government would take seriously were those backed by militant actions.

The strikes aggravated and were fueled by the poor economic performance that characterized Chamorro's first one hundred days in office. By August 1990—amid skyrocketing inflation, a dizzying spiral of currency devaluations and price hikes, and growing unemployment— the glittering campaign promises of prosperity had vanished and the population's confidence in the government's ability to address the economic crisis had seriously eroded.

Many factors caused the gulf that separated Mayorga's lofty promises and projections from the reality of the first one hundred days. The major ones were foreign aid shortfalls, last-minute wage demands, the growing budget deficit, and a thriving black market. Above all, the goals themselves had been grossly unrealistic, far out of line with the material conditions prevailing in the country. Even under ideal circumstances, Mayorga's projections would have been difficult to achieve.

The social polarization and production losses resulting from the stabilization measures and strikes set back by many months the timetable for economic recovery. Other factors, such as the faltering confidence of the private sector and potential investors in the plan's viability, also threatened to undermine essential elements of the plan.

Despite problems, a fragile consensus seems to be emerging within the government that the only way to maneuver around these and other dilemmas bound up with economic policy is through a broad process of national dialogue, incorporating the government, private enterprise, the unions, and the FSLN opposition. Although most observers see the move toward dialogue as positive, widespread doubts remain as to whether the Chamorro government has the will or the power to reach substantive accords and implement them.

Privatization

One of the most controversial aspects of the Chamorro government's economic policies, and the one that most forcefully signifies a rupture with the Sandinista past, has been privatization. All the key actors—the U.S. Embassy, the economic cabinet, COSEP and exiled Nicaraguan businessmen, the FSLN, and labor—have somewhat different views regarding the scope and speed of the ongoing privatization process. The delicate nature of the task and the difficulty of reaching minimal consensus among the various sectors have obstructed implementation of the projected policies. As a consequence, during Chamorro's first four months in office, privatization, defined as the selling of state enterprises, failed to proceed beyond the planning stages.

By August 1990 the nationalized sector of the Nicaraguan economy, the more than four hundred companies known as the Area of People's Property (APP), accounted for more than 40 percent of gross domestic product (GDP). Under the Sandinistas, the APP companies were attached to the appropriate government ministries. The UNO government, however, opted to concentrate all of the companies in a single entity, the National Corporation of the Public Sector (CORNAP), under the jurisdiction of Minister of the Presidency Antonio Lacayo. Lacayo's vice minister, Ervin Krügger, was named as CORNAP president and chairman of the General Committee of Corporations, the organization charged with overseeing the privatization process.

In practice, implementing privatization in Nicaragua required navigating a mine field of difficulties. Many of the potential Nicaraguan investors already had profitable businesses in other Central American countries and would have to find other motives to invest in risky Nicaragua. Likewise, foreign investors seeking profit margins through access to cheap labor could easily find opportunities in other countries of the region with less militant union movements and more stable political situations. Many sectors of the APP—for example, the manufacturing enterprises and the mining sector—were in need of large investments for modernization. For the government, selling off the most profitable companies quickly would mean forfeiting the revenues generated by them; closing down the unprofitable state companies to reduce the budget deficit would aggravate an already serious unemployment problem, estimated at between 35 percent and 45 percent of the economically active population.

Agriculture

Nicaragua is primarily an agrarian country. Agricultural production generates roughly 70 percent of the country's export earnings, and during the 1980s Nicaragua approached self-sufficiency in basic-grains production for domestic consumption. Despite a growing trend of migration to the urban areas, more than 40 percent of the economically active population has remained in agriculture. Historically, the overwhelming majority of Nicaragua's foreign-exchange earnings has come from the export of a few key products: coffee, cotton, beef, and sugar. Secondary exports like bananas, seafood, tobacco, and sesame trail far behind the "big four."

For the Sandinistas, applying the mixed-economy model meant trying to meet the varied needs of small and large private farms, cooperatives, and state-owned farms.[43] The Nicaraguan Agrarian Reform Law, promulgated in 1981 and then broadened in January 1986, was designed to meet the needs of the rural poor and increase production of food and export crops simultaneously. The law explicitly protected private farmers and ranchers, no matter how large their landholdings, provided they continued to farm productively and efficiently. Those who left their land idle, however, were subject to expropriation with compensation.

Despite a series of advances that benefited the Nicaraguan peasantry and rural workers, the Sandinista agrarian reform suffered from several key mistakes. In the first years of the revolution, there was resentment from the overemphasis on modernizing state farms, starting large-scale investment projects, and promoting cooperatives as the only acceptable form of *campesino* organization. Prior to 1986, artificially low prices on basic grains fixed by the state constituted another major factor in alienating sectors of the peasantry.

Finally, the Sandinista policy of giving *campesinos* "use" titles to their land as opposed to outright property titles created resentment among the recipients. The use titles allowed beneficiaries to pass their land on to children or to trade it for land elsewhere in the country, but not to sell it outright. The Sandinistas argued that such a step was necessary to avoid a future reconcentration of land in the hands of big private growers through the selling off of their property during hard times by desperate *campesinos*. Nonetheless, the *contras'* insistence that the use titles were worthless, and UNO's campaign promise to exchange them for "real" titles, had a significant impact among the peasantry.

Formally, the Chamorro administration was committed to respecting the land-tenure transformations undertaken by the Sandinista agrarian reform. In practice, however, things looked very different. On May 11, 1990, Chamorro announced two executive decrees, 10–90 and 11–90, which set the process of counterreform in motion. Under Decree 11–90, the former landowners would have six months to present petitions soliciting the return of their farms. Decree 10–90 empowered the state to lease lands that had been affected by the agrarian reform to private individuals. By the end of June the government had approved requests by fifty-seven former landowners to rent some 86,000 acres of land on state farms. As the former owners—for the most part businessmen who had returned from exile in Miami—began showing up at the farms, many faced the active resistance of the workers. As the conflicts spread throughout the countryside, growing numbers of state farms were seized by the workers. This momentum led to the July 1990 general strike.

Dismantling the APP is seen as a top priority by UNO and its U.S. backers for several reasons. Many of the 70,000 workers on the state farms are affiliated to the pro-Sandinista Association of Rural Workers (ATC) and the APP generally is seen as a key FSLN power base. In addition, the state farms came almost exclusively from confiscations and expropriations. Politically, UNO needs the allegiance of some of these former owners, and feels it can be won by returning their land.

The cooperative movement also found itself embroiled in various altercations after the arrival of the new government. The Chamorro administration's role has been less one of taking the initiative in dismembering the cooperatives set up under the Sandinistas than of remaining passive in the face of illegal takeovers of cooperatives by ex-*contras* and by forces aligned with the hard-line sector in UNO. In dozens of takeovers around the countryside, the government, fearful of provoking a backlash from the right wing, has failed to act on its promise to defend the rule of law and the integrity of the cooperative movement.

The unstable situation on the APP farms and cooperatives is aggravated by the persistent problem of landless *campesinos*. During the electoral campaign both the FSLN and UNO promised to address the needs of an estimated 40,000 landless families. To date the Chamorro administration has not unveiled a plan to meet this promise, and the ranks of the landless are growing rapidly as a result of *contra* demobilization, reductions in the army, and repatriation of refugees.

Meanwhile, uncertainty in the countryside provoked by the government's failure clearly to define its agrarian strategy, combined with high interest rates and a general apprehensiveness over the economy, have resulted in serious shortfalls in most crop projections. In particular, *campesino* producers of basic grains for the domestic market have for the most part decided not to risk planting anything beyond what is necessary for their subsistence needs.

Industry and Finance

The industrial sector, which was never very large or developed in Nicaragua, has suffered over the last two decades.[44] Dependent on exports to the Central American Common Market (CACM), Nicaraguan industry was severely wounded by the virtual collapse of the market in the 1970s. In the mid-1980s the Sandinista government's economic policy increasingly prioritized agricultural production, often to the detriment of industry. By 1988 industrial exports only amounted to about $20 million, down from a peak of $110 million in 1976.

The Sandinistas' mixed-economy model sought to provide incentives for private capital. The state, however, maintained control over the chief levers for regulating the economy, stimulating productive activities in all sectors, and distributing profits generated in the state's productive enterprises. In part, this was achieved through the nationalization of the banks, insurance, and foreign-trade enterprises. The Sandinistas believed that part of the profits gained through commercial transactions and international trade should be reinvested according to criteria mandated by the national development model and in accordance with the needs of all Nicaraguans. The nationalized banking and foreign-trade systems thus were seen as essential in effecting a redistribution of resources in favor of the poor majority, and ultimately, in allowing the country to move toward a socialist economy.

UNO's plans for the banking system contemplated privatization through the establishment of new financial institutions, which would gradually replace the nationalized banks. Major reforms also were planned on the foreign investment law. The law promulgated by the Sandinistas in 1987 contained virtually no restrictions, leaving most conditions and terms to be dealt with on a case-by-case basis with the Ministry of Foreign Cooperation. The new law would offer tax rebates and other incentives for enterprises exporting nontraditional products. The proposal, similar to the regulations existing in the other Central American countries, also included import-duty waivers for raw materials.

The Burden of Debt

A major problem inherited by the Chamorro government was the massive external debt that had accumulated in the 1980s. By the time the Sandinistas left office in 1990, the debt had mushroomed to $9.6 billion, a dramatic increase over the $1.6 billion debt that existed in 1979.[45] The key factor behind the growth of the debt was the government's need to finance the trade deficit, which averaged $400 million to $600 million per year after 1982.

Although the size of the foreign debt is staggering, one of the highest per capita in Latin America, Chamorro's economic policymakers will have two elements working in their favor when they sit down to renegotiate the debt with the banks, lending institutions, and governments involved. First, compared with other countries, the structure of Nicaragua's debt is more flexible because 59 percent is owed to governments (more than half of that is owed to the socialist and formerly socialist countries) and governments are more willing than financial institutions to renegotiate loan terms. Of the remainder, 13.6 percent is owed to commercial banks; 10.5 percent to multilateral organizations; others, including interest, cover the remaining 16.9 percent. Second, much of the international community, and in particular the governments to which the bulk of the debt is owed, recognize that Nicaragua's debt was incurred under unique circumstances and have expressed a willingness to treat it as a special case.

SOCIETY AND ENVIRONMENT

Popular Organizing

Despite widespread support for the revolution, there existed no extensive infrastructure of experienced popular organizations on which the new government could base its radical political and economic agenda. Until the FSLN helped organize the clandestine Association of Rural Workers in 1978, most rural organizing was linked to the popular education and social justice initiatives of the Catholic Church. And in the cities, where student and worker organizations were weak and repressed, the Sandinistas were able to spark the creation of the Civilian Defense Committees (CDCs) in the urban *barrios*.

The Sandinista victory sparked a flourishing of popular organizations. During the last two months of the Sandinista offensive, the CDCs were the only functioning civilian structure in many areas. They played an equally critical role following the change in government. Renamed the Sandinista Defense Committees (CDSs), these *barrio* organizations, which were highly regarded by their communities, coordinated relief operations and provided defense work for the new government.

With the creation of the Sandinista Workers Confederation (CST), there was an explosion of union organizing. By 1983 at least 40 percent of the country's workforce had become union members, rising to 56 percent by 1986. The two other major "mass organizations" associated with the new revolutionary government were the Nicaraguan Women's Association (AMNLAE) and the Sandinista Youth (JS).

The mass organizations were established with the dual function of serving as instruments of the revolutionary state and representing the sectoral interests of their own constituencies. During the first couple years of the Sandinista government they performed both functions well. With the assistance of the organized popular sectors, massive health and literacy programs were launched and new state structures were put into place. The mass organizations also proved critically important in propagating revolutionary analysis. Although the leaders of these organizations were FSLN militants, they were also strong advocates of the special interests of their respective organizations.

The government's economic project has been described as "development with redistribution."[46] During the first years of the Sandinista government that is exactly what happened: consumption levels increased for the poor and the economy was recovering from the war. At the same time the people were enthusiastic about the popular organizations. But as inflationary pressures mounted and production levels stagnated, the government began to intervene to defuse class-based confrontations. Marking the end of an era of aggressive popular organizing, the government issued the Social and Economic Emergency Law in September 1981. Strikes, lockouts, and spontaneous takeovers of private property were banned.[47]

The government, concerned about the stagnating economy, sought to avoid aggravating class conflicts while increasing production. With the escalation of the *contra* war, national defense became an even more powerful justification for clamping down on economic disruptions. Although there was some opposition, the priorities of economic stability and defense were largely accepted by the mass organizations. Increasingly, the focus of popular mobilizing was on the military effort to defeat the counterrevolution.

But it was the dual-purpose nature of the mass organizations that eventually proved to be their major weakness. Defining itself as the vanguard party, the FSLN expected the popular organizations to accept its formulation of priorities for revolutionary stability and progress. Since the directors of the mass organizations were themselves Sandinista militants, the particular needs and demands of the organizations they led were increasingly pushed to the side by the FSLN's own priorities. Confusion and contradictions developed because of the double role and dual responsibility. Since the party's hierarchy and discipline were superior to that of the popular organizations, their interests often got lost.

From its earliest days the Sandinista revolution pledged to create a participatory democracy that included the poor and workers not only in national policymaking but also in the decision-making in factories, agricultural estates, and schools. Women, students, peasants, workers, and neighborhood activists did gain an extraordinary new prominence in Nicaragua as a result of the revolution. But the new model of participatory democracy was limited and in the end seriously compromised by the ever-present control of the FSLN, itself a vertical and highly centralized political organization. The top-down working style of the Sandinistas also was closely reflected in the operations of the mass organizations, further inhibiting popular participation and limiting these organizations to Sandinista sympathizers.

The Grass-Roots Revolution

The election victory of the UNO slate raised popular expectations that the war would finally end and that U.S. dollars would flow into Managua. In fact, UNO promises that foreign aid would help reconstruct the economy partly explain the opposition coalition's impressive majority. With no war and the economic blockade lifted, the country's popular sectors felt that the new administration would address their needs and demands, postponed for so long as a result of the war and U.S. economic aggression; instead, they found themselves the victims of a new and still-harsher economic-stabilization program.

Ironically, it was these adverse circumstances—the defeat of the FSLN and the government's antipopular economic program—that sparked an explosion of popular organizing. The most dramatic evidence of this revival of the popular movement was the united peasant, worker, and student reaction to government attempts to roll back revolutionary gains and impose its stabilization program. Acting independently of the FSLN directorate, the ATC, CST, and other unions showed impressive mobilizing power during the first few months of the Chamorro administration. Integrating wage issues with demands addressing the broader social welfare, the newly formed National Workers Federation (FNT) forged widespread popular support for the general strikes of May and July 1990.

Still in question is the nature of the relationship between the popular movement and the FSLN. The loss of state power has made it impossible for the FSLN to maintain responsibility for the mass organizations. The party is having a difficult enough time maintaining itself financially without having to worry about the financial and institutional stability of these popular organizations.

The FSLN and the popular organizations are debating the party's role in setting the political and strategic direction for the entire progressive movement. Some leftist critics have charged that the FSLN is moving into an alliance with the "modern" bourgeois faction of government and giving its support to an economic-stabilization program contrary to the interests of the general public. During the strikes following Chamorro's inauguration, there also was criticism that the FSLN incorrectly assumed that it could step in and negotiate on behalf of the popular organizations. With their greater autonomy and need to respond to members' demands, the popular organizations may be more reluctant now to accept the FSLN's vanguard status. At the same time, there is widespread recognition of the FSLN's historical commitment to the poor and its proven leadership capacities.

The success of the FSLN's determination to "govern from below" and to regain political power in 1996 will be determined primarily by its ability to represent the interests of the popular sectors. Likewise the growth and influence of the mass organizations will depend on their ability to unite around common economic demands and political principles.

Labor and Unions

Labor organizing flourished under the Sandinista government, particularly during the early 1980s. When the FSLN took power, there were 183 workplace unions, representing less than 10 percent of all workers.[48] By the end of the 1980s there were more than two thousand workplace unions, more than a third of them in rural areas, with some 55 percent of the working population unionized.

Although the union movement was larger than ever, the economic circumstances of the working class had barely improved. When the FSLN left office more than 25 percent of the population was unemployed and real per capita income levels had regressed almost forty years—paralleling trends in Guatemala and El Salvador. Workers and peasants could, however, point to some fundamental gains, such as the right to review company financial records and participate in decision-making at state enterprises. The provision of new health, education, and social welfare services was also attributed to the government's basic commitment to assist the poor and working class. Along with the entire

popular movement, the war and economic crisis hit the union movement hard, creating new division and tensions.

Because of their institutional ties to the FSLN and their commitment
to the revolutionary process, the leading labor organizations during the
FSLN government were the CST and the ATC. Nearly two-thirds of the
country's organized workers were affiliated with either of these groups.
Other much smaller union confederations were found to the left and
the right of the Sandinista unions.

To the right of the ATC and CST stand the Confederation of Trade
Union Unity (CUS) and the Nicaraguan Workers Confederation
(CTN), both of which have received U.S. government funding through
the AIFLD. Only CUS, however, is organizationally linked to AIFLD.
Although representing only about 3 percent of the country's workforce,
the two unions had high international profiles during the 1980s. Although it had shied away from the political struggle against Somoza,
CUS became virulently anti-Sandinista, organizing several opposition
demonstrations in 1988 and 1989. Membership estimates have ranged
from two thousand, a figure given by the Sandinista Ministry of Labor,
to 35,000, claimed by CUS. While it has denied any formal relations
with political parties, CUS has been very close to the Social Democratic
party (PSD) and was a strong backer of the UNO campaign.

The other pillar of the right-wing labor movement has been the
CTN, which is affiliated with the Social Christian party (PSC). It has
some 20,000 members from sixty-three unions, ranging from metal
workers to bus drivers, *La Prensa* staff, and banana workers. A CTN
split in 1982 gave rise to the CTN-A, which affiliated with the Popular
Social Christian party (PPSC).

The General Confederation of Workers-Independent (CGT-I), along
with the Nicaraguan Socialist party (PSN), were generally supportive
of the FSLN for most of the 1980s, although the CGT-I strongly
criticized the government's austerity program and in 1987 joined the
opposition alliance Permanent Workers Congress (CPT). Strong in the
construction industry, the CGT-I organized important strikes during
the last year of the FSLN government.

The CPT was formed in late 1987 as an umbrella organization of
four confederations from left and right: CUS, CTN-A, CGT-I, and the
Trade Union Action and Unity Confederation (CAUS). With the initiation of the Esquipulas peace accords, negotiations with the *contras*, and
increased U.S. emphasis on building the internal opposition, there was
more political space available for organizing within the anti-Sandinista
labor movement. Like UNO itself, CPT was largely a product of U.S.-
sponsored unification efforts and benefited from large doses of advice

and financing from AIFLD, AID, and the NED. Despite the ideological diversity that separated them, the CPT unions managed to remain united around a series of demands, including revision of the labor code, elimination of preferential treatment for pro-FSLN unions, and restoration of full trade-union freedoms.

The New Labor Battlefield

The April 1990 inauguration of President Violeta Chamorro dramatically changed the configuration of the Nicaraguan labor movement. The political positions of the two contending union sectors were suddenly reversed. Subject to discrimination and a certain degree of repression during the 1980s, the anti-Sandinista unions counted on rapid growth after the FSLN government was voted out of office. No longer tied to defending the government, the CST and ATC moved easily into the opposition.

The CPT unions, which had so strongly backed the UNO campaign, found themselves torn in several directions at the start of the Chamorro administration. On one hand the CPT found itself in the same position formerly occupied by the Sandinista unions: defending the government against the political and economic challenges of the opposition. On the other hand the CPT, like the U.S. embassy, was extremely uncomfortable with the independent political stance taken by the Chamorro administration in its first months in power. Like the right-wing political parties and business organizations, the CPT unions for the most part are ardently anti-Sandinista and would like to see all vestiges of *sandinismo* destroyed. They fear that the Chamorro government, unwittingly perhaps, gave the Sandinistas a new lease on life.

To bolster their own positions, the CPT unions are seeking to move into workplaces long controlled by the Sandinista unions. Sandinista-sponsored revisions to the labor code, approved by the National Assembly in April 1990, opened up workplaces to more than one union. The FSLN advocated this change to protect its own associated unions from being displaced by unions installed by the UNO government; the CPT unions regarded this multiunion environment conducive to their own growth also. Member unions of CPT quickly moved to establish new anti-Sandinista unions in the private and public sectors, while the National Workers Federation charged that the government was firing thousands of public-sector employees only to replace many with UNO sympathizers.

The electoral defeat of the Sandinistas pushed the Nicaraguan labor movement to the forefront of the country's new economic and political struggles. Nowhere else in the region is the labor movement so strong. The absence of repressive security forces also means that the Nicaraguan labor movement enjoys a degree of freedom unique in the region. Although the government favors the CPT unions, the organizing environment is still extremely competitive. Union struggles in Nicaragua are highly politicized, but the success of one or another of the factions will likely depend more on its stand on economic issues than on its political affiliations.

Schools and Students

Any doubts about the priority the Chamorro government would place on transforming the national education system (guided by Cardinal Obando y Bravo) were removed during the president's inauguration. The new minister and vice minister of education, Sofonías Cisneros and Humberto Belli—close associates of Obando and members of the City of God charismatic Catholic sect—quickly set about the task of "depoliticizing" the nation's schools.[49] The changes being implemented in Nicaraguan schools seek to marginalize Sandinista influence and revolutionary ideology, replacing them with a traditionalist worldview more appropriate to the social and economic policies pursued by the UNO government.

Implementation of the new project has already generated conflict. The pro-Sandinista teachers' union ANDEN has a significant presence among the country's 30,000 teachers, many of whom are resisting efforts to make a radical break with the past. Many parents, particularly those who belong to protestant churches, are also expected to resist change. A glimpse of the struggles to come was provided early on in the Chamorro administration when a major battle was fought over proposed textbook changes. Within weeks of the government's inauguration, thousands of new primary-school readers—printed with funds furnished by AID—arrived in the country. The Ministry of Education's goal was to substitute the imported texts for the Nicaraguan-produced reader that had been used during the 1980s. Faced with an uproar from ANDEN, as well as from pedagogic experts who criticized the notion of changing books in mid-semester, the MED temporarily backed off.[50] Other bones of contention have been the firing of school directors and their replacement with UNO partisans, and MED-sponsored efforts to impose a parallel, progovernment teachers' union.

Popular reactions forced the UNO government to back off on another early initiative, the move to undermine university autonomy. The

University Autonomy Law, passed by the outgoing Sandinista-dominated National Assembly, guarantees "academic, financial, organic and administrative autonomy" for four state and two private universities and two centers of higher education. The law also stipulates that each university will be responsible for electing its own rector, faculty council, and other governing bodies. In mid-May 1990 Chamorro handed the legislature a bill of reforms to the autonomy law. The bill called for the immediate suspension of the electoral process for university authorities, already well under way at the time, pending review of the entire law.

The executive's action provoked a quick and massive response by students, professors, and administrators, many of whom had struggled for years in favor of university autonomy. In the face of the backlash, Chamorro changed tacks, asking the National Assembly to send the bill to committee for further discussion there and with the university community. The committee introduced only minor reforms and the bill was then passed by an overwhelming majority in the National Assembly.

Many in the university community predict that the law will come up for reforms again as UNO moves toward its goal of eliminating what it sees as a "Sandinista stronghold" in the universities. Meanwhile, Obando announced plans to counter progressive currents at Managua's Jesuit-run Central American University by constructing a new papally sanctioned university.

The provision of minimum educational opportunities, free of charge, to the Nicaraguan population constituted a central goal of the Sandinista government's project to extend social services to the majority. Efforts to extend educational opportunities to the population were initiated in earnest in 1980 with the launching of the National Literacy Crusade. The crusade, part of a larger project that aspired to provide 92 percent of the population with a functional literacy level by the year 2000, was billed as a "cultural insurrection," a sequel to the armed struggle against Somoza. The total pretriumph student population of about 300,000 had mushroomed to more than one million by 1989. Parallel to the greatly expanded public education system, Nicaragua had 247 private schools, mostly religious, of which 188 received partial financing from the Sandinista government until the onset of austerity measures in 1989.

After 1983 the education system as a whole suffered because of the diversion of national resources toward fighting the war and because schools and teachers were priority targets for the *contras*. By late 1987 the toll was substantial: 411 teachers killed and sixty-six kidnapped; fifty-nine students kidnapped; forty-six schools destroyed, twenty-one damaged, and 555 temporarily forced to close, leaving 45,000 students without classrooms.[51]

Communications Media

The Nicaraguan media has long been a hotbed of polemics. Even during the 1980s, when censorship of opposition media was imposed on several occasions, the country's radio waves and newspapers were vociferous defenders of opposing political projects.[52] Even the harshly anti-Sandinista *New York Times* conceded in a March 11, 1988, editorial that "there's more diversity of published and spoken opinion in Managua than in Guatemala, Honduras, and El Salvador."

At a deeper level, efforts throughout the 1980s to transform the country's media institutions constituted an integral part of the Sandinistas' project to empower the Nicaraguan masses. Such initiatives were based on a democratic model of media structure and access unique in Latin America. Its features included balance in the ownership of media outlets among public, private, and cooperative forms; political and ideological pluralism in media content; and the promotion of popular participation and horizontal communication through the mass media. The underlying philosophy was that the media, instead of serving the narrow interests of a wealthy elite, should become vehicles for expression of the opinions of the broad majority of society, and that notions of social responsibility should guide the media's activities as opposed to narrowly defined profit motives. Many of the resulting media experiments were cut short by war-related restrictions and economic constraints. Nonetheless, the media access gained by broad sectors of the population during the revolution is a major legacy, which the Chamorro government will have to confront.[53]

Formally, the government is committed to absolute freedom of expression, and much of Chamorro's reputation is built around her image as a resolute defender of press freedom. During the UNO government's tense first four months in office, the battle for public opinion was intense. Electronic and print media, bolstered by the addition of dozens of new shows, newsletters, and magazines, quickly came to reflect an increasingly fractured and polarized society.

The New Media Lineup

Not surprisingly, the April 1990 change of government was accompanied by major shakeups in the ownership and content of many of the country's existing media outlets, as well as the creation of dozens of new ones. Radio and television stations and newspapers staked out their positions in alliance with the Chamorro government or with the broad array of opposition forces to the left and right. There was little room for "independent" media projects.[54]

La Prensa found itself confronted with a serious dilemma. For decades the paper's reputation had been built on its image as the "bastion of opposition." In a political culture that thrives on criticizing those in power and opposing anything associated with the government, the paper suddenly became the semiofficial mouthpiece of the country's president.[55] La Prensa was forced to navigate through much murkier waters of conflicting political interests and shifting alliances. Accordingly, during the conflict-ridden first three months of Chamorro's administration, the pages of La Prensa became a portrait of contrasts. Lofty calls to patience and reconciliation appeared side by side with the crudest forms of Sandinista-bashing. For the most part, however, La Prensa weathered the transition well. Although the paper carried its share of progovernment stories and editorials, it largely avoided the excesses of "officialism," which had plagued the FSLN's Barricada during the 1980s. Like the other two dailies, La Prensa suffered a loss of readership due to the precipitous decline in purchasing power under UNO's economic-stabilization measures. The drop in income from lost advertising has hurt Barricada and El Nuevo Diario, the country's second- and third-largest dailies. Barricada has announced intentions to drop its status as the FSLN's paper.

Under the Sandinistas, the state maintained a monopoly on television broadcasting through ownership of the country's two stations (Channels 2 and 6). The UNO-appointed director of the network, Carlos Briceño, instituted a thoroughgoing change in programming and initiated a process of substituting pro-Sandinista staff members with UNO activists and exiles brought back from Miami. Reports indicated that several groups—including the FSLN, COSEP, and that of U.S. televangelist Pat Robertson—had been authorized to open new channels, but by late 1990 the Chamorro government's monopoly remained intact.

While the Chamorro faction of UNO had a distinct advantage through its television monopoly and La Prensa, its weakest presence was to be found in the medium that in many ways is Nicaragua's most important: radio. With newspapers beyond the budget of the majority of Nicaraguans, and television largely limited to advantaged sectors of the urban population, radio is the key medium for reaching the broader population. There are approximately forty radio stations currently operating in Nicaragua.

The three prerevolutionary stations, in addition to the network of community stations set up in other parts of the country, are all expected to feel the pinch as advertising revenues dry up. During the 1980s a large part of their operating budgets came from selling advertising to state companies, which are now either in the process of being privatized or have moved their ads to the right-wing stations.

The State of Health

Nicaraguans witnessed a dramatic increase in health care during the early years of the Sandinista revolution.[56] But the *contra* war and economic-austerity measures hit the health sector hard, and by the end of the 1980s key indicators showed public health in decline. These trends are likely to continue under the UNO government as the demand for health services increases in proportion to the declining public-health conditions brought on by growing poverty and unemployment. Minister of Health Ernesto Salmerón, the Chamorros' family physician, has established a positive working relationship with health workers including those belonging to the pro-Sandinista union FET-SALUD. He has, however, often found his hands tied in dealing with the growing health crisis because of the drastic budget restrictions prescribed by the economic-stabilization plan.

In Somoza's Nicaragua, access to health care was essentially a luxury for a privileged minority. Upon taking power, the Sandinista government embarked on a major program to revamp the health system based on the conviction that access to decent and affordable health services should be a basic human right guaranteed to every citizen. The long-range goal was to create a national, socialized health-care system. Given the shortage of resources, it was agreed that in the short term, private health care would continue to exist alongside an expanded public system of hospitals, primary-care clinics, and mass-based health campaigns. To streamline the public sector, a National Unified Health System was created under the jurisdiction of the Ministry of Health. Initially health care and medicines were provided free of charge, but as austerity policies deepened later in the 1980s, user fees were gradually introduced.

Substantial expansion was achieved in both curative and preventive medicine. More than four hundred new health clinics and posts were opened and several major hospitals were built. A new medical school was opened, expanding the capacity for doctor training from fifty to five hundred per year.

The major thrust of Nicaragua's initiatives to improve the nation's health, however, was based on direct participation of the population in health affairs. In 1981 and 1982 basic health training was given to some 80,000 *brigadistas*, volunteer paramedical health aides capable of carrying rudimentary services to even the most isolated corners of the nation. In coordination with the popular organizations and local health officials, the *brigadistas* carried out annual nationwide health-education campaigns, vaccination drives for the eradication of infectious diseases such as polio, and a malaria-control program.

Nearly all major health- and living-standard indicators showed considerable improvements from 1979 to 1983, when the combination of war and economic crisis began to turn many of the trends around. Infant mortality, which stood at 121 deaths per thousand live births before the triumph was cut almost in half by 1985, and both malaria and polio were completely eradicated. Even life expectancy, where improvements usually are spread out over long time periods, had gone from fifty-two years before 1979 to sixty-two years by 1988.

The growing economic crisis, however, has placed severe constraints on the country's general health situation, as dramatically exemplified in the case of diarrhea, the principal cause of death among children under five years of age. Most diarrhea in children is caused by low-quality drinking water or general unsanitary conditions in the home. In Managua, less than 50 percent of the population has access to safe water, in large measure due to the explosion of urban-squatter settlements. In the rural areas, the figure is less than 10 percent. In all urban areas of the country, sewer systems reach less than 40 percent of the homes.

Another worrisome trend tied to deteriorating economic conditions is the rise of malnutrition among children due to a decline in food consumption, particularly protein-rich staples such as beans, meat, and milk. One source estimates that 48 percent of all children are born into households with "inadequate living conditions."[57]

The control of epidemic diseases in 1990 has been complicated by economic and political factors. Some health workers feel that the central government is holding back on budget outlays to the Ministry of Health in an effort to starve out the hospitals and clinics, thus paving the way for their privatization. The reduction and elimination of government subsidies for basic medicines has placed them far beyond the reach of many people who could afford them before. The government contends that reduced funding is simply part of the general effort to cut spending. The minister of health also has announced plans to search abroad for funding for the crippled health-care system, apparently convinced that adequate resources will not be forthcoming from the central government.

Some see a potential hidden bonus in the process of budget cutbacks at the Ministry of Health. Although in the short run they will lead to a reduction of services as personnel are laid off and primary-care centers close down, this might stimulate a greater degree of community-level organizing around health needs. The reduction of dependence on the central government and increased reliance on people taking responsibility for their own solutions in the field of health could stimulate a broader dynamic of grass-roots empowerment.

Religion

Perhaps even more than the media or political parties, the religious terrain in Nicaragua was an ideological battlefield after 1979. Both the Catholic and evangelical churches were wracked by divisions between pro- and counterrevolutionary tendencies. In the end, the Catholic Church's unrelenting opposition to revolutionary changes in Nicaragua succeeded in severely eroding the Sandinistas' legitimacy.

The conflicts that would come to pervade the Catholic Church and create tense relations between the Sandinista government and the hierarchy were largely unforeseen in 1979.[58] Notwithstanding Cardinal Obando's last-minute collaboration in Carter-sponsored efforts to avoid a Sandinista victory, there was widespread optimism for a fruitful relationship on both sides after the triumph. The Church was assured a central role in national life as thousands of Christians took up the tasks of reconstruction, and several priests were appointed to high positions within the new government. In late 1980 the FSLN ratified the "Document on Religion," guaranteeing total freedom of worship and respect for all religious beliefs. Earlier that year, the National Literacy Crusade was kicked off, under the leadership of Jesuit priest Father Fernando Cardenal, with the blessing of both the pope and Cardinal Obando.

The adversarial stance later adopted by the Catholic Church hierarchy was touched off by a series of clashes with the Sandinista government in mid-1982. The confrontational posture was reinforced and legitimized during Pope John Paul II's March 1983 visit to Nicaragua, in which he came down squarely on the side of the bishops during an open-air mass attended by some 700,000 people in Managua.

The spiral of conflicts gave way to a gradual easing of tensions and dialogue after 1986. In 1987, with the momentum unleashed by the

Esquipulas peace process, the government turned to Obando, naming him head of the National Reconciliation Commission and then mediator in cease-fire talks with the *contras*. The Sandinistas felt that Obando's strong influence among the *contra* leadership and his broad legitimacy among the population would help pave the way for an authentic process of peace and reconciliation. Likewise, the FSLN government expected that the protagonist role given to Obando in the peace process would undermine anti-Sandinista sentiment among those sectors of the population who had followed the cardinal's lead in opposing the revolution. In the end, the FSLN's calculations proved wrong. Obando capitalized on the opening for his own anti-Sandinista agenda and played an unabashedly pro-*contra* role as "mediator" in their negotiations with the government. Later, with the process of *contra* demobilization effectively stalled, Obando became a major supporter of Chamorro's bid for the presidency.

With the Chamorro government firmly installed, the Catholic hierarchy wasted no time in moving forward with its ambitious agenda. "We have two themes," said Obando's spokesman Bismarck Carballo. "To promote the family in Nicaragua and unity within the Church. The pope has asked that we promote a new evangelism, with new priests and new methods. We want to purify the Church."[59] In essence, "promoting the family" means reimposing the traditional, conservative social order and moral values.

Despite the generally cozy relationship between Obando and Chamorro, there has been some friction. On several occasions, Obando and the Catholic Church hierarchy have criticized the government and tacitly given their approval and support to the Chamorro group's "tactical adversaries"—the right-wing extremists in UNO and the *contras*. In an effort to ensure the Church's continued influence in any potential confrontation, and to maximize positions in terms of isolating *sandinismo*, Obando has attempted to play with both sides at the same time.

City of God

Cardinal Obando's prominence in relation to the Chamorro government has overlapped with, and in some cases been overshadowed by, that of a little-known charismatic Catholic group, Ciudad de Dios (City of God). Prominent individuals from the group, estimated to have about eight hundred members, have taken influential cabinet and advisory posts in the Chamorro administration.

One observer described the groups this way: "They practice 'shepherding discipleship,' which requires a member's total submission to a hierarchy of command. Authority, submission, and a belief that they are specially chosen by God are combined with layers of secrecy and ritual that keep members aloof from the rest of society."[60] For City of God members, life revolves around the search for direct, personal communication with God.

City of God members opted to keep their distance from the anti-Somoza struggle, sticking to the belief that worldly injustice was divinely dictated. With the Sandinistas in power, however, many became active opponents, working in concert with Obando, COSEP, and *La Prensa* to topple the revolutionary government.

Evangelicalism on the Rise

Nicaragua's evangelical churches experienced rapid growth during the 1980s. By the end of the decade estimates of evangelical strength ran as high as one-fifth of the population.[61] This expansion was as much a product of the Sandinista government's policy of religious freedom as it was of the broader trend in Central America where the effects of war and economic crisis have provided fertile terrain for the growth of dozens of evangelical denominations. With the arrival of the UNO government, both conservative and progressive evangelicals openly expressed their fears that the close relationship between Chamorro and Obando, as well as the sizable presence of charismatic Catholics in Chamorro's cabinet, threatened to elevate Catholicism to the *de facto* position of official religion in Nicaragua. Progressive evangelicals felt doubly cornered with the initiation of a campaign by conservative denominations in Nicaragua and the United States to consolidate anti-Sandinista sentiment among all Nicaraguan Christians, regardless of their religious affiliation.

The largest and oldest of the 118 non-Catholic denominations and groups are the Moravians (concentrated on the Atlantic coast), the Assemblies of God, and the Baptist Convention of Nicaragua.[62] The recent evangelical boom is largely attributable to the rapid growth of such pentecostal churches as the Assemblies of God. Most of the country's pentecostal churches, which now account for some 85 percent of all Nicaraguan evangelicals, are recently arrived and are still relatively small. In part, this boom is explained by the fact that the evangelical religions offered a participatory, less hierarchical experience than did the traditional Roman Catholic Church.

Although evangelical pastors, following the guidance of private U.S. organizations and the U.S. embassy, became involved in counterrevolutionary activity, mainline protestant denominations like the Baptists

were more supportive of the revolution. The bulk of progressive protestants are grouped together under the Evangelical Committee for Aid
to Development (CEPAD), formed to assist relief efforts after the 1972
earthquake. CEPAD, which has grown to incorporate forty-nine member denominations, is an influential force at the national level and
sponsors a wide array of social-development projects in the countryside. On the other end of the spectrum, a smaller split from CEPAD,
the National Council of Evangelical Pastors of Nicaragua (CNPEN), is
organized around several hundred conservative pastors. CNPEN enjoys close ties with the Institute on Religion and Democracy (IRD) and
with numerous right-wing protestant groups in the United States.[63]
While CNPEN members are not monolithically reactionary, the organizational leadership consistently adopted a counterrevolutionary posture during the 1980s.

Women and Feminism

The most noticeable gains won by women as a result of the Sandinista
revolution took place in two areas: changes in the legal superstructure
and the incorporation of women into production and political life. The
Nicaraguan constitution, promulgated in January 1987, overturned
the historical legal discrimination against Nicaraguan women, establishing equality between the sexes as a fundamental right of all Nicaraguans. The constitution also obliges the state to remove, by all available
means, obstacles to full equality. Modifications proposed by the
women's movement, as well as input by women during open assemblies
held to enrich the draft constitution, were instrumental in reformulat-
ing earlier draft versions of the document.

In addition to the constitutional clauses, a host of Nicaraguan laws
passed since 1979 addressing women's issues are far more progressive
than most in the Americas. They cover such areas as adoption, divorce,
common-law marriage, and familial relations. These and other legal
modifications empowered Nicaraguan women in their struggle to
achieve greater equality.

The participation of women in the workforce and formal political life
of the nation increased dramatically in the 1980s. By 1989 women
represented 45 percent of the working population.[64] Nonetheless, for
the most part the jobs open to women remained concentrated in the
lower levels of the industrial pay scale, and women continued to pre-
dominate in commerce and the informal sector.

Despite the existence of a militant women's movement in Nicaragua,
backed during the 1980s by a government that was at least in principle

committed to the promotion of women's rights, several important factors constrained the pace of change. First, the Sandinistas' commitment to backing progressive change in favor of women was tempered by the hesitation to struggle against *machismo* within the party and government, and by the decision to place the defense effort above sector-specific demands.

Second, Nicaragua is a socially conservative country, particularly in the countryside. Despite many of the efforts sponsored by the Sandinistas and by the women's movement to promote an alternative vision of women's role in society, in the streets and in the homes attitudes often changed little. Third, the influential Catholic Church hierarchy tenaciously resisted many of the government's policies regarding women. It opposed reforms in the areas of family life and education and the participation of women in the military, as well as rigidly insisting on adherence to the papal encyclical stating that contraception is a sin.[65]

Despite some NED-funded pre-electoral outreach to women, during the first four months of the Chamorro administration it became clear to Nicaraguan women that having the first woman president in Central American history was not an advance for feminism. Violeta Chamorro in many ways epitomized the social conservatism of traditional Nicaragua, and her close ties to the Catholic Church hierarchy, together with the austerity policies of the UNO government, threatened to overturn many of the gains women had made during the 1980s.

Women soon were bearing a large part of the fallout from two broader trends initiated by the new government. First, as unemployment mushroomed, women became "last hired and first fired." The economic hardships faced by newly unemployed women, most of whom were heads of households, were aggravated by cutbacks and cost increases in social services, particularly in health and child care.

Second, the Catholic Church's ideological crusade, strongly endorsed by President Chamorro, sought to reimpose traditional, conservative social values. These changes were most graphically represented in the attack on reproductive rights. As part of the government's efforts to stamp out abortion—illegal but widely tolerated under the Sandinistas—Managua's women's hospital stopped the practice of performing therapeutic abortions, while progovernment media beamed powerful antiabortion messages. A television series on sex education, "Sex and Youth," was ordered taken off the air, and Ministry of Education officials engaged in a project to rewrite sex-education literature used in the nation's schools. According to numerous public declarations by Church and education authorities, the use of all contraceptives other than the rhythm method will be condemned.

In part as a response to the growing problem of unemployment among women, and to fill the void left by the government's cancellation of basic social services, a host of new nongovernmental organizations dedicated to women's issues have sprung up since April 1990. These groups are attempting to offer free or low-cost services to women, including legal assistance, sex education, family planning, and gynecologic care.

Native Peoples

Nicaragua's ethnic communities—Creoles, Miskitos, Sumus, Ramas, and Garifuna—share the vast expanses of the Atlantic coast with some 180,000 Spanish-speaking *mestizos*.[66] While the Atlantic coast region encompasses more than half of the nation's territory, its population of roughly 300,000 is less than one-tenth of the national total. The Miskitos are the most numerous native group, numbering around 67,000 according to conservative estimates. There are also about five thousand Sumus and fewer than six hundred Ramas. There are about 26,000 English-speaking Afro-Americans, or Creoles, while the small Afro-Indian Garifuna group numbers around 1,500.

The Sandinista victory in 1979 created, for the first time, the space and conditions in which Nicaragua's indigenous peoples could press for fulfillment of their historical demands. However, the FSLN's inexperience with ethnic politics and ignorance of the coast's complexities led to political clashes with Misurasata, an indigenous mass organization formed just after the Sandinista victory, that drove some to join the *contras* while thousands of others migrated to Costa Rica and Honduras.

By 1985 relations between the indigenous population and the Sandinistas had begun to improve, mainly as a result of reexamination by the government of its own views and policies.[67] The FSLN openly admitted many of its mistakes in its relations with the native population and rectified earlier policy shortcomings. The Miskito combatants, for their part, were tired of fighting, and the Indian population had had enough of war.

A lengthy process of negotiations with both political leaders and field commanders of the Indian fighters led to a gradual lessening of hostilities. The factor that finally tipped the balance in favor of peace on the Atlantic coast came in September 1987, when the National Assembly signed the Autonomy Statute into law. The product of two and a half years of grass-roots consultations among the coastal communities, the statute incorporated a series of demands put forth by the indigenous groups and was backed by guarantees in the Nicaraguan constitution.

The Autonomy Statute called for the installation of two forty-five member coastal governments—one in the north, known as the North Atlantic Autonomous Region (RAAN), the other in the south (RAAS)—comprising directly elected representatives from each ethnic group. These councils were to be responsible for governing regional trade with the Caribbean, distributing basic goods, and administrating health, education, and cultural services. They also were charged with developing a plan for the natural use of the region's resources. The intent of the autonomy statute was for the regional governments to have control over finances as well. The central government would transfer all financing authority for the Atlantic coast to the autonomy councils and the councils were empowered to design a taxation plan. In addition, the councils were to administer a special development fund for the region, composed of contributions from bilateral and multilateral sources as well as the central government.

In 1990 elections for the autonomous governments and the change in Managua from the FSLN to UNO opened up a new phase on the Atlantic coast.[68] Despite the tenacious continuity of old rivalries and the eruption of new ones, for the first time in a decade conflicts were now being played out politically rather than with military force. By mid-1990 peace, or at least the absence of shooting, had become a reality on the coast.

On May 9, 1990, the new regional government authorities, the North Atlantic Autonomous Region (RAAN) and the South "AA" Region (RAAS), were formally sworn in. The RAAN—whose February 1990 elections had resulted in twenty-two seats for Yatama (the Miskito Indian Organization), twenty-one for the FSLN, and two for UNO— elected moderate Yatama activist Leonel Pantin as coordinator of its Autonomous Council, the highest representative of the autonomous government. In the RAAS—twenty-three seats for UNO, eighteen for the FSLN, and four for Yatama—the post went to Alvin Guthrie, who also was elected as a UNO deputy in the National Assembly and is head of the right-wing trade-union federation CUS.[69]

The biggest threat to autonomy came not from internal dissensions, but from the central government in Managua. In April, Chamorro created the Institute for the Development of the Atlantic Coast (IN-DERA) and appointed Brooklyn Rivera as director. The creation of INDERA was not well received on the coast and many saw it as a direct attempt to undermine autonomy. The RAAS Autonomous Council sent a letter to Chamorro condemning INDERA as "antihistorical, illegal, and unconstitutional." They were fearful that Managua would attempt to use INDERA to usurp powers delegated to the regional governments, and that as head of the institute Rivera would be well placed to favor his followers, for the most part Miskitos from the RAAN.

Environment

The Sandinista government sponsored a variety of initiatives aimed at protecting the environment and conserving natural resources.[70] An integral part of this strategy was the attempt to transform the prevailing agricultural model and land-tenure patterns.

As a result of the agricultural expansion under way since the 1950s, large agroexport plantations and cattle ranches constantly ate away at Nicaragua's tropical rain forests. The Sandinista agrarian reform sought to break up many of the large plantations and to foster the creation of agricultural cooperatives and small family farms. It also sought to break the chronic dependence on a few export crops and to move toward national self-sufficiency in basic-grains production. This model, it was hoped, would help the country move away from the destructive and expensive "pesticide treadmill" to sustainable methods such as crop rotation and integrated pest management (IPM). Terracing and reforestation practices to foster soil and watershed conservation also received official backing from the government. However, after 1985 the Sandinistas' objective of promoting environmentally sound practices was deprioritized by three factors: the war, economic-austerity policies, and differences within the government over the relationship between development policies and environmentalism.

When economic reforms were introduced to fuel the defense effort, sharp cutbacks were made in all but the most essential social and economic projects; environmental programs were among the first to face the budget ax. DIRENA, which had been set up in 1979 to coordinate all aspects of natural-resource management, saw its mandate and budget gradually whittled away after 1983. Many of DIRENA's ambitious plans, such as the creation of a large national parks system, remained on the drawing board. Nicaragua's IPM program, regarded by many as the most advanced in Latin America, was similarly cut back in the wake of austerity policies.

Nicaragua's efforts to protect its forests, hindered by the effects of war and economic crisis, were dealt another heavy blow in October 1988 as Hurricane Joan destroyed some 10 percent of the country's tropical rain forests, advancing deforestation by fifteen years in the space of four short hours. With large quantities of wood felled by the hurricane located in and around the *contras'* Río San Juan development pole, *contra* leaders were enthusiastic about a plan to generate jobs and income through extracting and processing the trees. Some environmentalists, however, cautioned that the negative effects of such an operation could be devastating because the zone has few existing roads.

Beginning with President Violeta Chamorro's inauguration speech the UNO government has consistently professed a commitment to environmental protection. Chamorro appointed the country's best-known environmentalist, Jaime Incer, to head the Institute of Natural Resources and the Environment (IRENA, formerly DIRENA). Incer soon began speaking of ambitious plans to arrest environmental decay and to promote sustainable development practices.

Although willing to give the benefit of the doubt to Chamorro regarding her proclaimed commitment to conservation, many Nicaraguan environmentalists questioned the extent to which ecologically sound policies would be compatible with the broader thrust of the government's economic and agrarian policies. Early policy decisions including austerity measures, privatization, and a renewed emphasis on agroexport crops produced by large private producers indicated that the economic model being pursued could lead only to the perpetuation of environmentally destructive practices.

FOREIGN INFLUENCE

U.S. Foreign Policy

President Ronald Reagan quickly grasped the ideological threat that Sandinista Nicaragua represented. During his eight years in the White House, the campaign against the FSLN took the form of a crusade and obsession. The counterrevolution became a passion that pushed aside legal restraints and more pragmatic solutions. During the 1980s Washington directed considerable money and energy toward destroying the Sandinistas' revolutionary project—not toward furthering democracy and development in Nicaragua.

The extremes to which Washington was willing to go in pursuit of its objectives reflected the degree to which Nicaragua was a threat—not to its neighbors or to any real U.S. security interests, but to the way the U.S. government has traditionally viewed its interests in Latin America. Symbolically, revolutionary Nicaragua represented the antithesis of the U.S. vision of what reality should look like south of its borders. The small country held up an alternative model of socioeconomic change: one based on national sovereignty, political pluralism, a mixed economy, and improved living standards for the majority. The stakes of the conflict also rose to the extent that the White House, Pentagon, and CIA, spurred on by important forces from the New Right, conceived of the Nicaraguan counterrevolution as a litmus test for the Reagan doctrine and for the application of the precepts of low-intensity conflict in a counterrevolutionary context.

The original Reagan plan of counterrevolution sought to combine economic pressure, political manipulation, and support for the internal opposition. But the heart of the project consisted of military support for the armed *contras*. The goal was to throw the revolution into turmoil, provoking anti-Sandinista unrest and, eventually, an insurrection. When this approach failed to overturn the Sandinista revolution, the U.S.-sponsored *contra* forces began to wage a prolonged, grinding war of attrition against the government forces, while Washington increased pressures aimed at isolating the Sandinistas in the economic, diplomatic, and political arena. The attrition strategy—spearheaded by the massive destruction inflicted on the country by the *contra* army—was more successful than the earlier approach in advancing the United States toward its goals. For some Nicaraguans, economic hardships and war weariness began to make the revolution look like a no-win alternative. But the fruits of the attrition strategy would not be fully harvested until long after Ronald Reagan left the White House.

As Reagan's vice president, George Bush showed himself to be a strong supporter of the *contras* and the entire U.S. strategy of waging counterrevolutionary war against the Sandinista government. By the time Bush ascended to the presidency, however, the time had come to move away from the increasingly unproductive *contra* war and to focus on building a more effective internal opposition. President Bush abandoned Reagan's obsessive anti-Sandinista crusade but continued the fundamental policy of seeking to destroy the Sandinistas.

Upon becoming president, Bush shifted away from the more aggressive policies of his predecessor and slowly began distancing himself from the *contras*. The key tactical dilemmas hinged on what to do with the *contras* in light of Central America's resolve to disband them, and how best to build up an internal anti-Sandinista coalition. The bipartisan accord placed the *contras* on the back burner; it tacitly accepted the inevitability of their eventual disbanding, while allowing the Bush administration to use "humanitarian aid" to keep the *contra* threat alive until after the 1990 election. This continued assistance to the *contras*, which violated the Esquipulas agreements, reminded Nicaraguan voters that six more years of Sandinista rule could mean six more years of war.

Washington has not abandoned Nicaragua, but its commitment to support the new UNO government and rebuild the country is not commensurate with its decade-long campaign to destabilize the Sandinista revolution. The NED is still funding programs in the country, but no longer will millions of dollars be targeted for Nicaragua. AID has given Nicaragua special consideration in UNO's first year, but the country cannot expect a generous long-term commitment. Rather than giving the new administration a grace period, Washington has indicated that it will be hard-nosed in insisting that a neoliberal restructuring program be implemented, no matter what its social and political consequences.

In its new policy toward Nicaragua, Washington is not just taking aim at the vestiges of the revolution—from agrarian reform to government control over international trade—but also looking to destroy *sandinismo* as a political and social force. Winning elections had been only one aspect of Washington's strategy of creating and supporting a wide range of civic, political, media, business, and labor organizations.

Following UNO's election victory the U.S. Embassy, which had long coordinated the internal opposition, started to bustle with new activity. Down to fifteen staff members before the election, the embassy began to swell immediately after Chamorro's inauguration. Some officials have moved over from Honduras, where they were in charge of *contra* operations, but dozens more are coming from Washington to set up the new AID mission and Department of Commerce office.

U.S. Trade and Investment

Although some U.S. traders and investors were scared off by the revolution, the most damaging economic moves were made by Washington. In 1981 the Reagan administration cut off the trade and investment credits offered by the U.S. Export-Import Bank (Eximbank) and the Overseas Private Investment Corporation (OPIC). The next step in the escalating trade war came in 1983 when Washington slashed the country's sugar quota. That same year President Reagan ordered the closing of all Nicaraguan consular and commercial offices in the United States—an action that further obstructed U.S. trade and investment in Nicaragua. The final blow was delivered in 1985 when the president announced a complete embargo against Nicaragua. Under the provisions of the International Emergency Economic Powers Act, the president could declare an embargo in a situation involving "any unusual and extraordinary threat to the national security, foreign policy, or economy of the United States."[71]

The embargo declaration merely accelerated Nicaragua's efforts to diversify its trading partners. The diversification efforts, already well under way by 1985, were adopted as part of the government's non-alignment strategy and in expectation of an eventual U.S. embargo. When the embargo was announced, U.S. trade accounted for less than 15 percent of the country's commercial relations. Despite a direct plea launched by several private business groups in Nicaragua and backed by Cardinal Obando y Bravo, the Bush administration decided to renew the embargo in May 1989, and again in November of that year. It was not until March 1990 that the embargo was finally lifted—an action that the U.S. Department of Commerce asserted would allow the United States to "resume its role as Nicaragua's most vital trading partner."[72]

The U.S. Department of Commerce believes potential U.S. exports to Nicaragua could reach $1 billion annually for the next few years as the country reconstructs. All of Washington's usual array of incentives and trade weapons are being quickly put into place. Most important is the economic-aid program, which will be used, according to the agreements being signed with the Nicaraguan government, to buy mostly U.S. goods and services. Eximbank took Nicaragua off its blacklist of Marxist-Leninist countries and approved short-term trade insurance. More important than the usual Eximbank trade insurance will be the Trade Credit Insurance Program (TCIP), a program that allows AID to use taxpayer funds to guarantee high-risk trade with Central America.

Despite the increase in U.S. investment and trade, there certainly has not been a flood of new business. The first major corporations to enter Nicaragua have been airline and shipping companies such as Continental and Sea-Land. Mining, lumber, and ranching companies—including Rosario Resources (AMAX), Robinson Lumber, and Peterson Ranching—that were notorious for their exploitative practices during the Somoza era have expressed interest in reinvesting. Standard Fruit, a Castle & Cooke subsidiary, has visited its old banana estates and is considering reinvesting in Nicaragua, as is United Brands.

The U.S. Department of Commerce is advising potential U.S. investors that there are at least 160 state enterprises that will soon be privatized, "opening interesting opportunities for investors" in "publicly owned businesses ranging from a discotheque, hard-currency stores, and a luxury resort to sugar mills, beef slaughterhouses, a cement plant, textile factories, and beer and soft-drink processing

plants."[73] AID has promised to provide the technical assistance necessary to facilitate this immense privatization process. Nevertheless, while
the investment opportunities may be attractive at first glance, the transfer of government properties to U.S. corporations will likely set off
major labor conflicts and stir up the nationalist spirit of the Nicaraguan
populace.

U.S. Economic Aid

During the 1960s and 1970s Nicaragua was a favored recipient of U.S.
economic aid; AID's funds constituted as much as 15 percent of the
government's budget. After the Sandinista revolution, U.S. economic
aid to the government of Nicaragua was cut sharply under Carter and
ceased under Reagan. Although the cutoff in bilateral assistance from
the United States was a serious blow, Nicaragua was eventually able to
compensate by establishing aid programs with other countries, particularly in Western Europe and the Soviet Union. More painful were the
U.S. pressures against multinational bank assistance, because many of
these loans were destined for development projects that constituted an
essential element of the Sandinistas' long-term strategy for building an
economy able to meet its population's basic needs.

In mid-1981 Washington began systematically to use its voting
power as well as numerous delaying techniques to oppose all loans from
the multinational banks for Nicaraguan development projects. World
Bank and Inter-American Development Bank (IDB) lending to
Nicaragua gradually slowed to a trickle. By 1984 Nicaragua had become the only Latin American member country not to receive an IDB
loan. All told, between 1981 and 1984 Nicaragua lost $400 million in
loans and credits approved as bilateral and multilateral aid, subsequently blocked by the Reagan administration.[74]

The sources, recipients, and objectives behind U.S. funding for the
internal opposition have closely followed the twists and turns of Washington's overall strategy against the Sandinistas, and the fate of the
contras in particular. For the most part, aid to the internal opposition
was channeled through an international private network that was coordinated and largely funded by the U.S. government.

At first the *contras* were the focus of the U.S. network's assistance
programs. Working closely with the National Security Council and the
CIA, private groups raised funds to support the counterrevolution.
Groups such as the U.S. Council for World Freedom and Civilian
Material Assistance (CMA) provided the *contras* with military advisers,
equipment, and mercenaries. Most U.S. private groups, however, struc-

tured their fund-raising efforts along humanitarian lines, providing food, medicine, and other nonlethal supplies to the *contras* and their families.

Inside Nicaragua, direct and overt U.S. government aid to the Catholic Church hierarchy and the private-sector elite had been suspended in 1981. But U.S. economic support for the internal opposition was never completely shut off. In the early 1980s the CIA became the main backer of internal opposition groups, including the newspaper *La Prensa*.[75] In addition to this clandestine funding, the internal opposition counted on other sources of U.S. government and private support. The American Institute for Free Labor Development (AIFLD), for instance, kept the right-wing CUS labor federation alive through training and travel programs for its leaders and social-welfare services for its members.[76]

Beginning in 1984 the NED became a leading source of support for the internal opposition. From 1984 to 1988 NED funneled more than $2 million to opposition groups, ranging from human-rights organizations to the media. The primary recipients were UNO candidate Chamorro's *La Prensa*, the CUS, the CTN, the Nicaraguan Permanent Commission on Human Rights, and business associations and political parties associated with the Nicaraguan Democratic Coordinator (CDN). NED's patronage allowed these groups, most of which operated with little popular support, to remain viable until the time of the elections, when they were called upon to mobilize associated constituencies.

Between October 1988 and the elections in February 1990, NED supplied nearly $12 million for the electoral process in Nicaragua. Some of the money was used for election observer teams, the administrative costs of the pass-through grantees, and a required contribution to the Nicaraguan Supreme Electoral Council, which oversaw the elections. The bulk, however, went to UNO and to its network of civic groups. Such groups included the Nicaraguan Women's Movement (MMN), Youth Training Center (CEFOJ), *Vía Cívica*, and the Institute for Electoral Promotion and Training.

In addition to those mentioned above, the increased NED funding flowed through the National Republican Institute for International Affairs, National Democratic Institute for International Affairs, International Foundation for Electoral Systems, the Center for Democracy, America's Development Foundation, and the Pro-Democracy Association (based in Costa Rica). Other U.S. private organizations not part of the NED network also joined the effort to support the internal opposition and defeat the Sandinistas in the 1990 election. These included the

World Freedom Foundation and the Simón Bolívar Fund—each of which took care to demonstrate bipartisan consensus for their activities within Nicaragua.

Capitalizing on the devastation wreaked by nearly a decade of U.S. military and economic aggression, NED's electoral campaign helped to defeat the Sandinistas and elect a new government headed by U.S. allies. NED funds glued together a fragmented opposition, torn by ideological and personal rivalries and dominated by reactionary elements. Those parties that chose not to participate in the UNO coalition were excluded from NED support.

Stabilization and Private-Sector Support

Washington seemed as surprised as most observers by the electoral triumph of UNO: It had no economic-aid package waiting for the new administration. The Chamorro transition team said that it needed at least $1.8 billion over three years to stabilize the country's finances and begin moving its economy forward. Although UNO's victory did not result in the downpour of dollars that many Nicaraguans had expected, Washington's support was nonetheless critical in bolstering the new government and setting its economic-policy direction.

Immediately following the election, the Bush administration authorized $30 million in emergency aid that did not require congressional approval. As part of its supplemental appropriations for 1990, Congress later approved $300 million and another $200 million for 1991. This direct economic aid will be complemented by the trade credits and investment insurance offered by OPIC and Eximbank. The White House also renewed the sugar import quota for Nicaragua, worth about $8 million annually in higher sugar prices.

Administered largely by the Agency for International Development, the aid package reflects U.S. foreign-policy objectives in Nicaragua. Washington's foreign-aid policy in Nicaragua is multilayered and supports the various policy goals of destroying *sandinismo*, opening up the country to U.S. trade and investment, boosting the capitalist sector, stabilizing the economy, and shaping the new government. Although it is not necessarily an internally consistent program, it does show Washington's determination to use increasingly scarce resources to debilitate the FSLN, impose a neoliberal economic program, and create an infrastructure of U.S.-sponsored programs and institutions.

With the balance-of-payments assistance and private-sector support projects dominating the package, the economic aid scheduled for Nicaragua resembles AID funding for other Central American countries. Actual development aid forms a minor part of the funding package. The little assistance that is directed toward the poor is more political than developmental—designed to pacify the urban poor by partially easing the impact of AID-mandated structural-adjustment measures. As in the other Central American countries, AID also is sponsoring a "democracy-strengthening" program that provides funds and training to government institutions and private groups, most of which were part of the anti-Sandinista internal opposition.

The postelection aid package also includes more than $57 million for the repatriation and resettlement of the *contras*, their families, and other refugees.[77] A $1.4 million grant went to Cardinal Obando "for a monitoring network to assure the security of returning members of the resistance."[78] Of AID's 1990 grant of $300 million, $50 million is slated to pay part of Nicaragua's estimated $300 million in debt arrears. According to AID, a "considerable" portion of the 1991 aid package will go to covering debt arrears to the World Bank, IMF, and IDB.

The largest segment of the 1990 economic assistance, $125 million, is cash transfer for balance-of-payments support. This money goes directly to the country's Central Bank, where it is used to purchase imports, including petroleum, agricultural inputs, and goods requested by the private sector to stimulate new productive enterprises. As stipulated in AID contracts, most of these imports, with the exception of petroleum, will be purchased from U.S. suppliers.

It is still unclear to what extent NED will approve new funds to support anti-Sandinista organizations. Pulled by other target areas such as Eastern Europe and South Africa, NED will likely cut back on many of its former Nicaraguan programs and concentrate on the formation of new political institutes designed to shore up the counter-revolution's hold on government. Besides the projects described above, which used previously allocated funds, its only postinauguration grant thus far has gone to the Nicaragua Municipal Leadership Training Institute.[79]

Food aid is also part of the expanding U.S. presence in Nicaragua. There are two components of this program that reflect the two different types of U.S. food aid. The larger program, called Food for Progress, involves the donation of wheat, corn, and other commodities to the government, which then sells that food to private-sector millers and distributors who resell the commodities on the local market. Food for Progress does not pretend to be a development program but instead concentrates exclusively on inducing recipient governments to undertake free-market reforms. It serves as balance-of-payments support, by obviating the need to use foreign exchange to purchase foodstuffs, and as direct budgetary support, by creating a new source of governmental revenue.[80]

In contrast to Food for Progress, the Title II program is a food-distribution program. The initial food-distribution program was administered by the Adventist Development Relief Agency (ADRA) and COPROSA, the social-service agency of the archbishop's office in Managua. CARE/USA is setting up another large Title II program in the *barrios* of Managua. This modified food-for-work program will function as a public-works and employment-generation project. To pay project costs, CARE and the city of Managua will sell the food commodities on the local market and then use this generated revenue to pay temporary workers. Similar urban-employment projects backed by U.S. food aid in other Central American countries have the stated political objective of reducing urban unrest resulting from U.S.-supported structural-adjustment programs.

For AID, its assistance package serves as a lever to force governments to institute policy reforms. Since the beginning of the Reagan administration, the policy reforms that AID pushes have had a distinctly neoliberal bent. It uses its economic assistance and food aid to ensure that recipient governments adhere to structural-adjustment programs that reduce the size of the public sector, promote private-sector investment, and liberalize trade. This pattern is being repeated in Nicaragua with a special emphasis on the privatization of state enterprises. Among the conditions for its balance-of-payments support, AID has forced the government to liberalize agricultural prices, abolish state marketing boards, and sell state-owned enterprises to private bidders.

U.S. Military Aid

Immediately after their triumph in 1979 the Sandinistas petitioned Washington for military aid to shape the guerrilla force into a national army. Instead Washington chose to mount a war against the Sandinista government just as it had chosen to wage a counterinsurgency war on Sandino's peasant army half a century before. The centerpiece of the destabilization campaign was the *contra* army, initially drawn from the remnants of the National Guard. During fiscal years 1982 through 1989 the *contras* received $343.89 million in direct U.S. government aid, $40.5 million in aid coordinated by the National Security Council (mainly through the Oliver North network), and $6.3 million in U.S. insurance and loans, for a total of $390.69 million.[81] Hundreds of millions more were channeled to the *contras* through private organizations, foreign governments, and other indirect sources. In 1990 Washington allocated another $57 million for the repatriation of the *contras* and their families, including support for the new development poles.

Even with that war over and the Sandinistas out of power, U.S. military aid to the government of Nicaragua has not resumed. While bolstering the other armies in the region, despite their notorious human-rights records, the U.S. government refuses to renew its military-aid program to the Nicaraguan forces until they are unilaterally cut back, and cleansed of their Sandinista officer corps.

Although there were no immediate plans to begin a military-aid program, the Drug Enforcement Administration (DEA) began working with the government and the police on drug interdiction soon after Chamorro took office. The DEA is also helping the country set up a more comprehensive antidrug program that will work closely with DEA's regional office in Costa Rica.

REFERENCE NOTES

[1] "El Dráma de la Salud Infantil: Que No Se Apague Esta Sonrisa," *Pensamiento Propio*, October 1988, p. 46.

[2] Known originally as the National Opposition Union, UNO changed its name to the National Organized Union following its election victory in February 1990.

[3] For detailed expositions on the question of popular hegemony in the Nicaraguan revolution, see Susanne Jonas and Nancy Stein, "The Construction of Democracy in Nicaragua," *Latin American Perspectives*, Summer 1990, pp. 10–37; and Richard R. Fagen, Carmen Diana Deere, and José Luís Coraggio, eds., *Transition and Development: Problems of Third World Socialism* (New York: Monthly Review Press, 1986).

[4] For a detailed analysis of the constitution-drafting process and an analysis of the document itself, see Andrew Reding, "Nicaragua's New Constitution," *World Policy Journal*, Spring 1987.

[5] For textual reproduction of the most important articles in the constitution, see *Barricada Internacional*, April 7, 1990, pp. 6–7.

[6] Much of this information is taken from "Setting the Rules of the Game: Nicaragua's Reformed Electoral Law," *Envío*, Instituto Histórico Centroamericano, June 1989, p. 27. For more details on the division of state powers in Nicaragua and the democratic guarantees built into the model, see Alejandro Serrano Caldera, "Democracia y Estado de Derecho," *Pensamiento Propio*, July 1989, pp. 23–25.

[7] Losing presidential candidates are eligible to assume a seat in the legislature

upon receiving more than 1 percent of the vote. As a result, from 1984 to 1990, the National Assembly actually consisted of ninety-six representatives, and beginning in April 1990 it had ninety-two representatives.

[8] The official results were: FSLN, 67 percent; PCD, 13 percent; PLI, 9 percent; PPSC, 5 percent; and 2 percent each for the left parties PSN, PC de N, and MAP-ML.

[9] Including the smaller municipal councils, UNO won a total of one hundred municipalities and the FSLN, thirty-one. National Assembly seats were divided as follows: the fourteen parties belonging to UNO had a total of fifty-one seats; the FSLN, thirty-nine; one seat went to a Yatama (Miskito Indian organization) candidate who ran on the Social Christian party ticket; and the Revolutionary Unity Movement (MUR) had one seat. For the specific breakdown by party and region, see Latin American Studies Association, *Electoral Democracy Under International Pressure* (Pittsburgh: University of Pittsburgh, March 1990).

[10] See Jack Spence, "Will Everything Be Better?" *Socialist Review*, March 1990, pp. 115–132. This article sums up the main theories, and poses important questions regarding their general validity and implications. Also see Latin American Studies Association, *Electoral Democracy Under International Pressure*, op. cit.; James Petras, "Flawed Strategies Planted Seeds of Sandinista Defeat," *In These Times*, March 21, 1990; Carlos M. Vilas, "What Went Wrong" and George R. Vickers, "A Spider's Web," in *NACLA Report on the Americas*, June 1990; William M. LeoGrande, "Was the Left Wrong About Nicaragua?" and Paul Berman, "A Response to William M. LeoGrande," in *Tikkun*, May–June 1990; Julia Preston, "The Defeat of the Sandinistas," *New York Review of Books*, April 12, 1990; and Alma Guillermoprieto, "Letter from Managua," *The New Yorker*, March 26, 1990. A lengthy account of the FSLN's own reflections on its electoral defeat was included in the resolutions from a party assembly held in June 1990. The resolutions are reproduced in full as a special supplement in *Barricada Internacional*, July 14, 1990.

[11] This evidence is based on an analysis of poll data. See, for example, Spence, op. cit., pp. 127–129.

[12] For a book-length account of the history of elections and political parties in Nicaragua, see Oscar René Vargas, *Elecciones en Nicaragua* (Managua: Fundación Manolo Morales, 1989).

[13] The most important of these was the Revolutionary Patriotic Front (FPR), which lasted from 1980 until 1984, when it was dissolved as the different forces jockeyed for position vis-à-vis national elections. The FPR included the FSLN, the Independent Liberal party (PLI), the Popular Social Christian party (PPSC), and the Nicaraguan Socialist party (PSN).

[14] Martin Edwin Andersen and Willard Dupree, "Nicaragua's Municipal Elections: The Report of an NDI Survey Mission," National Democratic Institute for International Affairs, October 31, 1988, p. 3.

[15] Cited in "Chamorro Takes a Chance," *Time*, May 7, 1990.

[16] The Communists and Socialists, neither of which split, won three National Assembly seats each, also running on the UNO ticket.

[17] Most of the UNO parties were splinters from the existing main party currents. With the exception of the Social Democrats and the left-wing parties, different factions of the tendencies represented in UNO also ran in the 1990 elections independent of UNO. The Independent Liberal party, for example, won nearly 10 percent of the votes in the 1984 elections, but since then had divided into three factions, one of which remained outside UNO. One indication of the UNO parties' weak organizational base was the difficulty they had in finding poll-watchers to staff the 4,394 voting booths for election day. UNO leaders complained bitterly at the delays in arrival of U.S. funding, in part asserting that it constituted an obstacle in their efforts to mobilize poll-watchers. FSLN poll-watchers, as those in most countries, worked on a volunteer basis. Similarly, in four of the country's nine administrative regions, UNO was unable to fill candidate slates for municipal council posts.

[18] A lengthy exposition on this position can be found in Silvio De Franco, "Nicaragua en la Encrucijada: Reflexiones sobre las Tareas Críticas en su Nueva Etapa," *Pensamiento Centroamericano*, January–March 1990, pp. 64–72. De Franco was later named by Chamorro to the post of minister of economy and development.

[19] In fact, Chamorro had named two COSEP leaders to cabinet posts, but both refused the offer citing their opposition to her decision to allow General Humberto Ortega to remain in his post as head of the army. The political parties and COSEP had fully expected that the majority of ministerial posts would be assigned to them.

[20] CORDENIC was formed under the auspices of the International Commission for Central American Recovery and Development, better known as the Sanford Commission, in which Chamorro appointees Enrique Dreyfus and Francisco Mayorga were representatives. See International Commission for Central American Recovery and Development, *Poverty and Hope: A Turning Point in Central America* (Durham, NC: Duke University Press, 1989).

[21] The Chamorro government inherited a judiciary whose FSLN-appointed members' terms were set to expire in 1993. By late July 1990 Chamorro had dismissed the court's president, Rodrigo Reyes, replacing him with Orlando Trejos, who had served as labor minister under Somoza. Reforms to the Organic Law of Tribunals also had been approved by the National Assembly expanding the high court from seven to nine members. See "Not Another One, Violeta," *Barricada Internacional*, August 11, 1990, p. 19.

[22] The first was during the July 1990 general strike, and the second in late September when President Chamorro was outside the country.

[23] For a discussion of the FSLN's role as vanguard, see Bruce E. Wright,

"Pluralism and Vanguardism in the Nicaraguan Revolution," *Latin American Perspectives*, Summer 1990, pp. 38–54.

24 The amnesty bill proposed by Chamorro was reformed by UNO representatives before being passed into law by the National Assembly. The FSLN voted unanimously for the original bill, but the reformed version overturned the amnesty passed by the FSLN during the transition period. The amended bill passed with fifty-one UNO votes plus one from Moisés Hassan against thirty-seven FSLN votes.

25 In 1988 alone, military prosecutors brought charges against 3,519 members of the armed forces, many of these for human-rights abuses. More than 2,500 were found guilty and sentenced to jail terms. "Human Rights: Regional Commission Studies Nicaragua," *Envío*, July 1989, p. 12. Amnesty International also discusses the FSLN's policy and practices regarding these matters in *Amnesty International Report 1990* (London: Amnesty International Publications, 1990), pp. 175–178.

26 *Amnesty International Report 1988* (London: Amnesty International Publications, 1988); *Human Rights in Nicaragua: August 1987–August 1988* (New York: Americas Watch, 1988).

27 Paul Laverty, "Human Rights Report—The CPDH: Can It Be Trusted?" Scottish Medical Aid to Nicaragua, cited in *Envío*, March 1989. The CPDH receives no monies directly from the NED, but NED funds have been used to translate, publish, and distribute the group's bulletins.

28 For more on the National Guard, see Richard Millett, *Guardians of the Dynasty* (New York: Maryknoll, 1977).

29 These figures are from the International Institute of Strategic Studies, cited in *Barricada Internacional*, June 30, 1990, p. 12.

30 For an analysis of how the EPS views its role under the new circumstances, see Rodolfo Castro, "El General en su Laberinto," *Pensamiento Propio*, September 1990, pp. 25–27.

31 See Oswaldo Lacayo, second-in-command of the EPS chiefs of staff, cited in *La Crónica*, September 1–7, 1989; and an interview with EPS chiefs of staff head Joaquín Cuadra, "El Mayor Acierto: Un Ejército Popular," *Pensamiento Propio*, July 1989, pp. 6–9.

32 Throughout the 1980s as alliances in the anti-Sandinista camp were formed, broken, and reformed in accordance with the political exigencies of the moment, dozens of *contra* groups and front organizations came and went. From the beginning the *contra* landscape was dominated by the Nicaraguan Democratic Force (FDN), operating out of Honduras. In 1982, the Democratic Revolutionary Alliance (ARDE) was formed in Costa Rica. Armed groups on the Atlantic coast included Misura, Misurasata, Kisan and Yatama. The last of several *contra* umbrella organizations, the Nicaraguan Resistance (RN) oversaw demobilization of most *contra* forces in mid-1990.

33 In mid-1985 one study concluded that forty-six of forty-eight command positions in the *contra* movement were held by former National Guard

members. See "Who Are the Contras?", a report by the Arms Control and Foreign Policy Caucus of the U.S. Congress, April 18, 1985.

34 For an account of the transformation of the *contra* army and the rise of the new leadership, see Raúl Marín, "Los Ultimos 'Paladines,'" *Pensamiento Propio*, May 1990, pp. 26–28.

35 See David MacMichael, "The U.S. Plays the Contra Card," *The Nation*, February 5, 1990, pp. 162–166.

36 The new party was under the leadership of Oscar Sobalvarro. Former *contra* chief Israel Galeano complained at having been displaced, insisting that the full Nicaraguan Resistance command had not been present at the meeting in which Sobalvarro was "elected."

37 *Barricada*, August 16, 1990.

38 By 1983, when most of the major changes in ownership had already taken place, the structure of the mixed economy measured in terms of percent contribution to GDP was as follows: state, 40 percent; capitalist, 29 percent; and small producers, 31 percent. In the economy's two major productive areas, agroexports and industry, the capitalist sector was responsible for 42 percent and 49 percent of production, respectively. Cited in Eduardo Baumeister and Oscar Neira Cuadra, "The Making of a Mixed Economy: Class Struggle and State Policy in the Nicaraguan Transition," in Richard R. Fagen, Carmen Diana Deere, and José Luís Coraggio, eds., *Transition and Development: Problems of Third World Socialism* (New York: Monthly Review Press, 1986), p. 188.

39 In 1979 Nicaragua's GNP dropped by 26 percent as production ground to a near-standstill. Direct infrastructure damage alone was close to $500 million. Tom Barry and Debra Preusch, *The Soft War: The Uses and Abuses of U.S. Economic Aid in Central America* (New York: Grove Press, 1988), p. 219. Only $3.5 million in reserves, not enough to pay for two days of imports, was left behind after Somoza's looting. George Black, *Triumph of the People* (London: Zed Books, 1981), p. 201. The Sandinistas assumed responsibility for repaying the foreign debt accumulated by the dictatorship in the 1970s, calculated at roughly $1.6 billion.

40 World Bank, *Nicaragua: The Challenge of Reconstruction*, Report No. 3524-NI (Washington, D.C.: World Bank, 1981).

41 For a comprehensive discussion of the Sandinistas' efforts to achieve food self-sufficiency, see Joseph Collins et al., *What Difference Could a Revolution Make? Food and Farming in the New Nicaragua* (New York: Grove Press, 1986).

42 U.S. pressure resulted in a precipitous drop in financing to Nicaragua from multilateral development banks. In 1979, these sources provided 78 percent of all Nicaragua's contracted borrowing; by 1984 the figure was down to zero. See Stahler-Sholk, "Stabilization, Destabilization, and the Popular Classes in Nicaragua, 1979–1988," *Latin American Research Review*, Fall 1990, p. 56.

43 For lengthy expositions on Sandinista agrarian policies and land reform, see Wheelock, op. cit.; Laura J. Enriquez, "The Dilemmas of Agro-Export Planning in Revolutionary Nicaragua," in Thomas W. Walker, ed., *Nicaragua: The First Five Years* (New York: Praeger, 1985); and Carmen Diana Deere, Peter Marchetti, and Nola Reinhardt, "The Peasantry and the Development of Sandinista Agrarian Policy: 1979–1984," *Latin American Research Review*, Fall 1985, pp. 75–109.

44 A profile of the Nicaraguan industrial sector can be found in Richard L. Harris, "The Economic Transformation and Industrial Development of Nicaragua," in Richard L. Harris and Carlos M. Vilas, eds., *Nicaragua: a Revolution Under Siege* (London: Zed Books, 1985). Another excellent overview is provided in Claes Brundenius, "Industrial Development Strategies in Revolutionary Nicaragua," in Rose J. Spalding, ed., *The Political Economy of Revolutionary Nicaragua* (Boston: Allen and Unwin, Inc., 1987), pp. 85–104.

45 The statistics cited here on the foreign debt are the official ones used by Nicaragua's Central Bank. See "The Foreign Debt: Things Could be Worse," *Barricada Internacional*, June 16, 1990, p. 9.

46 E. V. K. Fitzgerald, "Stabilization and Economic Justice: The Case of Nicaragua," in Kwan S. Kim and David F. Ruccio, eds., *Debt and Development in Latin America* (Notre Dame, IN: University of Notre Dame Press, 1985).

47 For a broader discussion of class alliances in terms of the government's stabilization policies see Richard Stahler-Sholk, "Stabilization, Destabilization, and the Popular Classes in Nicaragua, 1979–1988," op. cit.

48 "Creating a New Power," *Barricada Internacional*, special supplement, May 1989. For information on the labor movement during the 1980s also see, Harris and Vilas, "The Workers' Movement in the Sandinista Revolution," op. cit., pp. 120–150; Richard Stahler-Sholk, "Nicaragua," in Gerald Michael Greenfield and Sheldon L. Maram, eds., *Latin America Labor Organizations* (Westport, CT: Greenwood Press, 1987); and Stahler-Sholk, "Stabilization, Destabilization, and the Popular Classes in Nicaragua, 1979–1988," op. cit.

49 Belli was instrumental in the propaganda war against the Sandinista government. He received financial and logistical support from the CIA for his anti-Sandinista volume, *Nicaragua: Christians Under Fire*. During the 1980s, Belli, a former *La Prensa* editor, was active with the Puebla Institute, an anti-Sandinista human-rights organization. See, for example, Edgar Chamorro, *Packaging the Contras: A Case of CIA Disinformation* (New York: Institute for Media Analysis, Inc., 1987).

50 The textbook change was opposed both for ideological reasons—many Sandinista educators asserted that the content of the AID-funded readers was inappropriate to Nicaraguan reality—as well as for pedagogical ones—

education professionals pointed out that, irrespective of the content, the two readers were based on fundamentally different teaching methodologies.

51 These statistics were included in a September 1987 letter sent by Fernando Cardenal, Nicaraguan minister of education, to the U.S. Secretary of Education, cited in *Update*, October 26, 1987, p. 2.

52 The FSLN was formally committed to freedom of the press, and the 1987 constitution forbids prior censorship. In exercising censorship against *La Prensa* during the mid 1980s, the Sandinistas argued that under wartime conditions, opposition forces aligned with the foreign power sponsoring the aggression—the United States government—could not be allowed to play the role of open accomplice to destabilization.

53 For more information on these themes, see "Nicaragua's New Media Law: Freedom and Social Responsibility," in *Envío*, July 1989, pp. 25–32; Armand Mattelart, ed., *Communicating in Popular Nicaragua* (New York: International General, 1986); and Carlos Fernando Chamorro, "Frontpage Battlefront," *Barricada Internacional*, July 8, 1989, p. 36.

54 One relative exception to this was the weekly newspaper *La Crónica*. The paper had a pluralist editorial staff and its content, although sharply anti-Sandinista, offered a broad range of opinions on current affairs. In mid-1990, *La Crónica* closed down operations amidst a scandal over misappropriated finances.

55 Violeta Chamorro is *La Prensa*'s publisher; her daughter Cristiana—who is the wife of top Chamorro aide and minister of the presidency, Antonio Lacayo—is codirector.

56 An extensive account of changes in health care under the Sandinistas can be found in Richard Garfield, *Health and Revolution: The Nicaraguan Experience* (London: Oxfam, 1989).

57 *Envío*, January 1989.

58 Informative accounts of the history of this conflict can be found in Alfonso Dubois, "La Iglesia en Nicaragua: El Proyecto Tras el Cardenal," *Pensamiento Propio*, March 1986, pp. 22–27; "Church-State Relations: A Chronology," *Envío*, November and December 1987; Penny Lernoux, "The Struggle for Nicaragua's Soul: The Church in Revolution and War," *Sojourners*, May 1989; and an interview with Monseñor Bosco Vivas, "Los Vericuetos de una Relación," *Pensamiento Propio*, July 1989, pp. 51–53.

59 Cited in "The Pope's Man Always Rings Twice," *Newsweek*, August 6, 1990.

60 Russ Bellant, "Nicaraguan Government Appointments Linked with U.S. Charismatic Group," *National Catholic Reporter*, July 27, 1990, p. 6.

61 For lengthy accounts on evangelicals in Nicaragua during the 1980s, see Abelino Martínez, *Las Sectas en Nicaragua: Oferta y Demanda de Salvación* (San José, Costa Rica: DEI, 1989); and David Stoll, *Is Latin America Turning*

Protestant? (Berkeley: University of California Press, 1990). Paul Jeffrey, "Church Fray Spurs Liberation Theology," *The Guardian* (New York), July 1989. Two brief accounts of the impact of evangelism in Nicaragua during the 1980s are "Pentecostals in Nicaragua," *Update*, Central American Historical Institute, March 10, 1987, p. 2; and Edwin Saballos, "Los Conservadores Tienen el Protagonismo," *Pensamiento Propio*, July 1989, pp. 54–56.

62 James and Margaret Goff, "The Church Confronting Change: Organized Religion and Liberation Theology in Revolutionary Society," *Nicaraguan Perspectives*, Summer–Fall 1989, p. 7.

63 Many of these sects form part of the "Shepherding" movement and include Chapel Hill Harvester Church in Atlanta, Georgia; the Crossroads Community Church in Vancouver, Washington; and congregations associated with Shepherding guru Dennis Peacocke.

64 Mónica Baltodano, "Women: Ten Years of Achievement and Hope," *Barricada Internacional*, July 8, 1989, p. 24.

65 Maxine Molyneux, "La Mujer: Activismo sin Emancipación," *Pensamiento Propio*, June–July 1985.

66 For a lengthy account of the situation of Nicaragua's ethnic communities during the 1980s, see Carlos M. Villas, *State, Class, and Ethnicity in Nicaragua: Capitalist Modernization and Revolutionary Change on the Atlantic Coast* (Boulder: Lynne Reinner, 1989).

67 For detailed accounts of the peace and autonomy processes, see "The Atlantic Coast: Peace Has Taken Hold," *Envío*, June 1988; and "From Separatism to Autonomy: Ten Years on the Atlantic Coast," *Envío*, April 1989.

68 For an early analysis of the elections' impact on the autonomy process, see "Será Ahora una Realidad la Autonomía?" *Pensamiento Propio*, June 1990, pp. 27–29.

69 For more details and analysis on the election results, see "Atlantic Coast: What Fate Autonomy?" *Envío*, March–April 1990, pp. 17–20.

70 Much of the information in this section is taken from David Henson, "Elections in Nicaragua: The Environmental Impact," *EPOCA Update*, Spring 1990, pp. 1–10.

71 For a complete summary of Washington's trade war see Tom Barry, *The Destabilization of Nicaragua* (Albuquerque: The Resource Center, 1986).

72 U.S. Department of Commerce, "Business Opportunities in Nicaragua," May 1990.

73 Ibid.

74 E. V. K. Fitzgerald, "Stabilization and Economic Justice: The Case of Nicaragua," in Kwan S. Kim and David F. Ruccio, eds., *Debt and Development in Latin America* (Notre Dame, IN: University of Notre Dame Press, 1985), pp. 195–213.

75 See, for example, Bob Woodward, *Veil: The Secret Wars of the CIA* (New York:

Simon and Schuster, 1987), p. 113; and John Spicer Nichols, "*La Prensa:* The CIA Connection," *Columbia Journalism Review*, July–August, 1988.

76 See, for example, "Nicaragua: Special Campesino Program" and "Exchange Trip to Central America, June 12–18, 1988," in quarterly report to the National Endowment for Democracy from the Free Trade Union Institute, second quarter 1988. Also see quarterly reports for the third quarter 1988 and July 1, 1989–September 30, 1989.

77 This $57 million-plus estimate comes from an information sheet distributed by AID. It includes $5.7 million from the Survival Assistance for Civilian Victims of Civil Strife program, $1.405 million earmarked for repatriation efforts by Cardinal Obando's office, $250,000 for a "Basic Support for the Resistance" program, $330,000 for rehabilitation programs for the resistance, and $3 million for the assistance provided to the *contras* by the Organization of American States and the United Nations High Commission of Refugees (UNHCR) through the International Commission for Assistance and Verification. Of AID's FY1990 supplemental grant, $47 million is scheduled for the repatriation of the resistance and refugees, of which $30 million is directly targeted for *contra* resettlement programs, including the new development poles.

78 U.S. Embassy, "Status of AID Programs in Nicaragua," no date.

79 Interview by Beth Sims with Peter Kosciewicz, NED Public Information Officer, September 19, 1990.

80 The high level of executive discretion in the allocation of Food for Progress makes this a highly politicized program. As described in National Security Council Memorandum No. 156 (January 1985), "This judicious use of aid . . . will reduce the political risks to leaders of the third world countries committed to undertaking agricultural reform during a transition period of economic hardship." NSDD Memorandum No. 167 (April 1985) stresses that before all other criteria, "U.S. strategic and foreign-policy interests must be served by the Food for Progress program."

81 "Previous U.S. and U.S.-Coordinated Aid to the Contras," Arms Control and Foreign Policy Caucus of the U.S. Congress, January 29, 1988, updated November 1989.

Chapter Seven
PANAMA

CHRONOLOGICAL HISTORY

1821   Panama declares independence from Spain and becomes a province of Great Colombia.

1834   The Congress of New Granada (Colombia) authorizes the construction of a canal, railroad, or road through the isthmus of Panama.

1840   Revolt gives Panama brief independence until 1842.

1846   U.S.–New Granada treaty; United States guarantees neutrality and the sovereign rights of New Granada on the isthmus.

1850–6   U.S. businessmen finance construction of forty-eight-mile Panama Railway, completed in 1855. U.S. troops protect the transisthmian railroad from possible attacks by Panamanian independence forces for next nine years.

1865   U.S. troops intervene three times in the next eight years to protect U.S. interests.

1878   French Panama Canal Company acquires exclusive right to build canal through Panama.

1882   Canal construction companies have financial problems for next decade.

1902   U.S. Congress authorizes the president to acquire from Colombia a strip of land in Panama to build an interoceanic canal.

1903   Secessionists declare the department of Panama an independent republic; the new flag is raised by a member of the U.S. Army Corps of Engineers as three U.S. gunboats prevent the landing of Colombian troops.

The Hay-Bunau-Varilla Treaty between United States and Panama is signed, authorizing the United States to construct, maintain, operate, protect, and sanitize an interoceanic canal through Panama "in perpetuity," and allowing

419

the United States to act in the Canal Zone "as if it were the sovereign of the territory." The Panamanian signatory lacked the full powers and credentials to sign the treaty.

1904   U.S. troops intervene to quash protests against the Hay-Bunau-Varilla Treaty.

New constitution promulgated, which grants the United States the right to intervene "in any part of Panama, to reestablish public peace and constitutional order." Panama informs the United States that the canal treaty does not entail a territorial grant or transfer of sovereignty.

National army disbanded and Panama establishes monetary system based on U.S. dollar.

1908   U.S. troops intervene in Panama for first of four times within the next decade.

1914   Panama Canal opens for operation.

1918   Constitutional crisis; U.S. troops intervene in Panama City and Colón during elections; liberal Porras installed as president.

U.S. troops intervene in the Chiriquí province and remain for next two years to protect United Fruit Company plantations.

1921   U.S. troops intervene in border conflicts between Panama and Costa Rica.

1925   A rent strike prompts the arrival of U.S. troops in Panama City.

1930   Government curtails labor organizing for next fifteen years.

1932   Election of Harmodio Arias Madrid.

1936   Election of J. D. Arosemena.

Panama and United States sign the General Treaty of Friendship and Cooperation, which maintains all stipulations of 1903 treaty except the guarantee of Panama's independence and right of the United States to intervene in Panama.

1939   Revised treaty ratified.

1940   National party candidate Arnulfo Arias Madrid elected.

1941   Adolfo de la Guardia replaces Arias in coup.

1942   Treaty with United States to allow U.S. stations and airfields on Panamanian territory; treaty is to expire in six years.

Many U.S. military bases built upon the entry of the United States into World War II.

1946   New constitution promulgated; Enrique Jiménez elected as provisional president.

1947   New treaty on U.S. military sites is rejected by the National Assembly after popular pressure.

1948   Constitutional crisis; Díaz Arosemena defeats Arias in national presidential elections.

        Colón free trade zone created in Panama based on a proposal by a New York banker.

1949   Death of Díaz Arosemena; succession by First Vice President Daniel Chanis, who attempts to dismiss National Guard Commander José Antonio Remón Cantera, but is ousted himself. Remón installs Arias.

1951   Arias ousted; formation of a coalition government led by Alcibiades Arosemena.

1952   National Patriotic Coalition candidate Remón elected president.

1953   United States creates the Panamanian National Guard modeled after Anastasio Somoza's Nicaraguan National Guard.

1955   Remón assassinated; First Vice President José Guizado inaugurated and then impeached due to suspicion of his involvement in Remón's death; Second Vice President Ricardo Arias Espinosa installed as president.

        Treaty of Mutual Understanding and Cooperation (Remón-Eisenhower Treaty) is signed.

1956   National Patriotic Coalition candidate Ernesto de la Guardia elected.

1960   National Opposition Union candidate Roberto Chiari elected.

1962   Presidents Chiari and Kennedy agree to designate negotiators to review the 1903 treaty; also agree to display the Panamanian flag in the Canal Zone.

1963   A joint Panamanian-U.S. statement advising that the Panamanian flag be flown alongside the U.S. flag in the Canal Zone.

1964   Students attempting to fly the Panamanian flag next to the U.S. flag at a high school are attacked by Canal Zone residents. During subsequent Flag Riots, 21 people are killed, more than three hundred wounded, and more than five hundred arrested; diplomatic relations with United States temporarily severed; negotiations begin to draft new treaties to resolve the conflicts.

Marco Aurelio Robles elected president.

1968   Constitutional crisis; Arnulfo Arias Madrid elected again but is deposed within ten days of being sworn in. Junta is formed, but power is assumed by the commander-in-chief of the defense forces, Colonel Omar Torrijos Herrera.

1970   Panamanian government assumes control of the U.S. military base of Río Hato after refusing to renew provisions of the 1955 treaty.

1972   New constitution promulgated; Torrijos named "Supreme Leader of the Panamanian Revolution" with virtually unlimited powers.

1974   Panama and United States agree to begin new treaty negotiations.

1977   Presidents Torrijos and Carter sign the Panama Canal treaties in Washington D.C. giving Panama control of the canal at noon on December 31, 1999. The accords replace the U.S. government agency Panama Canal Company with a jointly supervised Panama Canal Commission. A Panamanian is to take office as administrator of the commission on January 1, 1990. The canal treaties are approved in Panama.

1978   Canal treaties ratified by U.S. Senate with the provision that permits U.S. intervention if the canal's operation is interrupted, though such action shall not be interpreted as a right of intervention in Panama's sovereignty or internal affairs.

National Assembly elects Aristides Royo president.

1979   Panama canal treaties go into effect and U.S. control of the Canal Zone officially ends.

1981   Torrijos dies in an unexplained plane crash; Colonel Florencio Flores succeeds him as head of the National Guard.

1982   President Royo resigns under pressure from National Guard; Ricardo de la Espriella becomes president. Rubén Darío Paredes ousts Flores as head of National Guard.

1983   National Guard renamed Panamanian Defense Forces (PDF); General Manuel Antonio Noriega, CIA asset trained at the School of the Americas and head of military intelligence, becomes commander of the Panama Defense Forces.

The Contadora Group meets for the first time on the Panamanian island of Contadora to develop peace accords.

1984   PRD candidate Nicolás Ardito-Barletta narrowly defeats Arnulfo Arias Madrid in fraudulent elections.

New government inaugurated. Secretary of State George Shultz attends the inauguration ceremony and calls Ardito-Barletta "a longtime and respected friend."

1985   Dr. Hugo Spadafora, a former vice minister of health, is assassinated upon his return from a visit to Costa Rica. The military is accused of complicity in the assassination of Spadafora; Ardito-Barletta resigns; Noriega installs industrialist Eric Arturo Delvalle.

1986   U.S. newspapers allege that Noriega traffics in drugs and supplies arms to Colombian guerrillas.

Oliver North plans to frame the Sandinistas by "capturing" a ship with Eastern bloc arms in the canal; plan fails when Noriega seizes the ship and exposes the scheme.

1987   An ousted second-in-command of the Defense Forces accuses Noriega of rigging the 1984 elections and murdering Dr. Hugo Spadafora; antigovernment rioting results; ten-day "state of urgency" declared; constitutional guarantees suspended.

Panamanian government informs the United States and other creditor nations that it is stopping all principal and interest payments. Rumors of printing Panamanian currency lead to heavy bank withdrawals.

U.S. Senate calls for Noriega to step down and calls for new elections. U.S. embassy attacked by a hundred protesters; United States demands payment for damages to building.

All U.S. military and economic aid suspended; sugar quota suspended.

1988   U.S. Justice Department seals indictments charging Noriega and others with international drug trafficking. After a meeting with Elliott Abrams, President Delvalle attempts to fire Noriega. But Delvalle is himself ousted by the National Assembly, which then appoints Manuel Solís Palma. Delvalle goes into hiding but is recognized by the United States as Panama's president.

U.S. government withholds payments of the Panama Canal Commission and suspends trade preferences for Panama.

Coup attempt shuts down economy; massive power outages shut down transisthmian oil pipeline; transportation disrupted; two-week general strike.

Dignity battalions are formed and begin training to fight against a possible U.S. invasion.

CIA develops a coup plan, which might result in Noriega's assassination by dissident officers; plan nixed by Senate Select Committee on Intelligence and opposition is given a mobile transmitter instead.

1989   ADOC candidate Guillermo Endara apparently wins presidential election; election nullified by Noriega regime.

OAS forms a mediation commission with the foreign ministers of Ecuador, Guatemala, and Trinidad-Tobago.

OAS ministers propose that Noriega step down, a government of transition take power, and elections be held at a later date; they also call for an end to U.S. military and economic aggression, compliance with 1977 canal treaties, and OAS mediation during the negotiation process.

The U.S. commander in Panama, critical of Bush's escalating policies, is replaced by the aggressive General Maxwell R. Thurman, who is told to prepare for an invasion.

Noriega elected head of government with unlimited powers by National Assembly.

U.S. invasion with 26,000 troops; United States installs Endara as president; after two weeks in hiding and sanctuary in the Vatican embassy, Noriega turns himself over to U.S. officials.

1990   Noriega arraigned in Miami on drug charges.

Sources for the chronology include Tom Barry and Debra Preusch, *The Central America Fact Book* (New York: Grove Press, 1986); *Conflict in Central America* (London: Longman Group Ltd., 1987); *U.S. Embassy in Panama* (1975); *Encyclopedia of the Third World* (New York: Facts on File, 1987); *Labor Organizations in Latin America*, Gerald Greenfield and

Sheldon Maran, eds. (Westport, CT: Greenwood Press, 1987); *The Washington Post* (May 10, 1989); *The Nation* (March 12, 1988); Brecha, *CODEHUCA* (May–June 1989); *Central America Education Project* (Summer 1987); Regionews from Managua, *Pensamiento Propio*, September 1989; *Albuquerque Journal* (October 4, 1989).

TRENDS

- As the economic and political problems of the postinvasion government deepen, Panamanians begin to question the nature of the democracy that the U.S. invasion established and again confront the underlying class, race, and sovereignty issues that gave rise to the military regime installed in 1968.
- Long based on services and commerce associated with its status as an international crossroads, the Panamanian economy will find it difficult to develop a substantial nontraditional export-oriented agricultural and industrial sector as advocated by foreign lenders while at the same time stopping the dangerous decline in the levels of local food production and manufacturing.
- Major issues by the mid-1990s will be the future of U.S. bases and revisions of the 1977 canal treaties—both of which will be contingent on the related issues of the stability of the government and the ability of the newly constituted Public Force to operate independently from its U.S. advisers.
- The country's popular sectors, which fell under the sway of collaborationist leaders and were coopted by military populism, face the challenge of developing an alternative economic and political agenda that combines the principles of democracy, nationalism, and social justice.
- The 1989 invasion, having renewed and expanded the U.S. colonial role in Panama, was called a "liberation," but inadequate economic aid, the likely failure of the U.S.-sponsored government to return the country to the levels of economic progress experienced in the 1970s, and the contradictions of the country's dual power structure may become the foundations of a new cycle of U.S.-Panama tensions and conflict.

Panama, the southernmost country in the Central American isthmus, stands apart from its neighbors. Although geographically a Central American nation, Panama has not been included in regional bodies like the Central American Common Market. Neither has it been considered a South American nation even though it once was a province of Colombia. Panama owes its special and isolated character to its role as an international crossroad.

Panama, about the size of South Carolina, stands out as the country in the region with the highest per capita income, highest foreign investment, and most highly developed economic infrastructure. More than 85 percent of its 2.3 million inhabitants are literate and 82 percent have access to potable water.

Nationalism and anti-U.S. sentiments have been a constant feature of Panamanian society since independence in 1903. In 1964, twenty-one Panamanians lost their lives to U.S. bullets to gain the right to fly the Panamanian flag at schools in the Canal Zone. But there is also, especially among the middle and upper classes, a pattern of dependent behavior and identification with anything with a USA label—from consumer products and cultural values to language and politics. It was no surprise to see many middle-class Panamanians out in the streets waving U.S. flags after the December 1989 invasion.

By early 1991 the early enthusiasm for the government and the U.S. occupation had largely dissipated. Internal disputes in the ruling political coalition and the conservative economic policies of the new government turned popular opinion against the U.S.-installed administration; opinion polls showed that only 14 percent of the public supported President Guillermo Endara while unions, human-rights groups, the Catholic Church, journalists, and even the National Civic Crusade, which had led the campaign against Manuel Noriega, were all angered by the political direction of his administration.

Leading the popular protests against the government's neoliberal economic reforms were the unions. Workers who went out on strike were fired by the government on the grounds they were threatening the democratic system. Reacting to massive layoffs in the public sector and to deteriorating wage levels, private- and public-sector workers joined in a national coalition to protect their jobs and their right to organize.

The Noriega-associated National Liberation Coalition (COLINA) which was formed to contest the May 1989 elections won five of the nine contested seats in the Legislative Assembly in the first elections held since the invasion. Both the support for the opposition parties and the high abstention rate (over 50 percent) in these partial elections of January 1991 were widely intepreted as signs of popular discontent with the government and with the continued U.S. occupation.

Facing widespread criticism, President Endara chose to strike out against the country's news media, jailing and bringing legal suits

against reporters who accused him of corruption and money laundering. These crackdowns against the press earned the government the
condemnation of the Interamerican Press Society, along with censure
from the country's human-rights groups and the National Civic Crusade, the citizens' organization that had led the anti-Noriega movement.

The country's internal security was also being threatened, especially
by two small guerrilla groups apparently led by former members of
Noriega's special forces—the Movement of the 20th of December
(M-20) and the Popular National Liberation Army (EPLN)—which
were mounting occasional attacks against the Endara government and
U.S. targets. Furthermore, the government's continued dependence on
U.S. military forces to resolve internal problems was evidenced by the
use of five hundred U.S. troops to quell a December 1990 rebellion by
former police chief Colonel Eduardo Herrera and other dissidents
within the newly created Public Force.

Despite the continued presence of U.S. troops, relations between
Panama and the United States remained tense. Thousands of Panamanians were made homeless as a result of the U.S. invasion, and families
of civilian victims as well as owners of businesses damaged in the
invasion demanded financial compensation from the United States.
Also complicating relations between the two nations was Washington's
insistence upon the signing of a legal assistance agreement between
Panama and the United States. Such an agreement would jeopardize
the country's international finance center by changing the bank-
secrecy laws and by giving U.S. regulators increased access to account
records. Dispersal of promised U.S. aid was conditioned on such an
agreement, but the country's financiers said Panama would lose more
from decreased banking activity than it would benefit from U.S. economic aid.

More than a year after the December 1989 invasion by U.S. troops
and the removal of Noriega, uncertainty still characterized the country's political and economic climate. Although the country was enjoying
positive economic growth for the first time in several years, the combined effects of the trade embargo, invasion, and recessionary trends
in the world market meant that the economy was still functioning
at income levels of the mid-1970s. Neoliberal reforms were rapidly
instigated at the cost of continuing cutbacks in social services and
public-sector employment. Panama continued to be a center for drug
smuggling and money laundering, and drug use and crime were on the
upswing. Electoral democracy had been instituted, but public cynicism
toward the political institutions was spreading and military coups

remained a threat. Also worrisome were the continued presence of U.S. troops on the streets of Panama and the future of the U.S.-Panama canal treaties.

GOVERNMENT AND POLITICS

The swearing in of President Guillermo Endara on a U.S. military base in Panama on December 20, 1989, marked the beginning of a new era of governance in Panama. For the first time since 1968 a Panamanian government was not beholden to the country's military. Endara and his two vice presidents—the candidates of the Democratic Civic Opposition Alliance (ADOC)—were the apparent winners of the May 7, 1989, election that was annulled by General Manuel Antonio Noriega. Endara was then installed after Noriega was toppled. This left the new civilian government, while breaking the two-decade tradition of military rule, grounded in another more deeply rooted tradition in Panama: U.S. military intervention in the country's internal politics.

The Endara administration took office without real power and without an independent political platform. It was a government produced by a U.S. military invasion and one whose stability depended on a U.S. military occupation. The ADOC coalition had attracted more voters not because of the charisma or credibility of its candidates but rather as a result of the widespread unpopularity of Noriega and his puppets and the deep popular frustration with military governments. Furthermore, the government also lacked international legitimacy, with most Latin American governments declining to recognize the Panamanian government and calling upon President Endara to hold new elections to confirm his mandate.

According to the 1983 constitution, executive power is held by a president directly elected every five years and assisted by two elected vice presidents and an appointed cabinet. Legislative power is vested in a unicameral Legislative Assembly. The government's judiciary branch comprises the Supreme Court, subordinate tribunals, and district and municipal courts.

Another important instrument of government is the Electoral Tribunal, an autonomous institution with representatives from the legislative, executive, and judicial branches and three elected judges. The country is divided into nine provinces, each with a governor appointed by the president, and it has one semiautonomous Indian reservation. Each province is further divided into districts and municipalities.

Two months after the invasion the Electoral Tribunal, working on May 1989 election returns it deemed 83 percent accurate, confirmed the election of fifty-seven of the legislature's sixty-seven members. Of the fifty-seven seats, fifty-one went to the ADOC coalition, with twenty-seven of those going to the Christian Democratic party, fifteen to the National Liberal Republican Movement (MOLIRENA), and nine to the Authentic Liberal party of President Endara. Only six seats were awarded to the Revolutionary Democratic party (PRD), the leading party in the pro-Noriega National Liberation Coalition (COLINA). The Panamanian Labor party (PALA), also a member of the former government, was in line to receive one of the remaining ten seats, with the other nine to be decided by new elections.

Questions of legitimacy hounded the new government for months after the invasion. But the more serious threats to stability were the country's weak economy, weaknesses within the ruling coalition, and dependence on the U.S. military to maintain order. The Endara government inherited an unpayable external debt, a heavy burden of internal debt, recessionary conditions, and a huge gap between its costs and revenues. The high public expectations that accompanied the invasion created added pressure for the government to usher in an economic recovery. Although nationalism had been shunted aside in the enthusiasm for what the new government called the "liberation" by the "allied forces," the continuing presence of U.S. troops and many other signs of U.S. influence could spark a wave of new nationalist and anti-Yankee sentiment if social and economic conditions do not improve.

Military and the Government

For three decades after independence in 1903 the Panamanian security forces were kept at a lowly and largely subservient status, the United States assuming the responsibility for maintaining internal order and defending the newly independent country. As a result of a revised canal treaty in 1936, Washington relinquished its right to intervene militarily in the country's internal affairs. President Harmodio Arias appointed José Antonio Remón Cantera to be chief of police in 1943, and under Remón's reign the prestige and the power of the National Police Forces steadily increased. By the mid-1940s the national police was a power in its own right and had become the chief arbiter of power in the political arena.[1] The police (called the National Guard after 1953) did not participate directly in government but increasingly served in its repressive capacity as the guarantor of oligarchic rule.

Although the economy was expanding, Panama in the late 1960s was facing a hegemonic crisis.[2] The traditional political parties were badly divided and counted on little support among the increasingly restive popular sectors. The election of maverick politician Arnulfo Arias in 1968 was unhappily received by the National Guard and the traditional Liberal parties. The National Guard saw Arias as a threat to the power and privileges it had been accumulating through close relations with the oligarchy. Having heard that Arias planned to restructure it and remove many of its officers, the National Guard ousted the president.

In the jousting for dominance following 1968, Omar Torrijos Herrera emerged as the dominant figure. Torrijos, a son of middle-class educators in rural Panama, became the National Guard's third commander-in-chief and the first not linked familially to the oligarchy.[3] Under the provisions of the 1972 constitution, Torrijos became head of government. In 1978 Aristides Royo was elected by the National Assembly to become the country's figurehead president, but until Torrijos's death in a mysterious airplane crash in July 1981, Torrijos was the actual center of political and military power in Panama. With many of the characteristics of a traditional *caudillo*, Torrijos ruled Panama with a strong but considerate hand. Years after his death many Panamanians still had a photo of Torrijos hanging in a place of honor on the living-room wall.

Raising high the banners of nationalism and populism, Torrijos proceeded to restructure Panamanian government and politics. The traditional political parties and the Legislative Assembly were abolished. The National Guard, at least until the mid-1970s, became an autonomous political force that ruled the country with the consultation and assistance of leaders of the private and popular sectors. Progressives and communists were brought into government mainly in the ministries of education, labor, health, agricultural development, and foreign policy; representatives of the business sector were appointed to positions in planning, finance, and commerce and industry.[4]

For the first time, government institutions were opened up to participation by *mestizos*, blacks, and those with lower-class origins. Calling himself "*cholo* Omar," Torrijos won wide popular support from formerly disenfranchised sectors of the population. (*Cholo* is a slang term used in Panama to mean, among other things, a policeman of *mestizo* origins.)

Another characteristic of the Torrijos regime and subsequent governments in Panama is what some have called the "military-business complex."[5] Although he broke the stronghold of the oligarchy on government, Torrijos encouraged the participation and cooperation of

the industrial and financial sectors of the economic elite in his government. In return, the National Guard leadership corps enriched themselves with favors and bribes offered by the private sector.

The 1972 constitution made the National Guard's newfound power
the law of the land. Previously the National Guard was subject to the
civilian government, but the new constitution stipulated that "the three
governmental branches are obligated to act in harmonious collaboration with the public force [National Guard]." Among the important
new government institutions were the National Assembly of Community Representatives, the National Legislative Council, the Legislating
Commission, and local community boards under the direction of the
General Directorate for Community Development (DIGEDECOM).
The new institutions, especially the community boards and the National Assembly, permitted popular sectors to participate in government for the first time. Many political analysts, however, felt that the
Torrijos regime never committed itself to the popular sector, but coopted it while maintaining full control of the legislative and executive
power.

Responding to local and international pressure, Torrijos in 1978
took steps to return Panama to civilian rule. An official party, the
Revolutionary Democratic party (PRD), was created to compete in local
elections scheduled for 1980, and a presidential election was set for
1984. The PRD was conceived as a centrist political party that would
administer the Panamanian state with the politics of pragmatism and
cooptation much like the corporatist Institutional Revolutionary party
(PRI) of Mexico.

The PRD, however, quickly proved incapable of this challenge. In the
1980 elections for the Legislative Council the party faced a strong
antimilitarist challenge from the Christian Democratic party and re-
constituted Liberal factions. Arnulfo Arias and his *panameñista* movement also challenged the legitimacy of the National Guard–PRD
controlled state.[6] Although the popular sectors did not break with the
government, the gap between the regime's populist rhetoric and its
private-sector-oriented policies was widening.

After the 1981 death of Torrijos, the Panamanian government became steadily more conservative. Three National Guard officers—
Noriega, Rubén Darío Paredes, and Roberto Díaz Herrera—became
contenders for political and military leadership. Apparently the three
agreed to alternate in power. As National Guard commander, Paredes
challenged the independence of the PRD and in July 1982 removed
Torrijos's hand-picked president, Aristides Royo, and replaced him
with Ricardo de la Espriella. Paredes meanwhile also began to extend

his power base by trying to bring disaffected elements of the private sector, mainly the agricultural oligarchy, into a new political alliance. But when Paredes retired from the Guard to run for president, Noriega did not support his bid, which left Paredes marginalized and extremely bitter. As the new National Guard commander, Noriega engineered to have Nicolás Ardito-Barletta run for president as part of a five-party coalition. The power of the National Guard assured his victory. The fraudulent nature of democracy in Panama became obvious to all in the September 1984 inauguration of Ardito-Barletta as president after the country's first national election in sixteen years. And then in the face of rising public protest to his austerity program, Ardito-Barletta was deposed a year later by Noriega and replaced with Eric Arturo Delvalle. For three years Delvalle proved a faithful servant of Noriega.

In February 1988, however, Delvalle tried to replace Noriega as PDF commander. Instead it was Delvalle who was forced to step down and in his place, Noriega appointed Manuel Solís Palma to the presidency. Solís Palma finished out the five-year term started by Ardito-Barletta. In September 1989 Noriega appointed Francisco Rodríguez to be provisional president; and then in December 1989 Noriega was declared head of government by a newly appointed National Assembly.[7]

Government had come full circle by the end of the decade. Once again the commander of the military was also the country's top figure in government. To legitimize this new military government, Noriega, like Torrijos before him, identified himself with the politics of nationalism and populism. Noriega's credentials as a populist and nationalist leader were, however, even less convincing. A recent history of joint military maneuvers with U.S. forces, increased repression of workers, and his support for antipopular austerity measures all undermined Noriega's ability to portray himself as a leader in the *torrijista* tradition.

Oligarchy and the Government

Before 1968 politics in Panama was dominated by the country's small oligarchy—a grouping of a couple dozen families that are known disparagingly as *Rabiblancos* or white-tailed birds.[8] For the most part this elite represented the service and commercial sectors associated with the transit operations of the canal.

The oligarchy ruled with the backing of the U.S. authorities and relied on the might of the U.S. military to maintain the peace. Under these conditions political development was retarded. Political scientist John Weeks observed that, "the overwhelming dominance of American governments over Panama distorted political life both between the rulers and the ruled and within the elite itself. Relieved of the burden of consolidating its rule over the population, the Panamanian elite failed to develop effective, long-term institutions of political accommodation and cooptation."[9]

When the National Guard led by Torrijos took control over the government in 1968, it broke the dominance of the oligarchy but did not represent a class-based attack on the private sector. Instead it set about establishing a new economic alliance with the industrial and financial sectors, bypassing the interests of some of the more traditional oligarchic sectors. Many representatives of the private sector were brought into the Torrijos government as cabinet ministers and Torrijos worked closely with business leaders in developing the international financial center, expanding the Colón Free Zone, and developing the country's industrial and agricultural production capacity.

Torrijos succeeded in establishing a close alliance with the industrial bourgeoisie and those financial interests associated with the country's international services economy. After his death, representatives of the traditional parties were brought back into the government's political alliance for the 1984 elections. Joining the National Democratic Unity Coalition (UNADE) were the Liberal and Republican parties, the business-oriented and military-created Panamanian Labor party (PALA), and the Revolutionary Democratic party (PRD). The choice of Ardito-Barletta, while opposed by the *torrijista* factions of the PRD, was the choice of Noriega and widely supported by the business community. The replacement of Ardito-Barletta by misfit Vice President Eric Delvalle, a multimillionaire with interests in sugar, race horses, and television, also illustrated the close working relationship that existed between the government and oligarchy.

Beginning in mid-1987 the country's dominant economic forces began grouping around the National Civic Crusade and later the Democratic Opposition Alliance (ADO). The Civic Crusade was formed in June 1987 by a group of antigovernment business owners to capitalize on the spontaneous popular demonstrations that resulted from charges by Colonel Roberto Díaz Herrera linking Noriega to the torture and murder of former Vice Minister of Health Hugo Spadafora, and to the fraudulent 1984 elections.[10] The Civic Crusade brought together dozens of civic groups, business organizations, and professional associations. Three opposition political parties also were closely associated with the Civic Crusade: Christian Democratic party (PDC), Authentic *Panameñista* party (PPA), and the Popular Action party (PAPO). By 1988 it was also becoming clear that the country's powerful financial sector, which for so long had supported the military government, had moved into the opposition. It was not, however, the oligarchs who were the main activists of the Civic Crusade. Its most active supporters were found among the country's merchant and middle classes, landowners, and small-business entrepreneurs.

Despite the anger over the anti-Noriega U.S. economic sanctions, there was wide agreement among the oligarchy and those supporting the Civic Crusade that Noriega must go and that the Panama Defense Forces be returned to their barracks. All sectors of the oligarchy—except those directly linked with the PDF in business transactions—wanted the military to step down from its central role in government and resume its pre-1968 role as the armed guarantor of political stability and elite rule. With the installation of the Endara government, the country's economic elite again assumed direct control over the country's economic and political development.

Political Parties and Elections

The new administration installed after the U.S. invasion in December 1989 was that of the Democratic Civic Opposition Alliance (ADOC), an opposition alliance of three political parties and various civic organizations. ADOC represented the coming together of the Democratic Opposition Alliance (ADO); a coalition of the Authentic *Panameñista* party (PPA), the Christian Democratic party (PDC), and the National Liberal Republican Movement (MOLIRENA); and the National Civic Crusade for the May 1989 elections. President Guillermo Endara was a founding member of the PPA—a conservative populist party headed by Arnulfo Arias until his death in 1988—and the leader of the Authentic Liberal party, a 1988 splitoff from the PPA. In mid-1990 Endara's supporters organized an impressive signature drive to inscribe a new party known as the Arnulfista party. First Vice President Ricardo Arias Calderón is president of the Christian Democratic party (PDC). Second Vice President Guillermo Ford is leader of the National Liberal Republican Movement (MOLIRENA), a fusion of the traditional Liberal party factions of the oligarchy.

The ADOC coalition was also supported by dissidents from the Liberal party (Roderick Esquivel) and the Republican party (Eric Delvalle). In addition, ADOC counted on the strong support of the Catholic Church. The ADOC coalition apparently won the election by a wide margin based on a broad public rejection of Manuel Noriega.

The ADOC slate (Endara, Calderón, and Ford), installed as the new government of Panama in late 1989, has promised to rule by consensus. But having come together as a broad alliance of business, civic, and political groups with the goal of ousting Noriega, the coalition had never ironed out a common political platform. Upon taking power, the personal and political differences among the three parties and their powerful supporters immediately began to weaken the alliance. Although there was a certain commitment to maintain a unified front, the three factions also began to jockey for public favor by criticizing one another in an attempt to strengthen their own positions for the 1994 elections. Growing splits in the ruling coalitions also surfaced in the Assembly and obstructed the approval of the government's plan for privatization, strict structural adjustment, and changes in the banking laws, thereby jeopardizing the continual flow of U.S. economic aid. In this New Right political coalition, Calderón will likely emerge as the strongest figure.

The Christian Democratic party (PDC) is one of the most conservative Christian Democratic parties in the region. Led by Ricardo Arias Calderón, the PDC has closely associated itself with U.S. policy and strategy in Panama. The PDC's base is found among the middle class, professionals, and the financial community. The party's former commitment to the interests of the poor majority and to forging a new and more broadly based politics of national development have been dropped in favor of a private sector—oriented approach to economic development and a political direction that is closely associated with the U.S. State Department. The PDC has, however, adopted a more populist rhetoric so as to widen its appeal among the poor and working class.

In the postinvasion government the PDC is the most organized and powerful party. Not only does it have the most consistent and appealing political rhetoric and the most international support, it also counts on the majority of the national legislators and the ministries of government and justice, education, and housing and public works. The PDC also controls such state institutions as INTEL (National Telecommunications Institute), IRHE (Hydraulic Resources and Electrification Institute), IMA (Agricultural Marketing Institute), National Cultural Institute, and the immigration agency.

The National Liberal Republican Movement (MOLIRENA) formed the third pillar of the ADOC alliance. Represented by Guillermo Ford, MOLIRENA formed in 1984 as a coalition of traditional oligarchic political parties not associated with the government. A right-wing party, MOLIRENA brought together the factions of the Liberal, National, and Republican parties that stood outside the government's own political coalition. Ford and MOLIRENA will be the driving force behind the neoliberal economic policy of the Endara government. In the new government, MOLIRENA controls the ministries of planning and economy, treasury, labor, and social welfare. It also runs the government's general accounting department, the national lottery, and the ministries of health and foreign relations.

Besides ADOC and COLINA, the Authentic *Panameñista* party (PPA) also contended for power in the May 1989 elections. Following the death of party patriarch Arnulfo Arias in August 1988, the PPA split into two factions. The Endara faction left the party to form the Authentic Liberal party (PLA) and the Arnulfista party (PA), both of which joined the U.S.-backed opposition. The remnants of the party regrouped under the leadership of the party secretary, General Hildebrando Nicosia Pérez. The reconstructed party recognized the legitimacy of the Solís Palma government and was strongly critical of U.S. economic sanctions. It posed as the rightful heir of the legacy of nationalism and populism left by Arias.

Panama's Communist and Socialist parties were at the heart of most popular antigovernment and labor organizing from the 1920s to the late 1960s. But during the period of military rule (1969–1989) the organized left in Panama became closely associated with the government. Small, divided, and isolated it, for the most part, allowed itself and its associated popular organizations and unions to be coopted by the government. The left's failure to develop an independent and class-based political platform is in part responsible for the country's lack of a progressive alternative to the oligarchy and the military. By adhering to a narrow nationalism promoted by the PDF and by not raising strong demands for democratic changes, it allowed the oligarchy, the Church, and the New Right to lead the opposition to the military dictatorship.

Human Rights

Human-rights violations by the security forces and associated paramilitary groups have been widespread since 1987, although serious abuses, like torture, killings, and disappearances, have been rare. Violent suppression of demonstrations, arbitrary short-term detentions, sexual abuse of detainees, and sharp limitations on freedom of the press and of expression constituted the most common violations. As Latin America scholar Richard Millet noted, "Noriega managed to maintain power without resorting to the terror and massive human rights violations characteristic of so many Latin American military governments."[11]

It was not until the kidnapping and decapitation of Dr. Hugo Spadafora in 1985 that the human-rights situation in Panama became a

matter of great national and international concern. The mutilation and
death of Spadafora sparked internal criticism within the National
Guard, and popular protests. From June through August 1987, after
the revelations of Colonel Díaz Herrera, there were large demonstrations marking the anniversary of Spadafora's death and the fraudulent
1984 elections, in which protesters also complained about other
human-rights violations by the PDF. The protests were brutally crushed
by the "Dobermans," the PDF's antiriot squads. Human-rights violations increased steadily after June 1987, and harassment of journalists
and government control over the media became common.

Amnesty International charged the country's security forces with
"excessive use of force" in response to antigovernment demonstrations.[12] This included the common practice of beating arrested demonstrators and critics of the government. Demonstrators also were
subject to liberal use of birdshot by antiriot squads.

In early 1989 the Inter-American Commission on Human Rights
called for increased freedom of the press, demanding that all news
media be permitted to publish and broadcast without government
interference. It demanded that the government guarantee "complete
and unrestricted exercise of freedom of expression, right to assembly,
judicial guarantees, and personal liberties."[13]

The human-rights picture in Panama was further complicated by
the December 1989 U.S. invasion. Washington justified the action by
saying that it was necessary to protect U.S. lives. Prior to the invasion,
however, the 40,000 U.S. citizens living in Panama were in no special
danger. One U.S. soldier was killed when running a military roadblock
several days before the invasion, but this seemed an inappropriate
justification for an invasion that resulted in the deaths of three U.S.
civilians and twenty-three U.S. soldiers as well as at least several hundred Panamanians. Initially the Pentagon claimed that 324 PDF members were killed and only 202 civilians, but later reports reduced the
number of Panamanian soldiers killed to fifty. By official Pentagon
figures, therefore, the ratio of noncombatant to military deaths was
greater than four to one. These figures point to the indiscriminate
character of the invasion, especially considering that the actual number of civilian deaths was probably much higher.[14] Three months after
the invasion the U.S. military announced that it was investigating alleged misconduct by twenty-one U.S. soldiers that resulted in the
deaths of eight Panamanian noncombatants.

The Popular Coordinator of Human Rights in Panama (CO-
PODEHUPA) denounced the invasion and the subsequent wave of
detentions of civilian "prisoners of war" by the U.S. forces. Of the five

thousand Panamanians detained by U.S. troops, five hundred were civilians and the rest were PDF members. The Panama Civil Rights Commission, associated with the anti-Noriega opposition and later with the Endara government, praised the military action as "a surgical procedure to remove a cancer."[15]

MILITARY

For a long time the military and police forces of Panama operated under the tutelage of Washington. In fact, the U.S. government was instrumental in the creation of the National Guard and was, until 1987, the main source of funding and training for Panamanian police and military forces. The United States disbanded the country's small army in 1904 and its police force some ten years later, taking control over the internal and external security matters until the mid-1930s, when an end to the U.S. protectorate status was negotiated.[16]

During World War II the national police were militarized by the United States. In 1952, the year that former police chief José Antonio Remón Cantera became Panama's president, the National Police Force was modernized and the National Guard created. As part of its new effort to foster hemispheric security, the Pentagon started to train and aid the country's National Guard while establishing a strong foundation of counterinsurgency and national security doctrine among its ranks.[17] In the 1960s U.S. military and economic aid increased under the Alliance for Progress program.

When Torrijos toppled the Arias government in 1968 and established a populist military dictatorship, the National Guard became the country's main political institution. Torrijos broke oligarchic control of the National Guard and proceeded to make it the country's sponsor and protector of populist reforms—ranging from agrarian reform to the institution of a progressive labor code.[18]

From 1968 until his death in 1981, Torrijos served as the country's commander-in-chief. Colonel Florencio Flores assumed that position in 1981 followed by General Rubén Darío Paredes. When Paredes stepped down to run for president in 1983, General Manuel Antonio Noriega became commander-in-chief. A month later, the National Guard was restructured under Law 20 into the Panama Defense Forces (PDF). Aside from modernizing the structure of the police and military forces, Law 20 also instituted PDF control over many aspects of Panamanian public life, including the immigration department, civil aeronautics administration, railroads, traffic department, and the passport bureau.[19]

In 1987 Washington began encouraging dissident factions within the PDF to oust Noriega. Abortive coup attempts in March 1988 and October 1989 seriously depleted the PDF's officer corps, which had also been weakened by the forced retirement of many high officers suspected of harboring anti-Noriega sympathies.

It was the nationalist and reformist legacy of *torrijismo* that gave the PDF its credibility and sense of purpose. At the same time, however, the PDF was a corrupt institution that often put itself above law, morality, and government. Payoffs by businesses for special treatment were commonplace; the PDF raked in large sums in multinational business deals, and skimmed off profits from the international drug trade and arms smuggling. The PDF also had direct economic interests through its own national bank created in 1989. The PDF described the bank as a "private entity" that functioned as a branch of the Defense Forces Benevolent Society.

With the December 1989 invasion, the U.S. military resumed its historical role as the chief arbiter and guarantor of political power in Panama. Suddenly, after twenty-one years in which the military had served as the country's central institution, the National Guard/PDF ceased to exist. It was replaced by a new police organization called the Public Force (PF). In early 1990, under the supervision of the U.S. occupation army, the newly constituted security force, composed mainly of former PDF members, was in the process of gradually assuming control of some of the country's police functions. Widespread distrust of former PDF members who made up the PF, the disinclination of former army officers to do police work, and a postinvasion crime wave were among the many problems faced by the new security force.

The PF is a force of some 13,000, down from the 16,000 of the disbanded PDF. Its budget was cut from $150 million to $84 million for 1990. Unlike the PDF, the PF was placed under the civilian authority of the Ministry of Government and Justice. Initially the PF was divided into three branches: National Police, National Air Service, and National Maritime Service. In addition, there existed a prison police and a Technical Judicial Police unit that replaced the former National Department of Investigations (DENI), which functioned as a kind of secret police during the Noriega years. The government decree authorizing the PF also left open the possibility of creating new security forces that would be responsible for protecting the canal, guarding borders, and defending the country's democratic institutions.

An August 1990 poll conducted by a Costa Rican firm revealed that nearly three-quarters of the respondents believe that major changes in the PF are necessary to preclude a military coup in coming years. More than half expressed concern that the new security force was drawn almost exclusively from the former National Guard/PDF of the Torrijos and Noriega years.[20] In its May 1990 report on Panama, Americas Watch stated that it was "astonishing" that U.S. forces were permitting the PF to establish a new "intelligence and counter-intelligence" unit almost all of whose agents appeared to be former agents of General Noriega's notorious secret police.[21]

Panamanians were thrilled to be rid of the PDF, which had grown increasingly repressive and corrupt. But the dissolution of the PDF left a serious gap of authority in the country. As the country began its reconstruction efforts, it faced the challenge of creating a sovereign and ordered country without resorting to the use of U.S. troops. By late 1990 the PF seemed unable to control the postinvasion rise in crime, and some elements within the security force were accused of planning a coup. There was also the question of the Panama Canal's future now that the country was unable to protect the canal with its own forces.

In the shaping of the new Panama, Panamanians will have to come to terms with what the PDF was and exactly what kind of military and police force should emerge from its ashes. The Panamanian and U.S. governments have moved to create a security force with a wide range of functions, including counterinsurgency, intelligence operations, anti-riot response, and counterterrorism as well as normal police activities. But such a force, dependent on the United States for aid and training, could quickly become an instrument of repression of the popular movement and a threat to the political system.

ECONOMY

The State of the Economy

Panama began the 1990s with an economy badly shaken by U.S. economic sanctions (1987–1989) and smarting from the devastation and looting that accompanied the December 1989 invasion. In the two years prior to the invasion the gross national product had dropped 20 percent to 25 percent. The sanction had forced the per capita income back to the levels of the early 1980s. Government revenues were down about 44 percent, resulting in a similar drop in public services and investment. Industrial output had dropped by 40 percent, and tourism was down to 25 percent of capacity.

With credit so scarce, construction had ground to a standstill. Foreign-exchange revenues were down 50 percent, and debt arrears had risen to more than a half-billion dollars. Unemployment had doubled to more than 25 percent of the workforce. The political crisis and the U.S. campaign of economic destabilization had driven the country into a deep recession, a situation aggravated further by the invasion and accompanying devastation. The Panamanian business community estimated that the invasion and looting caused $1.5 billion in material losses; an official Panama-U.S. commission estimated that the invasion had cost Panama $600 million or about 11 percent of the gross domestic product.[22] In addition to direct economic losses, the havoc and destruction resulting from the invasion drove the unemployment rate up to 33 percent and caused a sharp drop in projected government revenues.

Even before the onset of the anti-Noriega campaign, the Panamanian economy had been reeling from a long-festering structural crisis. In the late 1970s the symptoms of the crisis were becoming increasingly apparent. Private and public investment rates were declining, the debt was unpayable, the international finance center, a multinational banking complex, was reaching its peak investment in Panama, budget deficits were expanding, and per capita food production was declining. In concert with international lending institutions, the military government responded to the crisis by imposing a structural-adjustment program that began to undo the social reforms and government services sponsored during the heyday of *torrijismo*.

Military Populism and Rising Debt

When the National Guard took power in 1968, the economy was sailing along at an 8 percent annual growth rate. World recession and rising oil prices, among other factors, caused this fast economic pace to slow down by 1974. The private sector, however, blamed the downturn on the populist bent of the Torrijos regime, and began its campaign to curb *torrijismo* and establish preeminence in the ruling alliance. As a result of this pressure and Torrijos's own efforts to win the oligarchy's support for revision of the canal treaties, the government shifted away from the popular sectors by the mid-1970s.

During the 1970s the government did, however, maintain its commitment to expanding government social services, especially health and education. It also continued to insist that a large public investment budget was necessary for an expanding economy. By the turn of the decade, however, even these remaining elements of *torrijismo* began to shrink in the face of an incipient coalition of the country's dominant economic forces with multilateral banks, foreign private banks, and the U.S. Agency for International Development (AID). A second jump in oil prices, another downturn in world trade, and the advent of the debt crisis combined to cause the collapse of the Torrijos development model.

Rising interest rates in the late 1970s precipitated the economic crisis of the 1980s. Government social services and the government's direct participation in the economy through more than three dozen state enterprises had been pushed forward primarily to strengthen the internal market. These economic stimulants had been financed not through progressive taxation but from funds borrowed from international banks. The borrowing spree of the 1970s, encouraged by foreign private banks, resulted in the largest per capita debt in Latin America.

By 1981 Panama could no longer keep up with the interest payments on its debt, let alone pay off the principal. This crisis in international accounts was paralleled by one in the government's own budget. Falling revenues and the burden of a large government payroll and social-service sector had caused the budget deficit to widen to crisis proportions.

The military government attempted to tackle the structural crisis with adjustment programs imposed by the World Bank and International Monetary Fund (IMF) and backed by the Inter-American Development Bank (IDB) and the U.S. Agency for International Development (AID). The structural-adjustment measures were an attempt to reshape the country's economic model along neoliberal lines by promoting exports, cutting government programs, pushing privatization, dropping protective tariffs, and liberalizing prices.

Although these programs had some success in easing the balance-of-payments crisis and closing budget deficits, they failed to spur significant new economic growth. Debt repayments continued to drain the national treasury and this decapitalization obstructed economic recovery. The government moved to liberalize the economy and promote exports but export growth proved disappointing.

At the same time that the new economic model was failing to achieve its initial promise, additional symptoms of the country's economic crisis surfaced during the 1980s. Per capita production of basic grains dropped, unemployment steadily rose, and the country's once-encouraging indices of health and education fell. The lack of adequate housing also threatened to precipitate new social unrest.

During the crisis of the late 1980s the Noriega regime suspended debt-servicing payments. These payments had previously soaked up about 40 percent of government revenues. By defaulting, Noriega was able, despite the U.S. embargo and declining tax revenues, to continue to meet most civilian and military payroll demands. But this was clearly a temporary solution to an increasingly grave financial crisis.

The economic and political crisis and the U.S. campaign of economic destabilization derailed the plans and projections of the structural-adjustment program. Following the invasion and the installation of the Endara government, steps were immediately taken to put the structural-adjustment program back on track. But adopting the conservative agenda of the multilateral lenders was not enough. Besides promising to privatize state corporations, liberalize trade, and cut the public workforce, the new government had to pay its large arrears to the Inter-American Development Bank and World Bank before new loans would begin to flow.

Economic Crisis As Nineties Begin

Some major characteristics of the Panamanian economy as the country entered the 1990s were

- An extremely open and dependent economy that does not even have its own Central Bank or an authentic national currency.
- An economy that depends on imports for most primary and personal consumption items, with a consequent history of wide trade imbalances since independence.
- High $2,200 per capita debt, which has made the country vulnerable to harsh structural-adjustment packages. Until debt payments were canceled in 1987, more capital was flowing out of the country in debt payments than into the country in new investment and adjustment capital.
- Austerity measures and a structural-adjustment program that have pushed forward a highly questionable economic development model based on export production, in a country where less than 20 percent of national income is generated by the productive agricultural and industrial sectors.[23]
- Relatively high per capita income but highly skewed income distribution. The bottom 20 percent of the population receive only 2.1 percent of national income, while the top 5 percent receive 17.8 percent.[24]
- After major advances in meeting basic needs and giving the poor access to health, education, and utilities in the 1970s, steadily falling socioeconomic indicators in the 1980s.

- A services and commerce sector that accounts for over 50 percent of the national product but for which benefits from this economic activity are limited by tax and tariff exemptions.
- An economy trying to recover from a vindictive U.S. destabilization campaign that cost the country $2 billion in reduced jobs and income, drove Panama into recession, and was followed by the U.S. invasion and accompanying looting with at least $600 million in losses.

It has been a challenge for the new Endara government to try to restore the economy to pre-1987 levels. It faced external debt payment arrears of $540 million and a devastated internal economy. Even if the debt arrears were cleared up, the country would still be confronted with one of the world's highest ratios of debt to gross national product. The debt crisis situation was aggravated by the fact that two-thirds of the country's $3.9 million public-sector debt is owed to high-interest commercial lenders.

A third of the workforce was unemployed, 44 percent of Panamanians lived in poverty, and projected government revenues were down by more than 40 percent from those collected in 1987. Besides the external debt, the new government was faced with an internal debt of more than $1 billion to private creditors. In early 1990 the economy was still reeling from sharp drops in trade and investment and the massive capital flight caused by the 1987–1989 crisis, with few signs that there would be an immediate recuperation of former levels of bank and business operations. Former president Ardito-Barletta estimated that for the country to return to pre-1988 levels would take fifteen years.[25]

The conservative direction of the Endara government's economic policies was immediately evident. The government promised to renew and broaden the structural-adjustment measures adopted by the previous regime. Although the governments of the 1980s did take steps to liberalize trade and prices, cut social services, and promote exports, the structural-adjustment program did not go far enough according to foreign lenders and the country's financial elite. With members of the right-wing MOLIRENA party placed as heads of the planning and financial ministries, the neoliberal economic direction of the new government was quickly established.

Although substantial, the approximately $500 million in credits and $420 million in promised economic aid fell far short of the $2 billion the government said it needed as a minimum to restore former prosperity. Under U.S. guidance the Endara government launched a recovery program that incorporated neoliberal economic formulas—including privatization of state enterprises, widespread firing of public employees, and an end to price subsidies—designed to spur private-sector investment and export production while narrowing fiscal deficits.

By mid-1990 the government could cite some positive economic indicators. For the first time in three years the economy began to inch forward, government revenues were increasing, and trade volume in the Colón free zone was rebounding. The government could also report that 85 percent of the businesses sacked during the invasion had reopened. But unemployment levels remained dangerously high, and there were no signs that the government could extricate itself from its weighty debt arrears.

Agriculture

Outside of the Panama City–Colón corridor, Panama is essentially an agricultural country. Together, agriculture, forestry, and fishing provide employment to 27 percent of working Panamanians—more than any other economic sector.[26] Beyond its contribution to employment, however, the agricultural sector plays a minor role in the economy: Its contribution dropped from 19 percent of the national income in the late 1960s to only 9 percent, with agroindustry (food processing) contributing another 4 percent to 5 percent. Agroexports account for only 28 percent of export revenues—less than any other Central American country.

The crisis in agriculture has been particularly severe in the last ten years as export revenues declined, per capita food production fell, and food imports increased. Among the main factors for this sectoral crisis are the structural-adjustment measures that deemphasize local food production; shrinking government support for farmers; inequities in land distribution; and low crop yields.[27] Over the last three decades many rural residents have left the countryside to seek a better living in the Panama City–Colón urban corridor.

Neither terrain nor soil quality favors agriculture in Panama. Over three-quarters of the land is hilly, and only 37 percent of these hillside zones have good, deep soils, compared with 50 percent in neighboring Costa Rica or 76 percent in El Salvador.[28] Only about 30 percent of the country's land is suitable for cropping and pasture. Of this, 8 percent of the land is cultivated and 15 percent is in pasture—leaving a large agricultural frontier in Darién and other isolated regions, although most of these areas are tropical forests.[29]

Agricultural land is unevenly divided among the country's farmers, with 1 percent of the farms covering more than 33 percent of the farm land. More than 90 percent of the farms are small holdings, representing only a third of the agricultural land. Only 4 percent of the farms are categorized as commercial, while 35 percent report no cash income at all. Clear land titles are held by just 10 percent of the country's farmers. Most of the estates larger than 500 hectares are dedicated to cattle and milk production.[30]

Slash-and-burn cultivation (known as *la roza*), machetes, and planting sticks still distinguish the agricultural practices of the small farm sector. As a result crop yields are extremely low—half the average for corn and beans production in South America.[31] Nonetheless, small and medium farmers produce most of the country's foodstuffs. The production increases that have occurred over the last couple decades have been more the result of expanding the land under production rather than improved production practices. It is only in the more organized export crops, such as bananas, sugar, and coffee, that there is substantial use of mechanization, fertilizers, and technical assistance.

As part of the structural-adjustment program sponsored by AID and international lending institutions, new emphasis was placed on agroexport production in the 1980s. Before suspending assistance in 1987, AID promoted increased export-oriented production of beef, fruit, and winter vegetables. With the renewal of U.S. economic aid, this development focus is now expected to be reinstituted. One private company that benefited from U.S. aid programs was Panama Agro Export, which exported cantaloupe, watermelon, and cucumber to the United States.

New U.S. credits and the probable incorporation of Panama into the Caribbean Basin Initiative (CBI) export-promotion program, as well as direct AID support for nontraditional production, will likely lead to increased nontraditional exports. But relatively high wage and worker benefit rates, uncompetitive transportation and shipping costs, and a lack of experience will hinder rapid growth in this sector. Even if the country does experience a spurt in nontraditional export production, these products will still compose only a small part of the country's export base. The prospects for significant increases in traditional agroexport production also appear dim.[32]

Colón Free Zone Booms

Unlike other Central American countries where the politics and economies have been dominated by a rural oligarchy, the Panamanian oligarchy has been largely based in services and commerce. At first, this service economy revolved almost exclusively around the Panama Canal. The increased canal traffic during World War II spurred further development of Panama as a transnational services platform. In 1948 the Colón Free Zone opened, established in part to stave off the postwar depression in Colón. Today, it is the second largest free zone in the world after Hong Kong. More than five hundred companies employ some five thousand people in warehousing, regional distribution, manufacturing, and wholesale trade. The targeted market for these free-port operations is Latin America and the Caribbean.

Companies locating in the free zone do not pay import duties or taxes and are not even required to secure a business license. They simply need to guarantee employment to at least ten Panamanians for the privilege of opening up business operations in one of the hundreds of prefabricated warehouses that line the free zone. This enclave of international trade, separated by high barbed-wire fence from the depressed city of Colón, accounts for 3 percent of the country's gross product.[33]

International Finance Center

Bank secrecy had been Panamanian law since 1959, but it was the 1970 banking law that created the ideal conditions for an international offshore financial center. Besides allowing numbered accounts, the 1970 law stipulated that bank deposits were not to be taxed, that no reserves were to be required, and that profits would be exempted from local income tax. The other essential element in building the international finance center in Panama was to use the U.S. dollar as the country's unit of exchange. A dollar-based economy means that there is no danger of currency devaluation and the inflation rate matches that of the United States.

The international finance center was thriving by the early 1980s with more than $35 billion in assets. Little of the profit from this banking complex, however, stays in Panama because the offshore transactions are not taxed. The employment of more than seven thousand Panamanians is the main benefit of the finance center. There are also many indirect benefits resulting from the presence of so many offshore banks.

The debt crisis, the opening up of offshore centers in Miami and other places, and assaults on the country's bank secrecy conditions by U.S. tax and drug enforcement agents combined to stifle the center's growth since 1982. When the crisis broke out in 1987, the center hosted more than 120 banks with $22 billion in assets and several dozen reinsurance companies with more than $175 million in premiums.

Although shaken by the crisis, in early 1990 Panama was still hosting 110 banks with about $15 billion in deposits.[34] The financial center will not recover fully, however, until "confidence" returns and the new rules of the game become clear. The chief obstacle to regaining this confidence is the U.S. pressure to rescind strict bank secrecy laws, which now keep the owners of the accounts out of the reach of U.S. drug enforcement and Internal Revenue Service agents. Nonetheless, it is and probably will remain, at least over the short term, a centerpiece in the Panamanian economy.

Paper Companies and a Pipeline

The registry of "paper" companies is another branch of the offshore industry found in Panama. The flexibility and ease of the country's 1927 incorporation law, based on that of the state of Delaware, has resulted in an estimated 100,000 company incorporations in Panama. Before the crisis, new companies were registering at the rate of 114 a day.[35] Corporation registry in Panama facilitates bookkeeping sleights of hand that enable companies and individuals to avoid taxation in their countries of operation.

The most recent addition to Panama's transnational service economy is the oil transshipment facility of the Panama Petroterminal company. This joint venture—60 percent owned by U.S. investors and 40 percent by the Panamanian government—was formed in 1977 to assist the crossisthmus transport of Alaska's North Slope oil.[36] Employing about four hundred workers, it contributes 3 percent of Panama's gross national income.[37] About one-third of Alaska's North Slope annual oil production flows through the pipeline. The completion of a transcontinental pipeline in the United States will eventually reduce the amount of oil (currently about 325,000 barrels per day, down from 575,000 barrels daily) pumped across the isthmus, as will the increase in consumption and new refining facilities in the United States.

The Business of the Canal

The Panama Canal, the foundation of the transnational services platform, is the source of the country's most important transshipment business. About 5 percent of all ocean-going trade passes through the canal; more than 70 percent of it originates in or is destined for the United States.

Every day thirty or more ships slowly make their way through the canal, paying high fees for the privilege of not having to make the long trip down and around Cape Horn. The average toll paid is $26,000 but the fees range as high as $107,000, paid by the *Queen Elizabeth II* luxury liner in early 1988.

The Panama Canal Commission, which administers the canal, employs more than one thousand U.S. citizens and six thousand Panamanians. More than 8 percent of the country's national product comes from the canal operations. Although canal traffic reached new peaks in the 1980s, its days as an essential link in world trade seem numbered unless it is upgraded and widened. All of the three main possibilities for upgrading the canal—widening the Culebra Cut, creating a third set of locks, and building a sea-level canal—have been put on hold because of U.S.-Panama tensions. The treaty stipulation that the canal has to be handed over to Panama "free of liens and debts" presents another obstacle to U.S. investment in canal improvement during the 1990s.

Because five of the nine members of the Panama Canal Commission's board of directors are appointed by Washington, decision-making about canal operations has remained largely in U.S. hands. In late 1989 U.S.-Panama tensions centered around the appointment of a new commission administrator. According to the provisions of the 1977 canal treaties, this post would be transferred on January 1, 1990, from a U.S. citizen to a Panamanian named by the Panamanian government and confirmed by the United States. President Bush rejected the nomination of newspaper publisher Tomás Altamirano Duque by the Noriega-controlled National Assembly on the grounds that Noriega's government was illegitimate and not recognized by the United States. Instead, Bush proposed the provisional appointment of a deputy administrator, Panamanian Fernando Manfredo. After the invasion, the U.S. Congress approved the selection of Gilberto Guardia to become the first Panamanian appointed by the Panamanian government to administer the Panama Canal.

Domestic Industry

Being an international crossroads, Panama has never developed a strong industrial sector of its own. Manufacturing and mining currently represent less than 9 percent of the gross national product and employ about the same percentage of the workforce. Today, the main components of Panama's manufacturing sector are food and beverage processing, textiles, petroleum products, chemicals, and construction materials.

During the 1980s the industrial sector experienced negative growth. As part of the structural-adjustment program imposed on Panama by international financial institutions and AID, tariff and quota barriers protecting the small manufacturing sector were removed and industries were encouraged to move to export-oriented production. The labor code also was revised to loosen restrictions on productivity premiums, piece work, and contract work in homes—measures designed to spur new investment in export-oriented manufacturing. Plans by the Endara government to reduce protection further for local industries have brought protests from the industrial sector.

The relatively high labor, energy, and transportation costs of doing business in Panama limit the prospects for export-oriented manufacturing in the country. After the invasion, Washington moved once again to integrate Panama into the Caribbean Basin Initiative (CBI), but expanding U.S. protectionism has largely counterbalanced the benefits from the export incentives offered by this regional program. By the middle of the decade, however, numerous Asian textile manufacturers began to establish assembly operations in Panama to take advantage of access to the U.S. market through the CBI.

SOCIETY AND ENVIRONMENT

Popular Organizing

Despite a tradition of political activism dating back to the Renters' Movement of 1925, the popular sectors of poor and working-class Panamanians played a passive role in the political crisis of the late 1980s. At a time of rapidly worsening economic conditions and intensifying U.S. pressure, the popular sectors remained unorganized and without a political agenda. Ideological differences, leadership struggles, the lack of good popular education programs, and the absence of a unified political program all weakened the popular movement.

This lack of political dynamism and militancy of the Panamanian majority can be attributed in part to the success of *torrijismo* in the 1970s. The reformism of the 1970s was not directed by the popular movement. Instead, the popular sectors formed the base of support for the government's own political and economic projects.[38] In the agrarian sector, the government sponsored colonization and land-distribution projects that targeted the most restive rural areas. The new labor code of 1972 increased employee rights and facilitated union organizing. Union activists and leaders of other popular sectors were coopted into the government as members of various public-sector commissions and committees, which resulted in the loss of their independence and militancy.

As part of its populist program, the government established hundreds of village "health committees" throughout the country. Health conditions did improve, but the government took measures to ensure that local committees did not become a catalyst for more independent community organizing. By establishing the new national political infrastructure of *corregimientos* (local councils) and a new National Assembly, the Torrijos regime undermined the local power of the old *patrones* only to substitute it with a system of political representation controlled by the central government.

Although the reformist character of *torrijismo* did have the effect of integrating most popular elements into the government's own stabilization plan, there also existed a more combative and independent edge to the popular movement in the 1970s. Within the Catholic Church, liberation theology inspired communities of "the poorest of the poor," base communities which constituted an important force for social activism.

One of the most militant sectors of the popular movement has been the urban land squatters known as *precaristas*. Since the 1950s poor Panamanians have increasingly resorted to illegal land occupations. At first, *precarismo* was limited to the Panama City area, but in the 1980s, land occupations have occurred in Colón and Chiriquí. These squatter settlements, known variously as *barriadas brujas* (underground/unofficial areas), *barriadas de emergencia* (emergency settlements), and *asentamientos espontáneos* (spontaneous settlements), are a response to the country's deficit of 200,000 houses.[39]

San Miguelito, a sprawling area on the outskirts of Panama City, is a product of this squatters' movement. Today, more than 9 percent of the nation's population and 20 percent of Panama City residents live in this collection of *barriadas*.[40] Representing these tens of thousands of squatters is the San Miguelito Coordinator of Spontaneous Settlements, which gained legal recognition in 1986. Its members fight for land titles and for the extension of city services into their communities. Although the squatters or *precaristas* represent a major social sector in Panama, they did not formulate their own political demands in the face of the crisis of the late 1980s. The military-controlled regime tried to manipulate their political sympathies by targeting these desperately poor communities for special government community-development projects and for PDF-sponsored civic action programs. While the residents of San Miguelito were certainly not the driving force behind the National Civic Crusade, many did support this elitist political opposition movement, feeling that an end of hostilities between the United States and Panama would mean more jobs.

As the country's crisis intensified in the late 1980s, there were several attempts to revitalize the popular movement. They were, however, unable to create an overall political vision that would encompass the broader and long-term needs of the poor majority. Appropriated by Noriega, nationalism and populism had become closely associated with a military dictatorship, while antimilitarism and democratic reforms had become the standards of the middle classes and private-sector elite. Those who purported to be the leaders of the popular movement, such as the country's labor hierarchy, were collaborationists beholden to state power, not to the popular sectors.

In this context of immobilization and absence of an independent political project, the popular sectors were manipulated by both Noriega and the Civic Crusade/ADOC opposition. As sociologist Raúl Leis concluded, "For the government and the opposition, the popular sectors are a crowd without faces, a docile and submissive mass that serves as a social base for each of their political projects."[41]

The U.S. invasion brought a violent close to the era of military-led populism in Panama. With the installation of the Endara administration, the popular sectors and the left wing could no longer look to the government and military for support. The military regime since 1968, and particularly during the late 1980s, had constructed a false dichotomy between democracy and nationalism. Noriega had robbed the historical nationalism and appropriated it to justify his personal rule. For Panamanians it became increasingly difficult to be an advocate of both nationalism and democracy. According to Leis, "The opposition put democracy ahead of nationalism," and the popular movement "was blackmailed by officialist nationalism. It was a false dichotomy, because in this country we need three things: democracy, nationalism, and popular measures."[42]

Several months after the invasion, opposition to the Endara government and the U.S. presence slowly began to emerge, mostly among the unions, leftist parties, the leftist human-rights organizations, and the Revolutionary Democratic party (PRD). In addition to these forces, which had mostly supported the Noriega regime during the U.S.-directed destabilization campaign, the new government also faced protests from those who were displaced or who otherwise suffered as a result of the invasion. The Catholic hierarchy also slowly began to distance itself from the Endara government, thereby opening up new space for popular opposition.

Nevertheless, in the 1990s the popular sectors face the challenge of building an independent movement and forging new alliances. The longtime leaders of the popular sectors and left-wing parties will be severely encumbered by their association with the Noriega regime, while emerging leaders and organizations will likely be handicapped by their lack of experience and ideology.

Labor and Unions

The Panamanian labor movement, like other components of the country's popular movement, was weak, fragmented, and without clear direction during the 1980s. Its longstanding and close ties to the military governments of Torrijos and Noriega handicapped its ability to formulate an independent and popular response to the political and economic crisis of the late 1980s. The country's economic downturn, which accelerated after 1987, caused thousands of unionized workers to lose their jobs. During this period there was a rapid decline in the strength of Panamanian unions.

Despite the labor movement's alliance with the military government, only 17 percent of the labor force was organized before the onset of the crisis.[43] As conditions worsened, the unions lost members and the numbers of unemployed and underemployed soared. By 1989 combined unemployment and underemployment estimates had risen to 50 percent.[44]

The 1990s present new challenges to the labor movement. Pushed back to a pre-1968 level, the unions will have to change their organizing methods and leadership if they hope to achieve the credibility needed to defend the rights and interests of Panamanian workers. With a conservative government in place, the union movement will need all the strength it can muster to fight further revisions in the labor code, privatization of state enterprises, the *solidarismo* movement, and the massive layoff of state employees.

The military coup of 1968 was a turning point for the country's labor movement. Until then the country's small labor unions were marginalized and repressed by the economic and political elite. As part of his shrewd maneuvering to win popular support, Torrijos encouraged union organizing and incorporated labor leaders into his government. The enactment of the prounion labor code of 1972 solidified union support for the military government. Although the labor code was subsequently revised because of pressure from the business community, it still guaranteed Panamanian workers more rights and privileges than did other Latin American countries.

There was a surge in union organizing in the 1970s but the end of the decade saw a new government-business alliance that made organizing increasingly difficult. Although organizing stagnated in the private sector, public-sector employees took up the banner of workplace organizing and in 1981 the labor movement united to overturn a 1976 conservative revision of the labor code. Yet soon thereafter labor unity broke down in the face of the historical divisiveness and political maneuvering of the union federations. Government and the private sector teamed up to prevent unionization in the international service sectors like the financial center and the Colón Free Zone, thereby blocking the union movement's access to some of the more dynamic economic sectors. In March 1986 the labor movement was unable to block further antilabor revisions in the labor code. Even a government commission, created in 1987 to formulate a new minimum wage, failed to enact a higher level.

Among the country's most important labor federations are the National Central of Panamanian Workers (CNTP), which has historically been associated with the country's Communist party; Panamanian Workers Federation (CRTP), which is the largest federation and linked to the International Confederation of Free Trade Unions (ICFTU) and supported by the American Institute for Free Labor Development (AIFLD); and the National Federation of Public Workers (FENASEP), which represents more than half of the country's 150,000 public-sector labor force. The Coordination of State Enterprise Workers (CSEE) is a smaller association of the employees of six autonomous public-sector agencies. In a new show of strength, nearly seventy unions joined together in late 1990 to form the Union Movement of the Private and Public Sectors (MSSPP) to protest the government's economic policies.

The majority of the more than 12,000 Panamanian employees and the several hundred U.S. citizens working in the Panama Canal area are represented not by Panamanian labor unions but by those directly affiliated with the AFL-CIO.[45] Among those unions are American Federation of State, County, and Municipal Employees (AFSCME), American Federation of Government Employees (AFGE), and the National Maritime Union (NMU). These unions remain independent of the government.

The country's labor movement generally supported the Noriega regime in the face of the U.S. campaign of destabilization. While increasingly critical of the military regime, labor leaders regarded the conservative political opposition and U.S. intervention as greater evils. When the Civic Crusade called for a general strike of workers and business owners in early 1988, unions for the most part refused to join. Important exceptions were the independent associations of educators and health workers as well as the canal workers.

Although not yet strong, the antiunion *solidarista* movement based in Costa Rica has made some inroads in Panama. This business-sponsored movement, which aims to establish labor-management mutual benefit associations, first appeared in the Coca-Cola Company of Panama.[46] With the labor movement having lost its privileged access to government, *solidarismo* may experience steady growth in the 1990s. As in the 1980s, it is likely that the public-sector unions will be in the forefront of labor struggles in the early 1990s as they struggle against privatization and budget cutbacks.

Education and Students

As a result of a higher per capita income and educational reforms implemented in the 1960s and 1970s, Panamanians as a whole are more literate and have better access to educational institutions than do many other Central Americans. In the mid-1980s the illiteracy rate was estimated to be 14 percent, with some 90 percent of the population having at least a grade-school education.[47]

These impressive achievements in extending education throughout the countryside have been undermined by the economic crisis and government cutbacks. From 1977 to 1987 the percentage of the national budget dedicated to education dropped from 19.8 to 10.3 percent.[48] Beginning in 1987 students were also victims of the political crisis as schools were closed by the government during strikes and states of emergency.

Panama has two national universities, the University of Panama (UP) and the Technological University of Panama (UTP), and one private university associated with the Catholic Church, University Santa María La Antigua (USMA). There is also the Panama Canal College, which is associated with the U.S. Department of Defense Dependents Schools.

Beginning in the 1940s a strong student movement promoting national sovereignty and educational opportunities for the poor developed in Panama. Unlike elsewhere in Latin America, the strongest force in this movement has been secondary school and not university students. Panamanian high school students gained their place in history with the Flag Riots of 1964, when twenty-one students were killed and three hundred wounded by Canal Zone police and U.S. soldiers.

The riots were set off when Panamanian students attempted to raise the nation's flag in front of Balboa High School in the Canal Zone.

Despite being quiet for most of the 1980s, the student movement became active on both sides of the preinvasion political conflict. Ad hoc student protest organizations like the Action Group and the Civil Student Movement formed to support the Civic Crusade and ADOC. Their protests were often brutally crushed by the military and police. Other student factions mounted protests in front of the U.S. embassy and denounced ADOC for being an instrument of the U.S. government.

Communications Media

Historically the media in Panama has been the domain of the country's oligarchy. Between 1968 and 1989, however, the military regime forged its own media empire of radio and television stations and newspapers while closely monitoring the private media.

Despite pervasive government control of the media in the 1980s, the independent press pushed forward with new papers like *La Prensa* and two new television stations. A wave of repression of the media followed the June 1987 revelations by Colonel Roberto Díaz Herrera. A state of emergency suspended freedom of the press, and the powerful Radio KW Continente was shut down by the military. As the crisis heated up, military repression of the press also intensified. In February 1989 Noriega, infuriated by all the bad publicity, again closed several radio stations and newspapers including *La Prensa*. The ouster of Noriega in December 1989 caused a flourishing of media operations with the newspapers *La Prensa*, *El Siglo*, and *El Extra* reopening, and *Crítica* being returned to its previous owners. At the same time, however, the newspapers and radio stations owned by the military regime were shut down. During the invasion, Radio Nacional was bombed off the air and U.S. troops occupied the headquarters of the Journalists Union.

Radio is the most important communications media in Panama. Virtually all Panamanians have one or two favorite radio stations among the some two dozen stations in the country. Unlike television, radio reaches even the most remote villages. Even in the cities, many Panamanians prefer radio to television. Especially popular are the lively morning talk shows broadcast by most stations. About a dozen radio stations were owned by politicians connected to the Noriega government.

Television, the most conservative communications media in Panama, is influential, especially in the Panama City area where an estimated 75 percent of homes have television sets.[49] Television fare has been limited by the political views of its oligarchic and government owners. The stations often ban certain movies and creative programming that deals with social issues, calling them "subversive" or "procommunist."

The State of Health

Health conditions in Panama compare favorably with those of most other Central American countries. As elsewhere in the region, Panama saw a steady improvement in health care in the 1970s that resulted in improving mortality rates and increased life expectancy.

The life expectancy at birth is seventy-three years (1986), compared to sixty years in Guatemala and seventy-five years in the United States. Infant mortality dropped from 105 per thousand births in 1960 to twenty-four per thousand in 1988.[50]

These sanguine statistics are somewhat shadowed by the widening gap between rural and urban health conditions. Areas with the least population density (Darién, Bocas del Toro, Veraguas, Los Santos, Colón) are the areas with the lowest levels of health care and the lowest per capita income. The difference between rural and urban areas is sometimes extreme, as in the case of the largely Indian town of Tolé in Chiriquí where the life expectancy in 1976 was only thirty-eight years.[51] In remote rural areas the causes of death are largely preventable; so too are the numerous illnesses related to poor diet and contaminated water supplies. In urban areas and more accessible rural areas, however, the most prevalent causes of death—cancer, accidents and other violent deaths, and heart failure—parallel patterns found in the industrial world.[52] In mid-1989 the Ministry of Health reported that Panama is among the countries most affected by AIDS. During the first six months of 1989, eighty-six AIDS-related deaths were reported.[53]

The 1968 coup by the National Guard signaled the beginning of a renewed and expanded government commitment to improving the country's health care. The Torrijos regime launched a national campaign, which included the formation of community "health committees" throughout the country. The government created a new Ministry of Health to coordinate and assist the grass-roots work of the health committees, which sponsored latrine, water, popular education, and communal vegetable projects. The health committees also developed productive economic projects designed to cover the costs of new health centers. The number of doctors doubled between 1970 and 1979 and the number of health-care facilities jumped 70 percent.[54] By 1988 there were 6.9 physicians per 10,000 inhabitants.[55]

The country's social security system also expanded rapidly in the 1970s, but is now in serious financial difficulty. Although the general population doubled during the decade, those covered by social security tripled, incorporating many aging workers into the system. Many of these workers are now retiring and represent a severe strain on the system. But the most serious problems facing social security have been its failure to contribute its fair share to the system, and the government's practice of dipping into its coffers to cover other government expenses. Corruption and the absence of a profitable investment policy have also weakened this important source of health care.[56] The country's social security system is likely to be one of the first targets of postinvasion austerity and structural-adjustment programs.

Religion

In 1981 it was estimated that 86 percent of the population identified themselves as Catholic and 12 percent were protestant/evangelical.[57] (In Panama, as elsewhere in Latin America, the term *evangélico* is frequently used to refer to all non-Catholic Christians.) Catholicism is taught in public schools, but the instruction in not obligatory. Despite its dominant position, the Catholic Church in Panama is a weak institution. Fewer than 20 percent of the country's self-identified Catholics regularly attend mass. And at least 75 percent of Catholic clergy are foreign missionaries.[58]

Although most of the Catholic clergy had from the beginning thrown their support to the Civic Crusade, it was not until after the May 1989 elections that the Church hierarchy aligned itself openly with the opposition. Church organizations had received U.S. funds to monitor the election, and circulated a pastoral letter condemning the election fraud. Archbishop Marcos McGrath even invited the Civic Crusade leaders to stand by him while he delivered his May 29, 1989, sermon accusing the Noriega regime of being illegitimate and repressive. After initially providing strong support for the U.S. invasion and the Endara government, McGrath and the Bishops' Conference gradually adopted a more critical stance. In an August 1990 press conference the Catholic bishops denounced continuing U.S. interference in Panamanian affairs and criticized the Endara administration for its lack of "direction and definition." The prelates charged that infighting among the political factions in the new government was indicative of the "age-old vices in the struggle to gain control" of the political process.[59]

Although not as strong as it was in the late 1970s, the popular Church associated with Christian base communities (CBCs) and liberation theology remains an influential sector within the Catholic Church. CBCs are especially active in Chiriquí, Darién, and San Miguelito near Panama City. Some protestant churches, especially the Lutheran and Methodist churches, also support the CBCs. A robust countervailing trend within the Catholic Church that has the support of the archbishop is the spiritualist charismatic movement, which has more in common with the emotion-charged Christianity of groups like the Full Gospel Business Men's Fellowship than with the socially committed popular Church.

Although protestant missionaries have been active in Panama since the early 1800s, the construction of the Panama Canal marked the beginning of the era of protestant evangelism.[60] Originally limited to the West Indians and U.S. citizens working on the canal, protestant missionaries later extended their mission to the country's *mestizo* population. Today more than two-thirds of the country's protestants are Spanish-speaking. In the 1950s extensive outreach work began in Indian communities. Among the most active groups has been the New Tribes Mission, with as many as sixty U.S. missionaries working among Panama's indigenous communities. Between 1960 and 1978 the overall rate of growth of Protestantism was 4.7 percent. Most of this growth has taken place among the *mestizo* population, and virtually all the increase has been among the new U.S. pentecostal churches that began establishing missions in the 1960s.

Nongovernmental Organizations

The first U.S. private, nongovernmental organization (NGO) that established operations in Panama was CARE; an NGO created to distribute U.S. food aid, it has been active in the country since 1953. But it was not until the 1960s that foreign NGOs, mainly from the United States, became common in Panama. This new influx of private charitable and development organizations was sparked by the Alliance for Progress program and the creation of the U.S. Agency for International Development (AID). Among those AID-linked NGOs that entered Panama in the 1960s were Catholic Relief Services (CRS), Partners of the Americas, American Institute for Free Labor Development (AIFLD), and the Pan American Development Foundation (PADF). By the early 1980s there were more than fifty U.S. NGOs and church organizations operating in Panama.

Until late 1987 when AID closed its offices in Panama, many U.S. and Panamanian NGOs received funding directly from the local AID mission. After the closing of AID offices, funding of several local

NGOs continued through the U.S. embassy's Office of Development Affairs. These include the Panamanian White Cross (CBP), Private Sector Council for Educational Assistance (COSPAE), and the National Charity for Rural Panamanian Youth (PANAJURU).[61] Another U.S. source of funding for local NGOs is the National Endowment for Democracy (NED), a quasiprivate foundation funded by the U.S. Information Agency (USIA) and AID. Also organizations like AIFLD, PADF, and International Executive Service Corps received funding for their Panama operations directly from AID's Washington office. It is expected that AID in 1990 will renew and probably increase support for NGOs through a variety of its funding channels.

The relief efforts following the U.S. invasion spurred a flurry of U.S. NGO activity in Panama. Among the main private organizations sending relief supplies were the American Red Cross, AmeriCares Foundation (through Knights of Malta), Catholic Relief Services, Direct Relief International, MAP International, Project Hope, and World Vision.[62]

Women and Feminism

Panama has a long and proud history of feminist activism. The Feminist National party (PNF), founded in 1923, was one of the first feminist parties in Latin America. The party spearheaded the women's suffrage campaign in Panama, and through its Women's Cultural School pushed for social reforms benefiting women and children. In the 1930s the PNF protested the government's issuing of citizenship identity cards only to men. The party's antigovernment positions made its leaders and members targets for government reprisals and led to all the PNF-associated university professors being terminated in 1938. In 1944 many former PNF members founded the National Women's Union, which renewed the struggle for women's right to vote. The fight finally bore fruit that year with a government decree allowing the female vote and another decree the next year establishing equal rights for women.[63]

The UN declaration in 1975 establishing International Women's Year sparked a new era of feminist organizing and consciousness-raising. Having won the right to vote, Panamanian women pushed aside the main legal impediment to their full participation in society and politics. But many other institutional and sociocultural obstacles kept full equality for women an unrealized goal.

Women constitute 57 percent of postsecondary school enrollment, but higher education levels do not necessarily mean equal pay. The International Labor Office (ILO) found that while median monthly income both of men and women in Panama increases significantly with increased education, the disparity between the monthly incomes of men and women increases rather than diminishes with the level of education.[64]

The economic crisis has hit poor women hard, forcing many mothers into the workforce. The female labor force is growing much faster than the male labor force, and the number of woman-headed households has also increased dramatically in the last decade. While 23 percent of higher-income women head households in the Panamanian urban sector, the percentage rises to 37 percent among lower-income women (compared with a corresponding 22 percent in neighboring Costa Rica)—one of the highest rates in Latin America.[65] Many lower-income women work as domestics, an occupation not protected by the labor code. Another common source of employment for working-class women is the export-oriented industrial sector. Laboring in sweatshop conditions, thousands of Panamanian women assemble clothes for export for such textile companies as Vanity Fair, Intimate, Gregor, and Durex.[66]

Although the feminist movement is largely leftist and anti-imperialistic, women played a major role in supporting the National Civic Crusade. In an analysis of this phenomenon, a 1987 article in the local *Diálogo Social* speculated that women were attracted to the anti-government, oligarchy-backed movement because of its tone of moral outrage. Churchwomen and housewives provided an important activist base for this movement.[67]

Minorities and Native Peoples

Spanish-speaking *mestizos* account for about 70 percent of the population. Blacks compose the largest minority—divided between those of colonial/slave descent (about 8 percent) and those of West Indian origin (about 5 percent), who are commonly called *antillanos*. A white creole sector, about 10 percent of the population, dominates the society's economic elite. The Indian population, divided among several different tribes, accounts for about 4 percent of the Panamanian population. The remaining 3 percent are from mixed social and ethnic backgrounds.

Although the black community is more integrated socially than in other Central American countries (with the exception of Belize), blacks are still widely considered second-class citizens. This treatment dates back to the early 1900s when during the construction of the Panama Canal white workers were paid in gold while the *antillanos* and many *mestizo* workers were compensated in silver.[68]

The advent of *torrijismo* in 1968 helped end the historical monopoly of power by white Panamanians. As a result of this new antioligarchic populism, blacks were more easily accepted into the government, security forces, and even business. Large numbers of blacks have become culturally Hispanicized and are now accepted as bona fide *panameños*. Throughout Panama blacks have fewer work opportunities than do whites and *mestizos*—in part for lack of good connections but also because of underlying racism.

Five different indigenous groups exist in Panama. The Guaymí, the most numerous with 54,000 tribal members, live in western Panama in Bocas del Toro on the Atlantic side and in the provinces of Chiriquí and Veraguas on the Pacific side. The Kuna, with an estimated 30,000 members, live mainly on the San Blas islands off the country's northeastern coast but are also found in settlements along the Gulf of Urabá (bordering Colombia) and in the Darién province. The Chocó Indians, with an estimated 25,000 members, live in the Pacific lowlands of the Darién province. Small numbers of Teribe and Bokota Indians live in the western *cordillera*.

Over the past two decades the Guaymí have organized to protect their land and culture. Through the Guaymí General Congress they have demanded that the government establish an autonomous Guaymí *comarca* (reserve)—a demand that was quashed in 1984 when the executive branch suspended talks and passed the problem to the National Assembly. The Guaymí continue to petition for the right to administer justice in their own language and based on their own laws. They have also asked for protection against the incursion of evangelical sects, which have further weakened their culture.[69]

The commercial exploitation of Guaymí land by non-Indians combined with the tribe's own slash-and-burn agriculture have degraded the environment, causing severe erosion in many areas, particularly in Chiriquí and Veraguas.[70] This environmental crisis has become one more cause of Guaymí poverty and unemployment. To make a living, many Guaymí males leave their homes to join the country's migrant workforce. On the coffee and banana plantations, they are generally relegated to the most dangerous and lowest-paying jobs.

In the 1960s the Chocó Indians, who migrated to Panama from Colombia in the late 1700s, gradually began to organize themselves into self-government communities and to demand government recognition of their land rights and access to government services. In 1983 the government recognized the *comarca* Embera-Drua, a reserve of 300,000 hectares, which overlaps with the area classified as the Darién Biosphere Reserve. This victory has been soured by the steady environmental degradation of the reserve. Much of the reserve, particularly the areas surrounding the recently established villages, is depleted of game animals and wild plants. Accustomed to a hunter-gatherer economy, the Chocó Indians have turned increasingly to cash crops. Aggravating the environmental crisis is the steady encroachment of lumber companies and agricultural colonists from the western provinces.[71]

The self-chosen isolation of the Kuna on the San Blas islands proved key to the preservation of their culture and the development of a self-directed economy. Strong local hierarchies developed on the occupied islands, and an elaborately organized political infrastructure developed.[72] The local governments were eventually integrated into the Kuna General Congress, which meets twice annually and establishes the direction of Kuna national politics. Three national chiefs preside over the congress and act as spokespeople to the Panamanian government and society.[73]

In 1938 the Kuna territory gained official status as a *comarca*.[74] The success story of the Kuna continues into the present with the development of a stable economy (based largely on tourism, crafts, coconuts, fishing, and cash transfers from Kunas employed in urban areas) and the maintenance of a strong cultural foundation. In 1985 the Kuna were the first Indian people to establish an internationally recognized forest reserve. The Kuna Wildlife Project, covering 60,000 hectares of rain forest within the *comarca* along the Caribbean coast, is being carefully preserved. Overall, the Kuna have been exceptional among Central American Indians. Not only did they survive the Spanish conquest, but they also seemed to have emerged stronger and better organized from the regional turmoil during the centuries that followed. Partially due to the relative inaccessibility of their territory, they have kept outside influence to a minimum, enabling them to protect and promote their culture and life-style.

Refugees and the Internally Displaced

Unlike other Central American countries, Panama does not have a significant refugee population. There are only about 1,400 official refugees under international protection; the UN High Commission on Refugees (UNHCR) reported in 1988 that it provides assistance to some two hundred Nicaraguans, 750 Salvadorans, and a small number of Guatemalans.[75] Under a cooperative program between UNHCR and the government, Salvadoran refugees were resettled in a remote jungle along the Atlantic coast where they cleared land and attempted to establish a self-sufficient community. By late 1990 the Salvadoran refugees began to repatriate under U.N. supervision.

At least 16,000 Panamanians were displaced by the U.S. invasion and ensuing conflict. Displaced families, mainly from the poor neighborhoods where the fighting was most intense, found temporary refuge in schools and churches. When the firing stopped most of the displaced moved in with families and friends, although several thousand were cared for by the U.S. military, AID, and U.S. private relief organizations. The U.S. government promised to rebuild the El Chorrillo neighborhood—located next to the Panamanian military high command—which was destroyed during the U.S. invasion. To provide new housing for the displaced, Washington has allocated $42 million mostly for private-sector construction programs.

The Chorrillo War Refugees Committee, along with the nongovernmental Panamanian Human Rights Commission, has charged that U.S. assistance has fallen far short of what is needed to compensate and shelter the displaced persons. Americas Watch concluded in its May 1990 report that U.S. emergency assistance was being distributed to only 2,500 of the more than 15,000 displaced and that the only resettlement project under way will provide homes to only 450 families.[76]

The Endara government in February 1990 announced a "voluntary repatriation" program to deport an estimated 25,000 people who illegally entered the country in the past five years. Apparently the Noriega regime had netted more than $200 million in the sale of visas and passports to foreigners, many of them Cubans.

Ecology and Environmentalism

Located below the hurricane belt and bathed in heavy rains, Panama hosts an abundance of tropical flora and fauna. More than eight hundred species of birds are found in Panama—more than are found in the entire Western hemisphere north of the Tropic of Cancer. The country is aflutter with aviary life, with three of the four major migration routes between North and South America converging on Panama.[77] With coral reefs on both sides and the most extensive mangrove area in Central America, Panama also hosts abundant sea life.[78]

Like other Central American countries, however, Panama faces severe environmental problems. This ecological crisis is most evident in the area of the canal and a small strip of Pacific lowlands west of the canal—the areas where 90 percent of Panamanians live. Most of the sewage from the two urban centers, Panama City and Colón, is discharged directly into coastal waters or canals and ditches that flow through the cities.

Long stretches of mangroves are being cut down to make room for new urban developments, shrimp farms, and resorts, causing immense losses for the commercially important seafood industry. Mangrove bark, useful in the tanning industry, is being exported to Costa Rica, where the harvesting of red mangrove bark is prohibited. Birds, especially brightly plumed macaws and yellow-crowned parrots, are also commercially shipped out of the country as part of the international trade in exotic house pets.[79]

More of the original forest cover remains in Panama than in any other Central American country except Belize. The country's low population density, the concentration of its population near the canal, and its diversified economic base have all contributed to the country's relatively large area of remaining tropical forest. About 60 percent of the country remains under some sort of forest cover.[80] Only 9 percent of the land base is dedicated to intensive annual cropping, but large areas are reserved for extensive livestock grazing. Deforestation, nonetheless, is a rising concern in Panama. Since 1983 the annual deforestation rate has been 2.3 percent. In the 1980s more than 97,000 acres of forest were lost each year, and only 9,000 acres were replanted annually.

Soil erosion is also raising concern in Panama: Fifty percent of the soil is of poor quality and 75 percent of the land is hillside terrain. Largely because of the severe rate of deforestation, about 20 percent of Panama has been categorized as being seriously eroded or degraded. Soil-erosion rates in some of the country's prime agricultural areas are thought to be among the highest in all of Latin America.

Reacting to the demands of environmentalists, the government in 1987 announced a five-year suspension of tree-felling. The law prohibits the cutting of any primary forest, or secondary forest more than five years old. The main culprits of deforestation have been the cattle ranchers, who have encouraged peasants, especially in the Darién region, to clear frontier lands for cattle grazing.[81] The pace of deforestation increased following the December 1989 invasion as thousands fled into the forests surrounding the city and as police protection for parks and forest reserves virtually ceased.

A major environmental concern for Panama and the United States alike is the threat to the canal watershed by deforestation in the canal area. To avert a calamity, two national parks, Soberanía and Chagres, were created in the canal watershed. Together they account for almost half the watershed of the canal or some six hundred square miles. As a result, the rate of deforestation in the canal watershed has slowed from

1,100 acres a year before 1976 to 540 acres a year between 1984 and 1987. Deforestation has also presented a threat to the country's hydro-electric system, which generates some 80 percent of the country's electricity, in the Bayano area and in Chiriquí.

International and local forces have combined to reserve a high per-centage (8.7 percent) of the Panamanian land area as environmentally protected territory. Most of this protected space is found within four large national parks. La Amistad covers the largest highland forest in Central America, extending into Costa Rica. Chagres covers the entire watershed of the Alajuela Lake, provides 40 percent of the water for the canal, and is a major source of drinking water. Soberanía is a highly regarded spot for tropical botanical studies as well as a favorite recre-ational site. The Darién national park encompasses a large stretch along the Darién border with Colombia; the largest protected area in Central America, the park has been declared a World Patrimony by UNESCO.[82]

FOREIGN INFLUENCE

U.S. Foreign Policy

Despite the constant aggravation of Panamanian nationalism, the United States has usually succeeded in getting what it wants from Panama. From President Theodore Roosevelt's boast, "I took the canal, and let the Congress debate" to presidential candidate Ronald Reagan's assertion in 1976 that the Canal Zone is "sovereign U.S. territory" and that it "is ours and we intend to keep it," U.S. arrogance has distin-guished U.S.-Panamanian relations.

The price of this arrogance has been a strong anti-U.S. sentiment —at times dormant but on occasion flaring up in violent protests and rhetoric. The long colonial-style relationship between Washington and Panama has also given rise to a contradictory history of collabo-rative and subservient behavior on the part of Panamanians. All three elements—U.S. arrogance and Panamanian nationalism and obsequiousness—were factors in the events leading up to the U.S. invasion. In all likelihood, they will continue to characterize U.S.-Panamanian interactions in the 1990s.

Since the first treaty in 1903 the United States resisted attempts by Panamanians to obtain more control over the canal and the Canal Zone. In the 1960s, however, U.S. military analysts reported that they no longer considered the canal of strategic military importance since at least twenty-four of the largest U.S. aircraft carriers could not fit through the canal.[83] Military experts also noted that the most likely threat to the operation of the canal would come from within Panama by insurgents frustrated with continued U.S. domination of the canal and the Canal Zone. The military generally agreed that the best defense of the canal would be a cooperative, protective contract involving Panama's National Guard (later called the Panamanian Defense Forces).

On October 1, 1979, the Panama Canal treaties signed in 1977 took effect. The first one, called simply the Panama Canal Treaty, governs the operation and defense of the canal by the United States through December 31, 1999. The second, Treaty on the Permanent Neutrality and Operation of the Panama Canal, guarantees the neutrality of the canal in peace and war. Among the provisions of the two treaties are the following:

- The United States has the right to manage and operate the canal until the year 2000.
- The United States retains primary responsibility for the canal's defense during the Panama Canal Treaty's term with increasing participation by the Panamanian Defense Forces.
- Although the primary responsibility to defend the canal will end in the year 2000, the United States retains perpetual authority to protect and defend the canal in the event that the neutrality of the canal is threatened.
- All key bases and training areas operated by the United States are to remain under U.S. control until the year 2000.
- In 1979 Panama was to appropriate territorial jurisdiction over the Canal Zone (five-mile area on either side of the canal).
- A nine-member board was to be established, composed of five U.S. members and four Panamanian members, to manage the newly created Panama Canal Commission.

The neutrality treaty, giving the United States the right to intervene without Panamanian permission, has no termination date. Under its provisions, the United States and Panama both guarantee the neutrality of the canal "in order that both in time of peace and in time of war it shall remain secure and open to peaceful transit by the vessels of all nations on terms of entire equality."

Posttreaty Relations: Calm After the Storm

Washington's relations with Panama significantly improved after the canal treaties went into effect in 1979. The flames of Panamanian nationalism were dampened as the fences that enclosed the Canal Zone were torn down. With the tensions around the control of the canal resolved for the time being, U.S. and other foreign investors found Panama a more stable place to do business. The American Chamber of Commerce in Panama formed in 1979, and the country's international servicing operations, particularly the offshore banking center and the Colón Free Zone, prospered.

After 1979, the U.S. Southern Command (SOUTHCOM), headquartered in the Canal Zone (now called the canal area), which had been one of the Pentagon's sleepiest military commands, suddenly started to buzz with activity.[84] Beginning in 1979, joint military maneuvers between U.S. forces and the National Guard deepened the relationship between the two armed forces. Broadly interpreting the treaty provision for defense of the canal, these maneuvers extended as far as the Costa Rican border. Some Nicaraguan *contras* were trained at U.S. bases, and aerial surveillance missions over Nicaragua and El Salvador took off daily from SOUTHCOM's air bases.

The cooperation between Panama and the United States that developed after the signing of the canal treaties continued after Torrijos's death in 1981. The new National Guard commander, General Rubén Darío Paredes, was by 1983 aligning himself with the U.S. anti-Sandinista counterrevolution. Under General Noriega, the PDF continued this shift away from the nonaligned foreign policy adopted by Torrijos. Panama even reactivated its observer status with the revived regional military alliance CONDECA, which was pushed forward by SOUTHCOM Commander General Paul Gorman as a way further to isolate Nicaragua.[85] This collaboration with U.S. military strategy in the region put the PDF at odds with the Foreign Ministry's promotion of the peace process through the Contadora Group, pointing to the growing contradictions between the PDF's profession of nationalism and populism and its uncritical cooperation with SOUTHCOM.[86]

An Old Affair Turns Bitter

The U.S. partnership with Noriega dated back to late 1959 when Noriega, then a student at a military academy in Peru, began supplying U.S. officials information about the leftist sympathies of fellow students.[87] This relationship did not become contractual until 1967 when, as intelligence officer under Major Omar Torrijos, Captain Noriega regularly supplied intelligence information to the CIA.[88] In 1967 Noriega also signed up for intelligence and counterintelligence training at

Fort Gulick. He then went to Fort Bragg, North Carolina, for a course in psychological operations (Psyops), where he learned the art of media manipulation to conquer adversaries and control internal enemies.[89]

In 1970 Noriega became the chief of intelligence for the Torrijos regime, which had seized power two years before. Using his new position to expand his intelligence work, he hired himself out to the Cubans, Israelis, and Taiwanese. Although aware of Noriega's double-dealing, the CIA insisted that his allegiance was first to the United States; the State Department called him the "rent-a-colonel."

By the beginning of the Carter administration the liabilities of dealing with Noriega, known to be raking in money from the drug trade since the late 1960s, were judged too great and his contract with U.S. intelligence agencies was withdrawn. The case against Noriega intensified in the late 1970s when U.S. intelligence found that Noriega was associated with Panamanians running guns to the Sandinista rebels in Nicaragua. In January 1980, however, the CIA pressured U.S. prosecutors to drop their plans to indict the Panamanian gun runners because the Torrijos regime had granted the shah of Iran asylum in Panama as a favor to the United States.

After Noriega maneuvered his way to the head of the PDF in 1983, the Reagan administration renewed his contracts with the CIA and Defense Intelligence Agency, which amounted to nearly $200,000 annually. Washington was not unaware that Noriega and the PDF were in league with the Medellín drug cartel but judged the PDF collaboration in U.S. foreign-policy objectives, especially the *contra* war, a more important concern. Some *contras* were trained in Panama, and in the spring of 1985 Noriega even helped arrange a sabotage attack on a Nicaraguan arsenal. In 1984 Noriega also provided at least $100,000 to a *contra* leader, according to a document released for Oliver North's trial. Any help for the *contra* cause blinded the Reagan administration to Noriega's transgressions, observed Senator Patrick Leahy, who then served on the Senate Intelligence Committee.[90]

By late 1985 relations between the United States and Panama's strongman grew increasingly testy. Washington had bestowed its blessings on the Ardito-Barletta government, which came to power after the 1984 fraudulent elections. But with the forced resignation of President Ardito-Barletta, a former World Bank president who was a U.S. favorite, and Noriega's appointment of Eric Delvalle as the new president, relations steadily deteriorated. Then Assistant Secretary of State Elliott Abrams and Senator Jesse Helms teamed up in attacking Noriega in congressional hearings in 1986, and the National Security Council (NSC) determined that Noriega was becoming less than fully coopera-

tive in U.S. efforts to topple the Sandinistas. The final links of cooperation between Noriega and Washington were broken in 1987 as a result
of the Iran-*contra* revelations and the crumbling of U.S. hopes for the
military counterrevolution against Nicaragua. The death of CIA chief
William Casey, a Noriega advocate, further isolated Noriega.

Destabilization and Invasion

To rid the country of Noriega, U.S. economic and military aid was cut
off, the propaganda war was intensified, economic sanctions were instituted, and federal indictments were handed down in Florida. These
measures paralleled U.S. support of the Civic Crusade and efforts to
promote a palace coup by dissident PDF officers. But psychological
operations, economic destabilization, political-opposition building,
and CIA plots all failed to topple Noriega. After the failed coup attempt of October 1989, the Bush administration stepped up plans for a
U.S. military invasion.

Washington gave many justifications for the invasion; it was needed
to protect U.S. lives, promote democracy, protect the canal. Bringing
Noriega to justice for drug trafficking was another reason given. Despite the invasion's violation of the charters of the United Nations and
Organization of American States, its willful and distorted interpreta-
tion of the 1977 canal treaties, and its disregard for the War Powers
Act, this act of war received wide bipartisan support.

. The invasion was unexpectedly costly. According to official U.S.
figures, twenty-three U.S. servicemen were killed and another 324
wounded; three U.S. civilians were killed and one injured; 314 PDF
members were killed and another 124 wounded; and 202 Panamanian
civilians died.[91] A *Miami Herald* account later revealed that the Southern Command had quietly revised downward to only fifty PDF and
Dignity Battalion members killed.[92] Another news report, citing interviews with U.S. troops, estimated that as many as sixty U.S. soldiers
were killed, mostly by friendly fire.[93] According to the weekly *Panorama Católico*, however, 655 Panamanians died in the invasion and
2,007 were wounded, most of whom were civilians.[94] The U.S. military,
conspicuously silent about the number of civilian deaths, finally reported that a couple hundred had been killed. In a visit to Panama to
investigate the civilian casualties, former Attorney General Ramsey
Clark estimated that at least 1,000 Panamanian civilians had died.[95]

In its May 1990 report *The Laws of War and the Conduct of the Invasion*,
Americas Watch concluded that the U.S. military failed to follow the
international laws of war as set forth in the 1949 Geneva Convention.

The human-rights group charged that the "U.S. forces violated their ever present duty to minimize harm to the civilian population." Although it found that civilian casualties were probably lower than alleged by local human-rights groups, Americas Watch stressed that a more conservative estimate of civilian victims—three hundred dead and three thousand wounded—calls into serious question boasts by the Bush administration that the invasion was a "surgical operation." "Indeed, civilian deaths now appear to have exceeded military deaths by a margin of four to one, using official figures, and possibly by as much as six to one."[96]

Americas Watch and other human-rights monitors were most critical of the attack on the PDF headquarters in the poor El Chorrillo neighborhood. Residents were given no warning of the attack, which resulted in the destruction of extensive areas of the neighborhood. Many residents "were burned alive in the wooden houses, were injured or killed trying to escape burning multistory buildings, or were killed in crossfire trying to flee."[97]

One foreign-policy headache was resolved by the invasion, but others were immediately created. The invasion was widely condemned throughout Latin America and revived fears of Yankee imperialism. As became obvious soon after the invasion, the arrest of Noriega was not the serious blow to narcotrafficking that Washington promised it to be. In fact, Noriega had largely cleaned up his act in terms of his collaboration with the Medellín cartel by the mid-1980s and had been cooperating with the Drug Enforcement Administration.[98] Also undermining Washington's case against Noriega were postinvasion revelations that the officials of the new government were connected to banks and individuals involved in the laundering of drug money.[99]

U.S. Trade and Investment

The United States historically has been Panama's single most important source of investment and trade. Literally hundreds of U.S. businesses are registered in Panama, but most are only "paper" companies with no operations in the country. Several such paper companies were, for example, established in the mid-1980s by the National Security Council's funding network for the *contras*.[100] About two-thirds of U.S. investment in Panama is nonproductive investment in the offshore banking center.

Nonetheless, U.S. productive investment, amounting to $1.5 billion, still dominates the economy.[101] Six of the top ten U.S. oil companies are active in Panama, one of which—Texaco—owns the country's main oil refinery. United Brands dominates the banana business, and Ralston Purina is the major investor in the seafood industry. Northville Terminal and CBI Industries own the transisthmian oil pipeline in a joint venture with the government. General Mills owns a flour mill, and Borden produces dairy products.[102] Until the 1987 political crisis, U.S. firms did exceedingly well in Panama despite the regional turmoil in Central America, enjoying a 20 percent rate of return and pulling in close to $300 million in profits in 1986 alone.[103] In the case of the oil pipeline, finished in 1982, U.S. investors were able to recoup their initial investment in just eighteen months. One-third of Alaskan North Slope oil flows through this profitable pipeline.[104]

U.S. trade and investment in Panama was adversely affected by the series of economic sanctions imposed by Washington—measures that were opposed by the American Chamber of Commerce and other representatives of U.S. traders and investors.[105] Unlike in most Central American countries, U.S. financial interest in Panama is considerable, even by U.S. terms; the book value of U.S. investment in the country was $4.8 billion in 1987, the third largest in Latin America.[106] According to the American Chamber of Commerce, about one-half of all private-sector business in Panama is U.S.-related.[107] The United States is Panama's single most important trading partner, with the U.S. receiving 60 percent of its exports and supplying 30 percent of its imports.[108] Another factor determining strong U.S. interest in Panama is the presence of some 40,000 U.S. citizens, both civilian and military, who live and work in the country.[109]

U.S. Economic Aid

Following the invasion, the Bush administration moved to provide economic support for the new government. The major elements of this planned assistance were to be disaster relief, trade credits, support for the private sector, balance-of-payments support, immediate debt relief, aid for a public-sector restructuring and investment program, and an emergency public-sector employment program.

An immediate $1 million in disaster relief for feeding programs, rubble removal, and temporary shelter for the displaced was sent to Panama following the invasion. This was to be supplemented by $42 million in humanitarian assistance, including funds for replacement housing for El Chorrillo residents, an emergency public works program, small business rehabilitation assistance, and technical assistance to the government.

Close to $500 million in aid was announced in loans, guarantees, and export assistance to strengthen Panama's private sector and create jobs. This included up to $400 million in trade guarantees for U.S. exporters to Panama through the Export-Import Bank and the affiliated Foreign Credit Insurance Association. AID was authorized to use $15 million in Trade Credit Insurance Program funds to support additional U.S. lending to private-sector borrowers. The Overseas Private Investment Corporation (OPIC) was told to reopen its programs to back U.S. foreign investment in Panama.

The U.S. Department of Agriculture was told to pitch in with $15 million in PL480 Title I food assistance and a $15 million Commodity Credit Program. Bush also told the U.S. Trade Representative to restore the country's suspended 1990 sugar quota and to compensate it for its foregone 1989 quota—together worth $28 million.

Another $420 million in direct economic aid was approved by Congress in June 1990 in Economic Support Funds (ESF), consisting of the following components: $185 million in balance-of-payments/business credit funds; a $145 million public-investment program; $20 million for public-sector restructuring; $20 million for private-sector export promotion and watershed protection for the canal; and $130 million to help erase more than $540 million in debt payment arrears.

Although part of the aid package is designed to provide immediate humanitarian relief and temporary jobs, the main thrust of the recovery aid is to stabilize the government by helping it meet its high debt payments and to support the country's business sector with credit and export-promotion programs. Despite early promises from the White House and Congress, budget constraints and a rising chorus of demand for U.S. aid by Eastern European countries and Nicaragua reduced the chances that Panama would receive the full $500 million in direct economic aid for 1990.

Even if the requested amount of aid were to be approved, it would fall far short of what the government and the Panamanian people had initially expected of Washington. The government estimated that some $2 billion was needed to jump-start the economy, and many Panamanians felt that Washington should compensate business owners whose stores were looted during the first few days of the U.S. occupation. There also was strong Panamanian desire to see compensation for families who lost members due to the violence. Another problem was that U.S. aid, with the exception of some immediate relief, came too slowly, placing the government in a severe financial pinch and leaving thousands of displaced people without adequate shelter. Washington's insistence that the release of large portions of the aid be contingent on the government's approval of numerous conditions, including a new banking law, designed to give U.S. regulators access to bank records, created new tensions between the United States and Panama.

U.S. Military Presence

Instead of the gradual reduction in U.S. military presence after the 1977 canal treaties, U.S. military operations expanded and intensified during the 1980s. When the canal treaties were signed, the Panama-based U.S. Southern Command (SOUTHCOM) was the least important of the four regional commands. Political upheaval in Central America and the formation of a revolutionary government in Grenada during the first half of the decade and the U.S. military involvement in antidrug operations in Peru, Bolivia, and Colombia in the late 1980s dramatically increased the strategic importance of the Southern Command. Central America was regarded as a laboratory for evolving counterinsurgency theory and tactics, and South America as a proving ground for the new low-intensity conflict (LIC) emphasis on counterterrorism and antidrug operations. As if overnight, SOUTHCOM changed from a sleepy command to one responsible for a region of "high probability conflict."[110]

SOUTHCOM suddenly buzzed with activity, providing intelligence for the Salvadoran military, training and coordinating the *contras*, and directing frequent military maneuvers. An estimated fifty intelligence-gathering sites were established in Panama, and from Howard Air Force Base the CIA and the National Security Agency launched high-altitude espionage missions over Nicaragua and El Salvador.[111]

SOUTHCOM: A Home in Panama

The smallest in a global network of four regional U.S. military commands, SOUTHCOM is responsible for U.S. military activities in Central and South America.[112] It is composed of components of three branches of the armed forces (army, navy, air force), a special command in Honduras, security-assistance operations for Latin America, and the Special Operations Command South. In addition, the U.S. military facilities in Panama host a wide range of military and intelligence operations not directly under SOUTHCOM authority.

Prior to the December 1989 invasion, approximately 11,000 U.S. troops were permanently stationed in Panama. In addition, SOUTHCOM employed 8,600 civilian employees and 70 percent of these workers were Panamanian. Under the provisions of the Treaty on the Permanent Neutrality and Operation of the Panama Canal, all U.S.

military personnel must leave the country by the year 2000 unless separate agreements are reached. Immediately following the ratification of the canal treaties, several U.S. military facilities were handed over to Panama while other facilities were designated military areas of coordination, for joint U.S.-Panamanian use.

In late 1988 the Department of Defense announced a preliminary proposal for the "orderly phased withdrawal" of all U.S. troops from Panama. This Treaty Implementation Plan, apparently drawn up as a contingency plan in the face of growing instability in Panama, specified no sites for the relocation but noted that SOUTHCOM would continue as a unified regional command beyond the end of the century.[113] After leaving their posts, the last four SOUTHCOM commanders have all called for SOUTHCOM's relocation.

Although SOUTHCOM probably will be relocating in the 1990s, there is little likelihood that the United States will close all its military bases in Panama. To keep a military presence in Panama, however, the United States will have to renegotiate the 1977 canal treaties to give it the right to maintain bases into the next decade. It is also possible that a separate agreement between Panama and the United States will be drawn up allowing the bases to remain in exchange for an annual fee, similar to arrangements in Spain and the Philippines.

U.S. Military Aid and Training

Historically the United States has exercised major influence and control over the Panamanian security forces. Most important among U.S. programs was the U.S. Army School of the Americas. More than five thousand members of the Panamanian National Guard were trained at the school before it was relocated to Fort Benning, Georgia, in 1984. Instruction in jungle warfare, intelligence operations, counterinsurgency, and psychological operations was made available to National Guard officers at other canal-area training facilities too. Among those who received this training were Omar Torrijos and his two successors, Rubén Darío Paredes and Manuel Noriega.

Although the National Guard relied on the U.S. military for training and supplies, the level of U.S. support was relatively small before 1979. Between 1946 and 1979 Panama received $13 million in U.S. supplies and training. Between 1980 and 1987, however, the level of U.S. support increased steadily. During that period Panama received $47.3 million in U.S. military aid and training. In addition, the Panamanian military also became a favored recipient of surplus U.S. military equipment and participated in annual joint military maneuvers with the

United States. The National Guard/PDF also benefited from the transfer of U.S. military property and the use of coordinated military areas as mandated by agreements associated with the canal treaties.[114]

The evolution of the National Guard from a police force into an army responsible for defending the canal and handling the growing regional turmoil was the result of the Reagan administration's interest in having a strong allied force in the region.

A High-Tech Invasion

The seismology station of the University of Panama reported 422 explosions in Panama City from just before 1 A.M. on December 20, 1989, until its monitors broke down thirteen hours later. This amounted to a bomb every two minutes in the capital, not counting the explosions in Colón and in the interior of the country.[115]

The U.S. invasion was a well-planned, high-tech venture that had the distinct advantage of being an inside job. Unlike earlier U.S. invasions of Grenada and the Dominican Republic, the U.S. forces were already in the country and had been planning the takeover for at least several months. The U.S. marines led the Panamanian occupation of December 1989 to avoid the communications fiasco of Grenada in 1983, which was a joint operation of the armed forces.

In line with low-intensity conflict doctrine, Operation Just Cause was to be a quick-strike mission designed to avoid the loss of U.S. lives. The U.S. military used the opportunity to try out some of its newest technology and combat gear. The billion-dollar super-secret F-11A Stealth was used to bomb the PDF's headquarters. Also used against the PDF were the night-flying AH-64 Apache attack helicopters and the new HM-MWV jeeps. The latest in bulletproof vests and helmets, as well as the military's new semidry rations, were also tested in Panama.[116]

Following the invasion U.S. troops became an occupying force, taking up police and judicial functions, and arresting suspected Noriega supporters and collaborators. Hundreds of specialists in psychological operations (Psyops) were immediately put to work to "bolster the image of the United States" and "to stamp American influence on almost every phase of the new government."[117] Military aid once again began flowing to Panama with some $9 million in redirected military aid being approved for the new Panamanian Public Force (PF).

REFERENCE NOTES

[1] Sharon Phillipps, "Labor Policy in an Inclusionary-Authoritarian Regime: Panama Under Torrijos," dissertation (University of New Mexico, July 1987), p. 47.

[2] For a discussion of the crisis of hegemony in Panamanian politics between 1968 and 1984 see Marco A. Gandásegui, "Militares y Crisis de los Partidos Políticos," *Tareas*, No. 66, June–September 1987.

[3] The first National Guard commander, José Antonio Remón Cantera (1943–1952), was an impoverished cousin of the Chiari family. His successor, Bolívar Vallarino (1952–1968), was a member of an important preindependence family.

[4] Renato Pereira, *Panamá: Fuerzas Armadas y Política* (Panama City: Ediciones Nueva Universidad, 1979), pp. 136–145.

[5] Raúl Leis, "Cousins' Republic," *NACLA Report on the Americas*, July–August 1988, p. 24.

[6] Gandásegui, "Militares y Crisis," op. cit., p. 30.

[7] Unlike the National Assembly of 1972, the one of 1989 was appointed, not elected. Like the 1972–1978 period, Panama had both a president and a head of government. The president from 1972 to 1978 was Demetrio Lakas.

[8] In addition to the use of the term *rabiblancos* Panamanians also use *rabiprietos* (mestizos) and *rabicolorados* (blacks).

[9] John Weeks, "Panama: The Roots of Current Political Instability," *Third World Quarterly*, July 1987, p. 769.

[10] John M. Zindar, "Opposition Outflanked," *NACLA Report on the Americas*, July–August 1988.

[11] Richard Millet, "Looking Beyond Noriega," *Foreign Policy*, Summer 1988.

[12] Amnesty International, *Amnesty International Report 1988*.

[13] *Central America Report*, March 31, 1989.

[14] Tom Wicker, "Panama and the Press," *New York Times*, April 18, 1990.

[15] *Washington Post*, January 7, 1990.

[16] See Steve Ropp, *Panamanian Politics: From Guarded Nation to National Guard* (New York: Praeger, 1982). Also see the following essays in *Revista Panameña de Sociología*, No. 5 (Universidad de Panamá, Departamento de Sociología): Marco A. Gandásegui, "Las FDP y el Año 2000"; Renato Pereira, "Fuerzas Armadas y Partidos Políticos"; Everardo Bósquez De León, "Fuerzas de Defensa y el Año 2000."

[17] Marco A. Gandásegui, *Panamá: Crisis Política y Agresión Económica* (Panama City: CELA, 1989), p. 16.

18 George Priestley, *Military Government and Popular Participation in Panama: The Torrijos Regime, 1968–1975* (Boulder: Westview Press, 1986).

19 Alfonso Villarreal, "Fuerzas Armadas de Panamá: Aspectos Históricos, Políticos, y Jurídicos de la Ley No. 20," in *Revista Panameña de Sociología*, No. 5 (Universidad de Panamá, Departamento de Sociología).

20 *La Prensa*, August 7, 1990; EFE News Service, August 7, 1990.

21 Americas Watch, *The Laws of War and the Conduct of the Invasion*, May 1990, p. 45.

22 *La Prensa*, January 23, 1990.

23 Charlotte Elton, "Serving Foreigners," *NACLA Report on the Americas*, July–August 1988, p. 30.

24 Ibid., p. 29.

25 *Central America Report*, January 26, 1990.

26 U.S. Embassy, *Foreign Economic Trends* (Washington, D.C.: U.S. Department of Commerce, August 1988).

27 *Este País Mes a Mes*, February 1989.

28 H. Jeffrey Leonard, *Natural Resources and Economic Development in Central America* (New Brunswick, NJ: Transaction Books, 1987), pp. 4, 16.

29 Ibid., pp. 18, 222.

30 Tom Barry, *Roots of Rebellion: Land and Hunger in Central America* (Boston: South End Press, 1987), p. 9; *Centro América 1988* (Guatemala City: Inforpress Centroamericana, 1989), pp. 235–236.

31 U.S. Agency for International Development, *Panama: Country Development Strategy Statement FY1988–1992* (Washington, D.C.: AID, February 1986), p. 15.

32 During the 1980s traditional agricultural and industrial exports (bananas, coffee, refined petroleum, sugar, clothing, and fish meal) experienced a $40 million decline.

33 Elton, op. cit., Kenneth Jones, ed., *Panama Now* (Panama City: Focus Publications, 1986), p. 62.

34 *New York Times*, February 6, 1989.

35 Elton, op. cit., p. 28.

36 Panama Petroterminal is a joint venture with the government holding 40 percent, Northville Industries 38.75 percent, and Chicago Bridge and Iron 21.25 percent.

37 Elton, op. cit., p. 28.

38 Lucía Luna, "La Clara Intervención Estadunidense, Dirigida Contra el Grupo de Los Ocho," *Proceso* (Mexico), March 7, 1988.

39 James Aparicio, "Las Barriadas Brujas," *Diálogo Social*, October 1986.

40 Virgilio Hernández, "El Más Jóven Distrito," *Diálogo Social*, January 1986.

[41] Raúl Leis, "Cuatro Ideas Sobre el Papel de Los Sectores Populares en la Coyuntura Actual," *Este País Mes a Mes*, October 1987.

[42] Raúl Leis, "Diez Ideas Sobre el Panamá de Hoy," *Este País Mes a Mes*, February 1990.

[43] *CIA World Factbook* (1988); U.S. Embassy, *Foreign Labor Trends: Panama* (Department of Labor, 1986).

[44] *CIA World Factbook*, ibid.; *Business Latin America*, January 23, 1989.

[45] The 1977 Panama Canal treaties and their U.S. implementing legislation, Public Law 96-70 of 1979, established a special labor-relations structure for U.S. military forces and the Panama Canal Commission, which places all their civilian employees under U.S. federal labor law. U.S. Embassy, *Foreign Labor Trends*, op. cit., p. 10.

[46] Victor Rodríguez, "La Coca-Cola de Panamá, *Diálogo Social*, June–July 1989.

[47] *Resumen Estadístico de UNESCO* (1987); Juan Bosco Bernal, "Estilos de Desarrollo, Educación, y Democracia," *Revista Panameña de Sociología*, VI Congreso Nacional de Sociología, 1989.

[48] Juana Camargo, "Hacia Dónde Va la Educación," *Diálogo Social*, August 1988. In reference to national income, expenditures in education dropped from 5.5 percent in 1977 to 5.2 percent in 1986.

[49] U.S. Embassy, "Country Data: Panama," January 1, 1989.

[50] Otto S. Wald, "Condiciones Generales de Salud en la República de Panamá," *Revista Panameña de Sociología*, No. 3 (Universidad de Panamá, Departamento de Sociología, 1987); *Central America Report*, February 26, 1988.

[51] Wald, op. cit.

[52] *Panama Now*, op. cit., p. 14.

[53] *Central America Report*, September 29, 1989.

[54] Wald, op. cit.

[55] World Health Organization, *World Health Statistics, Annual 1988*.

[56] Ernesto A. and Carmelo Mesa-Lago, *La Seguridad Social en Panamá: Avances y Problemas*, cited in Wald, op. cit.

[57] Clifton Holland, ed., *World Christianity, Volume 4: Central America and the Caribbean* (Monrovia, CA: Mission Advanced Research and Communication Center/World Vision International, 1981).

[58] Betrand de la Grange, "Church Drops Neutral Facade," *Miami Herald*, May 21, 1989.

[59] Latin America Data Base, August 11, 1990, from AFP release of August 2, 1990.

[60] The excellent overview of religion and churches, *World Christianity*, op. cit., was the source for most of this section on Protestantism in Panama.

[61] Letter from Office of Development Affairs, March 23, 1988.

[62] Interview by Debra Preusch with Gussie Daniels, U.S. Department of State, February 23, 1990.

[63] "La Situación y Luchas de la Mujer en Panamá," *Cuadernos Liberación de la Mujer* (Partido Socialista de Trabajadores, ca. 1984). Women's right to vote was incorporated into the country's constitution in 1946.

[64] International Labor Office, *Panamá: Situación y Perspectivas del Empleo Femenino* (Santiago, Chile: OIT, 1984), Table 7, cited in International Center for Research on Women, "Integrating Women into Development Programs: A Guide for Implementation for Latin America and the Caribbean," *Gender Issues in Latin America and the Caribbean* (Washington, D.C.: AID, May 1986), p. 10.

[65] United Nations, *La Mujer en el Sector Urbano* (Santiago, Chile: UN, 1985).

[66] *Cuadernos Liberación de la Mujer*, op. cit.

[67] Urania Ungo, "La Mujer y La Cruzada Civilista," *Diálogo Social*, August–September 1987.

[68] Michael L. Conniff, *Black Labor on a White Canal: Panama, 1904–1981* (Pittsburgh: University of Pittsburgh Press, 1985). For a discussion of blacks and black organizing in Panama, also see Gerardo Maloney, "El Movimiento Negro en Panamá," *Revista Panameña de Sociología*, No. 5 (Universidad de Panamá, Departamento de Sociología, 1989).

[69] Burton L. Gordon, *A Panama Forest and Shore: Natural History and Amerindian Culture in Bocas del Toro* (Pacific Grove, CA: Boxwood Press, 1982).

[70] The slash-and-burn agriculture requires a fallow period of twenty-five years—something no longer possible as the country's agricultural frontier shrinks.

[71] Peter H. Herlihy, "Indians and Rainforest Collide: The Cultural Parks of Darién," *Cultural Survival Quarterly*, Vol. 10, No. 3, pp. 57–61.

[72] James Howe, *The Kuna Gathering: Contemporary Village Politics in Panama* (Austin: University of Texas Press, 1986), pp. 10–13.

[73] Brian Houseal, Craig MacFarland, Guillermo Archibold, and Aurelio Chiari, "Indigenous Cultures and Protected Areas in Central America," *Cultural Survival Quarterly*, Vol. 9, No. 1, 1985, pp. 15–18.

[74] Howe, op. cit., pp. 24–28.

[75] U.S. General Accounting Office, "Central America: Conditions of Refugees and Displaced Persons," March 1989.

[76] Americas Watch, *The Laws of War and the Conduct of the Panama Invasion*, May 1990, pp. 48–49.

[77] Leonard, op. cit., pp. 26, 27.

[78] Ibid., p. 25; "Global Status of Mangrove Ecosystems," *Environmentalist*, Supplement 3, 1983.

[79] Leonard, op. cit., p. 156.

[80] Ibid., p. 18.

[81] *The Amicus Journal*, Fall 1988.

[82] *Ancon Boletín*, January 1989.

[83] *NACLA Report on the Americas*, September–October 1979, p. 4.

[84] Opposition to the 1977 canal treaties was instrumental in forging the U.S. New Right in the 1970s. Among its principal strategists were Paul Weyrich of the Free Congress Foundation, Howard Phillips of the Conservative Caucus, the late Terry Dolan, who founded the National Conservative Political Action Committee, and Dick Viguerie, the New Right's direct-mail expert. James Ridgeway, "The Canal Is Ours," *Village Voice*, June 14, 1988.

[85] Thomas John Bossert, "Panama," in Morris Blachman and William LeoGrande, eds., *Inside Central America: The Impact of U.S. Policy* (New York: Pantheon, 1987), p. 202.

[86] Ibid., p. 203.

[87] For good accounts of the U.S.-Noriega relationship see John Dinges, *Our Man in Panama* (New York: Random House, 1990), and Frederick Kempe, *Divorcing the Dictator* (New York: G.P. Putnam's Sons, 1990).

[88] Frederick Kempe, "U.S. Taught Noriega to Spy, But Pupil Bested His Teachers," *Wall Street Journal*, October 18, 1989. Much of the information in this section on Noriega's relationship with the U.S. government comes from this revealing article.

[89] Kempe, *Divorcing the Dictator*, op. cit.

[90] John Weeks and Andrew Zimbalist, "The Failure of Intervention in Panama," *Third World Quarterly*, January 1989, pp. 8–9; *New York Times Magazine*, May 19, 1988; Seymour Hersh, "Panama Strongman Said to Trade in Drugs, Arms, and Illicit Money," *New York Times*, June 12, 1986.

[91] Information from Major Kathy Wood, U.S. Department of Defense Public Affairs, February 23, 1989.

[92] "U.S. Admits Inflated Military Death Count," *Miami Herald*, March 27, 1990.

[93] Jonathan Franklin, "Hidden Body Count," *San Francisco Bay Guardian*, September 26, 1990.

[94] *Panorama Católico*, January 14, 1990.

[95] *Newsday*, January 10, 1990.

[96] Americas Watch, *The Laws of War and the Conduct of the Panama Invasion*, May 1990, p. 14.

[97] Ibid., p. 16.

[98] Dinges, op. cit; Michael Isikoff, "Analysts Challenge View of Noriega as Drug Lord," *The Washington Post*, January 7, 1990.

99 President Endara is a close friend of Carlos Eleta and was the attorney for several companies owned by Eleta, a political opposition figure arrested in April 1989 on the suspicion of smuggling hundreds of pounds of cocaine into the United States. Endara has for years been the director of Banco Oceánico, one of two dozen banks in Panama named by the FBI as laundering drug money. The new labor minister, Jorge Rubén Rosas, was Eleta's trial attorney. Vice President Guillermo Ford is part owner of the Dadeland Bank of Florida, which has received deposits from the Medellín cartel. Attorney General Rogelio Cruz, Chief Justice Carlos López, and Treasury Minister Mario Galindo all sat on the board of the Inter-Americas Bank, which was shut down in 1985 by Washington after its ownership by a leader of the Cali cartel was established. *New York Times*, February 6, 1990; *Washington Report on the Hemisphere*, February 21, 1990.

100 These included Lake Resources, Udall Research Corporation, and Human Development Foundation.

101 According to U.S. embassy figures, U.S. productive investment in Panama as of 1987 was in the following sectors: petroleum and pipeline, $750 million; agriculture and seafood, $330 million; banking, $200 million; commerce and medical care, $85 million; other manufacturing, $40 million; chemicals and pharmaceuticals, $35 million; food processing, $20 million; insurance and financial services, $20 million; shipping, communications, and transport, $15 million; and tourism, $5 million. The major U.S. firms doing business in Panama include Agro Marina, ALCOA Interamericana, Armour Company, Arthur Young & Co., Arthur Andersen, Black & Decker, Borden, Bristol Laboratories, Burroughs, Chiriquí Land Company (United Brands), Chrysler, Colgate-Palmolive, Coopers & Lybrand, Deloitte Haskins & Sells, Del Monte, Eastern Airlines, Ernst & Whinney, Esso Standard Oil, Firestone, Ford, General Mills, Gillette, Goodyear, IBM, Jenny Manufacturing, Johnson & Johnson, Kativo, Kimberly-Clark, Kodak, Nabisco Brands, NCR, Peat, Marwick, Mitchell & Co., Philip Morris, Price Waterhouse, Schering, Sherwin-Williams, Texaco, Touche Ross, and Wang, as well as the following banks: Citibank, Chase Manhattan, Bank of America, Marine Midland, American Express Bank, Merrill Lynch International Bank, Republic National Bank, Philadelphia National Bank, and Bank of Boston. U.S. Embassy, *Investment Climate Survey* (Washington, D.C.: U.S. Chamber of Commerce, February 1988).

102 Data from the Resource Center "Compilation of Corporations," 1985; Tom Barry and Debra Preusch, *The Central America Fact Book* (New York: Grove Press, 1986), p. 310.

103 "U.S. Transnationals Profit During Regional Crisis," *Central America Report*, December 11, 1987, citing data from the U.S. Department of Commerce.

104 Elton, op. cit.

105 *Latin American Weekly Report*, March 2, 1989.

106 U.S. Embassy, *Investment Climate Survey*, op. cit.; U.S. Department of Commerce, *Survey of Current Business*, June 1988.

107 Elton, op. cit.

108 U.S. Embassy, "Business Facts Sheets: Panama," October 1988.

109 Roger Millet, "Looking Beyond Noriega," *Foreign Policy*, Summer 1988, p. 58.

110 See special issue of *Military Review* (February 1989) on "U.S. SOUTH-COM: High-Probability Conflict" for the latest U.S. military thinking on the role of the Southern Command in low-intensity conflict. Also see Michael Klare, "Panama Signals New U.S. Military Mission in Third World," *Pacific News Service*, December 21, 1989.

111 Alfonso Chardy, "U.S. May Close Bases," *Miami Herald*, May 7, 1989.

112 SOUTHCOM covers 22 percent of the territories assigned to the four regional commands but only counts for 0.1 percent of the Pentagon's budget and 0.5 percent of its military personnel.

113 *Central America Report*, May 12, 1989; *Latin American Weekly Report*, January 5, 1989; Chardy, op. cit.

114 U.S. General Accounting Office, *Security Assistance: Update of Programs and Related Assistance* (Washington, D.C.: December 1988). Worth noting is that U.S. commercial military sales continued even after the June 1987 cutoff of U.S. military aid. These sales decreased in 1987 but rose to an unprecedented $8 million in 1988.

115 Estación Sismología e Instituto de Geociencia, "Reporte Especial de Actividad del Día 20 de Diciembre," *Este País Mes a Mes*, February 1990.

116 Leis, "Diez Ideas Sobre el Panamá de Hoy," op. cit.

117 Press reports cited by Noam Chomsky in "Post Cold War Cold War," *Z Magazine*, March 1990.

SELECTED
BIBLIOGRAPHY

The following periodicals are useful sources of information and analysis on Central America:

Alert! Focus on Central America, Committee in Solidarity with the People of El Salvador (Washington, D.C.), monthly, English.

Boletín Informativo, Centro de Documentación de Honduras (Tegucigalpa), monthly, Spanish.

Central America Bulletin, Central America Research Institute (Berkeley), monthly, English.

Central America Report, Inforpress Centroamericana (Guatemala City), weekly, English and Spanish.

Costa Rica: Balance de la Situación, Centro de Estudios para la Acción Social (San José), bimonthly, Spanish.

Envío, Central American Historical Institute (Washington, D.C.), monthly, English and Spanish.

Este País Mes a Mes, Centro de Estudios y Acción Social Panameño (Panama), monthly, Spanish.

Hondupress, Honduran Press Agency (Boulder and Managua), biweekly, English.

Mesoamérica, Institute for Central American Studies (San José), monthly, English.

NACLA Report on the Americas, North American Congress on Latin America (New York), bimonthly, English.

Pensamiento Propio, Coordinadora Regional de Investigaciones Económicas y Sociales (Managua), monthly, Spanish.

Proceso, Centro Universitario de Documentación e Información, Universidad Centroamericana (San Salvador), weekly, Spanish.

Washington Report on the Hemisphere, Council on Hemispheric Affairs (Washington, D.C.), bimonthly, English.

The following books contain valuable background on many issues important to understanding Central America:

Tom Barry, *Roots of Rebellion: Land and Hunger in Central America* (Boston: South End Press, 1987).

Tom Barry and Debra Preusch, *The Central America Fact Book* (New York: Grove Press, 1986).

————, *The Soft War: The Uses and Abuses of U.S. Economic Aid in Central America* (New York: Grove Press, 1988).

O. Nigel Bolland, *Belize: A New Nation in Central America* (Boulder: Westview Press, 1986).

Central American Recovery and Development Task Force Report to the International Commission for Central American Recovery and Development, William Ascher and Ann Hubbard, eds. (Durham, NC: Duke University Press, 1989).

The Costa Rica Reader, Marc Edelman and Joanne Kenen, eds. (New York: Grove Weidenfeld, 1989).

Richard Lapper and James Painter, *Honduras: State for Sale* (London: CIIR/ Latin American Bureau, 1985).

H. Jeffrey Leonard, *Natural Resources and Economic Development in Central America* (New Brunswick, NJ: Transaction Books, 1987).

James Painter, *Guatemala: False Hope, False Freedom* (London: CIIR/Latin America Bureau, 1988).

William I. Robinson and Kent Norsworthy, *David and Goliath: The U.S. War Against Nicaragua* (New York: Monthly Review Press, 1987).

Holly Sklar, *Washington's War on Nicaragua* (Boston: South End Press, 1988).

INDEX

THE RESOURCE CENTER

The Inter-Hemispheric Education Resource Center is a private, non-profit, research and policy institute located in Albuquerque, New Mexico. Founded in 1979, the Resource Center produces books, policy reports, and audiovisuals about U.S. foreign relations with Third World countries. For a catalogue of publications, write, The Resource Center, Box 4506, Albuquerque, NM 87196.